THE JFC Swing Tutorial

A Guide to Constructing GUIs

FOR CD-ROM

The Java™ Series

Lisa Friendly, Series Editor
Tim Lindholm, Technical Editor
Please see our web site (http://www.awl.com /cseng/javaseries) for more information on these titles.

Ken Arnold and James Gosling, *The Java™ Programming Language, Second Edition*
ISBN 0-201-31006-6

Mary Campione and Kathy Walrath, *The Java™ Tutorial, Second Edition: Object-Oriented Programming for the Internet* (Book/CD)
ISBN 0-201-31007-4

Mary Campione, Kathy Walrath, Alison Huml, and the Tutorial Team, *The Java™ Tutorial Continued: The Rest of the JDK™* (Book/CD)
ISBN 0-201-48558-3

Patrick Chan, *The Java™ Developers Almanac 1999*
ISBN 0-201-43298-6

Patrick Chan and Rosanna Lee, *The Java™ Class Libraries, Second Edition, Volume 2: java.applet, java.awt, java.beans*
ISBN 0-201-31003-1

Patrick Chan, Rosanna Lee, and Doug Kramer, *The Java™ Class Libraries, Second Edition, Volume 1: java.io, java.lang, java.math, java.net, java.text, java.util*
ISBN 0-201-31002-3

Patrick Chan, Rosanna Lee, and Doug Kramer, *The Java™ Class Libraries, Second Edition, Volume 1: Supplement for the Java™ 2 Platform, Standard Edition, v1.2*
ISBN 0-201-48552-4

Li Gong, *Inside the Java™ 2 Platform Security Architecture: Cryptography, APIs, and Implementation*
ISBN 0-201-31000-7

James Gosling, Bill Joy, and Guy Steele, *The Java™ Language Specification*
ISBN 0-201-63451-1

James Gosling, Frank Yellin, and The Java Team, *The Java™ Application Programming Interface, Volume 1: Core Packages*
ISBN 0-201-63453-8

James Gosling, Frank Yellin, and The Java Team, *The Java™ Application Programming Interface, Volume 2: Window Toolkit and Applets*
ISBN 0-201-63459-7

Jonni Kanerva, *The Java™ FAQ*
ISBN 0-201-63456-2

Doug Lea, *Concurrent Programming in Java™: Design Principles and Patterns*
ISBN 0-201-69581-2

Sheng Liang, *The Java™ Native Interface: Programmer's Guide and Specification*
ISBN 0-201-32577-2

Tim Lindholm and Frank Yellin, *The Java™ Virtual Machine Specification, Second Edition*
ISBN 0-201-43294-3

Henry Sowizral, Kevin Rushforth, and Michael Deering, *The Java™ 3D API Specification*
ISBN 0-201-32576-4

Kathy Walrath and Mary Campione, *The JFC Swing Tutorial: A Guide to Constructing GUIs*
ISBN 0-201-43321-4

Seth White, Maydene Fisher, Rick Cattell, Graham Hamilton, and Mark Hapner, *JDBC™ API Tutorial and Reference, Second Edition: Universal Data Access for the Java™ 2 Platform*
ISBN 0-201-43328-1

^{THE} JFC Swing Tutorial

A Guide to Constructing GUIs

Kathy Walrath
and
Mary Campione

ADDISON-WESLEY

An imprint of Addison Wesley Longman, Inc.

Reading, Massachusetts • Harlow, England • Menlo Park, California
Berkeley, California • Don Mills, Ontario • Sydney
Bonn • Amsterdam • Tokyo • Mexico City

Duke™ designed by Joe Palrang.

Sun Microsystems, Inc. has intellectual property rights relating to implementations of the technology described in this publication. In particular, and without limitation, these intellectual property rights may include one or more U.S. patents, foreign patents, or pending applications. Sun, Sun Microsystems, the Sun logo, and all Sun, Java, Jini, and Solaris based trademarks and logos are trademarks or registered trademarks of Sun Microsystems, Inc., in the United States and other countries. UNIX is a registered trademark in the United States and other countries, exclusively licensed through X/Open Company, Ltd.

Library of Congress Cataloging-in-Publication Data
Walrath, Kathy.
   The JFC Swing tutorial : a guide to constructing GUIs / Kathy
Walrath and Mary Campione.
     p. cm. -- (The Java series)
   Includes index.
   ISBN 0-201-43321-4
   1. Graphical user interfaces (Computer systems) 2. Java
foundation classes.   I. Campione, Mary. II. Title. III. Series.
QA76.9.U83W36   1998
005. 13'3--dc21   98-32305
                                  CIP

The publisher offers discounts on this book when ordered in quantity for special sales. For more information, please contact: Corporate, Government and Special Sales; Addison Wesley Longman, Inc.; One Jacob Way; Reading, Massachusetts 01867.

ISBN: 0-201-43321-4
1 2 3 4 5 6 7 8 9-CRS-0302010099
First Printing, June 1999

Contents

Preface

THIS volume of *The Java™ Tutorial* tells you how to write GUIs that use the Java™ Foundation Classes (JFC) "Swing" components. You can use the information in this book both with the Java 2 Platform (Standard Edition, v 1.2 and compatible versions) and with JDK™ 1.1 (with additional JFC 1.1 libraries).

The online form of *The Java™ Tutorial* has covered the Swing components since their first public early access release—Swing 0.2, which came out in July, 1997. Through the many early access releases, the Tutorial kept pace with API changes and additions. Readers and reviewers kept us on our toes, helping us improve each page tremendously. However, readers often requested a printed version of the online material. This book is that version.

About This Book's Structure

The hyperlinked origins of this book may be evident as you read it. For instance, underlined phrases throughout this book mimic online links. A link to material within this book is followed by the appropriate page number. A link to material outside this book, such as to the JDK API documentation, is accompanied by a footnote that contains a URL. Other evidence of this book's online origin can be found on the first page of each lesson and major section, which provides the URL where the lesson or section can be found in the online Tutorial.

You might be wondering why we use the terms "trails" and "lessons." We know that people don't learn linearly. People learn by posing a problem, solving it, uncovering other problems, solving them, and learning information as the need arises. Our original vision for the online Tutorial was to encourage and enable this type of thinking and learning. We envisioned a mountain of ski trails, where at any junction, a reader could choose the most interesting or appropriate path at that time. But we also needed some sort of structure and organization, so we created a two-tiered hierarchy: trails at the top level and lessons within them. This book consists of the largest Tutorial trail, Creating a GUI with JFC/Swing.

Acknowledgments

We would like to thank every member of the Swing project. They're a great team of people who do excellent work and are fun to be around.

For help with general technical issues, we depended on two people. Hans Muller, the Swing project lead, provided not only reviews of individual sections, but also gave sound advice and help with overall issues. Amy Fowler reviewed individual sections and, as someone with broad knowledge of both the AWT and Swing, helped us to correctly describe such architectural features as graphics support.

Reviewers of individual how-to sections include Philip Milne, who gave masterful reviews of the table and list portions and supplied the sorter example. Georges Saab reviewed the menu- and action-related discussions. Scott Violet provided invaluable help with the text and tree pages. Jeff Dinkins reviewed several sections and also provided quality-of-life enhancements such as tile samples and miniature phone lists.

Earl Johnson and Peter Korn, from the accessibility team, gently prodded us into covering accessibility well. Their demos, coaching, and careful review of the accessibility section helped us improve it greatly.

It's always a pleasure working with Pat Chan, whose early review of this book helped us determine its scope and approach.

Other reviewers and Swing team members that we'd like to thank include Mike Albers, Tim Prinzing, Tom Santos, Steve Wilson, Rich Schiavi, Tom Ball, Jim Graham, and Hania Gajewska. Rick Levenson, the original manager of the Swing project, was very supportive. We look forward to working with the new manager, Howard Rosen.

Alison Huml performed production duties on this book, juggling coursework, paid work, RSI, and a household move. Without her, this book wouldn't exist. She also drew most of the pictures in this book, with the exception of the cartoony ones, which were drawn by Kathy's sweetheart Nathan.

Jennifer Ball helped us at crucial points, doing such tasks as checking API tables and code snippets, and converting graphics examples.

Lisa Friendly, our manager and series editor, gave us the freedom and support necessary to do our work—and enjoy it. Stans Kleijnen and Jon Kannegaard, respectively the director of product engineering and the vice president of the Java platform, also contributed to an atmosphere that let everyone do their best.

We'd also like to thank the team at Addison-Wesley: Mike Hendrickson, Sarah Weaver, Evelyn Pyle, Jacquelyn Young, Marina Lang, and Julie DeBaggis. They've been a pleasure to work with.

Finally, thank you to our readers.

About the Authors

Kathy Walrath is a senior technical writer on the Swing team at Sun Microsystems. After graduating from UC Berkeley with a B.S. in Electrical Engineering and Computer Science, Kathy wrote extensively about UNIX, Mach, and NEXTSTEP. Since 1993, Kathy has been writing specifications and how-to guides for the Java platform. She and her family spend their free hours spelunking for books, coffee, and used furniture in San Francisco.

Mary Campione is a senior technical writer at Sun Microsystems, where she's been writing about the Java platform since 1995. Mary graduated from Cal Poly, San Luis Obispo, with a B.S. in Computer Science and has been a technical writer and programmer for 13 years. In addition to the tutorial books, she is the co-author of *PostScript by Example* (Addison-Wesley, 1992). Mary and her family enjoy summer weekends at the beach and winter weekends on the slopes.

Before You Start

$\mathbf{Y}$OU should read one or both of the following sections, according to your experience with the Java™ platform.

Getting Started (page 1) is for newbies. Skip this if you're comfortable writing and running programs with the Java platform.

Finding the Information You Want (page 2) is for all readers. It lists the navigational aids that can help you find your path through this book.

Getting Started

If you haven't written and run programs using the Java platform, then please close this book and go to the "Getting Started" trail of *The Java™ Tutorial*. That trail introduces you to the Java programming language and platform, and then leads you through writing and running a basic application and applet. You can find it either at the beginning of the first tutorial book, *The Java™ Tutorial, Second Edition*, or online at this URL:

```
http://java.sun.com/docs/books/tutorial/getStarted/index.html
```

At various points, the "Getting Started" trail suggests other sections that you might want to read. For example, it introduces you to objects and classes, and then tells you where you can find detailed information about them. Once you feel comfortable with the Java programming language and confident that you know your way around *The Java™ Tutorial*, please return to this book.

Finding the Information You Want

We try to make it easy for you to skip around this book, choosing exactly which lessons you want to read. That's why this book is heavily cross-referenced and why we provide self-contained lessons. We also provide the following navigational aids:

- Contents (page v) lists all the lessons in this book, and the major sections within them.

- The beginning of each lesson describes what you can expect to learn. Each lesson also has its own table of contents which lists the sections within it.

- Within each lesson, you can expect to find links to related information whenever appropriate.

- The Code Examples (page 607) contains full source code listings, along with links to where in this book each program is discussed.

- The Index (page 931) is a traditional book index.

The Java Tutorial CD-ROM pages at the end of this book list the contents of the CD-ROM. In particular, the CD-ROM includes *The Java*^{TM} *Tutorial* in HTML and all of the source code for the examples in this book. The CD-ROM also includes most of the resources referenced in this book, such as the API documentation and the online magazine, *The Swing Connection*. It's easy to translate the URLs in the book to their locations on the CD-ROM. For example, this URL for `JApplet` API documentation:

```
http://java.sun.com/products/jdk/1.2/docs/api/javax/swing/JApplet.html
```

can be found here on the CD-ROM:

```
/java2/docs/api/javax/swing/JApplet.html
```

Getting Started with Swing

THIS lesson gives you a brief introduction to using the Java™ Foundation Classes (JFC) Swing packages to create a program's GUI (graphical user interface). After telling you about the JFC and Swing, this lesson helps you get the necessary releases and use them to compile and run a program. Then this lesson shows you how to run applets that use the Swing packages. Finally, it takes you on a whirlwind tour of a simple Swing application.

If you're more interested in learning concepts than in running programs right now, feel free to skip part or all of this lesson and to go to the next lesson, Features and Concepts (page 25). Then return here when you're ready to start programming.

About the JFC and Swing (page 5)
This chapter gives you a little history about the JFC and Swing. If you've used AWT (Abstract Windowing Toolkit) components to develop programs, you'll probably be interested in the description of the differences between AWT and Swing components.

Compiling and Running Swing Programs (page 11)
To write programs using the Swing components, you must first download the appropriate releases of the Java platform and the JFC. Then you can follow this chapter's instructions to compile and run the small Swing application provided.

Running Swing Applets (page 17)
To write applets that use the Swing packages, you must first be able to run them. This chapter provides two applets, with instructions for running them.

3

A Quick Tour of a Swing Application's Code (page 19)
This chapter takes you through the code for a Swing application that uses the Swing packages. You'll see the code that a Swing application absolutely must have, and you'll learn about some commonly used Swing features.

About the JFC and Swing

THIS chapter answers four questions:

What Are the JFC and Swing?

JFC is short for Java™ Foundation Classes, which encompass a group of features to help people build graphical user interfaces (GUIs). The JFC was first announced at the 1997 JavaOne developer conference and is defined as containing the following features.

The Swing Components
Include everything from buttons to split panes to tables. You can see mugshots of all of the components in A Visual Index to Swing Components (page 63).

Pluggable Look & Feel Support
Gives any program that uses Swing components a choice of "look and feel." For example, the same program can use either the Java Look & Feel or the Windows Look & Feel. We expect many more look-and-feel packages—including some that use sound instead of a visual "look"—to become available from various sources.

Accessibility API

Enables assistive technologies, such as screen readers and Braille displays, to get information from the user interface.

Java™ 2D API (Java 2 Platform only)

Enables developers to easily incorporate high-quality 2D graphics, text, and images in applications and in applets.

Drag and Drop Support (Java 2 Platform only)

Provides the ability to drag and drop between a Java application and a native application.

The first three JFC features were implemented without any native code, relying only on the API defined in JDK™ 1.1. As a result, they could and did become available as an extension to JDK 1.1. This extension was released as JFC 1.1, which is sometimes called "the Swing release." The API in JFC 1.1 is often called "the Swing API."

Note: "Swing" was the code name of the project that developed the new components. Although it's an unofficial name, it's frequently used to refer to the new components and related API. It's immortalized in the package names for the Swing API, which begin with `javax.swing`.

This book concentrates on the Swing components. We help you choose the appropriate ones for your GUI, tell you how to use them, and give you the background information you need to use them effectively. We discuss the Pluggable Look & Feel and Accessibility support when they affect how you write Swing programs. This book does not cover the JFC features that appear only in the Java platform. For information about those, refer to 2D Graphics,[1] and to the JFC home page at `http://java.sun.com/products/jfc/index.html`.

Figure 1 shows three views of a GUI that uses Swing components. Each picture shows the same program, but with a different look and feel.

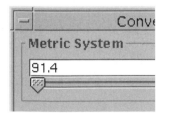 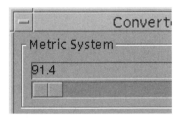 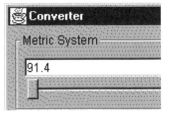

(a) Java Look & Feel   **(b) CDE/Motif Look & Feel**   **(c) Windows Look & Feel**

Figure 1   Three Look & Feel samples.

---

[1]   The "2D Graphics" trail is in the book *The Java Tutorial Continued*. It is also available online at http://java.sun.com/docs/books/tutorial/2d/index.html

The program, called `Converter`, is discussed in detail at the end of the next lesson, <u>Features and Concepts</u> (page 25).

Which Releases Contain the Swing API?

The Swing API is present in two releases:

- Java 2 Platform, Standard Edition, v 1.2
- JFC 1.1 (for use with JDK 1.1)

Which release you use depends on whether you need to use JDK 1.1 or the Java 2 platform. It's a bit simpler to use the Java 2 platform, because the JFC is built into it and you don't need to add libraries to be able to use the Swing API. However, if you need to use JDK 1.1, adding the Swing API (using JFC 1.1) isn't difficult. Instructions for doing both are in <u>Compiling and Running Swing Programs</u> (page 11).

This book describes the Swing 1.1 API, which is the version present in Java 2 platform, v 1.2, and in the release called "JFC 1.1 (with Swing 1.1)." The code in this book works, without any changes, with either release.

Sun has released many versions of JFC 1.1, which are identified by the version of Swing API they contain. One previous version, for example, was called "JFC 1.1 (with Swing 1.0.3)." The following table shows some of the important releases containing Swing API. Boldface type indicates the releases typically used in shipping products.

Table 1   Important Swing Releases

Swing API Version	Corresponding JFC 1.1 Release	Corresponding Java 2 Release	Comments
Swing 0.2	JFC 1.1 (with Swing 0.2)	None	The first public release of JFC 1.1.
Swing 1.0.3	**JFC 1.1 (with Swing 1.0.3)**	None	The release of JFC 1.1 included in **Java Plug-in**^{TM} **1.1.1**. Supported for use in shipping products.
Swing 1.1 Beta	JFC 1.1 (with Swing 1.1 Beta)	JDK 1.2 Beta 4	The first JDK 1.2 release that used the same Swing package names as the corres-ponding JFC 1.1 release.
Swing 1.1 Beta 3	JFC 1.1 (with Swing 1.1 Beta 3)	JDK 1.2 RC1	The first release with the final Swing package names.

Table 1   Important Swing Releases

Swing API Version	Corresponding JFC 1.1 Release	Corresponding Java 2 Release	Comments
Swing 1.1 **Note:** This is the API this book covers.	**JFC 1.1 (with Swing 1.1)**	**Java 2 SDK, Standard Edition, v 1.2**	The first releases containing the final Swing 1.1 API supported for use in shipping products. **Java Plug-in 1.1.2** and **Java Plug-in 1.2** provide applet support for JDK 1.1 + Swing 1.1 and Java 2, respectively.
Swing 1.1.1 Beta 2 **Note:** This book describes some HTML text functionality added in this release.	JFC 1.1 (with Swing 1.1.1 Beta 2)	None	

By the time you read this book, new versions of the JDK 1.1, JFC 1.1, and Java 2 Platform might be available. See the JFC home page[1] for the latest information on releases containing the Swing API.

What Swing Packages Should I Use?

The Swing API is powerful, flexible—and immense. For example, the Swing 1.1 API release has 15 public packages:

```
javax.accessibility        javax.swing.filechooser    javax.swing.table
javax.swing                javax.swing.plaf           javax.swing.text
javax.swing.border         javax.swing.plaf.basic     javax.swing.text.html
javax.swing.colorchooser   javax.swing.plaf.metal     javax.swing.tree
javax.swing.event          javax.swing.plaf.multi     javax.swing.undo
```

Fortunately most programs use only a small subset of the API. This book sorts out the API for you, giving you examples of common code and pointing you to methods and classes you're likely to need. Most of the code in this book uses only one or two Swing packages:

- `javax.swing`
- `javax.swing.event` (not always required)

---

[1]   You can find the JFC home page online at http://java.sun.com/products/jfc/index.html

How Are Swing Components Different from AWT Components?

If you don't care about the AWT components, skip to the next chapter. You can get a more general introduction to the Swing components from <u>A Quick Tour of a Swing Application's Code</u> (page 19) and from <u>Features and Concepts</u> (page 25).

The AWT components are those provided by the JDK 1.0 and 1.1 platforms. Although the Java 2 Platform still supports the AWT components, we strongly encourage you to use Swing components instead. You can identify Swing components because their names start with J. The AWT button class, for example, is named Button, whereas the Swing button class is named JButton. Additionally the AWT components are in the java.awt package, whereas the Swing components are in the javax.swing package.

The biggest difference between the AWT components and the Swing components is that the Swing components are implemented with absolutely no native code. Since Swing components aren't restricted to the least common denominator—the features that are present on every platform—they can have more functionality than AWT components. Because the Swing components have no native code, they can be shipped as an add-on to JDK 1.1, in addition to being part of the Java 2 Platform.

Even the simplest Swing components have capabilities far beyond what the AWT components offer:

- Swing buttons and labels can display images instead of or in addition to text.
- You can easily add or change the borders drawn around most Swing components. For example, it's easy to put a box around the outside of a container or a label.
- You can easily change the behavior or appearance of a Swing component by either invoking methods on it or creating a subclass of it.
- Swing components don't have to be rectangular. Buttons, for example, can be round.
- Assistive technologies, such as screen readers, can easily get information from Swing components. For example, a tool can easily get the text that's displayed on a button or a label.

The Swing API lets you specify which look and feel your program's GUI uses. By contrast, AWT components always have the look and feel of the native platform.

Another interesting feature is that Swing components with state use models to keep the state. A JSlider, for instance, uses a BoundedRangeModel object to hold its current value and range of legal values. Models are set up automatically, so you don't have to deal with them unless you want to take advantage of the power they can give you.

If you're used to using AWT components, you need to be aware of a few gotchas when using Swing components:

- Programs should not, as a rule, use "heavyweight" components alongside Swing components. Heavyweight components include all of the ready-to-use AWT components, such as `Menu` and `ScrollPane`, and all components that inherit from the AWT `Canvas` and `Panel` classes. This restriction exists because when Swing components (and all other "lightweight" components) overlap with heavyweight components, the heavyweight component is always painted on top.[1]

- Swing components aren't thread safe. If you modify a visible Swing component—invoking its `setText` method, for example—from anywhere but an event handler, you need to take special steps to make the modification execute on the event-dispatching thread. This is not an issue for most simple Swing programs, since component-modifying code is typically in event handlers.

- The containment hierarchy for any window or applet that contains Swing components must have a Swing top-level container at the root of the hierarchy. For example, a main window should be implemented as a `JFrame` instance rather than as a `Frame` instance.

- You don't add components directly to a top-level container such as a `JFrame`. Instead you add components to a container, called the *content pane*, that is itself contained by the `JFrame`.

Converting to Swing (page 575) tells you more about the differences between Swing components and AWT components.

---

[1] For more information, see "Mixing Heavy and Light Components," an article in the online magazine, *The Swing Connection*. *The Swing Connection* is available on the CD-ROM that accompanies this book and online at http://java.sun.com/products/jfc/tsc/index.html

2

Compiling and Running Swing Programs

THIS chapter tells you how to compile and run a Swing application. The compilation instructions work for all Swing programs—applets, as well as applications. If you're interested in Swing applets, you should also read <u>Running Swing Applets</u> (page 17). If you aren't yet interested in compiling and running Swing programs, you can skip directly to <u>A Quick Tour of a Swing Application's Code</u> (page 19), which guides you through the code for a simple application.

The instructions in this chapter assume that you're already comfortable with writing and compiling programs that use the Java platform. If you aren't, please read the <u>Getting Started</u> trail.[1]

How you compile and run Swing programs depends on whether you're using JDK 1.1 or the Java 2 Platform. Using the Java 2 Platform is a bit simpler, because Swing is built into the Java 2 Platform. Choose the instructions corresponding to the release you're using:

- Java 2 Platform
- JDK 1.1 plus the JFC/Swing release

Both instructions tell you how to run a simple program, called `SwingApplication` (see Figure 2).

---

[1] The "Getting Started" trail is included in the book, *The Java Tutorial*, and is also available in HTML on this book's CD-ROM and online at http://java.sun.com/docs/books/tutorial/getStarted/index.html. In particular, you'll need to successfully follow the instructions in "The 'Hello World' Application" before you attempt to compile and run any Swing programs.

Figure 2   The GUI of the SwingApplication.

Compiling and Running Swing Programs (Java 2 Platform)

Here are the steps for compiling and running your first Swing program with the Java 2 Platform:

1. Install the latest release of the Java 2 Platform, if you haven't already done so.
2. Create a program that uses Swing components.
3. Compile the program.
4. Run the program.

Install the Latest Release of the Java 2 Platform

You can download the Java 2 platform for free from http://java.sun.com. The JDK is also included on the CD-ROM that accompanies this book.

Create a Program that Uses Swing Components

You can use a simple program we provide, called SwingApplication.java (page 610).[1] When you run this program, you must match this spelling and capitalization of the file's name exactly.

Compile the Program

Your next step is to compile the program. Compiling a Swing program with the Java 2 platform is simple, since the Swing packages are part of the Java 2 platform. Here is an example:

```
javac -deprecation SwingApplication.java
```

---

[1] You can find SwingApplication.java on this book's CD-ROM and online at http://java.sun.com/docs/books/tutorial/uiswing/start/example-swing/SwingApplication.java

If you can't compile `SwingApplication.java`, it's probably because you're using either a JDK 1.1 rather than the Java 2 development environment, or because you're using a beta release of the Java 2 platform. Once you update to the most recent release, you should be able to use the programs in this book without change.

Run the Program

After you compile the program successfully, you can run it. Assuming that your program uses a standard look and feel—such as the Java Look & Feel, Windows Look & Feel, or CDE/Motif Look & Feel—you can use the interpreter to run the program without adding anything to your class path. For example:

```
java SwingApplication
```

If you use a nonstandard look and feel, you must make sure that its package is included in the class path. For example:

Solaris:
```
java -classpath .:/home/me/lnfdir/newlnf.jar SwingApplication
```

Win32:
```
java -classpath .;C:\java\lnfdir\newlnf.jar SwingApplication
```

Note: Don't include the Java 2 classes in the class path. The interpreter finds them automatically.

Compiling and Running Swing Programs (JDK 1.1)

Here are the steps for compiling and running your first Swing program with JDK 1.1 and JFC 1.1:

1. Install the latest JDK 1.1 release, if you haven't already done so.
2. Install the latest JFC 1.1 release.
3. Create a program that uses Swing components.
4. Compile the program.
5. Run the program.

Install the Latest JDK 1.1 Release

You can either use the version of JDK 1.1 provided on this book's CD-ROM or download the latest version from `http://java.sun.com/products/jdk/1.1/`.

Install the Latest JFC/Swing Release

You can either use the version of JFC 1.1 provided on this book's CD-ROM or download the latest JFC 1.1 release from the JFC home page.[1] This book describes the Swing 1.1 version of JFC 1.1.

Create a Program that Uses Swing Components

You can use a simple program we provide, called <u>SwingApplication.java</u> (page 610).[2] You must match the spelling and capitalization of the file's name exactly.

Compile the Program

Your next step is to compile the program. Here's a general explanation of how to compile a Swing application with JDK 1.1.

1. Make a note of where your copy of the JFC 1.1 (Swing 1.1) release is installed. The Swing class archive file, swing.jar, is in the top directory of this release. You might want to create an environment variable called SWING_HOME that contains the path of the top directory of the JFC 1.1 release.

Note: Don't bother unarchiving swing.jar!

---

2. Make a note of where your copy of the JDK release is installed. You'll need this to be able to find the proper versions of the JDK classes, the compiler and the interpreter. You might want to create an environment variable, JAVA_HOME, and set it to the top directory of the JDK release.[3]

   The JDK classes are in the lib directory of the JDK release, in a file called classes.zip. Don't uncompress that file! The compiler and interpreter are in the bin directory of the JDK release.

3. Compile the application, specifying a class path that includes the swing.jar file, the JDK classes.zip file, and the directory containing the program's classes (usually "."). Make sure that the JDK classes.zip file and the compiler you use are from exactly the same release of the JDK!

The following example shows how to compile SwingApplication on a UNIX system. The example assumes that you've set up the environment variables JAVA_HOME and SWING_HOME.

---

[1] You can find the JFC home page online at http://java.sun.com/products/jfc/index.html

[2] You can also find SwingApplciation.java on this book's CD-ROM and online at http://java.sun.com/docs/books/tutorial/uiswing/start/example-swing/SwingApplication.java

[3] For more information, see <u>Platform-Specific Details: Setting Environment Variables</u> (page 927).

```
$JAVA_HOME/bin/javac -classpath .:$SWING_HOME/swing.jar:$JAVA_HOME/lib/
classes.zip SwingApplication.java
```

If you choose not to use the environment variables, you might instead use a command like this:

```
javac -classpath .:/home/me/swing-1.1/swing.jar:/home/me/jdk1.1.8/lib/
classes.zip SwingApplication.java
```

Here's an example of compiling on Win32:

```
%JAVA_HOME%\bin\javac
    -deprecation
    -classpath .;%SWING_HOME%\swing.jar;%JAVA_HOME%\lib\classes.zip
    SwingApplication.java
```

Here's an alternative that doesn't use environment variables:

```
javac
    -deprecation
    -classpath .;C:\java\swing1.1\swing.jar;C:\java\jdk1.1.8\lib\
      classes.zip
    SwingApplication.java
```

Note: If you can't compile `SwingApplication.java`, it's probably due either to having the wrong files in your class path or to using a version of JFC 1.1 that has old Swing API. You should be able to use the programs in this book without change once you update to the most recent JFC 1.1 release.

Run the Program

Once the program has successfully compiled, you can run it. Make sure that the interpreter's class path includes not only what you needed to compile the file but also the archive file for the look and feel the program uses. The Java Look & Feel, which is the default, is in the `swing.jar` file. The Windows Look & Feel is in `windows.jar`, and the CDE/Motif Look & Feel is in `motif.jar`. You aren't limited to these look-and-feel options; you can use any look and feel designed for use with the Swing 1.1 API.

This application uses the Java Look & Feel, so you need only `swing.jar` in the class path. Thus the command for running it is similar to the command for compiling it. Just substitute `java` for `javac` and remove the `.java` suffix. For example, on UNIX:

```
java -classpath .:/home/me/swing-1.1/swing.jar:/home/me/jdk1.1.8/lib/
classes.zip SwingApplication
```

Here's an example of running an application that uses the Windows Look & Feel:

```
%JAVA_HOME%\bin\java
   -classpath
   .;%SWING_HOME%\swing.jar;%JAVA_HOME%\lib\classes.zip;%SWING_HOME%\
     windows.jar
   SomeClass
```

While you're developing your application, you can simplify the class path by using the swingall.jar file, which includes all of the classes in the JFC 1.1 release. So instead of putting swing.jar and windows.jar in your class path, for example, you can just put in swingall.jar.

Important: Avoid using swingall.jar in your final application. It contains information used by builders, as well as more look-and-feel packages than a typical application uses. You can save space by simply using the swing.jar file plus any look-and-feel archives that you need.

Running Swing Applets

THIS chapter explains how to run applets that use Swing components. For information on *writing* Swing applets, see <u>How to Make Applets</u> (page 99).

You can run Swing applets in any browser that has the appropriate version of Java™ Plug-in installed.[1] While you're developing your applets, we recommend running them using a tool such as Applet Viewer, which is provided in JDK 1.1 and Java 2 SDK v 1.2.

To test whether your browser can run applets, go to this page in the online tutorial:

```
http://java.sun.com/docs/books/tutorial/uiswing/start/
HelloSwingApplet.html
```

You should see a box that looks like this.

> You are successfully running a Swing applet!

Figure 3   A snapshot of the simple applet, `HelloSwingApplet`.

You can find the applet's source code in <u>HelloSwingApplet.java</u> (page 610), and the HTML code in <u>HelloSwingApplet.java</u> (page 610). The bad news is that the HTML code for including the applet is rather convoluted. The good news is that you can generate the HTML code automatically from a simple <APPLET> tag. See the Java Plug-in documentation for details on downloading a free HTML converter.[2]

---

[1]   The Java Plug-in is included on the CD-ROM that accompanies this book.

[2]   The Java Plug-in documentation is online at http://java.sun.com/products/plugin/index.html

The following more complex applet uses multiple class and image files.

Figure 4   A snapshot of the more complex applet, `AppletDemo`.

To run the applet, go to this page in the online tutorial:

```
http://java.sun.com/docs/books/tutorial/uiswing/start/
HelloSwingApplet.html
```

The applet's source code, in <u>AppletDemo.java</u> (page 608), uses the files `images/` `right.gif`, `images/middle.gif`, and `images/left.gif` as well.[1]

The rest of this chapter gives step-by-step instructions for running the preceding applets.

Step by Step: Running a Swing-Based Applet

1. Download Java Plug-in into a supported browser. You can do this by visiting the URL for either of the preceding applets. Another alternative is to use Applet Viewer (`appletviewer`). Java Plug-in supports certain versions of Netscape Navigator and Internet Explorer. See the Java Plug-in documentation on this book's CD-ROM for details.

2. If you're using JDK 1.1 Applet Viewer, you'll need to load the Swing JAR file. See <u>Platform-Specific Details: Setting the Browser's Class Path</u> (page 925) for an example.[2]

3. Point the browser at the online version of this section:

   ```
   http://java.sun.com/docs/books/tutorial/uiswing/start/
   swingApplet.html
   ```

   From that page, you can follow the links to visit the two applets described in this section.

---

[1] For a list of links to the image files, see http://java.sun.com/docs/books/tutorial/uiswing/components/ example-swing/index.html

[2] For examples of doing the same for Internet Explorer and Netscape Navigator, see "Make Your Browser Swing," an article in the online magazine, *The Swing Connection*. *The Swing Connection* is available on the CD-ROM that accompanies this book and online here: http://java.sun.com/products/jfc/tsc/index.html

A Quick Tour of a Swing Application's Code

THIS chapter takes you through the code for the `SwingApplication` program. The next lesson, <u>Features and Concepts</u> (page 25), provides full explanations of the topics introduced in this chapter. That lesson also provides a bigger, more realistic example that you can use to expand and test your Swing knowledge.

`SwingApplication` brings up a window that looks like this.

Figure 5 A snapshot of the simple GUI of `SwingApplication`.

Each time the user clicks the button, the label is updated. You can find the whole program in <u>SwingApplication.java</u> (page 610).

The following sections explain how the code in `SwingApplication.java` accomplishes various tasks.

Importing Swing Packages

The following line imports the main Swing package:

```
import javax.swing.*;
```

Note: Early beta releases used different names for the Swing packages. See <u>Swing Package Names</u> (page 927) for details.

Most Swing programs also need to import the two main AWT packages:

```
import java.awt.*;
import java.awt.event.*;
```

Choosing the Look and Feel

Swing allows you to specify which look and feel your program uses—Java Look & Feel, Windows Look & Feel, CDE/Motif Look & Feel, and so on. The code in boldface type in the following snippet shows you how SwingApplication specifies the look and feel:

```
public static void main(String[] args) {
    try {
        UIManager.setLookAndFeel(
            UIManager.getCrossPlatformLookAndFeelClassName());
    } catch (Exception e) { }
    ...//Create and show the GUI...
}
```

The preceding code essentially says, "I don't care whether the user has chosen a look and feel—use the cross-platform look and feel (the Java Look & Feel)." You already know what the Java Look & Feel looks like, since almost all of our screenshots show it.

For more information on specifying the look and feel, see <u>How to Set the Look and Feel</u> (page 428).

Setting Up the Top-Level Container

Every program that presents a Swing GUI contains at least one top-level Swing container. For most programs the top-level Swing containers are instances of JFrame, JDialog, or (for applets) JApplet. Each JFrame object implements a single main window, and each JDialog implements a secondary window. Each JApplet object implements an applet's display area within a browser window. A top-level Swing container provides the support that Swing components need to perform their painting and event handling.

The SwingApplication example has only one top-level container, a JFrame. When the user closes the frame, the application exits. Here is the code that sets up and shows the frame:

```
public class SwingApplication {
    ...
    public static void main(String[] args) {
        ...
        JFrame frame = new JFrame("SwingApplication");
        //...create the components to go into the frame...
        //...stick them in a container named contents...
        frame.getContentPane().add(contents,
                                BorderLayout.CENTER);
        //Finish setting up the frame, and show it.
        frame.addWindowListener(new WindowAdapter()) {
            public void windowClosing(...);
        }
        ...
        frame.pack();
        frame.setVisible(true);
    }
}
```

For more information about top-level containers, see <u>Components and Containment Hierarchies</u> (page 29).

Setting Up Buttons and Labels

Like most GUIs, the SwingApplication GUI contains a button and a label. (Unlike most GUIs, that's about all that SwingApplication contains.) Here's the code that initializes the button:

```
JButton button = new JButton("I'm a Swing button!");
button.setMnemonic('i');
button.addActionListener(...create an action listener...);
```

The first line creates the button. The second sets the letter "i" as the mnemonic that the user can use to simulate a click of the button. For example, in the Java Look & Feel, typing Alt-i results in a button click. The third line registers an event handler for the button click. You'll see the event-handling code for this program in <u>Handling Events</u> (page 23).

Here's the code that initializes and manipulates the label:

```
.../where instance variables are declared:
private static String labelPrefix = "Number of button clicks: ";
private int numClicks = 0;

.../in GUI initialization code:
final JLabel label = new JLabel(labelPrefix + "0     ");
...
label.setLabelFor(button);

.../in the event handler for button clicks:
label.setText(labelPrefix + numClicks);
```

The preceding code is pretty straightforward, except for the line that invokes the setLabel-For method. That code exists solely to hint to assistive technologies that the label describes the button. For more information, see Supporting Assistive Technologies (page 24).

For more information about such Swing components as buttons and labels, see Using Swing Components (page 57).

Adding Components to Containers

SwingApplication groups the label and the button in a container (a JPanel) before adding the components to the frame. Here's the code that initializes the panel:

```
JPanel pane = new JPanel();
pane.setBorder(BorderFactory.createEmptyBorder(...));
pane.setLayout(new GridLayout(0, 1));
pane.add(button);
pane.add(label);
```

The first line of code creates the panel. The second line adds a border to it. We'll discuss the border later.

The third line of code creates a layout manager that forces the panel's contents to be displayed in a single column. The last lines add the button and the label to the panel, so that they are controlled by the panel's layout manager. Specifically a container's layout manager determines the size and position of each component that's been added to the container.

Layout management concepts are discussed in Layout Management (page 33). To learn how to use individual layout managers, see Laying Out Components (page 341).

Adding Borders Around Components

Here again is the code that adds a border to the panel:

```
pane.setBorder(BorderFactory.createEmptyBorder(
                            30, //top
                            30, //left
                            10, //bottom
                            30) //right
                            );
```

This border simply provides some empty space around the panel's contents—30 extra pixels on the top, left, and right, and 10 extra pixels on the bottom. Borders are a feature that JPanel inherits from the JComponent class.

Border concepts are discussed in <u>Layout Management</u> (page 33). See <u>How to Use Borders</u> (page 408) for information about using the border API.

Handling Events

The SwingApplication example contains two event handlers. One handles button clicks (action events); the other handles window closing (window events). Here is the event-handling code from SwingApplication:

```
button.addActionListener(new ActionListener() {
    public void actionPerformed(ActionEvent e) {
        numClicks++;
        label.setText(labelPrefix + numClicks);
    }
});
...
    frame.addWindowListener(new WindowAdapter() {
        public void windowClosing(WindowEvent e) {
            System.exit(0);
        }
    });
```

You can read about Swing event handling in <u>Event Handling</u> (page 37) and <u>Writing Event Listeners</u> (page 439).

Dealing with Thread Issues

The SwingApplication program is thread safe. Once the application's GUI is visible, its only GUI manipulation (updating the label) occurs in an event handler. Because the event handler runs in the same thread that performs all event handling and painting for the application, there's no possibility that two threads will try to manipulate the GUI at once.

However, it can be all too easy to introduce thread problems into a program. See Threads and Swing (page 45) for information about thread safety in Swing.

Supporting Assistive Technologies

Support for assistive technologies—devices such as screen readers that provide alternative ways of accessing information in a GUI—is already included in every Swing component. In SwingApplication the only code that exists solely to support assistive technologies is this:

```
label.setLabelFor(button);
```

Assistive technologies can get plenty of information from Swing components, without any special code from you. For example, assistive technologies can automatically get the text information set by the following lines of code:

```
JButton button = new JButton("I'm a Swing button!");
label = new JLabel(labelPrefix + "0    ");
label.setText(labelPrefix + numClicks);
JFrame frame = new JFrame("SwingApplication");
```

See How to Support Assistive Technologies (page 393) for more information about how you can ensure that your programs work well with tools that use the Accessibility API to query components.

Features and Concepts

THIS lesson introduces Swing's features and explains all of the concepts you need to be able to use Swing components effectively. At the end of this lesson we dissect a Swing program as a means of reviewing everything you've learned.

Components and Containment Hierarchies (page 29)

This chapter describes the many standard GUI components Swing provides—such as buttons, lists, menus, and text areas—which you combine to create your program's GUI. Swing components also include containers, such as windows and tool bars.

Layout Management (page 33)

Containers use *layout managers* to determine the size and the position of the components they contain. This chapter describes layout managers and how borders can affect the layout of Swing GUIs by making Swing components larger. You can also use invisible components to affect layout.

Event Handling (page 37)

Event handling refers to how programs respond to external events, such as the user's pressing a mouse button. This chapter explains how Swing programs perform all painting and event handling in the event-dispatching thread.

Painting (page 41)

This chapter describes *painting*, or drawing the component on-screen. Although it's easy to customize a component's painting, most programs don't do anything more complicated than customizing a component's border.

Threads and Swing (page 45)

If you do something that might depend on or affect a visible component's state, you need to do it from the event-dispatching thread. This isn't an issue for many simple programs, which generally refer to components only in event-handling code. However, some programs need to use the `invokeLater` method to execute component-related calls in the event-dispatching thread.

More Swing Features and Concepts (page 49)

Many Swing features rely on features provided by the `JComponent` class. This chapter looks at some of the more interesting features: support for icons, actions, Pluggable Look & Feel technology, assistive technologies, and separate models.

The Anatomy of a Swing-Based Program (page 51)

This chapter provides a sample Swing application, named `Converter`, to show how Swing programs work and how the code hangs together.

Components and Containment Hierarchies

AGAIN, here is a picture of the `SwingApplication` program presented in <u>A Quick Tour of a Swing Application's Code</u> (page 19).

Figure 6   A screenshot of the `SwingApplication` program.

We use this program to introduce some commonly used Swing components and to show how the components in a GUI fit together into one or more containment hierarchies.

`SwingApplication` creates four commonly used Swing components:

- A *frame*, or main window (`JFrame`)
- A *panel*, sometimes called a *pane* (`JPanel`)
- A *button* (`JButton`)
- A *label* (`JLabel`)

The frame is a *top-level container*. It exists mainly to provide a place for other Swing components to paint themselves. The other commonly used top-level containers are dialogs (JDialog) and applets (JApplet).

The panel is an *intermediate container*. Its only purpose is to simplify the positioning of the button and the label. Other intermediate Swing containers, such as scroll panes (JScrollPane) and tabbed panes (JTabbedPane), typically play a more visible, interactive role in a program's GUI. As you'll see shortly, every top-level container indirectly contains a special intermediate container known as a *content pane*.

The button and the label are *atomic components*—components that exist not to hold random Swing components but rather as self-sufficient entities that present bits of information to the user. Often atomic components also get input from the user. The Swing API provides many atomic components, including combo boxes (JComboBox), text fields (JTextField), and tables (JTable).

Here is a diagram of the *containment hierarchy* for the window shown by SwingApplication. This diagram shows each container created or used by the program, along with the components it contains. Note that if we add a window—a dialog, for instance—the new window has its own component hierarchy, unattached to the hierarchy shown in this figure.

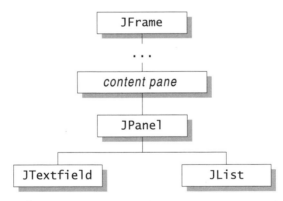

Figure 7   A diagram of the containment hierarchy for SwingApplication's window.

As the figure shows, even the simplest Swing program has multiple levels in its containment hierarchy. The root of the containment hierarchy is always a top-level container. The top-level container provides a place for its descendant Swing components to paint themselves.

Tip: To view the containment hierarchy for any frame or dialog, click its border to select it, and then press Control-Shift-F1. A list of the containment hierarchy will be written to the standard output stream.

As Figure 7 shows, the content pane generally contains, directly or indirectly, all of the visible components in its top-level container's GUI. The big exception to the rule is that if the top-level container has a menu bar, by convention the menu bar goes in a special place outside of the content pane. For most programs you don't need to know what's between a top-level container and its content pane.[1]

To add a component to a container, you use one of the various forms of the add method. The add method has at least one argument—the component to be added. Sometimes an additional argument is required to provide layout information. For example, the last line of the following code sample specifies that the panel should be in the center of the container (the content pane). For more information about the add method, see the how-to page for the container's layout-manager. Also see Table 8 (page 73), "Dealing with the Containment Hierarchy see Components and Containment Hierarchy."

Here is the code that adds the button and the label to the panel, and the panel to the content pane:

```
frame = new JFrame(...);
button = new JButton(...);
label = new JLabel(...);
pane = new JPanel();
pane.add(button);
pane.add(label);
frame.getContentPane().add(pane, BorderLayout.CENTER);
```

To see all of the Swing components, refer to <u>A Visual Index to Swing Components</u> (page 63).

---

[1] If you really want to know, see <u>How to Use Root Panes</u> (page 158).

6

Layout Management

THE following figure shows the GUIs of five programs, each of which displays five buttons. The buttons are identical, and the code for the programs is almost identical. So why do the GUIs look so different? Because they use different layout managers to control the size and the position of the buttons.

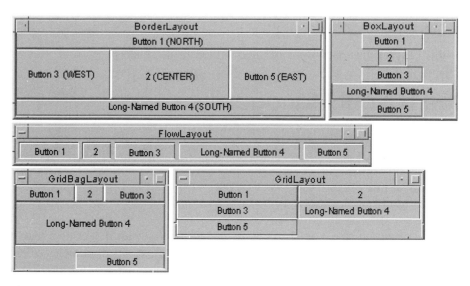

Figure 8   Several examples of layout management.

Layout management is the process of determining the size and the position of components. By default each container has a *layout manager*—an object that performs layout management for the components within the container. Components can provide size and alignment hints to layout managers, but layout managers have the final say on the size and the position of those components.

The Java™ platform supplies five commonly used layout managers: BorderLayout, Box-Layout, FlowLayout, GridBagLayout, and GridLayout. These layout managers are designed for displaying multiple components at once and are shown in the preceding figure. A sixth provided class, CardLayout, is a special-purpose layout manager used in combination with other layout managers. You can find details about each of these six layout managers, including hints for choosing the appropriate one, in Using Layout Managers (page 343).

Whenever you use the add method to put a component in a container, you must take the container's layout manager into account. Some layout managers, such as BorderLayout, require you to specify the component's relative position in the container, using an additional argument with the add method. Occasionally a layout manager, such as GridBagLayout, requires elaborate setup procedures. Many layout managers, however, simply place components on the basis of the order in which they were added to their container.

All this probably sounds more complicated than it is. You can usually either copy code from our examples in Using Swing Components (page 57) or look up the individual layout manager in Using Layout Managers (page 343). Generally, you set the layout manager of only two types of containers: content panes (which use BorderLayout by default) and JPanels (which use FlowLayout by default).

The rest of this chapter discusses some of the common layout tasks.

Setting the Layout Manager

You can easily change the layout manager that a container uses. Just invoke the container's setLayout method. For example, here's the code that makes a panel use BorderLayout:

```
JPanel pane = new JPanel();
pane.setLayout(new BorderLayout());
```

Although we recommend that you use layout managers, you can perform layout without them. By setting a container's layout property to null, you make the container use no layout manager. With this strategy, called *absolute positioning*, you must specify the size and the position of every component within that container. One drawback of absolute positioning is that it doesn't adjust well when the top-level container is resized; nor does it adjust well to differences between users and systems, such as different font sizes.

Providing Hints About a Component

Sometimes you need to customize the size hints that a component provides to its container's layout manager so that the component will be laid out well. You do this by specifying the minimum, preferred, and maximum sizes of the component. You can either invoke the component's methods for setting size hints—setMinimumSize, setPreferredSize, and setMaximumSize—or you can create a component subclass that overrides the appropriate getter methods— getMinimumSize, getPreferredSize, and getMaximumSize. Currently the only standard layout manager that pays attention to a component's requested maximum size is BoxLayout.

Besides providing size hints, you can also provide alignment hints. For example, you can specify that the top edges of two components should be aligned. You set alignment hints either by invoking the component's setAlignmentX and setAlignmentY methods or by overriding the component's getAlignmentX and getAlignmentY methods. Currently Box-Layout is the only standard layout manager that pays attention to alignment hints.

Putting Space Between Components

Three factors influence the amount of space between visible components in a container.

The layout manager
Some layout managers automatically put space between components; others don't. Some let you specify the amount of space between components. See Laying Out Components (page 341) for information about spacing support in layout managers.

Invisible components
You can create lightweight components that perform no painting but that can take up space in the GUI. Often you use invisible components in containers controlled by Box-Layout. See How to Use BoxLayout (page 350) for examples of using invisible components.

Empty borders
No matter what the layout manager, you can affect the apparent amount of space between components by adding empty borders to components. The best candidates for empty borders are components that typically have no default border, such as panels and labels. Some other components might not work well with borders in some look-and-feel implementations, because of the way their painting code is implemented. For information about borders, see How to Use Borders (page 408).

How Layout Management Occurs

Here's an example of a layout management sequence for a frame (JFrame).

1. After the GUI is constructed, the pack method is invoked on the JFrame. This specifies that the frame should be at its preferred size.

2. To find the frame's preferred size, the frame's layout manager adds the size of the frame's edges to the preferred size of the component directly contained by the frame. This is the sum of the preferred size of the frame's content pane and the size of the frame's menu bar, if any.

3. The content pane's layout manager is responsible for figuring out the content pane's preferred size. By default this layout manager is a BorderLayout object. However, let's assume that we replace it with a GridLayout object that's set up to create two columns, as in the bottom right of Figure 8. The interesting thing about grid layout is that it forces all components to be the same size, and it tries to make them as wide as the widest component's preferred width and as high as highest one's preferred height.

   First, the grid layout manager queries the content pane for its insets—the size of the content pane's border, if any. Next, the grid layout manager queries each component in the content pane for its preferred size, noting the largest preferred width and the largest preferred height. Then the grid layout manager calculates the content pane's preferred size.

4. When asked for its preferred size, each button first checks whether the user specified a preferred size. If so, the button reports that size. If not, the button queries its look and feel for the preferred size.

The end result is that to determine the best size for the frame, the system determines the sizes of the containers at the bottom of the containment hierarchy. These sizes then percolate up the containment hierarchy, eventually determining the frame's total size. Similar calculations occur when the frame is resized.

For more information about layout, see Laying Out Components (page 341).

Event Handling

EVERY time the user types a character or pushes a mouse button, an event occurs. Any object can be notified of the event. All the object has to do is implement the appropriate interface and be registered as an *event listener* on the appropriate *event source*. Swing components can generate many kinds of events. Table 2 lists a few examples.

Table 2   Examples of Events and Their Associated Event Listeners

Act that Results in the Event	Listener Type
User clicks a button, presses Return while typing in a text field, or chooses a menu item	`ActionListener`
User closes a frame (main window)	`WindowListener`
User presses a mouse button while the cursor is over a component	`MouseListener`
User moves the mouse over a component	`MouseMotionListener`
Component becomes visible	`ComponentListener`
Component gets the keyboard focus	`FocusListener`
Table or list selection changes	`ListSelectionListener`

Each event is represented by an object that gives information about the event and identifies the event source. Event sources are typically components, but other kinds of objects can also be event sources. As the following figure shows, each event source can have multiple listeners registered on it. Conversely a single listener can register with multiple event sources.

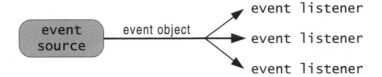

Figure 9　Multiple listeners can register to be notified of events of a particular type from a particular source.

Whenever you want to detect events from a particular component, first check the how-to section for that component in Using Swing Components (page 57). The how-to sections give examples of handling the events that you're most likely to care about. In How to Make Frames (page 82), for instance, you'll find an example of writing a window listener that exits the application when the frame closes.

How to Implement an Event Handler

Every event handler requires three pieces of code:

1. In the declaration for the event handler class, one line of code specifies that the class either implements a listener interface or extends a class that implements a listener interface. For example:

   ```
   public class MyClass implements ActionListener {
   ```

2. Another line of code registers an instance of the event handler class as a listener on one or more components. For example:

   ```
   someComponent.addActionListener(instanceOfMyClass);
   ```

3. In the event handler class, a few lines of code implement the methods in the listener interface. For example:

   ```
   public void actionPerformed(ActionEvent e) {
       ...//code that reacts to the action...
   }
   ```

Let's investigate a typical event-handling scenario by looking at how buttons (JButton) handle mouse clicks (see Figure 10). To detect when the user clicks an on-screen button (or does the keyboard equivalent), a program must have an object that implements the Action-Listener interface. The program must register this object as an action listener on the button (the event source), using the addActionListener method. When the user clicks the onscreen button, the button fires an action event. This results in the invocation of the action listener's `actionPerformed` method (the only method in the `ActionListener` interface). The single argument to the method is an `ActionEvent` object that gives information about the event and its source.

Figure 10 When the user clicks a button, the button's action listeners are notified.

Event handlers can be instances of any class. Often an event handler that has only a few lines of code is implemented using an *anonymous inner class*—an unnamed class defined inside of another class. Anonymous inner classes can be somewhat confusing at first, but once you're used to them, they make the code clearer by keeping the implementation of an event handler close to where the event handler is registered. For information about using inner classes, see Using Adapters and Inner Classes to Handle Events (page 449).

For more information about implementing event handlers, see Writing Event Listeners (page 439).

Threads and Event Handling

Event-handling code executes in a single thread, the *event-dispatching thread*. This ensures that each event handler finishes execution before the next one executes. For instance, the `actionPerformed` method in the preceding example executes in the event-dispatching thread. Painting code also executes in the event-dispatching thread. This means that while the `actionPerformed` method is executing, the program's GUI is frozen—it won't repaint or respond to mouse clicks, for example.

Important: The code in event handlers should execute very quickly! Otherwise your program's perceived performance will be poor. If you need to perform a lengthy operation as the result of an event, do it by starting up another thread (or somehow sending a request to another thread) to perform the operation. For help on using threads, see How to Use Threads (page 431).

Painting

YOU might not need the information in this chapter at all. However, if your components don't seem to be painting themselves correctly, understanding the concepts in this chapter might help you figure out what's wrong. If you plan to create custom painting code for a component, this chapter is required reading.

How Painting Works

When a Swing GUI needs to paint itself—whether for the first time, in response to becoming unhidden, or because it needs to reflect a change in the program's state—it starts with the highest component that needs to be repainted and works its way down the containment hierarchy. This process is orchestrated by the AWT painting system and is made more efficient and smooth by the Swing repaint manager and double-buffering code.

Swing components generally repaint themselves whenever necessary. When you invoke the `setText` method on a component, for example, the component should automatically repaint itself and, if appropriate, resize itself. If it doesn't, it's a bug. The workaround is to invoke the `repaint` method on the component to request that it be scheduled for painting. If the component's size or position needs to change but does not automatically, you should invoke `revalidate` on the component before invoking `repaint`.

Like event-handling code, painting code executes on the event-dispatching thread. While an event is being handled, no painting will occur. Similarly if a painting operation takes a long time, no events will be handled during that time.

Programs should paint only when the painting system tells them to, because each occurrence of a component painting itself must execute without interruption. Otherwise unpredictable results could occur.

For smoothness Swing painting is *double-buffered* by default—performed in an off-screen buffer and then flushed to the screen once finished. It might help performance slightly if you make a Swing component opaque, so that the Swing painting system can know not to paint anything behind the component. Invoke `setOpaque(true)` on the component to make a Swing component opaque.

Although their available painting area is always rectangular, nonopaque Swing components can appear to be any shape. A button, for instance, might display itself by painting a filled octagon. The component behind the button (its container, most likely) would then be visible, showing through at the corners of the button's bounds. The button would have to include special hit-detection code to avoid acting pressed if the user happens to click on its corners.

An Example of Painting

To illustrate painting, we'll use the `SwingApplication` program, explained in <u>A Quick Tour of a Swing Application's Code</u> (page 19). Here is the `SwingApplication`'s GUI.

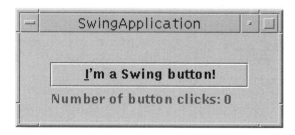

Figure 11 A screenshot of the `SwingApplication`'s GUI.

Here again is its containment hierarchy.

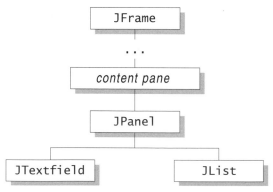

Figure 12 The containment hierarchy of the `SwingApplication`.

When the GUI for SwingApplication is painted, here's what happens:

1. The top-level container, JFrame, paints itself.
2. The content pane first paints its background, which is a solid gray rectangle. The content pane then tells the JPanel to paint itself. The content pane's background rectangle doesn't actually appear in the finished GUI, because the content pane is obscured by JPanel.

Note: It's important that the content pane be opaque. Otherwise messy repaints will result. Because the JPanel is opaque, we could make it the content pane (by substituting setContentPane for the existing code getContentPane().add). This would slightly simplify the containment hierarchy and painting by removing an unnecessary container.

---

3. The JPanel first paints its background, a solid gray rectangle, and next its border. The border is an EmptyBorder, which has no effect except for increasing the JPanel's size by reserving some space at the edge of the panel. Finally, the panel asks its children to paint themselves.
4. To paint itself, the JButton paints its background rectangle, if necessary, and then paints the text that it contains. If the button has the keyboard focus, meaning that any typing goes directly to the button for processing, the button does some look-and-feel-specific painting to make clear that it has the focus.
5. To paint itself, the JLabel paints its text.

Each component paints itself in this way before any of the components it contains. This ensures that the background of a JPanel, for example, is visible only where it isn't covered by painting performed by one of the components it contains. The following table illustrates the order in which each component that inherits from JComponent paints itself. For more information on how to paint, see Working with Graphics (page 533).

Table 3   Order in Which Components Are Painted

1. Background (if opaque)	2. Custom Painting (if any)	3. Border (if any)	4. Children (if any)

9

Threads and Swing

IF your program creates and refers to its GUI the right way, you might not need to worry about threads. For example, if your program is an applet, it's safe to construct its GUI in the `init` method. You're also safe if your program is an application with the following common pattern:

```
//Thread-safe example
public class MyApplication {
    public static void main(String[] args) {
        JFrame f = new JFrame(...);
        ...//Add components to the frame here...
        f.pack();
        f.setVisible(true);
        //Don't do any more GUI work here.
    }

    ...
    //All manipulation of the GUI -- setText, getText, etc. --
    //is performed in event handlers such as actionPerformed().
    ...
}
```

However, if your program creates threads to perform tasks that affect the GUI, or if it manipulates an already visible GUI in response to anything but a standard event, read on.

The Single-Thread Rule

Swing components can be accessed by only one thread at a time, generally, the event-dispatching thread. Thus, the single-thread rule is as follows.

Rule: Once a Swing component has been realized, all code that might affect or depend on the state of that component should be executed in the event-dispatching thread.

This rule might sound scary, but for many simple programs you don't have to worry about threads.

Before we go into detail about how to write Swing code, let's define the term *realized*. *Realized* means that the component has been painted on-screen or that it is ready to be painted. A Swing component that's a top-level window is realized by having one of these methods invoked on it: setVisible(true), show, or pack. Once a window is realized, all of the components it contains are realized. Another way to realize a component is to add it to a container that's already realized. You'll see examples of realizing components later.

Note: The show method does the same thing as setVisible(true).

Exceptions to the Rule

The rule that all code that might affect a realized Swing component must run in the event-dispatching thread has a few exceptions.

A few methods are thread safe.
In the Swing API documentation thread-safe methods are marked with this text:

This method is thread safe, although most Swing methods are not. Please see Threads and Swing (page 45) for more information.

An application's GUI can often be constructed and shown in the main thread.
As long as no Swing or other components have been realized in the current runtime environment, it's fine to construct and show a GUI in the main thread of an application. To help you see why, here's an analysis of the thread safety of the thread-safe example. To refresh your memory, here are the important lines from the example:

```
public static void main(String[] args) {
    JFrame f = new JFrame(...);
    ...//Add components to the frame here...
    f.pack();
    f.setVisible(true);
    //Don't do any more GUI work here.
}
```

1. The example constructs the GUI in the main thread. In general, you can construct (but not show) a GUI in any thread, as long as you don't make any calls that refer to or affect already realized components.

2. The components in the GUI are realized by the `pack` call.

3. Immediately afterward the components in the GUI are shown with the `setVisible` (or `show`) call. Technically the `setVisible` call is unsafe, because the components have already been realized by the `pack` call. However, because the program doesn't already have a visible GUI, it's exceedingly unlikely that a paint request will occur before `setVisible` returns.

4. The main thread executes no GUI code after the `setVisible` call. This means that all GUI work moves from the main thread to the event-dispatching thread, and the example is, in practice, thread safe.

An applet's GUI can be constructed and shown in the `init` method.
Existing browsers don't paint an applet until after its `init` and `start` methods have been called. Thus constructing the GUI in the applet's `init` method is safe, as long as you never call `show()` or `setVisible(true)` on the applet object.

These `JComponent` methods are safe to call from any thread: `repaint` and `revalidate`.
These methods queue requests to be executed on the event-dispatching thread.

Listener lists can be modified from any thread.
It's always safe to call the add*ListenerType*Listener and remove*ListenerType*Listener methods. The add/remove operations have no effect on an event dispatch that's under way.

How to Execute Code in the Event-Dispatching Thread

Most postinitialization GUI work naturally occurs in the event-dispatching thread. Once the GUI is visible, most programs are driven by events, such as button actions or mouse clicks, which are always handled in the event-dispatching thread.

However, some programs need to perform nonevent-driven GUI work after the GUI is visible. Here are two examples.

Programs that must perform a lengthy initialization operation before they can be used
This kind of program should generally show some GUI while the initialization is occurring and then update or change the GUI. The initialization should *not* occur in the event-dispatching thread; otherwise repainting and event dispatching would stop. However, after initialization the GUI update or change *should* occur in the event-dispatching thread, for thread-safety reasons.

Programs whose GUI must be updated as the result of nonstandard events

For example, suppose that a server program can get requests from other programs that might be running on different machines. These requests can come at any time, and they result in one of the server's methods being invoked in a possibly unknown thread. How can that method update the GUI? By executing the GUI-update code in the event-dispatching thread.

The `SwingUtilities`[1] class provides two methods to help you run code in the event-dispatching thread:

invokeLater

Requests that some code be executed in the event-dispatching thread. This method returns immediately, without waiting for the code to execute.

invokeAndWait

Acts like `invokeLater`, except that this method waits for the code to execute. As a rule, you should use `invokeLater` rather than this method.

For information on using `invokeLater` and `invokeAndWait`, and for other tips on writing multithreaded programs, see How to Use Threads (page 431).

---

[1] API documentation for this class is available on the CD-ROM that accompanies this book and online here:
http://java.sun.com/products/jdk/1.2/docs/api/javax/swing/SwingUtilities.html

More Swing Features and Concepts

THIS chapter has discussed some of the major concepts you need to know to build Swing GUIs—the containment hierarchy, layout management, event handling, painting, and threads. Along the way, we touched on related topics, such as borders. This chapter tells you about some of the other Swing features.

Features that JComponent Provides

Except for the top-level containers, all components that begin with J inherit from the JComponent class. They get many features from JComponent, such as the ability to have borders, tool tips, and a configurable look and feel. These components also inherit many convenient methods. For JComponent details, see The JComponent Class (page 67).

Icons

Many Swing components—notably buttons and labels—can display images.You specify these images as Icon objects. See How to Use Icons (page 417) for instructions and a list of examples that use icons.

Actions

With Action objects, the Swing API provides special support for sharing data and state between two or more components that can generate action events. For example, if you have a button and a menu item that perform the same function, consider using an `Action` object to coordinate the text, icon, and enabled state for the two components. For details, see How to Use Actions (page 389).

Pluggable Look & Feel

A single program can have any one of several looks and feels. You can let the user determine the look and feel, or you can specify the look and feel programatically. See How to Set the Look and Feel (page 428) for details.

Support for Assistive Technologies

Assistive technologies, such as screen readers, can use the Accessibility API to get information from Swing components. Because support for the Accessibility API is built into the Swing components, your Swing program will probably work just fine with assistive technologies, even if you do nothing special. With very little extra effort, however, you can make your program function even more smoothly with assistive technologies, which might well expand its market. See How to Support Assistive Technologies (page 393) for details.

Separate Data and State Models

Most noncontainer Swing components have models. A button (`JButton`), for example, has a model (`ButtonModel`) that stores the button's state—what its keyboard mnemonic is, whether it's enabled, selected, or pressed, and so on. Some components have multiple models. A list (`JList`), for example, uses a `ListModel` to hold the list's contents and a `ListSelectionModel` to track the list's current selection.

You don't usually need to know about the models that a component uses. For example, almost all programs that use buttons deal directly with the `JButton` object and don't deal at all with the `ButtonModel` object.

Why, then, do separate models exist? Because they give you the ability to work with components more efficiently and to easily share data and state between components. One common case is when a component, such as a list or table, contains lots of data. It can be much faster to a customized data model than to have a component store a copy of the data. For information about models, see the how-to pages for individual components. Also, the next chapter discusses some custom models used by that section's featured program, `Converter`.

The Anatomy of a Swing-Based Program

THIS chapter picks apart a program, called Converter, that has a Swing-based GUI. You can see how this program is implemented by looking at its source code, which is mainly in <u>Converter.java</u> (page 614) and <u>ConversionPanel.java</u> (page 612).[1] However, this chapter doesn't talk about individual lines of code, but concentrates on how the Converter program uses the GUI features provided by the Swing packages. If you get lost while looking at the Converter source code, you might want to refresh your memory by going to <u>A Quick Tour of a Swing Application's Code</u> (page 19).

The Converter is an application that converts distance measurements between metric and U.S. units. To run it, compile the following seven source files: Converter.java, ConversionPanel.java, ConverterRangeModel.java, FollowerRangeModel.java, DecimalField.java, FormattedDocument.java, and Unit.java. Once you've compiled the program, run it by invoking the interpreter on the Converter class. If you need help compiling or running Converter, see <u>Compiling and Running Swing Programs</u> (page 11).

Figure 13 shows an annotated snapshot of Converter's GUI.

---

[1] You can find the source files in the Code Appendix. You can also get them from the CD-ROM or the online tutorial by following this links from the HTML version of this chapter: http://java.sun.com/docs/books/tutorial/uiswing/overview/anatomy.html

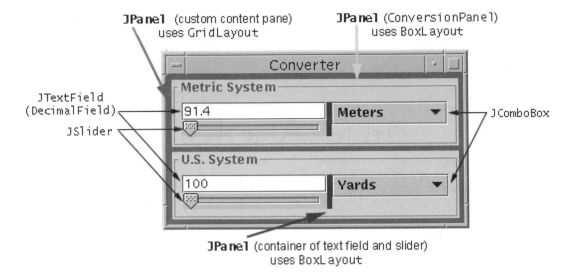

Figure 13 An annotated snapshot of the Converter's GUI.

Swing Components

As the preceding figure shows, Converter has the following visible components:

- One JFrame
- Two custom JPanels
- Two custom JTextFields
- Two JSliders
- Two JComboBoxes

The JFrame, the top-level container, provides the only window in the application. All of the other components in the application are contained by the JFrame.

Except for the top-level container, all of the visible components in Converter inherit from JComponent. The JComponent class provides such features as support for borders and accessibility. The two custom JPanels shown in the snapshot use the border support to provide titles (for example, "Metric System") and to paint boxes around themselves.

The Containment Hierarchy

The following figure shows the containment hierarchy for the JFrame.

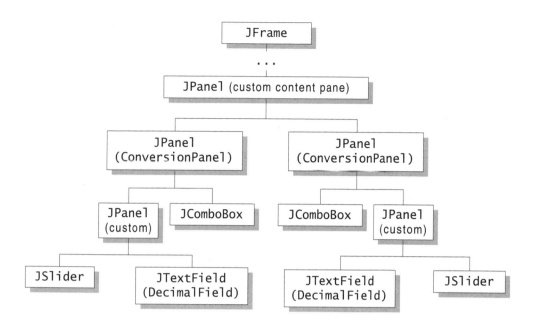

Figure 14 JFrame's containment hierarchy.

This diagram shows three components not labeled in Figure 13 because they don't paint anything noticeable on-screen:

- One JPanel that serves as the content pane
- Two custom JPanels that each hold a text field and a slider

These three components exist to affect layout. They do this either by simplifying layout or by adding "empty" borders that add space to the layout. Grouping components—whether in visible or invisible containers—also provides hints to assistive technologies. For example, grouping a text field and a slider in their own container gives assistive technologies the information that the text field and the slider might be closely related.

Under the content pane are two ConversionPanels. One holds the components related to metric distances; the other does the same for U.S. distances.

Each ConversionPanel contains three visible components: a text field, a slider, and a combo box. The text field and the slider are grouped together in a JPanel mainly to make layout simpler.

Layout Management and Borders

Figure 15 shows a shaded version of `Converter`. In this version each container has a background shade, so that you can easily see the parts of the containers that aren't covered by other components. Note that all of the containers are opaque; otherwise, the background shade would not automatically be painted for the container.

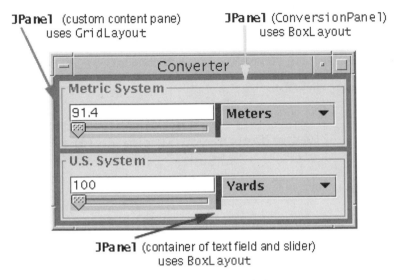

Figure 15 Shaded version of `Converter` with `JPanel`s labeled.

The `Converter` application creates five layout manager objects—one instance of `GridLayout` and four of `BoxLayout`.

The first `JPanel` (the custom content pane) uses `GridLayout` to make the `Conversion-Panel`s exactly equal in size. The code sets up the `GridLayout` so that it puts the `ConversionPanel`s in a single column (two rows), with five pixels between components. The `JPanel` is initialized to have an empty border that adds five pixels between the panel and the sides of the frame.

Each `ConversionPanel` has a compound border. On the outside is a titled border, and on the inside is an empty border. The titled border paints a look-and-feel-specific box around the `ConversionPanel` and places the panel's title in the box. The empty border puts some more space between the `ConversionPanel` and its contents.

Each `ConversionPanel` uses a `BoxLayout` manager to place its contents, a `JPanel` and a `JComboBox`, in a row. By setting the *Y* alignment of both the panel and the combo box, the program aligns the top of the panel with the top of the combo box.

The JPanel that groups the text field and the slider is implemented with an unnamed subclass of JPanel. This subclass overrides the getMinimumSize, getPreferredSize, and getMaximumSize methods so that they all return the same value: 150 pixels wide and the preferred height. This is how we ensure that both text-slider groups have the same width, even though they're controlled by different layout managers. We need to create a subclass of JPanel, instead of just calling the setXxxxSize methods, because the preferred height of components is determined at runtime, by the layout manager.

The JPanel that groups the text field and the slider uses a top-to-bottom BoxLayout manager so that the text field is placed on top of the slider. This panel also has an empty border that adds a bit of space to its right, between it and the combo box.

Separate Models

This program uses three custom models. The first is a data model for the text fields. Text data models are known as *document models*. The document model parses the value that the user enters into the text field and formats the number so that it looks nice. We borrowed this document model, without changing it, from the example presented in <u>Creating a Validated Text Field</u> (page 299).

The other two custom models are slider data models. They ensure that the data displayed by the application is kept in only one place—in the model for the top slider. The top slider's model is an instance of a custom class called ConverterRangeModel. The bottom slider uses a second custom class, FollowerRangeModel, which forwards all requests to get and set data to the top slider's model.

All slider data models must implement the BoundedRangeModel interface. We learned this by looking at the API section of <u>How to Use Sliders</u> (page 248). The API documentation for <u>BoundedRangeModel</u>[1] tells us that the interface has an implementing class named Default-BoundedRangeModel. The API documentation for <u>DefaultBoundedRangeModel</u>[2] shows that it's a general-purpose implementation of BoundedRangeModel.

We didn't use DefaultBoundedRangeModel directly, because it stores data as integers, and we need to store floating-point data. Thus we implemented ConverterRangeModel as a subclass of Object, checking it against the DefaultBoundedRangeModel source code (distributed with the JFC 1.1 and Java 2 SDK releases), to make sure that we implemented the model correctly. We then implemented FollowerRangeModel as a subclass of Converter-RangeModel.

---

[1] API documentation for this class is available on this book's CD-ROM and online at http://java.sun.com/products/jdk/1.2/docs/api/javax/swing/BoundedRangeModel.html

[2] http://java.sun.com/products/jdk/1.2/docs/api/javax/swing/DefaultBoundedRangeModel.html

Look and Feel

The Converter program sets itself up to use the Java Look & Feel. By changing the value of its LOOKANDFEEL variable, you can make it use a different look and feel. Three of its incarnations are pictured in Figure 1 (page 6).

Event Handling

The Converter program creates several event handlers.

Action listeners

Each combo box has an action listener. Whenever the user selects a new unit of measure, the action listener notifies the relevant slider's model and resets the maximum values of both sliders.

Each text field has an action listener that's notified when the user presses Return to indicate that typing has ended. This action listener updates the corresponding slider's model to reflect the text field's value.

Change listeners

Each slider model has a custom change listener. Whenever a slider's value changes, the custom change listener updates the appropriate text field. We didn't have to register the sliders as listeners on their own models, since Swing automatically does so. In other words, whenever a program sets a value in a slider's model, that slider is automatically updated to reflect the model's new state.

The model for the bottom slider adds a change listener to the top slider's model. This change listener fires a change event to the bottom slider model's change listeners, which are the bottom slider and the custom change listener described in the previous paragraph. The effect is that when the top slider's value changes, the value displayed in the bottom slider and the text field is updated. It isn't necessary to notify the top slider of changes in the bottom slider, since the bottom slider's model forwards all data-setting requests to the top slider's model.

Window listener

A window listener on the frame causes the application to exit when the window is closed.

Using Swing Components

THIS lesson describes every Swing component. All of the chapters in this lesson assume that you've successfully compiled and run a program that uses Swing components and that you're familiar with Swing concepts. These prerequisites are covered in <u>Getting Started with Swing</u> (page 3) and <u>Features and Concepts</u> (page 25).

<u>A Visual Index to Swing Components</u> (page 63)
This chapter has a picture of each Swing component, from top-level containers to intermediate containers to atomic components. The chapter in which the component is discussed is listed below the component's picture.

<u>The JComponent Class</u> (page 67)
Almost all Swing components inherit from the JComponent class. This chapter tells you about the features JComponent provides and gives tips on how to take advantage of those features.

<u>Using Top-Level Containers</u> (page 77)
This chapter discusses how to create windows and applets.

<u>Using Intermediate Swing Containers</u> (page 105)
This chapter discusses how to use intermediate containers to group or to add features to other components.

<u>Using Atomic Components</u> (page 167)
This chapter discusses the rest of the Swing components, which are generally the ones that users interact with when using your GUI.

57

12

A Visual Index to Swing Components

T HIS chapter gives a quick, visual reference of the Swing components. The components are broken down into six categories: top-level containers, general-purpose containers, special-purpose containers, basic controls, uneditable information displays, and editable displays of formatted information.

Top-Level Containers

The components at the top of any Swing containment hierarchy.

Applet **Dialog** **Frame**

   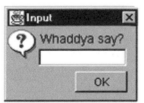 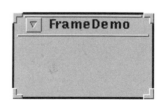

see How to Make Applets *see* How to Make Dialogs *see* How to Make Frames
(page 99) (page 87) (page 82)

General-Purpose Containers

Intermediate containers that can be used under many different circumstances.

Panel

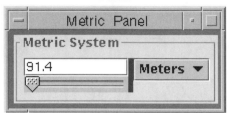

see <u>How to Use Panels</u> (page 107)

Scroll Pane

see <u>How to Use Scroll Panes</u> (page 112)

Split Pane

see <u>How to Use Split Panes</u>
(page 127)

Tabbed Pane

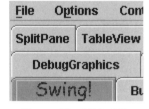

see <u>How to Use Tabbed Panes</u>
(page 134)

Tool Bar

see <u>How to Use Tool Bars</u> (page 138)

Special-Purpose Containers

Intermediate containers that play specific roles in the UI.

Internal Frame

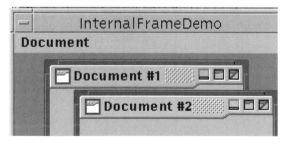

see <u>How to Use Internal Frames</u> (page 143)

Layered Pane

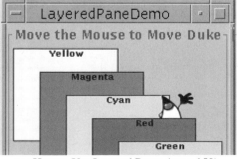

see <u>How to Use Layered Panes</u> (page 150)

Root Pane (representation)

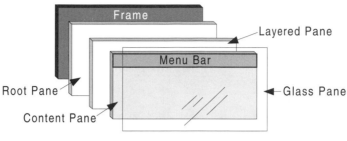

see How to Use Root Panes (page 158)

Basic Controls

Atomic components that exist primarily to get input from the user; they generally also show simple state.

Buttons

see How to Use Buttons, Check Boxes, and Radio Buttons (page 169)

Combo Box

see How to Use Combo Boxes (page 192)

List

see How to Use Lists (page 218)

Menu

see How to Use Menus (page 226)

Slider

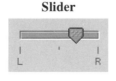

see How to Use Sliders (page 248)

Text Fields

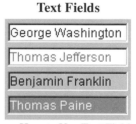

see How to Use Text Fields (page 298)

Uneditable Information Displays

Atomic components that exist solely to give the user information.

Label	Progress Bar	Tool Tip

see <u>How to Use Labels</u> (page 212)   *see* <u>How to Monitor Progress</u> (page 239)   *see* <u>How to Use Tool Tips</u> (page 317)

Editable Displays of Formatted Information

Atomic components that display highly formatted information that (if you choose) can be edited by the user.

Color Chooser	File Chooser

see <u>How to Use Color Choosers</u> (page 184)   *see* <u>How to Use File Choosers</u> (page 200)

Table	Text	Tree

First Na...	Last Name
Mark	Andrews
Tom	Ball
Alan	Chung
Jeff	Dinkins

With *styled text*, you can have multiple fonts, styles, colors, and **extras** such as embedded pictures and components.

see <u>How to Use Tables</u> (page 254)   *see* <u>How to Use Text Components</u> (page 275)   *see* <u>How to Use Trees</u> (page 320)

13

The JComponent Class

WITH the exception of top-level containers, all Swing components whose names begin with "J" descend from the JComponent[1] class. For example, JPanel, JScroll-Pane, JButton, and JTable all inherit from JComponent. However, JFrame doesn't, because it implements a top-level container.

Note: A few Swing components aren't top-level containers and yet don't inherit from JComponent. The one you're most likely to need is the Box.Filler class, which is a non-painting component designed for use with BoxLayout. The Box.Filler class doesn't inherit from JComponent, because it is so specialized that it needs no JComponent features, and because it is instantiated so often that it should be as small and as fast as possible.

The JComponent class extends the Container[2] class, which itself extends Component.[3] The Component class includes everything from providing layout hints to supporting painting and events. The Container class has support for adding components to the container and laying them out. This chapter's API tables, starting on pa ge70, summarize the most often used methods of Component and Container. Information about how to use the methods is scattered throughout this lesson.

---

[1] API documentation for JComponent is available on this book's CD-ROM and online at
   http://java.sun.com/products/jdk/1.2/docs/api/javax/swing/JComponent.html
[2] http://java.sun.com/products/jdk/1.2/docs/api/java/awt/Container.html
[3] http://java.sun.com/products/jdk/1.2/docs/api/java/awt/Component.html

JComponent Features

The JComponent class provides the following functionality to its descendants:

- Tool tips
- Borders
- Keyboard-generated actions
- Applicationwide Pluggable Look & Feel
- Properties
- Support for layout
- Support for accessibility
- Double buffering
- Methods to increase efficiency

Tool tips

By specifying a string with the setToolTipText method, you can provide help to users of a component. When the cursor pauses over the component, the specified string is displayed in a small window that appears near the component. See How to Use Tool Tips (page 317) for more information.

Borders

The setBorder method allows you to specify the border that a component displays around its edges. See How to Use Borders (page 408) for details.

Keyboard-generated actions

Using the registerKeyboardAction method, you can enable the user to use the keyboard, instead of the mouse, to operate the GUI.

Note: Some classes provide convenience methods for keyboard actions. For example, AbstractButton provides setMnemonic, which lets you specify the character that, in combination with a look-and-feel-specific modifier key, causes the button's action to be performed. See How to Use Buttons, Check Boxes, and Radio Buttons (page 169) for an example of using mnemonics in buttons.

The combination of character and modifier keys that the user must press to start an action is represented by a KeyStroke[1] object. The resulting action event must be handled by an action listener. Each keyboard action works under one of three conditions: only

---

[1] API documentation for KeyStroke is available on this book's CD-ROM and online at http://java.sun.com/products/jdk/1.2/docs/api/javax/swing/KeyStroke.html

when the component has the focus, only when the component or one of its containers has the focus, or any time that anything in the component's window has the focus.

Applicationwide pluggable look and feel

Behind the scenes, each `JComponent` object has a corresponding `ComponentUI` object that performs all of the drawing, event handling, size determination, and so on, for that `JComponent`. Exactly which `ComponentUI` object is used depends on the current look and feel, which you can set by using the `UIManager.setLookAndFeel` method. See How to Set the Look and Feel (page 428) for details.

Properties

You can associate one or more properties (name/object pairs) with any `JComponent`. For example, a layout manager might use properties to associate a `constraints` object with each `JComponent` it manages. You put and get properties by using the `putClientProperty` and `getClientProperty` methods. For general information about properties, see the section "Using Properties to Manage Program Attributes" in the trail "Essential Java Classes" in the book *The Java™ Tutorial, Second Edition,* and online at `http://java.sun.com/docs/books/tutorial/essential/attributes/properties.html`

Support for layout

Although the `Component` class provides layout hint methods, such as `getPreferredSize` and `getAlignmentX`, it doesn't provide any way to set these layout hints, short of creating a subclass and overriding the methods. To give you another way to set layout hints, the `JComponent` class adds setter methods—`setPreferredSize`, `setMinimumSize`, `setMaximumSize`, `setAlignmentX`, and `setAlignmentY`. See Layout Management (page 33) for more information.

Support for accessibility

The `JComponent` class provides API and basic functionality to help assistive technologies, such as screen readers, get information from Swing components. For more information about accessibility, see How to Support Assistive Technologies (page 393).

Double buffering

Double buffering smooths onscreen painting. For details, see Painting (page 41).

Methods to increase efficiency

`JComponent` has a few methods that provide more efficient ways to get information than the JDK 1.1 API allowed. The methods include `getX` and `getY`, which you can use instead of `getLocation`, and `getWidth` and `getHeight`, which you can use instead of `getSize`. `JComponent` also adds one-argument forms of `getBounds`, `getLocation`, and `getSize`; you specify the object to be modified and returned, thereby avoiding unnecessary object creation. These methods have been added to `Component` for the Java 2 Platform (JDK 1.2).

The JComponent API

The `JComponent` class provides many new methods and inherits many methods from `Component` and `Container`. The following tables summarize the methods we use the most. The tables are for reference only. Wherever possible, we provide links to where the API is discussed in more detail.

Table 4   Customizing Component Appearance

Method	Purpose

`void setBorder(Border)`
`Border getBorder()`
(*in JComponent*)
	Set or get the border of the component. See How to Use Borders (page 408) for details.

`void setForeground(Color)`
`Color getForeground()`
`void setBackground(Color)`
`Color getBackground()`
(*in java.awt.Component*)
	Set or get the foreground or background color for the component. The foreground is generally the color used to draw the text in a component. The background is (not surprisingly) the color of the background areas of the component, assuming that the component is opaque.

`void setOpaque(boolean)` (*in JComponent*)	Set whether the component is opaque. An opaque component fills its background with its background color.
`boolean isOpaque` (*in JComponent*)	Get whether the component is opaque. This method (but not `setOpaque`) was added to `Component` in Java 2.

`void setFont(Font)`
`Font getFont()`
(*in java.awt.Component*)
	Set or get the component's font. If a font has not been set for the component, the font of its parent is returned.

`FontMetrics getFontMetrics(Font)` (*in java.awt.Component*)	Get the font metrics for the specified font.

Table 5   Setting Component State

Method	Purpose
`void setToolTipText(String)` (*in JComponent*)	Set the text to display in a tool tip. See How to Use Tool Tips (page 317) for more information.

`void setEnabled(boolean b)`
`boolean isEnabled()`
(*in java.awt.Component*)
	Set or get whether the component is enabled. An enabled component can respond to user input and generate events.

Table 5   Setting Component State

Method	Purpose
void setLocale(Locale l) Locale getLocale() (*in* java.awt.Component)	Set or get the component's locale. If the component does not have a locale, the locale of its parent is returned. See the Internalization trail in *The Java Tutorial Continued* for information about locales. This trail is also available in HTML on this book's CD-ROM and online at http://java.sun.com/docs/books/tutorial/i18n/index.html
void setCursor(Cursor) Cursor getCursor() (*in* java.awt.Component)	Set or get the cursor image to display when the mouse is over the component.
void setVisible(boolean) boolean isVisible() (*in* java.awt.Component)	Set or get whether the component is visible. Components are initially visible, with the exception of top-level components.

Table 6   Handling Events

Method	Purpose
void addComponentListener(ComponentListener) void removeComponentListener(ComponentListener) (*in* java.awt.Component)	Add or remove a component listener to or from the component. Component listeners are notified when the listened-to component is hidden, shown, moved, or resized.
void addKeyListener(KeyListener) void removeKeyListener(KeyListener l) (*in* java.awt.Component)	Add or remove a key listener to or from the component. Key listeners are notified when the user types at the keyboard and the listened-to component has the keyboard focus.
addMouseListener(MouseListener l) void removeMouseListener(MouseListener) (*in* java.awt.Component)	Add or remove a mouse listener to or from the component. Mouse listeners are notified when the user uses the mouse to interact with the listened-to component.

void addMouseMotionListener(
    MouseMotionListener)
void removeMouseMotionListener(
    MouseMotionListener)
(*in* java.awt.Component)
	Add or remove a mouse-motion listener to or from the component. Mouse-motion listeners are notified when the user moves the mouse within the listened-to component's bounds.

void addContainerListener(ContainerListener) void removeContainerListener(ContainerListener) (*in* java.awt.Container)	Add or remove a container listener to or from the container. Container listeners are notified when a component is added to or removed from the listened-to container.
void addFocusListener(FocusListener) void removeFocusListener(FocusListener) (*in* java.awt.Component)	Add or remove a focus listener to or from the component. Focus listeners are notified when the listened-to component gains or loses keyboard focus.

Table 6   Handling Events

Method	Purpose

`Component getNextFocusableComponent()`
`void setNextFocusableComponent(Component)`
(*in JComponent*)
	Set or get the next focusable component: `null` indicates that the focus manager should choose the next focusable component automatically.

`void requestFocus()`
`boolean hasFocus()`
(*in java.awt.Component*)
	Request that the component get the keyboard focus or detect whether it has the focus.

`boolean contains(int, int)`
`boolean contains(Point p)`
(*in java.awt.Component*)
	Determine whether the specified point is within the component. The argument should be specified in terms of the component's coordinate system. The two `int` arguments specify *x* and *y* coordinates, respectively.

`Component getComponentAt(int, int)` (*in java.awt.Container*)	Return the component that contains the specified *x*, *y* position. The top-most child component is returned in the case where components overlap. This is determined by finding the component closest to the index 0 that claims to contain the given point via `Component.contains()`.

Table 7   Painting Components *see* Painting (page 41) *for details*

Method	Purpose

`void repaint()`
`void repaint(int, int, int, int)`
(*in java.awt.Component*)
	Request that all or part of the component be repainted. The four `int` arguments specify the bounds (*x*, *y*, width, height, in that order) of the rectangle to be painted.

`void repaint(Rectangle)` (*in JComponent*)	Repaint the specified area within the component.
`void revalidate()` (*in JComponent*)	Request that the component and its affected containers be laid out again. You shouldn't generally need to invoke this method unless you explicitly change a component's size/alignment hints after it's visible, change a containment hierarchy after it's visible, or perhaps change the data in a component's model directly (without going through the component's API). You might need to invoke `repaint` after `revalidate`.
`void paintComponent(Graphics)` (*in JComponent*)	Paint the component. Override this method to implement painting for custom components.

Table 8   Dealing with the Containment Hierarchy
see <u>Components and Containment Hierarchies</u> (page 29) *for more information*

Method	Purpose

`Component add(Component)`
`Component add(Component, int)`
`void add(Component, Object)`
(*in java.awt.Container*)
	Add the specified component to the container. The one-argument version of this method adds the component to the end of the container. When present, the `int` argument indicates the new component's position within the container. When present, the `Object` argument provides layout constraints to the current layout manager.

`void remove(int)`
`void remove(Component comp)`
`void removeAll()`
(*in java.awt.Container*)
	Remove one or all of the components from the container. When present, the `int` argument indicates the position within the container of the component to remove.

`JRootPane getRootPane()` (*in JComponent*)	Get the component's root pane ancestor.
`Container getParent()` (*in java.awt.Component*)	Get the component's parent.
`int getComponentCount()` (*in java.awt.Container*)	Get the number of components in the container.

`Component getComponent(int)`
`Component[] getComponents()`
(*in java.awt.Container*)
	Get one or all of the components in the container. The `int` argument indicates the position of the component to get.

Table 9   Laying Out Components
see <u>Laying Out Components</u> (page 341) *for more information*

Method	Purpose

`void setPreferredSize(Dimension)`
`void setMaximumSize(Dimension)`
`void setMinimumSize(Dimension)`
(*in JComponent*)
	Set the component's preferred, maximum, or minimum size, measured in pixels. The preferred size indicates the best size for the component. The component should be no larger than its maximum size and no smaller than its minimum size. Be aware that these are hints only and might be ignored by certain layout managers.

`Dimension getPreferredSize()`
`Dimension getMaximumSize()`
`Dimension getMinimumSize()`
(*in java.awt.Component*)
	Get the preferred, maximum, or minimum size of the component, measured in pixels. For non-`JComponent` subclasses, which don't have the corresponding setter methods, you can set a component's preferred, maximum, or minimum size by creating a subclass and overriding these methods.

Table 9   Laying Out Components

see <u>Laying Out Components</u> (page 341) *for more information*

Method	Purpose
void setAlignmentX(float) void setAlignmentY(float) (*in JComponent*)	Set the alignment along the *x*- or *y*-axis. These values indicate how the component would like to be aligned relative to other components. The value should be a number between 0 and 1, where 0 represents alignment along the origin, 1 is aligned the farthest away from the origin, 0.5 is centered, and so on. Be aware that these are hints only and might be ignored by certain layout managers.
float getAlignmentX() float getAlignmentY() (*in java.awt.Component*)	Get the preferred, maximum, or minimum size of the component. For non-JComponent subclasses, which don't have the corresponding setter methods, you can set a component's preferred, maximum, or minimum size by creating a subclass and overriding these methods.
void setLayout(LayoutManager) LayoutManager getLayout() (*in java.awt.Container*)	Set or get the component's layout manager. The layout manager is responsible for sizing and positioning the components within a container.

Table 10   Getting Size and Position Information

Method	Purpose
int getWidth() int getHeight() (*in java.awt.Component*)	Get the current width or height of the component, measured in pixels.
Dimension getSize() Dimension getSize(Dimension) (*in java.awt.Component*)	Get the component's current size, measured in pixels. When using the one-argument version of this method, the caller is responsible for creating the Dimension instance in which the result is returned.
int getX() int getY() (*in java.awt.Component*)	Get the current *x* or *y* coordinate of the component's origin relative to the parent's upper-left corner, measured in pixels.
Rectangle getBounds() Rectangle getBounds(Rectangle) (*in java.awt.Component*)	Get the bounds of the component, measured in pixels. The bounds specify the component's width, height, and origin relative to its parent. When using the one-argument version of this method, the caller is responsible for creating the Rectangle instance in which the result is returned.

Table 10   Getting Size and Position Information

Method	Purpose

`Point getLocation()`
`Point getLocation(Point)`
`Point getLocationOnScreen()`
(*in java.awt.Component*)
	Get the current location of the component relative to the parent's upper-left corner, measured in pixels. When using the one-argument version of `getLocation` method, the caller is responsible for creating the `Point` instance in which the result is returned. The `getLocationOnScreen` method returns the position relative to the upper-left corner of the screen.

`Insets getInsets()` (*in java.awt.Container*)	Get the insets of the component.

Table 11   Specifying Absolute Size and Position
see <u>Doing Without a Layout Manager (Absolute Positioning)</u> (page 383) *for more information*

Method	Purpose

`void setLocation(int, int)`
`void setLocation(Point)`
(*in java.awt.Component*)
	Set the location of the component, in pixels, relative to the parent's upper-left corner. The two `int` arguments specify *x* and *y*, in that order. Use these methods to position a component when you aren't using a layout manager.

`void setSize(int, int)`
`void setSize(Dimension)`
(*in java.awt.Component*)
	Set the size of the component, measured in pixels. The two `int` arguments specify width and height, in that order. Use these methods to size a component when you aren't using a layout manager.

`void setBounds(int, int,`
`                int, int)`
`void setBounds(Rectangle)`
(*in java.awt.Component*)
	Set the size and location of the component relative to the parent's upper-left corner, in pixels. The four `int` arguments specify *x*, *y*, width, and height, in that order. Use these methods to position and size a component when you aren't using a layout manager.

Using Top-Level Containers

BEFORE you try to use a top-level container, you should read and understand <u>Components and Containment Hierarchies</u> (page 29). In particular, you should know these facts:

- Swing provides three generally useful top-level container classes: `JFrame`,[1] `JDialog`,[2] and `JApplet`.[3]

Note: Swing contains a fourth top-level container, `JWindow`, which we don't cover because it isn't generally useful. `JWindow` is the Swing version of the AWT `Window` class, which provides a window with no controls or title that is always on top of every other window.

Swing also provides an intermediate container, `JInternalFrame`,[4] that mimics a frame. However, internal frames aren't top-level containers.

- To appear onscreen, every GUI component must be part of a containment hierarchy. Each containment hierarchy has a top-level container as its root.
- Each top-level container has a content pane that, generally speaking, contains the visible components in that top-level container's GUI.
- You can optionally add a menu bar to a top-level container. The menu bar is positioned within the top-level container but outside the content pane.

---

[1] API documentation for this class is available on this book's CD-ROM and online at
http://java.sun.com/products/jdk/1.2/docs/api/javax/swing/JFrame.html
[2] http://java.sun.com/products/jdk/1.2/docs/api/javax/swing/JDialog.html
[3] http://java.sun.com/products/jdk/1.2/docs/api/javax/swing/JApplet.html
[4] http://java.sun.com/products/jdk/1.2/docs/api/javax/swing/JInternalFrame.html

Here's a picture of a frame created by an application. The frame contains an empty menu bar and, in the frame's content pane, a large label.

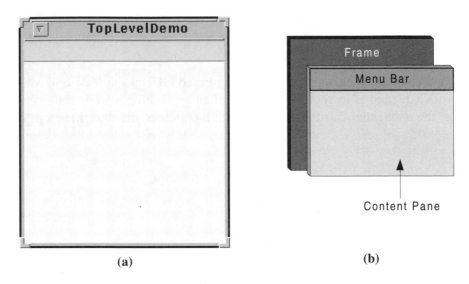

         (a)   **(b)**

Figure 16 (a) A simple application with a frame that contains a menu bar and a content pane.
      (b) The frame's contents.

You can find the entire source for this example in `TopLevelDemo.java` (page 762). Although the example uses a `JFrame`, the same concepts apply to `JApplets` and to `JDialogs`.

Here's the containment hierarchy for this example's GUI.

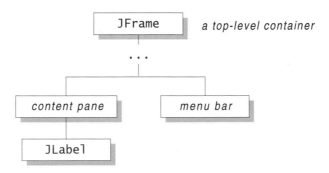

Figure 17 Containment hierarchy for example's GUI.

As the ellipses imply, we left some details out of this diagram. We reveal the missing details a bit later.

Top-Level Containers and Containment Hierarchies

Each program that uses Swing components has at least one top-level container. This top-level container is the root of a containment hierarchy—the hierarchy that contains all of the Swing components that appear inside the top-level container.

As a rule, a standalone application with a Swing-based GUI has at least one containment hierarchy with a JFrame as its root. For example, if an application has one main window and two dialogs, the application has three containment hierarchies and thus three top-level containers. One containment hierarchy has a JFrame as its root, and each of the other two has a JDialog object as its root.

A Swing-based applet has at least one containment hierarchy, exactly one of which is rooted by a JApplet object. For example, an applet that brings up a dialog has two containment hierarchies. The components in the browser window are in a containment hierarchy rooted by a JApplet object. The dialog has a containment hierarchy rooted by a JDialog object.

Adding Components to the Content Pane

Here's the code that the preceding example uses to get a frame's content pane and to add the yellow label to it:

```
frame.getContentPane().add(yellowLabel, BorderLayout.CENTER);
```

As the code shows, you find the content pane of a top-level container by calling the getContentPane method. The default content pane is a simple intermediate container that inherits from JComponent and that uses a BorderLayout as its layout manager.

It's easy to customize the content pane—setting the layout manager or adding a border, for example. However, there is one tiny gotcha. The getContentPane method returns a Container object, not a JComponent object. This means that if you want to take advantage of the content pane's JComponent features, you need to either typecast the return value or create your own component to be the content pane. Our examples generally take the second approach, since it's a little cleaner. Another approach we sometimes take is to simply add a customized component to the content pane, covering the content pane completely.

If you create your own content pane, make sure that it's opaque. A JPanel object makes a good content pane because it's simple and it's opaque, by default. Note that the default layout manager for JPanel is FlowLayout; you'll probably want to change it. To make a component the content pane, use the top-level container's setContentPane method. For example:

```
JPanel contentPane = new JPanel();
contentPane.setLayout(new BorderLayout());
contentPane.setBorder(someBorder);
contentPane.add(someComponent, BorderLayout.CENTER);
contentPane.add(anotherComponent, BorderLayout.SOUTH);
topLevelContainer.setContentPane(contentPane);
```

Note: Don't use nonopaque containers, such as `JScrollPane`, `JSplitPane`, and `JTabbed-Pane`, as content panes. A nonopaque content pane results in messy repaints. Although you can make any Swing component opaque by invoking `setOpaque(true)` on it, some components don't look right when they're completely opaque. For example, tabbed panes generally let part of the underlying container show through, so that the tabs look nonrectangular. So an opaque tabbed pane just tends to look bad.

Adding a Menu Bar

All top-level containers can, in theory, have a menu bar. In practice, however, menu bars usually appear only in frames and perhaps in applets. To add a menu bar to a frame or an applet, you create a `JMenuBar` object, populate it with menus, and then call `setJMenuBar`. The `TopLevelDemo` adds a menu bar to its frame with this code:

```
frame.setJMenuBar(cyanMenuBar);
```

For more information about implementing menus and menu bars, see How to Use Menus (page 226).

The Root Pane

Each top-level container relies on a reclusive intermediate container called the *root pane*. The root pane manages the content pane and the menu bar, along with a couple of other containers. You generally don't need to know about root panes to use Swing components. However, if you ever need to intercept mouse clicks or paint over multiple components, you should get acquainted with root panes.

Here's a glimpse at the components that a root pane provides to a frame (and to every other top-level container).

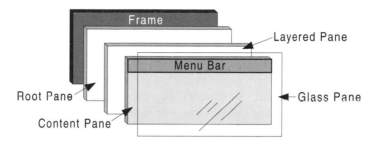

Figure 18 A representation of the components that a root pane provides to a frame.

We've already told you about the content pane and the optional menu bar. The two other components that a root pane adds are a layered pane and a glass pane. The layered pane contains the menu bar and the content pane and enables Z-ordering of other components you might add. The glass pane is often used to intercept input events occurring over the top-level container and can also be used to paint over multiple components.

For more information about the intricacies of root panes, see How to Use Root Panes (page 158).

How to Make Frames

A frame, implemented as an instance of the `JFrame`[1] class, is a window that has decorations, such as a border, a title, and buttons for closing and iconifying the window. Applications with a GUI typically use at least one frame. Applets also sometimes use frames.

To make a window that's dependent on another window—disappearing when the other window is iconified, for example—use a <u>dialog</u> (page 87) instead of a frame. To make a window that appears within another window, use an <u>internal frame</u> (page 143).

Here are two pictures of an empty-looking frame, each taken on a different platform.

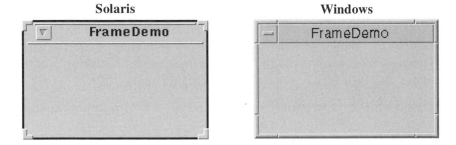

Figure 19 Screenshots of the `FrameDemo` on both Solaris and Windows platforms.

Note: The decorations on a frame are platform-dependent. You cannot change the decorations on a frame.

The Example Explained

The following code creates and sets up the frame from the previous figure and makes it visible onscreen. You can find the whole program in <u>`FrameDemo.java`</u> (page 653).

```
public static void main(String s[]) {
    JFrame frame = new JFrame("FrameDemo");
```

---

[1] API documentation for this class is available on this book's CD-ROM and online at http://java.sun.com/products/jdk/1.2/docs/api/javax/swing/JFrame.html

```
frame.addWindowListener(new WindowAdapter() {
    public void windowClosing(WindowEvent e) {
        System.exit(0);
    }
});

//...create a blank label, set its preferred size...

frame.getContentPane().add(emptyLabel, BorderLayout.CENTER);

frame.pack();
frame.setVisible(true);
}
```

The first line of code creates a frame with the constructor that lets you set the frame's title. The only other constructor provided by JFrame is a no-argument constructor.

Next, the code adds a window listener to the frame. The listener's implementation makes the program exit when the user closes the frame. This behavior is appropriate for this program because the program has only one frame, and closing the frame makes the program useless. If the program didn't exit, it would continue to run but have no visible GUI and no way of making any GUI visible. See the next section, Responding to Window-Closing Events (page 84), for more information.

The boldface line in the code segment adds a blank label to the frame's content pane. If you're not already familiar with content panes and how to add components to them, please read Adding Components to the Content Pane (page 79).

The next line gives the frame a size, using the pack method. The pack method sizes the frame so that all of its contents are at or above their preferred sizes. An alternative to pack is to establish a frame's size explicitly by calling setSize. In general, using pack is preferable to calling setSize, since pack leaves the frame's layout manager in charge of the frame's size, and layout managers are good at adjusting to platform dependencies and other factors that affect component size.

The last line uses the setVisible method to make the frame appear onscreen. Sometimes you might see the show method used instead of setVisible(true). The two uses are equivalent but we use setVisible(true) for consistency's sake.

Note: If any part of the frame has been realized, you should invoke pack and setVisible from the event-dispatching thread. For a definition of the term "realized" and information about the event-dispatching thread, refer to Threads and Swing (page 45).

Responding to Window-Closing Events

When the user closes a frame onscreen, the frame is hidden by default. Although invisible, the frame still exists, and the program can make it visible again. If you want different behavior, you need to either register a window listener that handles window-closing events, or you need to specify default close behavior by using the `setDefaultCloseOperation` method. You can even do both.

The argument to `setDefaultCloseOperation` must be one of the following values, which are defined in the `WindowConstants`[1] interface (which `JFrame` implements):

- `DO_NOTHING_ON_CLOSE`
  Don't do anything when the user requests that the frame close. Instead, the program should probably use a window listener that performs another action in its `windowClosing` method.

- `HIDE_ON_CLOSE` (the default)
  Hide the frame when the user closes it. This removes the frame from the screen.

- `DISPOSE_ON_CLOSE`
  Hide and dispose of the frame when the user closes it. This removes the frame from the screen and frees up any resources it used.

The default close operation is executed after the frame's window listeners, if any, handle the window-closing event. So, for example, assume that you specify that the default close operation is to dispose of the frame. You also implement a window listener that tests whether the frame is the last one and, if so, exits the application. Under these conditions, when the user closes a frame, the window listener will be called first. If it doesn't exit the application, the default close operation—disposing of the frame—will then be performed.

For more information about handling window-closing events, see How to Write a Window Listener (page 521). Besides handling window-closing events, window listeners can also react to other window state changes, such as iconification and activation.

The Frame API

The following tables list the commonly used `JFrame` constructors and methods. Other methods you're likely to call are defined by the java.awt.Frame[2] and java.awt.Window[3] classes, from which `JFrame` descends. These methods include `pack`, `setSize`, `setVisible`, `setTitle`, and `getTitle`.

---

[1]   API documentation for this interface is available on this book's CD-ROM and online at
     http://java.sun.com/products/jdk/1.2/docs/api/javax/swing/WindowConstants.html
[2]   http://java.sun.com/products/jdk/1.2/docs/api/java.awt.Frame.html
[3]   http://java.sun.com/products/jdk/1.2/docs/api/java.awt.Window.html

Because each `JFrame` object has a root pane, frames have support for interposing input and painting behavior in front of the frame's children, placing children on different "layers," and for Swing menu bars. These topics are introduced in Using Top-Level Containers (page 77) and are explained in detail in How to Use Root Panes (page 158).

The API for using frames falls into two categories.

Table 12   Creating and Setting Up a Frame

Method	Purpose
`JFrame()` `JFrame(String)`	Create a frame that is initially invisible. To make the frame visible, call `setVisible(true)`. The `String` argument provides a title for the frame. You can also use `setTitle` to set a frame's title.
`void setDefaultCloseOperation(int)` `int getDefaultCloseOperation()`	Set or get the operation that occurs when the user clicks on the close button on this frame. Possible choices are: `DO_NOTHING_ON_CLOSE`, `HIDE_ON_CLOSE` (the default), and `DISPOSE_ON_CLOSE`. These constants are defined in the `WindowConstants` interface, which `JFrame` implements.

Table 13   Methods Related to the Root Pane

Method	Purpose
`void setContentPane(Container)` `Container getContentPane()`	Set or get the frame's content pane. The content pane contains the frame's visible GUI components and should be opaque.
`JRootPane createRootPane()` `void setRootPane(JRootPane)` `JRootPane getRootPane()`	Create, set, or get the frame's root pane. The root pane manages the interior of the frame, including the content pane, the glass pane, and so on.
`void setJMenuBar(JMenuBar)` `JMenuBar getJMenuBar()`	Set or get the frame's menu bar to manage a set of menus for the frame.
`void setGlassPane(Component)` `Component getGlassPane()`	Set or get the frame's glass pane. You can use the glass pane to intercept mouse events.
`void setLayeredPane(JLayeredPane)` `JLayeredPane getLayeredPane()`	Set or get the frame's layered pane. You can use the frame's layered pane to put components on top of or behind other components.

Examples that Use Frames

All of our examples that are standalone applications use `JFrame`. The following table lists a few and tells you where each is discussed.

Table 14   Examples that Use Frames

Example	Where Described	Notes
FrameDemo.java	The Example Explained (page 82)	Displays a basic frame with one component.
Framework.java	–	A study in creating and destroying windows, in implementing a menu bar, and in exiting an application.
ColorChooser-Demo.java	How to Use Color Choosers (page 184)	A `JFrame` subclass that adds components to the default content pane.
TableDemo.java	How to Use Tables (page 254)	A `JFrame` subclass that sets the frame's content pane.
Layered-PaneDemo.java	How to Use Layered Panes (page 150)	Illustrates how to use a layered pane (but not the frame's layered pane).
GlassPaneDemo.java	The Glass Pane (page 159)	Illustrates the use of a frame's glass pane.
MenuDemo.java	How to Use Menus (page 226)	Shows how to put a `JMenuBar` in a `JFrame`.

How to Make Dialogs

Several classes support *dialogs*—windows that are more limited than frames. To create simple, standard dialogs, you use the `JOptionPane`[1] class. The `ProgressMonitor` class can put up a dialog that shows the progress of an operation. Two other classes, `JColorChooser` and `JFileChooser`, also supply standard dialogs. To bring up a print dialog, you can either use the `getPrintJob` method defined in the `Toolkit`[2] class or, if you're using Java 2, use the Java Printing API.[3] To create custom dialogs, use the `JDialog`[4] class directly.

The code for simple dialogs can be minimal. For example, here's an instructive dialog.

Figure 20 A simple dialog.

Here is the code that creates and shows that dialog:

```
JOptionPane.showMessageDialog(frame,
                        "Eggs aren't supposed to be green.");
```

An Overview of Dialogs

Every dialog is dependent on a frame. When that frame is destroyed, so are its dependent dialogs. When the frame is iconified, its dependent dialogs disappear from the screen. When the

---

[1] API documentation for this class is available on this book's CD-ROM and online at http://java.sun.com/products/jdk/1.2/docs/api/javax/swing/JOptionPane.html

[2] http://java.sun.com/products/jdk/1.2/docs/api/java/awt/Toolkit.html

[3] Refer to the trail "2D Graphics" in the book, *The Java Tutorial Continued*. This trail is also available in HTML on this book's CD-ROM and online at http://java.sun.com/docs/books/tutorial/2d/index.html

[4] http://java.sun.com/products/jdk/1.2/docs/api/javax/swing/JDialog.html

frame is deiconified, its dependent dialogs return to the screen. The AWT automatically provides this behavior.

A dialog can be *modal*. When a modal dialog is visible, it blocks user input to all other windows in the program. The dialogs that JOptionPane provides are modal. To create a non-modal dialog, you must use the JDialog class directly.

The JDialog class, a subclass of the AWT java.awt.Dialog[1] class, adds to Dialog a root pane and support for a default close operation. These are the same features that JFrame has, and using JDialog directly is very similar to using JFrame directly. If you're going to use JDialog directly, you should understand the material in the sections Using Top-Level Containers (page 77) and How to Make Frames (page 82), especially Responding to Window-Closing Events (page 84).

Even when you use JOptionPane to implement a dialog, you're still using a JDialog behind the scenes. The reason is that JOptionPane is simply a container that can automatically create a JDialog and add itself to the JDialog's content pane.

The DialogDemo Example

Here's a picture of an application that displays dialogs.

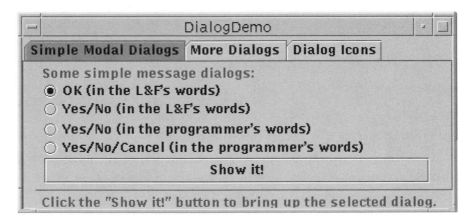

Figure 21 The DialogDemo application.

---

[1]   API documentation for this class is available on this book's CD-ROM and online at http://java.sun.com/
products/jdk/1.2/docs/api/java/awt/Dialog.html

Try this:

1. Compile and run the application.[1] The source file is `DialogDemo.java` (page 639).

2. Click the Show it! button. A modal dialog will appear. Until you close it, the application will be unresponsive, although it will repaint itself if necessary. You can close the dialog either by clicking a button in the dialog or explicitly, such as by using the dialog's window decorations.

3. Iconify the `DialogDemo` window while a dialog is showing. The dialog will disappear from the screen until you deiconify the `DialogDemo` window.

4. In the More Dialogs pane, click the bottom radio button and then the Show it! button. A nonmodal dialog will appear. Note that the `DialogDemo` window remains fully functional while the nonmodal dialog is up.

JOptionPane Features

Using `JOptionPane`, you can create and customize several kinds of dialogs. `JOptionPane` provides support for laying out standard dialogs, providing icons, specifying the dialog's title and text, and customizing the button text. Other features allow you to customize the components the dialog displays and to specify where the dialog should appear onscreen. You can even specify that an option pane put itself into an internal frame (`JInternalFrame`) instead of a `JDialog`.

Note: The internal frames that `JOptionPane` creates currently behave differently from modal dialogs. The internal frames don't behave modally, and in general seem more like frames than like dialogs. For this reason, we don't currently recommend their use.

When you create a `JOptionPane`, look-and-feel-specific code adds components to the `JOptionPane` and determines the layout of those components.

`JOptionPane`'s icon support lets you easily specify which icon the dialog displays. You can use a custom icon, no icon at all, or any one of four standard `JOptionPane` icons (question, information, warning, and error). Each look and feel has its own versions of the four standard icons. The following figure shows the icons used in the Java Look & Feel.

---

[1] See the chapter Getting Started with Swing (page 3) if you need help compiling or running this application.

| question | information | warning | error |

Figure 22 Icons provided by JOptionPane (Java Look & Feel shown).

Creating and Showing Simple Dialogs

For most simple modal dialogs, you create and show the dialog by using one of JOption-Pane's show*Xxx*Dialog methods. If your dialog should be an internal frame, add Internal after show—for example, showMessageDialog changes to showInternalMessageDialog. If you need to control the dialog's window-closing behavior or if the dialog isn't modal, you should directly instantiate JOptionPane and add it to a JDialog instance. Then invoke set-Visible(true) on the JDialog to make it appear.

The two most useful show*Xxx*Dialog methods are showMessageDialog and showOption-Dialog. The showMessageDialog method displays a simple, one-button dialog. The show-OptionDialog method displays a customized dialog—it can display a variety of buttons with customized button text and can contain a standard text message or a collection of components.

The other two show*Xxx*Dialog methods are used less often. The showConfirmDialog method asks the user to confirm something but has the disadvantage of having standard button text (Yes/No or the localized equivalent, for example) rather than button text customized to the user's situation (Start/Cancel, for example). A fourth method, showInputDialog, is designed to display a modal dialog that gets a string from the user, using either a text field or an uneditable combo box. However, input dialogs aren't very useful right now, since the text field doesn't let you perform validation before the dialog goes away, and combo boxes in dialogs don't yet work well.

Here are some examples, taken from DialogDemo.java, of using showMessageDialog, showOptionDialog, and the JOptionPane constructor. For more example code, see <u>Dialog-Demo.java</u> (page 639) and the other programs listed in <u>Examples that Use Dialogs</u> (page 98).

showMessageDialog
> Displays a modal dialog with one button, which is labeled "OK" (or the localized equivalent). You can easily specify the message, icon, and title that the dialog displays. Table 15 shows several examples that use showMessageDialog.

Table 15   Examples Using `showMessageDialog`

(Message dialog: "Eggs aren't supposed to be green.")	`//default title and icon`
	`JOptionPane.showMessageDialog(frame,`
	`    "Eggs aren't supposed to be green.");`

(Inane warning dialog: "Eggs aren't supposed to be green.")	`//custom title, warning icon`
	`JOptionPane.showMessageDialog(frame,`
	`    "Eggs aren't supposed to be green.",`
	`    "Inane warning",`
	`    JOptionPane.WARNING_MESSAGE);`

(Inane error dialog: "Eggs aren't supposed to be green.")	`//custom title, error icon`
	`JOptionPane.showMessageDialog(frame,`
	`    "Eggs aren't supposed to be green.",`
	`    "Inane error",`
	`    JOptionPane.ERROR_MESSAGE);`

(A plain message dialog: "Eggs aren't supposed to be green.")	`//custom title, no icon`
	`JOptionPane.showMessageDialog(frame,`
	`    "Eggs aren't supposed to be green.",`
	`    "A plain message",`
	`    JOptionPane.PLAIN_MESSAGE);`

(Inane custom dialog: "Eggs aren't supposed to be green.")	`//custom title, custom icon`
	`JOptionPane.showMessageDialog(frame,`
	`    "Eggs aren't supposed to be green.",`
	`    "Inane custom dialog",`
	`    JOptionPane.INFORMATION_MESSAGE,`
	`    icon);`

showOptionDialog

Displays a modal dialog with the specified buttons, icons, message, title, and so on. You can use this method to change the text that appears on the buttons of standard dialogs. You can also perform many other kinds of customization. Table 16 shows an example that uses `showOptionDialog`.

Table 16   An Example Using showOptionDialog

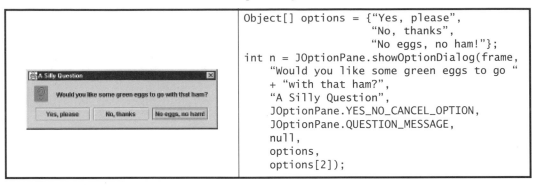

```
Object[] options = {"Yes, please",
                    "No, thanks",
                    "No eggs, no ham!"};
int n = JOptionPane.showOptionDialog(frame,
    "Would you like some green eggs to go "
    + "with that ham?",
    "A Silly Question",
    JOptionPane.YES_NO_CANCEL_OPTION,
    JOptionPane.QUESTION_MESSAGE,
    null,
    options,
    options[2]);
```

JOptionPane (constructor)

Creates a JOptionPane with the specified buttons, icons, message, title, and so on. You must then add the option pane to a JDialog, register a property-change listener on the option pane, and show the dialog. For an example that uses JOptionPane, see <u>Stopping Automatic Dialog Closing</u> (page 95) for details and the following table.

Table 17   An Example Using JOptionPane

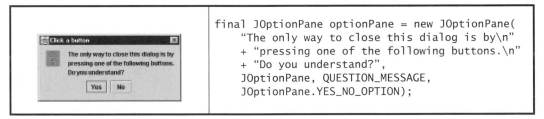

```
final JOptionPane optionPane = new JOptionPane(
    "The only way to close this dialog is by\n"
    + "pressing one of the following buttons.\n"
    + "Do you understand?",
    JOptionPane, QUESTION_MESSAGE,
    JOptionPane.YES_NO_OPTION);
```

The arguments to all of the showXxxDialog methods and JOptionPane constructors are standardized, although the number of arguments for each method and constructor varies. The following list describes each argument. To see the exact list of arguments for a particular method, see <u>The Dialog API</u> (page 96).

Component *parentComponent*

The first argument to each showXxxDialog method is always the parent component, which must be a frame, a component inside a frame, or null. If you specify a frame, the dialog will appear over the center of the frame and will depend on that frame. If you specify a component inside a frame, the dialog will appear over the center of that component and will depend on that component's frame. If you specify null, the look and feel picks an appropriate position for the dialog—generally the center of the screen— and the dialog doesn't depend on any visible frame.

The JOptionPane constructors do not include this argument. Instead you specify the parent frame when you create the JDialog that contains the JOptionPane, and you use the JDialog setLocationRelativeTo method to set the dialog's position.

Object *message*

This required argument specifies what the dialog should display in its main area. Generally you specify a string, which results in the dialog displaying a label with the specified text. You can split the message over several lines by putting new line (\n) characters inside the message string. For example:

```
"Complete the sentence:\"Green eggs and...\""
```

String *title*

This is the title of the dialog.

int *optionType*

This specifies the set of buttons that appears at the bottom of the dialog. You can choose one of the following four standard sets: DEFAULT_OPTION, YES_NO_OPTION, YES_NO_CANCEL_OPTION, OK_CANCEL_OPTION.

int *messageType*

This argument determines the icon displayed in the dialog. Choose from one of the following values: PLAIN_MESSAGE (no icon), ERROR_MESSAGE, INFORMATION_MESSAGE, WARNING_MESSAGE, QUESTION_MESSAGE.

Icon *icon*

This specifies the custom icon to display in the dialog.

Object[] *options*

This further specifies the option buttons to appear at the button of the dialog. Generally you specify an array of strings for the buttons. See Customizing Button Text (page 94) for more information.

Object *initialValue*

This specifies the default value to be selected. You can either let the default icon be used or specify the icon, using the messageType or the icon argument. By default a dialog created with showMessageDialog displays the information icon, and a dialog created with showConfirmDialog or showInputDialog displays the question icon. An option pane created with a JOptionPane constructor displays no icon, by default. To specify that the dialog display a standard icon or no icon, specify the message type. To specify a custom icon, use the icon argument. The icon argument takes precedence over the message type; as long as the icon argument has a non-null value, the dialog displays the specified icon.

Customizing Button Text

When you use JOptionPane to create a dialog, you can choose either to use the standard button text, which might vary by look and feel, or to specify different text. The code in Table 18,
taken from DialogDemo.java (page 639), creates two Yes/No dialogs. The first dialog is
implemented with showConfirmDialog, which uses the look-and-feel wording for the two
buttons. The second dialog uses showOptionDialog so it can customize the wording. With
the exception of wording changes, the dialogs are identical.

Table 18   Two Yes/No Dialog Examples

An Inane Question
Would you like green eggs and ham?
Yes   No
	```//default icon, custom title```
	 ```int n = JOptionPane.showConfirmDialog(frame,```
	 ``` "Would you like green eggs and ham?",```
	 ``` "An Inane Question",```
	 ``` JOptionPane.YES_NO_OPTION);```

A Silly Question
Would you like green eggs and ham?
Yes, please   No way!
	```Object[] options = {"Yes, please", "No way!"};```
	 ```int n = JOptionPane.showOptionDialog(frame,```
	 ``` "Would you like green eggs and ham?",```
	 ``` "A Silly Question",```
	 ``` JOptionPane.YES_NO_OPTION,```
	 ``` JOptionPane.QUESTION_MESSAGE,```
	 ``` null, //don't use a custom Icon```
	 ``` options, //the titles of buttons```
	 ``` options[0]); //title of the default button```

Getting the User's Input from a Dialog

As the code snippets in Tables 15, 16, and 18 showed, the showMessageDialog, showOptionDialog, showConfirmDialog methods return an integer indicating the user's choice.
The values for this integer are YES_OPTION, NO_OPTION, CANCEL_OPTION, OK_OPTION, and
CLOSED_OPTION. Each option, except for CLOSED_OPTION, corresponds to the button the user
pressed. When CLOSED_OPTION is returned, it indicates that the user closed the dialog window explicitly rather than by choosing a button inside the option pane.

Even if you change the strings that the standard dialog buttons display, the return value is
still one of the predefined integers. For example, a YES_NO_OPTION dialog always returns one
of the following values: YES_OPTION, NO_OPTION, or CLOSED_OPTION.

If you're designing a custom dialog, on the other hand, you need to design your dialog's API
so that you can query the dialog about what the user chose. For example, the dialog imple-

mented in <u>CustomDialog.java</u> (page 636) has a `getValidatedText` method that returns the text the user entered.

Stopping Automatic Dialog Closing

When the user clicks a `JOptionPane`-created button, the dialog closes by default. But what if you want to check the user's answer before closing the dialog? In this case you must implement your own property-change listener so that when the user clicks a button, the dialog doesn't automatically close.

`DialogDemo` contains two dialogs that implement a property-change listener. One of these dialogs is a custom modal dialog, implemented in <u>CustomDialog.java</u> (page 636), that uses `JOptionPane` both to get the standard icon and to get layout assistance. The other dialog, whose code follows, uses a standard Yes/No `JOptionPane`. Although this dialog is rather useless as written, its code is simple enough that you can use it as a template for more complex dialogs.

Besides setting the property-change listener, the following code also calls the `JDialog`'s `setDefaultCloseOperation` method and implements a window listener that handles the window-close attempt properly. If you don't care to be notified when the user closes the window explicitly, ignore the code in boldface type.

```
final JOptionPane optionPane = new JOptionPane(
                "The only way to close this dialog is by\n"
                + "pressing one of the following buttons.\n"
                + "Do you understand?",
                JOptionPane.QUESTION_MESSAGE,
                JOptionPane.YES_NO_OPTION);

final JDialog dialog = new JDialog(frame,
                        "Click a button",
                        true);
dialog.setContentPane(optionPane);
dialog.setDefaultCloseOperation(
    JDialog.DO_NOTHING_ON_CLOSE);
dialog.addWindowListener(new WindowAdapter() {
    public void windowClosing(WindowEvent we) {
        setLabel("Thwarted user attempt to close window.");
    }
});

optionPane.addPropertyChangeListener(
    new PropertyChangeListener() {
        public void propertyChange(PropertyChangeEvent e) {
```

```
            String prop = e.getPropertyName();
            if (dialog.isVisible()
             && (e.getSource() == optionPane)
             && (prop.equals(JOptionPane.VALUE_PROPERTY) ||
                 prop.equals(JOptionPane.INPUT_VALUE_PROPERTY))) {
                //If you were going to check something
                //before closing the window, you'd do
                //it here.
                dialog.setVisible(false);
            }
        }
    });
dialog.pack();
dialog.setLocationRelativeTo(frame);
dialog.setVisible(true);

int value = ((Integer)optionPane.getValue()).intValue();
if (value == JOptionPane.YES_OPTION) {
    setLabel("Good.");
} else if (value == JOptionPane.NO_OPTION) {
    setLabel("Try using the window decorations "
            + "to close the non-auto-closing dialog. "
            + "You can't!");
}
```

The Dialog API

The following tables list the commonly used JOptionPane and JDialog constructors and methods. Other methods you're likely to call on JDialog are defined by the Dialog, Window, and Component classes and include pack, setSize, and setVisible.

Table 19   Showing Standard Modal Dialogs, Using JOptionPane Class Methods

Method	Purpose

int showMessageDialog(Component, Object)
int showMessageDialog(Component, Object,
                      String, int)
int showMessageDialog(Component, Object,
                      String, int, Icon)
	Show a one-button modal dialog that gives the user some information. The arguments[a] specify (in order) the parent component, message, title, message type, and icon for the dialog.

int showOptionDialog(Component, Object, String,
                    int, int, Icon, Object[],
                    Object)
	Show a customized modal dialog. The arguments[a] specify (in order) the parent component, message, title, option type, message type, icon, options, and initial value for the dialog.

Table 19   Showing Standard Modal Dialogs, Using `JOptionPane` Class Methods

Method	Purpose

`int showConfirmDialog(Component, Object)`
`int showConfirmDialog(Component, Object,`
`                String, int)`
`int showConfirmDialog(Component, Object,`
`                String, int, int)`
`int showConfirmDialog(Component, Object,String,`
`                int, int, Icon)`
	Show a modal dialog that asks the user a question. The arguments[a] specify (in order) the parent component, message, title, option type, message type, and icon for the dialog.

`String showInputDialog(Object)`
`String showInputDialog(Component,Object)`
`String showInputDialog(Component, Object,`
`                String, int)`
`String showInputDialog(Component, Object, String,`
`                int, Icon, Object[],`
`                Object)`
	Show a modal dialog that prompts the user for input. The single-argument version specifies just the message, with the parent component assumed to be `null`. The arguments[a] for the other versions specify (in order) the parent component, message, title, message type, icon, options, and initial value for the dialog.

`int showInternalMessageDialog(...)`
`int showInternalOptionDialog(...)`
`int showInternalConfirmDialog(...)`
`String showInternalInputDialog(...)`
	Implement a standard dialog as an internal frame. See the `JOptionPane` API documentation[b] for the exact list of arguments.

a. See Creating and Showing Simple Dialogs (page 90) for a discussion of the arguments and their effects.
b. http://java.sun.com/products/jdk/1.2/docs/api/javax/swing/JOptionPane.html

Table 20   Methods for Using `JOptionPane`s Directly

Method or Constructor	Purpose

`JOptionPane()`
`JOptionPane(Object)`
`JOptionPane(Object, int)`
`JOptionPane(Object, int, int)`
`JOptionPane(Object, int, int, Icon)`
`JOptionPane(Object, int, int, Icon, Object[])`
`JOptionPane(Object, int, int, Icon, Object[], Object)`
	Create a `JOptionPane` instance. See Creating and Showing Simple Dialogs (page 90) for a discussion of the arguments and their effects.

`Frame getFrameForComponent(Component)` `JDesktopPane getDesktopPaneForComponent(Component)`	Handy `JOptionPane` class methods that find the frame or desktop pane, respectively, that the specified component is in.

Table 21   Frequently Used `JDialog` Constructors and Methods

Method/Constructor	Purpose

`JDialog()`
`JDialog(Frame)`
`JDialog(Frame, boolean)`
`JDialog(Frame, String)`
`JDialog(Frame, String, boolean)`
	Create a `JDialog` instance. The `Frame` argument, if any, is the frame (usually a `JFrame` object) that the dialog depends on. Make the boolean argument `true` to specify a modal dialog and `false` or absent to specify a nonmodal dialog. You can also specify the title of the dialog, using a string argument.

`Container getContentPane()` `void setContentPane(Container)`	Get and set the content pane, which is usually the container of all of the dialog's components. See Using Top-Level Containers (page 77) for more information.
`int getDefaultCloseOperation()` `void setDefaultCloseOperation(int)`	Get and set what happens when the user tries to close the dialog. Possible values: DISPOSE_ON_CLOSE, DO_NOTHING_ON_CLOSE, HIDE_ON_CLOSE (the default). See Responding to Window-Closing Events (page 84) for more information.
`void setLocationRelativeTo(Component)`	Center the dialog over the specified component.

Examples that Use Dialogs

Table 22 lists examples that use `JOptionPane` or `JDialog`. To find other examples that use dialogs, see the example lists for progress bars (page 239), color choosers (page 184), and file choosers (page 200).

Table 22   Examples that Use `Dialogs`

Example	Where Described	Notes
`DialogDemo.java`, `CustomDialog.java`	This section	Creates many kinds of dialogs, using `JOption-Pane` and `JDialog`.
`Framework.java`	–	Brings up a confirmation dialog when the user selects the Quit menu item.
`ListDialog.java`	How to Use BoxLayout (page 350)	Implements a modal dialog containing a scrolling list and two buttons. Doesn't use `JOptionPane`, except for the utility method `getFrameForComponent`.
`TableDemo.java`	How to Use Tables (page 254)	Brings up a warning dialog when the user types a nonnumber entry into a cell that must contain a number.

How to Make Applets

This section covers the JApplet class, which enables applets to use Swing components. JApplet is a subclass of <u>java.applet.Applet</u>,[1] which is covered in the "Writing Applets" trail.[2] If you've never written a regular applet before, we urge you to read that trail before proceeding with this section. The information provided in that trail applies to Swing applets, with a few exceptions that this section explains.

Any applet that contains Swing components must be implemented with a subclass of JApplet.[3] Here's a Swing version of one of the applets that helped make Java famous—an applet that animates our mascot, Duke, doing cartwheels.

Figure 23 One frame of the Duke tumbling applet.

The source code for this applet is in <u>TumbleItem.java</u> (page 773) and <u>SwingWorker.java</u> (page 720). The CD-ROM that accompanies this book includes the source code and the 17 images used in this applet.[4]

JApplet Features

JApplet adds two major features to the functionality that it inherits from java.applet.Applet. First, JApplet provides support for assistive technologies. Second, because JApplet is a top-level Swing container, each Swing applet has a root pane. The most

---

[1] API documentation for this class is available on this book's CD-ROM and online at http://java.sun.com/products/jdk/1.2/docs/api/java.applet.Applet.html

[2] You can find the "Writing Applets" trail in the book, *The Java™ Tutorial, Second Edition*, and online at http://java.sun.com/docs/books/tutorial/ui/applet/index.html

[3] API documentation for this class is available on this book's CD-ROM and online at http://java.sun.com/products/jdk/1.2/docs/api/javax/swing/JApplet.html

[4] The directory with the tumbling duke images on the CD-ROM is: tutorial/uiswing/components/example-swing/images/tumble/

noticeable results of the root pane's presence are support for adding a menu bar and the need to use a content pane.

As described in Using Top-Level Containers (page 77), each top-level container, such as JApplet, has a single content pane. The content pane makes Swing applets different from regular applets in the following ways:

- You add components to a Swing applet's content pane, not directly to the applet. Adding Components to the Content Pane (page 79) shows you how.

- You set the layout manager on a Swing applet's content pane, not directly on the applet.

- The default layout manager for a Swing applet's content pane is BorderLayout. This differs from the default layout manager for Applet, which is FlowLayout.

- You should not put painting code directly in a JApplet object. See Converting to Swing (page 575) for information on converting applet painting code, and Working with Graphics (page 533) for examples of how to perform custom painting in applets.

JDK 1.1 Note: If you run a Swing applet using JDK 1.1 and JFC 1.1, you might see an error message that looks like this:

```
Swing: checked access to system event queue.
```

You can often avoid this message by telling the applet not to check whether it has access to the system event queue. To do so, put the following code in the constructor for the applet class:

```
getRootPane().putClientProperty("defeatSystemEventQueueCheck",
                                Boolean.TRUE);
```

Threads in Applets

Because applets inherently use multiple threads and Swing components aren't thread safe, you should take care with threads in Swing applets. It's generally considered safe to create and to manipulate Swing components directly in the init method. However, the other milestone methods—start, stop, and destroy—might cause trouble when the browser invokes them after the applet's already visible. To avoid trouble, you should make these methods thread safe.

For example, when you implement a stop or a start method, be aware that the browser doesn't call them from the event-dispatching thread. Thus those methods shouldn't affect or query Swing components directly. Instead they should use such techniques as using the SwingUtilities.invokeLater method to affect components.

For more information about using threads, see Threads and Swing (page 45) and How to Use Threads (page 431).

Using Images in a Swing Applet

Recall that the `Applet` class provides the `getImage` method for loading images into an applet. The `getImage` method creates and returns an `Image` object that represents the loaded image. Because Swing components use `Icon`s rather than `Image`s to refer to pictures, Swing applets tend not to use `getImage`. Instead Swing applets usually create instances of `Image-Icon`—an icon loaded from an image file. `ImageIcon` comes with a code-saving benefit: It handles image tracking automatically. Refer to <u>How to Use Icons</u> (page 417).

The animation of Duke doing cartwheels requires 17 pictures, with one `ImageIcon` per picture. Because images can take a long time to load, the icons are loaded in a separate thread implemented by a `SwingWorker` object. The applet's `init` method starts the thread by creating the `SwingWorker` object. Here's the code:

```
public void init() {
    ...
    imgs = new ImageIcon[nimgs];
    final SwingWorker worker = new SwingWorker() {
        public Object construct() {
            URL baseURL = getCodeBase();
            String prefix = dir + "/T";
            //Images are numbered 1 to nimgs,
            //but fill array from 0 to nimgs-1
            for (int i = 0; i < nimgs; i++) {
                imgs[i] = new ImageIcon(getURL(baseURL,
                                           prefix + (i+1) + ".gif"));
            }
            finishLoading = true;
            return imgs;
        }
    };
    ...
}
```

To create an `ImageIcon` and load it with an image, you specify the image file's URL to the `ImageIcon`'s constructor. The preceeding applet defines a method named `getURL` to construct the URL for each image file. Here is the code:

```
protected URL getURL(URL codeBase, String filename) {
    URL url = null;
    try {
        url = new URL(codeBase, filename);
    } catch (java.net.MalformedURLException e) {
        System.out.println("Couldn't create image: badly specified URL");
        return null;
    }
    return url;
}
```

Providing an OBJECT/EMBED Tag for Java Plug-in

To run, an applet must be included in an HTML page. If you're using Applet Viewer to run a Swing applet, you include the applet by using an <APPLET> tag.[1] Here's the <APPLET> tag for the cartwheeling Duke applet:

```
<applet code="TumbleItem.class"
        codebase="example-swing/"
        archive="tumble.jar"
        width="600" height="95">
    <param name="maxwidth" value="120">
    <param name="nimgs" value="17">
    <param name="offset" value="-57">
    <param name="img" value="images/tumble">
Your browser is completely ignoring the &lt;APPLET&gt; tag!
</applet>
```

To make an applet work with the Java Plug-in, you need to convert the <APPLET> tag into <OBJECT> and <EMBED> tags so that an applet can be included in an HTML page. You can download a free tool that automatically generates the necessary tags from an <APPLET> tag. To download Java Plug-in and the HTML conversion tool, as well as related documentation, go to the Java Plug-in home page.[2]

Because the Java Plug-in can take a while to download and load into the browser, it's considerate to give users advance warning that a page contains an applet. You might have noticed that the tutorial's applets don't run the same page as the text that describes the applet. Instead we provide a screenshot of the applet running and a link that brings up a separate browser window in which to run the applet. We feel that this provides a better experience because users can choose whether to visit a page that contains an applet.

The JApplet API

The next table lists the interesting methods that JApplet adds to the applet API. They give you access to features provided by the root pane. Other methods you might use are defined

---

[1]   To find out about the various <APPLET> tag parameters, refer to "Test Driving an Applet" and "Using the <APPLET> Tag" found in the "Writing Applets" trail in the book, *The Java™ Tutorial, Second Edition*. This trail is also available in HTML on this book's CD-ROM and online at http://java.sun.com/docs/books/tutorial/applet/index.html

[2]   http://java.sun.com/products/plugin/index.html

by the `Component` and `Applet` classes. See <u>The JComponent Class</u> (page 67) for a list of commonly used `Component` methods, and <u>Taking Advantage of the Applet API</u>, a lesson in the "Writing Applets" trail, for help in using `Applet` methods.[1]

Table 23   Commonly Used Methods `JApplet` Adds to the Applet API

Method	Purpose
`void setContentPane(Container)` `Container getContentPane()`	Set or get the applet's content pane. The content pane contains the applet's visible GUI components and should be opaque.
`void setJMenuBar(JMenuBar)` `JMenuBar getJMenuBar()`	Set or get the applet's menu bar to manage a set of menus for the applet.

Applet Examples

Table 24 shows examples of Swing applets and where those examples are described.

Table 24   Examples that Use Swing Applets

Example	Where Described	Notes
`TumbleItem.java`	This section	An animation applet
`HelloSwingApplet.java`	<u>Running Swing Applets</u> (page 17)	The simplest of all Swing applets—it contains only a label.
`AppletDemo.java`	<u>Running Swing Applets</u> (page 17)	The applet version of the button demo.
`IconDemoApplet.java`	<u>How to Use Icons</u> (page 417)	An applet for showing photos.
Several examples.	<u>Using Layout Managers</u> (page 343)	You can run several applets from the section listed. Each applet demonstrates a different layout manager.
Several examples.	<u>Some Simple Event-Handling Examples</u> (page 443)	You can run several applets from the section listed. Each applet shows how to handle different types of events.

---

[1] You can find the "Writing Applets" trail in *The Java^TM Tutorial, Second Edition book*. This trail is also available in HTML on this book's CD-ROM and online at http://java.sun.com/docs/books/tutorial/applet/appletsonly/index.html

15

Using Intermediate Swing Containers

THIS chapter describes intermediate containers—Swing components that are not top-level containers but that instead exist solely to contain other components. To use intermediate containers, you should understand the concepts presented in Components and Containment Hierarchies (page 29). You can see all the intermediate containers in A Visual Index to Swing Components (page 63).

Swing provides several general-purpose intermediate containers, as listed in Table 25. Note that although technically menu bars are intermediate containers, we discuss them elsewhere, in How to Use Menus (page 226).

Table 25   General-Purpose Intermediate Containers

Container	**Purpose**
Panel	The most flexible, frequently used intermediate container. Implemented with the JPanel class, panels add almost no functionality beyond what all JComponent objects have. Panels are often used to group components, that are related or in order to make layout easier. A panel can use any layout manager, and you can easily give it a border. The content panes of top-level containers are often implemented as JPanel instances.
Scroll Pane	Provides scroll bars around a large or growable component.
Split Pane	Displays two components in a fixed amount of space, letting the user adjust the amount of space devoted to each component.
Tabbed Pane	Contains multiple components but shows only one at a time. The user can easily switch between components.
Tool Bar	Holds a group of components (usually buttons) in a row or a column, optionally allowing the user to drag the tool bar into various locations.

The rest of the Swing intermediate containers are more specialized. These specialized containers are listed in Table 26.

Table 26   Specialized Intermediate Containers

Container	Purpose
`Internal Frame`	Looks like a frame and has much the same API but must appear within another window.
`Layered Pane`	Provides a third dimension, depth, for positioning components. You specify the position and the size of each component. One type of layered pane, a desktop pane, is designed primarily to contain and to manage internal frames.
`Root Pane`	Provides behind-the-scenes support to top-level containers.

How to Use Panels

The JPanel[1] class provides general-purpose containers for lightweight components. By default panels paint nothing but their background; however, you can easily add borders to them and otherwise customize their painting. For information about using panels to perform custom painting, see Overview of Custom Painting (page 537).

By default panels are opaque. This makes them work well as content panes and can help painting efficiency, as described in Painting (page 41). You can make a panel transparent by invoking setOpaque(false). A transparent panel draws no background, so that any components underneath show through.

An Example

The Converter application described in The Anatomy of a Swing-Based Program (page 51) uses panels in several ways.

- One JPanel instance serves as a content pane for the application's frame. This content pane uses a two-row GridLayout[2] to lay out its contents and an empty border to put 5 pixels of space around them. See Using Top-Level Containers (page 77) for information about content panes.
- Two instances of ConversionPanel, a JPanel subclass, are used to both contain components and coordinate communication between components. The panels also have titled borders, which describe their contents and paint a line around them. The panels use left-to-right BoxLayout objects to lay out their contents.
- Two instances of an unnamed JPanel subclass are used to group components and to restrict their size. The panels use top-to-bottom BoxLayout[3] objects to lay out their contents.

In the following picture each panel in the Converter application has a different background color.

---

[1] API documentation for this class is available on this book's CD-ROM and online at http://java.sun.com/products/jdk/1.2/docs/api/javax/swing/JPanel.html
[2] GridLayout is discussed in How to Use GridLayout (page 368).
[3] BoxLayout is discussed in How to Use BoxLayout (page 350).

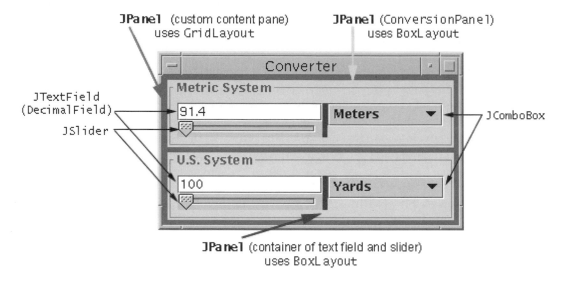

Figure 24 The Converter application uses panels to group components.

As the figure shows, panels are useful for grouping components, simplifying component layout, and putting borders around groups of components. The rest of this section gives hints on grouping and laying out components. For information about using borders, see How to Use Borders (page 408).

Setting the Layout Manager

Like other containers, a panel uses a layout manager to position and to size its components. By default, a panel's layout manager is an instance of FlowLayout,[1] which places the panel's contents in a row. You can easily make a panel use any other layout manager; you do so by invoking the setLayout method or by specifying a layout manager when creating the panel. Here is an example of the first approach:

```
JPanel aPanel = new JPanel();
aPanel.setLayout(new BorderLayout());
```

Here is an example of setting the layout manager at instantiation:

```
JPanel aPanel = new JPanel(new BorderLayout());
```

---

[1] See How to Use FlowLayout (page 366) for details on the FlowLayout manager.

For more information about choosing and using layout managers, see <u>Laying Out Components</u> (page 341).

Adding Components

When you add components to a panel, you use the add method. Exactly which arguments you specify to the add method depend on which layout manager the panel uses. When the layout manager is FlowLayout, BoxLayout, GridLayout, or GridBagLayout, you'll typically use the one-argument add method, like this:

```
aFlowPanel.add(aComponent);
aFlowPanel.add(anotherComponent);
```

When the layout manager is BorderLayout, you need to provide a second argument to specify the added component's position within the panel. For example:

```
aBorderPanel.add(aComponent, BorderLayout.CENTER);
aBorderPanel.add(anotherComponent, BorderLayout.SOUTH);
```

For information on the arguments to use with BorderLayout, see <u>How to Use BorderLayout</u> (page 347).

The Panel API

The API in the JPanel class itself is minimal. The methods you are most likely to invoke on a JPanel object are those it inherits from its superclasses—JComponent, Container, and Component. The following tables list the API you're most likely to use, with the exception of methods related to borders and layout hints. For more information about the API all JComponents can use, see <u>The JComponent API</u> (page 70).

Table 27   Creating a JPanel

Constructor	Purpose
JPanel() JPanel(LayoutManager)	Create a panel. The LayoutManager parameter provides a layout manager for the new panel. By default a panel uses a FlowLayout to lay out its components.

Table 28   Managing a Container's Components

Method	Purpose

`void add(Component)`
`void add(Component, int)`
`void add(Component, Object)`
`void add(Component, Object, int)`
`void add(String, Component)`
	Add the specified component to the panel. When present, the `int` parameter is the index of the component within the container. By default the first component added is at index 0, the second is at index 1, and so on. The `Object` parameter is dependent on the layout manager and typically provides information to the layout manager about positioning and other layout constraints for the added component. The `String` parameter is similar to the `Object` parameter.

`int getComponentCount()`	Get the number of components in this panel.

`Component getComponent(int)`
`Component getComponentAt(int, int)`
`Component getComponentAt(Point)`
`Component[] getComponents()`
	Get the specified component or components. You can get a component based on its index or *x, y* position.

`void remove(Component)`
`void remove(int)`
`void removeAll()`
	Remove the specified component(s).

Table 29   Setting/Getting the Layout Manager

Method	Purpose
`void setLayout(LayoutManager)` `LayoutManager getLayout()`	Set or get the layout manager for this panel. The layout manager is responsible for positioning the panel's components within the panel's bounds according to specified criteria.

Examples that Use Panels

Many examples contained in this section use `JPanel` objects. The following table lists a few.

Table 30   Examples that use `JPanel` objects

Example	Where Described	Notes
`Converter.java`, `ConversionPanel.java`, and other files	This section and The Anatomy of a Swing-Based Program (page 51)	Uses five panels, four of which use `Box-Layout` and one of which uses `GridLay-out`. The panels use borders and, as necessary, size and alignment hints to affect layout.

Table 30   Examples that use `JPanel` objects

Example	Where Described	Notes
`ListDemo.java`	How to Use Lists (page 218)	Uses a panel, with its default `FlowLay-out` manager, to center three components in a row.
`ToolBarDemo.java`	How to Use Tool Bars (page 138)	Uses a panel as a content pane. The panel contains three components, laid out by `BorderLayout`.
`BorderDemo.java`	How to Use Borders (page 408)	Contains many panels that have various kinds of borders. Several panels use `Box-Layout`.
`BoxLayoutDemo.java`	How to Use BoxLayout (page 350)	Illustrates the use of a panel with Swing's `BoxLayout` manager.

How to Use Scroll Panes

A `JScrollPane`[1] provides a scrollable view of a component. When screen real estate is limited, use a scroll pane to display a component that is large or one whose size can change dynamically.

The code to create a scroll pane can be minimal. For example, here's a picture of a demo program that puts a text area in a scroll pane because the text area's size grows dynamically as text is appended to it.

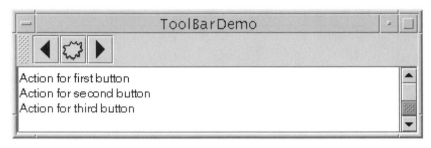

Figure 25 The `ToolBarDemo` applet features a scroll pane.

The following code creates the text area, makes it the scroll pane's client, and adds the scroll pane to the frame:

```
textArea = new JTextArea(5, 30);
JScrollPane scrollPane = new JScrollPane(textArea);
...
contentPane.setPreferredSize(new Dimension(400, 100));
...
contentPane.add(scrollPane, BorderLayout.CENTER);
```

The program provides the text area as an argument to `JScrollPane`'s constructor. This establishes the text area as the scroll pane's client. The scroll pane handles everything else: creating the scroll bars when necessary, redrawing the client when the user moves the scroll knobs, and so on.

---

[1] API documentation for this class is available on this book's CD-ROM and online at http://java.sun.com/products/jdk/1.2/docs/api/javax/swing/JScrollPane.html

Without the boldface line of code, the scroll pane would compute its preferred size so that the text area, at its preferred size, would fit entirely within the scroll pane. Consequently the scroll pane would have no scroll bars. The boldface line sets the preferred size of the scroll pane's container such that the scroll pane is forced into a shorter-than-preferred area. Thus when the program first appears onscreen, the scroll pane has a vertical scroll bar. Refer to Sizing a Scroll Pane (page 122) for information about using other techniques for making a scroll pane the size you want.

How a Scroll Pane Works

Here is a screenshot of an application that uses a customized scroll pane to view a large photograph.

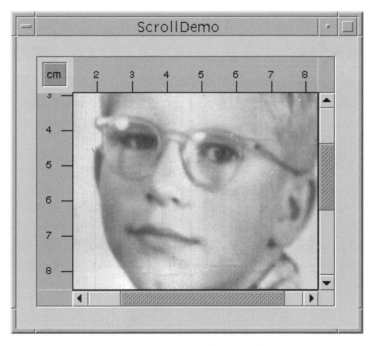

Figure 26 The ScrollDemo application uses a customized scroll pane.

The scroll pane in this application looks very different from the one in the previous demo program. Rather than displaying text, this scroll pane contains a large image. The scroll pane also has two scroll bars, a row header, a column header, and four corners, three of which have been customized.

Try this:

1. Compile and run the application. The main source file is <u>ScrollDemo.java</u> (page 702).[1] You also need <u>ScrollablePicture.java</u> (page 701), <u>Rule.java</u> (page 699), <u>Corner.java</u> (page 633) and youngdad.jpeg. All of these files are included on the CD-ROM that accompanies this book.

2. Move the knobs on the scroll bars. Watch the image scroll and the horizontal and vertical rulers scroll along.

3. Click the cm toggle in the upper-left corner of the scroll pane. The units on the row and the column headers change to inches (or back to centimeters).

4. Click the arrow buttons on the scroll bars. Also try clicking on the track above or below the knob on the vertical scroll bar, or to the left or right of the horizontal one.

5. Resize the window. Note that the scroll bars disappear when the scroll pane is large enough to display the entire image and that they reappear when the scroll pane is too small to show the entire client.

This program establishes the scroll pane's client when creating the scroll pane:

```
// where the member variables are declared:
private ScrollablePicture picture;
...
// where the GUI is created:
picture = new ScrollablePicture( ... );
JScrollPane pictureScrollPane = new JScrollPane(picture);
```

You can change a scroll pane's client dynamically by calling the setViewportView method. Note that JScrollPane has no corresponding getViewportView method, so you should cache the client object in a variable if you need to refer to it later.

When the user manipulates the scroll bars in a scroll pane, the area of the client that is visible changes accordingly. Figure 27 shows the relationship between the scroll pane and its client and indicates the classes that the scroll pane commissions to help.

A scroll pane uses a <u>JViewport</u>[2] instance to manage the visible area of the client. The viewport is responsible for computing the bounds of the current visible area, based on the positions of the scroll bars, and displaying it.

---

[1]   See <u>Getting Started with Swing</u> (page 3) if you need help with compiling and running applications.

[2]   API documentation for this class is available on this book's CD-ROM and online at http://java.sun.com/ products/jdk/1.2/docs/api/javax/swing/JViewport.html

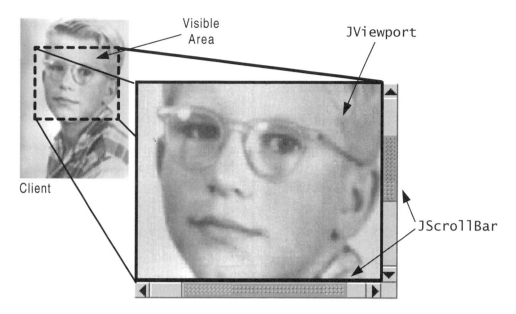

Figure 27 This figure shows the relationship between the scroll pane and its client. The classes that the scroll pane commissions to help, `JViewport` and `JScrollBar`, are also listed.

A scroll pane uses two separate instances of <u>`JScrollBar`</u>[1] for the scroll bars. The scroll bars provide the interface for the user to manipulate the visible area. The following figure shows the three areas of a scroll bar: the knob, the buttons, and the track.

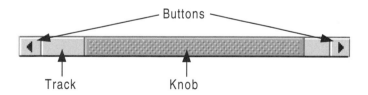

Figure 28 The three areas of a scroll bar: knob, buttons, and track.

When the user moves the knob on the vertical scroll bar up and down, the visible area of the client moves up and down. Similarly when the user moves the knob on the horizontal scroll bar to the right and left, the visible area of the client moves back and forth accordingly. The position of the knob relative to its track is proportionally equal to the position of the visible

---

[1] API documentation for this class is available on this book's CD-ROM and online at http://java.sun.com/products/jdk/1.2/docs/api/javax/swing/JScrollBar.html

area relative to the client. In the Java Look & Feel and some others, the size of the knob gives a visual clue as to how much of the client is visible.

By clicking a button, the user can scroll by a *unit increment*. By clicking within the track, the user can scroll by a *block increment*. Information about unit and block increments is in Implementing a Scrolling-Savvy Client (page 120).

Typical programs don't directly instantiate or call methods on a viewport or a scroll bar. Instead programs achieve their scrolling behavior by using the `JScrollPane` API and the API discussed in Implementing a Scrolling-Savvy Client (page 120). Some scrolling-savvy components, such as `JList`, `JTable`, and `JTree`, also provide additional API to help you affect their scrolling behavior.

Setting the Scroll Bar Policy

On startup the scroll pane in the `ScrollDemo` application has two scroll bars. If you make the window as large as your screen, both scroll bars disappear because they are no longer needed. If you then shrink the height of the window without changing its width, the vertical scroll bar reappears. Further experimentation will show that in this application both scroll bars disappear and reappear as needed. This behavior is controlled by the scroll pane's *scroll bar policy*. Actually, it's two policies—one for each scroll bar.

`ScrollDemo` doesn't explicitly set the scroll pane's scroll bar policies; instead it uses the default. But you can set the scroll bar policies when you create the scroll pane, or you can change the policies dynamically.

Of the constructors provided by `JScrollPane`, these two let you set the scroll bar policies when you create the scroll pane:

```
JScrollPane(Component, int, int)
JScrollPane(int, int)
```

The first `int` specifies the policy for the vertical scroll bar; the second specifies the policy for the horizontal scroll bar. You can set the policies dynamically with the `setHorizontal-ScrollBarPolicy` and `setVerticalScrollBarPolicy` methods. With both the constructors and the methods, use one of the constants defined in the ScrollPaneConstants[1] interface (which is implemented by `JScrollPane`) and listed in the following table.

---

[1] API documentation for this class is available on this book's CD-ROM and online at http://java.sun.com/products/jdk/1.2/docs/api/javax/swing/ScrollPaneConstants.html

Table 31   Scroll Bar Policy Constants Defined in the `ScrollPaneConstants` Interface

Constant	Description
`VERTICAL_SCROLLBAR_AS_NEEDED` `HORIZONTAL_SCROLLBAR_AS_NEEDED`	The default. The scroll bar appears when the viewport is smaller than the client and disappears when the viewport is larger than the client.
`VERTICAL_SCROLLBAR_ALWAYS` `HORIZONTAL_SCROLLBAR_ALWAYS`	Always display the scroll bar. The knob typically disappears if the viewport is large enough to show the whole client.
`VERTICAL_SCROLLBAR_NEVER` `HORIZONTAL_SCROLLBAR_NEVER`	Never display the scroll bar. Use this option if you don't want the user to directly control what part of the client is shown. Perhaps you have an application that requires all scrolling to occur programmatically.

Providing Custom Decorations

The area drawn by a scroll pane consists of up to nine parts: the center, four sides, and four corners. The center is the only component that is always present in all scroll panes. Besides scroll bars, the sides can contain column and row headers. A corner component is visible only if both sides that intersect at that corner contain visible components.

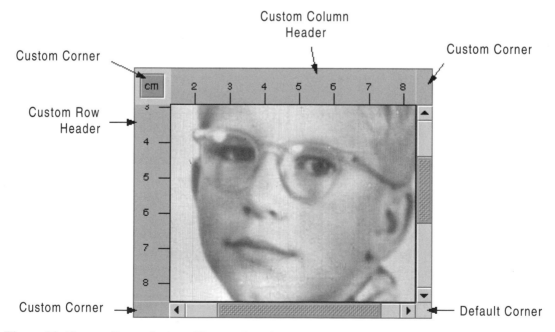

Figure 29 The scroll pane in `ScrollDemo.java` has custom row and column headers and custom corners.

As shown in Figure 29, the scroll pane in `ScrollDemo` has custom row and column headers. Additionally, because all four sides are populated, all four corners are present. The program customizes three of the corners—two just fill their area with the same color as the custom row and column headers, and the other contains a toggle button. The fourth corner, the lower-right corner, is the default provided by the scroll pane. Notice that because the row and column headers are always present in this example, the toggle button is also always present.

If a corner contains a control that the user needs access to all the time, make sure that the sides that intersect at the corner are always present. For example, if this application placed the toggle in the lower-right corner, where the scroll bars intersect, the toggle would disappear if the user resized the window and even one of the scroll bars disappeared.

The scroll pane's row and column headers are provided by a custom `JComponent` subclass, implemented in `Rule.java` (page 699), which draws a ruler in centimeters or in inches. Here's the code that creates and sets the scroll pane's row and column headers:

```
//...where the member variables are defined:
private Rule columnView;
private Rule rowView;
...
    //...where the GUI is initialized:
    ImageIcon david = new ImageIcon("images/youngdad.jpeg");
    ...
    // Create the row and column headers
    columnView = new Rule(Rule.HORIZONTAL, true);
    columnView.setPreferredWidth(david.getIconWidth());
    rowView = new Rule(Rule.VERTICAL, true);
    rowView.setPreferredHeight(david.getIconHeight());
    ...
    pictureScrollPane.setColumnHeaderView(columnView);
    pictureScrollPane.setRowHeaderView(rowView);
    ...
```

You can use any component for a scroll pane's row and column headers. The scroll pane puts the row and column headers in `JViewPorts` of their own. Thus when scrolling horizontally, the column header follows along, and when scrolling vertically, the row header follows along.

As a `JComponent` subclass, our custom `Rule` class puts its rendering code in its `paintCompo-nent` method. Careful scrutiny of the code reveals that special effort is taken to draw only within the current clipping bounds. Your custom row and column headers should do the same to ensure speedy scrolling.

You can also use any component for the corners of a scroll pane. `ScrollDemo` illustrates this by putting a toggle button in the upper-left corner and custom `Corner` objects in the upperright and lower-left corners. Here's the code that creates the Corner objects and calls set-Corner to place them:

```
// Create the corners.
JPanel buttonCorner = new JPanel();
isMetric = new JToggleButton("cm", true);
isMetric.setFont(new Font("SansSerif", Font.PLAIN, 11));
isMetric.setMargin(new Insets(2,2,2,2));
isMetric.addItemListener(new UnitsListener());
buttonCorner.add(isMetric); //Use the default FlowLayout
...
// Set the corners.
pictureScrollPane.setCorner(JScrollPane.UPPER_LEFT_CORNER,
                           buttonCorner);
pictureScrollPane.setCorner(JScrollPane.LOWER_LEFT_CORNER,
                           new Corner());
pictureScrollPane.setCorner(JScrollPane.UPPER_RIGHT_CORNER,
                           new Corner());
```

Remember that the size of each corner is determined by the size of the sides intersecting there. For some components you must take care that the specific instance of the component fits in its corner. For example, the program sets the font and margins on the toggle button so that it fits within the space established by the headers. It's not an issue with theCorner class, which colors its entire bounds, whatever they happen to be, with a solid color.

As you can see from the code, constants indicate the corner positions. This figure shows the constant for each position.

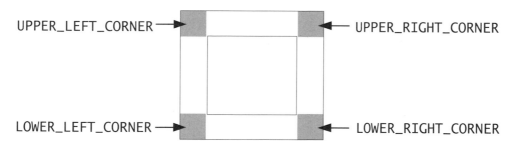

Figure 30 Constants defined in the ScrollPaneConstants interface indicate the corner positions.

The constants are defined in the <u>ScrollPaneConstants</u>[1] interface, which JScrollPane implements.

---

[1] API documentation for this class is available on this book's CD-ROM and online at http://java.sun.com/products/jdk/1.2/docs/api/javax/swing/ScrollPaneConstants.html

Implementing a Scrolling-Savvy Client

To customize the way that a client component interacts with its scroll pane, you can make the component implement the Scrollable[1] interface. By implementing Scrollable, a client can specify both the size of the viewport used to view it and the amount to scroll for clicks on the various parts of a scroll bar. Recall from Figure 28 (page 115) the three control areas of a scroll bar: the knob, the buttons, and the track.

When manipulating the scroll bars in ScrollDemo, you might have noticed that clicking the buttons scrolls the image to a tick boundary. You might also have noticed that clicking in the track scrolls the picture by a "screenful." More generally the button scrolls the visible area by a unit increment, and the track scrolls the visible area by a block increment. The behavior you see in the example is not the scroll pane's default behavior but rather is specified by the client in its implementation of the Scrollable interface.

The client for the ScrollDemo program is ScrollablePicture.java. ScrollablePicture is a subclass of JLabel that implements all five Scrollable methods:

- getScrollableBlockIncrement
- getScrollableUnitIncrement
- getPreferredScrollableViewportSize
- getScrollableTracksViewportHeight
- getScrollableTracksViewportWidth

ScrollablePicture implements the Scrollable interface primarily to affect the unit and block increments. However, it must provide implementations for all five methods. So it provides reasonable defaults for the other three methods that you might want to copy for your scrolling-savvy classes.

The scroll pane calls the client's getScrollableUnitIncrement method whenever the user clicks one of the buttons on the scroll bar. This method returns the number of pixels to scroll. An obvious implementation of this method returns the number of pixels between tick marks on the header rulers. But ScrollablePicture does something different: It returns the value required to position the image on a tick mark boundary. Here's the implementation:

```
public int getScrollableUnitIncrement(Rectangle visibleRect,
                                      int orientation,
                                      int direction) {
    //Get the current position.
    int currentPosition = 0;
    if (orientation == SwingConstants.HORIZONTAL) {
        currentPosition = visibleRect.x;
```

---

[1] API documentation for this class is available on this book's CD-ROM and online at http://java.sun.com/ products/jdk/1.2/docs/api/javax/swing/Scrollable.html

```
        } else {
            currentPosition = visibleRect.y;
        }
        //Return the number of pixels between currentPosition
        //and the nearest tick mark in the indicated direction.
        if (direction < 0) {
            int newPosition = currentPosition -
                              (currentPosition / maxUnitIncrement) *
                              maxUnitIncrement;
            return (newPosition == 0) ? maxUnitIncrement : newPosition;
        } else {
            return ((currentPosition / maxUnitIncrement) + 1) *
                   maxUnitIncrement - currentPosition;
        }
    }
}
```

If the image is already on a tick mark boundary, this method returns the number of pixels between ticks. Otherwise it returns the number of pixels from the current location to the nearest tick.

Likewise the scroll pane calls the client's getScrollableBlockIncrement method each time the user clicks on the track. Here's ScrollablePicture's implementation of this method:

```
    public int getScrollableBlockIncrement(Rectangle visibleRect,
                                           int orientation,
                                           int direction) {
        if (orientation == SwingConstants.HORIZONTAL) {
            return visibleRect.width - maxUnitIncrement;
        } else {
            return visibleRect.height - maxUnitIncrement;
        }
    }
```

This method returns the height of the visible rectangle minus a tick mark. This behavior is typical. A block increment should be slightly smaller than the viewport to leave a little of the previous visible area for context. For example, a text area might leave one or two lines of text for context, and a table might leave a row or a column, depending on the scroll direction.

These Swing components implement the Scrollable interface:

- lists (page 218)
- tables (page 254)
- text components (page 275)
- trees (page 320)

Sizing a Scroll Pane

Unless you explicitly set a scroll pane's preferred size, the scroll pane computes it based on the preferred size of its nine components (the viewport, and, if present, the two scroll bars, the row and column headers, and the four corners). The largest factor—the one most programmers care about—is the size of the viewport used to display the client.

If the client is not scrolling-savvy, the scroll pane sizes itself so that the client displays at its preferred size. For typical unsavvy clients, this makes the scroll pane redundant. That is, the scroll pane has no scroll bars because the client's preferred size is big enough to display the entire client. In this case, if the client doesn't change size dynamically, you should probably limit the size of the scroll pane by setting its preferred size or the preferred size of its container.

If the client is scrolling-savvy, the scroll pane uses the value returned by the client's `getPreferredScrollableViewportSize` method to compute the size of its viewport. Implementations of this method for scrolling generally report a preferred size that's smaller than the component's standard preferred size. For example, by default the value returned by `JList`'s implementation of `getPreferredScrollableViewportSize` is just big enough to display eight rows.

Scrolling-savvy classes, such as lists, tables, text components, and trees, often provide one or more methods that let programmers affect the size returned from `getPreferredScrollableViewportSize`. For example, you can set the number of visible rows in a list or a tree by calling `setVisibleRowCount`. The list or the tree takes care of figuring out the size needed to display that number of rows.

Refer to Table 35 (page 125) for information about scrolling-related methods provided by classes other than `JScrollPane`. And remember: If you don't like the value that `getPreferredScrollableViewportSize` returns, you can always set the preferred size of the scroll pane or its container.

Dynamically Changing the Client's Size

Changing the size of a scroll pane's client is a two-step process. First, set the client's preferred size. Then call `revalidate` on the client to let the scroll pane know that it should update itself and its scroll bars. Let's look at an example.

Here's a picture of an application that changes the client's size whenever the user places a circle whose bounds fall outside of the client's current bounds. The program also changes the client's size when the user clears the drawing area.

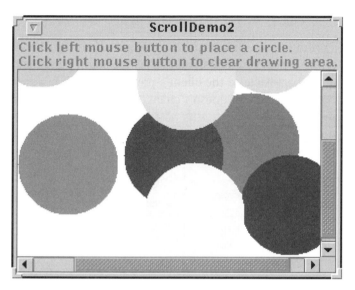

Figure 31 A screenshot of the ScrollDemo2 application.

You can find the full source code for this example in <u>ScrollDemo2.java</u> (page 704), which is based on an example provided by a *Java Tutorial* reader, John Vella.

Here's the code that changes the drawing area's size when necessary:

```
if (changed) {
    //Update client's preferred size because the area taken up
    //by the graphics has gotten larger or smaller (if cleared)
    drawingArea.setPreferredSize(.../* the new size */...);

    //Let the scroll pane know to update itself
    //and its scroll bars.
    drawingArea.revalidate();
}
```

Note that when the client changes size, the scroll bars adjust. Neither the scroll pane nor the viewport resizes.

Refer to <u>SplitPaneDemo2.java</u> (page 719) for another example in which the client object changes size.

The Scroll Pane API

The API for using scroll panes falls into four categories. These are shown in the following tables, which list the commonly used `JScrollPane` constructors and methods, as well as scrolling-related methods in other classes. Other methods you are most likely to invoke on a `JScrollPane` object are those, such as `setPreferredSize`, that its superclasses provide. See The JComponent API (page 70) for tables of commonly used inherited methods.

Table 32   Setting Up the Scroll Pane

Method	Purpose

`JScrollPane()`
`JScrollPane(Component)`
`JScrollPane(int, int)`
`JScrollPane(Component, int, int)`
	Create a scroll pane. The `Component` parameter, when present, sets the scroll pane's client. The two `int` parameters, when present, set the respective vertical and horizontal scroll bar policies.

`void setViewportView(Component)`	Set the scroll pane's client.
`void setVerticalScrollBarPolicy(int)` `int getVerticalScrollBarPolicy()`	Set or get the vertical scroll policy. `ScrollPaneConstants` defines three values for specifying this policy: `VERTICAL_SCROLLBAR_AS_NEEDED` (the default), `VERTICAL_SCROLLBAR_ALWAYS`, and `VERTICAL_SCROLLBAR_NEVER`.
`void setHorizontalScrollBarPolicy(int)` `int getHorizontalScrollBarPolicy()`	Set or get the horizontal scroll policy. `ScrollPaneConstants` defines three values for specifying this policy: `HORIZONTAL_SCROLLBAR_AS_NEEDED` (the default), `HORIZONTAL_SCROLLBAR_ALWAYS`, and `HORIZONTAL_SCROLLBAR_NEVER`.
`void setViewportBorder(Border)` `Border getViewportBorder()`	Set or get the border around the viewport.

Table 33   Decorating the Scroll Pane

Method	Purpose
`void setColumnHeaderView(Component)` `void setRowHeaderView(Component)`	Set the column or row header for the scroll pane.
`void setCorner(Component, int)` `Component getCorner(int)`	Set or get the corner specified. The `int` parameter specifies which corner and must be one of the following constants defined in `ScrollPaneConstants`: `UPPER_LEFT_CORNER`, `UPPER_RIGHT_CORNER`, `LOWER_LEFT_CORNER`, and `LOWER_RIGHT_CORNER`.

Table 34   Implementing the Scrollable Interface

Method	Purpose

`int getScrollableUnitIncrement(Rectangle,`
`                    int, int)`
`void getScrollableBlockIncrement(Rectangle,`
`                    int, int)`
	Get the unit or block increment, in pixels. The `Rectangle` parameter is the bounds of the currently visible rectangle. The first `int` parameter is either `SwingConstants.HORI-ZONTAL` or `SwingConstants.VERTICAL`, depending on what scroll bar the user clicked on. The second `int` parameter indicates which direction to scroll. A value less than 0 indicates up or left. A value greater than 0 indicates down or right.

`Dimension getPreferredScrollableViewportSize()`	Get the preferred size of the viewport. This allows the client to influence the size of the viewport in which it is displayed. If the viewport size is unimportant, implement this method to return `getPreferredSize`.
`boolean getScrollableTracksViewportWidth()` `boolean getScrollableTracksViewportHeight()`	Get whether the scroll pane should force the client to be the same width or height as the viewport. A return value of `true` from either of these methods effectively disallows horizontal or vertical scrolling, respectively.

Table 35   Methods in Other Classes Related to Scrolling

Method	Purpose
`void scrollRectToVisible(Rectangle)` (*in* `JComponent`)	If the component is in a container that supports scrolling, such as a scroll pane, calling this method scrolls the scroll pane such that the specified rectangle is visible.

`void setAutoscrolls(boolean)`
`boolean getAutoScrolls()`
(*in* `JComponent`)
	Set or get whether the component automatically scrolls when the user drags the component with the mouse. Even if autoscrolling is turned on, it works only when the component is in a container that supports scrolling.

`void setVisibleRowCount(int)`
`int getVisibleRowCount()`
(*in* `JList`)
	Set or get how many rows of the list are visible. The `get-PreferredScrollableViewportSize` method uses the visible row count to compute its return value.

`void ensureIndexIsVisible(int)` (*in* `JList`)	Scroll so that the row at the specified index is visible. This method calls `scrollRectToVisible` and works only if the list is in a container that supports scrolling.

Table 35   Methods in Other Classes Related to Scrolling

Method	Purpose
`void setVisibleRowCount(int)` `int getVisibleRowCount()` (*in* `JTree`)	Set or get how many rows of the tree are visible. The `get-PreferredScrollableViewportSize` method uses the visible row count to compute its return value.
`void scrollPathToVisible(TreePath)` `void scrollRowToVisible(int)` (*in* `JTree`)	Scroll so that the specified tree path or row at the specified index is visible. These methods call `scrollRectToVisible` and work only if the tree is in a container that supports scrolling.
`void setScrollsOnExpand(boolean)` `boolean getScrollsOnExpand()` (*in* `JTree`)	Set or get whether scrolling occurs automatically when the user expands a node. True by default. This feature works only when the tree is in a container that supports scrolling.
`void setPreferredScrollableViewportSize(Dimension)` (*in* `JTable`)	Set the value to be returned by `getPreferredScrollableViewportSize`.

Examples that Use Scroll Panes

This table shows the examples that use `JScrollPane` and where those examples are described.

Table 36   Examples that Use `JScrollPane`

Example	Where Described	Notes
`ToolBarDemo.java`	This section, How to Use Tool Bars (page 138)	Shows a simple yet typical use of a scroll pane.
`ScrollDemo.java`	This section	Uses many of scroll pane's bells and whistles.
`ScrollDemo2.java`	This section	Shows how to change the client's size.
`SplitPaneDemo.java`	How to Use Split Panes (page 127), How to Use Lists (page 218)	Puts a list and a label in a scroll pane. Also shows how to handle the case when a scroll pane's client changes size.
`TableDemo.java`	How to Use Tables (page 254)	Puts a table in a scroll pane.
`TextSamplerDemo.java`	An Example that Uses Each Text Component (page 276)	Puts a text area, an editor pane, and a text pane in a scroll pane.
`TreeDemo.java`	How to Use Trees (page 320)	Puts a tree in a scroll pane.

How to Use Split Panes

A `JSplitPane`[1] displays two components, either side by side or one on top of the other. By dragging the divider that appears between the components, the user can specify how much of the split pane's total area goes to each component. You can divide screen space among three or more components by putting split panes inside of split panes, as described in <u>Nesting Split Panes</u> (page 130).

Instead of adding the components of interest directly to a split pane, you often put each component into a scroll pane. You then put the scroll panes into the split pane. This allows the user to view any part of a component of interest, without requiring the component to take up a lot of screen space or to adapt to displaying itself in varying amounts of screen space.

Here's a picture of an application that uses a split pane to display a list and an image side by side.

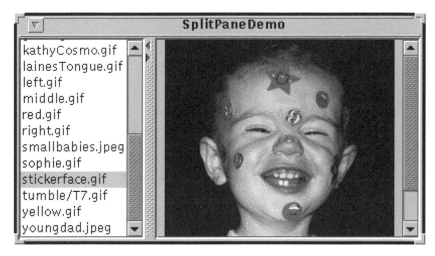

Figure 32 The `SplitPaneDemo` application uses a split pane to display a list and an image side by side.

---

[1] API documentation for this class is available on this book's CD-ROM and online at http://java.sun.com/products/jdk/1.2/docs/api/javax/swing/JSplitPane.html

127

Try this:

1. Compile and run the application.[1] The main source file is <u>SplitPaneDemo.java</u> (page 717). To run the demo you also need imagenames.properties, which provides the image names to put in the JList. You can find the listed image files online[2] and on this book's CD-ROM, or you can modify the properties file to list images you already have.

2. Drag the dimpled line that divides the list and the image to the left or right. Try to drag the divider all the way to the window's edge.

3. Click the tiny arrows on the divider to hide/expand the left or right component.

The following SplitPaneDemo code creates and sets up the split pane:

```
//Create a split pane with the two scroll panes in it.
splitPane = new JSplitPane(JSplitPane.HORIZONTAL_SPLIT,
                           listScrollPane, pictureScrollPane);
splitPane.setOneTouchExpandable(true);
splitPane.setDividerLocation(150);

//Provide minimum sizes for the two components in the split pane.
Dimension minimumSize = new Dimension(100, 50);
listScrollPane.setMinimumSize(minimumSize);
pictureScrollPane.setMinimumSize(minimumSize);
```

The constructor this example uses takes three arguments. The first indicates the split direction. The other arguments are the two components to put in the split pane. Refer to <u>Setting the Components in a Split Pane</u> (page 129) for information about JSplitPane methods that set the components dynamically.

The split pane in this example is split horizontally—the two components appear side by side—as specified by the JSplitPane.HORIZONTAL_SPLIT argument to the constructor. Another option that places one component above the other is specified with JSplit-Pane.VERTICAL_SPLIT. Use the setOrientation method to change the split direction after the split pane has been created.

Two small arrows appear at the top of the divider in the example's split pane. These arrows let the user collapse (and then expand) with a single click either of the components. The current look and feel determines whether these controls appear by default. In the Java Look & Feel, they are turned off by default. The example turned them on with a call to the method setOneTouchExpandable.

---

[1] See <u>Getting Started with Swing</u> (page 3) if you need help.
[2] For a list of links to the image files, see
http://java.sun.com/docs/books/tutorial/uiswing/components/example-swing/index.html

The range of a split pane's divider is determined in part by the minimum sizes of the components within the split pane. See Positioning the Divider and Restricting Its Range (page 129) for details.

Setting the Components in a Split Pane

A program can set a split pane's two components dynamically with these four methods:

- `setLeftComponent`
- `setRightComponent`
- `setTopComponent`
- `setBottomComponent`

You can use any of these methods at any time, regardless of the split pane's current split direction. Calls to `setLeftComponent` and `setTopComponent` are equivalent and set the specified component in the top or left position, depending on the split pane's current split orientation. Similarly calls to `setRightComponent` and `setBottomComponent` are equivalent. These methods replace whatever component is already in that position with the new one.

Like other containers, `JSplitPane` supports the add method. A split pane puts the first component added in the left or top position. The danger of using add is that you can inadvertently call it too many times, in which case the split pane's layout manager will throw a rather esoteric-looking exception. If you are using the add method and a split pane is already populated, you first need to use remove to get rid of the existing components. If you put only one component in a split pane, the divider will be stuck at the right side or the bottom of the split pane, depending on its split direction.

Positioning the Divider and Restricting Its Range

Use the `setDividerLocation` method to position the divider programmatically. You can specify the new position by pixel or by percentage. To get the current divider location specified in pixels, call `getDividerLocation`.

```
splitPane.setDividerLocation(150);//Set divider at pixel 150
splitPane.setDividerLocation(0.25);//25% of the space goes to left/top
```

Another handy method, `resetToPreferredSizes`, sets the divider location such that the two components are at their preferred sizes. This is the initial arrangement of a split pane, unless specified otherwise.

The user can set the divider location by dragging it. A split pane does not allow the user to make either of its components smaller than the component's minimum size by dragging the divider. Thus you can affect the divider's range by setting the minimum sizes of the two components in the split pane. For example, to ensure that a minimum amount of each component in a split is visible at all times, set the minimum size of each component. To allow the user to drag the divider all the way to the edge of the split pane, use 0 for the minimum size.

If you don't set the minimum size of the two components in a split pane, you might end up with a split pane whose divider won't move. By default a split pane sizes its components at their preferred sizes, which for many components is equal to the minimum size. This means that both components are already displayed at their minimum sizes and the divider is stuck. Most programs that put standard components in a split pane need to reduce the minimum sizes of the components in the split pane.

Nesting Split Panes

Here's a picture of a program that achieves a three-way split by nesting one split pane inside of another.

Figure 33 SplitPaneDemo2, an application with a nested split pane.

If the top portion of the split pane looks familiar to you, it's because the program puts the split pane created by SplitPaneDemo inside a second split pane. A simple JLabel is the other component in the second split pane. This is not the most practical use of a nested split pane, but it gets the point across. You can find the source code in <u>SplitPaneDemo2.java</u> (page 719). Here's the code that sets up the nested split panes:

```
//Create an instance of SplitPaneDemo.
SplitPaneDemo splitPaneDemo = new SplitPaneDemo();
JSplitPane top = splitPaneDemo.getSplitPane();
...
//Create a regular old label.
label = new JLabel("Click on an image name in the list.",
                   JLabel.CENTER);
//Create a split pane and put "top" (a split pane)
//and JLabel instance in it.
JSplitPane splitPane = new JSplitPane(JSplitPane.VERTICAL_SPLIT,
                                      top, label);
```

Refer to <u>Solving Common Component Problems</u> (page 337) for information about fixing a border problem that can appear when nesting split panes.

The Split Pane API

The following tables list the commonly used `JSplitPane` constructors and methods. Other methods you are most likely to invoke on a `JSplitPane` object are those, such as `setPreferredSize`, that its superclasses provide. See <u>The JComponent API</u> (page 70) for tables of commonly used inherited methods.

Table 37   Setting Up the Split Pane

Method	Purpose

`JSplitPane()`
`JSplitPane(int)`
`JSplitPane(int, boolean)`
`JSplitPane(int, Component, Component)`
`JSplitPane(int, boolean, Component, Component)`
	Create a split pane. When present, the `int` parameter indicates the split pane's orientation, either `HORIZONTAL_SPLIT` (the default) or `VERTICAL_SPLIT`. The `boolean` parameter, when present, sets whether the components continually repaint as the user drags the split pane. If left unspecified, this option, called *continuous layout*, is turned off. The `Component` parameters set the initial left and right, or top and bottom components, respectively.

`void setOrientation(int)` `int getOrientation()`	Set or get the split pane's orientation. Use either `HORIZONTAL_SPLIT` or `VERTICAL_SPLIT` defined in `JSplitPane`. If left unspecified, the split pane will be horizontally split.
`void setDividerSize(int)` `int getDividerSize()`	Set or get the size of the divider, in pixels.

Table 37   Setting Up the Split Pane

Method	Purpose
`void setContinuousLayout(boolean)` `boolean getContinuousLayout()`	Set or get whether the split pane's components are continually laid out and painted while the user is dragging the divider. By default continuous layout is turned off.
`void setOneTouchExpandable(boolean)` `boolean getOneTouchExpandable()`	Set or get whether the split pane displays a control on the divider to expand/collapse the divider. The default depends on the look and feel. In the Java Look & Feel it's off by default.

Table 38   Managing the Split Pane's Contents

Method	Purpose

`void setTopComponent(Component)`
 `void setBottomComponent(Component)`
 `void setLeftComponent(Component)`
 `void setRightComponent(Component)`
 `Component getTopComponent()`
 `Component getBottomComponent()`
 `Component getLeftComponent()`
 `Component getRightComponent()`
	Set or get the indicated component. Each method works regardless of the split pane's orientation. Top and left are equivalent, and bottom and right are equivalent.

`void remove(Component)` `void removeAll()`	Remove the indicated component(s) from the split pane.
`void add(Component)`	Add the component to the split pane. You can add only two components to a split pane. The first component added is the top/left component. The second component added is the bottom/right component. Attempts to add more components result in an exception.

Table 39   Positioning the Divider

Method	Purpose

`void setDividerLocation(double)`
 `void setDividerLocation(int)`
 `int getDividerLocation()`
	Set or get the current divider location. When setting the divider location, you can specify the new location as a percentage (`double`) or a pixel location (`int`).

`void resetToPreferredSizes()`	Move the divider such that both components are at their preferred sizes. This is how a split pane divides itself at startup, unless specified otherwise.

Table 39   Positioning the Divider

Method	Purpose
`void setLastDividerLocation(int)` `int getLastDividerLocation()`	Set or get the previous position of the divider.
`int getMaximumDividerLocation()` `int getMinimumDividerLocation()`	Get the minimum and maximum locations for the divider. These are set implicitly by setting the minimum sizes of the split pane's two components.

Examples that Use Split Panes

This table shows the examples that use `JSplitPane` and where those examples are described.

Table 40   Examples that Use Split Panes

Example	Where Described	Notes
`SplitPaneDemo.java`	This section and <u>How to Use Lists</u> (page 218)	Shows a split pane with a horizontal split.
`SplitPaneDemo2.java`	This section	Puts a split pane within a split pane to create a three-way split.
`TreeDemo.java`	<u>How to Use Trees</u> (page 320)	Uses a split pane with a vertical split. Does not use the one-touch expandable feature.

How to Use Tabbed Panes

You can use the <u>JTabbedPane</u>[1] class to have several components (usually panels) share the same space. The user chooses which component to view by selecting the tab corresponding to the desired component. If you want similar functionality without the tab interface, you might want to use a <u>card layout</u> (page 363) instead of a tabbed pane.

To create a tabbed pane, you simply instantiate JTabbedPane, create the components you wish it to display, and then add the components to the tabbed pane, using the addTab method.

Here is a picture of an application that has a tabbed pane with four tabs.

Figure 34 The TabbedPaneDemo application.

Try this:

1. Compile and run the application.[2] The full code is in <u>TabbedPaneDemo.java</u> (page 722).
2. Put the cursor over a tab. After a short time, you'll see the tool tip associated with the tab. As a convenience, you can specify tool tip text when you add a component to the tabbed pane.
3. Select a tab. The tabbed pane displays the component corresponding to the tab.

---

[1] API documentation for this class is available on this book's CD-ROM and online at http://java.sun.com/products/jdk/1.2/docs/api/javax/swing/JTabbedPane.html

[2] See <u>Getting Started with Swing</u> (page 3) if you need help compiling and running Swing applications.

As the TabbedPaneDemo example shows, a tab can have a tool tip and can display both text and an image. The example shows the tabs in their default positions, at the top of the tabbed pane. You can change the tab position to be at the left, right, or bottom of the tabbed pane.

Below is the code that creates the tabbed pane in the previous example. Note that no event-handling code is necessary. The JTabbedPane object takes care of mouse events for you.

```
ImageIcon icon = new ImageIcon("images/middle.gif");
JTabbedPane tabbedPane = new JTabbedPane();

Component panel1 = makeTextPanel("Blah");
tabbedPane.addTab("One", icon, panel1, "Does nothing");
tabbedPane.setSelectedIndex(0);

Component panel2 = makeTextPanel("Blah blah");
tabbedPane.addTab("Two", icon, panel2, "Does twice as much nothing");

Component panel3 = makeTextPanel("Blah blah blah");
tabbedPane.addTab("Three", icon, panel3, "Still does nothing");

Component panel4 = makeTextPanel("Blah blah blah blah");
tabbedPane.addTab("Four", icon, panel4, "Does nothing at all");
```

The Tabbed Pane API

The following tables list the commonly used JTabbedPane constructors and methods.

Table 41   Creating and Setting Up a Tabbed Pane

Method	Purpose
JTabbedPane() JTabbedPane(int)	Create a tabbed pane. The optional argument specifies where the tabs should appear. By default the tabs appear at the top of the tabbed pane. You can specify these positions (defined in the SwingConstants interface, which JTabbedPane implements): TOP, BOTTOM, LEFT, RIGHT.
addTab(String, Icon, Component, String) addTab(String, Icon, Component) addTab(String, Component)	Add a new tab to the tabbed pane. The first argument specifies the text on the tab. The optional icon argument specifies the tab's icon. The component argument specifies the component that the tabbed pane should show when the tab is selected. The fourth argument, if present, specifies the tool tip text for the tab.

Table 42   Inserting, Removing, Finding, and Selecting Tabs

Method	Purpose
`insertTab(String, Icon, Component, String, int)`	Insert a tab at the specified index, where the first tab is at index 0. The arguments are the same as for `addTab`.
`remove(Component)` `removeTabAt(int)`	Remove the tab corresponding to the specified component or index.
`removeAll()`	Remove all tabs.
`int indexOfComponent(Component)` `int indexOfTab(String)` `int indexOfTab(Icon)`	Return the index of the tab that has the specified component, title, or icon.
`void setSelectedIndex(int)` `void setSelectedComponent(Component)`	Select the tab that has the specified component or index. Selecting a tab has the effect of displaying its associated component.
`int getSelectedIndex()` `Component getSelectedComponent()`	Return the index or component for the selected tab.

Table 43   Changing Tab Appearance

Method	Purpose
`void setComponentAt(int, Component)` `Component getComponentAt(int)`	Set or get which component is associated with the tab at the specified index. The first tab is at index 0.
`void setTitleAt(int, String)` `String getTitleAt(int)`	Set or get the title of the tab at the specified index.
`void setIconAt(int, Icon)` `Icon getIconAt(int)` `void setDisabledIconAt(int, Icon)` `Icon getDisabledIconAt(int)`	Set or get the icon displayed by the tab at the specified index.
`void setBackgroundAt(int, Color)` `Color getBackgroundAt(int)` `void setForegroundAt(int, Color)` `Color getForegroundAt(int)`	Set or get the background or foreground color used by the tab at the specified index. By default a tab uses the tabbed pane's background and foreground colors. For example, if the tabbed pane's foreground is black, each tab's title is black except for any tabs for which you specify another color, using `setForegroundAt`.
`void setEnabledAt(int, boolean)` `boolean isEnabledAt(int)`	Set or get the enabled state of the tab at the specified index.

Examples that Use Tabbed Panes

This table lists examples that use JTabbedPane and where those examples are described.

Table 44   Examples that Use Tabbed Panes

Example	Where Described	Notes
TabbedPaneDemo.java	This section	Demonstrates a few tabbed-pane features, such as tool tips and icons in tabs. The frame's size is set by using setSize.
AlignmentDemo.java	How to Use BoxLayout (page 350)	Uses a JTabbedPane as the only child of a frame's content pane. The tab's components have different preferred sizes, and the frame uses pack rather than setSize to set its size.
BorderDemo.java	How to Use Borders (page 408)	Uses its tabbed pane in a manner similar to AlignmentDemo's usage.
DialogDemo.java	How to Make Dialogs (page 87)	Has a tabbed pane in the center of a frame's content pane, with a label below it. Uses pack, not setSize, to set the frame's size.

How to Use Tool Bars

A JToolBar[1] is a container that groups several components—usually buttons with icons— into a row or a column. Often tool bars provide easy access to functionality that is also in menus. How to Use Actions (page 389) explains how to provide the same functionality in menu items and tool bar buttons.

The following pictures show an application that contains a tool bar that's initially above a text area.

Figure 35 ToolBarDemo, an application that contains a tool bar and a text area.

By default the user can drag the tool bar to a different edge of its container or out into a window of its own. The next figure shows how the application looks after the user has dragged the tool bar to the right-hand edge of its container.

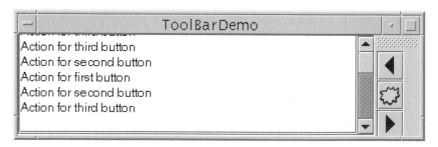

Figure 36 ToolBarDemo after tool bar was dragged to the right-hand edge of its container.

---

[1] API documentation for this class is available on this book's CD-ROM and online at http://java.sun.com/ products/jdk/1.2/docs/api/javax/swing/JToolBar.html

For the drag-out behavior to work correctly, the tool bar must be in a container that uses `Bor`-`derLayout`. The component that the tool bar affects is generally in the center of the container. The tool bar must be the only other component in the container; it must not be in the center.

The next figure shows how the application looks after the user has dragged the tool bar outside its window.

Figure 37 `ToolBarDemo` after the user has dragged the tool bar outside its window.

The following code implements the tool bar. You can find the entire program in `ToolBar-Demo.java` (page 759). It relies on these images: `left.gif`, `middle.gif`, and `right.gif`.[1]

Note: If any buttons in your tool bar duplicate functionality of other components, such as menu items, then you should probably create and add the toolbar buttons as described in How to Use Actions (page 389).

```
public ToolBarDemo() {
    ...
    JToolBar toolBar = new JToolBar();
    addButtons(toolBar);
    ...
    JPanel contentPane = new JPanel();
    contentPane.setLayout(new BorderLayout());
    ...
    contentPane.add(toolBar, BorderLayout.NORTH);
    contentPane.add(scrollPane, BorderLayout.CENTER);
    ...
}
```

---

[1] For a list of links to the image files online, see http://java.sun.com/docs/books/tutorial/uiswing/components/example-swing/index.html

```java
protected void addButtons(JToolBar toolBar) {
    JButton button = null;
    //first button
    button = new JButton(new ImageIcon("images/left.gif"));
    ...
    toolBar.add(button);

    //second button
    button = new JButton(new ImageIcon("images/middle.gif"));
    ...
    toolBar.add(button);

    //third button
    button = new JButton(new ImageIcon("images/right.gif"));
    ...
    toolBar.add(button);
}
```

By adding a few lines of code to the preceding example, we can demonstrate some more tool bar features:

- Using the `setFloatable(false)` method to make a tool bar immovable
- Adding a separator to a tool bar
- Adding a nonbutton component to a tool bar

Here is a picture of the new user interface, which is implemented in <u>ToolBarDemo2.java</u> (page 760).

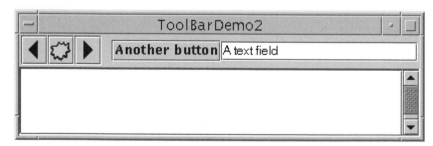

Figure 38 The revised `ToolBarDemo`, in which the tool bar can no longer be dragged and nonbutton components abound.

Because the tool bar can no longer be dragged, it no longer has bumps at its left edge. Here's the code that turns off dragging:

```java
toolBar.setFloatable(false);
```

The biggest visible difference is that the tool bar contains two new components, which are preceded by a blank space—a *separator*. Here is the code that adds the separator:

```
toolBar.addSeparator();
```

Here is the code that adds the new components:

```
.../add to where the first button is initialized:
button.setAlignmentY(CENTER_ALIGNMENT);
.../add to where the second button is initialized:
button.setAlignmentY(CENTER_ALIGNMENT);
.../add to where the third button is initialized:
button.setAlignmentY(CENTER_ALIGNMENT);
...
//fourth button
button = new JButton("Another button");
...
button.setAlignmentY(CENTER_ALIGNMENT);
toolBar.add(button);

//fifth component is NOT a button!
JTextField textField = new JTextField("A text field");
...
textField.setAlignmentY(CENTER_ALIGNMENT);
toolBar.add(textField);
```

The setAlignmentY calls are necessary to make the tool bar's components align nicely. If the code doesn't set the alignment, the text field is positioned too high. That happens because JToolBar uses BoxLayout as its layout manager and because buttons and text fields have different default *Y* alignments. If you encounter layout problems in a tool bar, see How to Use BoxLayout (page 350) for help.

The Tool Bar API

The following table lists the commonly used JToolBar constructors and methods. Other methods you might call are listed in the API tables in The JComponent API (page 70).

Table 45   The Tool Bar API

Method	Purpose
`JToolBar()`	Create a tool bar.
`JButton add(Action)` `Component add(Component)`	Add a component, usually a button, to the tool bar. If the argument to `add` is an `Action` object, the tool bar automatically creates a `JButton` and adds it.
`void addSeparator()`	Add a separator to the end of the tool bar.
`void setFloatable(boolean)` `boolean isFloatable()`	Indicate that the user can drag the tool bar out into a separate window. True by default. To turn off tool bar dragging, use `toolbar.setFloatable(false)`.

Examples that Use Tool Bars

This table lists examples that use `JToolBar` and where those examples are described.

Table 46   Examples that Use Tool Bars

Example	Where Described	Notes
`ToolBarDemo.java`	This section	A basic tool bar with icon-only buttons.
`ToolBarDemo2.java`	This section	Demonstrates a nonfloatable tool bar containing a separator and nonbutton components.
`ActionDemo.java`	How to Use Actions (page 389)	Implements a tool bar, using `Action` objects.

How to Use Internal Frames

With the `JInternalFrame`[1] class you can display a `JFrame`-like window within another window. Usually you add internal frames to a desktop pane, which in turn might be used as the content pane of a `JFrame`, see How to Make Frames (page 82). The desktop pane is an instance of `JDesktopPane`,[2] which is a subclass of `JLayeredPane`[3] that has added API for managing multiple overlapping internal frames.

You should consider carefully whether to base your program's GUI around frames or internal frames. Switching from internal frames to frames or vice versa isn't necessarily a simple task. By experimenting with both frames and internal frames, you can get an idea of the tradeoffs involved in choosing one over the other.

Here is a picture of an application that has two internal frames inside a regular frame.

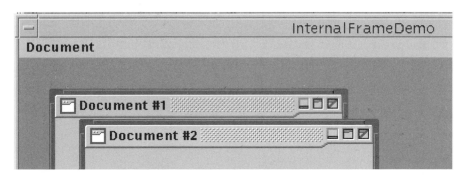

Figure 39 A partial screenshot of an application that uses an internal frame.

As the figure shows, the window decorations on the internal frames reflect the Java Look & Feel. However, the window that contains them has the decorations for the native look and feel (in this case, Motif).

---

[1] API documentation for this class is available on this book's CD-ROM and online at http://java.sun.com/products/jdk/1.2/docs/api/javax/swing/JInternalFrame.html

[2] http://java.sun.com/products/jdk/1.2/docs/api/javax/swing/JDesktopPane.html

[3] For more information on `JLayeredPane`, see How to Use Layered Panes (page 150).

Try this:

1. Compile and run the application.[1] The source files are <u>InternalFrameDemo.java</u> (page 668) and <u>MyInternalFrame.java</u> (page 689) included.

2. Create new internal frames, using the Create item in the Document menu. Each internal frame comes up 30 pixels lower and to the right of the place where the previous internal frame first appeared. This functionality is implemented in the MyInternalFrame class, which is a custom subclass of JInternalFrame.

The following code, taken from InternalFrameDemo.java, creates the desktop and internal frames in the previous example.

```
.../In the constructor of InternalFrameDemo, a JFrame subclass:
    desktop = new JDesktopPane();
    createFrame(); //Create first window
    setContentPane(desktop);
    ...
    //Make dragging faster:
    desktop.putClientProperty("JDesktopPane.dragMode", "outline");
...

protected void createFrame() {
    MyInternalFrame frame = new MyInternalFrame();
    desktop.add(frame);
    try {
        frame.setSelected(true);
    } catch (java.beans.PropertyVetoException e) {}
}

.../In the constructor of MyInternalFrame, a JInternalFrame subclass:
static int openFrameCount = 0;
static final int xOffset = 30, yOffset = 30;
public MyInternalFrame() {
    super("Document #" + (++openFrameCount),
            true, //resizable
            true, //closable
            true, //maximizable
            true);//iconifiable
    //...Create the GUI and put it in the window...
    //...Then set the window size or call pack...
    ...
    //Set the window's location.
    setLocation(xOffset*openFrameCount, yOffset*openFrameCount);
}
```

---

[1] See <u>Getting Started with Swing</u> (page 3), if you need help.

Internal Frames versus Regular Frames

The code for using internal frames is similar in many ways to the code for using regular Swing frames. Because internal frames have root panes, setting up the GUI for a JInternalFrame is very similar to setting up the GUI for a JFrame. In addition, JInternalFrame provides other API, such as pack, that makes it similar to JFrame.

Internal frames aren't windows or top-level containers, however, which makes them different from frames. For example, you must add an internal frame to a container (usually a JDesktopPane); an internal frame can't be the root of a containment hierarchy. Also, internal frames don't generate window events. Instead the user actions that would cause a frame to fire window events cause an internal frame to fire internal frame events.

Because internal frames are implemented with platform-independent code, they add some features that frames can't give you. One such feature is that internal frames give you more control over their state and capabilities than frames do. You can programmatically iconify or maximize an internal frame. You can also specify what icon goes in the internal frame's title bar. You can even specify whether the internal frame has the window decorations to support resizing, iconifying, closing, and maximizing.

Another feature is that internal frames are designed to work within desktop panes. The JInternalFrame API contains methods, such as moveToFront, that work only if the internal frame's container is a layered pane, such as a JDesktopPane.

Rules of Using Internal Frames

If you've built any programs using JFrame and the other Swing components, you already know a lot about how to use internal frames. The following list summarizes the rules for using internal frames. For additional information, see How to Make Frames (page 82) and The JComponent API (page 70).

You must set the size of the internal frame.
> If you don't set the size of the internal frame, it will have zero size and thus never be visible. You can set the size by using one of the following methods: setSize, pack, or setBounds.

You should, in general, set the location of the internal frame.
> If you don't set the location of the internal frame, it will come up at 0,0 (the upper-left of its container). You can use the setLocation or the setBounds method to specify the upper-left point of the internal frame, relative to its container.

To add components to an internal frame, you add them to its content pane.
> This is exactly like the JFrame situation. See Adding Components (page 109) for details.

Dialogs that are internal frames should be implemented by using `JOptionPane` or `JInternalFrame`, not `JDialog`.

To create a simple dialog, you can use the `JOptionPane showInternalXxxDialog` methods, as described in <u>How to Make Dialogs</u> (page 87).

You must add an internal frame to a container.

If you don't add the internal frame to a container (usually a `JDesktopPane`), the internal frame won't appear.

You don't usually need to call `show` or `setVisible` on internal frames.

Like a button, an internal frame automatically is shown either when it's added to a visible container or when its previously invisible container is made visible.

Internal frames fire internal frame events, not window events.

Handling internal frame events is almost identical to handling window events. See <u>How to Write an Internal Frame Listener</u> (page 480) for more information.

Performance Tip: Because dragging internal frames can be slow, Swing 1.1.1 adds a way to make it zippy: outline dragging. With outline dragging, only the outline of the internal frame is painted at the current mouse position while the window's being dragged. The internal frame's innards are not repainted at a new position until dragging stops. The default, slower behavior is to reposition and to repaint the entire internal frame continuously while it's being moved.

In a future release, the Swing team plans to add a method to let you specify outline dragging. Until that method is added, you can specify outline dragging by setting a client property of the desktop pane, like this:

```
desktop.putClientProperty("JDesktopPane.dragMode", "outline");
```

The preceding code has no effect in JFC implementations before Swing 1.1.1 Beta 1.

The Internal Frame API

The following tables list the commonly used `JInternalFrame` constructors and methods, as well as a few methods that `JDesktopPane` provides. Besides the API listed in this section, `JInternalFrame` inherits useful API from its superclasses: `JComponent`, `Component`, and `Container`. See <u>The JComponent Class</u> (page 67) for lists of methods from those classes.

Like `JInternalFrame`, `JDesktopPane` descends from `JComponent` and thus provides the methods described in <u>The JComponent API</u> (page 70). Because `JDesktopPane` extends `JLayeredPane`, it also supports the methods described in <u>The Layered Pane API</u> (page 156).

Table 47   Creating the Internal Frame

Constructor or Method	Purpose

`JInternalFrame()`
`JInternalFrame(String)`
`JInternalFrame(String, boolean)`
`JInternalFrame(String, boolean,`
`                    boolean)`
`JInternalFrame(String, boolean,`
`                    boolean, boolean)`
`JInternalFrame(String, boolean,`
`          boolean, boolean, boolean)`
	Create a `JInternalFrame` instance. The first argument specifies the title, if any, to be displayed by the internal frame. The rest of the arguments specify whether the internal frame should contain decorations allowing the user to resize, close, maximize, and iconify (specified in that order) the internal frame. The default value for each boolean argument is `false`, which means that the operation is not allowed.

`JOptionPane` class methods:
`  showInternalConfirmDialog(...)`
`  showInternalInputDialog(...)`
`  showInternalMessageDialog(...)`
`  showInternalOptionDialog(...)`
	Create a `JInternalFrame` that simulates a dialog. See How to Make Dialogs (page 87) for details.

Table 48   Adding Components to the Internal Frame

Method	Purpose
`void setContentPane(Container)` `Container getContentPane()`	Set or get the internal frame's content pane, which generally contains all of the internal frame's GUI, with the exception of the menu bar and window decorations.
`void setJMenuBar(JMenuBar)` `JMenuBar getJMenuBar()`	Set or get the internal frame's menu bar. Note that some early Swing releases do not include this method.

Table 49   Specifying the Internal Frame's Size and Location

Method	Purpose
`void pack()`	Size the internal frame so that its components are at their preferred sizes.
`void setLocation(Point)` `void setLocation(int, int)`	Set the position of the internal frame. (Inherited from Component.)
`void setBounds(Rectangle)` `void setBounds(int, int, int, int)`	Explicitly set the size and location of the internal frame. (Inherited from `Component`.)
`void setSize(Dimension)` `void setSize(int, int)`	Explicitly set the size of the internal frame. (Inherited from `Component`.)

Table 50   Performing Window Operations on the Internal Frame

Method	Purpose
`void setDefaultCloseOperation(int)` `int getDefaultCloseOperation()`	Set or get what the internal frame does when the user attempts to "close" the internal frame. The default value is `HIDE_ON_CLOSE`. Other possible values are `DO_NOTHING_ON_CLOSE` and `DISPOSE_ON_CLOSE`. See <u>Responding to Window-Closing Events</u> (page 84) for details.

`void addInternalFrameListener(`
`    InternalFrameListener)`
`void removeInternalFrameListener(`
`    InternalFrameListener)`
	Add or remove an internal frame listener (`JInternal-Frame`'s equivalent of a window listener). See <u>How to Write an Internal Frame Listener</u> (page 480) for more information.

`void moveToFront()` `void moveToBack()`	If the internal frame's parent is a layered pane, such as a desktop pane, moves the internal frame to the front or back, respectively, of its layer.
`void setClosed(boolean)` `boolean isClosed()`	Set or get whether the internal frame is currently closed.
`void setIcon(boolean)` `boolean isIcon()`	Iconify or deiconify the internal frame, or determine whether it's currently iconified.
`void setMaximum(boolean)` `boolean isMaximum()`	Maximize or restore the internal frame, or determine whether it's maximized.
`void setSelected(boolean)` `boolean isSelected()`	Set or get whether the internal frame is the currently "selected" (activated) internal frame.

Table 51   Controlling Window Decorations and Capabilities

Method	Purpose
`void setFrameIcon(Icon)` `Icon getFrameIcon()`	Set or get the icon displayed in the title bar of the internal frame (usually in the top-left corner).
`void setClosable(boolean)` `boolean isClosable()`	Set or get whether the user can close the internal frame.
`void setIconifiable(boolean)` `boolean isIconifiable()`	Set or get whether the internal frame can be iconified.
`void setMaximizable(boolean)` `boolean isMaximizable()`	Set or get whether the user can maximize this internal frame.
`void setResizable(boolean)` `boolean isResizable()`	Set or get whether the internal frame can be resized.
`void setTitle(String)` `String getTitle()`	Set or get the window title.

Table 52   Using the `JDesktopPane` API

Constructor or Method	Purpose
`JDesktopPane()`	Create a new instance of `JDesktopPane`.
`JInternalFrame[] getAllFrames()`	Return all `JInternalFrame` objects that the desktop contains.
`JInternalFrame[] getAllFramesInLayer(int)`	Return all `JInternalFrame` objects that the desktop contains that are in the specified layer. See How to Use Layered Panes (page 150) for information about layers.

Examples that Use Internal Frames

The following examples use internal frames. Because internal frames are similar to regular frames, you should also look at Examples that Use Frames (page 86).

Table 53   Examples that Use Internal Frames

Example	Where Described	Notes
`MyInternalFrame.java`	This section	Implements an internal frame that appears at an offset to the previously created internal frame.
`InternalFrameDemo.java`	This section	Lets you create internal frames (instances of `MyInternalFrame`) that go into the application's `JDesktopPane`.
`InternalFrameEvent-Demo.java`	How to Write an Internal Frame Listener (page 480)	Demonstrates listening for internal frame events. Also demonstrates positioning internal frames within a desktop pane.

How to Use Layered Panes

A layered pane is a Swing container that provides a third dimension for positioning components: *depth*, also known as *Z-order*. When adding a component to a layered pane, you specify its depth as an integer. The higher the number, the higher the depth. If components overlap, those at a higher depth are drawn on top of components at a lower depth. The relationship between components at the same depth is determined by their positions within the depth.

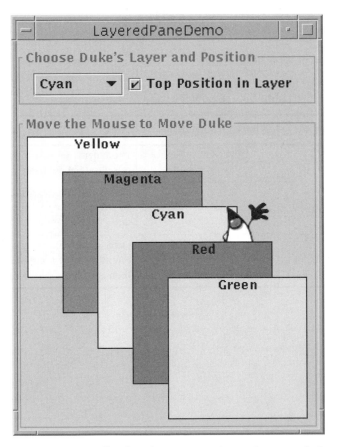

Figure 40 `LayeredPaneDemo`, an application that creates a layered pane and places overlapping, colored labels at various depths.

Every Swing container that has a root pane—such as `JFrame`,[1] `JApplet`,[2] `JDialog`,[3] or `JInternalFrame`[4]—automatically has a layered pane. Most programs don't explicitly use the root pane's layered pane, so we don't discuss it in this section. You can find information about it in The Root Pane (page 80), which provides an overview, and The Layered Pane API (page 156), which has further details. This section concentrates on telling you how to create your own layered pane and use it anywhere you might use a regular Swing container.

Swing provides two layered pane classes. The first, `JLayeredPane`, is the class that root panes use and is the class used by the example in this section. The second, `JDesktopPane`, is a `JLayeredPane` subclass, specialized for the task of holding internal frames. For examples of using `JDesktopPane`, see How to Use Internal Frames (page 143).

Try this:

1. Compile and run the `LayeredPaneDemo` application.[5] The source file is Layered-PaneDemo.java (page 671). You will also need the dukeWaveRed.gif image file.[6]

2. Move the mouse around in the lower part of the window. The image of Duke drags behind the green and red labels (layers three and four) but in front of the other three labels (which have lower depths).

3. Use the combo box at the top of the window to change Duke's depth. Use the check box to set whether Duke is in the top position—position 0—within the current depth.

Here's the code from the sample program that creates the layered pane:

```
layeredPane = new JLayeredPane();
layeredPane.setPreferredSize(new Dimension(300, 310));
layeredPane.setBorder(BorderFactory.createTitledBorder(
                    "Move the Mouse to Move Duke"));
layeredPane.addMouseMotionListener(new MouseMotionAdapter() {
    ...
});
```

The code uses `JLayeredPane`'s only constructor—the no-argument constructor—to create the layered pane. The rest of the code uses methods inherited from superclasses to give the layered pane a preferred size and a border and to add a mouse-motion listener to it. The mouse-motion listener just moves the Duke image around in response to mouse movement.

---

[1] See How to Make Frames (page 82) for more information.
[2] See How to Make Applets (page 99) for more information.
[3] See How to Make Dialogs (page 87) for more information.
[4] See How to Use Internal Frames (page 143) for more information.
[5] See Getting Started with Swing (page 3), if you need help.
[6] You can find this image on the CD-ROM or online at http://java.sun.com/docs/books/tutorial/uiswing/components/example-swing/index.html

Ultimately the example adds the layered pane to the frame's content pane:

```
Container contentPane = getContentPane();
contentPane.setLayout(...);
...
contentPane.add(layeredPane);
```

As we'll show you a bit later, you add components to a layered pane by using an add method. When adding a component to a layered pane, you specify the component's depth and optionally its position within its depth. The layered pane in the demo program contains six labels—the five colored labels and a sixth one that displays the Duke image. As the program demonstrates, both the depth of a component and its position within that depth can change dynamically.

Adding Components and Setting Component Depth

Here's the sample-program code that adds the colored labels to the layered pane:

```
for (int i = 0; i < ...number of labels...; i++) {
    JLabel label = createColoredLabel(...);
    layeredPane.add(label, new Integer(i));
    ...
}
```

You can find the implementation of the createColoredLabel method in the source code for the program. It just creates an opaque JLabel initialized with a background color, a border, some text, and a size.

The sample program uses a two-argument version of the add method. The first argument is the component to add, and the second is an Integer object specifying the depth. This program uses the for loop's iteration variable to specify depths. The actual values don't matter much. What matters is the relative value of the depths and that you are consistent within your program in how you use each depth.

Note: If you use the root pane's layered pane, be sure to use its depth conventions. Refer to The Layered Pane (page 162) for details. That section shows you how to modify LayeredPaneDemo to use the root pane's layered pane. With the modifications, you can see how the dragging Duke image relates to the combo box in the control panel.

As you can see from the sample program, if components overlap, those at a higher depth are on top of components at a lower depth. To change a component's depth dynamically, use the setLayer method. In the example the user can change Duke's layer by making a selection from the combo box. Here's the actionPerformed method of the action listener registered on the combo box:

```
public void actionPerformed(ActionEvent e) {
    int position = onTop.isSelected() ? 0 : 1;
    layeredPane.setLayer(dukeLabel, layerList.getSelectedIndex(),
                         position);
}
```

The setLayer method used here takes three arguments: the component whose depth is to be set, the new depth, and the position within the depth. JLayeredPane has a two-argument version of setLayer that takes only the component and the new depth. That method puts the component at the bottom position in its depth.

Note: When adding a component to a layered pane, you specify the layer with an Integer. When using setLayer to change a component's layer, you use an int. You might think that if you use an int instead of an Integer with the add method, the compiler would complain or that your program would throw an illegal argument exception. But the compiler says nothing, which results in a common layered pane problem. You can use the API tables at the end of this section to check the types of the arguments and return values for methods that deal with layers.

Setting a Component's Position Within Its Depth

The following code creates the label that displays Duke's image and then adds the label to the layered pane:

```
final ImageIcon icon = new ImageIcon("images/dukeWaveRed.gif");
...
dukeLabel = new JLabel(icon);
dukeLabel.setBounds(15, 225, icon.getIconWidth(), icon.getIconHeight());
layeredPane.add(dukeLabel, new Integer(2), 0);
```

This code uses the three-argument version of the add method. The third argument specifies the Duke label's position within its depth, which determines the component's relationship with other components at the same depth.

Positions are specified with an int between -1 and $(n - 1)$, where n is the number of components at the depth. Unlike layer numbers, the smaller the position number, the higher the component within its depth. Using -1 is the same as using $(n - 1)$; it indicates the bottommost position. Using 0 specifies that the component should be in the topmost position within its depth. As the following figure shows, with the exception of –1, a lower-position number indicates a higher position within a depth.

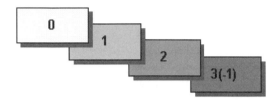

Figure 41 A lower-position number indicates a higher position within a depth.

A component's position within its layer can change dynamically. You can use the check box in the example to determine whether the Duke label is in the top position at its depth. Here's the `actionPerformed` method for the action listener registered on the check box:

```java
public void actionPerformed(ActionEvent e) {
    if (onTop.isSelected()) {
        layeredPane.moveToFront(dukeLabel);
    } else {
        layeredPane.moveToBack(dukeLabel);
    }
}
```

When the user selects the check box, the `moveToFront` method moves Duke to the front (position 0). And when the user deselects check box, the `moveToBack` method moves Duke to the back. You can also use the `setPosition` method or the three-argument version of `set-Layer` to change a component's position.

Laying Out Components in a Layered Pane

By default a layered pane has no layout manager. This means that you typically have to write the code that positions and sizes the components you put in a layered pane.

The example uses the `setBounds` method to set the size and the position of each of the labels:

```java
dukeLabel.setBounds(15, 225, icon.getIconWidth(), icon.getIconHeight());
...
label.setBounds(origin.x, origin.y, 140, 140);
```

When the user moves the mouse around, the program calls `setPosition` to change Duke's position:

```java
dukeLabel.setLocation(e.getX()-XFUDGE, e.getY()-YFUDGE);
```

Although by default a layered pane has no layout manager, you can still assign a layout manager to the layered pane. All of the layout managers provided by the Java platform arrange the components as if they were all on one layer. The following version of the previous demo sets the layered pane's layout manager to an instance of GridLayout, using that layout manager to lay out six colored labels.

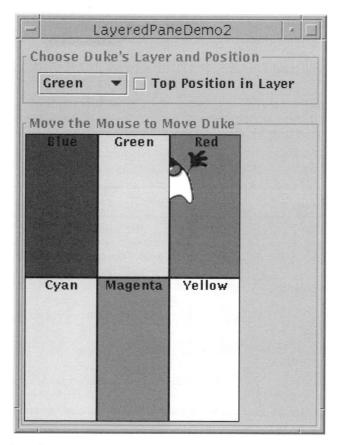

Figure 42 This version of LayeredPaneDemo sets the layered pane's layout manager to an instance of GridLayout, using that layout manager to lay out six colored labels.

You can find the code for this program in LayeredPaneDemo2.java (page 673).

Many programs use intermediate containers, such as panels, and their layout managers to lay out components on the same layer. However, to lay out components on *different* layers, use absolute positioning. For more information about absolute positioning, see Doing Without a Layout Manager (Absolute Positioning) (page 383).

The Layered Pane API

The following tables list the commonly used `JLayeredPane` constructors and methods. Other methods you are most likely to invoke on a `JLayeredPane` object are those it inherits from its superclasses, such as `setBorder`, `setPreferredSize`, and so on. See The JComponent API (page 70) for tables of commonly used inherited methods.

Table 54   Creating or Getting a Layered Pane

Method	Purpose
`JLayeredPane()`	Create a layered pane.
`JLayeredPane getLayeredPane()` (*in* `JApplet`, `JDialog`, `JFrame`, *and* `JInternalFrame`)	Get the automatic layered pane in an applet, dialog, frame, or internal frame.

Table 55   Layering Components

Method	Purpose

`void add(Component)`
 `void add(Component, Integer)`
 `void add(Component, Integer, int)`
	Add the specified component to the layered pane. The second argument, when present, indicates the layer. The third argument, when present, indicates the component's position within its layer. If you use the one-argument version of this method, the component is added to layer 0. If you use the one- or two-argument version of this method, the component is placed underneath all other components currently in the same layer.

`void setLayer(Component, int)` `void setLayer(Component, int, int)`	Change the component's layer. The second argument indicates the layer. The third argument, when present, indicates the component's position within its layer.
`int getLayer(Component)` `int getLayer(JComponent)`	Get the layer for the specified component.
`int getComponentCountInLayer(int)`	Get the number of components in the specified layer. The value returned by this method can be useful for computing position values.
`Component[] getComponentsInLayer(int)`	Get an array of all the components in the specified layer.
`int highestLayer()` `int lowestLayer()`	Compute the highest or lowest layer currently in use.

Table 56   Setting Components' Intralayer Positions

Method	Purpose
`void setPosition(Component, int)` `int getPosition(Component)`	Set or get the position for the specified component within its layer.
`void moveToFront(Component)` `void moveToBack(Component)`	Move the specified component to the front or back of its layer.

Examples that Use Layered Panes

This table shows the examples that use `JLayeredPane` and where those examples are described.

Table 57   Examples that Use Layered Panes

Example	Where Described	Notes
`LayeredPaneDemo.java`	This section	Illustrates layers and intralayer positions of a `JLayeredPane`.
`LayeredPaneDemo2.java`	This section	Uses a layout manager to help lay out the components in a layered pane.
No source provided	The Layered Pane (page 162)	The description explains how to change `LayeredPaneDemo` to use the root pane's layered pane.
`InternalFrameDemo.java`	How to Use Internal Frames (page 143)	Uses a `JDesktopFrame` to manage internal frames.

How to Use Root Panes

In general you don't directly create a `JRootPane`[1] object. Instead you get a `JRootPane` (whether you want it or not!) when you instantiate `JInternalFrame`[2] or one of the top-level Swing containers, such as `JApplet`,[3] `JDialog`,[4] and `JFrame`.[5]

Using Top-Level Containers (page 77) tells you the basics of using root panes—getting the content pane, setting its layout manager, and adding Swing components to it. This section tells you more about root panes, including the components that make up a root pane and how you can use them.[6]

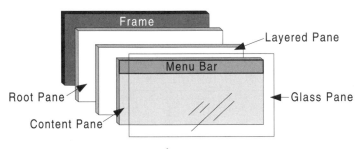

Figure 43 A root pane has four parts.

As the preceding figure shows, a root pane has four parts.

The glass pane

By default, hidden. If you make the glass pane visible, it's like a sheet of glass over all of the other parts of the root pane. It's completely transparent unless you implement the glass pane's `paint` method so that it does something, and it intercepts input events for the root pane. In the next section you'll see an example of using a glass pane.

---

[1] API documentation for this class is available on this book's CD-ROM and online at http://java.sun.com/ products/jdk/1.2/docs/api/javax/swing/JRootPane.html

[2] For details on `JInternalFrame`, see How to Use Internal Frames (page 143).

[3] For details on `JApplet`, see How to Make Applets (page 99).

[4] For details on `JDialog`, see How to Make Dialogs (page 87).

[5] For details on `JFrame`, see How to Make Frames (page 82).

[6] For more information, see "Understanding Containers," an article in the online magazine, *The Swing Connection. The Swing Connection* is available on this book's CD-ROM and online at http://java.sun.com/ products/jfc/tsc/index.html

The layered pane

Serves to position its contents, which consist of the content pane and the optional menu bar. Can also hold other components in a specified Z-order. For information, see The Layered Pane (page 162).

The content pane

The container of the root pane's visible components, excluding the menu bar. For information on using the content pane, see Using Top-Level Containers (page 77).

The optional menu bar

The home for the root pane's container's menus. If the container has a menu bar, you generally use the container's setJMenuBar method to put the menu bar in the appropriate place. For more information on using menus and menu bars, see How to Use Menus (page 226).

The Glass Pane

The glass pane is useful when you want to be able to catch events or to paint over an area that already contains one or more components. For example, you can deactivate mouse events for a multicomponent region by having the glass pane intercept the events. Or you can use the glass pane to display an image over multiple components.

Here's a picture of an application that demonstrates glass pane features. The glass pane contains a check box that lets you set whether the glass pane is "visible"—whether it can get events and paint itself onscreen. When the glass pane is visible, it blocks all input events from reaching the components in the content pane and also paints a red dot in the place where it last detected a mouse-pressed event.

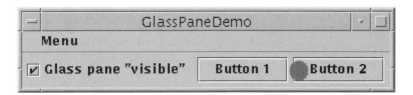

Figure 44 The GlassPaneDemo application.

Try this:

1. Compile and run the application.[1] The source file is GlassPaneDemo.java (page 661).

2. Click Button 1. The button's appearance changes to show that it's been clicked.

---

[1] See Getting Started with Swing (page 3), if you need help.

3. Click the check box so that the glass pane becomes "visible," and then click Button 1 again. The button does *not* detect the mouse-pressed event, because the glass pane intercepts it. When the glass pane detects the event, it beeps and paints a red circle where you clicked.

4. Click the check box again so that the glass pane is hidden. When it detects an event over the check box, the root pane forwards that event to the check box. Otherwise the check box would not respond to clicks.

The following code from `GlassPaneDemo.java` shows and hides the glass pane. This program happens to create its own glass pane, setting it by using the `JFramesetGlassPane` method. However, if a glass pane doesn't do any painting, the program might simply attach listeners to the default glass pane, as returned by `getGlassPane`.

```
...//where GlassPaneDemo's UI is initialized:
JCheckBox changeButton =
        new JCheckBox("Glass pane \"visible\"");
changeButton.setSelected(false);
changeButton.addItemListener(new ItemListener() {
    public void itemStateChanged(ItemEvent e) {
        myGlassPane.setVisible(e.getStateChange()
                               == ItemEvent.SELECTED);
    }
});
```

The next code snippet implements the mouse-event handling for the glass pane. If a mouse event occurs over the check box or the menu bar, the glass pane redispatches the event so that the check box or menu component receives it. So that the check box and menu behave properly, they also receive all drag events that started with a press in the button or menu bar.

```
...//In the implementation of the glass pane's mouse listener:
public void mouseMoved(MouseEvent e) {
    redispatchMouseEvent(e, false);
}

.../* The mouseDragged, mouseClicked, mouseEntered,
 * mouseExited, and mousePressed methods have the same
 * implementation as mouseMoved. */...

public void mouseReleased(MouseEvent e) {
    redispatchMouseEvent(e, true);
    inDrag = false;
}
```

```
private void redispatchMouseEvent(MouseEvent e, boolean repaint) {
    boolean inButton = false;
    boolean inMenuBar = false;
    Point glassPanePoint = e.getPoint();
    Component component = null;
    Container container = contentPane;
    Point containerPoint = SwingUtilities.convertPoint(
                                    glassPane,
                                    glassPanePoint,
                                    contentPane);
    int eventID = e.getID();
    if (containerPoint.y < 0) {
        inMenuBar = true;
        //...set container and containerPoint accordingly...
        testForDrag(eventID);
    }
    component = SwingUtilities.getDeepestComponentAt(
                                    container,
                                    containerPoint.x,
                                    containerPoint.y);
    if (component == null) {
        return;
    }
    if (component.equals(liveButton)) {
        inButton = true;
        testForDrag(eventID);
    }
    if (inMenuBar || inButton || inDrag) {
        ...//Redispatch the event to component...
    }
    if (repaint) {
        toolkit.beep();
        glassPane.setPoint(glassPanePoint);
        glassPane.repaint();
    }
}

private void testForDrag(int eventID) {
    if (eventID == MouseEvent.MOUSE_PRESSED) {
        inDrag = true;
    }
}
```

Here is the code that implements the painting for the glass pane:

```
...//where GlassPaneDemo's UI is initialized:
myGlassPane = new MyGlassPane(...);
frame.setGlassPane(myGlassPane);
...

/**
 * We have to provide our own glass pane so that it can paint.
 */

class MyGlassPane extends JComponent {
    Point point = null;
    public void paint(Graphics g) {
        if (point != null) {
            g.setColor(Color.red);
            g.fillOval(point.x - 10, point.y - 10, 20, 20);
        }
    }
    ...
}
```

The Layered Pane

A root pane places its menu bar and content pane in an instance of JLayeredPane—a container with depth—such that overlapping components can appear one on top of the other. This is useful for displaying popup menus above other components, for example. Your programs can also put components in the root pane's layered pane. If you do, you should be aware that certain depths are defined to be used for specific functions, and you should use the depths as intended. Otherwise your components might not play well with the others. Here's a diagram that shows the functional layers and their relationship.

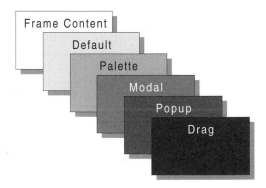

Figure 45 The functional layers and their relationship to one another.

The following table describes the intended use for each layer and the named constant defined in the `JLayeredPane` class that corresponds to it.

Table 58   Intended Use for Each Layer and Corresponding Constant in the `JLayeredPane` Class

Layer Name	Value	Description
FRAME_CONTENT_LAYER	new Integer(-30000)	This layer is used to position the frame's content pane and menu bar. Most programs won't use this layer. The root pane adds the menu bar and the content pane to its layered pane at this depth.
DEFAULT_LAYER	new Integer(0)	Most components go in this layer. If you don't specify a component's depth, the layered pane puts it at this depth.
PALETTE_LAYER	new Integer(100)	This layer is useful for floating tool bars and palettes.
MODAL_LAYER	new Integer(200)	Modal internalframe dialogs would belong in this layer.
POPUP_LAYER	new Integer(300)	Popups go in this layer because they need to appear above just about everything else.
DRAG_LAYER	new Integer(400)	Move a component to this layer when dragging. Return the component to its regular layer when dropped.

This tutorial does not provide an example of using the root pane's layered pane. However, by modifying a few lines of code in the example described in How to Use Layered Panes (page 150), you can make the program use the root pane's layered pane instead of creating one. The left column in the following table shows the code as it appears in `Layered-PaneDemo.java` (page 671). The right column shows how to change that code.

Table 59   Code Changes to Make a Program Use Root Pane's Layered Pane

From...	To...
layeredPane = new LayeredPane();	layeredPane = **getLayeredPane**();
final int YFUDGE = 57;	final int YFUDGE = **27**;
Point origin = new Point(10, 20);	Point origin = new Point(10, **70**);
contentPane.add(layeredPane);	//contentPane.add(layeredPane);
frame.pack();	frame.**setSize(new Dimension(310, 400))**;

Because the program now uses the root pane's layered pane, the Duke label can be dragged all around inside the window and over the components in the control panel. What do you suppose happens when you bring up the combo box? Will Duke be under the combo box's menu or over it?

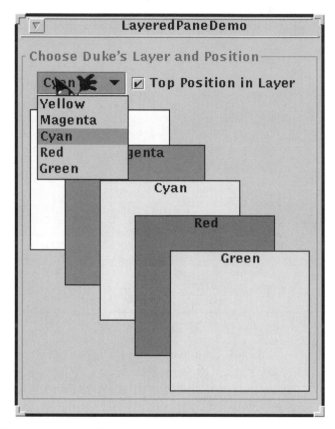

Figure 46   The modified `LayeredPaneDemo` application.

Notice that the layered pane's mouse listener is not notified of events when the mouse is over the combo box or the checkbox.

The Root Pane API

The tables that follow list the API for using root panes, glass panes, and content panes. The API for using other parts of the root pane is described in the sections <u>The Layered Pane API</u>

(page 156) and <u>The Menu API</u> (page 235). For more information on using content panes, go to <u>Using Top-Level Containers</u> (page 77).

Table 60   Using a Root Pane

Method	Purpose
JRootPane getRootPane() (*in* JApplet, JDialog, JFrame, JInternalFrame, *and* JWindow)	Get the root pane of the applet, dialog, frame, internal frame, or window.
JRootPane SwingUtilities.getRootPane(Component)	If the component contains a root pane, return that root pane. Otherwise return the root pane, if any, that contains the component.
JRootPane getRootPane() (*in* JComponent)	Invoke the SwingUtilities getRootPane method on the JComponent.
void setDefaultButton(JButton) JButton getDefaultButton()	Set or get which button, if any, is the default button in the root pane. A look-and-feel-specific action, such as pressing Enter, causes the button's action to be performed.

Table 61   Setting or Getting the Glass Pane

Method	Purpose
void setGlassPane(Component) Component getGlassPane() (*in* JApplet, JDialog, JFrame, JInternalFrame, JRootPane, *and* JWindow)	Set or get the glass pane.

Table 62   Setting or Getting the Content Pane

Method	Purpose
void setContentPane(Container) Container getContentPane() (*in* JApplet, JDialog, JFrame, JInternalFrame, JRootPane, *and* JWindow)	Set or get the content pane.

Examples that Use Root Panes

Every Swing program has a root pane, but few programs reference it directly. The table that follows lists examples of how to use features of `JRootPane` or the glass pane. Also see Examples that Use Layered Panes (page 157), Examples that Use Menus (page 238), and Examples that Use Frames (page 86).

Table 63   Examples that Use Root Panes

Example	Where Described	Notes
`GlassPaneDemo.java`	This section	Uses a glass pane. Redispatches events.
`ListDialog.java`	How to Use BoxLayout (page 350)	Sets the default button for a top-level container, using the root pane's `setDefaultButton` method.
`AppletDemo.java`	How to Make Applets (page 99)	Sets a property on the root pane, to try to avoid a security check that can cause disturbing messages in the console.

16

Using Atomic Components

THE rest of this lesson discusses the atomic components—those that exist solely to present and perhaps to accept information, rather than to contain other components. Although atomic components sometimes are implemented by combining components— for example, an editable combo box consists of such components as a text field, a button, and a menu—these combinations are look-and-feel-specific and thus not to be relied on or tampered with. An atomic component is a single entity, both to the user and to the programmer who uses its API. A Visual Index to Swing Components (page 63) presents pictures of all the atomic components.

All of the atomic components descend from the JComponent class. Thus they all support standard features, such as tool tips and borders. For more information about the API and features all atomic components support, see The JComponent Class (page 67).

The following atomic components exist primarily to get input from the user:

Button, Check Box, Radio Button (page 169)	Provide easy-to-use, easy-to-customize button implementations
Combo Box (page 192)	Provides both uneditable and editable combo boxes—buttons that bring up menus of choices
List (page 218)	Displays a group of items that the user can choose
Menu (page 226)	This section's coverage of menus includes menu bar, menu, and menu item implementations, including specialized menu items, such as check box menu items
Slider (page 248)	Lets the user choose one of a continuous range of values
Text Field (page 298)	Lets the user enter a single line of text data

Some atomic components exist only to give information:

Label (page 212)	Presents some text, an icon, or both
Progress Bar (page 239)	Displays progress toward a goal
Tool Tip (page 317)	Brings up a small window that describes another component

The rest of the atomic components provide formatted information and a way of editing it:

Color Chooser (page 184)	A UI for choosing colors; can be used inside or outside a dialog
File Chooser (page 200)	A UI for choosing files and directories
Table (page 254)	An extremely flexible component that displays data in a grid format
Text Support (page 275)	A framework including everything from simple text components, such as text fields, to a full-featured, extensible kit for building text editors
Tree (page 320)	A component that displays hierarchical data

The following sections discuss each of the atomic components, in alphabetical order.

How to Use Buttons, Check Boxes, and Radio Buttons

To create a button, you can instantiate one of the many classes that descend from the `AbstractButton`[1] class. The following table shows the Swing-defined `AbstractButton` subclasses that you might want to use.

Table 64   `AbstractButton` Subclasses

Class	Description	Where Described
JButton	A common button.	The Common Button API (page 170) and JButton Features (page 172)
JCheckBox	A check box button.	How to Use Check Boxes (page 177)
JRadioButton	One of a group of radio buttons.	How to Use Radio Buttons (page 180)
JMenuItem	An item in a menu.	How to Use Menus (page 226)
JCheckBoxMenuItem	A menu item that has a check box.	How to Use Menus (page 226) and How to Use Check Boxes (page 177)
JRadioButtonMenuItem	A menu item that has a radio button.	How to Use Menus (page 226) and How to Use Radio Buttons (page 180)
JToggleButton	Implements toggle functionality inherited by `JCheck-Box` and `JRadioButton`. Can be instantiated or subclassed to create two-state buttons.	Used to implement the crayon buttons in How to Use Color Choosers (page 184), the *cm* button in How to Use Scroll Panes (page 112), and Number-Button in the BINGO game.[a]

a. The BINGO game is featured in the "Putting It All Together" trail available online at http://java.sun.com/docs/books/tutorial/together/index.html

---

[1]   API documentation for `AbstractButton` is available online at http://java.sun.com/products/jdk/1.2/docs/api/javax/swing/AbstractButton.html

---

Note: If you want to collect a group of buttons into a row or column, then you should check out tool bars, discussed in <u>How to Use Tool Bars</u> (page 138).

First, this section explains the basic button API that AbstractButton defines—and thus all Swing buttons have in common. Next, this section describes the small amount of API that JButton adds to AbstractButton. Then this section shows you how to use specialized API to implement check boxes and radio buttons.

The Common Button API

Here is a picture of an application that displays three buttons.

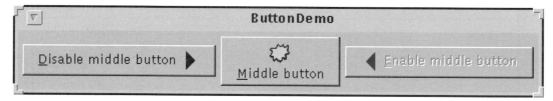

Figure 47   The ButtonDemo application.

Try this:

1. Compile and run the application.[1] The source file is <u>ButtonDemo.java</u> (page 625). You will also need to put three image files in a directory named images: left.gif, middle.gif, and right.gif.[2]
2. Click the left button. Doing so disables the middle button (and itself, since it's no longer useful) and enables the right button.
3. Click the right button. Doing so enables the middle and left buttons, and disables itself.

As the ButtonDemo example shows, a Swing button can display both text and an image. In ButtonDemo each button has its text in a different place, relative to its image. The underlined letter in each button's text shows the *mnemonic*—the keyboard alternative—for each button.

When a button is disabled, the look and feel automatically generates the button's disabled appearance. However, you could provide an image to be substituted for the normal image.

---

[1] See the lesson <u>Getting Started with Swing</u> (page 3) if you need help compiling or running this application.
[2] A directory of images used in the examples is available at http://java.sun.com/docs/books/tutorial/index.html

For example, you could provide gray versions of the images used in the left and right buttons.

How you implement event handling depends on the type of button you use and how you use it. Generally you implement an action listener, which is notified every time the user clicks the button. For check boxes you usually use an item listener, which is notified when the check box is selected or deselected.

The following code from ButtonDemo.java (page 625) creates the buttons in the previous example and reacts to button clicks. The code in boldface type is the code that would remain if the buttons had no images.

```java
//In initialization code:
    ImageIcon leftButtonIcon = new ImageIcon("images/right.gif");
    ImageIcon middleButtonIcon = new ImageIcon("images/middle.gif");
    ImageIcon rightButtonIcon = new ImageIcon("images/left.gif");
    b1 = new JButton("Disable middle button" , leftButtonIcon);
    b1.setVerticalTextPosition(AbstractButton.CENTER);
    b1.setHorizontalTextPosition(AbstractButton.LEFT);
    b1.setMnemonic('d');
    b1.setActionCommand("disable);
    b2 = new JButton("Middle button", middleButtonIcon);
    b2.setVerticalTextPosition(AbstractButton.BOTTOM);
    b2.setHorizontalTextPosition(AbstractButton.CENTER);
    b2.setMnemonic('m');
    b3 = new JButton("Enable middle button", rightButtonIcon);
    //Use the default text position of CENTER, RIGHT.
    b3.setMnemonic('e');
    b3.setActionCommand("enable");
    b3.setEnabled(false);
    //Listen for actions on buttons 1 and 3.
    b1.addActionListener(this);
    b3.addActionListener(this);

    . . .

public void actionPerformed(ActionEvent e) {
    if (e.getActionCommand().equals("disable")) {
        b2.setEnabled(false);
        b1.setEnabled(false);
        b3.setEnabled(true);
    } else {
        b2.setEnabled(true);
        b1.setEnabled(true);
        b3.setEnabled(false);
    }
}
```

JButton Features

Ordinary buttons—JButton objects—have just a bit more functionality than the Abstract-Button class provides. You can make a JButton be the default button, and if you're using the right release, you can specify the text and formatting of a button's label by using HTML.

At most one button in a top-level container can be the default button. The default button typically has a highlighted appearance and acts clicked whenever the top-level container has the keyboard focus and the user presses the Return or the Enter key. The exact implementation depends on the look and feel. Here is a picture of a dialog, implemented in ListDialog.java (page 678), in which the Set button is the default button.

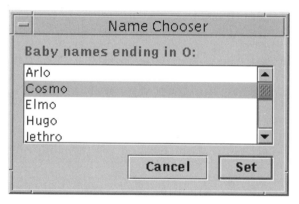

Figure 48   The ListDialog application.

You set the default button by invoking the setDefaultButton method on a top-level container's root pane. Here's the code that sets up the default button in the ListDialog example:

```
//In the constructor for a JDialog subclass:
getRootPane().setDefaultButton(setButton);
```

In the Swing 1.1.1 Beta 1 release of JFC 1.1, the Swing team added the ability to use HTML to specify a button's text. To do so, simply put the <HTML> tag at the beginning of a string, and then use any valid HTML in the remainder of the string. Using HTML can be useful for varying the text font or color within a button and for putting line breaks in a button.

Here's an example of specifying HTML for the buttons in ButtonDemo:

```
b1 = new JButton("<html><font size=-1><b><u>D</u>isable</b>"
                 + " middle button</font>",
                 leftButtonIcon);
...
```

```
b2 = new JButton("<html><font size=-1>Middle button</font>",
                  middleButtonIcon);
...
b3 = new JButton("<html><font size=-1><b><u>E</u>nable</b>"
                  + " middle button</font>",
                  rightButtonIcon);
```

Here is a picture of the buttons when the program is run in a platform that supports Swing 1.1.1 Beta 1 or a compatible release.

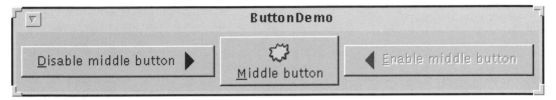

Figure 49 The ButtonDemo application run on the Swing 1.1.1 Beta 1 release.

Note that we had to use a <u> tag to cause the mnemonic character to be underlined in the button. The middle button has no underlined character because we didn't use the <u> tag in it. Note also that when a button is disabled, its HTML text remains dark, instead of becoming gray.

Warning: Don't use HTML in buttons unless you're absolutely sure that the program is running in a release that supports this feature. In releases such as Swing 1.1 that don't support HTML text, putting HTML in a button results in one ugly-looking button, whose label starts (not surprisingly) with <HTML>.

Here's an example of putting HTML in a button:

```
String htmlText =
       "<html>Click me if you like <font color=red>Red</font>";
JButton htmlButton = new JButton(htmlText);
```

For more information, see Using HTML on a Label (page 213).

The Button API

The following tables list the commonly used button-related API. You can see most of this API in action by playing with the Buttons, Radio Buttons, and Check Boxes panes in the SwingSet example that's part of the Swing release. See the release's top-level README file for help finding and using `SwingSet`. Other methods you might call are listed in the API tables in <u>The JComponent Class</u> (page 67).

Table 65   Setting or Getting the Button's Contents

Method or Constructor	Purpose

`JButton(String, Icon)`
`JButton(String)`
`JButton(Icon)`
`JButton()`
	Create a `JButton` instance, initializing it to have the specified text/image.

`void setText(String)` `String getText()`	Set or get the text displayed by the button.
`void setIcon(Icon)` `Icon getIcon()`	Set or get the image displayed by the button when it isn't selected or pressed.
`void setDisabledIcon(Icon)` `Icon getDisabledIcon()`	Set or get the image displayed by the button when it's disabled. If you don't specify a disabled image, the look and feel creates one by manipulating the default image.
`void setPressedIcon(Icon)` `Icon getPressedIcon()`	Set or get the image displayed by the button when it's being pressed.

`void setSelectedIcon(Icon)`
`Icon getSelectedIcon()`
`void setDisabledSelectedIcon(Icon)`
`Icon getDisabledSelectedIcon()`
	Set or get the image displayed by the button when it's selected. If you don't specify a disabled selected image, the look and feel creates one by manipulating the selected image.

`setRolloverEnabled(boolean)`
`boolean getRolloverEnabled()`
`void setRolloverIcon(Icon)`
`Icon getRolloverIcon()`
`void setRolloverSelectedIcon(Icon)`
`Icon getRolloverSelectedIcon()`
	Use `setRolloverEnabled(true)` and `setRollover-Icon(someIcon)` to make the button display the specified icon when the cursor passes over it.

Table 66   Fine Tuning the Button's Appearance

Method or Constructor	Purpose

`void setHorizontalAlignment(int)`
`void setVerticalAlignment(int)`
`int getHorizontalAlignment()`
`int getVerticalAlignment()`
	Set or get where content within the button should be placed. The `AbstractButton` class allows any one of the following values for horizontal alignment: LEFT, CENTER (the default), and RIGHT. For vertical alignment: TOP, CENTER (the default), and BOTTOM.

Table 66   Fine Tuning the Button's Appearance

Method or Constructor	Purpose

`void setHorizontalTextPosition(int)`
`void setVerticalTextPosition(int)`
`int getHorizontalTextPosition()`
`int getVerticalTextPosition()`
	Set or get where the button's text should be placed, relative to the button's image. The `AbstractButton` class allows any one of the following values for horizontal position: `LEFT`, `CENTER`, and `RIGHT` (the default). For vertical position: `TOP`, `CENTER` (the default), and `BOTTOM`.

`void setMargin(Insets)` `Insets getMargin()`	Set or get the number of pixels between the button's border and its contents.
`void setFocusPainted(boolean)` `boolean isFocusPainted()`	Set or get whether the button should look different when it has the focus.
`void setBorderPainted(boolean)` `boolean isBorderPainted()`	Set or get whether the border of the button should be painted.

Table 67   Implementing the Button's Functionality

Method or Constructor	Purpose
`void setMnemonic(char)` `char getMnemonic()`	Set or get the keyboard alternative to clicking the button.
`void setActionCommand(String)` `String getActionCommand(void)`	Set or get the name of the action performed by the button.
`void addActionListener(ActionListener)` `ActionListener removeActionListener()`	Add or remove an object that listens for action events fired by the button.
`void addItemListener(ItemListener)` `ItemListener removeItemListener()`	Add or remove an object that listens for item events fired by the button.
`void setSelected(boolean)` `boolean isSelected()`	Set or get whether the button is selected. Makes sense only for buttons that have on/off state, such as check boxes.
`void doClick()` `void doClick(int)`	Programmatically perform a "click." The optional argument specifies the amount of time in milliseconds that the button should look pressed.

Table 68   Commonly Used `ButtonGroup` Constructors/Methods

Constructor or Method	Purpose
`ButtonGroup()`	Create a `ButtonGroup` instance.
`void add(AbstractButton)` `void remove(AbstractButton)`	Add a button to the group or remove a button from the group.

Table 69   ToggleButton Constructors

Constructor	Purpose
JToggleButton(String) JToggleButton(String, boolean) JToggleButton(Icon) JToggleButton(Icon, boolean) JToggleButton(String, Icon) JToggleButton(String, Icon, boolean) JToggleButton()	Create a JToggleButton instance, which is similar to a JButton but with two states. Normally you use a JRadio-Button or a JCheckBox instead of directly instantiating JToggleButton, but JToggleButton can be useful when you don't want the typical radio button or check box appearance. The String argument specifies the text, if any, that the toggle button should display. Similarly the Icon argument specifies the image that should be used. Specifying the boolean argument as true initializes the toggle button to be selected. If the boolean argument is absent or false, the toggle button is initially unselected.

Examples that Use Buttons

The following examples use buttons. Also see Table 46, "Examples that Use Tool Bars" (page 142), which lists programs that add JButton objects to JToolBars.

Table 70   Examples that Use Buttons

Example	Where Described	Notes
ButtonDemo.java	The Common Button API (page 170)	Uses mnemonics and icons. Specifies the button text position, relative to the button icon. Uses action commands.
ListDialog.java	JButton Features (page 172)	Implements a dialog with two buttons, one of which is the default button.
AppletDemo.java	Running Swing Applets (page 17)	The same example as is explained in The Common Button API (page 170), but implemented as an applet.
DialogDemo.java	How to Make Dialogs (page 87)	Has Show It buttons whose behavior is tied to the state of radio buttons. Uses sizable, though anonymous, inner classes to implement the action listeners.
ProgressBarDemo.java	How to Monitor Progress (page 239)	Implements a button's action listener with a named inner class.

How to Use Check Boxes

The JCheckBox[1] class provides support for check box buttons. You can also put check boxes in menus, using the JCheckBoxMenuItem[2] class. Because JCheckBox and JCheckBoxMenuItem inherit from AbstractButton, Swing check boxes have all the usual button characteristics, as discussed earlier. For example, you can specify images to be used in check boxes.

Check boxes are similar to radio buttons, but by convention their selection models are different. Any number of check boxes in a group—none, some, or all—can be selected. A group of radio buttons, on the other hand, can have only one button selected.

Here is a picture of an application that uses four check boxes to customize a cartoon.

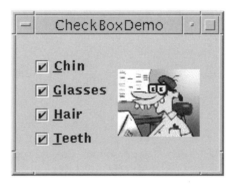

Figure 50   The CheckBoxDemo application.

Try this:

1. Compile and run the application.[3] The source file is CheckBoxDemo.java (page 626). You will also need to put 16 image files in a directory named /tutorial/images/geek.[4]

2. Click the Chin button or press Alt-c. The Chin check box becomes unselected, and the chin disappears from the picture. The other check boxes remain selected. This applica-

---

[1]   API documentation for this class is available on this book's CD-ROM and online at http://java.sun.com/products/jdk/1.2/docs/api/javax/swing/JCheckBox.html

[2]   http://java.sun.com/products/jdk/1.2/docs/api/javax/swing/JCheckBoxMenuItem.html

[3]   See the chapter Getting Started with Swing (page 3) if you need help compiling or running this application.

[4]   You can find the images by visiting: http://java.sun.com/docs/books/tutorial/uiswing/components/example-swing/index.html

tion has one item listener that listens to all the check boxes. Each time the item listener receives an event, the application loads a new picture that reflects the current state of the check boxes.

A check box generates one item event and one action event per click. Usually you listen only for item events, since they let you determine whether the click selected or deselected the check box. The following code from CheckBoxDemo.java (page 626) creates the check boxes in the previous example and reacts to clicks:

```
//In initialization code:
    chinButton = new JCheckBox("Chin");
    chinButton.setMnemonic('c');
    chinButton.setSelected(true);

    glassesButton = new JCheckBox("Glasses");
    glassesButton.setMnemonic('g');
    glassesButton.setSelected(true);

    hairButton = new JCheckBox("Hair");
    hairButton.setMnemonic('h');
    hairButton.setSelected(true);

    teethButton = new JCheckBox("Teeth");
    teethButton.setMnemonic('t');
    teethButton.setSelected(true);

    // Register a listener for the check boxes.
    CheckBoxListener myListener = new CheckBoxListener();
    chinButton.addItemListener(myListener);
    glassesButton.addItemListener(myListener);
    hairButton.addItemListener(myListener);
    teethButton.addItemListener(myListener);
...

class CheckBoxListener implements ItemListener {
    public void itemStateChanged(ItemEvent e) {
        ...
        Object source = e.getItemSelectable();
        if (source == chinButton) {
            //...make a note of it...
        } else if (source == glassesButton) {
            //...make a note of it...
        } else if (source == hairButton) {
            //...make a note of it...
        } else if (source == teethButton) {
            //...make a note of it...
        }
```

```
        if (e.getStateChange() == ItemEvent.DESELECTED)
            //...make a note of it...
        pictureLabel.setIcon( /* new icon */);
        ...
    }
}
```

Note: In a future release, we expect check boxes to support HTML text. See <u>Using HTML on a Label</u> (page 213) for information about HTML text support.

Table 71   Check Box Constructors

Constructor	Purpose

`JCheckBox(String)`
`JCheckBox(String, boolean)`
`JCheckBox(Icon)`
`JCheckBox(Icon, boolean)`
`JCheckBox(String, Icon)`
`JCheckBox(String, Icon, boolean)`
`JCheckBox()`
	Create a `JCheckBox` instance. The `String` argument specifies the text, if any, that the check box should display. The `Icon` argument specifies the image to be used instead of the look and feel's default check box image. Specifying the boolean argument as `true` initializes the check box to be selected. If the boolean argument is absent or `false`, the check box is initially unselected.

`JCheckBoxMenuItem(String)`
`JCheckBoxMenuItem(String, boolean)`
`JCheckBoxMenuItem(Icon)`
`JCheckBoxMenuItem(String, Icon)`
`JCheckBoxMenuItem(String, Icon, boolean)`
`JCheckBoxMenuItem()`
	Create a `JCheckBoxMenuItem` instance. The arguments are interpreted in the same way as the arguments to the `JCheckBox` constructors, except that any specified icon is shown in addition to the normal check box icon.

Examples that Use Check Boxes

The following examples use check boxes.

Table 72   Examples that Use Check Boxes

Example	Where Described	Notes
`CheckBoxDemo.java`	<u>How to Use Check Boxes</u> (page 177)	Uses check box buttons to determine which of 16 images it should display.
`ActionDemo.java`	<u>How to Use Actions</u> (page 389)	Uses check box menu items to set the state of the program.
`MenuDemo.java`	<u>How to Use Menus</u> (page 226)	Contains radio button menu items and check box menu items.

How to Use Radio Buttons

Radio buttons are groups of buttons in which, by convention, only one button at a time can be selected. The Swing API supports radio buttons with the <u>JRadioButton</u>[1] and <u>Button-Group</u>[2] classes. To put a radio button in a menu, use the <u>JRadioButtonMenuItem</u>[3] class. Other ways of displaying one-of-many choices are <u>combo boxes</u> (page 192) and <u>lists</u> (page 218). Radio buttons look similar to check boxes, but by convention check boxes place no limits on how many items can be selected at a time.

Because JRadioButton inherits from AbstractButton, Swing radio buttons have all of the usual button characteristics, as discussed in <u>The Common Button API</u> (page 170). For example, you can specify the image displayed in a radio button.

Here is a picture of an application that uses five radio buttons to let you choose which kind of pet is displayed.

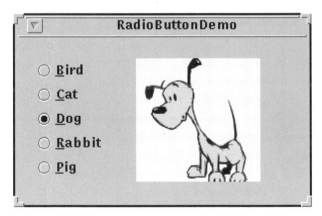

Figure 51 The RadioButtonDemo application.

---

[1] API documentation for this class is available on this book's CD-ROM and online at http://java.sun.com/products/jdk/1.2/docs/api/javax/swing/JRadioButton.html

[2] http://java.sun.com/products/jdk/1.2/docs/api/javax/swing/ButtonGroup.html

[3] http://java.sun.com/products/jdk/1.2/docs/api/javax/swing/JRadioButtonMenuItem.html

Try this:

1. Compile and run the application.[1] The source file is <u>RadioButtonDemo.java</u> (page 698). You will also need to put five image files in a directory named `images`: `Bird.gif`, `Cat.gif`, `Dog.gif`, `Rabbit.gif`, and `Pig.gif`.[2]

2. Click the Dog button or press Alt-d. The Dog button becomes selected, which makes the Bird button become unselected. The picture switches from a bird to a dog.

This application has one action listener that listens to all of the radio buttons. Each time the action listener receives an event, the application displays the picture for the radio button that was just clicked. Each time the user clicks a radio button—even if it was already selected—the button fires an action event. One or two item events also occur—one from the button that was just selected and one from the button that lost the selection, if any. Usually you handle radio button clicks by using an action listener.[3]

The following code from <u>RadioButtonDemo.java</u> (page 698) creates the radio buttons in the previous example and reacts to clicks:

//In initialization code:

```
// Create the radio buttons.
JRadioButton birdButton = new JRadioButton(birdString);
birdButton.setMnemonic(KeyEvent.VK_B);
birdButton.setActionCommand(birdString);
birdButton.setSelected(true);

JRadioButton catButton = new JRadioButton(catString);
catButton.setMnemonic(KeyEvent.VK_C);
catButton.setActionCommand(catString);

JRadioButton dogButton = new JRadioButton(dogString);
dogButton.setMnemonic(KeyEvent.VK_D);
dogButton.setActionCommand(dogString);

JRadioButton rabbitButton = new JRadioButton(rabbitString);
rabbitButton.setMnemonic(KeyEvent.VK_R);
rabbitButton.setActionCommand(rabbitString);
```

---

[1] See the chapter <u>Getting Started with Swing</u> (page 3) if you need help compiling or running this application.

[2] You can find the images by visiting: http://java.sun.com/docs/books/tutorial/uiswing/components/example-swing/index.html

[3] For more information on action listeners, see <u>How to Write an Action Listener</u> (page 459).

```
    JRadioButton pigButton = new JRadioButton(pigString);
    pigButton.setMnemonic(KeyEvent.VK_D);
    pigButton.setActionCommand(pigString);

    // Group the radio buttons.
    ButtonGroup group = new ButtonGroup();
    group.add(birdButton);
    group.add(catButton);
    group.add(dogButton);
    group.add(rabbitButton);
    group.add(pigButton);

    // Register a listener for the radio buttons.
    RadioListener myListener = new RadioListener();
    birdButton.addActionListener(myListener);
    catButton.addActionListener(myListener);
    dogButton.addActionListener(myListener);
    rabbitButton.addActionListener(myListener);
    pigButton.addActionListener(myListener);
...

class RadioListener implements ActionListener ... {
    public void actionPerformed(ActionEvent e) {
        picture.setIcon(new ImageIcon("images/" + e.getActionCommand()
                                                + ".gif"));
    }
}
```

For each group of radio buttons, you need to create a ButtonGroup instance and add each radio button to it. The ButtonGroup takes care of unselecting the previously selected button when the user selects another button in the group.

You should generally initialize a group of radio buttons so that one is selected. However, the API doesn't enforce this rule; a group of radio buttons can have no initial selection. Once the user has made a selection, exactly one button is selected from then on. There's no supported API for unselecting all of the buttons. However, if you really want to unselect all of the buttons—not that we recommend it—invoking setSelected(null, true) on the ButtonGroup should do the trick.

Note: In a future release, we expect radio buttons to support HTML text. See Using HTML on a Label (page 213) for information about HTML text support.

Table 73   Radio Button Constructors

Constructor	Purpose

`JRadioButton(String)`
 `JRadioButton(String, boolean)`
 `JRadioButton(Icon)`
 `JRadioButton(Icon, boolean)`
 `JRadioButton(String, Icon)`
 `JRadioButton(String, Icon, boolean)`
 `JRadioButton()`
	Create a `JRadioButton` instance. The `String` argument specifies the text, if any, that the radio button should display. Similarly the `Icon` argument specifies the image that should be used instead of the look and feel's default radio button image. Specifying the boolean argument as `true` initializes the radio button to be selected, subject to the approval of the `ButtonGroup` object. If the boolean argument is absent or `false`, the radio button is initially unselected.

`JRadioButtonMenuItem(String)`
 `JRadioButtonMenuItem(Icon)`
 `JRadioButtonMenuItem(String, Icon)`
 `JRadioButtonMenuItem()`
	Create a `JRadioButtonMenuItem` instance. The arguments are interpreted in the same way as the arguments to the `JRadioButton` constructors, except that any specified icon is shown in addition to the normal radio button icon.

Examples that Use Radio Buttons

The following examples use radio buttons. Also see Table 46, "Examples that Use Tool Bars" (page 142), which lists programs that add `JButton` objects to `JToolBars`.

Table 74   Examples that Use Radio Buttons

Example	Where Described	Notes
`RadioButtonDemo.java`	How to Use Radio Buttons (page 180)	Uses radio buttons to determine which of five images it should display.
`DialogDemo.java`	How to Make Dialogs (page 87)	Contains several sets of radio buttons, which it uses to determine which dialog to bring up.
`MenuDemo.java`	How to Use Menus (page 226)	Contains radio button menu items and check box menu items.

How to Use Color Choosers

Use the `JColorChooser`[1] class to provide users with a palette of colors to choose from. A color chooser is a component that you can place anywhere within your program's GUI. The `JColorChooser` API also makes it easy to bring up a dialog (modal or nonmodal) that contains a color chooser.

Here's a picture of an application that uses a color chooser to set the text color in a banner.

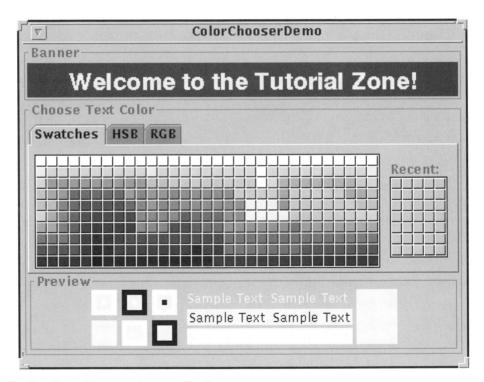

Figure 52   The `ColorChooserDemo` application.

The full code for the program is in <u>`ColorChooserDemo.java`</u> (page 628).

---

[1]   API documentation for this class is available on this book's CD-ROM and online at http://java.sun.com/products/jdk/1.2/docs/api/javax/swing/JColorChooser.html

The color chooser consists of everything within the box labeled Choose Text Color. This is what a standard color chooser looks like in the Java Look & Feel. The color chooser contains two parts: a tabbed pane and a preview panel. The three tabs in the tabbed pane select *chooser panels*. The *preview panel* below the tabbed pane displays the currently selected color.

The following code from the example creates a `JColorChooser` instance and adds it to the demo's window:

```
final JLabel banner = new JLabel("Welcome to the Tutorial Zone!",
                                 JLabel.CENTER);
banner.setForeground(Color.yellow);
...
final JColorChooser tcc = new JColorChooser(banner.getForeground());
...
Container contentPane = getContentPane();
contentPane.add(tcc, BorderLayout.SOUTH);
```

The `ColorChooser` constructor in the previous code snippet takes a `Color` argument, which specifies the chooser's initially selected color. If you don't specify the initial color, then the color chooser displays `Color.white`. See the <u>Color</u> API documentation[1] for a list of color constants you can use.

A color chooser uses an instance of <u>ColorSelectionModel</u>[2] to contain and to manage the current selection. The color selection model fires a change event whenever the user changes the color in the color chooser. The sample program registers a change listener with the color selection model so that it can update the banner at the top of the window.[3] The following code registers and implements the change listener:

```
tcc.getSelectionModel().addChangeListener(
    new ChangeListener() {
        public void stateChanged(ChangeEvent e) {
            Color newColor = tcc.getColor();
            banner.setForeground(newColor);
        }
    }
);
```

A basic color chooser, like the one used in the sample program, is sufficient for many programs. However, the color chooser API allows you to customize a color chooser by provid-

---

[1] API documentation for this class is available on this book's CD-ROM and online at http://java.sun.com/products/jdk/1.2/docs/api/java/awt/Color.html

[2] http://java.sun.com/products/jdk/1.2/docs/api/javax/swing/colorchooser/ColorSelectionModel.html

[3] See <u>How to Write a Change Listener</u> (page 464) for general information about change listeners and change events.

ing it with a preview panel of your own design, by adding your own chooser panels to it, or by removing existing chooser panels from the color chooser. Additionally the JColor-Chooser class provides two methods that make it easy to use a color chooser within a dialog.

Now turn your attention to ColorChooserDemo2, modified from the previous demo program to use more of the JColorChooser API. In addition to the main source file, ColorChooserDemo2.java (page 629), you need CrayonPanel.java (page 634) and the four crayon images (red.gif, yellow.gif, green.gif, and blue.gif) to run this program.[1]

Here's a picture of ColorChooserDemo2.

Figure 53   The ColorChooserDemo2 application.

---

[1]   You can find the images by visiting http://java.sun.com/docs/books/tutorial/uiswing/components/example-swing/index.html

This program customizes the banner's text color chooser in these ways:

- Removes the preview panel
- Removes all of the default chooser panels
- Adds a custom chooser panel

Replacing or Removing the Preview Panel (page 188) covers the first customization. Creating a Custom Chooser Panel (page 188) discusses the last two customizations.

This program also adds a button that brings up a color chooser in a dialog. You can use that button to set the banner's background color.

Showing a Color Chooser in a Dialog

The JColorChooser class provides two class methods to make it easy to use a color chooser in a dialog. ColorChooserDemo2 uses one of these methods, showDialog, to display the background color chooser when the user clicks the Show Color Chooser... button. Here's the single line of code that brings up the background color chooser in a dialog:

```
Color newColor = JColorChooser.showDialog(ColorChooserDemo2.this,
                                 "Choose Background Color",
                                 banner.getBackground());
```

The first argument is the parent component for the dialog, the second is the dialog's title, and the third is the initially selected color. The parent component affects the position of the dialog and the frame that the dialog depends on.

The dialog disappears if the user chooses a color and clicks the OK button, cancels the operation with the Cancel button, or dismisses the dialog with a frame control. If the user chooses a color, the showDialog method returns the new color. If the user cancels the operation or dismisses the window, the method returns null. Here's the code that updates the banner's background color according to the value returned by showDialog:

```
if (newColor != null) {
    banner.setBackground(newColor);
}
```

The dialog created by showDialog is modal. If you want a nonmodal dialog, you can use JColorChooser's createDialog method to create the dialog. This method also lets you specify action listeners for the OK and Cancel buttons in the dialog window. Use JDialog's show method to display the dialog created by this method. For an example that uses this method, see Specifying Other Editors (page 266) [in How to Use Tables (page 254)].

Replacing or Removing the Preview Panel

By default the color chooser displays a preview panel. The sample program removes the text color chooser's preview panel with this line of code:

```
tcc.setPreviewPanel(new JPanel());
```

This removes the preview panel because a plain `JPanel` has no size and no default view. To set the preview panel back to the default, use `null` as the argument to `setPreviewPanel`.

To provide a custom preview panel, you can also use `setPreviewPanel`. The component you pass into the method should inherit from `JComponent`, specify a reasonable size, and provide a customized view of the current color. To get notified when the user changes the color in the color chooser, the preview panel must register as a change listener on the color chooser's color selection model as already described.

Creating a Custom Chooser Panel

The default color chooser provides three chooser panels:

- Swatches—for choosing a color from a collection of swatches
- HSB—for choosing a color using the hue-saturation-brightness color model.
- RGB—for choosing a color using the red-green-blue color model.

You can extend the default color chooser by adding chooser panels of your own design with `addChooserPanel`, or you can limit it by removing chooser panels with `removeChooser-Panel`.

If you want to remove all of the default chooser panels and add one or more of your own, you can do so with a single call to `setChooserPanels`. <u>ColorChooserDemo2.java</u> (page 629) uses this method to replace the default chooser panels with an instance of <u>CrayonPanel</u> (page 634), a custom chooser panel. Here's the call to `setChooserPanels` from that example:

```
//Override the chooser panels with our own.
AbstractColorChooserPanel panels[] = { new CrayonPanel() };
tcc.setChooserPanels(panels);
```

The code is straightforward: It creates an array containing the `CrayonPanel`. Next, the code calls `setChooserPanels` to set the contents of the array as the color chooser's chooser panels.

CrayonPanel is a subclass of AbstractColorChooserPanel[1] and overrides the five abstract methods defined in its superclass.

void buildChooser()

Creates the GUI that comprises the chooser panel. The example creates four toggle buttons—one for each crayon—and adds them to the chooser panel.

void updateChooser()

This method is called whenever the chooser panel is displayed. The example's implementation of this method selects the toggle button that represents the currently selected color:

```
public void updateChooser() {
    Color color = getColorFromModel();
    if (color.equals(Color.red)) {
        redCrayon.setSelected(true);
    } else if (color.equals(Color.yellow)) {
        yellowCrayon.setSelected(true);
    } else if (color.equals(Color.green)) {
        greenCrayon.setSelected(true);
    } else if (color.equals(Color.blue)) {
        blueCrayon.setSelected(true);
    }
}
```

String getDisplayName()

Returns the display name of the chooser panel. The name is used on the tab for the chooser panel. Here's the example's getDisplayName method:

```
public String getDisplayName() {
    return "Crayons";
}
```

Icon getSmallDisplayIcon()

Returns a small icon to represent this chooser panel. This is currently unused. Future versions of the color chooser might use this icon or the large one to represent this chooser panel in the display. The example's implementation of this method returns null.

Icon getLargeDisplayIcon()

Returns a large icon to represent this chooser panel. This is currently unused. Future versions of the color chooser might use this icon or the small one to represent this chooser panel in the display. The example's implementation of this method returns null.

---

[1] API documentation is available on this book's CD-ROM and online at http://java.sun.com/products/jdk/1.2/docs/api/javax/swing/AbstractColorChooserPanel.html

The Color Chooser API

The following tables list the commonly used `JColorChooser` constructors and methods. Other methods you might call are listed in the API tables in The JComponent Class (page 67).

Table 75   Creating and Displaying the Color Chooser

Method	Purpose

`JColorChooser()`
`JColorChooser(Color)`
`JColorChooser(ColorSelectionModel)`
	Create a color chooser. The default constructor creates a color chooser with an initial color of `Color.white`. Use the second constructor to specify a different initial color. The `ColorSelectionModel` argument, when present, provides the color chooser with a color selection model.

`Color showDialog(Component,` `                  String, Color)`	Create and show a color chooser in a modal dialog. The `Component` argument is the dialog's parent, the `String` argument specifies the dialog's title, and the `Color` argument specifies the chooser's initial color.

`JDialog createDialog(Component,`
`                      String,boolean,`
`                      JColorChooser,`
`                      ActionListener,`
`                      ActionListener)`
	Create a dialog for the specified color chooser. As with `showDialog`, the `Component` argument is the dialog's parent, and the `String` argument specifies the dialog's title. The other arguments are as follows: `boolean` specifies whether the dialog is modal, `JColorChooser` is the color chooser to display in the dialog, the first `ActionListener` is for the OK button, and the second is for the Cancel button.

Table 76   Customizing the Color Chooser's GUI

Method	Purpose
`void setPreviewPanel(JComponent)` `JComponent getPreviewPanel()`	Set or get the component used to preview the color selection. To remove the preview panel, use `new JPanel()` as an argument. To specify the default preview panel, use `null`.

`void setChooserPanels(`
`    AbstractColorChooserPanel[])`
`AbstractColorChooserPanel[] getChooserPanels()`
	Set or get the chooser panels in the color chooser.

`void addChooserPanel(AbstractColorChooserPanel)`
`AbstractColorChooserPanel`
`    removeChooserPanel(AbstractColorChooserPanel)`
	Add a chooser panel to the color chooser, or remove a chooser panel from it.

Table 77 Setting or Getting the Current Color

Method	Purpose

`void setColor(Color)`
`void setColor(int, int, int)`
`void setColor(int)`
`Color getColor()`
	Set or get the currently selected color. The three-integer version of the `setColor` method interprets the three integers together as an RGB color. The single-integer version of the `setColor` method divides the integer into four 8-bit bytes and interprets the integer as an RGB color as follows:
	
	      `|
		R	G	B |`

`void setSelectionModel(`
   `ColorSelectionModel)`
`ColorSelectionModel`
   `getSelectionModel()`
	Set or get the selection model for the color chooser. This object contains the current selection and fires change events to registered listeners whenever the selection changes.

Examples that Use Color Choosers

This table shows the examples that use `JColorChooser` and where those examples are described.

Table 78 Examples that Use Color Choosers

Example	Where Described	Notes
`ColorChooserDemo.java`	This section	Uses a standard color chooser.
`ColorChooserDemo2.java`	This section	Uses one customized color chooser and one standard color chooser in a dialog created with `showDialog`.
`TableDialogEditDemo.java`	How to Use Tables (page 254)	Shows how to use a color chooser as a custom cell editor in a table. The color chooser used by this example is created with `createDialog`.

How to Use Combo Boxes

A `JComboBox`[1] comes in two very different forms: uneditable and editable.

By default a combo box is uneditable. An uneditable combo box looks like a button until the user interacts with it. When the user presses or clicks it, the combo box displays a menu of items to choose from. Use an uneditable combo box to display one-of-many choices when space is limited, when the number of choices is large, or when the menu items are computed at runtime. Other components that display one-of-many choices are lists (page 218) and groups of radio buttons (page 180).

An editable `JComboBox` looks like a text field with a small button abutting it. The user can type a value in the text field or click the button to choose a value from a menu. An editable combo box saves data-entry time by providing shortcuts to commonly entered values.

Using an Uneditable Combo Box

The application shown here uses an uneditable combo box for choosing a pet picture.

Figure 54   The `ComboBoxDemo` application.

---

[1]   API documentation for this class is available on this book's CD-ROM and online at http://java.sun.com/
products/jdk/1.2/docs/api/javax/swing/JComboBox.html

Try this:

1. Compile and run the program ComboBoxDemo.java (page 631).[1] You will also need to put five image files in a directory named images: Bird.gif, Cat.gif, Dog.gif, Rabbit.gif, and Pig.gif.[2]

2. Choose a pet name from the combo box to view the pet's picture.

3. Compile and run the program RadioButtonDemo.java (page 698) which uses a group of radio buttons instead of a combo box. Compare the source code, operation, and UI of the two programs.

The following code, taken from ComboBoxDemo.java (page 631), creates an uneditable combo box and sets it up:

```
String[] petStrings = { "Bird", "Cat", "Dog", "Rabbit", "Pig" };
// Create the combo box, select the pig.
JComboBox petList = new JComboBox(petStrings);
petList.setSelectedIndex(4);
...
```

The code initializes the combo box with an array of strings. You can also put icons in a combo box. To put other types of objects in a combo box or to customize how the items in a combo box look, you need to write a custom renderer. An editable combo box would need a custom editor, in addition. Refer to Providing a Custom Renderer (page 196) for information and an example.

Although not shown here, the program registers an action listener on the combo box. To see the code and learn about other types of listeners supported by combo box, see the next section.

No matter which constructor you use, a combo box uses a combo box model to contain and to manage the items in its menu. When you initialize a combo box with an array or a vector, the combo box creates a default model object for you. As with other Swing components, you can customize a combo box in part by implementing a custom model—an object that implements the ComboBoxModel[3] interface.

Note: Be careful when implementing a custom model for a combo box. The JComboBox methods, such as insertItemAt, that change the items in the combo box's menu work only if the data model implements the MutableComboBoxModel interface (a subinterface of ComboBox-Model). Refer to the API tables (page 198) to see which methods are affected.

---

[1] See the chapter Getting Started with Swing (page 3) if you need help compiling or running this application.

[2] You can find the images by visiting http://java.sun.com/docs/books/tutorial/uiswing/components/example-swing/index.html

[3] http://java.sun.com/products/jdk/1.2/docs/api/javax/swing/ComboBoxModel.html

Handling Events on a Combo Box

The following code from `ComboBoxDemo` registers and implements an action listener on the combo box:

```
petList.addActionListener(new ActionListener() {
    public void actionPerformed(ActionEvent e) {
        JComboBox cb = (JComboBox)e.getSource();
        String petName = (String)cb.getSelectedItem();
        picture.setIcon(new ImageIcon("images/" + petName + ".gif"));
    }
});
```

This action listener gets the newly selected item from the combo box, uses that item to compute the name of an image file, and updates a label to display the image. The combo box fires an action event when the user selects an item from the combo box's menu. See How to Write an Action Listener (page 459) for general information about implementing action listeners.

Combo boxes also generate item events, which are fired when any of the items' selection states change. Only one item at a time can be selected in a combo box, so when the user makes a new selection, the previously selected item becomes unselected. Thus two item events are fired each time the user selects an item from the menu. If the user chooses the same item, no item events are fired. Use `addItemListener` to register an item listener on a combo box. The section How to Write an Item Listener (page 484) gives general information about implementing item listeners.

Although `JComboBox` inherits methods to register listeners for low-level events—focus, key, and mouse events, for example—we recommend that you don't listen for low-level events on a combo box. Here's why: A combo box is a *compound component*, comprised of two or more other components. The combo box itself fires high-level events, such as action events. Its subcomponents fire low-level events, such as mouse, key, and focus events. The low-level events and the subcomponent that fires them are look-and-feel-dependent. To avoid writing look-and-feel-dependent code, you should listen only for high-level events on a compound component, such as a combo box. For information about events, including a discussion about high- and low-level events, refer to the chapter Writing Event Listeners (page 439).

Using an Editable Combo Box

In the following picture of a demo application, an editable combo box is used to enter a pattern with which to format dates.[1]

---

[1] The `ComboBoxDemo2` application was provided by our coworker Dale Green.

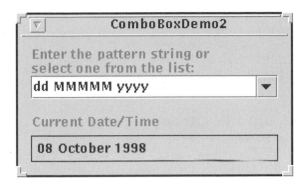

Figure 55 ComboBoxDemo2, an application that demonstrates the use of editable combo boxes.

Try this:

1. Compile and run the example: <u>ComboBoxDemo2.java</u> (page 632).[1]
2. Enter a new pattern by choosing one from the combo box's menu. The program reformats the current date and time.
3. Enter a new pattern by typing one in and pressing Return. The program again reformats the current date and time.

The following code, taken from ComboBoxDemo2.java, creates and sets up the combo box:

```
String[] patternExamples = { "dd MMMMM yyyy", "dd.MM.yy",
                             "MM/dd/yy", "yyyy.MM.dd G 'at' hh:mm:ss z",
                             "EEE, MMM d, ''yy", "h:mm a", "H:mm:ss:SSS",
                             "K:mm a,z", "yyyy.MMMMM.dd GGG hh:mm aaa"
                           } ;
. . .
JComboBox patternList = new JComboBox(patternExamples);
patternList.setEditable(true);
patternList.addActionListener(...);
. . .
```

This code is very similar to the previous example but warrants a few words of explanation. The line of code in boldface type explicitly turns on editing to allow the user to type values in. This is necessary because by default a combo box is not editable. This particular example allows editing on the combo box because its menu does not provide all possible date-formatting patterns, just shortcuts to frequently used patterns.

An editable combo box fires an action event when the user chooses an item from the menu and when the user presses Return. Note that the menu remains unchanged when the user

---

[1] See the chapter <u>Getting Started with Swing</u> (page 3) if you need help compiling or running this application.

enters a value into the combo box. If you want, you can easily write an action listener that adds a new item to the combo box's menu each time the user types in a unique value.

See the "Internationalization" trail in the book, *The Java Tutorial Continued*, to learn more about formatting dates and other types of data.[1]

Providing a Custom Renderer

A combo box uses a *renderer* to display each item in its menu. If the combo box is uneditable, it also uses the renderer to display the currently selected item. An editable combo box, on the other hand, uses an *editor* to display the selected item. A renderer for a combo box must implement the `ListCellRenderer`[2] interface. A combo box's editor must implement `ComboBoxEditor`.[3] This section shows how to provide a custom renderer for an uneditable combo box.

The default renderer knows how to render strings and icons. If you put other objects in a combo box, the default renderer calls the `toString` method to provide a string to display. You can implement your own `ListCellRenderer` to customize the way a combo box renders itself and its items.

Here's a picture of an application that uses a combo box with a custom renderer.

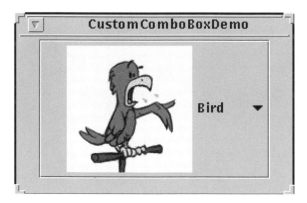

Figure 56   This application uses a combo box with a custom renderer.

---

[1] This trail is also available in HTML on this book's CD-ROM and online at http://java.sun.com/docs/ books/tutorial/i18n/index.html

[2] API documentation for this class is available on this book's CD-ROM and online at http://java.sun.com/ products/jdk/1.2/docs/api/javax/swing/ListCellRenderer.html

[3] http://java.sun.com/products/jdk/1.2/docs/api/javax/swing/ComboBoxEditor.html

You can find the full code for this example in <u>CustomComboBoxDemo.java</u> (page 635). You will also need the image files as described in <u>Using an Uneditable Combo Box</u> (page 192).

The following statements from the example create an instance of ComboBoxRenderer (a custom class) and set up the instance as the combo box's renderer:

```
JComboBox petList = new JComboBox(images);
ComboBoxRenderer renderer = new ComboBoxRenderer();
renderer.setPreferredSize(new Dimension(200, 130));
petList.setRenderer(renderer);
petList.setMaximumRowCount(3);
```

To see how the default renderer renders icons, just comment out the call to setRenderer, and compile and run the program again.

The code also sets the combo box's maximum row count. This attribute controls the number of items visible when the menu is displayed. If the number of items in the combo box is larger than its maximum row count, the menu has a scroll bar. The icons are pretty big for a menu, so the code limits the number of rows to three. Here's the complete implementation of ComboBoxRenderer, a renderer that puts an icon and text side by side:

```
class ComboBoxRenderer extends JLabel implements ListCellRenderer {
    public ComboBoxRenderer() {
        setOpaque(true);
        setHorizontalAlignment(CENTER);
        setVerticalAlignment(CENTER);
    }

    public Component getListCellRendererComponent(
        JList list,
        Object value,
        int index,
        boolean isSelected,
        boolean cellHasFocus) {
        if (isSelected) {
            setBackground(list.getSelectionBackground());
            setForeground(list.getSelectionForeground());
        } else {
            setBackground(list.getBackground());
            setForeground(list.getForeground());
        }
        ImageIcon icon = (ImageIcon)value;
        setText(icon.getDescription());
        setIcon(icon);
        return this;
    }
}
```

As a `ListCellRenderer`, ComboBoxRenderer implements a method called `getListCell-RendererComponent`, which returns a component whose `paintComponent` method is used to display the combo box and each of its items. The easiest way to display an image and an icon is to use a label. So ComboBoxRenderer is a subclass of `label` and returns itself. The implementation of `getListCellRendererComponent` configures the renderer to display the currently selected icon and its description.

These arguments are passed to `getListCellRendererComponent`:

- `JList list`—a list object used behind the scenes to display the items. The example uses this object's colors to set up foreground and background colors.
- `Object value`—the object to render: an `Icon` in this example.
- `int index`—the index of the object to render.
- `boolean isSelected`—indicates whether the object to render is selected. Used by the example to determine which colors to use.
- `boolean cellHasFocus`—indicates whether the object to render has the focus.

Note that combo boxes and lists use the same type of renderer—`ListCellRenderer`. You can save yourself some time by sharing renderers between combo boxes and lists, if it makes sense for your program.

The Combo Box API

The following tables list the commonly used `JComboBox` constructors and methods. Other methods you are most likely to invoke on a `JComboBox` object are those, such as `setPreferredSize`, that it inherits from its superclasses. See The JComponent Class (page 67) for tables of commonly used inherited methods.

Table 79   Setting or Getting the Items in the Combo Box's Menu

Method	Purpose

`JComboBox()`
`JComboBox(ComboBoxModel)`
`JComboBox(Object[])`
`JComboBox(Vector)`
	Create a combo box with the specified items in its menu. A combo box created with the default constructor has no items in the menu initially. Each of the other constructors initializes the menu from its argument: a model object, an array of objects, or a `Vector` of objects.

`void addItem(Object)`
`void insertItemAt(Object,`
                  `int)`
	Add or insert the specified object into the combo box's menu. The insert method places the specified object *at* the specified index, thus inserting it before the object currently at that index. These methods require that the combo box's data model be an instance of `MutableComboBoxModel`.

`Object getItemAt(int)` `Object getSelectedItem()`	Get an item from the combo box's menu.
`int getItemCount()`	Get the number of items in the combo box's menu.

Table 79   Setting or Getting the Items in the Combo Box's Menu

Method	Purpose

`void removeAllItems()`
`void removeItemAt(int)`
`void removeItem(Object)`
	Remove one or more items from the combo box's menu. These methods require that the combo box's data model be an instance of `MutableComboBoxModel`.

`void setModel(ComboBoxModel)` `ComboBoxModel getModel()`	Set or get the data model that provides the items in the combo box's menu.

Table 80   Customizing the Combo Box's Operation

Method	Purpose
`void addActionListener(` `        ActionListener)`	Add an action listener to the combo box. The listener's `actionPerformed` method is called when the user selects an item from the combo box's menu or presses Return in an editable combo box.
`void addItemListener(` `        ItemListener)`	Add an item listener to the combo box. The listener's `itemStateChanged` method is called when the selection state of any of the combo box's items change.
`void setEditable(boolean)` `boolean isEditable()`	Set or get whether the user can type in the combo box.

`void setRenderer(`
`        ListCellRenderer)`
`ListCellRenderer getRenderer()`
	Set or get the object responsible for painting the selected item in the combo box. The renderer is used only when the combo box is uneditable. If the combo box is editable, the editor is used to paint the selected item instead.

`void setEditor(`
`        ComboBoxEditor)`
`ComboBoxEditor getEditor()`
	Set or get the object responsible for painting and editing the selected item in the combo box. The editor is used only when the combo box is editable. If the combo box is uneditable, the renderer is used to paint the selected item instead.

Examples that Use Combo Boxes

This table shows the examples that use `JComboBox` and where those examples are described.

Table 81   Examples that Use Combo Boxes

Example	Where Described	Notes
`ComboBoxDemo.java`	This section	Uses an uneditable combo box.
`ComboBoxDemo2.java`	This section	Uses an editable combo box.
`CustomComboBoxDemo.java`	This section	Provides a custom renderer for a combo box.
`TableRenderDemo.java`	How to Use Tables (page 254)	Shows a combo box used as a table cell editor.

How to Use File Choosers

File choosers provide a GUI for navigating the file system and then either choosing a file or a directory from a list or entering a file name or a directory name. To display a file chooser, you can either add an instance of JFileChooser[1] to a container, or use the JFileChooser API to show a modal dialog that contains a file chooser. File choosers often appear within modal dialogs because file operations can be sensitive to changes within a program,

A JFileChooser object presents the GUI only for choosing files. Your program is responsible for doing something with the chosen file, such as opening or saving it.

Here's a snapshot of an application that brings up an open-file chooser and a save-file chooser.

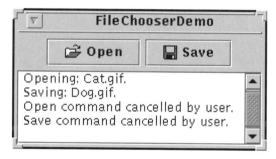

Figure 57   The FileChooserDemo application.

The look and feel will determine what the open and save dialogs look like and how they differ. In the Java Look & Feel the save-file chooser looks the same as the open-file chooser, except for the title on the dialog's window and the text on the button that approves the operation.

Figure 58 shows the file chooser that appears when the user clicks the Open a File... button. This is the Java Look & Feel's standard open-file chooser.

---

[1] API documentation for this class is available on this book's CD-ROM and online at http://java.sun.com/products/jdk/1.2/docs/api/javax/swing/JFileChooser.html

200

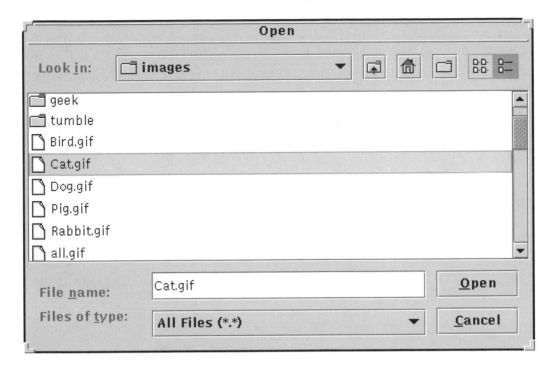

Figure 58   The `FileChooserDemo` application after a user has clicked the Open a File... button.

Try this:

1. Compile and run the program <u>FileChooserDemo.java</u> (page 650).[1] You will also need to put two image files in a directory named images: open.gif and save.gif.[2]

2. Click the Open a File... button. Navigate around the file chooser, choose a file, and click the dialog's Open button.

3. Use the Save a File... button to bring up a save-file chooser. Try to use all of the controls on the file chooser.

Bringing up a standard open-file chooser requires only two lines of code:

```
//Create a file chooser
final JFileChooser fc = new JFileChooser();
...
//In response to a button click:
int returnVal = fc.showOpenDialog(aComponent);
```

---

[1]   See the chapter <u>Getting Started with Swing</u> (page 3) if you need help compiling or running this application.

[2]   You can find the images by visiting: http://java.sun.com/docs/books/tutorial/uiswing/components/example-swing/index.html

The argument to the showOpenDialog method specifies the parent component for the dialog. The parent component affects the position of the dialog and the frame that the dialog depends on. For example, the Java Look & Feel places the dialog directly over the parent component. If the parent component is in a frame, the dialog is dependent on that frame, disappearing when the frame is iconified and reappearing when the frame is deiconified.

By default a file chooser that hasn't been shown before displays all files in the user's home directory. You can specify the file chooser's initial directory by using one of JFileChooser's other constructors, or you can set the directory by using the setCurrentDirectory method.

The call to showOpenDialog appears in the actionPerformed method of the Open a File... button's action listener, shown in full here:

```
public void actionPerformed(ActionEvent e) {
    int returnVal = fc.showOpenDialog(FileChooserDemo.this);
    if (returnVal == JFileChooser.APPROVE_OPTION) {
        File file = fc.getSelectedFile();
        //this is where a real application would open the file.
        log.append("Opening: " + file.getName() + "." + newline);
    } else {
        log.append("Open command cancelled by user." + newline);
    }
}
```

The showOpenDialog methods return an integer that indicates whether the user selected a file. The value returned is either CANCEL_OPTION or APPROVE_OPTION, both constants defined by JFileChooser. Use the return value to determine whether to perform the required operation. To get the chosen file, call getSelectedFile on the file chooser. This method returns an instance of File.

The sample gets the name of the file and uses it in the log message. You can call other methods on the File object, such as getPath, isDirectory, or exists, to get information about the file. You can also call other methods, such as delete and rename, to change the file in some way. Of course, you might also want to open or save the file, using one of the reader or writer classes provided by the JDK. See the "Reading and Writing" lesson in the book, *The Java™ Tutorial, Second Edition*, for information about using readers and writers to read and write data to the file system.[1]

The sample program uses the same instance of JFileChooser to display a standard save-file chooser. This time the program calls showSaveDialog:

```
int returnVal = fc.showSaveDialog(FileChooserDemo.this);
```

---

[1] This lesson is also available in HTML on this book's CD-ROM and online at http://java.sun.com/docs/books/tutorial/essential/index.html

By using the same file chooser instance to display its open- and save-file choosers, the program reaps these benefits:

- The chooser remembers the current directory between uses so the open and save versions automatically share the same current directory.
- You have to customize only one file chooser, and the customizations apply to both the open and save versions of it.

If you want to create a file chooser for a task other than opening or saving, or if you want to customize the file chooser, keep reading.

Another Example: FileChooserDemo2

Now let's look at `FileChooserDemo2.java` (page 651), a modified version of the previous demo program, that uses more of the `JFileChooser` API. This example uses a file chooser that has been customized in several ways. As in the original example, the user invokes a file chooser with the push of a button. Here's a picture of the file chooser.

Figure 59 The `FileChooser` application modified to permit previews of image files.

In addition to `FileChooserDemo2.java` (page 651), you need these source files to run this example: `ImageFilter.java` (page 667), `ImageFileView.java` (page 666), `ImagePre-`

<u>view.java</u> (page 667), and <u>Utils.java</u> (page 777). You will also need to put three image files in a directory named `images`: `gifIcon.gif`, `jpgIcon.gif`, and `tiffIcon.gif`.[1]

As the figure shows, this file chooser has been customized for a special task (attaching), provides a user-choosable file filter, uses a special file view for image files, and has an accessory component that displays a thumbnail sketch of the currently selected image file. We'll now show you the code that creates and customizes this file chooser.

Using a File Chooser for a Custom Task

As you've seen, `JFileChooser` provides `showOpenDialog` for displaying an open-file chooser and `showSaveDialog` for displaying a save-file chooser.

The class has another method, `showDialog`, for displaying a file chooser for a custom task in a dialog. In the Java Look & Feel the only difference between this file chooser and the others is the title on the dialog window and the label on the approve button. Here's the code that brings up the file chooser dialog for the Attach task:

```
JFileChooser fc = new JFileChooser();
int returnVal = fc.showDialog(FileChooserDemo2.this, "Attach");
```

The first argument to the `showDialog` method is the parent component for the dialog. The second argument is a `String` that provides both the title for the dialog window and the label for the approve button.

Once again, the file chooser doesn't do anything with the selected file. The program is responsible for implementing the custom task for which the file chooser was created.

Filtering the List of Files

By default a file chooser displays all of the files and directories that it detects, except hidden files. A program can apply one or more *file filters* to a file chooser so that the chooser shows only some files. The file chooser calls the filter's `accept` method for each file to determine whether it should be displayed. A file filter accepts or rejects a file, based on some criteria such as file type, size, ownership, and so on. Filters affect the list of files displayed by the file chooser. The user can enter the name of any file even if it's not displayed.

`JFileChooser` supports three kinds of filtering. The filters are checked in the order listed here. So a filter of the second type can filter only those files accepted by the first, and so on.

---

[1] You can find the images by visiting http://java.sun.com/docs/books/tutorial/uiswing/components/example-swing/index.html

Built-in filtering

Filtering is set up through specific method calls on a file chooser. Currently the only built-in filter available is for hidden files, such as those that begin with a period (.) on UNIX systems. By default hidden files are not shown. Call `setFileHidingEnabled(false)` to show hidden files.

Application-controlled filtering

The application determines which files are shown. Create a custom subclass of `File-Filter`,[1] instantiate it, and use the instance as an argument to `setFileFilter`. The file chooser shows only those files that the filter accepts.

User-choosable filtering

The file chooser GUI provides a list of filters that the user can choose from. When the user chooses a filter, the file chooser shows only those files accepted by that filter. `FileChooserDemo2` adds a custom file filter to the list of user-choosable filters:

```
fc.addChoosableFileFilter(new ImageFilter());
```

The custom file filter is implemented in `ImageFilter.java` and is a subclass of `FileFilter`. The `ImageFilter` class implements the `getDescription` method to return a string to put in the list of user-choosable filters. As the following code shows, `ImageFilter` implements the `accept` method to accept all directories and any file that has the filename extension `.jpg`, `.jpeg`, `.gif`, `.tif`, or `.tiff`.

```
public boolean accept(File f) {
    if (f.isDirectory()) {
        return true;
    }

    String extension = Utils.getExtension(f);
    if (extension != null) {
        if (extension.equals(Utils.tiff) ||
            extension.equals(Utils.tif) ||
            extension.equals(Utils.gif) ||
            extension.equals(Utils.jpeg) ||
            extension.equals(Utils.jpg)) {
            return true;
        } else {
            return false;
        }
    }

    return false;
}
```

---

[1] API documentation for this class is available on this book's CD-ROM and online at http://java.sun.com/products/jdk/1.2/docs/api/javax/swing/FileFilter.html

By accepting all directories, this filter allows the user to navigate around the file system. If the lines in boldface type were omitted from this method, the user would be limited to the directory with which the chooser was initialized.

The preceding code sample uses the `getExtension` method and several string constants from the `Utils` class, shown here:

```
public class Utils {

    public final static String jpeg = "jpeg";
    public final static String jpg = "jpg";
    public final static String gif = "gif";
    public final static String tiff = "tiff";
    public final static String tif = "tif";


    /*
     * Get the extension of a file.
     */
    public static String getExtension(File f) {
        String ext = null;
        String s = f.getName();
        int i = s.lastIndexOf('.');

        if (i > 0 &&  i < s.length() - 1) {
            ext = s.substring(i+1).toLowerCase();
        }
        return ext;
    }
}
```

Customizing the File View

In the Java Look & Feel the chooser's list shows each file's name and displays a small icon that represents whether the file is a true file or a directory. You can customize this *file view* by creating a custom subclass of `FileView` and using an instance of the class as an argument to `setFileView`. The example uses an instance of a custom class, `ImageFileView`, as the file chooser's file view.

```
fc.setFileView(new ImageFileView());
```

`ImageFileView` shows a different icon for each type of image accepted by the image filter described previously.

The `ImageFileView` class overrides the five abstract methods defined in `FileView` as follows.

String getTypeDescription(File f)

Returns a description of the file type. This is not yet used by any current look and feel. The intent is to provide information about the file's type. Here is ImageFileView's implementation of this method:

```
public String getTypeDescription(File f) {
    String extension = Utils.getExtension(f);
    String type = null;

    if (extension != null) {
        if (extension.equals(Utils.jpeg) || extension.equals(Utils.jpg)) {
            type = "JPEG Image";
        } else if (extension.equals(Utils.gif)){
            type = "GIF Image";
        } else if (extension.equals(Utils.tiff) ||
                    extension.equals(Utils.tif)) {
            type = "TIFF Image";
        }
    }
    return type;
}
```

Icon getIcon(File f)

Returns an icon representing the file or its type. Here is ImageFileView's implementation of this method:

```
public Icon getIcon(File f) {
    String extension = Utils.getExtension(f);
    Icon icon = null;

    if (extension != null) {
        if (extension.equals(Utils.jpeg) ||
            extension.equals(Utils.jpg)) {
            icon = jpgIcon;
        } else if (extension.equals(Utils.gif)) {
            icon = gifIcon;
        } else if (extension.equals(Utils.tiff) ||
                    extension.equals(Utils.tif)) {
            icon = tiffIcon;
        }
    }
    return icon;
}
```

String getName(File f)

Returns the name of the file. Most implementations of this method should return null to indicate that the look and feel should figure it out. Another common implementation returns f.getName().

String getDescription(File f)

Returns a description of the file. This is not yet used by any current look and feel. The intent is to describe individual files more specifically. A common implementation of this method returns null to indicate that the look and feel should figure it out.

Boolean isTraversable(File f)

Returns whether a directory is traversable. Most implementations of this method should return null to indicate that the look and feel should figure it out. Some applications might want to prevent users from descending into a certain type of directory because it represents a compound document. The isTraversable method should never return true for a nondirectory.

The ImageFileView implementation of both the getTypeDescription and getIcon methods uses a custom method, called getExtension, implemented as follows:

```
private String getExtension(File f) {
    String ext = null;
    String s = f.getName();
    int i = s.lastIndexOf('.');
    if (i > 0 &&  i < s.length() - 1) {
        ext = s.substring(i+1).toLowerCase();
    }
    return ext;
}
```

Providing an Accessory Component

The customized file chooser in FileChooserDemo2 has an accessory component. If the currently selected item is a JPEG, TIFF, or GIF image, the accessory component displays a thumbnail sketch of the image. Otherwise the accessory component is empty. Aside from a previewer, probably the most common use for the accessory component is a panel with more controls on it—say, check boxes that toggle some features.

The example calls the setAccessory method to establish an instance of ImagePreview as the chooser's accessory component:

```
fc.setAccessory(new ImagePreview(fc));
```

Any object that inherits from JComponent can be an accessory component. The component should have a preferred size that looks good in the file chooser.

The file chooser fires a property-change event when the user selects an item in the list. So a program with an accessory component must register to receive these events to update the accessory component whenever the selection changes. In the example the `ImagePreview` object itself registers for these events. This keeps all of the code related to the accessory component together in one class.

Here is the example's implementation of the `propertyChange` method, which is the method called when a property-change event is fired:

```
//where member variables are declared
File file = null;
...
public void propertyChange(PropertyChangeEvent e) {
    String prop = e.getPropertyName();
    if (prop.equals(JFileChooser.SELECTED_FILE_CHANGED_PROPERTY)) {
        file = (File) e.getNewValue();
        if (isShowing()) {
            loadImage();
            repaint();
        }
    }
}
```

If `SELECTED_FILE_CHANGED_PROPERTY` is the property that changed, this method gets a `File` object from the file chooser. The `loadImage` method loads the image from the specified file, and then the accessory component paints the image.

The File Chooser API

The API for using file choosers falls into four categories as shown in the following tables. File choosers also inherit the API listed in <u>The JComponent Class</u> (page 67).

Table 82   Creating and Showing the File Chooser

Method	Purpose

`JFileChooser()`
 `JFileChooser(File)`
 `JFileChooser(String)`
	Create a file chooser instance. The `File` and `String` arguments, when present, provide the initial directory.

`int showOpenDialog(Component)`
 `int showSaveDialog(Component)`
 `int showDialog(Component, String)`
	Show a modal dialog containing the file chooser. These methods return `APPROVE_OPTION` if the user approved the operation and `CANCEL_OPTION` if the user canceled it.

Table 83　　Selecting Files and Directories

Method	Purpose
`void setSelectedFile(File)` `File getSelectedFile()`	Set or get the currently selected file.
`void setSelectedFiles(File[])` `File[] getSelectedFiles()`	Set or get the currently selected files.

`void setFileSelectionMode(int)`
`int getFileSelectionMode()`
`boolean isDirectorySelectionEnabled()`
`boolean isFileSelectionEnabled()`
	Set the file selection mode. Acceptable values are `FILES_ONLY` (the default), `DIRECTORIES_ONLY`, and `FILES_AND_DIRECTORIES`.

`void setMultiSelectionEnabled(boolean)` `boolean isMultiSelectionEnabled()`	Set or get whether multiple files can be selected at once. By default a user can choose only one file.

Table 84　　Navigating the File Chooser's List

Method	Purpose
`void ensureFileIsVisible(File)`	Scroll the file chooser's list such that the indicated file is visible.
`void setCurrentDirectory(File)` `File getCurrentDirectory()`	Set or get the directory whose files are displayed in the file chooser's list.
`void changeToParentDirectory()`	Change the list to display the current directory's parent.
`void rescanCurrentDirectory()`	Check the file system and update the chooser's list.

Table 85　　Customizing the File Chooser

Method	Purpose
`JComponent getAccessory()` `void setAccessory(JComponent)`	Set or get the file chooser's accessory component.
`void setFileFilter(FileFilter)` `FileFilter getFileFilter()`	Set or get the file chooser's primary file filter.
`void setFileView(FileView)` `FileView getFileView()`	Set or get the chooser's file view.

`FileFilter[] getChoosableFileFilters()`
`void setChoosableFileFilters(FileFilter[])`
`void addChoosableFileFilter(FileFilter)`
`boolean removeChoosableFileFilter(FileFilter)`
`void resetChoosable(FileFilter)`
`FileFilter getAcceptAllFileFilter()`
	Set, get, or modify the list of user-choosable file filters.

`void setFileHidingEnabled(boolean)` `boolean isFileHidingEnabled()`	Set or get whether hidden files are displayed.

Examples that Use File Choosers

This table shows the examples that use `JFileChooser` and where those examples are described.

Table 86   Examples that Use File Choosers

Example	Where Described	Notes
`FileChooserDemo.java`	This section	Displays an open-file chooser and a save-file chooser.
`FileChooserDemo2.java`	This section	Uses a file chooser with custom filtering, a custom file view, and an accessory component.

How to Use Labels

You can use the JLabel[1] class to display unselectable text and images. If you need to create a component that displays a string or an image (or both), optionally reacting to user input, you can do so by using or extending JLabel. If the interactive component has state, you should probably use a button instead of a label.

Here's a picture of an application that displays three labels. The window is divided into three rows of equal height; the label in each row is as wide as possible.

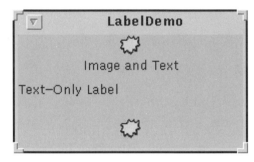

Figure 60 The LabelDemo application with three labels.

Try this:

1. Compile and run the application. The full code is in LabelDemo.java (page 670), and the image is middle.gif. Both files are available on this book's CD-ROM. See the chapter the lesson Getting Started with Swing (page 3) if you need help compiling or running this application.

2. Resize the window so you can see how the labels' contents are placed with the labels' drawing area.

All the label contents have the default vertical alignment: The label contents are centered vertically in the label's drawing area. The top label, which contains both image and text, is specified to have horizontal center alignment. The second label, which contains just text, has

---

[1] API documentation for this class is available on this book's CD-ROM and online at http://java.sun.com/products/jdk/1.2/docs/api/javax/swing/JLabel.html

the left alignment, the default for text-only labels. The third label, which contains just an image, has horizontal center alignment, the default for image-only labels.

The following code from <u>LabelDemo.java</u> (page 670) creates the labels in the previous example:

```
ImageIcon icon = new ImageIcon("images/middle.gif");
. . .
label1 = new JLabel("Image and Text", icon, JLabel.CENTER);

//Set the position of the text, relative to the icon:
label1.setVerticalTextPosition(JLabel.BOTTOM);
label1.setHorizontalTextPosition(JLabel.CENTER);
label2 = new JLabel("Text-Only Label");
label3 = new JLabel(icon);

//Add labels to the JPanel.
add(label1);
add(label2);
add(label3);
```

Note that label alignment is different from *X* and *Y* alignment. *X* and *Y* alignment are used by layout managers and can affect the way any component—not just a label—is sized or positioned. Label alignment, on the other hand, has no effect on a label's size or position but rather simply determines where, inside the label's painting area, the label's contents are positioned. In the usual case the label's painting area is exactly the size needed to paint the label, and thus label alignment is irrelevant. For more information about *X* and *Y* alignment, see the section <u>How to Use BoxLayout</u> (page 350).

Often a label describes another component. When this is true, you can improve your program's accessibility by using the setLabelFor method to identify the component the label describes. For example:

```
amountLabel.setLabelFor(amountField);
```

The preceding code, taken from the TextFieldDemo example discussed in <u>How to Use Text Fields</u> (page 298), lets assistive technologies know that the label (amountLabel) provides information about the text field (amountField). For more information about assistive technologies, see <u>How to Support Assistive Technologies</u> (page 393).

Using HTML on a Label

Note: The information in this section documents a feature available only in Swing 1.1.1 Beta 1 or compatible releases. It is not present in Java 2 SDK v 1.2 or v 1.2.1, but we expect it to be present in a forthcoming SDK release.

Have you ever wanted to put multiple lines on a label? Have you ever wanted to make part of a label bold or italic? Now you can. As of Swing 1.1.1 Beta 1, `JLabel` supports multiple lines, multiple fonts, and a whole lot more by letting you use HTML to specify a label's text.

Here's an application that dynamically sets the text on a label.

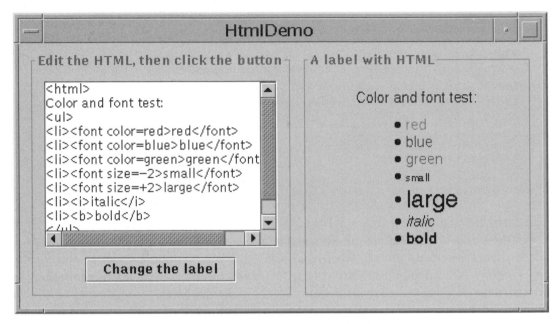

Figure 61   An application that dynamically sets the text on a label.

Try this:

1. Compile and run the application.[1] The full code is in `HtmlDemo.java` (page 664). Make sure that you run this program using Swing 1.1.1 Beta 1 or a compatible release.

2. Edit the HTML in the text area at the left and click the Change the label button. The label at the right shows the result.

3. Remove <html> from the text area on the left. The label at the right shows the result.

The action listener for the button executes this single line of code:

```
theLabel.setText(htmlTextArea.getText());
```

---

[1]   See the chapter <u>Getting Started with Swing</u> (page 3) if you need help compiling or running this application.

If the string in the text area on the left begins with <html>, the label parses it as HTML. Otherwise the label assumes that it's straight text. If you specify an invalid HTML tag, the program brings up a waring dialog. Fix your HTML and try again.

The Swing 1.1.1 Beta 1 release of JFC 1.1 added HTML support to JLabel and JButton. Swing 1.1.1 Beta 2 added HTML support to all menu items to tabbed panes, and to tool tips in the near future we expect radio buttons and check boxes to support HTML, as well.

Warning: There is no programmatic way to test whether a component supports HTML text. Do not specify HTML text unless you are absolutely sure that your program is running in a release that supports HTML text in the desired component.

The Label API

The following tables list the commonly used JLabel constructors and methods. Other methods you're likely to call are defined by the Component and JComponent classes. They include setFont, setForeground, setBorder, setOpaque, and setBackground. See the lesson The JComponent Class (page 67) for details.

Table 87   Setting or Getting the Label's Contents

Method or Constructor	Purpose
JLabel(Icon) JLabel(Icon, int) JLabel(String) JLabel(String, Icon, int) JLabel(String, int) JLabel()	Create a JLabel instance, initializing it to have the specified text/image/alignment. The int argument specifies the horizontal alignment of the label's contents within its drawing area. The horizontal alignment must be one of the following constants defined in the SwingConstants interface (which JLabel implements): LEFT, CENTER, RIGHT, LEADING, or TRAILING.
void setText(String) String getText()	Set or get the text displayed by the label.
void setIcon(Icon) Icon getIcon()	Set or get the image displayed by the label.
void setDisplayedMnemonic(char) char getDisplayedMnemonic()	Set or get the letter that should look like a keyboard alternative. This is handy when a label describes a component, such as a text field, that has a keyboard alternative but can't display it.
void setDisabledIcon(Icon) Icon getDisabledIcon()	Set or get the image displayed by the label when it's disabled. If you don't specify a disabled image, the look-and-feel creates one by manipulating the default image.

Table 88   Fine Tuning the Label's Appearance

Method	Purpose
void setHorizontalAlignment(int) void setVerticalAlignment(int) int getHorizontalAlignment() int getVerticalAlignment()	Set or get where content within the label should be placed. The SwingConstants interface defines five possible values for horizontal alignment: LEFT (the default for text-only labels), CENTER (the default for image-only labels), RIGHT, LEADING, and TRAILING. For vertical alignment: TOP, CENTER (the default), and BOTTOM.
void setHorizontalTextPosition(int) void setVerticalTextPosition(int) int getHorizontalTextPosition() int getVerticalTextPosition()	Set or get where the button's text should be placed, relative to the button's image. The SwingConstants interface defines three possible values for horizontal position: LEFT, CENTER, RIGHT (the default), LEADING and TRAILING. For vertical position: TOP, CENTER (the default), and BOTTOM.
void setIconTextGap(int) int getIconTextGap()	Set or get the number of pixels between the label's text and its image.

Table 89   Supporting Accessibility

Method	Purpose
void setLabelFor(component) Component getLabelFor()	Set or get which component the label describes.

Examples that Use Labels

The following table lists some of the many examples that use labels.

Table 90   Examples that Use Labels

Example	Where Described	Notes
LabelDemo.java	This section	Shows how to specify horizontal and vertical alignment, as well as aligning a label's text and image.
HtmlDemo.java	This section	Lets you experiment with specifying HTML text for a label.
AlignmentDemo.java	Fixing Alignment Problems (page 357)	Demonstrates a possible alignment problem when using a label in a vertical box layout. Shows how to solve the problem.

Table 90 Examples that Use Labels

Example	Where Described	Notes
`DialogDemo.java`	How to Make Dialogs (page 87)	Uses a changeable label to display instructions and provide feedback.
`SplitPaneDemo.java`	How to Use Split Panes (page 127) and How to Use Lists (page 218)	Displays an image using a label inside of a scroll pane.
`SliderDemo2.java`	How to Use Sliders (page 248)	Uses `JLabel` to provide labels for a slider.
`TableDialogEditDemo.java`	How to Use Tables (page 254)	Implements a label subclass, `ColorRenderer`, to display colors in table cells.
`TextFieldDemo.java`	How to Use Text Fields (page 298)	Has four rows, each containing a label and the text field it describes.
`TextComponentDemo.java`	General Rules for Using Text Components (page 282)	Has an inner class (`CaretListenerLabel`) that extends `JLabel` to provide a label that listens for events, updating itself based on the events. To run the example, you also need `LimitedStyledDocument.java` (page 675).
`ColorChooserDemo.java`	How to Use Color Choosers (page 184)	Uses an opaque label to display the currently chosen color against a fixed-color background.

How to Use Lists

A `JList`[1] presents the user with a group of items, displayed in a column, to choose from. Lists can have many items, so they are often put in scroll panes (page 112).

Other Swing components also present multiple selectable items to the user: combo boxes (page 192), menus (page 226), tables (page 226), and groups of check boxes (page 177) or radio buttons (page 180). Only tables, lists, and groups of check boxes allow multiple items to be selected at the same time.

The following figure shows an application that uses a `JList` to display a list of image names. When the user clicks on an image name, the application displays the image.

Figure 62   This application uses a `JList` to display a list of image names.

Try this:

1. Compile and run the application. The main source file is `SplitPaneDemo.java` (page 717). The file `imagenames.properties` provides the image names to put in the `JList`. These files and several image files are included on this book's CD-ROM; how-

---

[1]   API documentation for this class is available on this book's CD-ROM and online at http://java.sun.com/ products/jdk/1.2/docs/api/javax/swing/JList.html

218

ever, you can modify the properties file to use your own images.[1] Put the image files in a directory named images.

2. Choose an image from the list. Use the scroll bar to see more names.

Refer to <u>How to Use Split Panes</u> (page 127) to find out about this demo's use of a split pane.

Working with a List's Model

Here is the SplitPaneDemo code that creates and sets up the list:

```
//...where member variables are declared:
private Vector imageList;
//...initialize the vector from a properties file...//
...
//...where the GUI is created:
// Create the list of images and put it in a scroll pane
private JList list;
...
list = new JList(imageNames);
list.setSelectionMode(ListSelectionModel.SINGLE_SELECTION);
...
JScrollPane listScrollPane = new JScrollPane(list);
```

The code passes a Vector to the list's constructor. The vector is filled with strings that were read in from a properties file. Each string contains the name of an image file.

Other JList constructors let you initialize a list from an array of objects or from an object that adheres to the <u>ListModel</u>[2] interface. If you initialize a list with an array or a vector, the constructor implicitly creates a list model. This list model is immutable: You cannot add, remove, or replace items in the list. To create a list whose items can be changed individually, set the list's model to an instance of a mutable list model class, such as an instance of <u>DefaultListModel</u>.[3] You can set a list's model when you create the list or by calling the setModel method. See <u>Adding Items to and Removing Items from a List</u> (page 221) for an example.

Selecting Items in a List

A list uses an instance of <u>ListSelectionModel</u>[4] to manage its selection. By default a list selection model allows any combination of items to be selected at a time. You can specify a

---

[1] You can also find the images by visiting http://java.sun.com/docs/books/tutorial/uiswing/components/example-swing/index.html

[2] API documentation for this class is available on this book's CD-ROM and online at http://java.sun.com/products/jdk/1.2/docs/api/javax/swing/ListModel.html

[3] http://java.sun.com/products/jdk/1.2/docs/api/javax/swing/DefaultListModel.html

[4] http://java.sun.com/products/jdk/1.2/docs/api/javax/swing/ListSelectionModel.html

different selection mode by calling the setSelectionMode method on the list. For example, SplitPaneDemo sets the selection mode to SINGLE_SELECTION (a constant defined by ListSelectionModel) so that only one item in the list can be selected. The following table describes the three list selection modes.

Table 91   List Selection Modes

Mode	Description	Example
SINGLE_SELECTION	Only one item can be selected at a time. When the user selects an item, any previously selected item is deselected first.	
SINGLE_INTERVAL_SELECTION	Multiple, contiguous items can be selected. When the user begins a new selection range, any previously selected items are deselected first.	
MULTIPLE_INTERVAL_SELECTION	The default. Any combination of items can be selected. The user must explicitly deselect items.	

No matter which selection mode your list uses, the list fires list selection events whenever the selection changes. You can process these events by adding a list selection listener to the list, using the addListSelectionListener method. A list selection listener must implement one method: valueChanged. Here's the valueChanged method for the listener in SplitPaneDemo:

```
public void valueChanged(ListSelectionEvent e) {
    if (e.getValueIsAdjusting())
        return;
    JList theList = (JList)e.getSource();
    if (theList.isSelectionEmpty()) {
        picture.setIcon(null);
```

```
        } else {
            int index = theList.getSelectedIndex();
            ImageIcon newImage = new ImageIcon("images/" +
                                    (String)imageList.elementAt(index));
            picture.setIcon(newImage);
            picture.setPreferredSize(new Dimension(
                        newImage.getIconWidth(),
                        newImage.getIconHeight() ));
            picture.revalidate();
        }
    }
```

Many list selection events can be generated from a single user action, such as a mouse click. The getValueIsAdjusting method returns true if the user is still manipulating the selection. This particular program is interested only in the final result of the user's action, so the valueChanged method updates the image only if getValueIsAdjusting returns false.

Because the list is in single-selection mode, this code can use getSelectedIndex to get the index of the item just selected. JList provides other methods for setting or getting the selection when the selection mode allows more than one item to be selected. If you want, you can listen for events on the list's list selection model rather than on the list itself. Examples that Use List Selection Listeners (page 497) shows how to listen for list selection events on the list selection model and lets you change the selection mode of a list dynamically.

Adding Items to and Removing Items from a List

Here's an application that lets a user modify a list of employees by hiring and firing them.

Figure 63 The ListDemo application.

Try this:

1. Compile and run the application. The source file is <u>ListDemo.java</u> (page 676).

2. Select a name from the list and click the Fire button.

3. Type in a new name and click the Hire button.

Here's the ListDemo code that creates a mutable list model object, puts the initial items in it, and uses the list model to create a list:

```
listModel = new DefaultListModel();
listModel.addElement("Alison Huml");
listModel.addElement("Kathy Walrath");
listModel.addElement("Lisa Friendly");
listModel.addElement("Mary Campione");
list = new JList(listModel);
```

This particular program uses an instance of DefaultListModel, a class provided by Swing. In spite of the name, a list does not have a DefaultListModel unless your program explicitly makes it so. If this class doesn't suit your needs, you can write a custom list model, which must adhere to the ListModel interface.

Here's the actionPerformed method for the action listener registered on the Fire button:

```
public void actionPerformed(ActionEvent e) {
    int index = list.getSelectedIndex();
    listModel.remove(index);
    int size = listModel.getSize();
    //Nobody's left, disable firing
    if (size == 0) {
        fireButton.setEnabled(false);
    //Adjust the selection
    } else {
        if (index == listModel.getSize())//removed item in last position
            index--;
        list.setSelectedIndex(index);   //otherwise select same index
    }
}
```

The line of code in boldface type removes the selected item in the list. The remaining lines in the method disable the fire button (if the list is now empty) and make another selection.

Here's the actionPerformed method for the action listener shared by the Hire button and the text field:

```
public void actionPerformed(ActionEvent e) {
    //User didn't type in a name...
    if (employeeName.getText().equals("")) {
        Toolkit.getDefaultToolkit().beep();
```

```
            return;
        }
        int index = list.getSelectedIndex();
        int size = listModel.getSize();

        //If no selection or if item in last position is selected,
        //add the new hire to end of list, and select new hire
        if (index == -1 || (index+1 == size)) {
            listModel.addElement(employeeName.getText());
            list.setSelectedIndex(size);
        //Otherwise insert the new hire after the current selection,
        //and select new hire
        } else {
            listModel.insertElementAt(employeeName.getText(), index+1);
            list.setSelectedIndex(index+1);
        }
    }
}
```

This code uses the list model's addElement method to add the new name to the end of the list if the last item in the list is selected or if there's no selection. Otherwise the code calls insertElementAt to insert the new name after the current selection.

Writing a Custom Cell Renderer

A list uses an object called a cell renderer to display each of its items. The default cell renderer knows how to display strings and icons. If you want to put any other Object in a list or if you want to change the way the default renderer displays icons or strings, you can implement a custom cell renderer. Take these steps to provide a custom cell renderer for a list:

1. Write a class that implements the <u>ListCellRenderer</u>[1] interface.
2. Create an instance of your class and call the list's setCellRenderer, using the instance as an argument.

We don't provide an example of a list with a custom cell renderer, but we do have an example of a combo box with a custom renderer, and combo boxes use the same type of renderer as lists. See the example described in <u>Providing a Custom Renderer</u> (page 196).

The List API

The following tables list the commonly used JList constructors and methods. Other methods you are most likely to invoke on a JList object are those, such as setPreferredSize, that its superclasses provide. See <u>The JComponent Class</u> (page 67) for tables of commonly used inherited methods.

---

[1] API documentation for this class is available on this book's CD-ROM and online at http://java.sun.com/products/jdk/1.2/docs/api/javax/swing/ListCellRenderer.html

Much of the operation of a list is managed by other objects. The items in the list are managed by a list model object, the selection is managed by a list selection model object, and most programs put a list in a scroll pane to handle scrolling. For the most part, you don't need to worry about the models, because `JList` creates them as necessary, and you interact with them implicitly with `JList`'s convenience methods.

Table 92   Setting the Items in the List

Method	Purpose

`JList(ListModel)`
`JList(Object[])`
`JList(Vector)`
	Create a list with the initial list items specified. The second and third constructors implicitly create an immutable `ListModel`.

`void setModel(ListModel)` `ListModel getModel()`	Set or get the model that contains the contents of the list.
`void setListData(Object[])` `void setListData(Vector)`	Set the items in the list. These methods implicitly create an immutable `ListModel`.

Table 93   Managing the List's Selection

Method	Purpose
`void addListSelectionListener(` `        ListSelectionListener)`	Register to receive notification of selection changes.

`void setSelectedIndex(int)`
`void setSelectedIndices(int[])`
`void setSelectedValue(Object, boolean)`
`void setSelectedInterval(int, int)`
	Set the current selection as indicated. Use `setSelectionMode` to set what ranges of selections are acceptable. The boolean argument specifies whether the list should attempt to scroll itself so that the selected item is visible.

`int getSelectedIndex()`
`int getMinSelectionIndex()`
`int getMaxSelectionIndex()`
`int[] getSelectedIndices()`
`Object getSelectedValue()`
`Object[] getSelectedValues()`
	Get information about the current selection as indicated.

`void setSelectionMode(int)` `int getSelectionMode()`	Set or get the selection mode. Acceptable values are: `SINGLE_SELECTION`, `SINGLE_INTERVAL_SELECTION`, or `MULTIPLE_INTERVAL_SELECTION` (the default), which are defined in `ListSelectionModel`.
`void clearSelection()` `boolean isSelectionEmpty()`	Set or get whether any items are selected.
`boolean isSelectedIndex(int)`	Determine whether the specified index is selected.

Table 94   Working with a Scroll Pane

Method	Purpose
`void ensureIndexIsVisible(int)`	Scroll so that the specified index is visible within the viewport that this list is in.
`int getFirstVisibleIndex()` `int getLastVisibleIndex()`	Get the index of the first or last visible item.
`void setVisibleRowCount(int)` `int getVisibleRowCount()`	Set or get how many rows of the list are visible.

Examples that Use Lists

The following table shows the examples that use `JList` and where those examples are described.

Table 95   Examples that Use Lists

Example	Where Described	Notes
`SplitPaneDemo.java`	This section and <u>How to Use Split Panes</u> (page 127)	Contains a single selection, immutable list.
`ListDemo.java`	This section	Demonstrates how to add and remove items from a list at runtime.
`ListDialog.java`	<u>How to Use BoxLayout</u> (page 350)	Implements a modal dialog with a single-selection list.
`ListSelectionDemo.java`	<u>How to Write a List Selection Listener</u> (page 494)	Contains a list and a table that share the same selection model. You can dynamically choose the selection mode.
`SharedModelDemo.java`	–	Modifies `ListSelectionDemo` so that the list and the table share the same data model.
`CustomComboBox-Demo.java`	<u>Providing a Custom Renderer</u> (page 196)	Shows how to provide a custom renderer for a combo box. Because lists and combo boxes use the same type of renderer, you can use what you learn there an apply it to lists. In fact, a list and a combo box can share a renderer.

How to Use Menus

A menu provides a space-saving way to let the user choose one of several options. Other components that let the user make a one-of-many choice are <u>combo boxes</u> (page 192), <u>lists</u> (page 218), <u>radio buttons</u> (page 177), and <u>tool bars</u> (page 138). If any of your menu items performs an action that is duplicated by another menu item or by a toolbar button, you should also read <u>How to Use Actions</u> (page 389).

Menus are unique in that by convention, they aren't placed with the other components in the UI. Instead a menu usually appears either in a *menu bar* or as a *popup menu*. A menu bar contains one or more menus and has a customary, platform-dependent location—usually along the top of a window. A popup menu, by contrast, is invisible until the user makes a platform-specific mouse action, such as pressing the right mouse button, over a popup-enabled component. The popup menu then appears under the cursor.

The following figure shows the Swing components that implement each part of the menu system.

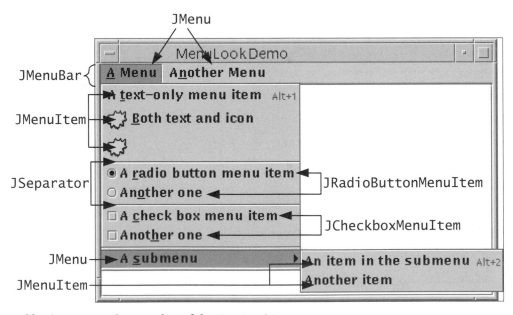

Figure 64   An annotated screenshot of the MenuLookDemo menu.

The Menu Component Hierarchy

The following picture shows the inheritance hierarchy for the menu-related classes.

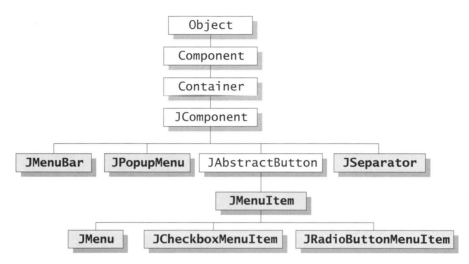

Figure 65   The menu component hierarchy.

As the figure shows, menu items, including menus, are simply buttons. You might be wondering how a menu, if it's only a button, shows its menu items. The answer is that when a menu is activated, it automatically brings up a popup menu that displays the menu items.

Creating Menus

The following code creates the menus shown in Figure 64. The lines of code in boldface type create and connect the menu objects; the other code sets up or customizes the menu objects. You can find the entire program in MenuLookDemo.java (page 687). To run the program, you need to have the following image file: images/middle.gif.[1]

> **Note:** Because this code has no event handling, the menus do nothing useful except look like they should. If you run the example, you'll notice that despite the lack of custom event handling, menus and submenus appear when they should, and the check boxes and the radio buttons respond appropriately when the user chooses them.

---

[1]   You can find the images by visiting: http://java.sun.com/docs/books/tutorial/uiswing/components/example-swing/index.html

```java
//in the constructor for a JFrame subclass:
JMenuBar menuBar;
JMenu menu, submenu;
JMenuItem menuItem;
JCheckBoxMenuItem cbMenuItem;
JRadioButtonMenuItem rbMenuItem;
...

//Create the menu bar.
menuBar = new JMenuBar();
setJMenuBar(menuBar);

//Build the first menu.
menu = new JMenu("A Menu");
menu.setMnemonic('a');
menu.getAccessibleContext().setAccessibleDescription(
        "The only menu in this program that has menu items");
menuBar.add(menu);

//a group of JMenuItems
menuItem = new JMenuItem("A text-only menu item",
                         KeyEvent.VK_T);
menuItem.setAccelerator(KeyStroke.getKeyStroke(
        KeyEvent.VK_1, ActionEvent.ALT_MASK));
menuItem.getAccessibleContext().setAccessibleDescription(
        "This doesn't really do anything");
menu.add(menuItem);
menuItem = new JMenuItem("Both text and icon",
                         new ImageIcon("images/middle.gif"));
menuItem.setMnemonic(KeyEvent.VK_B);
menu.add(menuItem);

menuItem = new JMenuItem(new ImageIcon("images/middle.gif"));
menuItem.setMnemonic('d');
menu.add(menuItem);

//a group of radio button menu items
menu.addSeparator();
ButtonGroup group = new ButtonGroup();
rbMenuItem = new JRadioButtonMenuItem("A radio button menu item");
rbMenuItem.setSelected(true);
rbMenuItem.setMnemonic('r');
group.add(rbMenuItem);
menu.add(rbMenuItem);

rbMenuItem = new JRadioButtonMenuItem("Another one");
rbMenuItem.setMnemonic('o');
group.add(rbMenuItem);
menu.add(rbMenuItem);
```

```
//a group of check box menu items
menu.addSeparator();
cbMenuItem = new JCheckBoxMenuItem("A check box menu item");
cbMenuItem.setMnemonic('c');
menu.add(cbMenuItem);

cbMenuItem = new JCheckBoxMenuItem("Another one");
cbMenuItem.setMnemonic('h');
menu.add(cbMenuItem);

//a submenu
menu.addSeparator();
submenu = new JMenu("A submenu");
submenu.setMnemonic('s');

menuItem = new JMenuItem("An item in the submenu");
menuItem.setAccelerator(KeyStroke.getKeyStroke(
        KeyEvent.VK_2, ActionEvent.ALT_MASK));
submenu.add(menuItem);

menuItem = new JMenuItem("Another item");
submenu.add(menuItem);
menu.add(submenu);

//Build second menu in the menu bar.
menu = new JMenu("Another Menu");
menu.setMnemonic('n');
menu.getAccessibleContext().setAccessibleDescription(
        "This menu does nothing");
menuBar.add(menu);
```

As the code shows, to set the menu bar for a JFrame, you use the setJMenuBar method. To add a JMenu to a JMenuBar, you use the add(JMenu) method. To add menu items and submenus to a JMenu, you use the add(JMenuItem) method. Other methods in the preceding code include setAccelerator and setMnemonic, which are discussed in Enabling Keyboard Operation (page 231). The setAccessibleDescription method is discussed in How to Support Assistive Technologies (page 393).

Handling Events from Menu Items

To detect when the user selects a JMenuItem, you can listen for action events, just as you would for a JButton. To detect when the user selects a JRadioButtonMenuItem, you can listen for either action events or item events, as described in How to Use Radio Buttons (page

180). For `JCheckBoxMenuItems` you generally listen for item events, as described in How to Use Check Boxes (page 177).

The following picture shows a program that adds event detection to the preceding example. The program's code is in MenuDemo.java (page 682). Like MenuLookDemo, MenuDemo uses the images/middle.gif image file.[1]

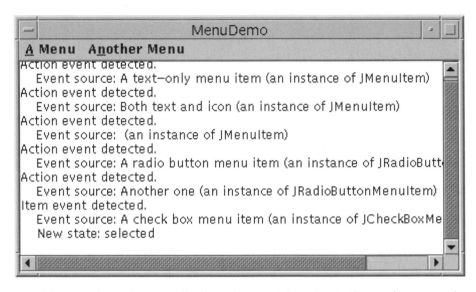

Figure 66   This revised MenuDemo application adds event detection to the previous example.

Here is the code that implements the event handling:

```
public class MenuDemo ... implements ActionListener, ItemListener {
    ...
    public MenuDemo() {
        //...for each JMenuItem instance:
        menuItem.addActionListener(this);
        ...
        //for each JRadioButtonMenuItem:
        rbMenuItem.addActionListener(this);
        ...
        //for each JCheckBoxMenuItem:
        cbMenuItem.addItemListener(this);
        ...
    }
```

---

[1]   You can find the images by visiting http://java.sun.com/docs/books/tutorial/uiswing/components/example-swing/index.html

```
    public void actionPerformed(ActionEvent e) {
        //...Get information from the action event...
        //...Display it in the text area...
    }

    public void itemStateChanged(ItemEvent e) {
        //...Get information from the item event...
        //...Display it in the text area...
    }
}
```

For examples of handling action and item events, see <u>How to Use Buttons, Check Boxes, and Radio Buttons</u> (page 169), as well as Table 100, "Examples that Use Menus" (page 238).

Enabling Keyboard Operation

Menus support two kinds of keyboard alternatives: mnemonics and accelerators. *Mnemonics* offer a way to use the keyboard to *navigate* the menu hierarchy, increasing the accessibility of programs. *Accelerators*, on the other hand, offer keyboard shortcuts to *bypass* navigating the menu hierarchy. Mnemonics are for all users; accelerators are for power users.

A mnemonic is a character that makes an already visible menu item be chosen. For example, the first menu in MenuDemo has the mnemonic 'a', and its second menu item has the mnemonic 'b'. This means that when you run MenuDemo with the Java Look & Feel, pressing the Alt and A keys makes the first menu appear. Pressing the B key (with or without Alt) while the first menu is visible makes the second menu item be chosen. A menu item generally displays its mnemonic by underlining the first occurrence of the mnemonic character in the menu item's text, as the following snapshot shows.

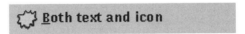

Figure 67 A menu item automatically underlines the first occurence of its mnemonic.

An accelerator is a key combination that causes a menu item to be chosen, whether or not it's visible. For example, pressing the Alt and 2 keys in MenuDemo makes the first item in the first menu's submenu be chosen, without bringing up any menus. Only leaf menu items—menus that don't bring up other menus—can have accelerators. The following snapshot shows how the Java Look & Feel displays a menu item that has an accelerator.

An item in the submenu   Alt+2

Figure 68 A menu item with an accelerator, "Alt+2".

You can specify a mnemonic either when constructing the menu item or with the setMne-monic method. To specify an accelerator, use the setAccelerator method. Here are examples of setting mnemonics and accelerators:

```
//Setting the mnemonic when constructing a menu item:
menuItem = new JMenuItem("A text-only menu item",
                        KeyEvent.VK_T);

//Setting the mnemonic after creation time (two versions):
menuItem.setMnemonic('t');

  or

menuItem.setMnemonic(KeyEvent.VK_T);

//Setting the accelerator:
menuItem.setAccelerator(KeyStroke.getKeyStroke(
        KeyEvent.VK_T, ActionEvent.ALT_MASK));
```

As you can see, you can set a mnemonic by specifying either a character or the KeyEvent[1] constant corresponding to the character. To specify an accelerator, you must use a Key-Stroke[2] object, which combines a key (specified by a KeyEvent constant) and a modifier-key mask (specified by an ActionEvent[3] constant).

Bringing Up a Popup Menu

To bring up a popup menu (JPopupMenu), you must register a mouse listener on each component that the popup menu should be associated with. The mouse listener must detect user requests that the popup menu be brought up. On Win32 and Motif platforms the user brings up a popup menu by pressing the right-mouse button while the cursor is over a component that is popup enabled.

The mouse listener brings up the popup menu by invoking the show method on the appropriate JPopupMenu instance. The following code, taken from PopupMenuDemo.java (page 692), shows how to create and show popup menus:

```
//...where instance variables are declared:
JPopupMenu popup;
    //...where the GUI is constructed:
    //Create the popup menu.
    popup = new JPopupMenu();
```

---

[1] API documentation for KeyEvent is available on this book's CD-ROM and online at http://java.sun.com/
   products/jdk/1.2/docs/api/java/awt/event/KeyEvent.html
[2] http://java.sun.com/products/jdk/1.2/docs/api/javax/swing/KeyStroke.html
[3] http://java.sun.com/products/jdk/1.2/docs/api/java/awt/event/ActionEvent.html

```
        menuItem = new JMenuItem("A popup menu item");
        menuItem.addActionListener(this);
        popup.add(menuItem);
        menuItem = new JMenuItem("Another popup menu item");
        menuItem.addActionListener(this);
        popup.add(menuItem);


        //Add listener to components that can bring up popup menus.
        MouseListener popupListener = new PopupListener();
        output.addMouseListener(popupListener);
        menuBar.addMouseListener(popupListener);
    ...
    class PopupListener extends MouseAdapter {
        public void mousePressed(MouseEvent e) {
            maybeShowPopup(e);
        }
        public void mouseReleased(MouseEvent e) {
            maybeShowPopup(e);
        }
        private void maybeShowPopup(MouseEvent e) {
            if (e.isPopupTrigger()) {
                popup.show(e.getComponent(),
                            e.getX(), e.getY());
            }
        }
    }
}
```

Popup menus have a few interesting implementation details. One is that every menu has an associated popup menu. When the menu is activated, it uses its associated popup menu to show its menu items.

Another detail is that a popup menu itself uses another component to implement the window containing the menu items. Depending on the circumstances under which the popup menu is displayed, it might implement its "window" by using a lightweight component (such as a JPanel), a "mediumweight" component (such as a <u>Panel</u>[1]), or a heavyweight window (something that inherits from <u>Window</u>[2]).

Lightweight popup windows are more efficient than heavyweight windows, but they don't work well if you have any heavyweight components inside your GUI. Specifically, when the lightweight popup's display area intersects the heavyweight component's display area, the heavyweight component is drawn on top. This is one of the reasons we recommend against mixing heavyweight and lightweight components. If you absolutely need to use a heavy-

---

[1] http://java.sun.com/products/jdk/1.2/docs/api/java/awt/Panel.html
[2] http://java.sun.com/products/jdk/1.2/docs/api/java/awt/Window.html

weight component in your GUI, you can invoke `JPopupMenu.setLightWeightPopupEn-abled(false)` to disable lightweight popup windows.[1]

Customizing Menu Layout

Because menus are made up of ordinary Swing components, you can easily customize them. For example, you can add any lightweight component to a `JMenu` or a `JMenuBar`. And because `JMenuBar` uses <u>BoxLayout</u> (page 350), you can customize a menu bar's layout just by adding invisible components to it. Here is an example of adding a glue component to a menu bar, so that the last menu is at the rightmost edge of the menu bar:

```
//...create and add some menus...
menuBar.add(Box.createHorizontalGlue());
//...create the rightmost menu...
menuBar.add(rightMenu);
```

Here is a picture of the result, which you can duplicate by compiling and running <u>MenuGlue-Demo.java</u> (page 685).

Figure 69   A glue component is between Menu 2 and Menu 3.

Another way of changing the look of menus is to change the layout managers used to control them. For example, you can change a menu bar's layout manager from the default left-to-right `BoxLayout` to something such as `GridLayout`. You can also change how an activated menu or other popup menu lays out its items, as <u>MenuLayoutDemo.java</u> (page 686) demonstrates. Here's a picture of the menu layout that `MenuLayoutDemo` creates.

Figure 70   This `MenuLayoutDemo` application uses `GridLayout` to display the menus vertically.

---

[1]   For more information, see "Mixing Heavy and Light Components," an article in the online magazine, *The Swing Connection. The Swing Connection* is available on the CD-ROM that accompanies this book and online at http://java.sun.com/products/jfc/tsc/index.html

The Menu API

The following tables list the commonly used menu constructors and methods.

Table 96   Creating and Setting Up Menu Bars

Constructor or Method	Purpose
`JMenuBar()`	Create a menu bar.
`JMenu add(JMenu)`	Create a menu bar.

`void setJMenuBar(JMenuBar)`
`JMenuBar getJMenuBar()`
`(in JApplet, JDialog, JFrame,`
`  JInternalFrame, JRootPane)`
	Set or get the menu bar of an applet, dialog, frame, internal frame, or root pane.

Table 97   Creating and Populating Menus

Constructor or Method	Purpose
`JMenu()` `JMenu(String)`	Create a menu. The string specifies the text to display for the menu.

`JMenuItem add(JMenuItem)`
`JMenuItem add(Action)`
`JMenuItem add(String)`
	Add a menu item to the current end of the menu. If the argument is an `Action` object, the menu creates a menu item as described in <u>How to Use Actions</u> (page 389). If the argument is a string, the menu automatically creates a `JMenuItem` object that displays the specified text.

`void addSeparator()`	Add a separator to the current end of the menu.

`JMenuItem insert(JMenuItem, int)`
`JMenuItem insert(Action, int)`
`void insert(String, int)`
`void insertSeparator(int)`
	Insert a menu item or a separator into the menu at the specified position. The first menu item is at position 0, the second at position 1, and so on. The `JMenuItem`, `Action`, and `String` arguments are treated the same as in the corresponding add methods.

`void remove(JMenuItem)`
`void remove(int)`
`void removeAll()`
	Remove the specified item(s) from the menu. If the argument is an integer, it specifies the position of the menu item to be removed.

Table 98   Creating and Populating Popup Menus

Constructor or Method	Purpose
`JPopupMenu()` `JPopupMenu(String)`	Create a popup menu. The optional string argument specifies the title that a look and feel might display as part of the popup window.

`JMenuItem add(JMenuItem)`
`JMenuItem add(Action)`
`JMenuItem add(String)`
	Add a menu item to the current end of the popup menu. If the argument is an `Action` object, the popup menu creates a menu item as described in <u>How to Use Actions</u> (page 389). If the argument is a string, the menu automatically creates a `JMenuItem` object that displays the specified text.

`void addSeparator()`	Add a separator to the current end of the popup menu.
`void insert(Component, int)`	Insert a menu item into the menu at the specified position. The first menu item is at position 0, the second at position 1, and so on. The `Component` argument specifies the menu item to add.

`void remove(JMenuItem)`
`void remove(int)`
`void removeAll()`
	Remove the specified item(s) from the menu. If the argument is an integer, it specifies the position of the menu item to be removed.

`static void`
    `setLightWeightPopupEnabled(`
    `boolean)`
	By default Swing implements a menu's window, using a lightweight component. This can cause problems if you use any heavyweight components in your Swing program, as described in <u>Bringing Up a Popup Menu</u> (page 232). (This is one of several reasons to avoid using heavyweight components.) As a workaround, invoke `JPopupMenu.setLightWeightPopupEnabled(false)`.

`void show(Component, int, int)`	Display the popup menu at the specified *X*, *Y* position (specified in that order by the integer arguments) in the coordinate system of the specified component.

Table 99   Implementing Menu Items

Constructor or Method	Purpose

`JMenuItem()`
`JMenuItem(String)`
`JMenuItem(Icon)`
`JMenuItem(String, Icon)`
`JMenuItem(String, int)`
	Create an ordinary menu item. The icon argument, if present, specifies the icon that the menu item should display. Similarly the `String` argument specifies the text that the menu item should display. The integer argument specifies the keyboard mnemonic to use. You can specify any of the relevant VK constants defined in the `KeyEvent` class. For example, to specify 'a' as the constant, you can use `KeyEvent.VK_A`.

Table 99   Implementing Menu Items

Constructor or Method	Purpose

`JCheckBoxMenuItem()`
`JCheckBoxMenuItem(String)`
`JCheckBoxMenuItem(Icon)`
`JCheckBoxMenuItem(String, Icon)`
`JCheckBoxMenuItem(String, boolean)`
`JCheckBoxMenuItem(String, Icon, boolean)`
	Create a menu item that looks and acts like a check box. The `String` argument, if any, specifies the text that the menu item should display. If you specify `true` for the boolean argument, the menu item is initially selected (checked). Otherwise the menu item is initially unselected.

`JRadioButtonMenuItem()`
`JRadioButtonMenuItem(String)`
`JRadioButtonMenuItem(Icon)`
`JRadioButtonMenuItem(String, Icon)`
`JRadioButtonMenuItem(String, boolean)`
`JRadioButtonMenuItem(Icon, boolean)`
`JRadioButtonMenuItem(String, Icon, boolean)`
	Create a menu item that looks and acts like a radio button. The `String` argument, if any, specifies the text that the menu item should display. If you specify `true` for the boolean argument, the menu item is initially selected. Otherwise the menu item is initially unselected.

`void setState(boolean)`
`boolean getState()`
(in `JCheckBoxMenuItem`)
	Set or get the selection state of a check box menu item.

`void setEnabled(boolean)`	If the argument is `true`, enable the menu item. Otherwise disable the menu item.
`void setMnemonic(char)` `void setMnemonic(int)`	Set the mnemonic that enables keyboard navigation to the menu or menu item. If you specify an integer argument, use one of the VK constants defined in the `KeyEvent` class.
`void setAccelerator(KeyStroke)`	Set the accelerator that activates the menu item.
`void setActionCommand(String)`	Set the name of the action performed by the menu item.
`void addActionListener(ActionListener)` `void addItemListener(ItemListener)`	Add an event listener to the menu item. See Handling Events from Menu Items (page 229) for details.
Many of the preceding methods are inherited from `AbstractButton`. See How to Use Color Choosers (page 184) for information about other useful methods that `AbstractButton` provides.	

Examples that Use Menus

A few of our examples use menus.

Table 100　Examples that Use Menus

Example	Where Described	Notes
MenuLookDemo.java	This section, especially <u>Creating Menus</u> (page 227)	A simple example that creates all kinds of menus except popup menus but doesn't handle events from the menu items.
MenuDemo.java	This section, especially <u>Handling Events from Menu Items</u> (page 229)	Add event handling to MenuLookDemo.
MenuGlueDemo.java	This section, especially <u>Customizing Menu Layout</u> (page 234)	Demonstrates affecting menu layout by adding invisible components to the menu bar.
MenuLayoutDemo.java	This section, especially <u>Customizing Menu Layout</u> (page 234)	Implements sideways-opening menus arranged in a vertical menu bar.
ActionDemo.java	<u>How to Use Actions</u> (page 389)	Uses Action objects to implement menu items that duplicate functionality provided by tool bar buttons.
Framework.java	–	Brings up multiple identical frames, each with a menu in its menu bar.
InternalFrameDemo.java	<u>How to Use Internal Frames</u> (page 143)	Uses a menu item to create windows.

How to Monitor Progress

Sometimes a task running within a program might take a while to complete. A user-friendly program gives the user some indication as to how long the task might take and how much work has already been done. Swing provides the following three classes to help you create GUIs that monitor and display the progress of a long-running task.

JProgressBar

A visible component to graphically display how much of a total task has completed. See How to Use Progress Bars (page 239) for information and an example of using a progress bar.

ProgressMonitor

Not a visible component. Instead, an instance of this class monitors the progress of a task and pops up a dialog if necessary. See How to Use Progress Monitors (page 241) for details and an example of using a progress monitor.

ProgressMonitorInputStream

An input stream with an attached progress monitor, which monitors reading from the stream. You use an instance of this stream like any of the other input streams described in the "Reading and Writing" lesson in the book, *The Java™ Tutorial, Second Edition*, for information about using readers and writers to read and write data to the file system.[1] You can get the stream's progress monitor with a call to getProgressMonitor and configure it as described in How to Use Progress Monitors (page 241).

After you see a progress bar and a progress monitor in action, Deciding Whether to Use a Progress Bar or a Progress Monitor (page 243) can help you figure out which is appropriate for your application.

How to Use Progress Bars

Figure 71 shows a small demo application that uses a progress bar to measure the progress of a task that runs in its own thread.

---

[1] This trail is also available in HTML on this book's CD-ROM and online at http://java.sun.com/docs/books/tutorial/essential/index.html

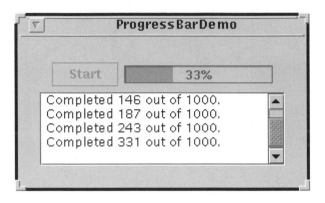

Figure 71 The `ProgressBarDemo` application.

Try this:

1. Compile and run the application.[1] The main source file is <u>ProgressBarDemo.java</u> (page 695). You will also need <u>LongTask.java</u> (page 681) and <u>SwingWorker.java</u> (page 720).

2. Click the Start button. Watch the progress bar as the task proceeds. The task displays its output in the text area at the bottom of the window.

The following code, excerpted from <u>ProgressBarDemo.java</u> (page 695), creates and sets up the progress bar:

```
//Where member variables are declared:
JProgressBar progressBar;
    //...in the constructor for the demo's frame:
    progressBar = new JProgressBar(0, task.getLengthOfTask());
    progressBar.setValue(0);
    progressBar.setStringPainted(true);
```

The constructor that creates the progress bar sets the progress bar's minimum and maximum values. You can also set these values with `setMinimum` and `setMaximum`. The minimum and maximum values used in this program are 0 and the length of the task, which is typical of many programs and tasks. However, a progress bar's minimum and maximum values can be any value, even negative. The code snippet also sets the progress bar's current value to 0.

The call to `setStringPainted` causes the progress bar to display, within its bounds, a textual indication of the percentage of the task that has completed. By default the progress bar displays the value returned by its `getPercentComplete` method formatted as a percent, such

---

[1] See the chapter <u>Getting Started with Swing</u> (page 3) if you need help compiling or running this application.

as 33%. Alternatively you can replace the default with a different string by calling set-
String. For example,

```
if (/*...half way done...*/)
    progressBar.setString("Half way there!");
```

You start this example's task by clicking the Start button. Once the task has begun, a timer
(an instance of the Timer class) fires an action event every second. See How to Use Timers
(page 436) for information about using Timer objects. Here's the ActionPerformed method
of our timer's action listener:

```
public void actionPerformed(ActionEvent evt) {
    progressBar.setValue(task.getCurrent());
    taskOutput.append(task.getMessage() + newline);
    taskOutput.setCaretPosition(taskOutput.getDocument().getLength());
    if (task.done()) {
        Toolkit.getDefaultToolkit().beep();
        timer.stop();
        startButton.setEnabled(true);
        progressBar.setValue(progressBar.getMinimum());
    }
}
```

The line of code in boldface type gets the amount of work completed by the task and updates
the progress bar with that value. So this example's progress bar measures the *progress* made
by the task each second, *not* the elapsed time. The rest of the code appends a message to the
output log (a text area named taskOutput) and, if the task is done, turns the timer off and
resets the other controls.

As mentioned, the long-running task in this program runs in a separate thread. Generally it's
a good idea to isolate a potentially long-running task in its own thread so that the task
doesn't block the rest of the program. The long-running task is implemented in Long-
Task.java (page 681), which uses a SwingWorker class to ensure that the thread runs safely.
See Using the SwingWorker Class (page 432) for information about that class.

How to Use Progress Monitors

Now let's rewrite the previous example to use a progress monitor instead of a progress bar.
Figure 72 shows the new demo program, which is implemented in ProgressMonitor-
Demo.java (page 696).

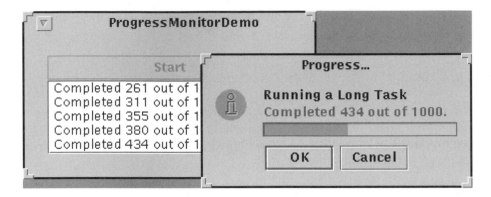

Figure 72 The ProgressMonitorDemo program uses progress monitor instead of a progress bar.

Try this:

1. Compile and run the application.[1] The main source file is ProgressMonitor-Demo.java (page 696). You will also need LongTask.java (page 681) and Swing-Worker.java (page 720).

2. Click the Start button. After a set amount of time, the program shows a progress dialog.

3. Click the OK button. Note that the task continues even though the dialog is gone.

4. Start another task. After the dialog pops up, click the Cancel button. The dialog goes away and the task stops.

A progress monitor cannot be used again, so a new one must be created each time a new task is started. This program creates a progress monitor each time the user starts a new task with the Start button.

Here's the statement that creates the progress monitor:

```
progressMonitor = new ProgressMonitor(ProgressMonitorDemo.this,
                                      "Running a Long Task",
                                      "", 0, task.getLengthOfTask());
```

This code uses ProgressMonitor's only constructor to create the monitor and to initialize several arguments.

- The first argument provides the parent component to the dialog popped up by the progress monitor.

- The second argument is a string that describes the nature of the task being monitored. This string is displayed on the dialog. See The Progress Monitoring API (page 244) for details about this argument.

---

[1] See the chapter Getting Started with Swing (page 3) if you need help compiling or running this application.

- The third argument is another string that provides a changeable status note. The example uses an empty string to indicate that the dialog should make space for a changeable status note but that the note is initially empty. If you provide null for this argument, the note is omitted from the dialog. The example updates the note each time the timer fires an action event and updates the monitor's current value at the same time:

```
progressMonitor.setNote(task.getMessage());
progressMonitor.setProgress(task.getCurrent());
```

- The last two arguments provide the minimum and maximum values, respectively, for the progress bar displayed in the dialog.

After creating the progress monitor, the example configures the monitor further:

```
progressMonitor.setProgress(0);
progressMonitor.setMillisToDecideToPopup(2 * ONE_SECOND);
```

The first line sets the current position of the progress bar on the dialog. The second tells the progress monitor to wait two seconds before deciding whether to bring up a dialog. If, after two seconds, the progress monitor's progress is less than its maximum, the monitor will bring up the dialog.

By the simple fact that this example uses a progress monitor, it adds a feature that wasn't present in the version of the program that uses a progress bar. The user can cancel the task by clicking the Cancel button on the dialog. Here's the code in the example that checks to see whether the user canceled the task or whether the task exited normally:

```
if (progressMonitor.isCanceled() || task.done()) {
    progressMonitor.close();
    task.stop();
    Toolkit.getDefaultToolkit().beep();
    timer.stop();
    startButton.setEnabled(true);
}
```

Note that the progress monitor doesn't itself cancel the task. It provides the GUI and API to allow the program to do so easily.

Deciding Whether to Use a Progress Bar or a Progress Monitor

Use a *progress bar* in the following situations:

- You want more control over the configuration of the progress bar. If you are working directly with a progress bar, you can make it display vertically, you can provide a string for it to display, you can register change listeners on it, and you can provide it with a bounded range model to control the progress bar's minimum, maximum, and current values.

- The program needs to display other components along with the progress bar.

- You need more than one progress bar. With some tasks, you need to monitor more than one parameter. For example, an installation program might monitor disk space usage in addition to how many files have been successfully installed.

- You need to reuse the progress bar. A progress bar can be reused; a progress monitor cannot. Once the progress monitor has decided to display a dialog (or not), the progress monitor cannot do it again.

Use a *progress monitor* in these situations:

- You want an easy way to display progress in a dialog.

- The running task is secondary and the user might not be interested in the progress of the task. A progress monitor provides a way for the user to dismiss the dialog while the task is still running.

- The task can be canceled. A progress monitor provides a GUI for the user to cancel the task. All you have to do is call the progress monitor's `isCanceled` method to find out whether the user clicked the Cancel button.

- Your task displays a short message periodically while running. The progress monitor dialog provides the `setNote` method so that the task can provide further information about what it's doing. For example, an installation task might report the name of each file as it's installed.

- The task might not take a long time to complete. You decide at what point a running task is taking long enough to warrant letting the user know about it. A progress monitor won't pop up a dialog if the task completes within the timeframe you set.

If you decide to use a progress monitor *and* the task you are monitoring is reading from an input stream, use the `ProgressMonitorInputStream` class.

The Progress Monitoring API

The following tables list the commonly used API for using progress bars and progress monitors. Because `JProgressBar` is a subclass of `JComponent`, other methods you are likely to call on a `JProgressBar` are listed in <u>The JComponent Class</u> (page 67). Note that `Progress-Monitor` is a subclass of `Object` and is not a visual component.

Table 101   Creating the Progress Bar

Constructor	Purpose
`JProgressBar()` `JProgressBar(int min, int max)`	Create a horizontal progress bar. The default constructor initializes the progress bar with a minimum and initial value of 0 and a maximum of 100. Use the `min` and `max` arguments to specify other values.

`JProgressBar(int orientation)`
`JProgressBar(int orientation,`
`              int min, int max)`
	Create a progress bar with the specified orientation, which can be either `JProgressBar.HORIZONTAL` or `JProgressBar.VERTICAL`. Use the `min` and `max` arguments to specify minimum and maximum values.

`JProgressBar(BoundedRangeModel)`	Create a horizontal progress bar with the specified range model.

Table 102   Setting or Getting the Progress Bar's Constraints/Values

Method or Constructor	Purpose
`void setValue(int)` `int getValue()`	Set or get the current value of the progress bar. The value is constrained by the minimum and maximum values.
`double getPercentComplete()`	Get the percent complete for the progress bar.
`void setMinimum(int)` `int getMinimum()`	Set or get the minimum value of the progress bar.
`void setMaximum(int)` `int getMaximum()`	Set or get the maximum value of the progress bar.
`void setModel(BoundedRangeModel)` `BoundedRangeModel getMaximum()`	Set or get the model used by the progress bar. The model establishes the progress bar's constraints and values, so you can use this method as an alternative to using the individual set/get methods listed previously.

Table 103   Fine Tuning the Progress Bar's Appearance

Method	Purpose
`void setOrientation(int)` `int getOrientation()`	Set or get whether the progress bar is vertical or horizontal. Acceptable values are `JProgressBar.VERTICAL` or `JProgressBar.HORIZONTAL`.
`void setBorderPainted(boolean)` `boolean isBorderPainted()`	Set or get whether the progress bar has a border.

Table 103   Fine Tuning the Progress Bar's Appearance

Method	Purpose
`void setStringPainted(boolean)` `boolean isStringPainted()`	Set or get whether the progress bar displays a percent string. By default the value of the percent string is the value returned by `getPercentComplete` formatted as a percent. You can set the string to be displayed with `setString`.
`void setString(String)` `String getString()`	Set or get the percent string.

Table 104   Creating the Progress Monitor

Method or Constructor	Purpose
`ProgressMonitor(Component, Object, String, int, int)`	Create a progress monitor. The `Component` argument is the parent for the monitor's dialog. The `Object` argument is a message to put on option pane within the dialog. The value of this object is typically a `String`. The `String` argument is a changeable status note. The final two `int` arguments set the minimum and maximum values, respectively, for the progress bar used in the dialog.
`ProgressMonitor getProgressMonitor()` (in `ProgressMonitorInputStream`)	Get a progress monitor that monitors reading from an input stream.

Table 105   Configuring the Progress Monitor

Method	Purpose
`void setMinimum(int)` `int getMinimum()`	Set or get the minimum value of the progress monitor. This value is used by the monitor to set up the progress bar in the dialog.
`void setMaximum(int)` `int getMaximum()`	Set or get the maximum value of the progress monitor. This value is used by the monitor to set up the progress bar in the dialog.
`void setProgress(int)`	Update the monitor's progress.
`void setNote(String)` `String getNote()`	Set or get the status note. This note is displayed on the dialog. To omit the status note from the dialog, provide `null` as the third argument to the monitor's constructor.
`void setMillisToDecideToPopup(int)` `int getMillisToDecideToPopup()`	Set or get the time after which the monitor should decide whether to popup a dialog.

Table 106   Terminating the Progress Monitor

Method	Purpose
`close()`	Close the progress monitor. This disposes of the dialog.
`boolean isCanceled()`	Determine whether the user clicked the Cancel button.

Examples that Monitor Progress

This table shows the examples that use `JProgressBar`, `ProgressMonitor`, or `ProgressMonitorInputStream` and indicates where those examples are described.

Table 107   Examples that Monitor Progress

Example	Where Described	Notes
`ProgressBarDemo.java`	This section and How to Use Timers (page 436)	Uses a basic progress bar to show progress on a task running in a separate thread.
`ProgressMonitorDemo.java`	This section	Modification of the previous example that uses a progress monitor instead of a progress bar.

How to Use Sliders

Use a `JSlider`[1] to let the user enter a numeric value bounded by a minimum and a maximum value. By using a slider instead of a text field, you eliminate input errors.

Here's a picture of an application that uses a slider to control animation speed.

Figure 73　The `SliderDemo` application.

Try this:

1. Compile and run the application.[2] The source file is `SliderDemo.java` (page 713). You will also need the 14 image files that make up the animation.[3]

2. Use the slider to adjust the animation speed.

3. Push the slider to 0 to stop the animation.

---

[1]　http://java.sun.com/products/jdk/1.2/docs/api/javax/swing/JSlider.html

[2]　See the chapter <u>Getting Started with Swing</u> (page 3) if you need help compiling or running this application.

[3]　You can find the images by visiting
http://java.sun.com/docs/books/tutorial/uiswing/components/example-swing/index.html

The following code from <u>SliderDemo.java</u> (page 713) creates the slider in the previous example:

```
JSlider framesPerSecond = new JSlider(JSlider.HORIZONTAL, 0, 30,
                                      FPS_INIT);
framesPerSecond.addChangeListener(new SliderListener());
framesPerSecond.setMajorTickSpacing(10);
framesPerSecond.setMinorTickSpacing(1);
framesPerSecond.setPaintTicks(true);
framesPerSecond.setPaintLabels(true);
framesPerSecond.setBorder(BorderFactory.createEmptyBorder(0,0,10,0));
. . .
//add the slider to the content pane
contentPane.add(framesPerSecond);
```

Spacing for major and minor tick marks is zero by default. To see tick marks, you must explicitly set the spacing for either major or minor tick marks (or both) to a nonzero value and call setPaintTicks(true). Just calling setPaintTicks(true) is not enough. To display standard, numeric labels at major tick mark locations, set the major tick spacing and then call setPaintLabels(true). The sample program provides labels for its slider this way. But you don't have to settle for these labels. <u>Customizing Labels on a Slider</u> (page 250) shows you how to customize slider labels.

When you move the slider's knob, the stateChanged method of the slider's ChangeListener is called. For information about change listeners, refer to <u>How to Write a Change Listener</u> (page 464). Here is the code for this example's change listener:

```
class SliderListener implements ChangeListener {
    public void stateChanged(ChangeEvent e) {
        JSlider source = (JSlider)e.getSource();
        if (!source.getValueIsAdjusting()) {
            int fps = (int)((JSlider)e.getSource()).getValue();
            if (fps == 0) {
                if (!frozen) stopAnimation();
            } else {
                delay = 1000 / fps;
                timer.setDelay(delay);
                timer.setInitialDelay(delay * 10);
                if (frozen) startAnimation();
            }
        }
    }
}
```

Note that our `stateChanged` method changes the animation speed only if `getValueIsAd-justing` returns `false`. Many change events are fired as the user moves the slider knob. This program is interested only in the final result of the user's action.

Customizing Labels on a Slider

Here is a modified version of the previous program that uses a slider with custom labels.

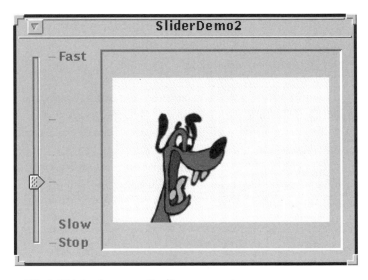

Figure 74   The modified `SliderDemo` application.

You can find the source for this program in `SliderDemo2.java` (page 715). As with the other example, you also need the 14 image files that make up the animation.[1]

The following code creates the slider and customizes its labels:

```
//Create the slider
JSlider framesPerSecond = new JSlider(JSlider.VERTICAL, 0, 30, FPS_INIT);
framesPerSecond.addChangeListener(new SliderListener());
framesPerSecond.setMajorTickSpacing(10);
framesPerSecond.setPaintTicks(true);

//Create the label table
Hashtable labelTable = new Hashtable();
```

---

[1] You can find the images by visiting: http://java.sun.com/docs/books/tutorial/uiswing/components/ example-swing/index.html

```
labelTable.put( new Integer( 0 ), new JLabel("Stop") );
labelTable.put( new Integer( 3 ), new JLabel("Slow") );
labelTable.put( new Integer( 30 ), new JLabel("Fast") );
framesPerSecond.setLabelTable( labelTable );
framesPerSecond.setPaintLabels(true);
framesPerSecond.setBorder(BorderFactory.createEmptyBorder(0,0,0,10));
```

Each key-value pair in a `Hashtable` specifies the position and the value of one label. The hashtable key must be an `Integer` and is a value within the slider's range at which to place the label. The hashtable value must be a `Component`. This program uses `JLabel` instances with text only. An interesting variation would be to use `JLabel` instances with icons, or perhaps buttons that move the knob to the label's position.

If you want a set of numeric labels positioned at a specific interval, you can use `JSlider`'s `createStandardLabels` method to create the `Hashtable` for you. You can also modify the table returned by `createStandardLabels` to then customize it.

The Slider API

The following tables list the commonly used `JSlider` constructors and methods. See <u>The JComponent Class</u> (page 67) for tables of commonly used inherited methods.

Table 108   Creating the Slider

Constructor	Purpose
`JSlider()`	Create a horizontal slider with the range 0 to 100 and an initial value of 50.
`JSlider(int min, int max)` `JSlider(int min, int max, int value)`	Create a horizontal slider with the specified minimum and maximum values. The third `int` argument, when present, specifies the slider's initial value.

`JSlider(int orientation)`
`JSlider(int orientation, int min,`
`       int max, int value)`
	Create a slider with the specified orientation, which must be either `JSlider.HORIZONTAL` or `JSlider.VERTICAL`. The last three `int` arguments, when present, specify the slider's minimum, maximum, and initial values, respectively.

`JSlider(BoundedRangeModel)`	Create a horizontal slider with the specified model, which manages the slider's minimum, maximum, and current values and their relationship.

Table 109   Fine Tuning the Slider's Appearance

Method	Purpose
`void setValue(int)` `int getValue()`	Set or get the slider's current value. This method also positions the slider's knob.
`void setOrientation(int)` `int getOrientation()`	Set or get the orientation of the slider. Possible values are `JSlider.HORIZONTAL` or `JSlider.VERTICAL`.
`void setInverted(boolean)` `boolean getInverted()`	Set or get whether the maximum is shown at the left of a horizontal slider or at the bottom of a vertical one, thereby inverting the slider's range.

`void setMinimum(int)`
`int getMinimum()`
`void setMaximum(int)`
`int getMaximum()`
	Set or get the minimum or maximum values of the slider. Together these methods set or get the slider's range.

`void setMajorTickSpacing(int)`
`int getMajorTickSpacing()`
`void setMinorTickSpacing(int)`
`int getMinorTickSpacing()`
	Set or get the range between major and minor ticks. You must call `setPaintTicks(true)` for the tick marks to appear.

`void setPaintTicks(boolean)` `boolean getPaintTicks()`	Set or get whether tick marks are painted on the slider.
`void setPaintLabels(boolean)` `boolean getPaintLabels()`	Set or get whether labels are painted on the slider. You can provide custom labels with `setLabelTable` or get automatic labels by setting the major tick spacing to a nonzero value.
`void setLabelTable(Dictionary)` `Dictionary getLabelTable()`	Set or get the labels for the slider. You must call `setPaintLabels(true)` for the labels to appear. A convenience method for creating a standard set of labels is `createStandardLabels`.
`Hashtable createStandardLabels(int)` `Hashtable createStandardLabels(int, int)`	Create a standard set of numeric labels. The first `int` argument specifies the increment; the second `int` argument specifies the starting point. When left unspecified, the slider's minimum is used as the starting point.

Table 110   Watching the Slider Operate

Method	Purpose
`void addChangeListener(ChangeListener)`	Register a change listener with the slider.
`boolean getValueIsAdjusting()`	Determine whether the user gesture to move the slider's knob is complete.

Examples that Use Sliders

The following table shows the examples that use JSlider and where those examples are described.

Table 111   Examples that Use Sliders

Example	Where Described	Notes
SliderDemo.java	This section	Shows a slider with labels at major tick marks.
SliderDemo2.java	This section	Shows a vertical slider with custom labels.
Converter.java	The Anatomy of a Swing-Based Program (page 51)	Features two sliders that share data and have a custom BoundedRangeModel.

How to Use Tables

You can use the `JTable`[1] class to display tables of data, optionally allowing the user to edit the data. `JTable` doesn't contain or cache data; it's simply a view of your data. Here's a picture of a typical table displayed within a scroll pane.

TableDemo				
First Name	Last Name	Sport	# of Years	Vegetarian
Mary	Campione	Snowboarding	5	☐
Alison	Huml	Rowing	3	☑
Kathy	Walrath	Chasing toddl...	2	☐
Mark	Andrews	Speed reading	20	☑

Figure 75   The `TableDemo` displays a table within a scroll pane.

The rest of this section tells you how to accomplish some common table-related tasks.

Creating a Simple Table

Here is a snapshot of an application with a simple table. Although similar to the preceding table, this table has some differences, as we'll explain shortly.

SimpleTableDemo				
First Name	Last Name	Sport	# of Years	Vegetarian
Mary	Campione	Snowboarding	5	false
Alison	Huml	Rowing	3	true
Kathy	Walrath	Chasing toddl...	2	false
Mark	Andrews	Speed reading	20	true

Figure 76   The `SimpleTableDemo` application.

---

[1]   http://java.sun.com/products/jdk/1.2/docs/api/javax/swing/JTable.html

Try this:

1. Compile and run `SimpleTableDemo`. The source file is `SimpleTableDemo.java` (page 709).[1]

2. Click the cell "Snowboarding." Doing so selects the entire first row; you have selected Mary Campione's data. A special highlight indicates that the "Snowboarding" cell is editable. Generally you begin editing a text cell by double-clicking it.

3. Position the cursor over "First Name." Now press the mouse button and drag to the right. As you can see, users can rearrange columns in tables.

4. Position the cursor just to the right of a column header. Now press the mouse button and drag to the right or left. The column changes size, and the other columns adjust to fill the remaining space.

5. Resize the window containing the table so that it's bigger than necessary to display the whole table. All of the table cells become larger, expanding to fill the extra space.

Here is the code that implements the table in `SimpleTableDemo`:

```
Object[][] data = {
    {"Mary", "Campione",
     "Snowboarding", new Integer(5), new Boolean(false)},
    {"Alison", "Huml",
     "Rowing", new Integer(3), new Boolean(true)},
    {"Kathy", "Walrath",
     "Chasing toddlers", new Integer(2), new Boolean(false)},
    {"Mark", "Andrews",
     "Speed reading", new Integer(20), new Boolean(true)},
    {"Angela", "Lih",
     "Teaching high school", new Integer(4), new Boolean(false)}
};

String[] columnNames = {"First Name",
                        "Last Name",
                        "Sport",
                        "# of Years",
                        "Vegetarian"};
final JTable table = new JTable(data, columnNames);
```

The `SimpleTableDemo` example uses one of two `JTable` constructors that directly accept data:

- `JTable(Object[][] rowData, Object[] columnNames)`
- `JTable(Vector rowData, Vector columnNames)`

---

[1] See the chapter Getting Started with Swing (page 3) if you need help compiling or running this application.

The advantage of these constructors is that they're easy to use. However, they also have disadvantages.

- They automatically make every cell editable.
- They treat all data types the same. For example, if a table column has `Boolean` data, the table can display the data in a check box. However, if you use one of the two `JTable` constructors listed previously, your `Boolean` data will be displayed as a string. You can see this difference in the last columns of Figure 75 and Figure 76.
- They require that you put all of the table's data in an array or a vector, which isn't appropriate for some data. For example, if you're instantiating a set of objects from a database, you might want to query the objects directly for their values, rather than copying all of their values into an array or a vector.

If you want to get around these restrictions, you need to implement your own table model, as described in Creating a Table Model (page 259).

Adding a Table to a Container

It's easy to put a table in a scroll pane. You need just one or two lines of code:

```
JScrollPane scrollPane = new JScrollPane(table);
table.setPreferredScrollableViewportSize(new Dimension(500, 70));
```

The scroll pane automatically gets the table's header, which displays the column names, and puts it on top of the table. Even when the user scrolls down, the column names remain visible at the top of the viewing area. The scroll table also tries to make its viewing area the same as the table's preferred viewing size. The previous code snippet sets the table's preferred viewing size with the `setPreferredScrollableViewportSize` method.

Note: If you're using a table without a scroll pane, you must get the table header component and place it yourself. For example:

```
container.setLayout(new BorderLayout());
container.add(table.getTableHeader(), BorderLayout.NORTH);
container.add(table, BorderLayout.CENTER);
```

Setting and Changing Column Widths

All columns in a table start out with equal width by default and the columns automatically fill the entire width of the table. When the table becomes wider or narrower, which might happen when the user resizes the window containing the table, all of the column widths change appropriately.

When the user resizes a column by dragging its right border, either other columns must change size or the table's size must change. The table's size remains the same by default, and all columns to the right of the drag point resize to accommodate space added or removed from the column to the left of the drag point.

The following figures illustrate the default resizing behavior. Initially, the columns have equal width as shown in this figure.

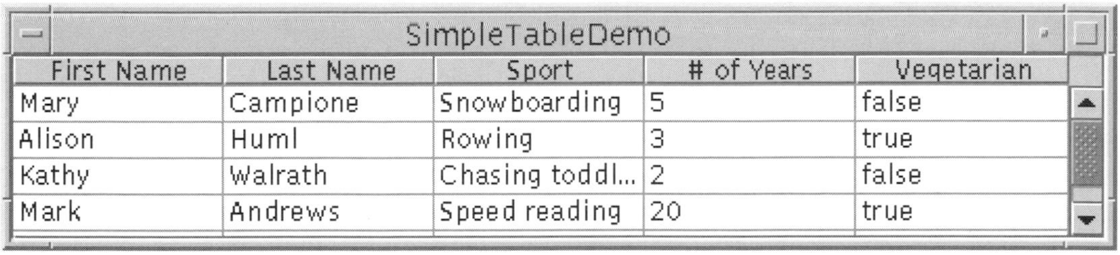

Figure 77 By default, the columns in SimpleTableDemo have the same width.

When the user resizes a column, some of the other columns must adjust size for the table to stay the same size.

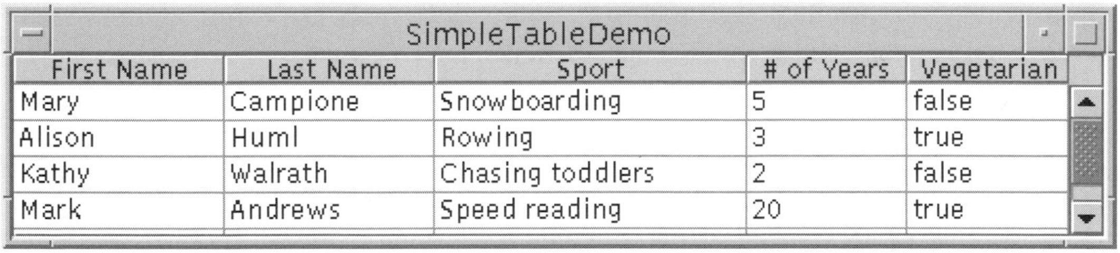

Figure 78 In this screenshot, the width of the "Sport" column is increased while the widths of the last two columns decreases.

When the entire table is resized, all of the columns are resized, as follows.

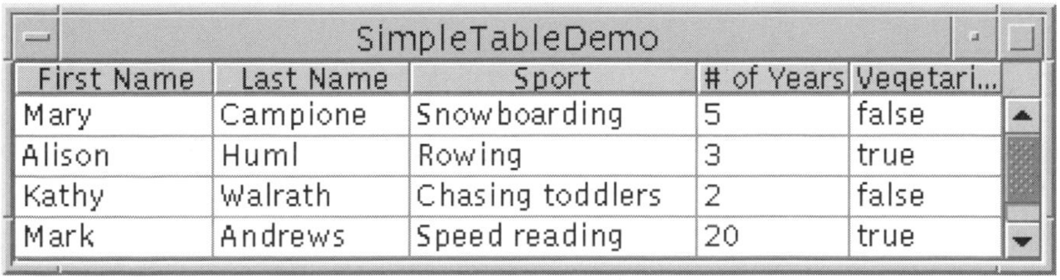

Figure 79 In this screenshot, the width of the entire table is decreased, and the widths of all the columns is decreased proportionally.

To customize initial column widths, you can invoke `setPreferredWidth` on each of your table's columns. This sets both the preferred widths of the columns and their approximate relative widths. For example, adding the following code to `SimpleTableDemo.java` makes the third column bigger than the other columns:

```
TableColumn column = null;
for (int i = 0; i < 5; i++) {
    column = table.getColumnModel().getColumn(i);
    if (i == 2) {
        column.setPreferredWidth(100); //sport column is bigger
    } else {
        column.setPreferredWidth(50);
    }
}
```

As the preceding code shows, each column in a table is represented by a <u>TableColumn</u>[1] object. Besides `setPreferredWidth`, `TableColumn` also supplies methods for getting and setting the minimum, current, and maximum width of a column. For an example of setting cell widths based on the actual amount of space needed to draw the cells' contents, see the `initColumnSizes` method in <u>TableRenderDemo.java</u> (page 733), which is discussed in <u>Further Customizing Table Display and Event Handling</u> (page 267).

When the user explicitly resizes columns, the new sizes become not only the columns' new *current* widths but also their new *preferred* widths. However, when columns are resized as the result of changing the table width, the columns' preferred widths do not change.

You can change a table's resize behavior by invoking the `setAutoResizeMode` method. The method's argument should have one of these values (defined as constants in `JTable`).

AUTO_RESIZE_SUBSEQUENT_COLUMNS
> The default. In addition to resizing the column to the left of the drag point, this argument adjusts the sizes of all columns to the right of the drag point.

AUTO_RESIZE_NEXT_COLUMN
> Adjusts only the columns immediately to the left and right of the drag point.

AUTO_RESIZE_OFF
> Adjust the table size instead.

Note: Another resize mode exists: `AUTO_RESIZE_ALL_COLUMNS`. However, this mode isn't intuitive, so we don't recommend its use.

---

[1] API documentation for this class is available on this book's CD-ROM and online at http://java.sun.com/products/jdk/1.2/docs/api/javax/swing/table/TableColumn.html

Detecting User Selections

The following code snippet shows how to detect when the user selects a table row. By default a table allows the user to select multiple rows—not columns or individual cells—and the selected rows need not be adjacent. The following code uses the setSelectionMode method to specify that only one row at a time can be selected. You can find the entire program in SimpleTableSelectionDemo.java (page 711).

```
table.setSelectionMode(ListSelectionModel.SINGLE_SELECTION);
...
ListSelectionModel rowSM = table.getSelectionModel();
rowSM.addListSelectionListener(new ListSelectionListener() {
    public void valueChanged(ListSelectionEvent e) {
        ListSelectionModel lsm = (ListSelectionModel)e.getSource();
        if (lsm.isSelectionEmpty()) {
            ...//no rows are selected
        } else {
            int selectedRow = lsm.getMinSelectionIndex();
            ...//selectedRow is selected
        }
    }
});
```

SimpleTableSelectionDemo.java also has code (not included in the preceding snippet) that changes the table's selection orientation. By changing a couple of boolean values, you can make the table allow either column selections or individual cell selections, instead of row selections.

For more information and examples of implementing selection, see How to Write a List Selection Listener (page 494).

Creating a Table Model

As the following figure shows, every table gets its data from an object that implements the TableModel[1] interface.

Figure 80 Every table gets its data from TableModel.

---

[1] API documentation for TableModel is available on this book's CD-ROM and online at
http://java.sun.com/products/jdk/1.2/docs/api/javax/swing/table/TableModel.html

The `JTable` constructor used by `SimpleTableDemo` creates its table model with code like this:

```
new AbstractTableModel() {
    public String getColumnName(int col) {
        return columnNames[col].toString();
    }
    public int getRowCount() { return rowData.length; }
    public int getColumnCount() { return columnNames.length; }
    public Object getValueAt(int row, int col) {
        return rowData[row][col];
    }
    public boolean isCellEditable(int row, int col) { return true; }
    public void setValueAt(Object value, int row, int col) {
        rowData[row][col] = value;
        fireTableCellUpdated(row, col);
    }
}
```

As the preceding code shows, implementing a table model can be simple. Generally you implement your table model in a subclass of the <u>AbstractTableModel</u>[1] class.

Your model might hold its data in an array, a vector, or a hashtable, or it might get the data from an outside source, such as a database. The model might even generate the data at execution time. For examples of getting data from a database, see the `examples/Table` or `examples/TableExamples` directory in the JFC 1.1 release or the Java 2 SDK.

Here again is a picture of a table implemented by `TableDemo`, which has a custom table model.

TableDemo				
First Name	Last Name	Sport	# of Years	Vegetarian
Mary	Campione	Snowboarding	5	☐
Alison	Huml	Rowing	3	☑
Kathy	Walrath	Chasing toddl...	2	☐
Mark	Andrews	Speed reading	20	☑

Figure 81   The table implemented by `TableDemo`.

---

[1]   API documentation for `AbstractTableModel` is available on this book's CD-ROM and online at http://java.sun.com/products/jdk/1.2/docs/api/javax/swing/table/AbstractTableModel.html

This table is different from the `SimpleTableDemo` table in the following ways:

- `SimpleTableDemo`'s table model, having been created automatically by `JTable`, isn't smart enough to know that the # of Years column contains numbers (which should generally be right aligned). It also doesn't know that the Vegetarian column contains boolean values, which can be represented by check boxes. `TableDemo`'s custom table model, even though it's simple, can easily determine the data's type, helping the `JTable` display the data in the best format.

- All cells in `SimpleTableDemo` are editable. In `TableDemo` we implemented the custom table model so that it doesn't let you edit the name columns; it does, however, let you edit the other columns.

The following code from `TableDemo.java` (page 723) is different from the code in `SimpleTableDemo.java` (page 709). Code in boldface type makes this table's model different from that defined automatically for `SimpleTableDemo`:

```
public TableDemo() {
    ...
    MyTableModel myModel = new MyTableModel();
    JTable table = new JTable(myModel);
    table.setPreferredScrollableViewportSize(new Dimension(500, 70));
    //Create the scroll pane and add the table to it.
    JScrollPane scrollPane = new JScrollPane(table);
    //Add the scroll pane to this window.
    getContentPane().add(scrollPane,BorderLayout.CENTER);
    ...
}

class MyTableModel extends AbstractTableModel {
    final String[] columnNames = ...//same as before...
    final Object[][] data = ...//same as before...
    public int getColumnCount() {
        return columnNames.length;
    }

        public int getRowCount() {
        return data.length;
    }

    public String getColumnName(int col) {
        return columnNames[col];
    }

    public Object getValueAt(int row, int col) {
        return data[row][col];
    }
```

```
public Class getColumnClass(int c) {
    return getValueAt(0, c).getClass();
}

/*
 * Don't need to implement this method unless your table's
 * editable.
 */
public boolean isCellEditable(int row, int col) {
    //Note that the data/cell address is constant,
    //no matter where the cell appears onscreen.
    if (col  < 2) {
        return false;
    } else {
        return true;
    }
}

/*
 * Don't need to implement this method unless your table's
 * data can change.
 */
public void setValueAt(Object value, int row, int col) {
    ...//debugging code not shown...
    ...//ugly class cast code for Integers not shown...
    data[row][col] = value;
    ...//debugging code not shown...
}
...
```

Detecting Data Changes

A table and its model automatically detect whenever the user edits the table's data. However, if the data changes for another reason, you must take special steps to notify the table and its model of the data change. Also, if you don't implement a table model, as in SimpleTable-Demo, you must take special steps to find out when the user edits the table's data.

An example of updating a table's data without directly editing it is in the BINGO application. The BINGO application, presented in "Putting It All Together,"[1] has a table that displays some information about each user who is signed up to play the game. When a new user signs up to play, the table needs to add a new row for that user. More precisely, the table model needs to get the data for the new user, and then the table model needs to tell the table to display the new data.

---

[1] The BINGO! game is featured in the trail, *Putting It All Together*, available in HTML on the CD-ROM and online here: http://java.sun.com/docs/books/tutorial/together/index.html

To notify the table model about a new user, the BINGO application invokes the table model's updatePlayer method. You can see the code for that method in PlayerInfoModel.java,[1] which contains the implementation of the table model. The updatePlayer method records the new user's data and fires a table-model event. Because every table listens for table-model events from its model, the user-information table automatically detects the change and displays the new data.

To fire the table-model event, the model invokes the fireTableRowsInserted method, which is defined by the AbstractTableModel class. Other fireXxxx methods that AbstractTableModel defines to help you fire table-model events are fireTableCellUpdated, fireTableChanged, fireTableDataChanged, fireTableRowsDeleted, fireTableRowsInserted, fireTableRowsUpdated, and fireTableStructureChanged.

If you have a class, such as SimpleTableDemo, that isn't a table or a table model but that needs to react to changes in a table model, you need to do something special to find out when the user edits the table's data. Specifically you need to register a table-model listener on the table model. The boldface code in the following snippet would make SimpleTableDemo react to table data changes:

```
public class SimpleTableDemo ... implements TableModelListener {
    ...
    public SimpleTableDemo() {
        ...
        model = table.getModel();
        model.addTableModelListener(this);
        ...
    }

    public void tableChanged(TableModelEvent e) {
        ...
        int row = e.getFirstRow();
        int column = e.getColumn();
        String columnName = model.getColumnName(column);
        Object data = model.getValueAt(row, column);

        ... // Do something with the data...
    }
    ...
}
```

---

[1] You can download all the code needed to play Bingo! from: http://java.sun.com/docs/books/tutorial/together/bingo/letsplay.html#download

Concepts: Cell Editors and Renderers

Before going on to the next few tasks, you need to understand how tables draw their cells. You might expect each cell in a table to be a component. For performance reasons, however, Swing tables aren't implemented that way.

Instead a single *cell renderer* is used to draw all of the cells in a column. Often this cell renderer is shared among all columns that contain the same type of data. You can think of the renderer as a configurable ink stamp that the table uses to stamp appropriately formatted data onto each cell. When the user starts to edit a cell's data, a *cell editor* takes over the cell, controlling the cell's editing behavior.

For example, each cell in the # of Years column in `TableDemo` contains `Number` data—specifically an `Integer` object. By default the cell renderer for a `Number`-containing column uses a single `JLabel` instance to draw the appropriate numbers, right-aligned, on the column's cells. If the user begins editing one of the cells, the default cell editor uses a right-aligned `JTextField` to control the cell editing.

To choose the renderer that displays the cells in a column, a table first determines whether you specified a renderer for that particular column. (We'll tell you how to specify renderers a bit later.) If you didn't, the table invokes the table model's `getColumnClass` method, which gets the data type of the column's cells. Next, the table compares the column's data type with a list of data types for which cell renderers are registered. This list is initialized by the table, but you can add to it or change it. Currently tables put the following types of data in the list:

- `Boolean`—rendered with a check box
- `Number`—rendered by a right-aligned label
- `ImageIcon`—rendered by a centered label
- `Object`—rendered by a label that displays the object's string value

The table uses a similar algorithm to choose cell editors.

Note: Swing 1.1.1 Beta 1 and compatible releases allow you to specify HTML tags in the table cell data since these releases support HTML labels. See <u>Using HTML on a Label</u> (page 213) for details.

Remember that if you let a table create its own model, it uses `Object` as the type of every column. <u>TableDemo.java</u> (page 723) shows how to specify more precise column types.

The next few sections tell you how to customize cell display and editing by specifying cell renderers and editors either by column or by data type.

Validating User-Entered Text

In the table examples you've seen so far, the user can enter any text into the # of Years column. SimpleTableDemo doesn't check the data's value, at all. The TableDemo example is slightly improved in that when the user is done editing, the code checks whether the entry can be parsed as an integer. However, TableDemo must use a bit of ugly code to convert the string returned by the default cell editor into an Integer. If it didn't do the conversion, the type of the data would change from Integer to String.

What we'd really like to do is to check the user's input *while* the user is typing and to have the cell editor return an Integer instead of a string. You can accomplish one or both of these tasks by using a custom text field to control the cell editing.

A custom text field can check the user's input either while the user is typing or after the user has indicated the end of typing, such as by pressing Return. We call these two types of checking *change* validation and *action* validation, respectively.

The following code, taken from TableEditDemo.java (page 730), sets up a change-validated text field. The boldface line of code makes the text field the editor for all columns that contain data of type Integer.

```
final WholeNumberField integerField = new WholeNumberField(0, 5);
integerField.setHorizontalAlignment(WholeNumberField.RIGHT);
DefaultCellEditor integerEditor = new DefaultCellEditor(integerField) {

        //Override DefaultCellEditor's getCellEditorValue method
        //to return an Integer, not a String:
        public Object getCellEditorValue() {
            return new Integer(integerField.getValue());
        }
    };
table.setDefaultEditor(Integer.class, integerEditor);
```

The WholeNumberField class, defined in WholeNumberField.java (page 777), is a custom JTextField subclass that allows the user to enter only digits. Its getValue method returns the int value of the WholeNumberField's contents. See How to Use Text Fields (page 298) for more information about WholeNumberField. That section also provides a more general-purpose validating text field, called DecimalField, that you can customize to validate any number format that you specify.

Using a Combo Box as an Editor

The following example sets up a combo box editor. The boldface line of code sets up the combo box as the editor for a column rather than for a specific data type.

```
        setupSportColumn(table.getColumnModel().getColumn(2));
        ...
        public void setupSportColumn(TableColumnModel sportColumn) {
            JComboBox comboBox = new JComboBox();
            comboBox.addItem("Snowboarding");
            comboBox.addItem("Rowing");
            comboBox.addItem("Chasing toddlers");
            comboBox.addItem("Speed reading");
            comboBox.addItem("Teaching high school");
            comboBox.addItem("None");
            sportColumn.setCellEditor(new DefaultCellEditor(comboBox));
        }
```

Figure 82 shows the combo box editor in use.

Figure 82   The `TableRenderDemo` application.

The combo box editor is implemented in `TableRenderDemo.java` (page 733), which is discussed some more in <u>Further Customizing Table Display and Event Handling</u> (page 267).

Specifying Other Editors

As the previous sections showed, you can set the editor for an entire column by using the `TableColumn setCellEditor` method, or for a specific type of data by using the `JTable setDefaultEditor` method. For both methods you must specify an argument that implements the <u>TableCellEditor</u>[1] interface. Fortunately the <u>DefaultCellEditor</u>[2] class implements this interface and provides constructors to let you specify an editing component that's a `JTextField`, a `JCheckBox`, or a `JComboBox`. You usually don't have to explicitly specify a check box as an editor, since columns with boolean data automatically use a check box renderer and editor.

---

[1] API documentation for `TableCellEditor` is available on this book's CD-ROM and online at
    http://java.sun.com/products/jdk/1.2/docs/api/javax/swing/table/TableCellEditor.html
[2] http://java.sun.com/products/jdk/1.2/docs/api/javax/swing/DefaultCellEditor.html

What if you want to specify an editor that isn't a text field, a check box, or a combo box? Well, because `DefaultCellEditor` doesn't support other types of components, you must do a little more work. You need to create a subclass of the desired editor component, and the subclass must implement the `TableCellEditor` interface. Then you set up the component as an editor for a data type or a column, using the `setDefaultEditor` or the `setCellEditor` method, respectively.

Following is a picture of a table with a dialog that serves, indirectly, as a cell editor. When the user begins editing a cell in the Favorite Color column, a button (the true cell editor) appears and brings up the dialog with which the user can choose a different color.

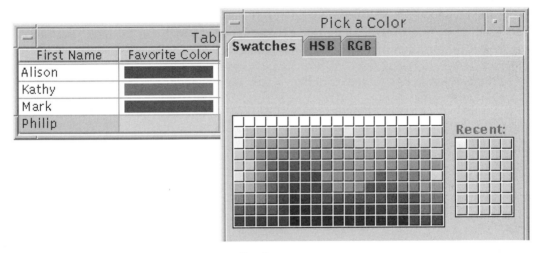

Figure 83 The `TableDialogEditDemo` application.

You can find the code in <u>TableDialogEditDemo.java</u> (page 725). The example also requires <u>WholeNumberField.java</u> (page 777).

Further Customizing Table Display and Event Handling

You've already seen how to specify cell *editors*. You can also specify *renderers* for cells and for column headers. Customizing renderers lets you display data in custom ways and specify tool tip text for the table to display.

Although renderers determine how each cell or column header looks, they don't handle events. To pick up the events that take place inside a table, you should choose the appropriate technique for the sort of event you're interested in. For a cell that's being edited, the editor should process events. To detect row/column/cell selections and deselections, use a selection listener, as described in <u>Detecting User Selections</u> (page 259). To detect mouse clicks on a column header, you can register a mouse listener on the table header; see `TableSorter.java` (page 737) for an example. To detect other events, you can register the appropriate listener on the JTable object.

Creating a custom renderer can be as easy as creating a subclass of an existing component and then implementing the single method in the <u>TableCellRenderer</u>[1] interface. In the preceding figure the color renderer used for Favorite Color cells is a subclass of JLabel. You can find the code for the renderer in the ColorRenderer inner class in <u>TableDialogEdit-Demo.java</u> (page 725). Here is the code that registers a ColorRenderer instance as the default renderer for all Color data:

```
table.setDefaultRenderer(Color.class, new ColorRenderer(true));
```

You can even specify a cell-specific renderer, if you like. To do this, you need to define a JTable subclass that overrides the getCellRenderer method. For example, the following code makes the first cell in the first column of the table use a custom renderer:

```
TableCellRenderer weirdRenderer = new WeirdRenderer();
table = new JTable(...) {
    public TableCellRenderer getCellRenderer(int row, int column) {
        if ((row == 0) && (column == 0)) {
            return weirdRenderer;
        }
        // else... {
        return super.getCellRenderer(row, column);
        }
    }
};
```

To add tool tips to cells or column headers, you need to get or create the cell or header renderer and then use the setToolTipText method of the renderer's component. <u>TableRender-Demo.java</u> (page 733) adds tool tips to both the cells and header for the Sport column with the following code:

```
//Set up tool tips for the sport cells.
DefaultTableCellRenderer renderer = new DefaultTableCellRenderer();
renderer.setToolTipText("Click for combo box");
sportColumn.setCellRenderer(renderer);

//Set up tool tip for the sport column header.
TableCellRenderer headerRenderer = sportColumn.getHeaderRenderer();
if (headerRenderer instanceof DefaultTableCellRenderer) {
    ((DefaultTableCellRenderer)headerRenderer).setToolTipText(
            "Click the sport to see a list of choices");
}
```

---

[1]   API documentation for TableCellRenderer is available on this book's CD-ROM and online at
http://java.sun.com/products/jdk/1.2/docs/api/javax/swing/table/TableCellRenderer.html

An interesting feature of TableRenderDemo is how it determines the sizes of its columns. For each column, TableRenderDemo gets the components used to render that column's header and cells. It then asks the components how much space they need. Finally it uses the space information to set the column's width.

```
TableColumn column = null;
Component comp = null;
int headerWidth = 0;
int cellWidth = 0;
Object[] longValues = model.longValues;

for (int i = 0; i < 5; i++) {
    column = table.getColumnModel().getColumn(i);

    comp = column.getHeaderRenderer().getTableCellRendererComponent(
                                null, column.getHeaderValue(),
                                false, false, 0, 0);
    headerWidth = comp.getPreferredSize().width;

    comp = table.getDefaultRenderer(model.getColumnClass(i)).
                getTableCellRendererComponent(table, longValues[i],
                                        false, false, 0, i);
    cellWidth = comp.getPreferredSize().width;
    ...//debugging code not shown...
    column.setPreferredWidth(Math.max(headerWidth, cellWidth));
}

...//In the model:
public final Object[] longValues = {"Angela", "Andrews",
                                "Teaching high school",
                                new Integer(20), Boolean.TRUE};
```

Sorting and Otherwise Manipulating Data

One way to perform data manipulation, such as sorting, is to use one or more specialized table models (*data manipulators*) in addition to the table model that provides the data (the data model). The data manipulators should sit between the table and the data model, as the following picture shows.

Figure 84 Data manipulators sit between the table and the data model.

You can use the `TableMap` and the `TableSorter` classes when implementing your data manipulator. `TableMap.java` (page 732) implements `TableModel` and serves as a superclass for data manipulators. `TableSorter.java` (page 737) is a `TableMap` subclass that sorts the data provided by another table model. You can either change these classes, using them as a basis for writing your own data manipulator, or use the classes as-is to provide sorting functionality.

To use `TableSort`, you need just three lines of code. The following code shows the differences between `TableDemo` and its sorting cousin, TableSorterDemo.java (page 742).

```
TableSorter sorter = new TableSorter(myModel); //ADDED THIS
//JTable table = new JTable(myModel);          //OLD
JTable table = new JTable(sorter);             //NEW
sorter.addMouseListenerToHeaderInTable(table); //ADDED THIS
```

The `addMouseListenerToHeaderInTable` method adds a mouse listener that detects clicks over the column headers. When the listener detects a click, it sorts the rows, based on the clicked column. As the following snapshot shows, when you click the Last Name column, the rows are reordered so that the row with "Andrews" becomes the first row. When you press Shift and click a column header, the rows are sorted in reverse order.

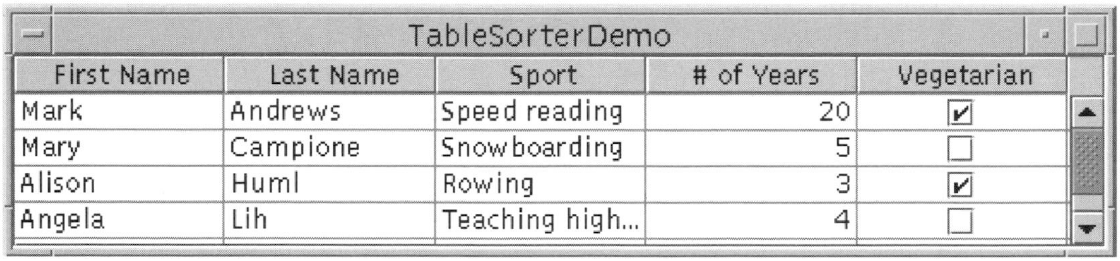

First Name	Last Name	Sport	# of Years	Vegetarian
Mark	Andrews	Speed reading	20	✔
Mary	Campione	Snowboarding	5	☐
Alison	Huml	Rowing	3	✔
Angela	Lih	Teaching high...	4	☐

Figure 85   The `TableSorterDemo` application.

The Table API

The tables in this section cover just part of the table API. For more information about the table API, see the API documentation for `JTable`[1] and for the various classes and interfaces in the table package. Also see The JComponent Class (page 67), which describes the API that `JTable` inherits from `JComponent`.

---

[1] API documentation for `JTable` is available on this book's CD-ROM and online at http://java.sun.com/products/jdk/1.2/docs/api/javax/swing/JTable.html

Table 112   Table-Related Classes and Interfaces

Class/Interface	Purpose
`JTable`	The component that presents the table to the user.
`JTableHeader`[a]	The component that presents the column names to the user. By default the table generates this component automatically.
`TableModel`, `AbstractTableModel`	Respectively, the interface that a table model must implement and the usual superclass for table model implementations.
`TableCellRenderer`, `DefaultTableCellRenderer`[b]	Respectively, the interface that a table cell renderer must implement and the usual implementation used.
`TableCellEditor`, `DefaultCellEditor`	Respectively, the interface that a table cell editor must implement and the usual implementation used.
`TableColumnModel`,[c] `DefaultTableColumnModel`[d]	Respectively, the interface that a table column model must implement and the usual implementation used. You don't usually need to deal with the table column model directly unless you need to get the column selection model or get a column index or an object.
`TableColumn`	Controls all of the attributes of a table column, including resizability; minimum, preferred, current, and maximum widths; and an optional column-specific renderer/editor.
`DefaultTableModel`[e]	A `Vector`-based table model used by `JTable` when you construct a table specifying no data model and no data.

a. API documentation for `JTableHeader` can be found at http://java.sun.com/products/jdk/1.2/docs/api/javax/ swing/table/JTableHeader.html

b. http://java.sun.com/products/jdk/1.2/docs/api/javax/swing/table/DefaultTableCellRenderer.html

c. http://java.sun.com/products/jdk/1.2/docs/api/javax/swing/table/TableColumnModel.html

d. http://java.sun.com/products/jdk/1.2/docs/api/javax/swing/table/DefaultTableColumnModel.html

e. http://java.sun.com/products/jdk/1.2/docs/api/javax/swing/table/DefaultTableModel.html

Table 113   Creating and Setting Up a Table

JTable Constructor/Method	Purpose
`JTable(TableModel)` `JTable(TableModel, TableColumnModel)` `JTable(TableModel, TableColumnModel,` `ListSelectionModel)` `JTable()` `JTable(int, int)` `JTable(Object[][], Object[])` `JTable(Vector, Vector)`	Create a table. The optional `TableModel` argument specifies the model that provides the data to the table. The optional `TableColumnModel` and `ListSelectionModel` arguments let you specify the table column model and the row selection model. As an alternative to specifying a table model, you can supply data and column names, using arrays or vectors. Another option is to specify no data, optionally specifying the number of rows and columns (both integers) to be in the table.

Table 113　Creating and Setting Up a Table

JTable Constructor/Method	Purpose
`void setPreferredScrollableViewportSize(` 　　　`Dimension)`	Set the size of the visible part of the table when it's viewed within a scroll pane.
`JTableHeader getTableHeader(Dimension)`	Get the component that displays the column names.

Table 114　Manipulating Columns

Constructor/Method	Purpose
`TableColumnModel getColumnModel()` (in `JTable`)	Get the table's column model.

`TableColumn getColumn(int)`
`Enumeration getColumns()`
(in `TableColumnModel`)
	Get one or all of the `TableColumn` objects for the table.

`void setMinWidth(int)`
`void setPreferredWidth(int)`
`void setMaxWidth(int)`
(in `TableColumn`)
	Set the minimum, preferred, or maximum width of the column.

`int getMinWidth(int)`
`int getPreferredWidth()`
`int getMaxWidth()`
`int getWidth()`
(in `TableColumn`)
	Get the minimum, preferred, maximum, or current width of the column.

Table 115　Using Editors and Renderers

Method	Purpose

`void setDefaultRenderer(Class,`
　　　　　　`TableCellRenderer)`
`void setDefaultEditor(Class, TableCellEditor)`
(in `JTable`)
	Set the renderer or editor used by default for all cells in all columns that return objects of the specified type.

`void setCellRenderer(TableCellRenderer)`
`void setCellEditor(TableCellEditor)`
(in `TableColumn`)
	Set the renderer or editor used for all cells in this column.

`TableCellRenderer getHeaderRenderer()` (in `TableColumn`)	Get the header renderer for this column, which you can then customize.

Table 116 Implementing Selection

JTable Method	Purpose
`void setSelectionMode(int)`	Set the selection intervals allowed in the table. Valid values are defined in `ListSelectionModel` as `SINGLE_SELECTION`, `SINGLE_INTERVAL_SELECTION`, and `MULTIPLE_INTERVAL_SELECTION` (the default).
`void setSelectionModel(ListSelectionModel)` `ListSelectionModel getSelectionModel()`	Set or get the model used to control row selections.
`void setRowSelectionAllowed(boolean)` `void setColumnSelectionAllowed(boolean)` `void setCellSelectionEnabled(boolean)`	Set the table's selection orientation. The boolean argument specifies whether that particular type of selection is allowed. By default row selection is allowed, and column and cell selection are not.

Examples that Use Tables

This table lists examples that use `JTable` and where those examples are described.

Table 117 Examples that Use Tables

Example	Where Described	Notes
`SimpleTableDemo.java`	Creating a Simple Table (page 254)	A basic table with *no* custom model. Does not include code to specify column widths or detect user editing.
`SimpleTable-SelectionDemo.java`	Detecting User Selections (page 259)	Adds single selection and selection detection to `SimpleTableDemo`. By modifying the program's `ALLOW_COLUMN_SELECTION` and `ALLOW_ROW_SELECTION` constants, you can experiment with alternatives to the table default of allowing only rows to be selected.
`TableDemo.java`	Creating a Table Model (page 259)	A basic table with a custom model.
`TableEditDemo.java`	Validating User-Entered Text (page 265)	

Table 117   Examples that Use Tables

Example	Where Described	Notes
`TableRenderDemo.java`	Using a Combo Box as an Editor (page 265), Further Customizing Table Display and Event Handling (page 267)	Modifies `TableDemo` to use a custom editor (a combo box) for all data in the Sport column. Also intelligently picks column sizes. Uses renderers to display tool tips for the Sport column (both cells and header).
`TableDialogEditDemo.java`	Specifying Other Editors (page 266), Validating User-Entered Text (page 265)	Modifies `TableEditDemo` to have a cell renderer and an editor that display a color and let you choose a new one, using a color chooser dialog.
`TableSorterDemo.java`	Sorting and Otherwise Manipulating Data (page 269)	Sorts column data by interposing a data-manipulating table model between the data model and the table. Detects user clicks on column headers.
`ListSelectionDemo.java`	How to Write a List Selection Listener (page 494)	Shows how to use all list selection modes, using a list selection listener that's shared between a table and a list.
`SharedModelDemo.java`	–	Builds on `ListSelectionDemo`, making the data model be shared between the table and the list. If you edit an item in the first column of the table, the new value is reflected in the list.
`TreeTable, TreeTable II`	"Creating TreeTables in Swing"[a] and "Creating TreeTables: Part 2"[b]	Examples that combine a tree and table to show detailed information about a hierarchy, such as a file system. The tree is a renderer for the table.

a. This article is available in the online magazine, *The Swing Connection*, available at http://java.sun.com/products/jfc/tsc/tech_topics/tables-trees/tables-trees.html.

b. This article is available in the online magazine, *The Swing Connection*, available at:http://java.sun.com/products/jfc/tsc/tech_topics/tables_trees_2/tables_trees_2.html.

How to Use Text Components

Swing's text components display text and optionally allow the user to edit the text. Programs need text components for tasks ranging from the straightforward (enter a word and press Return) to the complex (display and edit styled text with embedded images in an Asian language).

Swing text components can be divided into three groups, as shown in the following table.

Table 118   The Three Groups of Text Components

Group	Description	Swing Classes
Text Controls	Also known simply as text fields, text controls can display and edit only one line of text and are action-based, like buttons. Use text controls to get a small amount of textual information from the user and take some action after the text entry is complete.	`JTextField`[a] and its subclass `JPasswordField`[b]
Plain Text Areas	`JTextArea` can display and edit multiple lines of text. Although a text area can display text in any font, all of the text is in the same font. Use a text area to allow the user to enter unformatted text of any length or to display unformatted help information.	`JTextArea`[c]
Styled Text Areas	A styled text component can display and edit text using more than one font. Some styled text components allow embedded images and even embedded components. Styled text components are powerful, multifaceted components suitable for high-end needs and offer more avenues for customization than the other text components. They therefore typically require more up-front programming to set up and use. The one exception is that editor panes can be easily loaded with formatted text from a URL, which makes them useful for displaying uneditable help information.	`JEditorPane`[d] and its subclass `JTextPane`[e]

a. API documentation for `JTextField` can be found at http://java.sun.com/products/jdk/1.2/docs/api/javax/swing/JTextField.html

b. http://java.sun.com/products/jdk/1.2/docs/api/javax/swing/JPasswordField.html

c. http://java.sun.com/products/jdk/1.2/docs/api/javax/swing/JTextArea.html

d. http://java.sun.com/products/jdk/1.2/docs/api/javax/swing/JEditorPane.html

e. http://java.sun.com/products/jdk/1.2/docs/api/javax/swing/JTextPane.html

The five text components, along with supporting classes and interfaces, in these three groups meet even the most complex text requirements. In spite of their various uses and capabilities, all of Swing's text components inherit from the same superclass, `JTextComponent`,[1] which provides a highly configurable and powerful foundation for text manipulation.

The following figure shows the `JTextComponent` hierarchy and places each text component class into one of the three groups.

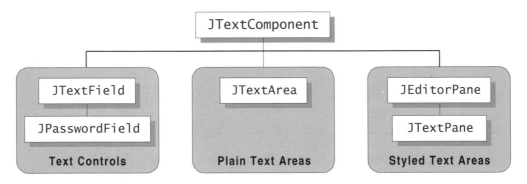

Figure 86   The `JTextComponent` hierarchy.

The next section, An Example that Uses Each Text Component (page 276), shows an application that creates one of each of the Swing text components. By studying this example, you can learn the basics of creating and including each text component in a program, what each component can and cannot do, and how the components differ.

Note: In this tutorial we give you information about the foundation laid by `JTextComponent` and tell you how to accomplish some common text-related tasks. Because `JTextComponent` and its subclasses have too many features to be described completely in this tutorial, please periodically search the online magazine, *The Swing Connection,* for pointers to more information. *The Swing Connection* is available on the CD-ROM that accompanies this book and online at `http://java.sun.com/products/jfc/tsc/index.html`.

An Example that Uses Each Text Component

Here's a picture of an application that shows one of each of Swing's text components.

---

[1]   API documentation for `JTextComponent` is available on this book's CD-ROM and online at
      http://java.sun.com/products/jdk/1.2/docs/api/javax/swing/text/JTextComponent.html

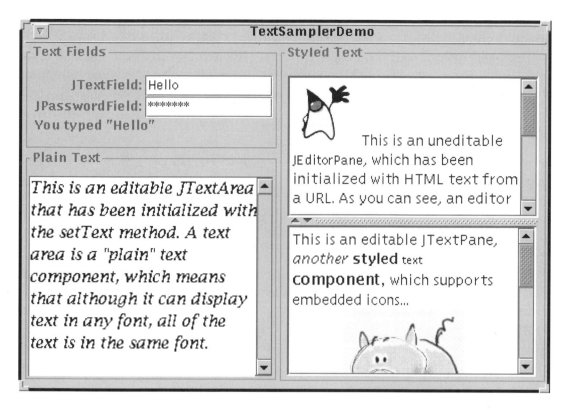

Figure 87   The TextSamplerDemo demonstrates each Swing text component in a single application.

Try this:

1. Compile and run the application.[1] The source code is in TextSamplerDemo.java (page 754). You will also need TextSamplerDemo.html (page 758) and three image files: images/Pig.gif, images/dukeWaveRed.gif, and images/sound.gif.[2]

2. Type some text into the text field and press Return. Do the same with the password field.

3. Select and edit text in the text area and the text pane. Use special keyboard keys to cut, copy, and paste text.

4. Try to edit the text in the editor pane, which has been made uneditable with a call to setEditable.

5. Scroll the text pane to find an example of an embedded component.

---

[1]   See the chapter Getting Started with Swing (page 3) if you need help compiling or running this application.

[2]   You can find the images by visiting http://java.sun.com/docs/books/tutorial/uiswing/components/example-swing/index.html

The `TextSamplerDemo` program is fairly basic in how it uses the text components: It simply creates each one, configures it, and adds it to the frame's content pane. This section looks at the `TextSamplerDemo` code that creates each text component. With the information in this short section alone, you can quickly learn everything necessary to include the various text components in a program and to interact with them on a basic level.

Using a Text Field

`TextSamplerDemo` contains a text field in the upper-left corner of the main frame. Here's the code that creates the text field:

```
JTextField textField = new JTextField(10);
textField.setActionCommand(textFieldString);
textField.addActionListener(this);
```

As with buttons, you can set an action command and register an action listener on a text field. Here's the `actionPerformed` method implemented by the text field's action listener, which is shared with the program's password field. This `actionPerformed` method copies the text field's contents to a label.

```
public void actionPerformed(ActionEvent e) {
    String prefix = "You typed \"";
    if (e.getActionCommand().equals(textFieldString)) {
        JTextField source = (JTextField)e.getSource();
        actionLabel.setText(prefix + source.getText() + "\"");
    } else {
        JPasswordField source = (JPasswordField)e.getSource();
        actionLabel.setText(prefix + new String(source.getPassword())
            + "\"");
    }
}
```

For descriptions of the constructor and the `getText` method used by this program, refer to <u>How to Use Text Fields</u> (page 298). That section also includes information and examples of customized text fields, including how to write a validated field.

Using a Password Field

`JPasswordField` is a subclass of `JTextField` that instead of showing the actual character the user types, shows another character, such as an asterisk (*). This type of field is useful for prompting users to enter passwords when logging in or validating identity. Here's the `Text-SamplerDemo` code that creates the password field and registers an action listener on it:

```
JPasswordField passwordField = new JPasswordField(10);
passwordField.setActionCommand(passwordFieldString);
passwordField.addActionListener(this);
```

This code is similar to that used to create the text field. The password field shares the text field's action listener, which uses these three lines of code to copy the password field's content to a label:

```
String prefix = "You typed \"";
...
JPasswordField source = (JPasswordField)e.getSource();
actionLabel.setText(prefix + new String(source.getPassword()) + "\"");
```

Note that this code uses the getPassword method instead of getText to get the contents of the password field. <u>Providing a Password Field</u> (page 306) explains why and provides additional information about password fields. Remember that password fields are text fields, so the information covered in <u>How to Use Text Fields</u> (page 298) pertains to password fields as well.

Using a Text Area

This is the only section provided in this book about using text areas, because JTextArea is a straightforward class to use and is largely backward compatible with the AWT TextArea class. If you are interested in customizing a text area, you can apply what you learn in <u>General Rules for Using Text Components</u> (page 282). The sample program described there uses a standard text area as a log. Be sure to check the <u>Summary of the Text Component API</u> (page 309) section for relevant API and other examples that use text areas.

A text area displays multiple lines of text and allows the user to edit the text with the keyboard and the mouse. Here's the TextSamplerDemo code that creates its text area:

```
JTextArea textArea = new JTextArea(
    "This is an editable JTextArea " +
    "that has been initialized with the setText method. " +
    "A text area is a \"plain\" text component, " +
    "which means that although it can display text " +
    "in any font, all of the text is in the same font."
);
textArea.setFont(new Font("Serif", Font.ITALIC, 16));
textArea.setLineWrap(true);
textArea.setWrapStyleWord(true);
```

The constructor used in this example initializes the text area with some text. Next, the code sets the text area's font.

By default a text area doesn't wrap lines but instead shows all of the text on one line. If the text area is within a scroll pane, the text area allows itself to be scrolled horizontally. This example turns line wrapping on with a call to `setLineWrap` and then calls `setWrapStyle-Word` to indicate that the text area should wrap lines at word boundaries rather than at character boundaries.

To provide scrolling capability, the example puts the text area in a scroll pane.

```
JScrollPane areaScrollPane = new JScrollPane(textArea);
areaScrollPane.setVerticalScrollBarPolicy(
    JScrollPane.VERTICAL_SCROLLBAR_ALWAYS);
areaScrollPane.setPreferredSize(new Dimension(250, 250));
areaScrollPane.setBorder(...create border...);
```

A text area is typically managed by a scroll pane. If you put a text area in a scroll pane, be sure to set the scroll pane's preferred size or use a text area constructor that sets the number of rows and columns for the text area.

Using an Editor Pane to Display Text from a URL

`JEditorPane` is the foundation for Swing's styled text components and provides the mechanism through which you can add support for custom text formats. `TextSamplerDemo` doesn't begin to exercise `JEditorPane`'s capability but does illustrate a very handy, easy-to-use editor pane feature: displaying uneditable help information loaded from a URL. Here's the code that creates the editor pane in `TextSamplerDemo`:

```
JEditorPane editorPane = new JEditorPane();
editorPane.setEditable(false);
...Create a URL object for the TextSamplerDemoHelp.html file...
try {
    editorPane.setPage(url);
} catch (IOException e) {
    System.err.println("Attempted to read a bad URL: " + url);
}
```

The code uses the default constructor to create the editor pane and then calls `setEditable(false)` so the user cannot edit the text. Next, the code creates the URL object and uses it to call the `setPage` method. The `setPage` method opens the resource pointed to by the URL and figures out the format of the text (which in the example is HTML). If the text format is known, the editor pane initializes itself with the text found at the URL. A standard editor pane can understand plain text, HTML, and RTF.

The code that creates the URL is missing from the previous code sample and is interesting in and of itself.

```
String s = null;
try {
    s = "file:"
        + System.getProperty("user.dir")
        + System.getProperty("file.separator")
        + "TextSamplerDemoHelp.html";
    URL helpURL = new URL(s);
    /* ...  use the URL to initialize the editor pane  ... */
} catch (Exception e) {
    System.err.println("Couldn't create help URL: " + s);
}
```

This code uses system properties to compute a file URL for the help file. Owing to security restrictions, this code won't work in untrusted applets. Instead use the applet's codebase to compute an http URL.

Like text areas, editor panes are typically managed by a scroll pane:

```
JScrollPane editorScrollPane = new JScrollPane(editorPane);
editorScrollPane.setVerticalScrollBarPolicy(
    JScrollPane.VERTICAL_SCROLLBAR_ALWAYS);
editorScrollPane.setPreferredSize(new Dimension(250, 150));
```

This short section shows a typical and basic use of an editor pane. However, many programs need to use editor panes in more sophisticated ways. To find out the types of things you can do with editor panes and how they differ from text panes, refer to Concepts: About Editor Panes and Text Panes (page 295).

Using a Text Pane

The final text component in our tour is JTextPane, which is a JEditorPane subclass. Here's TextSamplerDemo code that creates and initializes a text pane:

```
JTextPane textPane = new JTextPane();
String[] initString = { /* ...  fill array with initial text  ... */ };

String[] initStyles = { /* ...  fill array with names of styles  ... */ };

//Create the styles we need.
initStylesForTextPane(textPane);

Document doc = textPane.getDocument();

//Load the text pane with styled text.
try {
```

```
    for (int i=0; i < initString.length; i++) {
        textPane.setCaretPosition(doc.getLength());
        doc.insertString(doc.getLength(), initString[i],
            textPane.getStyle(initStyles[i]));
        textPane.setLogicalStyle(textPane.getStyle(initStyles[i]));
    }
} catch (BadLocationException ble) {
    System.err.println("Couldn't insert initial text.");
}
```

The preceding snippet hard codes the initial text into an array and creates and hard codes several *styles*—objects that represent various paragraph and character formats—into another array. Next, the code loops over the arrays, inserts the text into the text pane, and specifies the style to use for the inserted text. Although this makes for an interesting example and concisely shows off several features of JTextPane, "real-world" programs aren't likely to initialize a text pane this way. Instead the program would use a text pane to save out a document, which would then be used to intialize the text pane.

To find out the types of things you can do with text panes and how they differ from editor panes, refer to <u>Concepts: About Editor Panes and Text Panes</u> (page 295).

Now that you've seen all of the text components in action, it's time to learn about JTextComponent and the features it provides to all of its subclasses.

General Rules for Using Text Components

As the foundation for Swing's text components, JTextComponent provides these customizable features for all of its descendants:

- A separate model, known as a *document*, to manage the component's content
- A separate view, which is in charge of displaying the component onscreen
- A separate controller, known as an *editor kit*, that can read and write text and that implements editing capabilities with actions
- Customizable keymaps and key bindings
- Support for infinite undo and redo
- Pluggable caret and support for caret change listeners

We use the following application to explore each of these capabilities. Although the demo application contains a customized instance of JTextPane, the capabilities discussed here are inherited by all of JTextComponent's subclasses.

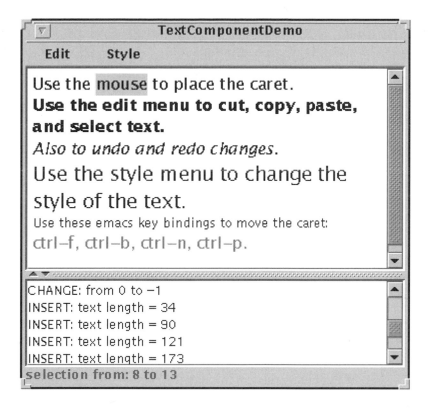

Figure 88 The TextComponentDemo application.

The upper text component is the customized text pane. The lower text component is an instance of JTextArea, which serves as a log that reports all changes made to the contents of the text pane. The status line at the bottom of the window reports either the location of the selection or the position of the caret, depending on whether text is selected.

Try this:

1. Compile and run the application.[1] The source is in <u>TextComponentDemo.java</u> (page 744) and <u>LimitedStyledDocument.java</u> (page 675).

2. Use the mouse to select text and to place the cursor in the text pane. Information about the selection and cursor is displayed at the bottom of the window.

3. Enter text by typing at the keyboard. You can move the caret around by using four emacs key bindings: Control-B (backward one character), Control-F (forward one character), Control-N (down one line), and Control-P (up one line).

---

[1]   See the chapter <u>Getting Started with Swing</u> (page 3) if you need help compiling or running this application.

4. Bring up the Edit menu and use its various menu items to perform editing on the text in the text pane. Make a selection in the text area at the bottom of the window. Because the text area is uneditable, only some of the Edit menu's commands, like copy-to-clipboard, work. It's important to note, though, that the menu operates on both text components.

5. Use the items in the Style menu to apply different styles to the text in the text pane.

Concepts: About Documents

Like other Swing components, a text component separates its data (known as the *model*) from its view of the data. If you are not yet familiar with the model-view split used by Swing components, refer to Separate Data and State Models (page 50).

A text component's model is known as a *document* and is an instance of a class that implements the Document[1] interface. A document provides the following services for a text component:

- Contains the text. A document stores the textual content in Element objects, which can represent any logical text structure, such as paragraphs, text runs that share styles, and so on. We do not cover Elements. However, the online magazine, *The Swing Connection*, has at least one article on the subject.[2]

- Provides support for editing the text through the remove and the insertString methods.

- Notifies document listeners and undoable edit listeners of changes to the text.

- Manages Position objects, which track a particular location within the text even as the text is modified.

- Allows you to get information about the text, such as its length, and segments of the text as a string.

The Swing text package contains a subinterface of Document, StyledDocument,[3] that adds support for marking up the text with styles. One JTextComponent subclass, JTextPane, requires that its document be a StyledDocument rather than merely a Document.

The javax.swing.text package provides the following hierarchy of document classes, which implement specialized documents for the various JTextComponent subclasses.

---

[1] http://java.sun.com/products/jdk/1.2/docs/api/javax/swing/text/Document.html
[2] *The Swing Connection* is available on the CD-ROM that accompanies this book and online at http://java.sun.com/products/jfc/tsc/index.html
[3] API documentation for StyledDocument is available on this book's CD-ROM and online at http://java.sun.com/products/jdk/1.2/docs/api/javax/swing/text/StyledDocument.html

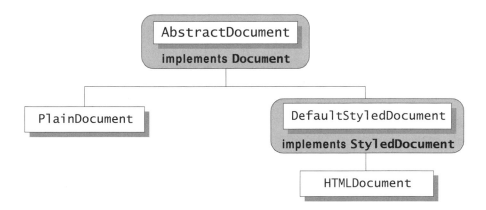

Figure 89   The hierarchy of document classes that the `javax.swing.text` package provides.

A `PlainDocument`[1] is the default document for text fields, password fields, and text areas. `PlainDocument` provides a basic text container where all of the text is displayed in the same font. Even though an editor pane is a styled text component, it uses an instance of `PlainDocument` by default. The default document for a standard `JTextPane` is an instance of `DefaultStyledDocument`[2]—a container for text of an unnamed custom text format provided by Swing. However, the document instance used by any particular editor pane or a text pane depends on the type of content bound to it. If you use `setPage` to load text into an editor pane or a text pane, the document instance used by the pane might change. Refer to Concepts: About Editor Panes and Text Panes (page 295) for details.

Text components inherit the `setDocument` method, which you can use to dynamically change a component's document. Also most `JTextComponent` subclasses provide constructors that set the document when creating the component. By replacing a text component's document with one of your own, you can implement certain customizations. For example, the text pane in `TextComponentDemo` has a custom document that limits the number of characters it can contain.

Customizing a Document

The `TextComponentDemo` application has a custom document, LimitedStyledDocument.java (page 675), that limits the number of characters that the text pane can contain. `LimitedStyledDocument` is a subclass of `DefaultStyledDocument`, the default document for `JTextPane`. The example needs to use a subclass of `DefaultStyledDocument` because `JTextPane` requires its document to be of that type. If you changed the superclass to `Plain-`

---

[1]   http://java.sun.com/products/jdk/1.2/docs/api/javax/swing/text/PlainDocument.html
[2]   http://java.sun.com/products/jdk/1.2/docs/api/javax/swing/text/DefaultStyledDocument.html

Document, the document would work for a text field or a text area—any text component except a text pane. No other code changes would be required, although you would probably remove Styled from the class name, for clarity.

Here's the sample program code that creates a LimitedStyledDocument and makes it the document for the text pane:

```
...where the member variables are declared...
JTextPane textPane;
static final int MAX_CHARACTERS = 300;
    ...in the constructor for the frame...
  //Create the document for the text area
  LimitedStyledDocument lsd = new LimitedStyledDocument(MAX_CHARACTERS);
  ...
  //Create the text pane and configure it
  textPane = new JTextPane();
  textPane.setDocument(lsd);
  ...
```

To limit the characters allowed in the document, LimitedStyledDocument overrides its superclass's insertString method, which is called each time text is inserted into the document. Text insertion can be the result of the user's typing or pasting text in or because of a call to setText. Here is LimitedStyledDocument's implementation of insertString:

```
public void insertString(int offs, String str, AttributeSet a)
             throws BadLocationException {
    if ((getLength() + str.length()) <= maxCharacters)
        super.insertString(offs, str, a);
    else
        Toolkit.getDefaultToolkit().beep();
}
```

In addition to insertString, custom documents commonly override the remove method, which is called each time text is removed from the document.

One common use of a custom document is to create a change-validated text field (a field whose value is checked each time its text changes). For two examples of validated text fields, refer to Creating a Validated Text Field (page 299).

Listening for Changes on a Document

You can register two types of listeners on a document: document listeners and undoable edit listeners. Here we cover document listeners. For information about undoable edit listeners, refer to Implementing Undo and Redo (page 292).

A document notifies registered document listeners of changes to the document. Use a document listener to react when text is inserted or removed from a document or when the style of some of the text changes.

The TextComponentDemo program uses a document listener to update the change log whenever a change is made to the text pane. The following line of code registers an instance of MyDocumentListener as a listener on the LimitedStyledDocument used in the example:

```
lsd.addDocumentListener(new MyDocumentListener());
```

Here's the implementation of MyDocumentListener:

```
protected class MyDocumentListener implements DocumentListener {
    public void insertUpdate(DocumentEvent e) {
        displayEditInfo(e);
    }

    public void removeUpdate(DocumentEvent e) {
        displayEditInfo(e);
    }

    public void changedUpdate(DocumentEvent e) {
        //Display the type of edit that occurred
        changeLog.append(e.getType().toString() +
                    ": from " + e.getOffset() +
                    " to " + (e.getOffset() + e.getLength() - 1) +
                    newline);
    }

    private void displayEditInfo(DocumentEvent e) {
        //Display the type of edit that occurred and
        //the resulting text length
        changeLog.append(e.getType().toString() +
                    ": text length = " +
                    e.getDocument().getLength() + newline);
    }
}
```

The listener implements three methods for handling three types of document events: insertion, removal, and style changes. StyledDocuments can fire all three types of events. Plain-Documents fire events only for insertion and removal. For general information about document listeners and document events, see How to Write a Document Listener (page 472).

Remember that the document for this text pane limits the number of characters allowed in the document. If you try to add more text than the document allows, the document blocks the change, and the listener's `insertUpdate` method is not called. Document listeners are notified of changes only if the change has already occurred.

Sometimes, you might be tempted to change the document's text from within a document listener. For example, if you have a text field that should contain only integers and the user enters another type of data, you might want to change the text to 0. However, you should *never* modify the contents of text component from within a document listener. In fact, if you do, your program will likely deadlock! Instead provide a custom document and override the `insertString` and `remove` the methods as needed.

Concepts: About Editor Kits

All Swing text components support standard editing commands, such as cut, copy, paste, and inserting characters. Each editing command is represented and implemented by an `Action` object. Actions (page 389) make it easy for you to associate a command with a GUI component, such as a menu item or a button, and therefore build a GUI around a text component.

Under the hood, text components use an `EditorKit`[1] to create and to manage actions. Besides managing a set of actions for a text component, an editor kit also knows how to read and to write documents of a particular format. Although all text components use editor kits, some components hide theirs. You can't set or get the editor kit used by a text field, a password field, or a text area. Editor panes and text panes provide the `getEditorKit` method to get the current editor kit and the `setEditorKit` to change it.

For all components, `JTextComponent` provides API for you to indirectly invoke or customize some editor kit capabilities. For example, `JTextComponent` provides `read` and `write` methods, which invoke the editor kit's `read` and `write` methods. `JTextComponent` also provides a `getActions` method that returns all of the actions supported by a component.

The Swing text package provides the following editor kits:

`DefaultEditorKit`[2]

> Reads and writes plain text. Provides a basic set of editing commands. All of the other editor kits descend from this one.

`StyledEditorKit`[3]

> Reads and writes styled text and provides a minimal set of actions for styled text. This class is a subclass of `DefaultEditorKit` and is the editor kit `JTextPane` uses by default.

---

[1]   API documentation for this class is available on this book's CD-ROM and online at http://java.sun.com/products/jdk/1.2/docs/api/javax/swing/text/EditorKit.html

[2]   http://java.sun.com/products/jdk/1.2/docs/api/javax/swing/text/DefaultEditorKit.html

[3]   http://java.sun.com/products/jdk/1.2/docs/api/javax/swing/text/StyledEditorKit.html

HTMLEditorKit[1]

Reads, writes, and edits HTML. This is a subclass of StyledEditorKit.

RTFEditorKit[2]

Reads, writes, and edits RTF. This is a subclass of StyledEditorKit.

Each of these editor kits has been registered with the JEditorPane class and associated with the text format that the kit reads, writes, and edits. When a file is loaded into an editor pane, the pane checks the format of the file against its registered kits. If a registered kit that supports that file format is found, the pane uses the kit to read, display, and edit the file. Thus the editor pane effectively transforms itself into an editor for that text format. You can extend JEditorPane to support your own text format by creating an editor kit for it and then using JEditorPane's registerEditorKitForContentType to associate your kit with your text format.

Associating Text Actions with Menus and Buttons

As we mentioned before, you can call the getActions method on any text component to get an array containing all of the actions supported by it. Often it's convenient to load the array of actions into a Hashtable so your program can retrieve an action by name. Here's the TextComponentDemo code that gets the actions from the text pane and loads them into a Hashtable:

```
private void createActionTable(JTextComponent textComponent) {
    actions = new Hashtable();
    Action[] actionsArray = textComponent.getActions();
    for (int i = 0; i < actionsArray.length; i++) {
        Action a = actionsArray[i];
        actions.put(a.getValue(Action.NAME), a);
    }
}
```

And here's a convenient method for retrieving an action by its name from the hashtable:

```
private Action getActionByName(String name) {
    return (Action)(actions.get(name));
}
```

You can use both methods verbatim in your programs.

---

[1] http://java.sun.com/products/jdk/1.2/docs/api/javax/swing/text/html/HTMLEditorKit.html
[2] http://java.sun.com/products/jdk/1.2/docs/api/javax/swing/text/rtf/RTFEditorKit.html

Now let's look at how the Cut menu item is created and associated with the action of removing text from the text component:

```
protected JMenu createEditMenu() {
    JMenu menu = new JMenu("Edit");
    ...
    menu.add(getActionByName(DefaultEditorKit.cutAction));
    ...
```

This code gets the action by name, using the handy method shown previously. The code then adds the action to the menu. That's all you need to do. The menu and the action take care of everything else. You'll note that the name of the action comes from `DefaultEditorKit`. This kit provides actions for basic text editing and is the superclass for all of the editor kits Swing provides. Thus its capabilities are available to all text components unless overridden by a customization.

For efficiency, text components share actions. The `Action` object returned by `getAction-ByName(DefaultEditorKit.cutAction)` is shared by the uneditable `JTextArea` at the bottom of the window. This has two important ramifications:

1. Generally speaking, you shouldn't modify `Action` objects you get from editor kits. If you do, the changes affect all text components in your program.

2. `Action` objects can operate on other text components in the program, perhaps more than you intended. In this example, even though it's uneditable, the `JTextArea` shares actions with the `JTextPane`. (Select some text in the text area, then choose the cut-to-clipboard menu item. You'll hear a beep because the text area is uneditable.) If you don't want to share, consider instantiating the `Action` object yourself. `DefaultEditorKit` defines a number of useful `Action` subclasses.

Here's the code that creates the Style menu and puts the Bold menu item in it:

```
protected JMenu createStyleMenu() {
    JMenu menu = new JMenu("Style");
    Action action = new StyledEditorKit.BoldAction();
    action.putValue(Action.NAME, "Bold");
    menu.add(action);
    ...
```

The `StyledEditorKit` class provides `Action` subclasses to implement editing commands for styled text. You'll note that instead of getting the action from the editor kit, this code creates an instance of the `BoldAction` class. Thus this action is not shared with any other text component, and changing its name won't affect any other text component.

In addition to associating an action with a GUI component, you can also associate an action with a keystroke. <u>Associating Text Actions with Keystrokes</u> (page 291) shows you how.

Concepts: About Keymaps

This section assumes that you understand actions and how to get them from the editor kit. If you don't, read <u>Concepts: About Editor Kits</u> (page 288) and <u>Associating Text Actions with Menus and Buttons</u> (page 289).

Every text component has one or more *keymaps*—each of which is an instance of the <u>Key-map</u>[1] class. A keymap contains a collection of name-value pairs, where the name is a <u>Key-Stroke</u>[2] and the value is an `Action`. Each pair *binds* the keystroke to the action such that when the user types the keystroke, the action occurs.

By default a text component has one keymap, named `JTextComponent.DEFAULT_KEYMAP`. This keymap contains standard, basic key bindings. For example, the arrow keys are mapped to caret movement, and so on. You can enhance or modify the default keymap in the following ways:

- Add a custom keymap to the text component, using `JTextComponent`'s `addKeymap` method.
- Add key bindings to the default keymap, using `Keymap`'s `addActionForKeyStroke` method. The default keymap is shared among text components, so use this with caution.
- Remove key bindings from the default keymap, using `Keymap`'s `removeKeyStroke-Binding` method. The default keymap is shared among text components, so again, use this with caution.

When resolving a keystroke to its action, the text component checks the keymaps in the order they are added to the text component. Thus the binding for a specific keystroke in a keymap that you add to a text component overrides any binding for the same keystroke in the default keymap.

Associating Text Actions with Keystrokes

The text pane in the `TextComponentDemo` supports four key bindings not provided by the default keymap.

- Control-B for moving the caret backward one character
- Control-F for moving the caret forward one character
- Control-N for moving the caret down one line
- Control-P for moving the caret up one line

---

[1] API documentation for `Keymap` is available on this book's CD-ROM and online at http://java.sun.com/products/jdk/1.2/docs/api/javax/swing/text/Keymap.html

[2] http://java.sun.com/products/jdk/1.2/docs/api/javax/swing/KeyStroke.html

The following code adds a new keymap to the text pane and adds the Control-B key binding to it. The code for adding the other three is similar.

```
Keymap keymap = textPane.addKeymap("MyEmacsBindings",
                                    textPane.getKeymap());

Action action = getActionByName(StyledEditorKit.backwardAction);
KeyStroke key = KeyStroke.getKeyStroke(KeyEvent.VK_B, Event.CTRL_MASK);
keymap.addActionForKeyStroke(key, action);
```

The code first adds a keymap to the component's hierarchy. The addKeymap method creates the keymap for you with the name and parent provided in the method call. In the example the parent is the text pane's default keymap. Next, the code gets the backward action from the editor kit and gets a KeyStroke object representing the Control-B key sequence. Finally, the code adds the action and keystroke pair to the keymap, thereby binding the key to the action.

Implementing Undo and Redo

Implementing undo and redo has two parts: remembering the undoable edits that occur and implementing the undo and redo commands and providing a user interface for them.

Note: The implementation of undo and redo in TextComponentDemo was taken from the Note-Pad demo that comes with the JFC 1.1 release and the Java 2 Platform. Many programmers will also be able to copy this implementation of undo/redo without modification.

Part 1: Remembering Undoable Edits

To support undo and redo, a text component must remember each edit that occurs, the order of edits, and what it takes to undo each edit. TextComponentDemo uses an instance of the UndoManager[1] class to manage its list of undoable edits. The undo manager is created where the member variables are declared:

```
protected UndoManager undo = new UndoManager();
```

Now let's look at how the program finds out about undoable edits and adds them to the undo manager.

---

[1] API documentation for UndoManager is available on this book's CD-ROM and online at
    http://java.sun.com/products/jdk/1.2/docs/api/javax/swing/undo/UndoManager.html

A document notifies interested listeners whenever an undoable edit occurs on its content. An important step in implementing undo and redo is to register an undoable edit listener on the document of the text component. The following code adds an instance of `MyUndoable-EditListener` to the text pane's document:

```
lsd.addUndoableEditListener(new MyUndoableEditListener());
```

The undoable edit listener used in our example adds the edit to the undo manager's list:

```
protected class MyUndoableEditListener implements UndoableEditListener {
    public void undoableEditHappened(UndoableEditEvent e) {
        //Remember the edit and update the menus
        undo.addEdit(e.getEdit());
        undoAction.updateUndoState();
        redoAction.updateRedoState();
    }
}
```

Note that this method updates two objects: `undoAction` and `redoAction`. These are the action objects attached to the Undo and Redo menu items, respectively. The next step shows you how the menu items are created and the implementation of the two actions. For general information about undoable edit listeners and undoable edit events, see <u>How to Write an Undoable Edit Listener</u> (page 519).

Part 2: Implementing the Undo/Redo Commands

The first step in this part of implementing undo and redo is to create the actions to put in the Edit menu.

```
JMenu menu = new JMenu("Edit");

//Undo and redo are actions of our own creation
undoAction = new UndoAction();
menu.add(undoAction);
redoAction = new RedoAction();
menu.add(redoAction);
...
```

The undo and redo actions are implemented by custom <u>AbstractAction</u>[1] subclasses: `Undo-Action` and `RedoAction`, respectively. These classes are inner classes of the example's primary class.

---

[1] API documentation for `AbstractAction` is available on this book's CD-ROM and online at http://java.sun.com/products/jdk/1.2/docs/api/javax/swing/AbstractAction.html

When the user invokes the Undo command, UndoAction's `actionPerformed` method, shown here, gets called:

```
public void actionPerformed(ActionEvent e) {
    try {
        undo.undo();
    } catch (CannotUndoException ex) {
        System.out.println("Unable to undo: " + ex);
        ex.printStackTrace();
    }
    updateUndoState();
    redoAction.updateRedoState();
}
```

This method calls the undo manager's `undo` method and updates the menu items to reflect the new undo/redo state. Similarly, when the user invokes the Redo command, the `action-Performed` method in RedoAction gets called:

```
public void actionPerformed(ActionEvent e) {
    try {
        undo.redo();
    } catch (CannotRedoException ex) {
        System.out.println("Unable to redo: " + ex);
        ex.printStackTrace();
    }
    updateRedoState();
    undoAction.updateUndoState();
}
```

This method is similar except that it calls the undo manager's `redo` method. Much of the code in the `UndoAction` and `RedoAction` classes is dedicated to enabling and disabling the actions as appropriate for the current state and to changing the names of the menu items to reflect the edit to be undone or redone.

Listening for Caret and Selection Changes

The `TextComponentDemo` program uses a caret listener to display the current position of the caret or, if text is selected, the extent of the selection. The caret listener class in this example is a `JLabel` subclass. Here's the code that creates the caret listener label and makes it a caret listener of the text pane:

```
//Create the status area
CaretListenerLabel caretListenerLabel = new CaretListenerLabel(
                                            "Caret Status");
...
textPane.addCaretListener(caretListenerLabel);
```

A caret listener must implement one method, caretUpdate, which is called each time the caret moves or the selection changes. Here's the CaretListenerLabel implementation of caretUpdate:

```
public void caretUpdate(CaretEvent e) {
    //Get the location in the text
    int dot = e.getDot();
    int mark = e.getMark();
    if (dot == mark) {  // no selection
        try {
            Rectangle caretCoords = textPane.modelToView(dot);
            //Convert it to view coordinates
            setText("caret: text position: " + dot +
                    ", view location = [" +
                    caretCoords.x + ", " + caretCoords.y + "]" +
                    newline);
        } catch (BadLocationException ble) {
            setText("caret: text position: " + dot + newline);
        }
    } else if (dot < mark) {
        setText("selection from: " + dot + " to " + mark + newline);
    } else {
        setText("selection from: " + mark + " to " + dot + newline);
    }
}
```

As you can see, this listener updates its text label to reflect the current state of the caret or selection. The listener gets the information to display from the caret event object. For general information about caret listeners and caret events, see How to Write a Caret Listener (page 462).

As with document listeners, a caret listener is passive. It reacts to changes in the caret or in the selection but does not change the caret or the selection. If you want to change the caret or selection, you should use a custom caret instead. To create a custom caret, write a class that implements the Caret[1] interface, and then provide an instance of your class as an argument to setCaret on a text component.

Concepts: About Editor Panes and Text Panes

Two Swing classes support styled text: JEditorPane and its subclass JTextPane. Several facts about editor panes and text panes were sprinkled throughout previous sections. Here we collect the facts in one place and provide a bit more detail. The information here should help

---

[1] API documentation for Caret is available on this book's CD-ROM and online at http://java.sun.com/products/jdk/1.2/docs/api/javax/swing/text/Caret.html

you understand the differences between editor panes and text panes and know when to use which.

- An editor pane or a text pane can easily be loaded with text from a URL, using the `set-Page` method. The `JEditorPane` class also provides constructors that let you initialize an editor pane from a URL. `JTextPane` has no such constructors. See <u>Using an Editor Pane to Display Text from a URL</u> (page 280) for an example of using this feature to load an uneditable editor pane with HTML.

- Be aware that the document and the editor kit might change when the `setPage` method is used. For example, if an editor pane contains plain text (the default) and you load it with HTML, the document will change to an `HTMLDocument` instance, and the editor kit will change to an `HTMLEditorKit` instance. If your program uses the `setPage` method, make sure that the code adjusts for possible changes to the pane's document and editor kit instances (reregister document listeners on the new document, and so on).

- By default editor panes know how to read, write, and edit plain, HTML, and RTF text. Text panes inherit this capability but impose certain limitations. A text pane insists that its document implement the `StyledDocument` interface. <u>HTMLDocument</u>[1] is a `Styled-Documents`, so HTML works as expected within a text pane. If you load a text pane with plain text, though, the text pane's document is not a `PlainDocument` as you might expect but rather a `DefaultStyledDocument`.

- To support a custom text format, implement an editor kit that can read, write, and edit text of that format. Then call the `registerEditorKitForContentType` method to register your kit with the `JEditorPane` class. By registering an editor kit in this way, all editor panes in your program will be able to read, write, and edit the new format.

- As mentioned previously, a text pane requires that its document be an instance of a class that implements the `StyledDocument` interface. The Swing text package provides a default implementation of this interface, `DefaultStyledDocument`. A text pane also requires that its editor kit be an instance of a `StyledEditorKit` (or a subclass), which can read, write, and edit text of an unnamed custom text format provided by Swing. The actual format doesn't matter, because the editor kit and the document understand text of this format. This makes text pane a good choice for a plug-and-play-style text component, if you want styled text and don't care what format it's in.

- Through its styled document and styled editor kit, text panes provide support for named styles and logical styles. The `JTextPane` class itself contains many methods for working with styles that simply call methods in its document or editor kit.

---

[1]   API documentation for `HTMLDocument` is available on this book's CD-ROM and online at
http://java.sun.com/products/jdk/1.2/docs/api/javax/swing/text/html/HTMLDocument.html

- Through the API provided in the JTextPane class, you can embed images and components in a text pane. You can embed images in an editor pane, too, but only by including the images in an HTML or an RTF file.

Examples that Use Text Components

This table shows some of the examples that use text components and where those examples are described. To get started with text components, you might want to run these programs and examine their code to find one that does something similar to what you want to do. For text and password field examples, don't forget to look at Examples that Use Text Fields and Password Fields (page 309).

Table 119   Examples that Use Text Components

Example	Where Described	Notes
TextSamplerDemo.java	An Example that Uses Each Text Component (page 276)	Uses one of each of Swing's text components.
TextComponentDemo.java	General Rules for Using Text Components (page 282)	Provides a customized text pane. Illustrates many text component features.
ToolBarDemo2.java	How to Use Tool Bars (page 138)	Puts a text field in a tool bar.
CustomDialog.java	How to Make Dialogs (page 87)	Puts a validated text field in a dialog. Part of DialogDemo (under the More Dialogs tab).
TreeDemo.java	How to Use Trees (page 320)	Uses an editor pane to display help loaded from an HTML file.

How to Use Text Fields

A text field is a basic text control that lets the user enter a small amount of text. When the user indicates that text entry is complete (usually by pressing Return), the text field fires an action event. Generally you use the `JTextField`[1] class to provide text fields. If you need to provide a *password field*—an editable text field that doesn't show the characters the user types—use the `JPasswordField`[2] class instead. This section discusses both text fields and password fields.

If you want a text field that also provides a menu of strings to choose from, consider using an editable combo box. If you need to obtain more than one line of input from the user, you should use one of the classes that implements a general-purpose text area.

The following applet displays a basic text field and a text area. The text field is editable; the text area isn't. When the user presses Return in the text field, the applet copies the text field's contents to the text area and then selects all of the text in the text field.

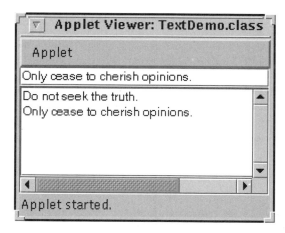

Figure 90   The `TextDemo` application.

---

[1]   API documentation for `JTextField` is available on this book's CD-ROM and online at
http://java.sun.com/products/jdk/1.2/docs/api/javax/swing/JTextField.html

[2]   http://java.sun.com/products/jdk/1.2/docs/api/javax/swing/JPasswordField.html

You can find the source for the program in <u>TextDemo.java</u> (page 750). Here's the TextDemo code that creates the text field in the applet:

```
textField = new JTextField(20);
textField.addActionListener(this);
...
contentPane.add(textField);
```

The integer argument passed to the JTextField constructor, 20 in the example, indicates the number of columns in the field. This number is used along with metrics provided by the field's current font to calculate the field's preferred width. This number does not limit how many characters the user can enter. To do that, you need to implement a custom document, as described in <u>General Rules for Using Text Components</u> (page 282).

The next lines of code register the applet as an action listener for the text field and add the text field to the applet's content pane. Here's the actionPerformed method that handles action events from the text field:

```
public void actionPerformed(ActionEvent evt) {
    String text = textField.getText();
    textArea.append(text + newline);
    textField.selectAll();
}
```

Note the use of JTextField's getText method to retrieve the text currently contained by the text field. The text returned by this method does *not* include a new-line character for the Return key that fired the action event.

This example illustrates using a basic, off-the-shelf text field for entering textual data and performing a task when the text field fires an action event. This is sufficient for many programs. Other programs, however, need more advanced behavior. As a subclass of <u>JTextComponent</u>,[1] JTextField can be configured and customized. One common customization is to provide a text field whose contents are validated.

This section covers several advanced text field topics. To get the most out of the information, you need to understand the material presented in <u>General Rules for Using Text Components</u> (page 282).

Creating a Validated Text Field

Many programs require users to enter textual data of a certain type or format. For example, a program might provide a text field for entering a date, a decimal number, or a phone number.

---

[1] http://java.sun.com/products/jdk/1.2/docs/api/javax/swing/text/JTextComponent.html

The contents of such a text field must be validated before being used for any purpose. A text field can be *action* validated or *change* validated.

The data in an action-validated field is checked each time the field fires an action event (each time the user presses the Return key). An action-validated field might, at any given time, contain invalid data. However, the data is validated before it's used for anything. To create an action-validated field, provide an action listener for your field, and implement its `action-Performed` method as follows:

1. Use `getText` to get the contents of the text field, or use `getPassword` if you're using a password field.
2. Evaluate the value returned.
3. If the value is valid, do whatever task or calculation is required. If the value is invalid, report an error, and return without performing a task or a calculation.

`PasswordDemo.java` (page 690), described later in this section, action-validates a password field in this manner.

The data in a change-validated field is checked each time the field changes. A field that is change validated can never contain invalid data, because every change (keystroke, cut, copy, and so on) that might cause the data to be invalid is rejected. To create a change-validated text field, you need to provide a custom document for your text field. If you aren't familiar with documents yet, see Concepts: About Documents (page 284).

Warning: Do not use a document listener for change validation. By the time a document listener has been notified of a change, it's too late; the change has already taken place. See Listening for Changes on a Document (page 286) for more information.

The application shown in the following figure has three change-validated text fields. The user enters loan information into the first three text fields. Each time the user types a character, the program validates the input and updates the result in the fourth text field.

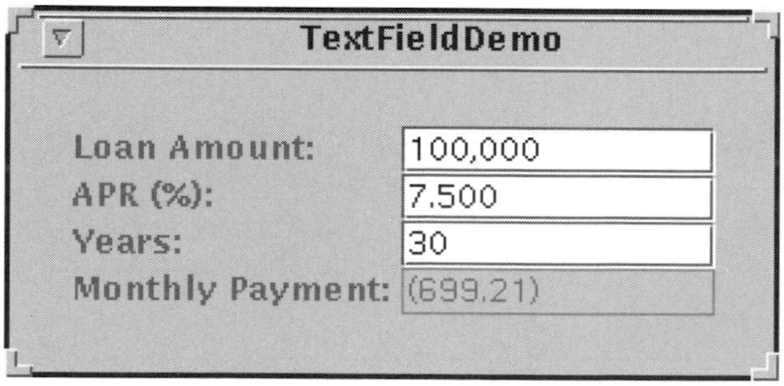

Figure 91   The `TextFieldDemo` application.

Try this:

1. Compile and run the application.[1] The source files are <u>TextFieldDemo.java</u> (page 751), <u>WholeNumberField.java</u> (page 777), <u>DecimalField.java</u> (page 638), and <u>FormattedDocument.java</u> (page 652).

2. Enter information into the text fields and see the results. If you attempt to enter invalid data, the program beeps.

3. Try to type into the fourth text field. You can't, because it isn't editable. However, you can select the text.

4. Resize the window. Note how the labels and the text fields remain aligned. <u>Laying Out Label–Text Field Pairs</u> (page 305) talks more about this feature of the program.

The Years field is an instance of WholeNumberField, which is a subclass of JTextField. By overriding the createDefaultModel method, WholeNumberField establishes a custom Document subclass—an instance of WholeNumberDocument—as the document for each WholeNumberField created:

```
protected Document createDefaultModel() {
    return new WholeNumberDocument();
}
```

Here's the implementation of WholeNumberDocument:

```
protected class WholeNumberDocument extends PlainDocument {
    public void insertString(int offs, String str, AttributeSet a)
                        throws BadLocationException {
        char[] source = str.toCharArray();
        char[] result = new char[source.length];
        int j = 0;
        for (int i = 0; i < result.length; i++) {
            if (Character.isDigit(source[i]))
                result[j++] = source[i];
            else {
                toolkit.beep();
                System.err.println("insertString: " + source[i]);
            }
        }
        super.insertString(offs, new String(result, 0, j), a);
    }
}
```

---

[1] See the chapter <u>Getting Started with Swing</u> (page 3) if you need help compiling or running this application.

This class overrides the `insertString` method, which is called every time any string or character is about to be inserted into the document. `WholeNumberDocument`'s implementation of `insertString` evaluates each character to be inserted into the text field. If the character is a digit, the document allows it to be inserted. Otherwise the method beeps and prints an error message. Thus `WholeNumberDocument` allows the numbers in the range 0, 1, 2, ...

An interesting implementation detail is that our custom document class does not have to override the `remove` method. The `remove` method is called each time a character or group of characters is removed from the text field. Because removing a digit from an integer cannot produce an invalid result, this class does not pay attention to removals.

The other two input fields in the example, as well as the uneditable Monthly Payment field, are all instances of <u>DecimalField</u> (page 620), a custom `JTextField` subclass. `DecimalField` uses a custom document, <u>FormattedDocument</u> (page 652), that allows only data of a particular format to be entered.

`FormattedDocument` has no knowledge of the format of its content. Instead, `FormattedDocument` relies on a format, an instance of a subclass of <u>Format</u>,[1] to accept or reject a proposed change. The text field that uses the `FormattedDocument` must specify which format the `FormattedDocument` uses.

The Loan Amount and Monthly Payment text fields use a <u>NumberFormat</u>[2] object created like this:

```
moneyFormat = NumberFormat.getNumberInstance();
```

The following code creates the APR text field's format:

```
percentFormat = NumberFormat.getNumberInstance();
percentFormat.setMinimumFractionDigits(3);
```

As the code shows, the same class (`NumberFormat`) can support various formats. Furthermore `Format` and its subclasses are locale-sensitive, so a decimal field can be made to support formats for specific countries and regions. Refer to the "Formatting" lesson in the "Internationalization" trail for detailed information about formats.[3]

---

[1] API documentation for `Format` is available on this book's CD-ROM and online at http://java.sun.com/products/jdk/1.2/docs/api/java/text/Format.html

[2] http://java.sun.com/products/jdk/1.2/docs/api/java/text/NumberFormat.html

[3] The "Internationalization" trail is included in the book, *The Java Tutorial Continued*, and in HTML on this book's CD-ROM and online at http://java/sun/com/docs/books/tutorial/i18n/index.html

Here is FormattedDocument's implementation of insertString:

```
public void insertString(int offs, String str, AttributeSet a)
                throws BadLocationException {
    String currentText = getText(0, getLength());
    String beforeOffset = currentText.substring(0, offs);
    String afterOffset = currentText.substring(offs,
                                        currentText.length());
    String proposedResult = beforeOffset + str + afterOffset;
    try {
        format.parseObject(proposedResult);
        super.insertString(offs, str, a);
    } catch (ParseException e) {
        Toolkit.getDefaultToolkit().beep();
        System.err.println("insertString: could not parse: " +
                            proposedResult);
    }
}
```

The method uses the format to parse the result of the proposed insertion. If the result is properly formatted, this method calls its superclass's insert method to do the insertion. If the result is not properly formatted, the program beeps.

In addition to overriding insertString, FormattedDocument also overrides the remove method. Recall that the remove method is called each time a character or group of characters is to be removed from the document.

```
public void remove(int offs, int len) throws BadLocationException {
    String currentText = getText(0, getLength());
    String beforeOffset = currentText.substring(0, offs);
    String afterOffset = currentText.substring(len + offs,
                                        currentText.length());
    String proposedResult = beforeOffset + afterOffset;
    try {
        if (proposedResult.length() != 0)
            format.parseObject(proposedResult);
        super.remove(offs, len);
    } catch (ParseException e) {
        Toolkit.getDefaultToolkit().beep();
        System.err.println("remove: could not parse: " + proposedResult);
    }
}
```

The FormattedDocument implementation of the remove method is similar to its implementation of the insertString method. The format parses the result of the proposed change and performs the removal or not, depending on whether the result is valid.

Note: The solution provided by this example is not a general solution for all types of formats. Some formats—most notably `DateFormat`—can't be change validated simply by calling the `parseObject` method. Here's an example to help you understand why. Suppose that you have a text field that contains the date "May 25, 1996" and want to change it to "June 11, 1996". You would select May and begin typing "June". As soon as you've typed the "J", the field won't parse, because "J 25, 1996" is not a valid date, even though it's a valid change. A number of solutions are possible for dates and other types of data where a partially completed change creates an invalid result. You can change the change validation such that it rejects all definitely invalid changes (typing "X" into a date, for example) but allows all possibly valid changes. Or you can switch to an action-validated field.

Using a Document Listener on a Text Field

If you can't use a document listener for field validation, what can you use it for? Use it to listen to, but not interfere with, changes to the document's content. The loan calculator uses the following document listener to update the monthly payment after every change:

```java
class MyDocumentListener implements DocumentListener {
    public void insertUpdate(DocumentEvent e) {
        calculateValue(e);
    }

    public void removeUpdate(DocumentEvent e) {
        calculateValue(e);
    }

    public void changedUpdate(DocumentEvent e) {
        // we won't ever get this with a PlainDocument
    }

    private void calculateValue(DocumentEvent e) {
        Document whatsup = e.getDocument();
        if (whatsup.getProperty("name").equals("amount"))
            amount = amountField.getValue();
        else if (whatsup.getProperty("name").equals("rate"))
            rate = rateField.getValue();
        else if (whatsup.getProperty("name").equals("numPeriods"))
            numPeriods = numPeriodsField.getValue();
        payment = computePayment(amount, rate, numPeriods);
        paymentField.setValue(payment);
    }
}
```

This is an appropriate use of a document listener. For general information about document listeners, see <u>Listening for Changes on a Document</u> (page 286) and <u>How to Write a Document Listener</u> (page 472).

Laying Out Label-Text Field Pairs

This section describing how the label and the text fields in the example are aligned requires some knowledge of layout managers. Rows of label–text field pairs, such as those found in the loan calculator, are quite common on preference panels and panels that implement forms. Here's the code that lays out the label–text field pairs:

```
. . .
//Layout the labels in a panel
JPanel labelPane = new JPanel();
labelPane.setLayout(new GridLayout(0, 1));
labelPane.add(amountLabel);
labelPane.add(rateLabel);
labelPane.add(numPeriodsLabel);
labelPane.add(paymentLabel);

//Layout the text fields in a panel
JPanel fieldPane = new JPanel();
fieldPane.setLayout(new GridLayout(0, 1));
fieldPane.add(amountField);
fieldPane.add(rateField);
fieldPane.add(numPeriodsField);
fieldPane.add(paymentField);

//Put the panels in another panel, labels on left,
//text fields on right
JPanel contentPane = new JPanel();
contentPane.setBorder(BorderFactory.createEmptyBorder(20, 20, 20, 20));
contentPane.setLayout(new BorderLayout());
contentPane.add(labelPane, BorderLayout.CENTER);
contentPane.add(fieldPane, BorderLayout.EAST);
setContentPane(contentPane);
. . .
```

You may be surprised to find that the labels are laid out without reference to the text fields and, in fact, are in a different panel, yet align correctly with them. This is a side effect of the layout managers used by the program.

As the following screenshot shows, the program uses two GridLayout managers: one to lay out the column of labels and one for the column of text fields.

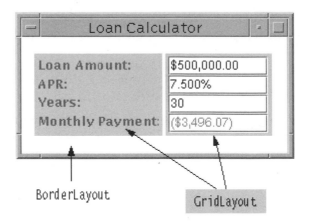

Figure 92　An annotated screenshot of the TextFieldDemoWithLayout application.

GridLayout guarantees that all of its components are the same size, so all of the text fields are the same height and all of the labels are the same height. But the text fields are not the same height as the labels. This difference is achieved with a third layout manager, Border-Layout. With just two components, at East and Center, BorderLayout guarantees that the columns are the same height. Now the labels and the text fields are the same height, and thus they are aligned.

Another way to get labels and text fields to align is to use GridBagLayout. For more information see <u>How to Use GridBagLayout</u> (page 370) and refer to <u>TextSamplerDemo.java</u> (page 754) for an example. In particular, look at the example's handy addLabelTextRows method, which you can probably copy verbatim into your programs.

Providing a Password Field

Swing provides the JPasswordField class, a subclass of JTextField, to use in place of a text field for password entry. For security reasons, a password field doesn't show the characters the user types. Instead the field displays another character, such as an asterisk (*). As another security precaution, the password field stores its value as an array of characters, rather than as a string.

The sample <u>PasswordDemo.java</u> (page 690) uses a JPasswordField. The program brings up a small window to prompt the user to type in a password, as shown here.

Figure 93 The PasswordDemo application.

Here's the PasswordDemo code that creates and sets up the password field:

```
JPasswordField password = new JPasswordField(10);
password.setEchoChar('#');
password.addActionListener(showSwingWorkerDialog);
```

As with text fields, the argument passed into the JPasswordField constructor indicates that the field should be 10 columns wide. By default a password field displays an asterisk (*) for each character typed. The call to setEchoChar changes it to a pound sign (#). Finally, the code adds an action listener to the password field, which action validates the value typed in by the user:

```
public void actionPerformed(ActionEvent e) {
    JPasswordField input = (JPasswordField)e.getSource();
    char[] password = input.getPassword();
    if (isPasswordCorrect(password))
        JOptionPane.showMessageDialog(f, worker.get());
    else
      JOptionPane.showMessageDialog(f, new JLabel("Invalid password."));
}
```

Note that getPassword returns a character array. Password information should not be stored or passed around in strings, because strings are not secure.

A program using a password field typically validates the password before completing any actions requiring the password. This program calls a custom method, isPasswordCorrect, that compares the value returned by getPassword to a value stored in a character array.

The Text Field and Password Field API

The following tables list the commonly used JTextField and JPasswordField constructors and methods. Other methods you are likely to call are defined in JTextComponent. Refer to the API tables in Summary of the Text Component API (page 309).

You might also invoke methods on a text field or password field that it inherits from its other ancestors, such as setPreferredSize, setForeground, setBackground, setFont, and so on. See The JComponent Class (page 67) for tables of commonly used inherited methods.

Table 120   Setting or Getting the Field's Contents

Method or Constructor	Purpose
JTextField() JTextField(String) JTextField(String, int) JTextField(int) JTextField(Document, String, int)	Create a text field. When present, the int argument specifies the desired column width. The String argument contains the field's initial text. The Document argument provides a custom document for the field.
JPasswordField() JPasswordField(String) JPasswordField(String, int) JPasswordField(int) JPasswordField(Document, String, int)	Create a password field. When present, the int argument specifies the desired field width in columns. The String argument contains the field's initial text. The Document argument provides a custom document for the field.
void setText(String) String getText()	Set or get the text displayed by the text field. Note that getText is deprecated for password fields in Swing 1.0.3 and higher releases.
char[] getPassword() (in JPasswordField)	Set or get the text displayed by the text field. Note that this method does not exist in Swing 1.0.3 and lower releases.

Table 121   Fine Tuning the Field's Appearance

Method or Constructor	Purpose
void setEditable(boolean) boolean isEditable()	Set or get whether the user can edit the text in the text field.
void setColumns(int); int getColumns()	Set or get the number of columns displayed by the text field. This is really just a hint for computing the field's preferred width.
int getColumnWidth()	Get the width of the text field's columns. This value is established implicitly by the font.
void setHorizontalAlignment(int); int getHorizontalAlignment()	Set or get how the text is aligned horizontally within its area. You can use JTextField.LEFT, JTextField.CENTER, and JTextField.RIGHT for arguments.
void setEchoChar(char) char getEchoChar() (in JPasswordField)	Set or get the echo character—the character displayed instead of the characters typed by the user.

Table 122 Implementing the Field's Functionality

Method or Constructor	Purpose
`void addActionListener(ActionListener)` `void removeActionListener(ActionListener)`	Add or remove an action listener.
`Document createDefaultModel()`	Override this method to provide a subclass with a custom document.

Examples that Use Text Fields and Password Fields

This table shows the examples that use `JTextField` or `JPasswordField` and where those examples are described.

Table 123 Examples that Use Text Fields and Password Fields

Example	Where Described	Notes
`TextDemo.java`	This section	An applet that uses a basic text field with an action listener.
`TextFieldDemo.java`	This section	Uses and provides implementations for two types of change-validated fields.
`PasswordDemo.java`	This section and <u>Using the Swing-Worker Class</u> (page 432)	Uses an action-validated password field.
`ControlPane.java,` `Utilities.java`	<u>Let's Play</u>ᵃ	Uses a grid bag layout to align labels with text fields. See the `addParameterRow` method in `Utilities.java`. Part of the BINGO player application.
`CustomDialog.java`	<u>How to Make Dialogs</u> (page 87)	Includes a text field whose value is checked. Part of `DialogDemo` (under the More Dialogs tab).

a. "Let's Play," is a section of the *Putting It All Together* trail available in HTML on the CD-ROM and online here: http://java.sun.com/docs/books/tutorial/together/index.html

Summary of the Text Component API

Because `JTextComponent` and its subclasses have too many features to be described completely in this tutorial, please periodically search *The Swing Connection* for pointers to other text documentation.[1] Also, check our `book.html` file for references to further documenta-

---

[1] *The Swing Connection* is available on the CD-ROM that accompanies this book and online at http://java.sun.com/products/jfc/tsc/index.html

tion and examples. For API tables and examples of text fields and password fields, see The Text Field and Password Field API (page 307) and Examples that Use Text Fields and Password Fields (page 309).

The tables in this section cover just part of the text API. For more information, see the API documentation for `JTextComponent` and for the various classes and interfaces in the text package.[1] Also see The JComponent Class (page 67), which describes the API that the text components inherit from `JComponent`.

Table 124　　Swing Text Component Classes

Class	Description
JTextComponent	The abstract superclass of all Swing text components. See General Rules for Using Text Components (page 282).
JTextField	An optionally editable, single-line, plain text component. See How to Use Text Fields (page 298).
JPasswordField	An optionally editable, single-line, plain text component that masks its content. See Providing a Password Field (page 306).
JTextArea	An optionally editable, multi-line, plain text component. See Using a Text Area (page 279).
JEditorPane	An optionally editable, multi-line, styled text component. See Concepts: About Editor Panes and Text Panes (page 295).
JTextPane	An optionally editable, multi-line, styled text component with support for named attributes. See Concepts: About Editor Panes and Text Panes (page 295).

Table 125　　Setting Attributes

Method	Description
void setDisabledTextColor(Color) Color getDisabledTextColor() (*in JTextComponent*)	Set or get the color used to display text when the text component is disabled.
void setOpaque(boolean) boolean getOpaque() (*in JTextComponent*)	Set or get whether the text component is completely opaque.

---

[1]　http://java.sun.com/products/jdk/1.2/docs/api/javax/swing/text/package-summary.html

Table 125   Setting Attributes

Method	Description
void setMargin(Insets) Insets getMargin() (*in JTextComponent*)	Set or get the margin between the text and the text component's border.
void setEditable(boolean) boolean isEditable() (*in JTextComponent*)	Set or get whether the user can edit the text in the text component.

Table 126   Converting Positions Between the Model and the View

Method	Description
int viewToModel(Point) (*in JTextComponent*)	Convert the specified point in the view coordinate system to a position within the text.
Rectangle modelToView(int) (*in JTextComponent*)	Convert the specified position within the text to a rectangle in the view coordinate system.

Table 127   Classes and Interfaces that Represent Documents

Interface or Class	Description
Document (*an interface*)	Defines the API that must be implemented by all documents.
AbstractDocument (*an interface*)	An abstract superclass implementation of the Document interface. This is the superclass for all documents provided by the Swing text package.
PlainDocument (*a class*)	Implements the Document interface. This is the default document for the plain text components (text field, password field, and text area). Additionally used by the editor pane and the text pane when loading plain text or text of an unknown format.
StyledDocument (*an interface*)	A Document subinterface. Defines the API that must be implemented by documents that support styled text. JText-Pane requires that its document be of this type.
DefaultStyledDocument (*a class*)	Implements the StyledDocument interface. The default document for JTextPane.

Table 128   Useful Methods for Working with Documents

Method	Description

`setDocument(Document)`
`Document getDocument()`
(*in JTextComponent*)
	Set or get the document for a text component.

`Document createDefaultModel()` (*in JTextField*)	Override this method in text field and its subclasses to create a custom document instead of the default `PlainDocument`. Creating a Validated Text Field (page 299) has an example of overriding this method.

`void insertString(int, String, AttributeSet)`
`void remove(int, int)`
(*in Document*)
	These methods are commonly overridden by custom documents. For an example of a custom document that overrides both of these methods, see Creating a Validated Text Field (page 299).

`void addDocumentListener(DocumentListener)`
`void removeDocumentListener(DocumentListener)`
(*in Document*)
	Add or remove a document listener to a document. See Listening for Changes on a Document (page 286).

`void addUndoableEditListener(UndoableEditListener)`
`void removeUndoableEditListener(UndoableEditlistener)`
(*in Document*)
	Add or remove an undoable edit listener to a document. See Implementing Undo and Redo (page 292).

`int getLength()`
`Position getStartPosition()`
`Position getEndPosition()`
`String getText(int, int)`
(*in Document*)
	`Document` methods that return useful information about the document.

`Object getProperty(Object)`
`void putProperty(Object, Object)`
(*in Document*)
`Dictionary getDocumentProperties()`
`void setDocumentProperties(Dictionary)`
(*in AbstractDocument*)
	A `Document` maintains a set of properties that you can manipulate with these methods. The example described in Using a Document Listener on a Text Field (page 304) uses a property to name text components so that a shared document listener can identify the document that generated the event.

Table 129   Manipulating the Current Selection

Method	Description
`String getSelectedText()`	Get the currently selected text.

`void selectAll()`
`void select(int, int)`
(*in JTextComponent*)
	Select all text or select text within a start and end range.

`void setSelectionStart(int)`
`void setSelectionEnd(int)`
`int getSelectionStart()`
`int getSelectionEnd()`
(*in JTextComponent*)
	Set or get extent of the current selection by index.

`void setSelectedTextColor(Color)`
`Color getSelectedTextColor()`
(*in JTextComponent*)
	Set or get the color of selected text.

`void setSelectionColor(Color)`
`Color getSelectionColor()`
(*in JTextComponent*)
	Set or get the background color of selected text.

Table 130   Manipulating Carets and Selection Highlighters

Interface, Class, or Method	Description
`Caret` (*an interface*)	Defines the API for objects that represent an insertion point within documents.
`DefaultCaret` (*a class*)	The default caret used by all text components.

`void setCaret(Caret)`
`Caret getCaret()`
(*in JTextComponent*)
	Set or get the caret object used by a text component.

`void setCaretColor(Color)`
`Color getCaretColor()`
(*in JTextComponent*)
	Set or get the color of the caret.

`void setCaretPosition(Position)`
`void moveCaretPosition(int)`
`Position getCaretPosition()`
(*in JTextComponent*)
	Set or get the current position of the caret within the document.

`void addCaretListener(CaretListener)`
`void removeCaretListener(CaretListener)`
(*in JTextComponent*)
	Add or remove a caret listener to a text component.

Table 130 Manipulating Carets and Selection Highlighters

Interface, Class, or Method	Description
Highlighter (*an interface*)	Defines the API for objects used to highlight the current selection.
DefaultHighlighter (*a class*)	The default highlighter used by all text components.
void setHighlighter(Highlighter) Highlighter getHighlighter() (*in JTextComponent*)	Set or get the highlighter used by a text component.

Table 131 Text Editing Commands

Class or Method	Description
void cut() void copy() void paste() void replaceSelection(String) (*in JTextComponent*)	Cut, copy, and paste text, using the system clipboard.
EditorKit (*a class*)	Edit, read, and write text of a particular format.
DefaultEditorKit (*a class*)	A concrete EditorKit subclass that provides the basic text-editing capabilities.
StyledEditorKit (*a class*)	A DefaultEditorKit subclass that provides additional editing capabilities for styled text.
String xxxxAction (*in DefaultEditorKit*)	The names of all of the actions supported by the default editor kit.
BeepAction CopyAction CutAction DefaultKeyTypedAction InsertBreakAction InsertContentAction InsertTabAction PasteAction (*in DefaultEditorKit*)	Inner classes that implement various text-editing commands.

Table 131 Text Editing Commands

Class or Method	Description

`AlignmentAction`
`BoldAction`
`FontFamilyAction`
`FontSizeAction`
`ForegroundAction`
`ItalicAction`
`StyledTextAction`
`UnderlineAction`
(*in StyledEditorKit*)
	Inner classes that implement various editing commands for styled text.

`Action[] getActions()` (*in JTextComponent*)	Get the actions supported by this component. This method gets the array of actions from the editor kit if one is used by the component.

Table 132 Binding Keystrokes to Actions

Interface or Method	Description
`Keymap` (*an interface*)	An interface for managing a set of key bindings. A key binding is represented by a keystroke/action pair.

`Keymap addKeymap(nm, Keymap)`
`Keymap removeKeymap(nm)`
`Keymap getKeymap(nm)`
(*in JTextComponent*)
	Add or remove a keymap to the keymap hierarchy. Also get a keymap by name. Note that these are class methods. The keymap hierarchy is shared by all text components.

`void loadKeymap(Keymap, KeyBinding[],`
`Action[])`
(*in JTextComponent*)
	Add a set of key bindings to the specified keymap. This is a class method.

`void setKeymap(Keymap)`
`Keymap getKeymap()`
(*in JTextComponent*)
	Set or get the currently active keymap for a particular text component.

`void addActionForKeyStroke(KeyStroke, Action)`
`Action getAction(KeyStroke)`
`KeyStroke[] getKeyStrokesForAction(Action)`
(*in Keymap*)
	Set or get keystroke/action binding from a keymap.

`boolean isLocallyDefined(KeyStroke)` (*in Keymap*)	Get whether the specified keystroke is bound to an action in a keymap.

`void removeKeyStrokeBinding(KeyStroke)`
`void removeBindings()`
(*in Keymap*)
	Remove one or all key bindings from a keymap.

Table 132   Binding Keystrokes to Actions

Interface or Method	Description

`void setDefaultAction(Action)`
`Action getDefaultAction()`
(*in Keymap*)
	Set or get the default action. This action is fired if a keystroke is not explicitly bound to an action.

`Action[] getBoundActions()`
`KeyStroke[] getBoundKeyStrokes()`
(*in Keymap*)
	Get an array containing all of the bound actions or keystrokes in a keymap.

Table 133   Reading and Writing Text

Method	Description

`void JTextComponent.read(Reader, Object)`
`void JTextComponent.write(Writer)`
(*in JTextComponent*)
	Read or write text.

`void read(Reader, Document, int)`
`void read(InputStream, Document, int)`
(*in EditorKit*)
	Read text from a stream into a document.

`void write(Writer, Document, int, int)`
`void write(OutputStream, Document, int, int)`
(*in EditorKit*)
	Write text from a document to a stream.

Table 134   Displaying Text from a URL

Method or Constructor	Description

`JEditorPane(URL)`
`JEditorPane(String)`
(*in JEditorPane*)
	Create an editor pane loaded with the text at the specified URL.

`setPage(URL)`
`setPage(String)`
(*in JEditorPane*)
	Load an editor pane (or text pane) with the text at the specified URL.

`URL getPage()` (*in JEditorPane*)	Get the URL for the editor pane's (or text pane's) current page.

How to Use Tool Tips

Creating a tool tip for any JComponent is easy. You just use the setToolTipText method to set up a tool tip for the component. For example, to add tool tips to three buttons, you add only three lines of code:

```
b1.setToolTipText("Click this button to disable the middle button.");
b2.setToolTipText("This middle button does nothing when you click it.");
b3.setToolTipText("Click this button to enable the middle button.");
```

When the user pauses with the cursor over any of the program's buttons, the tool tip for the button comes up. You can see this by running the ButtonDemo example, which is explained in <u>How to Use Buttons, Check Boxes, and Radio Buttons</u> (page 169). Here's a picture of the tool tip that appears when the cursor pauses over the left button in ButtonDemo.

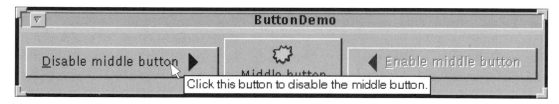

Figure 94 When the cursor pauses over the ButtonDemo's left button, a tool tip appears.

For components that have multiple parts, such as tabbed panes, it often makes sense to vary the tool tip text to reflect the part of the component under the cursor. For example, a tabbed pane might use this feature to explain what will happen when you click the tab under the cursor. When you implement a tabbed pane, you specify the tab-specific tool tip text in an argument to the addTab method.

Even in components that have no API for setting part-specific tool tip text, you can generally do the job yourself. If the component supports renderers, you can set the tool tip text on a custom renderer. An alternative that works for all JComponents is creating a subclass of the component and overriding its getToolTipText(MouseEvent)method.

As of Swing 1.1.1 Beta 2, you can specify HTML text in tool tips, similarly to specifying HTML text in labels. See <u>Using HTML on a Label</u> (page 213) for more information.

The Tool Tip API

Most of the API you need to set up tool tips is in the `JComponent` class and thus is inherited by most Swing components. More tool tip API is in individual classes, such as JTabbed-Pane. Those APIs are generally sufficient for specifying and displaying tool tips; you usually don't need to deal directly with the implementing classes, `JToolTip`[1] and `ToolTipManager`.[2]

The following table lists the `JComponent` tool tip API. For information on individual components' support for tool tips, see the how-to section for the component in question.

Table 135 Tool Tip API in `JComponent`

Method	Purpose
`setToolTipText(String)` (in JComponent)	If the specified string is nonnull, this method registers the component as having a tool tip and makes it, when displayed, have the specified text. If the argument is null, this method turns off tool tips for this component.
`String getToolTipText()` (in JComponent)	Returns the string that was previously specified with `setToolTipText`.
`String getToolTipText(MouseEvent)` (in JComponent)	By default returns the same value returned by `getToolTipText()`. Multipart components, such as JTabbedPane, JTable, and JTree, override this method to return a string associated with the mouse event location. For example, each tab in a tabbed pane can have different tool tip text.
`setToolTipLocation(Point)` `Point getToolTipLocation()` (in JComponent)	Set or get the location (in the receiving component's coordinate system) where the upper-left corner of the component's tool tip will appear. The default value is null, which tells the Swing system to choose a location.

Examples that Use Tool Tips

Table 136 shows some examples that use tool tips and where those examples are described.

---

[1] API documentation for `JToolTip` is available on this book's CD-ROM and online at http://java.sun.com/products/jdk/1.2/docs/api/javax/swing/JToolTip.html

[2] http://java.sun.com/products/jdk/1.2/docs/api/javax/swing/ToolTipManager.html

Table 136   Examples that Use Tool Tips

Example	Where Described	Notes
`ButtonDemo.java`	This section and <u>How to Use Buttons, Check Boxes, and Radio Buttons</u> (page 169)	Uses a tool tip to provide instructions for a button.
`IconDemoApplet.java`	<u>How to Use Icons</u> (page 417)	Uses a tool tip in a label to provide name and size information for an image.
`TabbedPaneDemo.java`	<u>How to Use Tabbed Panes</u> (page 134)	Uses an argument to the `addTab` method to specify tool tip text for each tab.
`TableRenderDemo.java`	<u>Further Customizing Table Display and Event Handling</u> (page 267)	Adds tool tips to a table using custom renderers and editors.
`TreeIconDemo2.java`	<u>Customizing a Tree's Display</u> (page 324)	Adds tool tips to a tree using a custom renderer.
`ActionDemo.java`	<u>How to Use Actions</u> (page 389)	Adds tool tips to buttons created using `Actions`.

How to Use Trees

With the `JTree`[1] class, you can display hierarchical data. A `JTree` object doesn't actually contain your data; it simply provides a view of the data. Like any nontrivial Swing component, the tree gets data by querying its data model. Here's a picture of a tree.

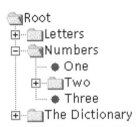

Figure 95   A simple tree application.

As the preceding figure shows, `JTree` displays its data vertically. Each row displayed by the tree contains exactly one item of data, or *node*. Every tree has a *root* node from which all nodes descend. By default the tree displays the root node, but you can decree otherwise. A node can either have children or not. We refer to nodes that can have children—whether or not they currently *have* children—as *branch* nodes. Nodes that can't have children are *leaf* nodes.

Branch nodes can have any number of children. Typically the user can expand and collapse branch nodes—making their children visible or invisible—by clicking them. By default all branch nodes except the root node start out collapsed. A program can detect changes in branch nodes' expansion state by listening for tree expansion events, as described in Responding to Node Selection (page 323).

Creating a Tree

Here is a picture of an application, the top half of which displays a tree in a scroll pane.

---

[1]   API documentation for `JTree` is available on this book's CD-ROM and online at http://java.sun.com/products/jdk/1.2/docs/api/javax/swing/JTree.html

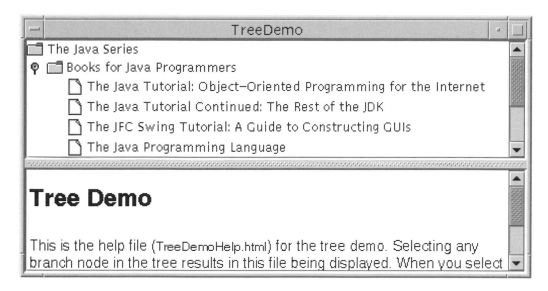

Figure 96 The `TreeDemo` application in which the top half displays a tree in a scroll pane.

Try this:

1. Compile and run the application.[1] The source file is <u>TreeDemo.java</u> (page 763). The program also looks for several HTML files—TreeDemoHelp.html, tutorial.html, tutorialcont.html, swingtutorial.html, arnold.html, faq.html, chanlee.html, thread.html, vm.html, and jls.html.[2]

2. Expand one or more nodes. You can do this by clicking the circle to the left of the item.

3. Collapse a node. You do this by clicking the circle to the left of an expanded node.

The following code, taken from `TreeDemo`, creates the `JTree` object:

```
DefaultMutableTreeNode top =
                    new DefaultMutableTreeNode("The Java Series");
createNodes(top);
final JTree tree = new JTree(top);
...
JScrollPane treeView = new JScrollPane(tree);
```

The code creates an instance of <u>DefaultMutableTreeNode</u>[3] to serve as the root node for the tree. The code then creates the rest of the nodes in the tree. After that it creates the tree, spec-

---

[1] See the chapter <u>Getting Started with Swing</u> (page 3) if you need help compiling or running this application.

[2] You can find these html files by visiting http://java.sun.com/docs/books/tutorial/uiswing/components/example-swing/index.html

[3] API documentation for `DefaultMutableTreeNode` is available on this book's CD-ROM and online at http://java.sun.com/products/jdk/1.2/docs/api/javax/swing/tree/DefaultMutableTreeNode.html

ifying the root node as an argument to the `JTree` constructor. Finally, the code puts the tree in a scroll pane, a common tactic because showing the full, expanded tree would otherwise require too much space.

Here is the code that creates the nodes under the root node:

```
private void createNodes(DefaultMutableTreeNode top) {
    DefaultMutableTreeNode category = null;
    DefaultMutableTreeNode book = null;
    category = new DefaultMutableTreeNode("Books for Java Programmers");
    top.add(category);

    //original Tutorial
    book = new DefaultMutableTreeNode(new BookInfo
      ("The Java Tutorial: Object-Oriented Programming for the Internet",
        "tutorial.html"));
    category.add(book);

    //Tutorial Continued
    book = new DefaultMutableTreeNode(new BookInfo
        ("The Java Tutorial Continued: The Rest of the JDK",
         "tutorialcont.html"));
    category.add(book);

    //JFC Swing Tutorial
    book = new DefaultMutableTreeNode(new BookInfo
        ("The JFC Swing Tutorial: A Guide to Constructing GUIs",
         "swingtutorial.html"));
    category.add(book);

    //...add many more books for programmers...
    category = new DefaultMutableTreeNode("Books for Java Implementers");
    top.add(category);
    //VM
    book = new DefaultMutableTreeNode(new BookInfo
        ("The Java Virtual Machine Specification",
         "vm.html"));
    category.add(book);

    //Language Spec
    book = new DefaultMutableTreeNode(new BookInfo
        ("The Java Language Specification",
         "jls.html"));
    category.add(book);
}
```

The argument to the `DefaultMutableTreeNode` constructor is the *user object*—an object that contains or points to the data associated with the tree node. The user object can be either a string or a custom object. If you implement a custom object, you should implement its toString method so that it returns the string to be displayed for that node.

For example, BookInfo, used in the previous code snippet, is a custom class that holds two pieces of data: the name of a book and the URL for an HTML file describing the book. The toString method is implemented to return the book name. Thus each node associated with a BookInfo object displays a book name.

Note: Swing 1.1.1 Beta 1 introduced the ability to specify HTML text for the string displayed by tree nodes. See <u>Using HTML on a Label</u> (page 213) for details.

To summarize, you can create a tree by invoking the JTree constructor, specifying the root node as an argument. You should probably put the tree inside a scroll pane so that the tree won't take up too much space. You don't have to do anything to make the tree nodes expand and collapse in response to user clicks. However, you do have to add some code to make the tree respond when the user selects a node—by clicking the node, for example.

Responding to Node Selection

Responding to tree node selections is simple. You implement a tree selection listener and register it on the tree. The following code shows the selection-related code from the TreeDemo program:

```
tree.getSelectionModel().setSelectionMode
        (TreeSelectionModel.SINGLE_TREE_SELECTION);

//Listen for when the selection changes.
tree.addTreeSelectionListener(new TreeSelectionListener() {
    public void valueChanged(TreeSelectionEvent e) {
        DefaultMutableTreeNode node = (DefaultMutableTreeNode)
                            tree.getLastSelectedPathComponent();

        if (node == null) return;

        Object nodeInfo = node.getUserObject();
        if (node.isLeaf()) {
            BookInfo book = (BookInfo)nodeInfo;
            displayURL(book.bookURL);
        } else {
            displayURL(helpURL);
        }
    }
});
```

The preceding code performs these tasks:

- Gets the default <u>`TreeSelectionModel`</u>[1] for the tree and then sets it up so that at most one tree node at a time can be selected.
- Creates an event handler and registers it on the tree. The event handler is an object that implements the <u>`TreeSelectionListener`</u>[2] interface.
- In the event handler, determines which node is selected by invoking the tree's `getLastSelectedPathComponent` method.
- Uses the `getUserObject` method to get the data associated with the node.

For more details about handling tree selection events, see <u>How to Write a Tree Selection Listener</u> (page 514).

Customizing a Tree's Display

Here is a picture of some tree nodes, as drawn by the Java, Windows, and Motif Look & Feel implementations.

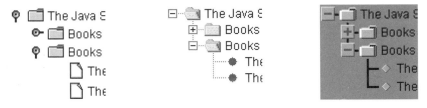

Figure 97   Three examples of tree nodes drawn by Java, Windows, and Motif Look & Feel
                implementations.

As the preceding figure shows, a tree conventionally displays an icon and some text for each node. You can customize these, as we'll show shortly.

A tree typically also performs some look-and-feel-specific painting to indicate relationships between nodes. You can customize this painting in a limited way. First, you can use `tree.setShowsRootHandles(true)` to request that a tree's top-level nodes—the root node (if it's visible) or its children (if not)—have handles that let them be expanded or collapsed. Second, if you're using the Java Look & Feel, you can customize whether lines are drawn to show relationships between tree nodes.

---

[1]   API documentation for `TreeSelectionModel` is available on this book's CD-ROM and online at
      http://java.sun.com/products/jdk/1.2/docs/api/javax/swing/tree/TreeSelectionModel.html
[2]   http://java.sun.com/products/jdk/1.2/docs/api/javax/swing/event/TreeSelectionListener.html

By default the Java Look & Feel draws no lines between nodes. By setting the `JTree.line-Style` client property of a tree, you can specify a different convention. For example, to request that the Java Look & Feel use horizontal lines to group nodes (as shown in Figure 98), use the following code:

```
tree.putClientProperty("JTree.lineStyle", "Horizontal");
```

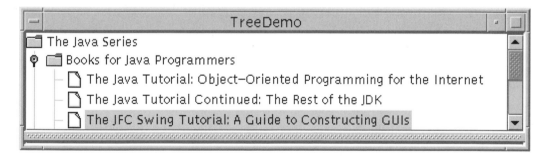

Figure 98 The `TreeDemo` application with horizontal lines to group nodes.

To specify that the Java Look & Feel should draw lines detailing the relationships between nodes (as shown in Figure 99), use this code:

```
tree.putClientProperty("JTree.lineStyle", "Angled");
```

Figure 99 The `TreeDemo` application with lines to show the hierarchy of nodes.

No matter what the look and feel, the default icon displayed by a node is determined by whether the node is a leaf and, if not, whether it's expanded. For example, in the Windows and Motif Look & Feel implementations the default icon for each leaf node is a dot; in the Java Look & Feel the default leaf icon is a paper-like symbol. In all of the look-and-feel implementations we've shown, branch nodes are marked with folder-like symbols. The Windows Look & Feel even has different icons to distinguish between expanded branches and collapsed branches.

You can easily change the default icon used for leaf, expanded branch, or collapsed branch nodes. To do so, you first create an instance of `DefaultTreeCellRenderer`.[1] Next, specify the icons to use by invoking one or more of the following methods on the renderer: `set-LeafIcon` (for leaf nodes), `setOpenIcon` (for expanded branch nodes), `setClosedIcon` (for collapsed branch nodes). If you want the tree to display no icon for a type of node, specify `null` for the icon. Once you've set up the icons, use the tree's `setCellRenderer` method to specify that the `DefaultTreeCellRenderer` paint its nodes.

Here is an example, taken from `TreeIconDemo.java` (page 766):

```
DefaultTreeCellRenderer renderer = new DefaultTreeCellRenderer();
    renderer.setLeafIcon(new ImageIcon("images/middle.gif"));
    tree.setCellRenderer(renderer);
```

Here is what the resulting UI looks like.

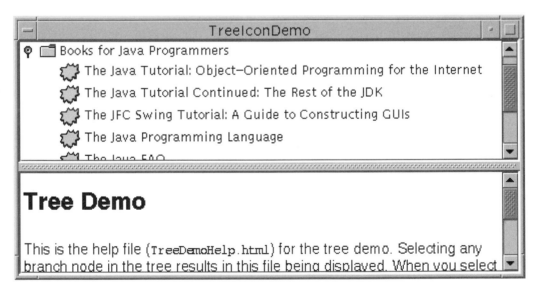

Figure 100 The `TreeIconDemo` application.

If you want finer control over the node icons or you want to provide tool tips, you can do so by creating a subclass of `DefaultTreeCellRenderer` and overriding the `getTreeCellRen-`

---

[1] API documentation for `DefaultTreeCellRenderer` is available on this book's CD-ROM and online at
     http://java.sun.com/products/jdk/1.2/docs/api/javax/swing/tree/DefaultTreeCellRenderer.html

dererComponent method. Because DefaultTreeCellRenderer is a subclass of JLabel, you can use any JLabel method—such as setIcon—to customize the DefaultTreeCellRenderer. Here is an example of creating a cell renderer that varies the leaf icon, depending on whether the word "Tutorial" is in the node's text data. The renderer also specifies tool tip text, as the boldface lines show. You can find the entire example in TreeIconDemo2.java (page 769).

```
//...where the tree is initialized:
//Enable tool tips.
ToolTipManager.sharedInstance().registerComponent(tree);
...
tree.setCellRenderer(new MyRenderer());
...

class MyRenderer extends DefaultTreeCellRenderer {
    ImageIcon tutorialIcon;

    public MyRenderer() {
        tutorialIcon = new ImageIcon("images/middle.gif");
    }

    public Component getTreeCellRendererComponent(
                        JTree tree,
                        Object value,
                        boolean sel,
                        boolean expanded,
                        boolean leaf,
                        int row,
                        boolean hasFocus) {
        super.getTreeCellRendererComponent(
                        tree, value, sel,
                        expanded, leaf, row,
                        hasFocus);
        if (leaf && isTutorialBook(value)) {
            setIcon(tutorialIcon);
            setToolTipText("This book is in the Tutorial series.");
        } else {
            setToolTipText(null); //no tool tip
        }
        return this;
    }

    protected boolean isTutorialBook(Object value) {
        DefaultMutableTreeNode node =
                (DefaultMutableTreeNode)value;
        BookInfo nodeInfo =
                (BookInfo)(node.getUserObject());
```

```
        String title = nodeInfo.bookName;
        if (title.indexOf("Tutorial") >= 0) {
            return true;
        }
        return false;
    }
}
```

The following screenshot shows the result.

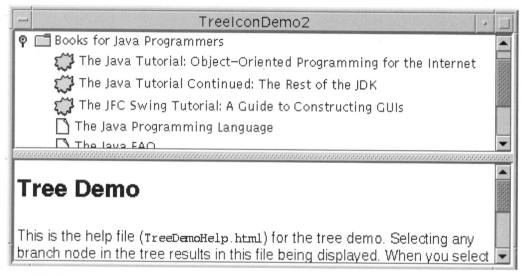

Figure 101 The `TreeIconDemo2` application.

You might be wondering how a cell renderer works. When a tree paints each node, neither the `JTree` nor its look-and-feel-specific implementation contains the code that paints the node. Instead the tree uses the cell renderer's painting code to paint the node. For example, to paint a leaf node that has the string "The Java Programming Language," the tree asks its cell renderer to return a component that can paint a leaf node with that string. If the cell renderer is a `DefaultTreeCellRenderer`, it returns a label that paints the default leaf icon followed by the string.

Note: Swing 1.1.1 Beta 1 and compatible releases allow you to specify HTML tags for tree nodes since these releases support HTML labels. See Using HTML on a Label (page 213) for details.

A cell renderer only paints; it cannot handle events. If you want to add event handling to a tree, you need to register your handler on either the tree or, if the handling occurs only when a node is selected, the tree's *cell editor*. For information about cell editors, see <u>Concepts:</u> <u>Cell Editors and Renderers</u> (page 264), which discusses table cell editors and renderers, which are similar to tree cell editors and renderers.

Dynamically Changing a Tree

The following figure shows an application that lets you add nodes to and remove nodes from a visible tree.[1] You can also edit the text in each node.

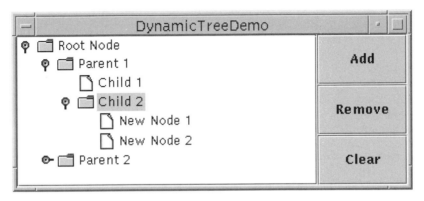

Figure 102 The `DynamicTreeDemo` application.

You can find the source code in <u>DynamicTreeDemo.java</u> (page 648) and <u>DynamicTree.java</u> (page 646). Here is the code that initializes the tree:

```
rootNode = new DefaultMutableTreeNode("Root Node");
treeModel = new DefaultTreeModel(rootNode);
tree = new JTree(treeModel);
tree.setEditable(true);
tree.getSelectionModel().setSelectionMode
        (TreeSelectionModel.SINGLE_TREE_SELECTION);
tree.setShowsRootHandles(true);
```

By explicitly creating the tree's model, the code guarantees that the tree's model is an instance of <u>DefaultTreeModel</u>.[2] Thus we know all of the methods that the tree model supports. For example, we know that we can invoke the model's `insertNodeInto` method, even though that method is not required by the `TreeModel` interface.

---

[1] The application is based on an example provided by tutorial reader Richard Stanford.
[2] API documentation for `DefaultTreeModel` is available on this book's CD-ROM and online at
    http://java.sun.com/products/jdk/1.2/docs/api/javax/swing/tree/DefaultTreeModel.html

To make the text in the tree's nodes editable, we invoke setEditable(true) on the tree. When the user has finished editing a node, the model generates a tree model event that tells any listeners that tree nodes have changed. To catch this event, we can implement a Tree-ModelListener. Here is an example of a tree model listener we implemented to detect when the user has typed in a new name for a tree node:

```
treeModel.addTreeModelListener(new MyTreeModelListener());
...
class MyTreeModelListener implements TreeModelListener {

    public void treeNodesChanged(TreeModelEvent e) {
        DefaultMutableTreeNode node;
        node = (DefaultMutableTreeNode)
                (e.getTreePath().getLastPathComponent());
        /*
         * If the event lists children, then the changed
         * node is the child of the node we've already
         * gotten.  Otherwise, the changed node and the
         * specified node are the same.
         */
        try {
            int index = e.getChildIndices()[0];
            node = (DefaultMutableTreeNode)
                    (node.getChildAt(index));
        } catch (NullPointerException exc) {}
        System.out.println("The user has finished editing the node.");
        System.out.println("New value: " + node.getUserObject());
    }

    public void treeNodesInserted(TreeModelEvent e) {
    }

    public void treeNodesRemoved(TreeModelEvent e) {
    }

    public void treeStructureChanged(TreeModelEvent e) {
    }
}
```

Here is the code that the Add button's event handler uses to add a new node to the tree:

```
public void actionPerformed(ActionEvent e) {
    treePanel.addObject("New Node " + newNodeSuffix++);
}
...

public DefaultMutableTreeNode addObject(Object child) {
    DefaultMutableTreeNode parentNode = null;
    TreePath parentPath = tree.getSelectionPath();
```

```
        if (parentPath == null) {
            //There's no selection. Default to the root node.
            parentNode = rootNode;
        } else {
            parentNode = (DefaultMutableTreeNode)
                        (parentPath.getLastPathComponent());
        }
        return addObject(parentNode, child, true);
    }
    ...

    public DefaultMutableTreeNode addObject(DefaultMutableTreeNode parent,
                                            Object child,
                                            boolean shouldBeVisible) {
        DefaultMutableTreeNode childNode =
            new DefaultMutableTreeNode(child);
        ...
        treeModel.insertNodeInto(childNode, parent,
                            parent.getChildCount());
        // Make sure the user can see the lovely new node.
        if (shouldBeVisible) {
            tree.scrollPathToVisible(new TreePath(childNode.getPath()));
        }
        return childNode;
    }
```

The code creates a node, inserts it into the tree model, and then, if appropriate, requests that the nodes above it be expanded and the tree scrolled so that the new node is visible. To insert the node into the model, the code uses the insertNodeInto method provided by the DefaultTreeModel class.

Creating a Data Model

If DefaultTreeModel doesn't suit your needs, you'll need to write a custom data model. Your data model must implement the TreeModel[1] interface. TreeModel specifies methods for getting a particular node of the tree, getting the number of children of a particular node, determining whether a node is a leaf, notifying the model of a change in the tree, and adding and removing tree model listeners.

Interestingly the TreeModel interface accepts any kind of object as a tree node. It doesn't require that nodes be represented by DefaultMutableTreeNode objects or even that nodes

---

[1] http://java.sun.com/products/jdk/1.2/docs/api/javax/swing/tree/TreeModel.html

implement the <u>TreeNode</u>[1] interface. Thus if the TreeNode interface isn't suitable for your tree model, feel free to devise your own representation for tree nodes.

The following figure shows an application that displays the descendants or ancestors of a particular person.[2]

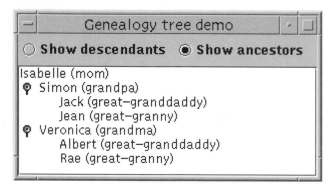

Figure 103 The GenealogyModel application.

You can find the custom tree model implementation in <u>GenealogyModel.java</u> (page 658). A simple JTree subclass that works with GenealogyModel is in <u>GenealogyTree.java</u> (page 660). The tree node class is defined in <u>Person.java</u> (page 691), and the application's GUI is created by the main method in <u>GenealogyExample.java</u> (page 656).

The Tree API

The tree API is quite extensive. The following tables list just a bit of the API, concentrating on the main categories. For more information about the tree API, see the API documentation for <u>JTree</u>[3] and for the various classes and interfaces in the <u>tree package</u>.[4] Also refer to <u>The JComponent Class</u> (page 67) for information on the API JTree inherits from its superclass.

---

[1] API documentation for TreeNode is available on this book's CD-ROM and online at http://java.sun.com/products/jdk/1.2/docs/api/javax/swing/tree/TreeNode.html

[2] Thanks to tutorial reader Olivier Berlanger for providing this example.

[3] http://java.sun.com/products/jdk/1.2/docs/api/javax/swing/JTree.html

[4] http://java.sun.com/products/jdk/1.2/docs/api/javax/swing/tree/package-summary.html

Table 137   Tree-Related Classes and Interfaces

Class/Interface	Purpose
`JTree`	The component that presents the tree to the user.
`MutableTreeNode,` `DefaultMutableTreeNode`	The interfaces that the default tree model expects its tree nodes to implement and the implementation used by the default tree model.
`TreeModel, DefaultTreeModel`	Respectively, the interface that a tree model must implement and the usual implementation used.
`TreeCellRenderer,` `DefaultTreeCellRenderer`	Respectively, the interface that a tree cell renderer must implement and the usual implementation used.
`TreeCellEditor,`[a] `DefaultTreeCellEditor`[b]	Respectively, the interface that a tree cell editor must implement and the usual implementation used.
`TreeSelectionModel,` `DefaultTreeSelectionModel`[c]	Respectively, the interface that the tree's selection model must implement and the usual implementation used.
`TreeSelectionListener,` `TreeSelectionEvent`[d]	The interface and event type used for detecting tree selection changes. For more information, see How to Write a Tree Selection Listener (page 514).
`TreeModelListener,` [e] `TreeModelEvent`[f]	The interface and event type used for detecting tree model changes. For more information, see How to Write a Tree Model Listener (page 512).
`TreeExpansionListener,`[g] `TreeWillExpandListener,`[h] `TreeExpansionEvent`[i]	The interfaces and event type used for detecting tree expansion and collapse. For more information, see How to Write a Tree-Will-Expand Listener (page 516).
`ExpandVetoException`[j]	An exception that a `TreeWillExpandListener` can throw to indicate that the impending expansion/collapse should not happen. For more information, see How to Write a Tree-Will-Expand Listener (page 516).

a. http://java.sun.com/products/jdk/1.2/docs/api/javax/swing/tree/TreeCellEditor.html
b. http://java.sun.com/products/jdk/1.2/docs/api/javax/swing/tree/DefaultTreeCellEditor.html
c. http://java.sun.com/products/jdk/1.2/docs/api/javax/swing/tree/DefaultTreeSelectionModel.html
d. http://java.sun.com/products/jdk/1.2/docs/api/javax/swing/event/TreeSelectionEvent.html
e. http://java.sun.com/products/jdk/1.2/docs/api/javax/swing/event/TreeModelListener.html
f. http://java.sun.com/products/jdk/1.2/docs/api/javax/swing/event/TreeModelEvent.html
g. http://java.sun.com/products/jdk/1.2/docs/api/javax/swing/event/TreeExpansionListener.html
h. http://java.sun.com/products/jdk/1.2/docs/api/javax/swing/event/TreeWillExpandListener.html
i. http://java.sun.com/products/jdk/1.2/docs/api/javax/swing/event/TreeExpansionEvent.html
j. http://java.sun.com/products/jdk/1.2/docs/api/javax/swing/tree/ExpandVetoException.html

Table 138   Creating and Setting Up a Tree

JTree Constructor/Method	Purpose

`JTree(TreeNode)`
`JTree(TreeNode, boolean)`
`JTree(TreeModel)`
`JTree()`
`JTree(Hashtable)`
`JTree(Object[])`
`JTree(Vector)`
	Create a tree. The `TreeNode` argument specifies the root node, to be managed by the default tree model. The `Tree-Model` argument specifies the model that provides the data to the table. The `boolean` argument specifies how the tree should determine whether a node can have children. The no-argument version of this constructor is for use in builders; it creates a tree that contains some sample data. If you specify a `Hashtable`, array of objects, or `Vector` as an argument, the argument is treated as a list of nodes under the root node (which is not displayed), and a model and tree nodes are constructed accordingly.

`void setCellRenderer(TreeCellRenderer)`	Sets the renderer that draws each node.
`void setEditable(boolean),` `void setCellEditor(TreeCellEditor)`	The first method sets whether the user can edit tree nodes. By default tree nodes are not editable. The second sets which customized editor to use.
`void setShowsRootHandles(boolean)`	Sets whether the tree shows handles for its leftmost nodes, letting you expand and collapse the nodes. The default is `false`. If the tree doesn't show the root node, you should invoke `setShowsRootHandles(true)`.

Table 139   Implementing Selection

Method	Purpose
`void addTreeSelectionListener(` `TreeSelectionListener)`	Register a listener to detect when the a node is selected or deselected.

`void setSelectionModel(`
`    TreeSelectionModel)`
`TreeSelectionModel getSelectionModel()`
	Set or get the model used to control node selections.

`void setSelectionMode(int)`
`int getSelectionMode()`
(in `TreeSelectionModel`)
	Set or get the selection mode. The value can be `CONTIGUOUS_TREE_SELECTION`, `DISCONTIGUOUS_TREE_SELECTION`, or `SINGLE_TREE_SELECTION` (all defined in `TreeSelectionModel`).

`Object getLastSelectionPathComponent()`	Get the object representing the currently selected node. This is equivalent to invoking `getLastPathComponent` on the value returned by `tree.getSelectionPath()`.
`void setSelectionPath(TreePath)` `TreePath getSelectionPath()`	Set or get the path to the currently selected node.

Table 139 Implementing Selection

Method	Purpose
void setSelectionPaths(TreePath[]) TreePath[] getSelectionPaths()	Set or get the paths to the currently selected nodes.
void setSelectionPath(TreePath) TreePath getSelectionPath()	Set or get the path to the currently selected node.

Table 140 Showing and Hiding Nodes

Method	Purpose

void addTreeExpansionListener(
    TreeExpansionListener)
void addTreeWillExpandListener(
    TreeWillExpandListener)
	Register a listener to detect when the tree nodes *have* expanded or collapsed, or *will be* expanded or collapsed, respectively. To veto an impending expansion or collapse, a TreeWillExpandListener can throw a ExpandVetoException.

void expandPath(TreePath) void collapsePath(TreePath)	Expand or collapse the specified tree path.
void scrollPathToVisible(TreePath)	Ensure that the node specified by the path is visible—that the path leading up to it is expanded and the node is in the scroll pane's viewing area.
void makeVisible(TreePath)	Ensure that the node specified by the path is viewable—that the path leading up to it is expanded. The node might not end up within the viewing area.
void setScrollsOnExpand(boolean) boolean getScrollsOnExpand()	Set or get whether the tree attempts to scroll to show previous hidden nodes. The default value is true.

Examples that Use Trees

This table lists examples that use JTree and where those examples are described.

Table 141 Examples that Use Trees

Example	Where Described	Notes
TreeDemo.java	Creating a Tree (page 320), Responding to Node Selection (page 323) and Customizing a Tree's Display (page 324)	Creates a tree that responds to user selections. It also has code for customizing the line style for the Java Look & Feel.
TreeIconDemo.java	Customizing a Tree's Display (page 324)	Adds a custom leaf icon to TreeDemo.

Table 141   Examples that Use Trees

Example	Where Described	Notes
TreeIconDemo2.java	<u>Customizing a Tree's Display</u> (page 324)	Customizes certain leaf icons and also provides tool tips for certain tree nodes.
DynamicTree.java, DynamicTreeDemo.java	<u>Dynamically Changing a Tree</u> (page 329)	Illustrates adding and removing nodes from a tree. Also allows editing of node text.
GenealogyTree.java, GenealogyModel.java	<u>Creating a Data Model</u> (page 331)	Implements a custom tree model.
TreeTable, TreeTable II	"Creating TreeTables in Swing," "Creating TreeTables: Part 2"[a]	Examples that combine a tree and table to show detailed information about a hierarchy such as a file system. The tree is a renderer for the table.

a. These articles are available in the online magazine, *The Swing Connection*, available at http://java.sun.com/products/jfc/tsc/index.html.

17

Solving Common Component Problems

THIS chapter discusses problems that you might encounter while using components. If you don't find your problem in this chapter, consult the following sections:

-
-
-
-
-

Problem: I can't make HTML tags work in my labels or buttons, etc. See JButton Features (page 172) for an example.

- Make sure your program is running in a release that supports HTML text in the desired component. Table 142 shows which releases support HTML in which components.

- `JCheckBox` and `JRadioButton` don't support HTML yet. We don't know yet when that support will be added.

- If you can't guarantee that your program will be executed only with a release that supports HTML text in the desired component, *don't use that feature!*

Table 142   Swing Releases and Component Support for HTML

Swing API Version	Corresponding JFC 1.1 Release	Corresponding Java 2 Release	Comments
Swing 1.1	JFC 1.1 (with Swing 1.1)	Java 2 v 1.2, Java 2 v 1.2.1	HTML supported in styled text components only.
Swing 1.1.1 Beta 1	JFC 1.1 (with Swing 1.1.1 Beta 1)	None	HTML support added for `JButton` and `JLabel`. Because table cells and tree nodes use labels to render strings, tables and trees automatically support HTML, as well.
Swing 1.1 Beta 2	JFC 1.1 (with Swing 1.1.1 Beta 2)	None	HTML support added for `JMenuItem`, `JMenu`, `JCheckBoxMenuItem`, `JRadioButtonMenuItem`, `JTabbedPane`, and `JToolTip`.
Swing 1.1.1 (*expected*)	JFC 1.1 (with Swing 1.1.1) (*expected*)	Java 2 v 1.2.2 (*expected*)	Same as Swing 1.1.1 Beta 2.

Problem: Certain areas of the content pane look weird when they're repainted.

- If you set the content pane, make sure it's opaque. `JPanel` and `JDesktopPane` make good content panes because they're opaque by default. See Adding Components to the Content Pane (page 79) for details.

- If one or more of your components performs custom painting, make sure you implemented it correctly. See Solving Common Graphics Problems (page 573) for help.

- You might have a thread safety problem. See the next entry.

Problem: My program is exhibiting weird symptoms that sometimes seem to be related to timing.

- Make sure your code is thread-safe. See Threads and Swing (page 45) for details.

Problem: The scroll bar policies don't seem to be working as advertised.

- Some Swing releases contain bugs in the implementations for the `VERTICAL_SCROLLBAR_AS_NEEDED` and the `HORIZONTAL_SCROLLBAR_AS_NEEDED` policies. If feasible for your project, use the most recent release of Swing.

- If the scroll pane's client can change size dynamically, the program should set the client's preferred size and then call `revalidate` on the client.

- Make sure you specified the policy you intended for the orientation you intended.

Problem: My scroll pane has no scroll bars.

- If you want a scroll bar to appear all the time, specify either `VERTICAL_SCROLLBAR_ALWAYS` or `HORIZONTAL_SCROLLBAR_ALWAYS` for the scroll bar policy as appropriate.

- If you want the scroll bars to appear as needed, and you want to force the scroll bars to be needed when the scroll pane is created, you have two choices: either set the preferred size of scroll pane or its container, or implement a scroll-savvy class and return a value smaller than the component's standard preferred size from the `getPreferred-ScrollableViewportSize` method. Refer to Sizing a Scroll Pane (page 122) for information.

Problem: The divider in my split pane won't move!

- You need to set the minimum size of at least one of the components in the split pane. Refer to Positioning the Divider and Restricting Its Range (page 129) for information.

Problem: The `setDividerLocation` method doesn't work.

- In some releases of Swing, there is a bug whereby a call to `setDividerLocation` doesn't work unless the split pane is already on screen. For information and possible workarounds, see bug #4101306 and bug #4182558 in the *Bug Parade* at the Java Developer's Connection at `http://developer.java.sun.com/`.

Problem: The borders on nested split panes look too wide.

- If you nest split panes, the borders accumulate—the border of the inner split panes display next to the border of the outer split pane causing borders that look extra wide. The problem is particularly noticeable when nesting many split panes. The workaround is to set the border to null on any split pane that is placed within another split pane. For information, see bug #4131528 in the *Bug Parade* at the Java Developer's Connection online at `http://developer.java.sun.com/`.

Problem: The buttons in my tool bar are too big.

- Try reducing the margin for the buttons. For example:
  ```
  button.setMargin(new Insets(0,0,0,0));
  ```

Problem: The components in my layered pane aren't layered correctly. In fact, the layers seem to be inversed—the lower the depth the higher the component.

- This can happen if you use an `int` instead of an `Integer` when adding components to a layered pane. To see what happens, make the following change to `Layered-PaneDemo`:

Change this...	to this...
`layeredPane.add(label, new Integer(i));`	`layeredPane.add(label, i);`

Problem: The method call *colorChooser*.`setPreviewPanel(null)` does not remove the color chooser's preview panel as expected.

- A `null` argument specifies the default preview panel. To remove the preview panel, specify a standard panel with no size, like this: *colorChooser*.`setPreview-Panel(new JPanel());`

Laying Out Components

THIS lesson tells you how to use layout managers that the Java™ platform provides. The lesson also tells you how to use absolute positioning (no layout manager) and gives two examples of writing custom layout managers. For each layout manager (or lack thereof), this lesson provides an example that can run either as an applet or as an application. By resizing the window the example brings up, you can see how size changes affect the layout.

Before reading this lesson, you should understand basic layout management concepts, which you can find in <u>Layout Management</u> (page 33).

<u>Using Layout Managers</u> (page 343)
This chapter gives both general rules and detailed instructions on using each of the layout managers that the Java™ platform provides.

<u>Creating a Custom Layout Manager</u> (page 379)
Instead of using one of the Java platform's layout managers, you can write your own. Layout managers must implement the `LayoutManager` interface, which specifies the five methods every layout manager must define. Optionally layout managers can implement `LayoutManager2`, which is a subinterface of `LayoutManager`.

<u>Doing Without a Layout Manager (Absolute Positioning)</u> (page 383)
If necessary, you can position components without using a layout manager. Generally this solution is used to specify absolute sizes and positions for components.

18

Using Layout Managers

BY default every container has a layout manager—an object that implements the LayoutManager interface. If a container's default layout manager doesn't suit your needs, you can easily replace it with another one. The Java platform supplies layout managers that range from the very simple (FlowLayout and GridLayout) to the special purpose (BorderLayout and CardLayout) to the very flexible (GridBagLayout and BoxLayout).

This chapter gives you an overview of some layout managers that the Java platform provides, gives you some general rules for using layout managers, and then tells you how to use each of the provided layout managers. The chapter also points to examples of using each layout manager.

Here's a quick summary of the various layout managers.

BorderLayout

> BorderLayout is the default layout manager for every content pane. As described in Using Top-Level Containers (page 77), the content pane is the main container in all frames, applets, and dialogs. A BorderLayout has five areas available to hold components: north, south, east, west, and center. All extra space is placed in the center area. See How to Use BorderLayout (page 347).

BoxLayout

> The BoxLayout class puts components in a single row or column. This class respects the components' requested maximum sizes and also lets you align components. See How to Use BoxLayout (page 350).

CardLayout

> The CardLayout class lets you implement an area that contains different components at different times. Tabbed panes are intermediate Swing containers that provide

similar functionality but with a predefined GUI. A `CardLayout` is often controlled by a combo box, with the state of the combo box determining which panel (group of components) the `CardLayout` displays. See <u>How to Use CardLayout</u> (page 363).

FlowLayout

`FlowLayout` is the default layout manager for every `JPanel`. This layout manager simply lays out components from left to right, starting new rows, if necessary. See <u>How to Use FlowLayout</u> (page 366).

GridLayout

`GridLayout` simply makes a bunch of components equal in size and displays them in the requested number of rows and columns. See <u>How to Use GridLayout</u> (page 368).

GridBagLayout

`GridBagLayout` is the most sophisticated, flexible layout manager the Java platform provides. This layout manager aligns components by placing them within a grid of cells, allowing some components to span more than one cell. The rows in the grid aren't necessarily all the same height; similarly grid columns can have different widths. See <u>How to Use GridBagLayout</u> (page 370).

Note: In JDK^{TM} 1.1 a second interface, `LayoutManager2`, was introduced. It extends `LayoutManager`, providing support for maximum size and alignment. Currently only `BoxLayout` implements `LayoutManager2`. All of the other layout managers that we discuss implement only `LayoutManager`.

General Rules for Using Layout Managers

As a rule, the only time you have to think about layout managers is when you create a `JPanel` or add components to a content pane. If you don't like the default layout manager that a panel or content pane uses, you can change it to a different one. When you add components to a panel or a content pane, the arguments you specify to the `add` method depend on the layout manager that the panel or content pane is using.

The other Swing containers are more specialized and tend to hide the details of which layout manager, if any, they use. For example, a scroll pane relies on a layout manager named `ScrollPaneLayout`, but you don't need to know that to use a scroll pane. Most Swing containers provide API that you can use instead of the `add` method. For example, instead of adding a component directly to a scroll pane (or, rather, to its viewport), you either specify the component in the `JScrollPane` constructor or use `setViewportView`. For information about how to add components to a specific container, see the how-to section for the container. Use <u>A Visual Index to Swing Components</u> (page 63) to find the how-to sections.

Choosing a Layout Manager

Layout managers have different strengths and weaknesses. This section discusses some common layout scenarios and which layout managers might work for each scenario. If none of the layout managers we discuss is right for your situation, feel free to use other layout managers that you write or find.

Scenario: Display a component in as much space as it can get.

Consider using `BorderLayout` or `GridBagLayout`. If you use `BorderLayout`, you'll need to put the space-hungry component in the center. If you use `GridBagLayout`, you'll need to set the constraints for the component so that `fill=GridBagConstraints.BOTH`. Another possibility is to use `BoxLayout`, making the space-hungry component specify very large preferred and maximum sizes.

Scenario: Display a few components at their natural size in a compact row.

Consider using a `JPanel` to group the components and using either the `JPanel`'s default `FlowLayout` manager or the `BoxLayout` manager.

Scenario: Display a few components of the same size in rows and columns.

`GridLayout` is perfect for this.

Scenario: Display a few components in a row or column, possibly with varying amounts of space between them, custom alignment, or custom component sizes.

`BoxLayout` is perfect for this.

Scenario: A complex layout has many components.

Consider either using `GridBagLayout` or grouping the components into one or more `JPanel`s to simplify layout. Each `JPanel` might use a different layout manager.

Creating a Layout Manager and Associating It with a Container

As mentioned in <u>Layout Management</u> (page 33), each container either has a layout manager or uses absolute positioning. All `JPanel` objects are use a `FlowLayout` by default Content panes (the main containers in `JApplet`, `JDialog`, and `JFrame` objects) use `BorderLayout` by default.

If you want to use a container's default layout manager, you don't have to do a thing. The constructor for the container creates a layout manager instance and initializes the container to use it.

To use a layout manager other than the default layout manager, you must create an instance of the desired layout manager class and tell the container to use it. The following statement creates a `BorderLayout` manager and sets it up as the layout manager for a panel:

```
aJPanel.setLayout(new BorderLayout());
```

Here is an example of making a `FlowLayout` object the layout manager for an applet's content pane:

```
//In a JApplet subclass:
Container contentPane = getContentPane();
contentPane.setLayout(new FlowLayout());
```

For examples of creating each layout manager, see the how-to section for the particular layout manager.

When Is a Layout Manager Consulted?

A container's layout manager is automatically consulted each time the container might need to change its appearance. For example, the layout manager is consulted whenever the user adds a component to a container. Most layout managers don't require programs to directly call their methods.

Only a few component methods result in a layout manager's actually performing layout: the `JComponent revalidate` method, the `Window pack` method, and the `Window show` and `setVisible` methods. Other methods that result in calls to a container's layout manager (but don't trigger a new layout) include the `Container add`, `remove`, `removeAll`, `getAlignmentX`, `getAlignmentY`, `getPreferredSize`, `getMinimumSize`, and `getMaximumSize` methods.

If you change the size of a component, even indirectly by changing its font, for example, the component should automatically resize and repaint itself. If that doesn't happen—because you made the change to the component's data model instead of the component, for example—you should invoke the `revalidate` method on the component.

When you invoke `revalidate` on a component, a request is passed up the containment hierarchy until it encounters a container, such as a scroll pane or a top-level container, that shouldn't be affected by the component's resizing. (This is determined by calling the container's `isValidateRoot` method.) The container is then laid out, which has the effect of adjusting the revalidated component's size and the size of all affected components.

After calling `revalidate` on a component, you can invoke `repaint` on it to make the change appear on-screen. Both `revalidate` and `repaint` are thread safe; you needn't invoke them from the event-dispatching thread.

How to Use BorderLayout

Here's an applet that shows a <u>BorderLayout</u>[1] in action.

Figure 104 An applet that uses BorderLayout.

As the preceding applet shows, a BorderLayout has five areas: north, south, east, west, and center. If you enlarge the window, the center area gets as much of the available space as possible. The other areas expand only as much as necessary to fill all available space. Often a container uses only one or two of the areas of the BorderLayout—just the center or just the center and south, for example.

The following code creates the BorderLayout and the components it manages. You can find the whole program in <u>BorderWindow.java</u> (page 786). The program runs either within an applet (with the help of AppletButton) or as an application.

```
Container contentPane = getContentPane();

//Use the content pane's default BorderLayout.
//contentPane.setLayout(new BorderLayout()); //unnecessary

contentPane.add(new JButton("Button 1 (NORTH)"),
                BorderLayout.NORTH);
contentPane.add(new JButton("2 (CENTER)"),
                BorderLayout.CENTER);
contentPane.add(new JButton("Button 3 (WEST)"),
                BorderLayout.WEST);
```

---

[1] http://java.sun.com/products/jdk/1.2/docs/api/java/awt/BorderLayout.html

```
contentPane.add(new JButton("Long-Named Button 4 (SOUTH)"),
                BorderLayout.SOUTH);
contentPane.add(new JButton("Button 5 (EAST)"),
                BorderLayout.EAST);
```

Important: When adding a component to a container that uses `BorderLayout`, specify the component's location as one of the arguments to the `add` method. Do not rely on the component's being added by default to the center. If you find that a component is missing from a container controlled by a `BorderLayout`, make sure that you specified the component's location and that you didn't put another component in the same location.

All of our examples that use `BorderLayout` specify the component as the first argument to the `add` method. For example:

```
add(component, BorderLayout.CENTER)  //preferred
```

However, in other programs you might see code that specifies the component second. For example, the following are alternative ways of writing the preceding code:

```
add(BorderLayout.CENTER, component)  //valid but old-fashioned
```

or

```
add("Center", component)             //valid but error prone
```

The BorderLayout API

By default a `BorderLayout` puts no gap between the components it manages. In the preceding applet any apparent gaps are the result of the buttons' reserving extra space around their apparent display areas. You can specify gaps, in pixels, using the following constructor:

```
BorderLayout(int horizontalGap, int verticalGap)
```

You can also use the following methods to set the horizontal and vertical gaps, respectively:

```
void setHgap(int)
void setVgap(int)
```

Examples that Use BorderLayout

The following table lists some of the many examples that use `BorderLayout`.

Table 143   Examples that Use `BorderLayout`

Example	Where Described	Notes
`BorderWindow.java`	This section	Puts a component in each of the five possible locations.
`TabbedPaneDemo.java`	How to Use Tabbed Panes (page 134)	One of many examples that puts a single component in the center of a content pane, so that the component is as large as possible.
`CheckBoxDemo.java`	How to Use Check Boxes (page 177)	Creates a `JPanel` that uses a `BorderLayout` and puts components into the west and center locations.

How to Use BoxLayout

The Swing packages include a general-purpose layout manager named <u>BoxLayout</u>.[1] Box-Layout either stacks its components on top of each other (with the first component at the top) or places them in a tight row from left to right—your choice. You might think of it as a full-featured version of FlowLayout. Here is an applet that demonstrates using BoxLayout to display a centered column of components.

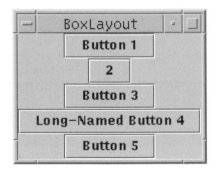

Figure 105 An applet that uses BoxLayout.

By creating one or more lightweight containers that use BoxLayout, you can achieve some layouts for which the more complex GridBagLayout is often used. BoxLayout is also useful in some situations in which you might consider using GridLayout or BorderLayout. One big difference between BoxLayout and the existing AWT layout managers is that BoxLayout respects each component's maximum size and *X*, *Y* alignment. We'll discuss that later.

The following figure shows a GUI that uses two instances of BoxLayout. In the top part of the GUI, a top-to-bottom box layout places a label above a scroll pane. In the bottom part of the GUI, a left-to-right box layout places two buttons next to each other. A BorderLayout combines the two parts of the GUI and ensures that any excess space is given to the scroll pane.

---

[1] http://java.sun.com/products/jdk/1.2/docs/api/javax/swing/BoxLayout.html

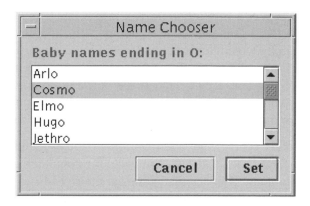

Figure 106 An applet that uses two instances of BoxLayout.

The following code, taken from <u>ListDialog.java</u> (page 678), lays out the GUI. This code is in the constructor for the dialog, which is implemented as a JDialog subclass. The boldface lines of code set up the box layouts and add components to them.

```
JScrollPane listScroller = new JScrollPane(list);
listScroller.setPreferredSize(new Dimension(250, 80));
listScroller.setMinimumSize(new Dimension(250, 80));
listScroller.setAlignmentX(LEFT_ALIGNMENT);
...

//Lay out the label and scroll pane from top to bottom.
JPanel listPane = new JPanel();
listPane.setLayout(new BoxLayout(listPane, BoxLayout.Y_AXIS));
JLabel label = new JLabel(labelText);
listPane.add(label);
listPane.add(Box.createRigidArea(new Dimension(0,5)));
listPane.add(listScroller);
listPane.setBorder(BorderFactory.createEmptyBorder(10,10,10,10));

//Lay out the buttons from left to right.
JPanel buttonPane = new JPanel();
buttonPane.setLayout(new BoxLayout(buttonPane, BoxLayout.X_AXIS));
buttonPane.setBorder(BorderFactory.createEmptyBorder(0, 10, 10, 10));
buttonPane.add(Box.createHorizontalGlue());
buttonPane.add(cancelButton);
buttonPane.add(Box.createRigidArea(new Dimension(10, 0)));
buttonPane.add(setButton);

//Put everything together, using the content pane's BorderLayout.
Container contentPane = getContentPane();
contentPane.add(listPane, BorderLayout.CENTER);
contentPane.add(buttonPane, BorderLayout.SOUTH);
```

The first boldface line creates a top-to-bottom box layout and sets it up as the layout manager for `listPane`. The two arguments to the `BoxLayout` constructor are the container that it manages and the axis along which the components will be laid out. The next three boldface lines add the label and the scroll pane to the container, separating them with a *rigid area*—an invisible lightweight component used to add space between components. In this case the rigid area has no width and puts exactly 5 pixels between the label and the scroll pane. Rigid areas are discussed later, in <u>Invisible Components as Filler</u> (page 355).

The next chunk of boldface code creates a left-to-right box layout and sets it up for the `buttonPane` container. Then the code adds two buttons to the container, using a rigid area to put 10 pixels between the buttons. To place the buttons at the right-hand side of their container, the first component added to the container is *glue*. This glue is an invisible lightweight component that grows as necessary to absorb any extra space in its container. Glue is discussed in <u>Invisible Components as Filler</u> (page 355).

As an alternative to using invisible components, you can sometimes use empty borders to create space around components. For example, the preceding code snippet uses empty borders to put 10 pixels between all sides of the dialog and its contents, and between the two parts of the contents. Borders are completely independent of layout managers. They're simply how Swing components draw their edges. See <u>How to Use Borders</u> (page 408) for more information.

Don't let the length of the `BoxLayout` discussion intimidate you. You can probably use `BoxLayout` with the information you already have. If you run into trouble or you want to take advantage of `BoxLayout`'s power, read on.

BoxLayout Features

As we said before, a `BoxLayout` arranges components either from top to bottom or from left to right. As it arranges components, `BoxLayout` takes the components' alignments and minimum, preferred, and maximum sizes into account. In this section, we'll talk about top-to-bottom (*Y*-axis) layout. The same concepts apply to left-to-right layout. You simply substitute *X* for *Y*, height for width, and so on.

When a `BoxLayout` lays out components from top to bottom, it tries to size each component at the component's preferred height. If the amount of vertical space is not ideal, `BoxLayout` tries to adjust each component's height so that the components fill the available amount of space. However, the components might not fit exactly, since `BoxLayout` respects each component's requested minimum and maximum heights. Any extra space appears at the bottom of the container.

A top-to-bottom `BoxLayout` tries to make all of its container's components equally wide— as wide as the largest preferred width. If the container is forced to be wider than that, `Box-`

Layout tries to make all of the components as wide as the container. If the components aren't all the same width (due to restricted maximum size or to any of them having strict left or right alignment), *X* alignment comes into play.

Components' *X* alignments affect not only the components' positions relative to each other but also the location of the components, as a group, within their container. The following figure illustrates alignment of components that have restricted maximum widths.

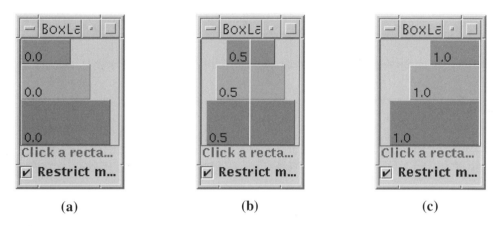

Figure 107 Left (a), center (b), and right (c) alignment of components with restricted maximum widths.

In left alignment, all three components have an *X* alignment of 0.0 (`Compo-nent.LEFT_ALIGNMENT`). This means that the components' left sides should be aligned. Furthermore it means that all three components are positioned as far left in their container as possible.

In center alignment, all three components have an *X* alignment of 0.5 (`Compo-nent.CENTER_ALIGNMENT`). This means that the components' centers should be aligned and that the components should be positioned in the horizontal center of their container.

In right alignment, the components have an *X* alignment of 1.0 (`Compo-nent.RIGHT_ALIGNMENT`). You can guess what that means for the components' alignment and position relative to their container.

You might be wondering what happens when the components have both restricted maximum sizes and different *X* alignments. The next figure shows an example of this.

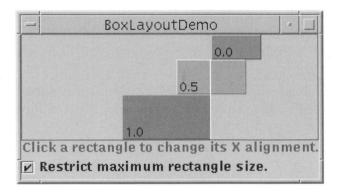

Figure 108 The components have both restricted maximum sizes and different *X* alignments.

As you can see, the left-hand side of the component with an *X* alignment of 0.0 (`Compo-nent.LEFT_ALIGNMENT`) is aligned with the center of the component that has the 0.5 *X* alignment (`Component.CENTER_ALIGNMENT`), which is aligned with the right-hand side of the component that has an *X* alignment of 1.0 (`Component.RIGHT_ALIGNMENT`). Mixed alignments like this are further discussed in Fixing Alignment Problems (page 357).

What if none of the components has a maximum width? Well, if all of the components have identical *X* alignment, they all are made as wide as their container. If the *X* alignments are different, then any component with an *X* alignment of 0.0 (left) or 1.0 (right) will be smaller. All components with an intermediate *X* alignment (such as center) will be as wide as their container. Figure 109 shows two examples.

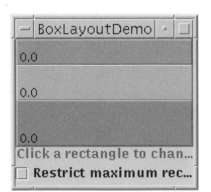 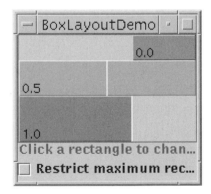

Figure 109 Two examples in which the components do not have set maximum widths.

To get to know `BoxLayout` better, you can run your own experiments with `BoxLayoutDemo`. Try this:

1. Compile and run `BoxLayoutDemo`.[1] The source files are `BoxLayoutDemo.java` (page 787) and `BLDComponent.java` (page 782). You'll see a window that contains three rectangles. Each rectangle is an instance of `BLDComponent`, which is a `JComponent` subclass.

2. Click inside one of the rectangles. This is how you change the rectangle's *X* alignment.

3. Click the check box at the bottom of the window. This turns off restricted sizing for all of the rectangles.

4. Make the window taller. This makes the rectangles' container larger than the sum of the rectangles' preferred sizes. The container is a `JPanel` that has a red outline, so that you can tell where the container's edges are.

Invisible Components as Filler

Each component controlled by a `BoxLayout` butts up against its neighboring components. If you want to have space between components, you can either add an empty border to one or both components, or you can insert invisible components to provide the space. You can create invisible components with the help of the `Box`[2] class.

The `Box` class provides an inner class, `Box.Filler`,[3] that provides invisible components. The `Box` class provides convenience methods to help you create common kinds of filler. The following table gives details about creating invisible components with `Box` and `Box.Filler`.

Table 144   How to Create Invisible Components with `Box` and `Box.Filler`

Type	Size Constraints	How to Create
Rigid area	▢	`Box.createRigidArea(size)`
Glue	◀—●—▶	`Box.createHorizontalGlue()`
	▲●▼	`Box.createVerticalGlue()`
Custom `Box.Filler`	as specified	`new Box.Filler(minSize, prefSize, maxSize)`

---

[1]   See the chapter Getting Started with Swing (page 3) if you need help compiling or running this application.
[2]   http://java.sun.com/products/jdk/1.2/docs/api/javax/swing/Box.html
[3]   http://java.sun.com/products/jdk/1.2/docs/api/javax/swing/Box.Filler.html

Here's how you generally use each type of filler.

Rigid area

Use this when you want a fixed-size space between two components. For example, to put 5 pixels between two components in a left-to-right box, you can use this code:

```
container.add(firstComponent);
container.add(Box.createRigidArea(new Dimension(5,0)));
container.add(secondComponent);
```

Figure 110 With and without a rigid area.

Note: The Box class provides another kind of filler for putting fixed space between components: a vertical or horizontal strut. Unfortunately struts have unlimited maximum heights or widths (for horizontal and vertical struts, respectively). This means that if you use a horizontal box within a vertical box, for example, the horizontal box can sometimes become too tall. Therefore we recommend that you use rigid areas instead of struts.

Glue

Use this to specify where excess space in a layout should go. Think of glue as semi-wet paste—stretchy and expandable yet taking up no space unless you pull apart the components that it's sticking to. For example, by putting horizontal glue between two components in a left-to-right box, you make any extra space go between those components, instead of to the right of all the components. Here's an example of making the space in a left-to-right box go between two components instead of to the right of the components:

```
container.add(firstComponent);
container.add(Box.createHorizontalGlue());
container.add(secondComponent);;
```

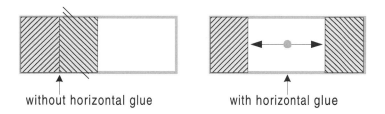

Figure 111 With and without horizontal glue.

Custom Box.Filler

Use this to specify a component with whatever minimum, preferred, and maximum sizes you want. For example, to create some filler in a left-to-right layout that puts at least 5 pixels between two components and ensures that the container has a minimum height of 100 pixels, you could use this code:

```
container.add(firstComponent);
Dimension minSize = new Dimension(5, 100);
Dimension prefSize = new Dimension(5, 100);
Dimension maxSize = new Dimension(Short.MAX_VALUE,100);
container.add(new Box.Filler(minSize, prefSize, maxSize));
container.add(secondComponent);
```

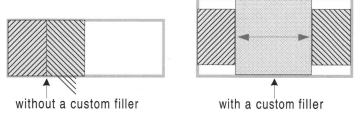

Figure 112 With and without a custom filler.

Fixing Alignment Problems

Two types of alignment problems sometimes occur with BoxLayout:

- A group of components all have the same alignment, which you want to change to make them look better. For example, instead of having the centers of a group of left-to-right buttons all in a line, you might want the bottoms of the buttons to be aligned. Figure 113 shows an example.

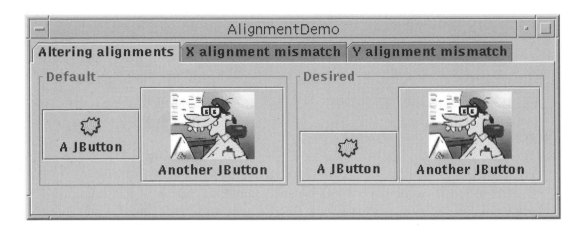

Figure 113 You can alter the default alignment of components.

- Two or more components controlled by a BoxLayout have different default alignments, which causes them to be misaligned. For example, as the following shows, if a
  label and a panel are in a top-to-bottom box layout, the label's left edge is, by default,
  aligned with the center of the panel.

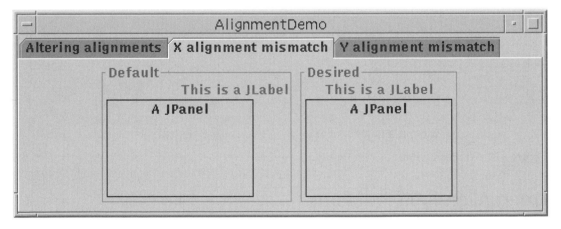

Figure 114 Misalignment can occur when two or more components controlled by a BoxLayout have
           different default alignments.

In general, all of the components controlled by a top-to-bottom BoxLayout object should
have the same *X* alignment. Similarly all of the components controlled by a left-to-right
BoxLayout should generally have the same *Y* alignment. You can set a JComponent's *X*
alignment by invoking its setAlignmentX method. An alternative available to all compo-

nents is to override the getAlignmentX method in a custom subclass of the component class. Similarly you set the *Y* alignment of a component by invoking the setAlignmentY method or by overriding getAlignmentY.

Here is an example, taken from AlignmentDemo.java (page 779), of changing the *Y* alignments of two buttons so that their bottoms are aligned:

```
button1.setAlignmentY(Component.BOTTOM_ALIGNMENT);
button2.setAlignmentY(Component.BOTTOM_ALIGNMENT);
```

By default most components have center *X* and *Y* alignment. However, buttons, combo boxes, labels, and menu items have a different default *X* alignment value: LEFT_ALIGNMENT. The previous picture shows what happens if you put a left-aligned component, such as a label, together with a center-aligned component in a container controlled by a top-to-bottom BoxLayout.

The AlignmentDemo.java program gives examples of fixing mismatched alignment problems. Usually it's as simple as making an offending button or label be center aligned. For example:

```
label.setAlignmentX(Component.CENTER_ALIGNMENT);
```

Specifying Component Sizes

As we mentioned before, BoxLayout pays attention to a component's requested minimum, preferred, and maximum sizes. While you're fine tuning the layout, you might need to adjust these sizes.

Sometimes the need to adjust the size is obvious. For example, a button's maximum size is generally the same as its preferred size. If you want the button to be drawn wider when additional space is available, you need to change its maximum size.

Sometimes, however, the need to adjust size is not so obvious. You might be getting unexpected results with a box layout, and you might not know why. In this case it's usually best to treat the problem as an alignment problem first. If adjusting the alignments doesn't help, you might have a size problem. We'll discuss this further a bit later.

Note: Although BoxLayout pays attention to a component's maximum size, most layout managers do not. For example, if you put a button in the south part of a BorderLayout, the button will probably be wider than its preferred width, no matter what the button's maximum size is. BoxLayout, on the other hand, never makes a button wider than its maximum size.

You can change the minimum, preferred, and maximum sizes in two ways:

- By invoking the appropriate set*Xxx*Size method, which is defined by the JComponent class. For example:

```
comp.setMinimumSize(new Dimension(50, 25));
comp.setPreferredSize(new Dimension(50, 25));
comp.setMaximumSize(new
        Dimension(Short.MAX_VALUE, Short.MAX_VALUE));
```

- By overriding the appropriate get*Xxx*Size method. For example:

```
...//in a subclass of a component class:
public Dimension getMaximumSize() {
    size = getPreferredSize();
    size.width = Short.MAX_VALUE;
    return size;
}
```

If you're running into trouble with a BoxLayout and you've ruled out alignment problems, the trouble might well be size-related. For example, if the container controlled by the Box-Layout is taking up too much space, one or more of the components in the container probably needs to have its maximum size restricted.

You can use two techniques to track down size trouble in a BoxLayout:

- Add a garish line border to the outside of the components in question. This lets you see what size they really are. For example:

```
comp.setBorder(BorderFactory.createCompoundBorder(
        BorderFactory.createLineBorder(Color.red), comp.getBorder()));
```

- Use good old System.out.println to print the components' minimum, preferred, and maximum sizes, and perhaps their bounds.

The BoxLayout API

The following tables list the commonly used BoxLayout and Box constructors and methods.

Table 145   Creating BoxLayout Objects

Constructor or Method	**Purpose**
BoxLayout(Container, int)	Create a BoxLayout instance that controls the specified Container. The integer argument specifies whether the container's components should be laid out left to right(Box-Layout.X_AXIS) or top to bottom (BoxLayout.Y_AXIS).

Table 145   Creating BoxLayout Objects

Constructor or Method	Purpose
Box(int)	Create a Box—a lightweight container that uses a BoxLayout with the specified alignment (BoxLayout.X_AXIS or Box-Layout.Y_AXIS). Note that a Box is *not* a JComponent—it's implemented as a subclass of Container. This makes it as lightweight as possible, but it lacks JComponent features, such as borders. If you want a simple JComponent as a container, use JPanel.
static Box createHorizontalBox()	Create a Box that lays out its components from left to right.
static Box createVerticalBox()	Create a Box that lays out its components from top to bottom.

Table 146   Creating Space Fillers

Constructor or Method	Purpose
Component createHorizontalGlue() Component createVerticalGlue() Component createGlue()	Create a glue lightweight component. Horizontal glue and vertical glue can be very useful.
Component createRigidArea()	Create a rigid area lightweight component.
Component createHorizontalStrut() Component createVerticalStrut()	Create a "strut" lightweight component. We recommend using rigid areas instead of struts.
Box.Filler(Dimension, Dimension, Dimension)	Create a lightweight component with the specified minimum, preferred, and maximum sizes, with the arguments specified in that order. See the custom Box.Filler discussion, earlier in this section, for details.

Table 147   Other Useful Methods

Method	Purpose
void changeShape(Dimension, Dimension, Dimension) (in Box.Filler)	Change the minimum, preferred, and maximum sizes of the recipient Box.Filler object. The layout changes accordingly.

Examples that Use Box Layouts

The following table lists some of the many examples that use BoxLayouts.

Table 148   Examples that Use BoxLayout

Example	Where Described	Notes
BoxWindow.java	This section	Uses a BoxLayout to create a centered column of components.
AlignmentDemo.java	This section	Demonstrates how to fix common alignment problems. Uses two image files: images/middle.gif and images/geek-cght.gif.
BoxLayoutDemo.java	This section	Lets you play with alignments and maximum sizes.
ListDialog.java	This section	A simple yet realistic example of using both a top-to-bottom BoxLayout and a left-to-right one. Uses horizontal glue, rigid areas, and empty borders. Also sets the *X* alignment of a component.
InternalFrameEventDemo.java	How to Write an Internal Frame Listener (page 480)	Uses a top-to-bottom layout to center buttons and a scroll pane in an internal frame.
MenuGlueDemo.java	Customizing Menu Layout (page 234)	Shows how to right-align a menu in the menu bar, using a glue component.
MenuLayoutDemo.java	Customizing Menu Layout (page 234)	Shows how to customize menu layout by changing the menu bar to use a top-to-bottom BoxLayout, and the pop-up menu to use a left-to-right BoxLayout.
ConversionPanel.java	Layout Management and Borders (page 54)	Aligns two components in different BoxLayout-controlled containers by setting the components' widths to be the same and their containers' widths to be the same.

How to Use CardLayout

Here's the GUI of a program that shows a <u>CardLayout</u>[1] in action.

Figure 115 A simple GUI that uses CardLayout.

As the preceding program shows, the CardLayout class helps you manage two or more components (usually JPanel instances) that share the same display space. Another way to accomplish the same thing is to use a tabbed pane. Here's what the preceding applet looks like when rewritten to use a tabbed pane.

Figure 116 The GUI reworked to use a tabbed pane rather than CardLayout.

Because a tabbed pane provides a GUI, using a tabbed pane is simpler than using CardLayout. For example, reimplementing the preceding applet to use a tabbed pane results in a program with 12 fewer lines of code. You can see the program's revised code in <u>TabWindow.java</u> (page 804). The CardLayout version of the program is in <u>CardWindow.java</u> (page 789).

---

[1] http://java.sun.com/products/jdk/1.2/docs/api/java/awt/CardLayout.html

Conceptually, each component that a `CardLayout` manages is like a playing card or a trading card in a stack, with only the top card visible at any time. You can choose the card that's showing in any of the following ways:

- By asking for either the first or last card, in the order it was added to the container.
- By flipping through the deck backward or forward.
- By specifying a card with a specific name. This is the scheme the sample program uses. Specifically the user can choose a card (component) by selecting it by name from a pop-up list of choices.

The following code creates the `CardLayout` and the components it manages. The program runs either within an applet, with the help of `AppletButton.java` (page 783), or as an application.

```java
//Where instance variables are declared:
JPanel cards;
final static String BUTTONPANEL = "JPanel with JButtons";
final static String TEXTPANEL = "JPanel with JTextField";

//Where the container is initialized:
cards = new JPanel();
cards.setLayout(new CardLayout());

...//Create a Panel named p1. Put buttons in it.
...//Create a Panel named p2. Put a text field in it.

cards.add(p1, BUTTONPANEL);
cards.add(p2, TEXTPANEL);
```

When you add a component to a container that a `CardLayout` manages, you must specify a string that identifies the component being added. In the preceding code snippet the first panel has the string `"JPanel with JButtons"`, and the second panel has the string `"JPanel with JTextField"`. As the next snippet shows, those strings are also used in the combo box.

To choose which component a `CardLayout` shows, you need some additional code. Here's the code that does this:

```java
//Where the container is initialized:
...
    //Put the JComboBox in a JPanel to get a nicer look.
    String comboBoxItems[] = { BUTTONPANEL, TEXTPANEL };
    JPanel cbp = new JPanel();
    JComboBox c = new JComboBox(comboBoxItems);
    c.setEditable(false);
```

```
        c.addItemListener(this);
        cbp.add(c);
        contentPane.add(cbp, BorderLayout.NORTH);
        ...
        contentPane.add(cards, BorderLayout.CENTER);
        ...

    public void itemStateChanged(ItemEvent evt) {
        CardLayout cl = (CardLayout)(cards.getLayout());
        cl.show(cards, (String)evt.getItem());
    }
```

This example shows that you can use the `CardLayout` `show` method to set the currently showing component. The first argument to the `show` method is the container the `CardLayout` controls, that is, the container of the components the `CardLayout` manages. The second argument is the string that identifies the component to show. This string is the same as was used when adding the component to the container.

The CardLayout API

The following `CardLayout` methods let you choose a component. The first argument for each method is the container for which the `CardLayout` is the layout manager (the container of the cards the `CardLayout` controls).

```
    void first(Container)
    void next(Container)
    void previous(Container)
    void last(Container)
    void show(Container, String)
```

Examples that Use CardLayout

Only one example in this tutorial uses `CardLayout`: <u>CardWindow.java</u> (page 789). Generally our examples use tabbed panes instead of `CardLayout`, since tabbed panes conveniently provide a nice GUI for the same functionality.

How to Use FlowLayout

The FlowLayout[1] class provides a very simple layout manager that JPanels use by default. Here's a program that shows a FlowLayout in action.

Figure 117 A simple GUI that uses FlowLayout.

FlowLayout puts components in a row, sized at their preferred size. If the horizontal space in the container is too small to put all of the components in one row, FlowLayout uses multiple rows. Within each row, components are centered (the default), left-aligned, or right-aligned as specified when the FlowLayout is created.

The following code creates the FlowLayout and the components it manages. You can find the whole program in FlowWindow.java (page 794). The program runs either within an applet (with the help of AppletButton) or as an application.

```
Container contentPane = getContentPane();
contentPane.setLayout(new FlowLayout());
contentPane.add(new JButton("Button 1"));
contentPane.add(new JButton("2"));
contentPane.add(new JButton("Button 3"));
contentPane.add(new JButton("Long-Named Button 4"));
contentPane.add(new JButton("Button 5"));
```

The FlowLayout API

The FlowLayout class has three constructors:

```
public FlowLayout()
public FlowLayout(int alignment)
public FlowLayout(int alignment,
                  int horizontalGap, int verticalGap)
```

---

[1] http://java.sun.com/products/jdk/1.2/docs/api/java/awt/FlowLayout.html

The *alignment* argument must have the value `FlowLayout.LEFT`, `FlowLayout.CENTER`, or `FlowLayout.RIGHT`. The *horizontalGap* and *verticalGap* arguments specify the number of pixels to put between components. If you don't specify a gap value, `FlowLayout` uses 5 for the default gap value.

Examples that Use FlowLayout

The following table lists some of the examples that use `FlowLayout`.

Table 149   Examples that Use `FlowLayout`

Example	Where Described	Notes
`FlowWindow.java`	This section	Sets up a content pane to use `Flow-Layout`.
`ButtonDemo.java`	How to Use Buttons, Check Boxes, and Radio Buttons (page 169)	Uses the default `FlowLayout` of a `JPanel`.

How to Use GridLayout

Here's a program that shows a <u>GridLayout</u>[1] in action.

Figure 118 A simple GUI that uses GridLayout.

A GridLayout places components in a grid of cells. Each component takes all of the available space within its cell, and all cells are exactly the same size. If you resize the GridLayout window, you'll see that the GridLayout changes the cell size so that the cells are as large as possible, given the space available to the container.

The following code creates the GridLayout and the components it manages. You can find the whole program in <u>GridWindow.java</u> (page 802). The program runs either within an applet (with the help of AppletButton) or as an application.

```
Container contentPane = getContentPane();
contentPane.setLayout(new GridLayout(0,2));
contentPane.add(new JButton("Button 1"));
contentPane.add(new JButton("2"));
contentPane.add(new JButton("Button 3"));
contentPane.add(new JButton("Long-Named Button 4"));
contentPane.add(new JButton("Button 5"));
```

The constructor tells the GridLayout class to create an instance that has two columns and as many rows as necessary.

The GridLayout API

The GridLayout class has two constructors:

---

[1] http://java.sun.com/products/jdk/1.2/docs/api/java/awt/GridLayout.html

```
public GridLayout(int rows, int columns)
public GridLayout(int rows, int columns,
                  int horizontalGap, int verticalGap)
```

At least one of the *rows* and *columns* arguments must be nonzero. The *horizontalGap* and *verticalGap* arguments to the second constructor allow you to specify the number of pixels between cells. If you don't specify gaps, their values default to 0. In the preceding applet, any apparent gaps are the result of the buttons' reserving extra space around their apparent display area.

Examples that Use GridLayout

The following table lists some of the examples that use `GridLayout`.

Table 150 Examples that Use `GridLayout`

Example	Where Described	Notes
GridWindow.java	This section	Uses a 2-column grid.
LabelDemo.java	How to Use Labels (page 212)	Uses a 3-row grid.
Converter.java	The Anatomy of a Swing-Based Program (page 51)	Uses the 4-argument `GridLayout` constructor.

How to Use GridBagLayout

Here's a program that shows a <u>GridBagLayout</u>[1] in action.

Figure 119 A simple GUI that uses GridBagLayout.

GridBagLayout is the most flexible—and complex—layout manager the Java platform provides. A GridBagLayout places components in a grid of rows and columns, allowing specified components to span multiple rows or columns. Not all rows necessarily have the same height, and not all columns necessarily have the same width. GridBagLayout places components in rectangles (cells) in a grid and then uses the components' preferred sizes to determine how big the cells should be.

Figure 120 shows the grid for the preceding applet. As you can see, the grid has three rows and three columns. The button in the second row spans all of the columns; the button in the third row spans the two right columns.

If you enlarge the window as shown in the figure, you'll notice that the bottom row, which contains Button 5, gets all of the new vertical space. The new horizontal space is split evenly among all the columns. This resizing behavior is based on weights the program assigns to individual components in the GridBagLayout. You'll also notice that each component takes up all of the available horizontal space—but not (as you can see with Button 5) all of the available vertical space. This behavior is also specified by the program individual components in the GridBagLayout. You'll also notice that each component takes up all of the

---

[1] API documentation for GridBagLayout is available on this book's CD-ROM and online at: http://java.sun.com/products/jdk/1.2/docs/api/java/awt/GridBagLayout.html

available horizontal space—but not (as you can see with Button 5) all of the available vertical space. This behavior is also specified by the program.

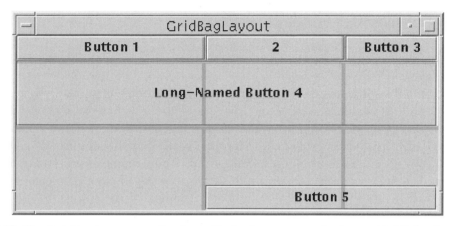

Figure 120 The GridBagLayout application with the three rows and columns highlighted.

The way the program specifies the size and position characteristics of its components is by specifying *constraints* for each component. To specify constraints, you set instance variables in a GridBagConstraints object and use the setConstraints method to tell the Grid-BagLayout to associate the constraints with the component.

Specifying Constraints

The following code is typical of what goes in a container that uses a GridBagLayout.[1] You'll see a more detailed example in the next section.

```
GridBagLayout gridbag = new GridBagLayout();
GridBagConstraints c = new GridBagConstraints();
JPanel pane = new JPanel();
pane.setLayout(gridbag);

//For each component to be added to this container:
//...Create the component...
//...Set instance variables in the GridBagConstraints instance...
gridbag.setConstraints(theComponent, c);
pane.add(theComponent);
```

---

[1] API documentation for GridBagLayout is available on this book's CD-ROM and online at: http://java.sun.com/products/jdk/1.2/docs/api/java/awt/GridBagLayout.html

As you might have guessed from the preceding example, you can reuse the same GridBag-Constraints instance for multiple components, even if they have different constraints. The GridBagLayout extracts the constraint values and doesn't use the GridBagConstraints again. You must be careful, however, to reset the GridBagConstraints instance variables to their default values when necessary.

You can set the following GridBagConstraints[1] instance variables:

gridx, gridy

Specify the row and column at the upper left of the component. The leftmost column has address gridx=0, and the top row has address gridy=0. Use GridBagCon-straints.RELATIVE (the default value) to specify that the component be placed just to the right of (for gridx) or just below (for gridy) the component that was added to the container just before this component was added. We recommend specifying the gridx and gridy values for each component; this tends to result in more predictable layouts.

gridwidth, gridheight

Specify the number of columns (for gridwidth) or rows (for gridheight) in the component's display area. These constraints specify the number of cells the component uses, *not* the number of pixels it uses. The default value is 1. Use GridBagCon-straints.REMAINDER to specify that the component be the last one in its row (for gridwidth) or column (for gridheight). Use GridBagConstraints.RELATIVE to specify that the component be the next to last one in its row (for gridwidth) or column (for gridheight).

Note: GridBagLayout doesn't allow components to span multiple rows unless the component is in the leftmost column or you've specified positive gridx and gridy values for the component.

---

fill

Used when the component's display area is larger than the component's requested size to determine whether and how to resize the component. Valid values (defined as GridBag-Constraints constants) are NONE (the default), HORIZONTAL (make the component wide enough to fill its display area horizontally, but don't change its height), VERTICAL (make the component tall enough to fill its display area vertically, but don't change its width), and BOTH (make the component fill its display area entirely).

---

[1] API documentation for GridBagConstraints is available on this book's CD-ROM and online at:
http://java.sun.com/products/jdk/1.2/docs/api/java/awt/GridBagConstraints.html

ipadx, ipady

Specifies the internal padding: how much to add to the minimum size of the component. The default value is 0. The width of the component will be at least its minimum width plus `ipadx*2` pixels, since the padding applies to both sides of the component. Similarly the height of the component will be at least its minimum height plus `ipady*2` pixels.

insets

Specifies the external padding of the component—the minimum amount of space between the component and the edges of its display area. The value is specified as an `Insets`[1] object. By default each component has no external padding.

anchor

Used when the component is smaller than its display area to determine where (within the area) to place the component. Valid values (defined as `GridBagConstraints` constants) are `CENTER` (the default), `NORTH`, `NORTHEAST`, `EAST`, `SOUTHEAST`, `SOUTH`, `SOUTHWEST`, `WEST`, and `NORTHWEST`.

weightx, weighty

Specifying weights is an art that can have a significant impact on the appearance of the components a `GridBagLayout` controls. Weights are used to determine how to distribute space among columns (`weightx`) and among rows (`weighty`); this is important for specifying resizing behavior.

Unless you specify at least one nonzero value for `weightx` or `weighty`, all of the components clump together in the center of their container. The reason is that when the weight is 0.0 (the default), the `GridBagLayout` puts any extra space between its grid of cells and the edges of the container.

Generally weights are specified with 0.0 and 1.0 as the extremes; the numbers in between are used as necessary. Larger numbers indicate that the component's row or column should get more space. For each column, the weight is related to the highest `weightx` specified for a component within that column, with each multicolumn component's weight being split somehow between the columns the component is in. Similarly each row's weight is related to the highest `weighty` specified for a component within that row. Extra space tends to go toward the rightmost column and bottom row.

The next section discusses constraints in depth, in the context of explaining how the sample program works.

The GridBagLayout Example Explained

Here again is the program that shows a `GridBagLayout` in action.

---

[1] API documentation for `Insets` is available on this book's CD-ROM and online at http://java.sun.com/products/jdk/1.2/docs/api/java/awt/Insets.html

Figure 121 A simple program that uses `GridBagLayout`.

The following code creates the `GridBagLayout` and the components it manages. You can find the entire source file in <u>GridBagWindow.java</u> (page 801). The program runs either within an applet (with the help of `AppletButton`) or as an application.

```
JButton button;
Container contentPane = getContentPane();
GridBagLayout gridbag = new GridBagLayout();
GridBagConstraints c = new GridBagConstraints();
contentPane.setLayout(gridbag);
if (shouldFill) { c.fill = GridBagConstraints.HORIZONTAL; }

button = new JButton("Button 1");
if (shouldWeightX) { c.weightx = 0.5; }
c.gridx = 0;
c.gridy = 0;
gridbag.setConstraints(button, c);
contentPane.add(button);

button = new JButton("2");
c.gridx = 1;
c.gridy = 0;
gridbag.setConstraints(button, c);
contentPane.add(button);

button = new JButton("Button 3");
c.gridx = 2;
c.gridy = 0;
gridbag.setConstraints(button, c);
contentPane.add(new JButton("Button 3"));
button = new JButton("Long-Named Button 4");
c.ipady = 40;        //make this component tall
c.weightx = 0.0;
c.gridwidth = 3;
c.gridx = 0;
c.gridy = 1;
```

Table 151   Constraints for Each Component the `GridBagLayout` Handles

Component	Constraints
Button 2	weightx = 0.5 *gridx = 1* gridy = 0
Button 3	weightx = 0.5 *gridx = 2* gridy = 0
Button 4	*ipady = 40* weightx = 0.0 *gridwidth = 3* *gridx = 0* *gridy = 1*
Button 5	ipady = 0 weightx = 0.0 *weighty = 1.0* *anchor = GridBagConstraints.SOUTH* *insets = new Insets(10,0,0,0)* *gridwidth = 2* *gridx = 1* *gridy = 2*

All of the components in this container are as wide as possible, given the cells that they occupy. The program accomplishes this by setting the `GridBagConstraints fill` instance variable to `GridBagConstraints.HORIZONTAL`, leaving it at that setting for all of the components. If the program didn't specify the fill, the buttons would be at their natural width, as in Figure 122.

Figure 122 The `GridBagLayout` application without the fill specified.

```
gridbag.setConstraints(button, c);
contentPane.add(button);

button = new JButton("Button 5");
c.ipady = 0;          //reset to default
c.weighty = 1.0;      //request any extra vertical space
c.anchor = GridBagConstraints.SOUTH; //bottom of space
c.insets = new Insets(10,0,0,0);  //top padding
c.gridx = 1;          //aligned with button 2
c.gridwidth = 2;      //2 columns wide
c.gridy = 2;          //third row
gridbag.setConstraints(button, c);
contentPane.add(button);
```

This example uses one `GridBagConstraints` instance for all of the components the Gr BagLayout manages. Just before each component is added to the container, the code set: resets to default values) the appropriate instance variables in the `GridBagConstrai` object. Then the code uses the `setConstraints` method to record all of the constraint ues for that component.

For example, to make Button 4 be extra tall, the example has this code:

```
c.ipady = 40;
```

And before setting the constraints of the next component, the code resets the value of ip to the default:

```
c.ipady = 0;
```

The following table shows all of the constraints for each component the `GridBagLay` handles. Values that aren't the default are marked in boldface type. Values that are diffe from those in the previous table entry are marked in italic.

Table 151   Constraints for Each Component the `GridBagLayout` Handles

Component	Constraints
All components	ipadx = 0 **fill = GridBagConstraints.HORIZONTAL**
Button 1	ipady = 0 **weightx = 0.5** weighty = 0.0 gridwidth = 1 anchor = GridBagConstraints.CENTER insets = new Insets(0,0,0,0) **gridx = 0** **gridy = 0**

This program has two components that span multiple columns (Buttons 4 and 5). To make Button 4 tall, we added internal padding (ipady) to it. To put space between Buttons 4 and 5, we used insets to add a minimum of 10 pixels above Button 5. We also specified a SOUTH anchor to make Button 5 hug the bottom edge of its cell, with any extra space going above the button.

When you enlarge the window the program brings up, the columns grow proportionately. The reason is that each component in the first row, where each component is one column wide, has weightx = 1.0. The value of these components' weightx is unimportant. What matters is that all of the components, and consequently all of the columns, have an equal weight that is greater than 0. If no component managed by the GridBagLayout had weightx set, the components would stay clumped together in the center of the container when the components' container was made wider, as shown in Figure 123.

Figure 123 None of the components in this example has weightx specified.

Note that if you enlarge the window, the last row is the only one that gets taller. The reason is that only Button 5 has weighty greater than 0.

The GridBagLayout API

The GridBagLayout and GridBagConstraints classes each have only one constructor, with no arguments. Instead of invoking methods on a GridBagConstraints object, you manipulate its instance variables, as described in Specifying Constraints (page 371). Generally the only method you invoke on a GridBagLayout object is setConstraints, as demonstrated in The GridBagLayout Example Explained (page 373).

Examples that Use GridBagLayout

You can find examples of using GridBagLayout throughout this tutorial. The following table lists a few.

Table 152   Examples that Use GridBagLayout

Example	Where Described	Notes
GridBagWindow.java	This section	Uses many features—weights, insets, internal padding, horizontal fill, exact cell positioning, multi-column cells, and anchoring (component positioning within a cell).
TextSamplerDemo.java	How to Use Text Components (page 275)	Aligns two pairs of labels and text fields and adds a label across the full width of the container.
ContainerEventDemo.java	How to Write a Container Listener (page 469)	Positions five components within a container, using weights, fill, and relative positioning.

Creating a Custom Layout Manager

TO create a custom layout manager, you must create a class that implements the <u>Lay-outManager</u>[1] interface. You can either implement it directly or implement its subinterface, <u>LayoutManager2</u>.[2]

Note: Before you start creating a custom layout manager, make sure that no existing layout manager will work. In particular, GridBagLayout and BoxLayout are flexible enough to work in many cases. You can also find layout managers from other sources, such as the Internet. Finally, you can simplify layout by grouping components into containers, such as invisible panels.

Every layout manager must implement at least the following five methods, which are required by the LayoutManager interface.

void addLayoutComponent(String, Component)

Called by the Container add methods. Layout managers that don't associate strings with their components generally do nothing in this method.

---

[1] API documentation for LayoutManager is available on this book's CD-ROM and online at:
http://java.sun.com/products/jdk/1.2/docs/api/java/awt/LayoutManager.html

[2] http://java.sun.com/products/jdk/1.2/docs/api/java/awt/LayoutManager2.html

void removeLayoutComponent(Component)

Called by the `Container` remove and removeAll methods. Many layout managers do nothing in this method, relying instead on querying the container for its components, using the `Container` getComponents method.

Dimension preferredLayoutSize(Container)

Called by the `Container` getPreferredSize method, which is itself called under a variety of circumstances. This method should calculate and return the ideal size of the container, assuming that the components it contains will be at or above their preferred sizes. This method must take into account the container's internal borders, which are returned by the `getInsets` method.

Dimension minimumLayoutSize(Container)

Called by the `Container` getMinimumSize method, which is itself called under a variety of circumstances. This method should calculate and return the minimum size of the container, assuming that the components it contains will be at or above their minimum sizes. This method must take into account the container's internal borders, which are returned by the `getInsets` method.

void layoutContainer(Container)

Called when the container is first displayed and each time its size changes. A layout manager's `layoutContainer` method doesn't draw components. It simply invokes each component's `resize`, `move`, and `reshape` methods to set the component's size and position. This method must take into account the container's internal borders, which are returned by the `getInsets` method. You can't assume that the `preferredLayoutSize` or `minimumLayoutSize` method will be called before `layoutContainer` is called.

Besides implementing the preceding five methods, layout managers generally implement at least one public constructor and the `toString` method.

If you wish to support component constraints, maximum sizes, or alignment, your layout manager should implement the `LayoutManager2` interface. That interface adds five methods to those required by `LayoutManager`:

- `addLayoutComponent(Component, Object)`
- `getLayoutAlignmentX(Container)`
- `getLayoutAlignmentY(Container)`
- `invalidateLayout(Container)`
- `maximumLayoutSize(Container)`

For more information about these methods, see the LayoutManager2[1] API documentation. Also see the source code for BoxLayout, to see how it implements the LayoutManager2 interface.

When implementing a layout manager, you might want to use SizeRequirements[2] objects to help you determine the size and position of components. See the source code for BoxLayout for an example of using SizeRequirements.

DiagonalLayout.java (page 791) provides the source code for a custom layout manager. DiagonalLayout lays out components diagonally, from left to right, with one component per row. Here's an example of DiagonalLayout in action.

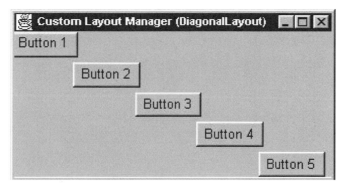

Figure 124 The DiagonalLayout program.

You can find another example of a custom layout manager in GraphPaperLayout.java (page 795).[3] GraphPaperLayout lays out components in a grid. Each component's size and location are specified, using grid units rather than absolute locations, when the component is added to its container. You can set the relative grid size, horizontal space between components, and vertical space between components when initializing the layout manager. You can also change component locations and the grid size dynamically. For an example of using GraphPaperLayout, see GraphPaperTest.java (page 800).

---

[1]   API documentation for LayoutManager2 is available on this book's CD-ROM and online at:
     http://java.sun.com/products/jdk/1.2/docs/api/java/awt/LayoutManager2.html
[2]   API documentation for SizeRequirements is available on this book's CD-ROM and online at:
     http://java.sun.com/products/jdk/1.2/docs/api/javax/swing/SizeRequirements.html
[3]   GraphPaperLayout was written by Michael Martak.

Here's a snapshot of `GraphPaperTest` that shows `GraphPaperLayout` in action.

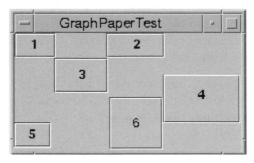

Figure 125 The `GraphPaperTest` application

Doing Without a Layout Manager (Absolute Positioning)

ALTHOUGH it's possible to do without a layout manager, you should use one if at all possible. A layout manager makes it easy to adjust to look-and-feel-dependent component appearances, to various font sizes, and to a container's changing size. Layout managers also can be reused easily by other containers as well as other programs.

If a container holds components whose size isn't affected by the container's size or by font and look-and-feel changes, absolute positioning might make sense. Desktop panes, which contain internal frames, are in this category. The size and the position of internal frames don't depend directly on the desktop pane's size. The programmer determines the initial size and placement of internal frames within the desktop pane, and then the user can move or resize the frames. A layout manager is unnecessary in this situation.

Another situation in which absolute positioning might make sense is that of a custom container that performs size and position calculations that are particular to the container and that perhaps require knowledge of the container's specialized state. This is the situation with split panes.

Figure 126 shows an applet that brings up a window whose content pane uses absolute positioning.

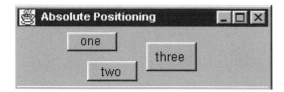

Figure 126 A simple applet that uses absolute positioning.

Following are the instance variable declarations and constructor implementation of the window class. You can find the entire program in <u>NoneWindow.java</u> (page 803). The program runs either within an applet (with the help of AppletButton) or as an application.

```
public class NoneWindow extends JFrame {
    . . .
    private boolean laidOut = false;
    private JButton b1, b2, b3;
    public NoneWindow() {
        Container contentPane = getContentPane();
        contentPane.setLayout(null);

        b1 = new JButton("one");
        contentPane.add(b1);

        b2 = new JButton("two");
        contentPane.add(b2);

        b3 = new JButton("three");
        contentPane.add(b3);

        Insets insets = contentPane.getInsets();
        b1.setBounds(25 + insets.left, 5 + insets.top, 75, 20);
        b2.setBounds(55 + insets.left, 35 + insets.top, 75, 20);
        b3.setBounds(150 + insets.left, 15 + insets.top, 75, 30);
        . . .
    }
    . . .
}
```

Solving Common
Layout Problems

Problem: How do I specify a component's exact size?

- First, make sure that you really need to set the component's exact size. Each Swing component has a different preferred size, depending on the font it uses and the look and feel. Therefore it often doesn't make sense to specify a Swing component's exact size.

- If the component isn't controlled by a layout manager, you can set its size by invoking the `setSize` or the `setBounds` method on it. Otherwise you need to provide size hints and then make sure that you're using a layout manager that respects the size hints.

- If you extend a Swing component class, you can give size hints by overriding the component's `getMinimumSize`, `getPreferredSize`, and `getMaximumSize` methods. What's nice about this approach is that each get*Xxxx*Size method can get the component's default size hints by invoking `super.get`*Xxxx*`Size()`. Then it can adjust the size, if necessary, before returning it.

- Another way to give size hints is to invoke the component's `setMinimumSize`, `setPreferredSize`, and `setMaximumSize` methods.

If you specify new size hints for a component that's already visible, you then need to invoke the `revalidate` method on it, to make sure that its containment hierarchy is laid out again. Then invoke the `repaint` method.

> **Note:** No matter how you specify your component's size, be sure that your component's container uses a layout manager that respects the requested size of the component. The `FlowLayout` and `GridBagLayout` managers use the component's preferred size (the latter depending on the constraints that you set), but `BorderLayout` and `GridLayout` usually don't. The `BoxLayout` manager generally uses a component's preferred size (although components can be larger), and is the only layout manager that respects the component's maximum size.

Problem: My custom component is being sized too small.

- Does the component implement the `getPreferredSize` and the `getMinimumSize` methods? If so, do they return the right values?

- Are you using a layout manager that can use as much space as is available? See <u>General Rules for Using Layout Managers</u> (page 344) for some tips on choosing a layout manager and specifying that it use the maximum available space for a particular component.

If you don't see your problem in this list, see <u>Solving Common Component Problems</u> (page 337).

Using Other Swing Features

THIS lesson consists of how-to sections to help you use miscellaneous Swing features.

How to Use Actions (page 389)
With Action objects you can coordinate the state and event handling of two or more components that generate action events. For example, you can use a single Action to create and coordinate a tool bar button and a menu item that perform the same function.

How to Support Assistive Technologies (page 393)
Swing components have built-in support for assistive technologies. Your program can provide even better support by following a few rules.

How to Use Borders (page 408)
Borders are very handy for drawing lines, titles, and empty space around the edges of components. This section tells you how to add a border to any JComponent.

How to Use Icons (page 417)
Many Swing components can display icons. Usually icons are implemented as instances of the ImageIcon class.

How to Set the Look and Feel (page 428)
You can specify the look and feel of your Swing components.

How to Use Threads (page 431)

Read this section if you need access to the GUI from any thread except the event-dispatching thread.

How to Use Timers (page 436)

Use the `Timer` class to implement a thread that performs an action after a delay and, optionally, continues to repeat the action. The action executes in the event-dispatching thread.

How to Use Actions

If you have two or more components that perform the same function, consider using an Action[1] object to implement the function. An Action object is an ActionListener[2] that provides not only action-event handling, but also centralized handling of the text, icon, and enabled state of tool bar buttons or menu items. By adding an Action to a JToolBar, JMenu, or JPopupMenu, you get the following features:

- A new JButton (for JToolBar) or JMenuItem (for JMenu and JPopupMenu) that is automatically added to the tool bar or the menu. The button or the menu item automatically uses the icon and the text specified by the Action.

- A registered action listener (the Action object) for the button or the menu item.

- Centralized handling of the enabled state of the button or the menu item.

In the following example an Action is used to create a tool bar button and a menu item that perform the same function:

```
Action leftAction = new <a class that implements Action>(...);
JButton button = toolBar.add(leftAction);
JMenuItem menuItem = mainMenu.add(leftAction);
```

For a button or a menu item to get the full benefit of using an Action, you must create the component by using the add(Action) method of JToolBar, JMenu, or JPopupMenu. Currently no API beyond addActionListener(ActionListener) exists to connect an Action to an already existing component. For example, although you can add an Action object as an action listener to any button, the button won't be notified when the action is disabled.

To create an Action object, you generally create a subclass of AbstractAction[3] and then instantiate it. In your subclass you must implement the actionPerformed method to react appropriately when the action event occurs. Here's an example of creating and instantiating an AbstractAction subclass:

---

[1] API documentation for Action is available on this book's CD-ROM and online at http://java.sun.com/products/jdk/1.2/docs/api/javax/swing/Action.html

[2] http://java.sun.com/products/jdk/1.2/docs/api/java/awt/ActionListener.html

[3] http://java.sun.com/products/jdk/1.2/docs/api/javax/swing/AbstractAction.html

```
leftAction = new AbstractAction("Go left",
                              new ImageIcon("images/left.gif")) {
    public void actionPerformed(ActionEvent e) {
        displayResult("Action for first button/menu item", e);
    }
};
```

The following demo application uses actions to implement three features.

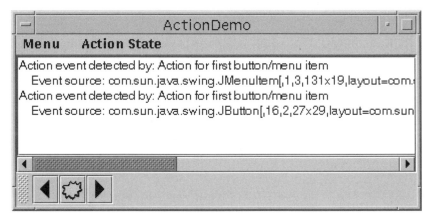

Figure 127 The `ActionDemo` application.

Try this:

1. Compile and run the application.[1] The source file is <u>ActionDemo.java</u> (page 808). You will also need to put three image files in a directory named `images`: `left.gif`, `middle.gif`, and `right.gif`.[2]

2. Choose the top item from the left menu (Menu > Go left). The text area displays some text identifying both the event source and the action listener that received the event.

3. Click the leftmost button in the tool bar. The text area again displays information about the event. Note that although the source of the events is different, both events were detected by the same action listener: the `Action` object with which the components were created.

4. Choose the top item from the Action State menu. This disables the Go left `Action` object, which in turn disables its associated menu item and button.

---

1   See the chapter <u>Getting Started with Swing</u> (page 3) if you need help compiling or running this application.
2   You can find the images by visiting http://java.sun.com/docs/books/tutorial/uiswing/components/ example-swing/index.html

Figure 128 shows what the user sees when the action Go left is disabled.

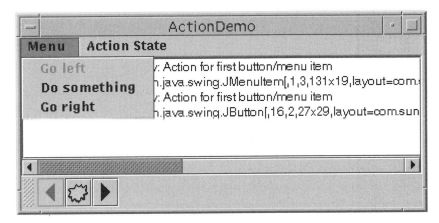

Figure 128 The `ActionDemo` application when the action Go left is disabled.

Here's the code that disables the action Go left:

```
boolean selected = ...// true if the action should be enabled
                     //false, otherwise
leftAction.setEnabled(selected);
```

After you create components by using an `Action`, you might well need to customize them. For example, you might want to set the tool tip text for a button. Or you might want to customize the appearance of one of the components by adding or deleting the icon or text. For example, `ActionDemo` has no icons in its menus, no text in its buttons, and tool tips for its buttons. Here's the code that accomplishes this:

```
button = toolBar.add(leftAction);
button.setText(""); //an icon-only button
button.setToolTipText("This is the left button");
menuItem = mainMenu.add(leftAction);
menuItem.setIcon(null); //arbitrarily chose not to use icon in menu
```

The Action API

The following tables list the commonly used `Action` constructors and methods.

Table 153   Common Action Constructors and Methods

Constructor or Method	Purpose
AbstractAction() AbstractAction(String) AbstractAction(String, Icon)	Create an Action object. You use arguments to specify the text and the icon to be used in the components that the action controls.
void setEnabled(boolean) boolean isEnabled()	Set or get whether the components the action controls are enabled. Invoking setEnabled(false) disables all of the components that the action controls. Invoking setEnabled(true) enables the action's components.

Table 154   Creating an Action-Controlled Component

Method	Purpose
JMenuItem add(Action) JMenuItem insert(Action, int) (in JMenu and JPopupMenu)	Create a JMenuItem object and put it in the menu or the pop up menu. See the discussion in this section and in How to Use Menus (page 226) for details.
JButton add(Action) (in JToolBar)	Create a JButton object and put it in the tool bar. See the discussion in this section and in How to Use Tool Bars (page 138) for details.

Examples that Use Actions

The following examples use Action objects.

Table 155   Examples that Use Actions

Example	Where Described	Notes
ActionDemo.java	This section	Uses actions to bind buttons and menu items to the same function.
TextComponentDemo.java	General Rules for Using Text Components (page 282)	Uses text actions to create menu items for text-editing commands, such as cut, copy, and paste, and to bind keystrokes to caret movement. Also implements custom AbstractAction subclasses to implement undo and redo. See Concepts: About Editor Kits (page 288).

How to Support Assistive Technologies

You might be wondering what exactly assistive technologies are and why you should care. Assistive technologies exist primarily to enable people with permanent or temporary disabilities to use the computer. For example, if you get carpal tunnel syndrome, you can use assistive technologies to accomplish your work without using your hands.

Assistive technologies—voice interfaces, screen readers, alternative input devices, and so on—are useful not only for people with disabilities but also for people using computers in nonoffice environments. For example, if you're stuck in a traffic jam, you might use assistive technologies to check your e-mail, using only voice input and output. The information that enables assistive technologies can be used for other tools as well, such as automated GUI testers. Assistive technologies get information from components by using the Accessibility API, which is defined in the `javax.accessibility`[1] package.

Because support for the Accessibility API is built into the Swing components, your Swing program will probably work just fine with assistive technologies, even if you do nothing special. For example, assistive technologies can automatically get the text information that is set by the following lines of code:

```
JButton button = new JButton("I'm a Swing button!");
label = new JLabel(labelPrefix + "0      ");
label.setText(labelPrefix + numClicks);
JFrame frame = new JFrame("SwingApplication");
```

Assistive technologies can also automatically grab the tool tip text, if any, associated with a component and use that text to describe the component to the user.

With very little extra effort, however, you can make your program function even more smoothly with assistive technologies. This might well expand your product's market.

---

[1] API documentation for this package is available on this book's CD-ROM and online at http://java.sun.com/products/jdk/1.2/docs/api/javax/accessibility/package-summary.html

Rules for Supporting Accessibility

Here are a few things you can do to make your program work as well as possible with assistive technologies.

- Set tool tip text for components whenever it makes sense to do so. For example:

```
aJComponent.setToolTipText("Clicking this component causes " +
                            "XYZ to happen.");
```

- If you don't provide a tool tip for a component, use the `setAccessibleDescription` method to provide a description that assistive technologies can give the user. For example:

```
aJComponent.getAccessibleContext().setAccessibleDescription(
        "Clicking this component causes XYZ to happen.");
```

- Specify keyboard alternatives wherever possible. You should be able to use your program with only the keyboard. Try hiding your mouse!

  Buttons support keyboard alternatives with the `setMnemonic` method. Menus inherit the button mnemonic support and also support accelerators, as described in <u>Enabling Keyboard Operation</u> (page 231). Mnemonics and accelerators are special cases of keyboard-generated actions, which are described in <u>The JComponent Class</u> (page 67).

- Use the `setDescription` method to provide a text description for all `ImageIcon` objects in your program.

- If a component doesn't display a short string, which serves as its default name, specify a name with the `setAccessibleName` method. You might want to do this for image-only buttons, panels that provide logical groupings, text areas, and so on.

- If a bunch of components form a logical group, try to put them into one container. For example, use a `JPanel` to contain all of the radio buttons in a radio button group.

- Whenever you have a label that describes another component, use the `setLabelFor` method so that assistive technologies can find the component the label is associated with. This is especially important when the label displays a mnemonic for another component, such as a text field.

- Make sure that your custom components support the accessibility API. In particular, be aware that subclasses of `JComponent` do not automatically do so. Custom components that are descendants of other Swing components should override inherited accessibility information as necessary. For more information, see <u>Concepts: How Accessibility Works</u> (page 398) and <u>Making Custom Components Accessible</u> (page 400).

- Use the examples provided with the Accessibility utilities to test your program. The Accessibility utilities area set of classes that help assistive technologies to provide access to GUI toolkits, such as JFC/Swing, that implement the Accessibility API. Although the primary purpose of these examples is to show programmers how to use the Accessibility API when implementing assistive technologies, these examples are also quite useful for testing application programs for accessibility. <u>Testing for Accessibility</u> (page 402) shows `ScrollDemo` running with `Monkey`—one of the Accessibility utilities examples. `Monkey` shows the tree of accessible components in a program and lets you interact with them.

- Finally, don't break what you get for free! If your GUI has an inaccessible container—for example, an AWT `Panel` or any other container that doesn't implement the `Accessible` interface—any components inside that container become inaccessible. For example, if you put a `JButton` inside a `Panel`, the `JButton` becomes inaccessible.

- We've always recommended against mixing lightweight and heavyweight components anyway. Its impact on accessibility is just another reason to avoid this practice.

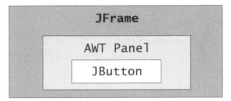

Figure 129 Swing components within AWT containers are inaccessible.

Setting Accessible Names and Descriptions on Components

Here's a picture of one of our demo programs, called `ScrollDemo`.

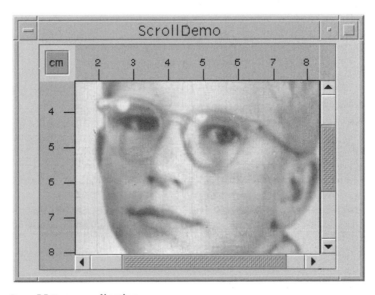

Figure 130 The `ScrollDemo` application.

You can find all of the files necessary to compile and run the program in <u>How to Use Scroll Panes</u> (page 112). Let's compare the original version of `ScrollDemo` to a version of the program to which the rules for supporting assistive technologies have been applied.

Try this:

1. Compile and run the accessible version of the application. The main source file is <u>AccessibleScrollDemo.java</u> (page 806). You also need <u>ScrollablePicture.java</u> (page 825), <u>Rule.java</u> (page 822), <u>Corner.java</u> (page 815) and youngdad.jpeg.[1] See <u>Getting Started with Swing</u> (page 3) if you need help compiling or running this application.

2. Run the accessible version alongside the original, and compare them. The only noticeable difference is that the cm toggle button and the photograph have tool tips in the accessible version.

3. Now run the two versions under `Monkey` as described in <u>Testing for Accessibility</u> (page 402). You can see detailed information for the various components. The inaccessible custom components (rules and corners) in the original version are accessible in the modified version. This can make quite a difference to assistive technologies.

Following is a complete listing of `AccessibleScrollDemo`'s constructor, which creates the scroll pane and the custom components it uses. The statements in boldface type give components names, and descriptions that assistive technologies can use.

```
public AccessibleScrollDemo() {
    //Load the photograph into an image icon.
    ImageIcon david = new ImageIcon("images/youngdad.jpeg");
    david.setDescription("Photograph of David McNabb in his youth.");

    //Create the row and column headers
    columnView = new Rule(Rule.HORIZONTAL, true);
    columnView.setPreferredWidth(david.getIconWidth());
    columnView.getAccessibleContext().setAccessibleName(
                                            "Column Header");
    columnView.getAccessibleContext().
        setAccessibleDescription("Displays horizontal ruler for " +
                                "measuring scroll pane client.");
    rowView = new Rule(Rule.VERTICAL, true);
    rowView.setPreferredHeight(david.getIconHeight());
    rowView.getAccessibleContext().setAccessibleName("Row Header");
    rowView.getAccessibleContext().
        setAccessibleDescription("Displays vertical ruler for " +
                                "measuring scroll pane client.");
```

---

[1] http://java.sun.com/docs/books/tutorial/uiswing/misc/example-swing/images/youngdad.jpeg

```
        //Create the corners
        JPanel buttonCorner = new JPanel();
        isMetric = new JToggleButton("cm", true);
        isMetric.setFont(new Font("SansSerif", Font.PLAIN, 11));
        isMetric.setMargin(new Insets(2,2,2,2));
        isMetric.addItemListener(new UnitsListener());
        isMetric.setToolTipText("Toggles rulers' unit of measure " +
                                "between inches and centimeters.");
        buttonCorner.add(isMetric); //Use the default FlowLayout
        buttonCorner.getAccessibleContext().
                setAccessibleName("Upper Left Corner");

        String desc = "Fills the corner of a scroll pane " +
                "with color for aesthetic reasons.";
        Corner lowerLeft = new Corner();
        lowerLeft.getAccessibleContext().
                setAccessibleName("Lower Left Corner");
        lowerLeft.getAccessibleContext().setAccessibleDescription(desc);

        Corner upperRight = new Corner();
        upperRight.getAccessibleContext().
                setAccessibleName("Upper Right Corner");
        upperRight.getAccessibleContext().setAccessibleDescription(desc);

        //Set up the scroll pane
        picture = new ScrollablePicture(david, columnView.getIncrement());
        picture.setToolTipText(david.getDescription());
        picture.getAccessibleContext().setAccessibleName(
                                                "Scroll pane client");

        JScrollPane pictureScrollPane = new JScrollPane(picture);
        pictureScrollPane.setPreferredSize(new Dimension(300, 250));
        pictureScrollPane.setViewportBorder(BorderFactory.createLineBorder(
                                                Color.black));

        pictureScrollPane.setColumnHeaderView(columnView);
        pictureScrollPane.setRowHeaderView(rowView);
        pictureScrollPane.setCorner(JScrollPane.UPPER_LEFT_CORNER,
                                buttonCorner);
        pictureScrollPane.setCorner(JScrollPane.LOWER_LEFT_CORNER,
                                lowerLeft);
        pictureScrollPane.setCorner(JScrollPane.UPPER_RIGHT_CORNER,
                                upperRight);
        setLayout(new BoxLayout(this, BoxLayout.XAXIS));
        add(pictureScrollPane);
        setBorder(BorderFactory.createEmptyBorder(20,20,20,20));
    }
```

Often the program sets a component's name and description directly through the component's accessible context. Other times the program sets an accessible description indirectly with tool tips. In the case of the cm toggle button, the program gives the component an accessible name as a side effect of creating it.

Concepts: How Accessibility Works

An object is accessible if it implements the Accessible[1] interface. The Accessible interface defines just one method, getAccessibleContext, which returns an AccessibleContext object. The AccessibleContext[2] object is an intermediary that contains the accessible information for an accessible object. The following figure shows how assistive technologies get the accessible context from an accessible object and query it for information.

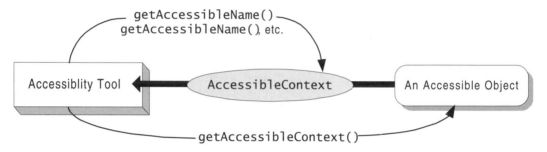

Figure 131 How assistive technologies get the accessible context from an accessible object.

AccessibleContext is an abstract class that defines the minimum set of information an accessible object must provide about itself. The minimum set includes name, description, role, state set, and so on. To identify its accessible object as having particular capabilities, an accessible context can implement one or more of the following interfaces:

- AccessibleAction[3]—indicates that the object can perform actions. By implementing this interface, the accessible context can give information about what actions the accessible object can perform and can tell the accessible object to perform them.

- AccessibleComponent[4]—indicates that the accessible object has an on-screen presence. Through this interface, an accessible object can provide information about its size, position, visibility, and so on. The accessible contexts for all standard Swing com-

---

[1] API documentation for this interface is available on this book's CD-ROM and online at
http://java.sun.com/products/jdk/1.2/docs/api/javax/accessibility/Accessible.html
[2] http://java.sun.com/products/jdk/1.2/docs/api/javax/accessibility/AccessibleContext.html
[3] http://java.sun.com/products/jdk/1.2/docs/api/javax/accessibility/AccessibleAction.html
[4] http://java.sun.com/products/jdk/1.2/docs/api/javax/accessibility/AccessibleComponent.html

ponents implement this interface. The accessible contexts for your custom components should do the same.

- `AccessibleHypertext`[1]—indicates that the accessible object contains hyperlinks. Through this interface, an accessible object can provide information about its links and allow them to be traversed.

- `AccessibleSelection`[2]—indicates that the accessible object is selectable. Accessible contexts that implement this interface can report information about the current selection and can modify it.

- `AccessibleText`[3]—indicates that the accessible object displays text. This interface provides methods for returning all or part of the text, attributes applied to it, and other information about the text, such as its length.

- `AccessibleValue`[4]—indicates that the object has a numeric value. An accessible objec uses this interface to provide information about the current value and its minimum and maximum.

Because `JComponent` class itself does not implement the `Accessible` interface, instances of its direct subclasses are inaccessible. If you write a custom component that inherits directly from `JComponent`, you need to explicitly make it implement the `Accessible` interface. `JComponent` does have an accessible context, called `AccessibleJComponent`,[5] that implements the `AccessibleComponent` interface and provides a minimal amount of accessible information. You can provide an accessible context for your custom components by creating a subclass of `AccessibleJComponent` and overriding important methods. The next section, Making Custom Components Accessible (page 400), shows two examples of doing this.

All of the other standard Swing components implement the `Accessible` interface and have an accessible context that implements one or more of the preceding interfaces as appropriate. The accessible contexts for Swing components are implemented as inner classes and have names of this style:

Component.`Accessible`*Component*

If you create a subclass of a standard Swing component and your subclass is substantially different from its superclass, you should provide a custom accessible context for it. The easiest way is to create a subclass of the superclass's accessible context class and to override methods as necessary. For example, if you create a `JLabel` subclass substantially different

---

[1] API documentation for `AccessibleHypertext` is available on this book's CD-ROM and online at http://java.sun.com/products/jdk/1.2/docs/api/javax/accessibility/AccessibleHypertext.html

[2] http://java.sun.com/products/jdk/1.2/docs/api/javax/accessibility/AccessibleSelection.html

[3] http://java.sun.com/products/jdk/1.2/docs/api/javax/accessibility/AccessibleText.html

[4] http://java.sun.com/products/jdk/1.2/docs/api/javax/accessibility/AccessibleValue.html

[5] http://java.sun.com/products/jdk/1.2/docs/api/javax/accessibility/AccessibleJComponent.html

from JLabel, then your JLabel subclass should contain an inner class that extends Accessible JLabel. The next section shows you how to do so, using examples in which JComponent subclasses extend AccessibleJComponent.

Making Custom Components Accessible

The scroll demo program uses three custom component classes. ScrollablePicture is a subclass of JLabel, and Corner and Rule are both subclasses of JComponent.

The ScrollablePicture class relies completely on accessibility inherited from JLabel through JLabel.AccessibleJLabel. The code that creates an instance of Scrollable-Picture sets the tool tip text for the scrollable picture. The context uses the tool tip text as the component's accessible description. This behavior is provided by AccessibleJLabel.

The accessible version of the Corner class contains just enough code to make its instances accessible. We implemented accessibility support by adding the code shown in boldface type to the original version of Corner.

```
public class Corner extends JComponent implements Accessible {
    public void paintComponent(Graphics g) {
        //fill me with dirty brown/orange
        g.setColor(new Color(230, 163, 4));
        g.fillRect(0, 0, getWidth(), getHeight());
    }
    public AccessibleContext getAccessibleContext() {
        if (accessibleContext == null) {
            accessibleContext = new AccessibleCorner();
        }
        return accessibleContext;
    }

    protected class AccessibleCorner extends AccessibleJComponent {
        //Inherit everything, override nothing.
    }
}
```

All of the accessibility provided by this class is inherited from AccessibleJComponent. This approach is fine for Corner because AccessibleJComponent provides a reasonable amount of default accessibility information and because corners are uninteresting—they exist only to take up a little bit of space on-screen. Other classes, such as Rule, need to provide more information so as to differentiate themselves from other components.

Rule provides an accessible context for itself in the same manner as Corner, but the context overrides two methods to provide details about the component's role and state:

```
protected class AccessibleRuler extends AccessibleJComponent {
    public AccessibleRole getAccessibleRole() {
        return AccessibleRuleRole.RULER;
    }
    public AccessibleStateSet getAccessibleStateSet() {
        AccessibleStateSet states = super.getAccessibleStateSet();
        if (orientation == VERTICAL) {
            states.add(AccessibleState.VERTICAL);
        } else {
            states.add(AccessibleState.HORIZONTAL);
        }
        if (isMetric) {
            states.add(AccessibleRulerState.CENTIMETERS);
        } else {
            states.add(AccessibleRulerState.INCHES);
        }
        return states;
    }
}
```

AccessibleRole[1] is an enumeration of objects that identify roles that components can play. It contains predefined roles, such as label, button, and so on. The rulers in our example don't fit well into any of the predefined roles, so the program invents a new one in a subclass of AccessibleRole:

```
class AccessibleRuleRole extends AccessibleRole {
    public static final AccessibleRuleRole RULER
        = new AccessibleRuleRole("ruler");
    protected AccessibleRuleRole(String key) {
        super(key);
    }
    //Should really provide localizable versions of these names
    public String toDisplayString(String resourceBundleName,
                                  Locale locale) {
        return key;
    }
}
```

Any component that has state can provide state information to accessibility tools by overriding the getAccessibleStateSet method. A rule has two sets of states: Its orientation can

---

[1] API documentation for AccessibleRole is available on this book's CD-ROM and online at
     http://java.sun.com/products/jdk/1.2/docs/api/javax/accessibility/AccessibleRole.html

be either vertical or horizontal, and its units of measure can be either centimeters or inches. AccessibleState[1] is an enumeration of predefined states. This program uses its predefined states for vertical and horizontal orientation. Because AccessibleState contains nothing for centimeters and inches, the program makes a subclass to provide appropriate states.

```
class AccessibleRulerState extends AccessibleState {
    public static final AccessibleRulerState INCHES
        = new AccessibleRulerState("inches");
    public static final AccessibleRulerState CENTIMETERS
        = new AccessibleRulerState("centimeters");
    protected AccessibleRulerState(String key) {
        super(key);
    }

    //Should provide localizable versions of these names
    public String toDisplayString(String resourceBundleName,
                                  Locale locale) {
        return key;
    }
}
```

You've seen how to implement accessibility for two simple components, which exist only to paint themselves on-screen. Components that do more, such as responding to mouse or keyboard events, need to provide more elaborate accessible contexts. You can find examples of implementing accessible contexts by delving in the source code for the Swing components.

Testing for Accessibility

The examples that come with the Accessibility utilities can give you an idea of how accessible your program is. You can download the Accessibility utilities and the examples for free from

```
http://java.sun.com/products/jfc/#download-access
```

Follow the instructions in the Accessibility utilities documentation for setting up the Java Virtual Machine to run one or more of the utilities automatically.

For example, to get an idea of the benefit gained by rewriting ScrollDemo, you can run Monkey on the original program and its accessible cousin, AccessibleScrollDemo. Here's a snapshot of Monkey running on ScrollDemo.

---

[1] API documentation for AccessibleState is available on this book's CD-ROM and online at http://java.sun.com/products/jdk/1.2/docs/api/javax/accessibility/AccessibleState.html

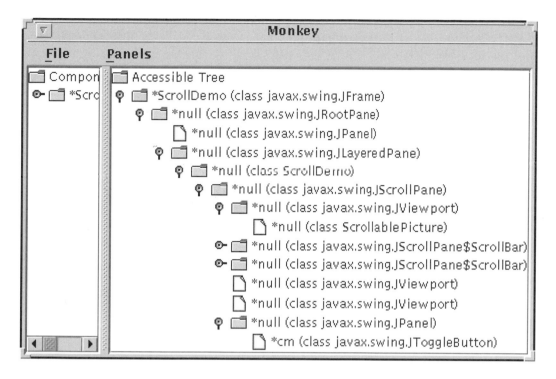

Figure 132 Many components in the original version of ScrollDemo don't show up in Monkey.

The left side of the split pane shows the component hierarchy for the program. The right side shows the accessible components in the hierarchy, which is what interests us.

The first thing to notice is that even with no explicit support in ScrollDemo, many of the components are accessible—they appear as nodes in the accessible tree. The accessible children of accessible components also appear in the tree. However, the names for most of the components are empty (null), which is rather unhelpful. The descriptions are also empty.

Further trouble comes with the program's custom components. The two rulers are inaccessible, so they are not included in the accessible tree. The viewports that contain the rulers are displayed as leaf nodes because they have no accessible children. The custom corners are also missing from the accessible tree.

Now here's a picture of the Monkey window for AccessibleScrollDemo (see Figure 133).

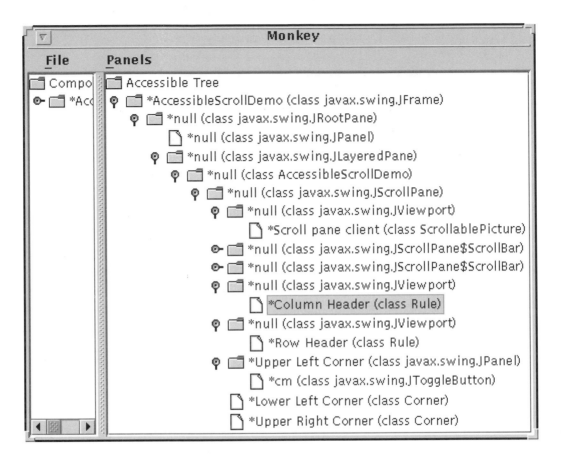

Figure 133 After improvements to the code, custom components appear in Monkey and other components provide better information.

The rules are now listed as children of the viewports, and the corners are listed as children of the scroll pane. Furthermore, many of the components now have non-null names.

In Figure 134, the Column Header item is selected. Monkey highlights the corresponding component in AccessibleScrollDemo.

With an item selected, you can bring up one of four panels that let you interact with the selected component in different ways. Use Monkey's Accessibility API panel menu item to bring up a panel like the one shown in Figure 135. This panel displays information available through methods defined in the AccessibleContext base class and the AccessibleComponent interface.

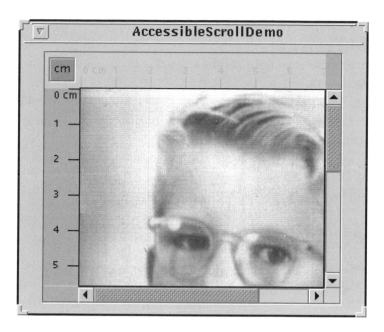

Figure 134 AccessibleScrollDemo with the column header selected.

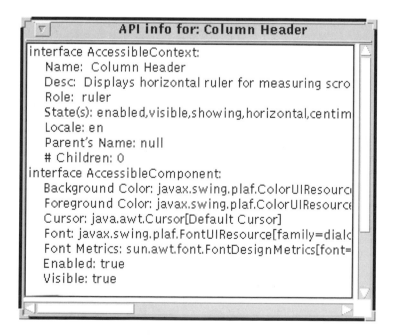

Figure 135 Monkey's Accessibility API panel.

Monkey has three other panels:

- `AccessibleAction`—shows the actions supported by an accessible component and lets you invoke the action. Works only with an accessible component whose context implements the `AccessibleAction` interface.
- `AccessibleSelection`—shows the current selection of an accessible component and lets you manipulate the selection. Works only with an accessible component whose context implements the `AccessibleSelection` interface.
- `AccessibleHypertext`—shows any hyperlinks contained within an accessible component and lets you traverse them. Works only with an accessible component whose context implements the `AccessibleHypertext` interface.

The Accessibility API

The tables in this section cover just part of the Accessibility API. For more information, see the API documentation for the classes and packages in the Accessibility package.[1] Also, refer to the API documentation for the accessible contexts for individual Swing components.

Table 156 Setting Accessible Names and Descriptions

Method	Purpose

`getAccessibleContext().setAccessibleName(`
`String)`
`getAccessibleContext().setAccessibleDescription(`
`String)`
(on a `JComponent` or `Accessible` object)
	Provide an accessible name or description for an accessible object.

`void setToolTipText(String)` (in `JComponent`)	Set a component's tool tip. Many accessible contexts use this as the default accessible description.
`void setLabelFor(Component)` (in `JLabel`)	Associate a label with a component. This tells assistive technologies that a label describes another component.
`void setDescription(String)` (in `ImageIcon`)	Provide a description for an image icon.

---

[1] API documentation for the accessibility package is available on this book's CD-ROM and online at http://java.sun.com/products/jdk/1.2/docs/api/javax/accessibility/package-summary.html

Table 157 Implementing an Accessible Custom Component

Method, Interface, or Class	Purpose
`Accessible` (an interface)	Components that implement this interface are accessible. Subclasses of `JComponent` must implement this explicitly.
`AccessibleContext getAccessibleContext()` (in `Accessible`)	Get the accessible context for an accessible object. Custom components should implement this method to return a custom accessible context.
`AccessibleContext` *Component.*`Accessible`*Component* (an abstract class and its subclasses)	The base class defines the minimal set of information required of accessible objects. The accessible context for each Swing component is a subclass of this and is named as shown. To provide custom accessible contexts, custom components should contain an inner class that descends from `AccessibleContext`. Typically the accessible context for a custom component is a subclass of one of the Swing component's accessible context classes.
`AccessibleAction` `AccessibleComponent` `AccessibleHypertext` `AccessibleSelection` `AccessibleText` `AccessibleValue` (interfaces)	Interfaces that accessible contexts can implement to identify particular behaviors.
`AccessibleRole` `AccessibleStateSet` (classes)	Define the objects returned by an `AccessibleContext` object's `getAccessibleRole` and `getAccessibleStateSet` methods, respectively.

Examples that Use the Accessibility API

The following table lists two examples that have good support for assistive technologies.

Table 158 Examples that Use the Accessibility API

Example	Where Described	Notes
`AccessibleScrollDemo`	This section	Contains two custom components that implement the `Accessible` interface. This program is a modified version of the `ScrollDemo` program featured in How to Use Scroll Panes (page 112).
`ButtonDemo.java`	The Common Button API (page 170)	Uses three buttons. Supports assistive technologies through button text, mnemonics, and tool tips.

How to Use Borders

Every JComponent can have one or more borders. Borders are incredibly useful objects that, while not themselves components, know how to draw the edges of Swing components. Borders are useful not only for drawing lines and fancy edges, but also for providing titles and empty space around components.

To put a border around a JComponent, you use its setBorder method. You can use the BorderFactory[1] class to create most of the borders that Swing provides. Here is an example of code that creates a bordered container:

```
JPanel pane = new JPanel();
pane.setBorder(BorderFactory.createLineBorder(Color.black));
```

Here's a picture of the container, which contains a label component. The black line drawn by the border marks the edge of the container.

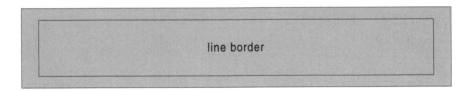

Figure 136 A bordered container.

The BorderDemo Example

The following application, called BorderDemo, displays the borders Swing provides. We show the code for creating these borders a little later, in the next section, Using the Borders Provided by Swing (page 411).

---

[1] API documentation for BorderFactory is available on this book's CD-ROM and online at
http://java.sun.com/products/jdk/1.2/docs/api/javax/swing/BorderFactory.html

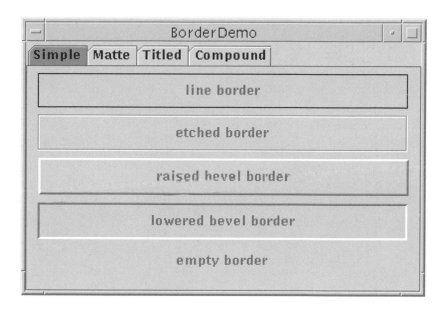

Figure 137 A version of the BorderDemo application.

Figure 138 shows some matte borders. When creating a matte border, you specify how many pixels it occupies at the top, left, bottom, and right of a component. You then specify either a color or an icon for the matte border to draw. You need to be careful when choosing the icon and determining your component's size; otherwise, the icon might get chopped off or have mismatch at the component's corners.

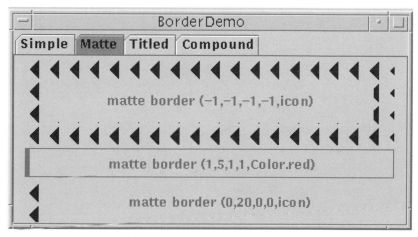

Figure 138 A version of the BorderDemo application.

Figure 139 shows titled borders. Using a titled border, you can convert any border into one that displays a text description. If you don't specify a border, a look-and-feel-specific border is used. For example, the default titled border in the Java Look & Feel uses a gray line, and the default titled border in the Windows Look & Feel uses an etched border. By default the title straddles the upper-left of the border, as shown at the top of Figure 139.

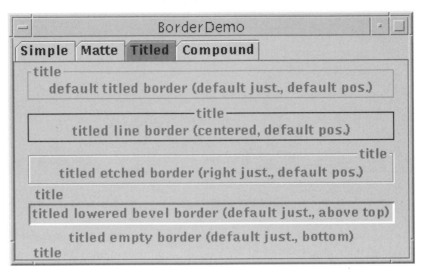

Figure 139 A version of the BorderDemo application.

Figure 140 shows compound borders. Compound borders let you combine any two borders, which can themselves be compound borders.

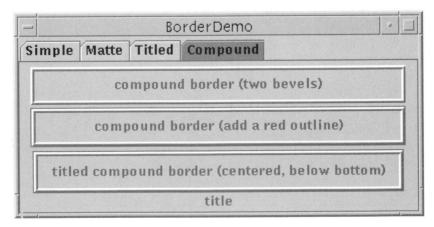

Figure 140 A version of the BorderDemo application.

Using the Borders Provided by Swing

The code that follows shows how to create and set the borders you saw in the preceding figures. You can find the program's code in <u>BorderDemo.java</u> (page 812).

```
//Keep references to the next few borders, for use in titles
//and compound borders.
Border blackline, etched, raisedbevel, loweredbevel, empty;
blackline = BorderFactory.createLineBorder(Color.black);
etched = BorderFactory.createEtchedBorder();
raisedbevel = BorderFactory.createRaisedBevelBorder();
loweredbevel = BorderFactory.createLoweredBevelBorder();
empty = BorderFactory.createEmptyBorder();

//Simple borders
jComp2.setBorder(blackline);
jComp3.setBorder(raisedbevel);
jComp4.setBorder(loweredbevel);
jComp5.setBorder(empty);

//Matte borders
ImageIcon icon = new ImageIcon("images/left.gif"); //20x22
jComp6.setBorder(BorderFactory.createMatteBorder(-1, -1, -1, -1, icon));
jComp7.setBorder(BorderFactory.createMatteBorder(1, 5, 1, 1,
Color.red));
jComp8.setBorder(BorderFactory.createMatteBorder(0, 20, 0, 0, icon));

//Titled borders
TitledBorder title1, title2, title3, title4, title5;
title1 = BorderFactory.createTitledBorder("title");
jComp9.setBorder(title1);
title2 = BorderFactory.createTitledBorder(
                    blackline, "title");
title2.setTitleJustification(TitledBorder.CENTER);
jComp10.setBorder(title2);
title3 = BorderFactory.createTitledBorder(
                    etched, "title");
title3.setTitleJustification(TitledBorder.RIGHT);
jComp11.setBorder(title3);
title4 = BorderFactory.createTitledBorder(
                    loweredbevel, "title");
title4.setTitlePosition(TitledBorder.ABOVETOP);
jComp12.setBorder(title4);
title5 = BorderFactory.createTitledBorder(
                    empty, "title");
title5.setTitlePosition(TitledBorder.BOTTOM);
jComp13.setBorder(title5);
```

```
//Compound borders
Border compound1, compound2, compound3;
Border redline = BorderFactory.createLineBorder(Color.red);

//This creates a nice frame.
compound1 = BorderFactory.createCompoundBorder(
                       raisedbevel, loweredbevel);
jComp14.setBorder(compound1);

//Add a red outline to the frame.
compound2 = BorderFactory.createCompoundBorder(
                       redline, compound1);
jComp15.setBorder(compound2);
//Add a title to the red-outlined frame.
compound3 = BorderFactory.createTitledBorder(
                       compound2, "title",
                       TitledBorder.CENTER,
                       TitledBorder.BELOWBOTTOM);
jComp16.setBorder(compound3);
```

As you probably noticed, the code uses the `BorderFactory` class to create each border. The `BorderFactory` class, which is in the `javax.swing` package, returns objects that implement the <u>Border</u>[1] interface.

The `Border` interface, as well as its Swing-provided implementations, is in the <u>javax.swing.border</u>[2] package. You often don't need to directly use anything in the border package, except when specifying constants that are specific to a particular border class or when referring to the `Border` type.

Creating Custom Borders

If `BorderFactory` doesn't offer you enough control over a border's form, you might need to directly use the API in the border package—or even define your own border. In addition to containing the `Border` interface, the border package contains the classes that implement the borders you've already seen: `LineBorder`, `EtchedBorder`, `BevelBorder`, `EmptyBorder`, `MatteBorder`, `TitledBorder`, and `CompoundBorder`. The border package also contains a class named `SoftBevelBorder`, which produces a result similar to `BevelBorder` but with softer edges.

---

[1] API documentation for this interface is available on this book's CD-ROM and online at
   http://java.sun.com/products/jdk/1.2/docs/api/javax/swing/border/Border.html
[2] http://java.sun.com/products/jdk/1.2/docs/api/javax/swing/border/package-summary.html

If none of the Swing borders is suitable, you can implement your own border. Generally you do this by creating a subclass of the `AbstractBorder` class. In your subclass you must implement at least one constructor and the following two methods:

- `paintBorder`, which contains the drawing code that a `JComponent` executes to draw the border
- `getBorderInsets`, which specifies the amount of space the border needs to draw itself

In addition, if your border is opaque, you might be able to decrease component drawing time by overriding the border's `isBorderOpaque` method so that it returns `true`. For examples of implementing borders, see the source code for the classes in the `javax.swing.border` package.

Adding a Border to a Bordered Swing Component

Many of the ready-to-use Swing components use borders to draw the outline of the component. If you want to draw an additional border around an already bordered component—to provide some extra space above a scroll pane, for example—you need to add the new border to the existing border. Be sure to test the component to make sure that it works well with your extra border; components that change their border depending on their state probably aren't good candidates for additional borders. Here's an example of adding to an existing border:

```
aJComponent.setBorder(
    BorderFactory.createCompoundBorder(
                BorderFactory.createEmptyBorder(20,0,0,0),
                aJComponent.getBorder())
);
```

The new border returned by `createEmptyBorder` adds 20 pixels of empty space above any component that uses it. The code uses the `createCompoundBorder` method to combine the new border with the existing border, which is returned by `getBorder`.

The Border API

The following tables list the commonly used border methods.

Table 159 Creating a Border with `BorderFactory`

Method	Purpose
`Border createLineBorder(Color)` `Border createLineBorder(Color, int)`	Create a line border. The first argument is a `java.awt.Color` object that specifies the color of the line. The optional second argument specifies the width, in pixels, of the line.
`Border createEtchedBorder()` `Border createEtchedBorder(Color, Color)`	Create an etched border. The optional arguments specify the highlight and shadow colors to be used.
`Border createLoweredBevelBorder()`	Create a border that gives the illusion of the component's being lower than the surrounding area.
`Border createLoweredBevelBorder()`	Create a border that gives the illusion of the component's being higher than the surrounding area.

`Border createBevelBorder(int, Color, Color)`
`Border createBevelBorder(int, Color, Color,`
`                          Color, Color)`
	Create a raised or a lowered beveled border, specifying the colors to use. The integer argument can be either RAISED or LOWERED (constants defined in `BevelBorder`). With the three-argument constructor, you specify the highlight and shadow colors. With the five-argument constructor, you specify the outer highlight, inner highlight, outer shadow, and inner shadow colors, in that order.

`Border createEmptyBorder()` `Border createEmptyBorder(int, int, int, int)`	Create an invisible border. If you specify no arguments, the border takes no space, which is useful when creating a titled border with no visible boundary. The optional arguments specify the number of pixels that the border occupies at the top, left, bottom, and right, in that order, of whatever component uses it.

`MatteBorder createMatteBorder(int, int, int,`
`                               int, Color)`
`MatteBorder createMatteBorder(int, int, int,`
`                               int, Icon)`
	Create a matte border. The integer arguments specify the number of pixels that the border occupies at the top, left, bottom, and right, in that order, of whatever component uses it. The `Color` argument specifies the color with which the border should fill its area. The `Icon` argument specifies the icon with which the border should title its area.

Table 159 Creating a Border with `BorderFactory`

Method	Purpose

`TitledBorder createTitledBorder(String)`
`TitledBorder createTitledBorder(Border)`
`TitledBorder createTitledBorder(Border,`
`                          String)`
`TitledBorder createTitledBorder(Border,`
`                    String, int, int)`
`TitledBorder createTitledBorder(Border,`
`              String, int, int, Font)`
`TitledBorder createTitledBorder(Border,`
`        String, int, int, Font, Color)`
	Create a titled border. The `String` argument specifies the title to be displayed. The optional `Font` and `Color` arguments specify the font and color to be used for the title's text. The `Border` argument specifies the border that should be displayed along with the title. If no border is specified, a look-and-feel-specific default border is used.
	
	By default the title straddles the top of its companion border and is left-justified. The optional integer arguments specify the title's position and justification, in that order. `TitledBorder` defines these possible positions: `ABOVE_TOP`, `TOP` (the default), `BELOW_TOP`, `ABOVE_BOTTOM`, `BOTTOM`, and `BELOW_BOTTOM`. You can specify the justification as `LEFT` (the default), `CENTER`, or `RIGHT`.

`CompoundBorder createCompoundBorder(Border,` `                          Border)`	Combine two borders into one. The first argument specifies the outer border; the second, the inner border.

Table 160 Setting or Getting a Component's Border

Method	Purpose
`void setBorder(Border)` `Border getBorder()`	Set or get the border of the receiving `JComponent`.

`void setBorderPainted(boolean)`
`boolean isBorderPainted()`
(in `AbstractButton`, `JMenuBar`, `JPopup-`
`Menu`, `JProgressBar`, and `JToolBar`)
	Set or get whether the border of the component should be painted.

Examples that Use Borders

Many examples in this lesson use borders. The following table lists a few interesting cases.

Table 161   Examples that Use Borders

Example	Where Described	Notes
`BorderDemo.java`	This section	Shows an example of each type of border that `BorderFactory` can create. Also uses an empty border to add breathing space between each pane and its contents.
`AlignmentDemo.java`	How to Use BoxLayout (page 350)	Uses titled borders.
`BoxLayoutDemo.java`	How to Use BoxLayout (page 350)	Uses a red line to show where the edge of a container is, letting you see how the extra space in a `BoxLayout` is distributed.
`ComboBoxDemo2.java`	How to Use Combo Boxes (page 192)	Uses a compound border to combine a line border with an empty border. The empty border provides space between the line and the component's innards.

How to Use Icons

Some Swing components, such as JLabel and JButton, can be decorated with an *icon*—a fixed-sized picture. An icon is an object that adheres to the Icon[1] interface. Swing provides a particularly useful implementation of the Icon interface: ImageIcon,[2] which paints an icon from a GIF or a JPEG image.

Here's a snapshot of an application that decorates two labels with an splat icon.

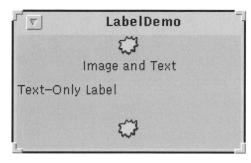

Figure 141 The LabelDemo application.

The program uses one image icon to contain and paint the splats. In the following code excerpt one statement creates the image icon, and two more statements include the image icon on each of the two labels:

```
ImageIcon icon = new ImageIcon("images/middle.gif",
                               "a pretty but meaningless splat");
...
label1 = new JLabel("Image and Text", icon, JLabel.CENTER);
...
label3 = new JLabel(icon);
```

The first argument to the ImageIcon constructor specifies the file to load, relative to the directory containing the application's class file. The second argument provides a description

---

[1] API documentation for Icon is available on this book's CD-ROM and online at http://java.sun.com/
    products/jdk/1.2/docs/api/javax/swing/Icon.html

[2] http://java.sun.com/products/jdk/1.2/docs/api/javax/swing/ImageIcon.html

of the icon, to be used by assistive technologies. This description might be used, for example, to help a visually impaired user understand what information the icon conveys.

Applets generally load image data from the computer that served up the applet. There are two reasons for this. First, untrusted applets can't read from the file system on which they're running. Second, it just makes sense to put an applet's class and data files together on the server. To load image data from the server, an applet uses a URL, as shown in the following example:

```java
public class SomeClass extends JApplet ... {
    protected String leftButtonFilename = "images/left.gif";
    ...
    public void init() {
        ...
        URL leftButtonURL = getURL(leftButtonFilename);
        ...
        leftButtonIcon = new ImageIcon(leftButtonURL,
                                      "an arrow pointing left");
        ...
    }
    ...
    protected URL getURL(String filename) {
        URL codeBase = getCodeBase();
        URL url = null;
        try {
            url = new URL(codeBase, filename);
        } catch (java.net.MalformedURLException e) {
            System.err.println("Couldn't create image: " +
                               "badly specified URL");
            return null;
        }

        return url;
    }
    ...
}
```

If you're writing an applet, you might want to copy the getURL method for use in your applet. For more information on specifying the source of image data, see Specifying the Image Source (page 420).

When you specify a filename or a URL to an ImageIcon constructor, the constructor returns only after the image data is completely loaded. Thus you can be sure that the image icon is usable following the call to the constructor. If you want more information while the image is loading, you can register an observer on an image icon by calling its setImageObserver method.

Under the covers, each image icon uses an Image object to hold the image data and a Media-Tracker object, which is shared by all image icons in the same program, to keep track of the image's loading status. If you're curious about Image objects, image observers, media trackers, and other image topics, see <u>Using Images</u> (page 555).

A More Complex Image Icon Example

Here's an applet that uses eight image icons. In Figure 142 you can see three of them: one displays the photograph, and two decorate the buttons at the bottom of the applet window with small arrows.

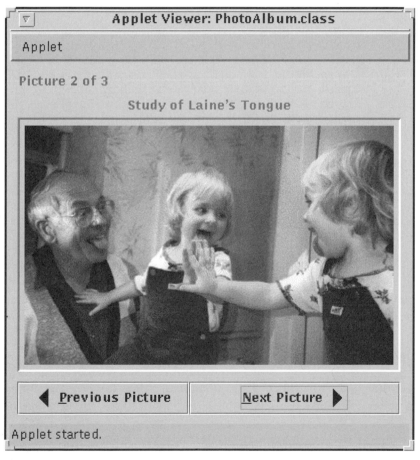

Figure 142 The IconDemoApplet applet.

Try this:

1. Run the applet.[1] The source code for the program is in <u>IconDemoApplet.java</u> (page 816), <u>Photo.java</u> (page 821), and <u>SwingWorker.java</u> (page 720). The applet also uses these image files: right.gif, left.gif, dimmedRight.gif, dimmed-Left.gif, ewanPumpkin.gif, kathyCosmo.gif, lainesTongue.gif, and stickerface.gif.[2]

2. Click the Previous Picture and Next Picture buttons to view the photographs.

3. Hold the mouse over a photograph. A tool tip appears that indicates the filename of the current photograph and its width and height.

4. To view your own photographs, modify the applet parameters. Here's the applet tag used for the preceding applet:

```
<applet code="IconDemoApplet.class"
        codebase="example-swing/"
        archive="icon.jar"
        width="400" height="360">
    <param NAME="IMAGEDIR" VALUE="images">
    <param NAME="IMAGE0" VALUE="stickerface.gif">
    <param NAME="CAPTION0" VALUE="StickerFace">
    <param NAME="WIDTH0" VALUE="230">
    <param NAME="HEIGHT0" VALUE="238">
    ...
</applet>
```

Note: We converted the <applet> tags to the <OBJECT> and <EMBED> tags required by the Java Plug-in, as described in <u>How to Make Applets</u> (page 99).

The IMAGEDIR parameter indicates that the image files should be in a directory named images relative to the applet's code base. Four parameters are required for each photograph, and the applet uses four photographs. The preceding tag shows the parameters for only the first photograph.

Specifying the Image Source

Most often, an image icon's data comes from an image file. You can specify the location of the file with either a filename or a <u>URL</u>[3] object. For applications, the filename or the URL is

---

[1] See the chapter <u>Getting Started with Swing</u> (page 3) if you need help compiling or running this application.

[2] You can find the images by visiting: http://java.sun.com/docs/books/tutorial/uiswing/components/example-swing/index.html

[3] http://java.sun.com/products/jdk/1.2/docs/api/java/net/URL.html

generally relative either to the directory containing the application's class files or to the class path. Applets generally use a URL that is constructed relative to the applet's code base (the directory containing the applet's class files).

You've already seen how to specify a filename relative to the directory containing the application's class files. To specify a URL relative to an application's class path, you can use the `ClassLoader getSystemResource` method. Here is an example:

```
ImageIcon icon = null1;
URL iconURL = ClassLoader.getSystemResource("images/middle.qif");
if (iconURL != null) {
    icon = new ImageIcon(iconURL,
                         "a beautiful yet meaningless icon");
}
```

The `getSystemResource` method looks through the directories and JAR (Java ARchive) files in the program's class path, returning a URL as soon as it finds the desired file. For example, assume that you put a JAR file named `icons.jar` in your program's class path. If the JAR file contains `images/middle.gif`, the class loader will definitely return a URL for `images/middle.gif`. However, the URL might not be relative to `icons.jar`, if another JAR file or a directory in the class path contains `images/middle.gif`. The URL will point to the *first* JAR file or directory in the class path that contains `images/middle.gif`.

The `IconDemoApplet` program initializes each of its image icons from GIF files whose locations are specified with URLs. Because `IconDemoApplet` is designed to be an untrusted applet, we must place the image files under the applet's code base. The following figure shows the locations of files for `IconDemoApplet`.

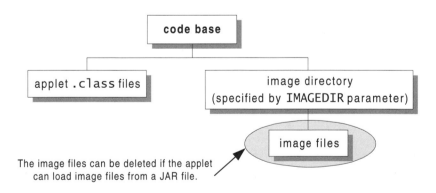

Figure 143 Locations of files for `IconDemoApplet`.

Note: Applets are supposed to be able to load images from JAR files. Currently, however, some browsers can't read images from a JAR file, although they do successfully get classes from a JAR file. With our applets, we currently hedge our bets by both putting the image files in the applet's archive file (the JAR file containing the applet's class files) and by putting the image files in the file system on the server.

Improving Perceived Performance When Loading Image Icons

Because the photograph images are large and because the applet uses multiple images, `IconDemoApplet` uses several techniques to improve the performance of the program as perceived by the user.

- Dimmed icons: The applet provides dimmed versions of the arrows for the buttons:

```
imagedir = getParameter("IMAGEDIR");
if (imagedir != null)
    imagedir = imagedir + "/";
    ...
    ImageIcon dimmedNextIcon = new ImageIcon(getURL(
                                    imagedir + "dimmedRight.gif"));

    ImageIcon dimmedPreviousIcon = new ImageIcon(getURL(
                                    imagedir + "dimmedLeft.gif"));
    ...
    nextButton.setDisabledIcon(dimmedNextIcon);

...
previousButton.setDisabledIcon(dimmedPreviousIcon);
```

  Without this code, the dimmed versions of the arrows would be computed, which (at least on our slow computers) causes a slight delay the first time each button is dimmed. This technique trades a noticeable delay when the user clicks the buttons for a smaller, less noticeable delay in the `init` method.

  This applet uses four separate image files just to display arrows on two buttons. The performance impact of these little images can add up, especially if the browser in which the applet is running uses a separate HTTP connection to load each one. A better alternative is to implement a custom `Icon` that paints the arrows. See the next section, Creating a Custom Icon Implementation (page 424), for an example.

- Lazy image loading: The applet's initialization code loads only the first photograph. Each other photograph gets loaded when the user first requests to see it. By loading images if and when needed, the applet avoids a long initialization. The downside is that the user has to wait to see each photograph. We try to make this wait less noticeable by providing feedback about the image loading and allowing the user to use the GUI while the image is loading.

Not all programs can benefit from lazy loading. For example, the `TumbleItem.java` (page 773) applet performs an animation, so all of the images are needed up-front. That applet's initialization code causes the images to be loaded in a background thread, so that the applet can present a GUI (a Loading Images... label) before the images have loaded.

- Background image loading: The applet uses a `SwingWorker` to load each photograph image in a background thread. Because the image is loaded in a separate thread, the user can still click the buttons and otherwise interact with the applet while the image is loading.

Here's the code to load each image:

```
private void loadImage(final String imagePath, final int index) {
    final SwingWorker worker = new SwingWorker() {
        ImageIcon icon = null;

        public Object construct() {
            icon = new ImageIcon(getURL(imagePath));
            return icon;
        }

        public void finished() {
            Photo pic = (Photo)pictures.elementAt(index);
            pic.setIcon(icon);
            if (index == current)
                updatePhotograph(index, pic);
        }
    };
}
```

The `construct` method, which creates the image icon for the photograph, is invoked by the thread that's created and started by the `SwingWorker` constructor. After the image icon is fully loaded, the `finished` method is called. The `finished` method is guaranteed to execute on the event-dispatching thread, so it can safely update the GUI to display the photograph.

- Status updates: While the image is loading in the background, the applet displays a status message:

```
photographLabel.setIcon(null);
photographLabel.setText("Loading image...");
```

This lets the user know that the program is doing something. After the image is loaded, the applet displays the photograph in the viewing area.

- Caching: After each photograph is viewed for the first time, the applet caches the image icon for later use. Thus if the user revisits a photograph, the program can use the same image icon and display the photograph quickly.

If you write a program without caching image icons, it may appear that some implicit image caching is going on within the Java platform. However, this is a side effect of the implementation and is not guaranteed. If your program uses one image many times, you can create the image icon once and use the same instance multiple times.

As with all performance-related issues, these techniques work in some situations and not others. These are not general recommendations for all programs, but they do provide some techniques you can use to try to improve the user's experience. Furthermore the techniques described here are designed to improve the program's perceived performance but don't necessarily impact its real performance.

Creating a Custom Icon Implementation

If you use a simple image repeatedly, consider implementing a custom `Icon` class to paint the image. The really nice thing about a custom icon is that you can easily change the icon's appearance to reflect its host component's state.

Look-and-feel implementations often use custom icons. For example, the Metal Look & Feel uses a single `MetalCheckBoxIcon` object to paint all of the check boxes in the GUI. The `MetalCheckBoxIcon` paints itself differently, depending on whether its host component is enabled, pressed, or selected.

In this section we'll convert a program called `ButtonDemo` so that it uses a custom icon to paint these two arrows:

You can see a picture of `ButtonDemo` in <u>The Common Button API</u> (page 170). The source code is in <u>ButtonDemo.java</u> (page 625). The following code loads the arrows from GIF files and put the arrows into buttons:

```
ImageIcon leftButtonIcon = new ImageIcon("images/right.gif");
...
ImageIcon rightButtonIcon = new ImageIcon("images/left.gif");
b1 = new JButton("Disable middle button", leftButtonIcon);
...
b3 = new JButton("Enable middle button", rightButtonIcon);
```

Here is the new code, which uses a custom icon class named `ArrowIcon`. Only the boldface lines have changed. You can find the entire program in CustomIconDemo.java (page 815).

```
Icon leftButtonIcon = new ArrowIcon(SwingConstants.RIGHT);
...
Icon rightButtonIcon = new ArrowIcon(SwingConstants.LEFT);

b1 = new JButton("Disable middle button", leftButtonIcon);
...
b3 = new JButton("Enable middle button", rightButtonIcon);
```

You can find the implementation of the custom icon class in ArrowIcon.java (page 811). Here are the interesting parts of its code:

```
class ArrowIcon implements Icon, SwingConstants {
    ...
    public void paintIcon(Component c, Graphics g, int x, int y) {
        int length = xPoints.length;
        int adjustedXPoints[] = new int[length];
        int adjustedYPoints[] = new int[length];
        for (int i = 0; i < length; i++) {
            adjustedXPoints[i] = xPoints[i] + x;
            adjustedYPoints[i] = yPoints[i] + y;
        }
        if (c.isEnabled()) {
            g.setColor(Color.black);
        } else {
            g.setColor(Color.gray);
        }
        g.fillPolygon(adjustedXPoints, adjustedYPoints, length);
    }
}
```

Note that the icon sets the current color. If you don't do this, the icon's painting might not be visible. For more information about performing custom painting, see Working with Graphics (page 533). The `fillPolygon` method is discussed in Painting Shapes (page 545).

Using a custom icon to paint the arrows has a few implications:

- Because the icon's appearance is determined dynamically, the icon painting code can use any information—component and application state, for example—to determine what to paint.

- Because we specified a non-`ImageIcon` icon for a button, the button doesn't bother to calculate the dimmed (disabled) version of the icon. Instead the button lets the icon paint its disabled self. This can reduce computation time and save space that would otherwise be used to hold the dimmed image.

- Depending on the platform, we might get a performance boost with custom icons, since painting polygons is often faster than painting images.
- Instead of loading all of the GIF files for the arrows (left and right, and perhaps dimmed left and dimmed right), we load a single class file (ArrowIcon). The performance implications of this depend on such factors as the platform, the size of the files, and the overhead for loading each type of file.

The Image Icon API

The following tables list the commonly used ImageIcon constructors and methods. Note that ImageIcon is not a descendant of JComponent or even of Component.

Table 162   Setting, Getting, and Painting the Image Icon's Image

Method or Constructor	Purpose
ImageIcon() ImageIcon(byte[]) ImageIcon(byte[], String) ImageIcon(Image) ImageIcon(Image, String) ImageIcon(String) ImageIcon(String, String) ImageIcon(URL) ImageIcon(URL, String)	Create an ImageIcon instance, initializing it to contain the specified image. The first argument indicates the source—image, byte array, filename, or URL—from which the image icon's image should be loaded. The source must be in a format supported by the java.awt.Image class: namely, GIF or JPEG. The second argument, when present, provides a description for the image. The description, a short textual description of the image, could be used in a variety of ways, such as alternative text for the image.
void setImage(Image) Image getImage()	Set or get the image displayed by the image icon.

void paintIcon(Component,
                           Graphics,
                                  int, int)
	Paint the image icon's image in the specified graphics context. You would do this only if you're implementing a custom component that performs its own painting. The Component object is used as an image observer. You can rely on the default behavior provided by Component class and pass in any component. The two int arguments specify the x and y coordinates, respectively.

Table 163   Setting or Getting Information About the Image Icon

Method	Purpose
void setDescription(String) String getDescription()	Set or get a description of the image. This description is intended for use by assistive technologies.
int getIconWidth() int getIconHeight()	Get the width or height of the image icon, in pixels.

Table 164 Watching the Image Icon's Image Load

Method	Purpose
`void setImageObserver(ImageObserver)` `ImageObserver getImageObserver()`	Set or get an image observer for the image icon.
`int getImageLoadStatus()`	Get the loading status of the image icon's image. The set of values returned by this method are defined by `Media-Tracker`.

Examples that Use Icons

The following table lists just a few of the many examples that use `ImageIcon`.

Table 165 Examples that Use Icons

Example	Where Described	Notes
`LabelDemo.java`	This section and How to Use Labels (page 212)	Demonstrates using icons in an application's label, with and without accompanying text.
`IconDemoApplet.java`	This section	An applet. Uses a label to show large images; uses buttons that have both images and text.
`TumbleItem.java`	How to Make Applets (page 99)	Uses image icons in an animation. Shows how to use `ImageIcon`'s `paintIcon` method.
`ButtonDemo.java`	How to Use Buttons, Check Boxes, and Radio Buttons (page 169)	Shows how to use icons in an application's buttons.
`CheckBoxDemo.java`	How to Use Check Boxes (page 177)	Uses multiple GIF images.
`TabbedPaneDemo.java`	How to Use Tabbed Panes (page 134)	Demonstrates adding icons to tabs in a tabbed pane.
`DialogDemo.java,` `CustomDialog.java`	How to Make Dialogs (page 87)	Shows how to use standard icons in dialogs.
`TreeIconDemo.java`	How to Use Trees (page 320)	Shows how to change the icons displayed by a tree's nodes.
`ActionDemo.java`	How to Use Actions (page 389)	Shows how to specify the icon in a tool bar button or a menu item, using an `Action`.

How to Set the Look and Feel

If you don't care which look and feel your program uses, you can skip this section entirely. For example, since most of the programs in this book don't specify the look and feel, you can easily run the programs with your preferred look and feel.

When a program does not set its look and feel, the Swing UI manager must figure out which look and feel to use. The UI manager first checks whether the user has specified a preferred look and feel and attempts to use that one. If the user hasn't specified one, or if the user's choice isn't valid, the UI manager chooses the Java Look & Feel.

Setting the Look and Feel

To programmatically specify a look and feel, use the `UIManager.setLookAndFeel` method. For example, the boldface code in the following snippet makes the program use the Java Look & Feel:

```
public static void main(String[] args) {
    try {
        UIManager.setLookAndFeel(
            UIManager.getCrossPlatformLookAndFeelClassName());
    } catch (Exception e) { }
    new SwingApplication(); //Create and show the GUI.
}
```

The argument to `setLookAndFeel` is the fully qualified name of the appropriate subclass of `LookAndFeel`. To specify the Java Look & Feel, we used the `getCrossPlatformLookAnd-FeelClassName` method. If you want to specify the native look and feel for whatever platform the user runs the program on, use `getSystemLookAndFeelClassName` instead. To specify a particular UI, you can use the actual class name. For example, if you design a program to look best with the Windows Look & Feel, you can use this code to set the look and feel:

```
UIManager.setLookAndFeel(
        "com.sun.java.swing.plaf.windows.WindowsLookAndFeel");
```

Here are some of the arguments you can use for `setLookAndFeel`.

`UIManager.getCrossPlatformLookAndFeelClassName()`
Returns the string for the one look and feel guaranteed to work—the Java Look & Feel.

`UIManager.getSystemLookAndFeelClassName()`
Specifies the look and feel for the current platform. On Win32 platforms this specifies the Windows Look & Feel. On Mac OS platforms this specifies the Mac OS Look & Feel. On Sun™ platforms it specifies the CDE/Motif Look & Feel.

`"javax.swing.plaf.metal.MetalLookAndFeel"`
Specifies the Java Look & Feel. (The code name for this look and feel was *Metal*.) This string is the value returned by the `getCrossPlatformLookAndFeelClassName` method.

`"com.sun.java.swing.plaf.windows.WindowsLookAndFeel"`
Specifies the Windows Look & Feel. Currently you can use this look and feel only on Win32 systems.

`"com.sun.java.swing.plaf.motif.MotifLookAndFeel"`
Specifies the CDE/Motif Look & Feel. This look and feel can be used on any platform.

`"javax.swing.plaf.mac.MacLookAndFeel"`
Specifies the Mac OS Look & Feel, which can be used only on Mac OS platforms.

You aren't limited to the preceding arguments. You can specify the name for any look and feel that is in your program's class path.

How the UI Manager Chooses the Look and Feel

Here are the look-and-feel determination steps that occur when the UI manager first initializes itself.

1. If the program sets the look and feel before any components are created, the UI manager tries to create an instance of the specified look-and-feel class. If successful, all components use that look and feel.

2. If the program hasn't successfully specified a look and feel, before the first component's UI is created, the UI manager tests whether the user specified a look and feel in a file named `swing.properties`. The UI manager looks for the file in the `lib` directory of the Java release. For example, if you're using the Java interpreter in *javaHomeDirectory*\bin, the `swing.properties` file is in *javaHomeDirectory*\lib (if it exists). If the user specified a look and feel, again the UI manager tries to instantiate the specified class. Here is an example of the contents of a `swing.properties` file:

```
# Swing properties
swing.defaultlaf=com.sun.java.swing.plaf.motif.MotifLookAndFeel
```

3. If neither the program nor the user successfully specifies a look and feel, the program uses the Java Look & Feel.

Changing the Look and Feel After Startup

You can change the look and feel with `setLookAndFeel` even after the program's GUI is visible. To make existing components reflect the new look and feel, invoke the `SwingUtilities` `updateComponentTreeUI` method once per top-level container. Then you might wish to resize each top-level container to reflect the new sizes of its contained components. For example:

```
UIManager.setLookAndFeel(lnfName);
SwingUtilities.updateComponentTreeUI(frame);
frame.pack();
```

How to Use Threads

The first rule of using threads is this: Avoid them if you can. Threads can be difficult to use, and they tend to make programs more difficult to debug. To avoid the possibility of deadlock, you must take extreme care that any threads you create don't invoke any methods on Swing components. Remember, once a Swing component has been realized, only the event-dispatching thread should affect or query the component. If you aren't familiar with the role of the event-dispatching thread, please read Threads and Swing (page 45) and Threads and Event Handling (page 39).

Despite the dangers, threads can be invaluable. You can use them to improve your program's perceived performance. And sometimes threads can simplify a program's code or architecture. Here are some typical situations in which threads are used:

- To move a time-consuming initialization task out of the main thread, so that the GUI comes up faster. Examples of time-consuming tasks include making extensive calculations and blocking for network or disk I/O (loading images, for example).

- To move a time-consuming task out of the event-dispatching thread, so that the GUI remains responsive.

- To perform an operation repeatedly, usually with a predetermined period of time between operations.

- To wait for messages from other programs.

If you need to create a thread, you can avoid some common pitfalls by implementing the thread with a utility class such as `SwingWorker.java` (page 720) or `Timer`.[1] A `SwingWorker` object creates a thread to execute a time-consuming operation. After the operation is finished, `SwingWorker` gives you the option of executing additional code in the event-dispatching thread. A `Timer` object implements a thread that spawns one or more action events after a specified delay. If you need to implement your own threads, you can find information on doing so in Doing Two or More Tasks At Once: Threads.[2]

You can use several techniques to make multithreaded Swing programs work well.

- If you need to update a component but your code isn't executing in an event handler, use one of these two `SwingUtilities` methods: `invokeLater` (preferred) or `invoke-`

---

[1] API documentation for `Timer` is available on this book's CD-ROM and online at http://java.sun.com/products/jdk/1.2/docs/api/javax/swing/Timer.html

[2] http://java.sun.com/docs/books/tutorial/essential/threads/index.html

AndWait. These methods let you specify that some code be executed in the event-dispatching thread.

- If you aren't sure whether your code is executing in an event handler, you should analyze your program's code and document which thread each method is (and can be) called from. Failing that, you can use the SwingUtilities.isEventDispatchThread() method, which returns true if your code is executing in the event-dispatching thread. You can safely call invokeLater from any thread, but invokeAndWait throws an exception if it's called from the event-dispatching thread.

- If you need to update a component after a delay (whether or not your code is currently executing in an event handler), use a timer to do so.

- If you need to update a component at a regular interval, use a timer.

The rest of this section discusses SwingWorker and the SwingUtilities invoke methods. For information and examples of using timers, see How to Use Timers (page 436).

Using the SwingWorker Class

The SwingWorker class is implemented in SwingWorker.java (page 720), which is *not* in the Swing release. To use the SwingWorker class, you first create a subclass of it. The subclass must implement the construct method so that it contains the code to perform your lengthy operation. When you instantiate your SwingWorker subclass, the SwingWorker creates a thread that calls your construct method.

Here is an example of using a SwingWorker to move a time-consuming task from an action event handler into a background thread, so that the GUI remains responsive:

```
//OLD CODE:
public void actionPerformed(ActionEvent e) {
    ...
    //...code that might take a while to execute is here...
    ...
}
//BETTER CODE:
public void actionPerformed(ActionEvent e) {
    ...
    final SwingWorker worker = new SwingWorker() {
        public Object construct() {
            //...code that might take a while to execute is here...
            return someValue;
        }
    };
    ...
}
```

The value that `construct` returns can be any object. If you need to get the value, you can do so by invoking the `get` method on your `SwingWorker` object. Be careful about using `get`. Because it blocks, it can cause deadlock. If necessary, you can interrupt the thread (causing `get` to return) by invoking `interrupt` on the `SwingWorker`.

If you need to detect when the time-consuming operation completes, you can do so either by using `get` (which is dangerous, as we noted) or by overriding the `finished` method in your `SwingWorker` subclass. The `finished` method runs after the `construct` method returns. Because the `finished` method executes in the event-dispatching thread, you can safely use it to update Swing components. Of course, you shouldn't put time-consuming operations in your `finished` implementation.

The following example of implementing `finished` is taken from `IconDemoApplet.java` (page 816). For a full discussion of this applet, including how it improves perceived performance by using background threads to load images, see How to Use Icons (page 417).

```
public void actionPerformed(ActionEvent e) {
    ...
    if (icon == null) {    //haven't viewed this photo before
        loadImage(imagedir + pic.filename, current);
    } else {
        updatePhotograph(current, pic);
    }
}
...

//Load an image in a separate thread.
private void loadImage(final String imagePath, final int index) {
    final SwingWorker worker = new SwingWorker() {
        ImageIcon icon = null;
        public Object construct() {
            icon = new ImageIcon(getURL(imagePath));
            return icon; //return value not used by this program
        }

        //Runs on the event-dispatching thread.
        public void finished() {
            Photo pic = (Photo)pictures.elementAt(index);
            pic.setIcon(icon);
            if (index == current)
                    updatePhotograph(index, pic);
        }
    };
}
```

For more examples of using SwingWorker, go to <u>How to Monitor Progress</u> (page 239). Also, <u>TumbleItem.java</u> (page 773), which is discussed in <u>How to Make Applets</u> (page 99), uses both a SwingWorker and a Timer.

Using the invokeLater Method

You can call invokeLater from any thread to request the event-dispatching thread to run certain code. You must put this code in the run method of a Runnable object and specify the Runnable object as the argument to invokeLater. The invokeLater method returns immediately, without waiting for the event-dispatching thread to execute the code. Here's an example of using invokeLater:

```
Runnable updateAComponent = new Runnable() {
    public void run() { component.doSomething(); }
};
SwingUtilities.invokeLater(updateAComponent);
```

Using the invokeAndWait Method

The invokeAndWait method is just like invokeLater, except that invokeAndWait doesn't return until the event-dispatching thread has executed the specified code. Whenever possible, you should use invokeLater instead of invokeAndWait. If you use invokeAndWait, make sure that the thread that calls invokeAndWait does not hold any locks that other threads might need while the call is occurring.

Here's an example of using invokeAndWait:

```
void showHelloThereDialog() throws Exception {
    Runnable showModalDialog = new Runnable() {
        public void run() {
            JOptionPane.showMessageDialog(myMainFrame,
                                          "Hello There");
        }
    };
    SwingUtilities.invokeAndWait(showModalDialog);
}
```

Similarly a thread that needs access to GUI state, such as the contents of a pair of text fields, might have the following code:

```
void printTextField() throws Exception {
    final String[] myStrings = new String[2];
    Runnable getTextFieldText = new Runnable() {
```

```
        public void run() {
            myStrings[0] = textField0.getText();
            myStrings[1] = textField1.getText();
        }
    };
    SwingUtilities.invokeAndWait(getTextFieldText);
    System.out.println(myStrings[0] + " " + myStrings[1]);
}
```

For more examples of using the invoke methods, see the BINGO example, especially the following classes: CardWindow,[1] ControlPane,[2] Player,[3] and OverallStatusPane.[4]

For more information about Swing thread issues, see *The Swing Connection* articles "Threads and Swing" and "Using a Swing Worker Thread."[5]

---

[1] http://java.sun.com/docs/books/tutorial/together/bingo/example-swing/bingo/CardWindow.java
[2] http://java.sun.com/docs/books/tutorial/together/bingo/example-swing/bingo/ControlPane.java
[3] http://java.sun.com/docs/books/tutorial/together/bingo/example-swing/bingo/player/Player.java
[4] http://java.sun.com/docs/books/tutorial/together/bingo/example-swing/bingo/OverallStatusPane.java
[5] *The Swing Connection* is available on the CD-ROM that accompanies this book and online at
   http://java.sun.com/products/jfc/tsc/index.html

How to Use Timers

A Timer[1] object fires one or more action events after a specified delay. You can use a timer in either of two ways:

- To perform a task once, after a delay. For example, the tool tip manager uses timers to determine when to show a tool tip and when to hide it.

- To perform a task repeatedly. For example, you might perform animation or update a component that displays progress toward a goal. See Creating an Animation Loop with Timer (page 562) for an example and discussion of using a timer for animation.

Note that the timer's task is performed in the event-dispatching thread. This means that the task can safely manipulate components, and it also means that the task should execute quickly. If the task might take a while to execute, consider using a SwingWorker instead of or in addition to the timer. See How to Use Threads (page 431) for instructions about using the SwingWorker class and information on using Swing components in multithreaded programs.

Let's look at an example of using a timer to periodically update a component that displays progress toward a goal. Here's a picture of an application that uses a timer and a progress bar to display the progress of a long-running task.

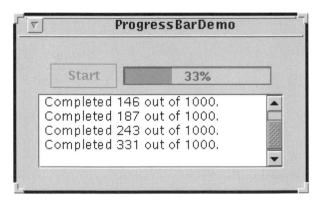

Figure 144 The ProgressBarDemo application.

---

[1] API documentation for Timer is available on this book's CD-ROM and online at http://java.sun.com/products/jdk/1.2/docs/api/javax/swing/Timer.html

Try this:

1. Compile and run the application.[1] The main source file is <u>ProgressBarDemo.java</u> (page 695).

2. Push the Start button. Watch the progress bar as the task proceeds.

Here's the code that creates a timer that "goes off" every second. Each time a timer goes off, it fires an action event. Conveniently the constructor also takes an action listener, which is implemented as an anonymous inner class. The action listener contains the code that implements the timer's task.

```
public final static int ONE_SECOND = 1000;
...
timer = new Timer(ONE_SECOND, new ActionListener() {
    public void actionPerformed(ActionEvent evt) {
        //...Perform a task...
    }
});
```

When the user presses the Start button, the program starts the timer:

```
timer.start();
```

When the task is finished, the timer's action listener stops the timer:

```
if (/* task is done */) {
    ...
    timer.stop();
    ...
}
```

The Timer API

The following tables list the commonly used Timer constructors and methods.

Table 166   Creating and Initializing the Timer

Method or Constructor	Purpose
Timer(int, ActionListener)	Create a timer. The int argument specifies the number of milliseconds to pause between action events. Use setDelay to change the delay after construction. The second argument is an action listener, which the constructor registers with the timer. You can also register action listeners with addActionListener and remove them with removeActionlistener.

---

[1] See the chapter <u>Getting Started with Swing</u> (page 3) if you need help compiling or running this application.

Table 166   Creating and Initializing the `Timer`

Method or Constructor	Purpose
`void setDelay(int)` `int getDelay()`	Set or get the number of milliseconds between action events.
`void setInitialDelay(int)` `int getInitialDelay()`	Set or get the number of milliseconds to wait before firing the first action event. By default the initial delay is equal to the regular delay.
`void setRepeats(boolean)` `boolean isRepeats()`	Set or get whether the timer repeats. By default this value is `true`. Call `setRepeats(false)` to set up a timer that fires a single action event and then stops.
`void setCoalesce(boolean)` `boolean isCoalesce()`	Set or get whether the timer coalesces multiple, pending action events into a single action event. By default this value is `true`.

Table 167   Running the Timer

Method	Purpose
`void start()` `void restart()`	Turn the timer on. Note that `restart` also cancels any pending action events.
`void stop()`	Turn the timer off.
`boolean isRunning()`	Get whether the timer is running.

Examples that Use Timer

This table shows the examples that use `Timer` and where those examples are described.

Table 168   Examples that Use Timer

Example	Where Described	Notes
`ProgressBarDemo.java`	This section and How to Monitor Progress (page 239)	Uses a timer to show periodic progress.
`AnimatorApplicationTimer.java` and `AnimatorAppletTimer.java`	Creating an Animation Loop with Timer (page 562)	Uses a timer to control an animation loop.
`SliderDemo.java`	How to Use Sliders (page 248)	An animation program that uses a timer. Allows the user to change the timer's delay dynamically. Also shows how to use the initial delay and `restart` to create a longer pause between certain frames in an animation.

Writing Event Listeners

THIS lesson gives you details about writing event listeners. It assumes you've already read and understood <u>Event Handling</u> (page 37), which gives an overview of the event model.

In fact, you might not need to read this lesson at all. Your first source of information for event information should be the how-to section for the component in question. You can find the appropriate section by referring to <u>A Visual Index to Swing Components</u> (page 63). Each component's section shows code for handling the events most commonly needed when implementing the component. For example, <u>How to Use Check Boxes</u> (page 177) shows you how to use an item listener to handle mouse clicks on check boxes.

The sections in this lesson rage from a gentle introduction to how-to reference sections.

<u>Some Simple Event-Handling Examples</u> (page 443)
Read this chapter if you're not comfortable with basic event-handling concepts. By running the applets in this chapter and viewing their source code, you can get a feel for how events work.

<u>General Rules for Writing Event Listeners</u> (page 447)
This chapter provides information that's useful for handling all types of events. One of the topics is how to reduce unnecessary code by using adapters and inner classes to implement event handlers.

Listeners Supported by Swing Components (page 453)
This is *the* place to find out which Swing components can fire which kinds of events. This chapter contains a handy quick-reference table.

Implementing Listeners for Commonly Handled Events (page 457)
This chapter has detailed information and examples of writing each common kind of event listener.

Summary of Listener API (page 527)
This chapter features a quick-reference table that shows each listener, its adapter class (if any), and its methods.

Solving Common Event-Handling Problems (page 531)
If you're having some hard-to-debug problems related to handling events, you might find the solution here.

Some Simple Event-Handling Examples

HERE is a bare-bones applet that illustrates event handling. It contains a single button that beeps when you click it.

Figure 145 The simple `Beeper` applet. You can see this applet online at `http://java.sun.com/docs/books/tutorial/uiswing/events/Beeper.html`

You can find the entire program in `Beeper.java` (page 826). Here's the code that implements the event handling for the button:

```
public class Beeper ... implements ActionListener {
    ...
    //where initialization occurs:
        button.addActionListener(this);
    ...
    public void actionPerformed(ActionEvent e) {
        ...//Make a beep sound...
    }
}
```

Isn't that simple? The `Beeper` class implements the <u>`ActionListener`</u>[1] interface, which contains one method: `actionPerformed`. Since `Beeper` implements `ActionListener`, a `Beeper` object can register as a listener for the action events that buttons fire. Once the `Beeper` has been registered by using the `Button addActionListener` method, the `Beeper`'s `actionPerformed` method is called every time the button is clicked.

A More Complex Example

The event model, which you saw at its simplest in the preceding example, is quite powerful and flexible. Any number of event listener objects can listen for all kinds of events from any number of event source objects. For example, a program might create one listener per event source. Or a program might have a single listener for all events from all sources. A program can even have more than one listener for a single kind of event from a single event source.

The following applet gives an example of using multiple listeners per object. The applet contains two event sources (`JButton` instances) and two event listeners. One of the event listeners—an instance of a class called `MultiListener`—listens for events from both buttons. When it receives an event, the event listener adds the event's "action command"—the text on the button's label—to the top text area. The second event listener—an instance of a class called `Eavesdropper`—listens for events on only one of the buttons.

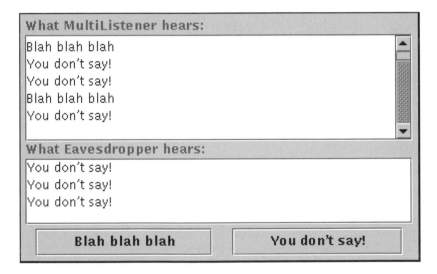

Figure 146 The `MultiListener` applet. You can see this applet online at `http://java.sun.com/docs/books/tutorial/uiswing/events/MultiListener.html`

---

[1]   See <u>How to Write an Action Listener</u> (page 459) for more information on the `ActionListener` interface.

When it receives an event, it adds the action command to the bottom text area.

You can find the entire program in MultiListener.java (page 849). Here's the code that implements the event handling for the button:

```
public class MultiListener ... implements ActionListener {

    ...
    //where initialization occurs:
        button1.addActionListener(this);
        button2.addActionListener(this);
        button2.addActionListener(new Eavesdropper(bottomTextArea));
    }

    public void actionPerformed(ActionEvent e) {
        topTextArea.append(e.getActionCommand() + newline);
    }
}

class Eavesdropper implements ActionListener {
    ...
    public void actionPerformed(ActionEvent e) {
        myTextArea.append(e.getActionCommand() + multiListener.newline);
    }
}
```

In the preceding code both MultiListener and Eavesdropper implement the ActionListener interface and register as action listeners, using the JButton addActionListener method. Both classes' implementations of the actionPerformed method are similar: They simply add the event's action command to a text area.

An Example of Handling Another Event Type

So far in this lesson, you've seen only action events. Let's take a look at a program that handles another kind of event: mouse events.

The following applet displays a rectangle-edged area and a text area. Whenever a mouse event—a click, press, release, enter, or exit—occurs on either the rectangle-edged area (BlankAreaMouseEventDemo), the text area displays a string describing the event.

You can find the entire program in MouseEventDemo.java (page 847) and BlankArea.java (page 827).

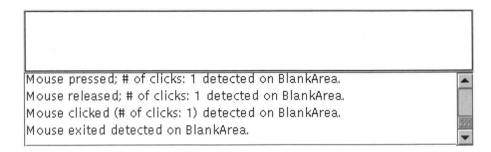

Figure 147   The MouseEventDemo applet. You can see this applet online at http://java.sun.com/
docs/books/tutorial/uiswing/events/MouseEventDemo.html

Here's the code that implements the event handling:

```
public class MouseEventDemo ...  implements MouseListener {
    ...
    //where initialization occurs:
        //Register for mouse events on blankArea and applet
        blankArea.addMouseListener(this);
        addMouseListener(this);
    ...
    public void mousePressed(MouseEvent e) {
        saySomething("Mouse pressed; # of clicks: "
                    + e.getClickCount(), e);
    }
    public void mouseReleased(MouseEvent e) {
        saySomething("Mouse released; # of clicks: "
                    + e.getClickCount(), e);
    }
    public void mouseEntered(MouseEvent e) {
        saySomething("Mouse entered", e);
    }
    public void mouseExited(MouseEvent e) {
        saySomething("Mouse exited", e);
    }
    public void mouseClicked(MouseEvent e) {
        saySomething("Mouse clicked (# of clicks: "
                    + e.getClickCount() + ")", e);
    }
    void saySomething(String eventDescription, MouseEvent e) {
        textArea.append(eventDescription + " detected on "
                        + e.getComponent().getClass().getName()
                        + "." + newline);
    }
}
```

You'll see the code explained in <u>How to Write a Mouse Listener</u> (page 498).

23

General Rules for Writing Event Listeners

FROM <u>Event Handling</u> (page 37), you should already know the basics of event listeners. For example, you know that you can attach multiple listeners to a single event source. Most important, you know that event-listener methods should execute quickly. Because all event-handling and drawing methods are executed in the same thread, a slow event-listener method can make the program seem unresponsive and slow to repaint itself.

This chapter first introduces you to event objects—small objects that describe each event. In particular, we talk about `EventObject`, the superclass for all AWT and Swing events. Then this chapter describes two major categories of events and gives you hints for avoiding clutter in your code.

Getting Event Information: Event Objects

Every event-listener method has a single argument—an object that inherits from the `EventObject`[1] class. Although the argument always descends from `EventObject`, its type is generally specified more precisely. For example, the argument for methods that handle mouse events is an instance of `MouseEvent`, where `MouseEvent` is an indirect subclass of `EventObject`.

---

[1] API documentation for `EventObject` is available on this book's CD-ROM and online at http://java.sun.com/products/jdk/1.2/docs/api/java/util/EventObject.html

The `EventObject` class defines one very useful method.

Object getSource()
　　Returns the object that fired the event.

Note that the `getSource` method returns an `Object`. Event classes sometimes define methods that, although similar to `getSource`, have more restricted return types. For example, the `ComponentEvent` class defines a `getComponent` method that—just like `getSource`—returns the object that fired the event. The difference is that `getComponent` always returns a `Component`. Each how-to section in this lesson describes whether you should use `get-Source` or another method to get the event source.

Often an event class defines methods that return information about the event. For example, you can query a `MouseEvent` object for information about where the event occurred, how many clicks the user made, which modifier keys were pressed, and so on.

Concepts: Low-Level Events and Semantic Events

Events can be divided into two groups: *low-level* events and *semantic* events. Low-level events represent window-system occurrences, or low-level input. Everything else is a semantic event.

Mouse and key events—both of which result directly from user input—are low-level events. Other low-level events are component, container, focus, and window events. Component events let you track changes to a component's position, size, and visibility. Container events let you know when any component is added to or removed from a particular container. Focus events tell you when a component gains or loses the *keyboard focus*—the ability to receive characters typed at the keyboard. Window events keep you informed of the basic status of any kind of `Window`, such as a `Dialog` or a `Frame`.

Examples of semantic events are action events, item events, and list selection events. The trigger for a semantic event can differ by component. For example, a button customarily fires an action event when the user clicks it, but a text field fires an action event when the user presses Return. The trigger can also vary by look and feel. For example, an audio look and feel might implement a button that fires an action event when the user says a certain phrase. Some semantic events aren't triggered by low-level events at all. For example, a table-model event might be fired when a table model receives new data from a database.

Whenever possible, you should listen for semantic events rather than for low-level events. That way you can make your code as robust and portable as possible. For example, listening for action events on buttons, rather than mouse events, means that the button will react appropriately when the user tries to activate the button by using a keyboard alternative or a look-and-feel-specific gesture. When dealing with a compound component, such as a combo box, it's imperative that you stick to semantic events, since you have no reliable way of registering listeners on all of the look-and-feel-specific components that might be used to form the compound component.

Using Adapters and Inner Classes to Handle Events

This section tells you how to use adapters and inner classes to reduce clutter in your code. If you don't care about this subject, feel free to skip to the next section Listeners Supported by Swing Components (page 453).

Most listener interfaces contain more than one method. For example, the `MouseListener` interface contains five methods: `mousePressed`, `mouseReleased`, `mouseEntered`, `mouseExited`, and `mouseClicked`. If your class directly implements `MouseListener`, you must implement all five `MouseListener` methods, even if you care only about mouse clicks. Methods for those events you don't care about can have empty bodies. Here's an example:

```
//An example with cluttered but valid code.
public class MyClass implements MouseListener {
    ...
    someObject.addMouseListener(this);
    ...
    /* Empty method definition. */
    public void mousePressed(MouseEvent e) {
    }

    /* Empty method definition. */
    public void mouseReleased(MouseEvent e) {
    }

    /* Empty method definition. */
    public void mouseEntered(MouseEvent e) {
    }

    /* Empty method definition. */
    public void mouseExited(MouseEvent e) {
    }

    public void mouseClicked(MouseEvent e) {
    ...//Event handler implementation goes here...
    }
}
```

Unfortunately the resulting collection of empty method bodies can make code more difficult to read and to maintain. To help you avoid cluttering your code with empty method bodies, the API generally includes an *adapter* class for each listener interface with more than one method. [For a list of listeners and adapters, see Implementing Listeners for Commonly Handled Events (page 457).] For example, the `MouseAdapter` class implements the `MouseListener` interface. An adapter class implements empty versions of all of its interface's methods.

To use an adapter, you create a subclass of it instead of directly implementing a listener interface. For example, by extending `MouseAdapter`, your class inherits empty definitions of all five of the methods that `MouseListener` contains.

```
/*
 * An example of extending an adapter class instead of
 * directly implementing a listener interface.
 */
public class MyClass extends MouseAdapter {
    ...
    someObject.addMouseListener(this);
    ...

    public void mouseClicked(MouseEvent e) {
        ...//Event handler implementation goes here...
    }
}
```

What if you don't want your event-handling class to inherit from an adapter class? For example, suppose that you write an applet and want your `JPanel` subclass to contain some code to handle mouse events. Since the Java programming language doesn't permit multiple inheritance, your class can't extend both the `JPanel` and the `MouseAdapter` classes. The solution is to define an *inner class*—a class inside of your `JPanel` subclass—that extends the `Mouse-Adapter` class.

```
//An example of using an inner class.
public class MyClass extends JPanel {
    ...
    someObject.addMouseListener(new MyAdapter());
    ...

    class MyAdapter extends MouseAdapter {
        public void mouseClicked(MouseEvent e) {
            ...//Event handler implementation goes here...
        }
    }
}
```

Here's an example of using an inner class with no name:

```
//An example of using an anonymous inner class.
public class MyClass extends JPanel {
    ...
        someObject.addMouseListener(new MouseAdapter() {
            public void mouseClicked(MouseEvent e) {
                ...//Event handler implementation goes here...
            }
        });
    ...
}
```

Inner classes work well even if your event handler needs access to private instance variables from the enclosing class. As long as you don't declare an inner class to be `static`, an inner class can refer to instance variables and methods just as if its code were in the containing class. To make a local variable available to an inner class, just save a copy of the variable as a `final` local variable.

Note: Some 1.1 compilers don't let an inner class use private instance variables of the enclosing class. A workaround is to remove the `private` specifier from the instance variable's declaration.

To refer to the enclosing instance, you can use `EnclosingClass.this`. For more information about inner classes, see "Implementing Nested Classes" in the book, *The Java™ Tutorial, Second Edition.*[1]

---

[1] This trail is also available in HTML on this book's CD-ROM and online at http://java.sun.com/docs/books/tutorial/java/more/nested.html

Listeners Supported by Swing Components

 $\mathbf{Y}$ OU can tell what kinds of events a component can fire by looking at the kinds of event listeners you can register on it. For example, the Component class defines these listener registration methods:

- addComponentListener
- addFocusListener
- addKeyListener
- addMouseListener
- addMouseMotionListener

Thus every component supports component, focus, key, mouse, and mouse-motion listeners. However, a component fires only those events for which listeners have registered on it. For example, if a mouse listener is registered on a particular component but the component has no other listeners, the component will fire only mouse events—no component, focus, key, or mouse-motion events.

Listeners supported by Swing components fall into two categories: those that all Swing components support and other listeners that Swing components support.

Listeners that All Swing Components Support

Because all Swing components descend from the AWT `Component` class, you can register the following listeners on any Swing component.

Component listener

Listens for changes in the component's size, position, or visibility.

Focus listener

Listens for whether the component has gained or lost the ability to receive keyboard input.

Key listener

Listens for key presses; key events are fired only by the component that has the current keyboard focus.

Mouse events

Listens for mouse clicks and mouse movement into or out of the component's drawing area.

Mouse-motion events

Listens for changes in the cursor's position over the component.

All Swing components descend from the AWT `Container` class, but many of them aren't used as containers. So, technically speaking, any Swing component can fire container events, which notify listeners that a component has been added to or removed from the container. Realistically speaking, however, only containers, such as panels and frames, and compound components, such as combo boxes, fire container events.

`JComponent` provides support for three more listener types. You can register an ancestor listener[1] to be notified when a component's containment ancestors are added to or removed from a container, hidden, made visible, or moved. This listener type is an implementation detail and can generally be ignored. Swing components are JavaBeans™-compliant. Among other things, this means that Swing components support bound and constrained properties and notify listeners of changes to the properties. Property-change listeners[2] listen for changes to bound properties, and vetoable change listeners[3] listen for changes to constrained properties. These listeners are used primarily by Beans-aware builder tools. For more information about Beans properties, refer to the "Properties" section in the "JavaBeans" lesson. This lesson can be found in the book, *The Java™ Tutorial Continued.*[4]

---

[1] API documentation for `AncestorListener` is available on this book's CD-ROM and online at
http://java.sun.com/products/jdk/1.2/docs/api/javax/swing/event/AncestorListener.html

[2] http://java.sun.com/products/jdk/1.2/docs/api/java/beans/PropertyChangeListener.html

[3] http://java.sun.com/products/jdk/1.2/docs/api/java/beans/VetoableChangeListener.html

[4] This trail is also available in HTML on this book's CD-ROM and online at http://java.sun.com/docs/
books/tutorial/javabeans/properties/index.html

Other Listeners that Swing Components Support

The following table lists Swing components and the listeners they support. In many cases the events are fired directly from the component. In other cases the events are fired from the component's data or selection model. To find out the details for the particular component and listener you're interested in, go first to the component how-to section, and then if necessary to the listener how-to section.

Table 169   Swing Components and the Listeners They Support

Component	action	caret	change	document, undoable edit	item	list selection	window	other
button	X		X		X			
check box	X		X		X			
color chooser			X					
combo box	X				X			
dialog							X	
editor pane		X		X				hyperlink
file chooser	X							
frame							X	
internal frame								internal frame
list						X		list data
menu								menu
menu item	X		X		X			menu key menu drag mouse
option pane								
password field	X	X		X				
popup menu								popup menu
progress bar			X		X			
radio button	X		X					
slider			X					
tabbed pane			X					

Table 169   Swing Components and the Listeners They Support

Component	Listener							
	action	caret	change	document, undoable edit	item	list selection	window	other
table						X		table model table column model cell editor
text area		X		X				
text field	X	X		X				
text pane		X		X				hyperlink
toggle button	X		X		X			
tree								tree expansion tree will expand tree model tree selection
viewport (used by scroll pane)			X					

Implementing Listeners for Commonly Handled Events

Now we turn to the details about implementing specific kinds of event listeners. We don't have a how-to section for every single kind of event listener that you can write. Rather, we cover the listeners we think you're most likely to need. If you're interested in other listeners, you can find some information in the section Summary of Listener API (page 527).

- How to Write an Action Listener (page 459)
- How to Write a Caret Listener (page 462)
- How to Write a Change Listener (page 464)
- How to Write a Component Listener (page 466)
- How to Write a Container Listener (page 469)
- How to Write a Document Listener (page 472)
- How to Write a Focus Listener (page 476)
- How to Write an Internal Frame Listener (page 480)
- How to Write an Item Listener (page 484)
- How to Write a Key Listener (page 486)
- How to Write a List Data Listener (page 491)
- How to Write a List Selection Listener (page 494)
- How to Write a Mouse Listener (page 498)
- How to Write a Mouse-Motion Listener (page 503)
- How to Write a Table Model Listener (page 507)

How to Write an Action Listener

Action listeners are probably the easiest—and most common—event handlers to implement. You implement an action listener to respond to the user's indication that an implementation-dependent action should occur.

When the user clicks a button (page 169), chooses a menu item (page 226), or presses Return in a text field (page 298), an action event occurs. The result is that an `actionPerformed` message is sent to all action listeners that are registered on the relevant component.

Here is the action event–handling code from an applet named `Beeper`:

```
public class Beeper ...  implements ActionListener {
    ...
    //where initialization occurs:
        button.addActionListener(this);
    ...

    public void actionPerformed(ActionEvent e) {
        Toolkit.getDefaultToolkit().beep();
    }
}
```

The `Beeper` applet is described in Some Simple Event-Handling Examples (page 443). You can find the entire program in `Beeper.java` (page 826).

The Action Event API

The `ActionListener`[1] interface contains a single method and thus has no corresponding adapter class. Here is the lone `ActionListener` method.

void actionPerformed(ActionEvent)
Called just after the user informs the listened-to component that an action should occur.

The `actionPerformed` method has a single parameter: an `ActionEvent`[2] object. The `ActionEvent` class defines two useful methods.

---

[1] API documentation for `ActionListener` is available on this book's CD-ROM and online at
http://java.sun.com/products/jdk/1.2/docs/api/java/awt/event/ActionListener.html

[2] API documentation for `ActionListener` is available on this book's CD-ROM and online at
http://java.sun.com/products/jdk/1.2/docs/api/java/awt/event/ActionEvent.html

`String getActionCommand()`

Returns the string associated with this action. Most objects that can fire action events support a method called `setActionCommand` that lets you set this string. If you don't set the action command explicitly, it's generally the text displayed in the component. For objects with multiple items, and thus multiple possible actions, the action command is generally the name of the selected item.

`int getModifiers()`

Returns an integer representing the modifier keys the user was pressing when the action event occurred. You can use the `ActionEvent`-defined constants `SHIFT_MASK`, `CTRL_MASK`, `META_MASK`, and `ALT_MASK` to determine which keys were pressed. For example, if the user Shift-selects a menu item, the following expression is nonzero: `actionEvent.getModifiers() & ActionEvent.SHIFT_MASK`.

Also useful is the `getSource` method, which `ActionEvent` inherits from `EventObject`.[1]

Examples that Use Action Listeners

The following table lists some of the many examples that use action listeners.

Table 170   Examples that Use Action Listeners

Example	Where Described	Notes
`Beeper.java`	This section and Some Simple Event-Handling Examples (page 443)	Contains one button with one action listener that beeps when you click the button.
`MultiListener.java`	Some Simple Event-Handling Examples (page 443)	Registers two action listeners on one button. Also registers the same action listener on two buttons.
`RadioButtonDemo.java`	How to Use Radio Buttons (page 180)	Registers the same action listener on five radio buttons. The listener uses the `getActionCommand` method to determine which radio button fired the event.
`MenuDemo.java`	How to Use Menus (page 226)	Shows how to listen for action events on menu items.
`TextDemo.java`	How to Use Text Fields (page 298)	An applet that registers an action listener on a text field.
`ActionDemo.java`	How to Use Actions (page 389)	Uses actions to bind buttons and menu items to the same function.

---

1   http://java.sun.com/products/jdk/1.2/docs/api/java/util/EventObject.html

Table 170   Examples that Use Action Listeners

Example	Where Described	Notes
IconDemoApplet.java	How to Use Icons (page 417)	Loads an image in an action listener. Because loading an image can take a while, this program uses a Swing-Worker to load the image in a background thread.
TableDialogEdit-Demo.java	How to Use Tables (page 254)	Registers an action listener through a factory method on the OK button of a color chooser dialog.
SliderDemo.java	How to Use Sliders (page 248)	Registers an action listener on a timer that controls an animation loop.

How to Write a Caret Listener

Caret events occur when the caret in a text component moves or when the selection in a text component changes. You can attach a caret listener to an instance of any `JTextComponent` subclass, using the `addCaretListener` method.

If your program has a custom caret, you might find it more convenient to attach a listener to the caret object rather than to the text component for which it is a caret. A caret fires change events rather than caret events, so you would need to write a change listener rather than a caret listener.

Here is the caret event–handling code from an application called `TextComponentDemo`:

```
...
//where initialization occurs
CaretListenerLabel caretListenerLabel =
                  new CaretListenerLabel("Caret Status");
...
textPane.addActionListener(caretListenerLabel);
...
protected class CaretListenerLabel extends JLabel
                                   implements CaretListener {
    ...
    public void caretUpdate(CaretEvent e) {
        //Get the location in the text
        int dot = e.getDot();
        int mark = e.getMark();
        ...
    }
}
```

You can find the full source code for the program and instructions for compiling and running it in <u>General Rules for Using Text Components</u> (page 282). For a discussion about the caret listener aspect of the program, see <u>Listening for Caret and Selection Changes</u> (page 294).

The Caret Event API

The `CaretListener` interface has just one method, so it has no corresponding adapter class.

void caretUpdate(CaretEvent)
> Called when the caret in the listened-to component moves or when the selection in the listened-to component changes.

The caretUpdate method has a single parameter: a <u>CaretEvent</u>[1] object. To get the text component that fired the event, use the getSource method, which CaretEvent inherits from <u>EventObject</u>.[2]

The CaretEvent class defines two useful methods.

int getDot()
> Returns the current location of the caret. If text is selected, the caret marks one end of the selection.

int getMark()
> Returns the other end of the selection. If nothing is selected, the value returned by this method is equal to the value returned by getDot. Note that the dot is not guaranteed to be less than the mark.

Examples that Use Caret Listeners

The following table lists the examples that use caret listeners.

Table 171   Examples that Use Caret Listeners

Example	Where Described	Notes
TextComponentDemo.java	<u>Listening for Caret and Selection Changes</u> (page 294)	Uses a "listener label" to display caret and selection status.

---

[1]   API documentation for CaretEvent is available on this book's CD-ROM and online at
    http://java.sun.com/products/jdk/1.2/docs/api/javax/swing/event/CaretEvent.html

[2]   http://java.sun.com/products/jdk/1.2/docs/api/java/util/EventObject.html

How to Write a Change Listener

Change events occur whenever a component changes state. For example, a button fires a change event every time the button is clicked. The look-and-feel implementation of the button listens for change events so that it can react appropriately to the state change (repainting itself, for example). Although nothing's stopping you from registering for change events on a button, most programs don't need to do so.

Two Swing components—sliders (page 248) and color choosers (page 184)—rely on change events for basic functionality. To learn when the value in a slider changes, you need to register a change listener. Similarly you need to register a change listener on a color chooser to be informed when the user chooses a new color.

Here is an example of change event–handling code for a slider:

```
//...where initialization occurs:
framesPerSecond.addChangeListener(new SliderListener());
...

class SliderListener implements ChangeListener {
    public void stateChanged(ChangeEvent e) {
        JSlider source = (JSlider)e.getSource();
        if (!source.getValueIsAdjusting()) {
            int fps = (int)source.getValue();
            ...
        }
    }
}
```

This snippet is from a program named SliderDemo. You can find the source and image files for the program, along with instructions for compiling and running it, in How to Use Sliders (page 248).

The Change Event API

The ChangeListener[1] interface has just one method, so it has no corresponding adapter class.

---

[1] API documentation for ChangeListener is available on this book's CD-ROM and online at http://java.sun.com/products/jdk/1.2/docs/api/javax/swing/event/ChangeListener.html

void stateChanged(ChangeEvent)
Called when the listened-to component changes state.

The stateChanged method has a single parameter: a ChangeEvent[1] object. To get the component that fired the event, use the getSource method, which ChangeEvent inherits from EventObject. The ChangeEvent class defines no additional methods.

Examples that Use Change Listeners

The following table lists the examples that use change listeners.

Table 172 Examples that Use Change Listeners

Example	Where Described	Notes
SliderDemo.java and SliderDemo2.java	How to Use Sliders (page 248)	Register a change listener on a slider that controls animation speed. The change listener ignores the change events until the user releases the slider.
ColorChooserDemo.java and ColorChooserDemo2.java	How to Use Color Choosers (page 184)	Use a change listener on the selection model of a color chooser to learn when the user changes the current color.
ConverterRangeModel.java and its subclass, FollowerRangeModel.java	The Anatomy of a Swing-Based Program (page 51)	Implement custom models for the sliders used in the Converter demo. Both models explicitly fire change events when necessary.

---

[1] API documentation for ChangeEvent is available on this book's CD-ROM and online at http://java.sun.com/products/jdk/1.2/docs/api/javax/swing/event/ChangeEvent.html

How to Write a Component Listener

One or more component events are fired by a `Component` object just after the component is hidden, made visible, moved, or resized. An example of a component listener might be in a GUI builder tool that's displaying information about the size of the currently selected component and that needs to know when the component's size changes. You shouldn't need to use component events to manage basic layout and rendering.

The component-hidden and component-shown events occur only as the result of calls to a `Component`'s `setVisible` method (or its deprecated equivalents, `show` and `hide`). For example, a window might be miniaturized into an icon (iconified) without a component-hidden event being fired.

The following applet demonstrates component events. The applet contains a button that brings up a window (`JFrame`). The window contains a panel that has a label and a check box. The check box controls whether the label is visible. When you leave the applet's page, the window disappears; it reappears when you return to the applet's page. A text area displays a message every time the window, panel, label, or check box fires a component event.

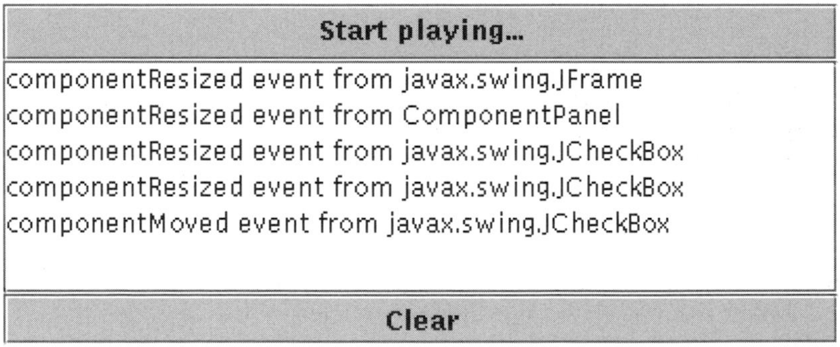

Start playing...

componentResized event from javax.swing.JFrame
componentResized event from ComponentPanel
componentResized event from javax.swing.JCheckBox
componentResized event from javax.swing.JCheckBox
componentMoved event from javax.swing.JCheckBox

Clear

Figure 148 The `ComponentEventDemo` applet. You can see this applet online at `http://java.sun.com/docs/books/tutorial/uiswing/events/ComponentEventDemo.html`

Try this:

1. Click the button labeled "Start playing...". The window comes up, generating one or more component-shown and component-moved events.

2. Click the check box to hide the label. The label fires a component-hidden event.

3. Click the check box again to show the label. The label fires a component-shown event.

4. Iconify and then deiconify the window that contains the label. You do *not* get component-hidden or -shown events. If you want to be notified of iconification events, you should use a window listener.

5. Resize the window that contains the label. You'll see component-resized (and possibly component-moved) events from all four components—label, check box, panel, and window. If the window and panel's layout manager didn't make every component as wide as possible, the panel, label, and check box wouldn't have been resized.

You can find the applet's code in `ComponentEventDemo.java` (page 827). Here is just the code related to handling component events:

```java
public class ComponentEventDemo ... implements ComponentListener,
                                                ActionListener {
    ...
    //where initialization occurs:
        aFrame = new JFrame("A Frame");
        ComponentPanel p = new ComponentPanel(this);
        aFrame.addComponentListener(this);
        p.addComponentListener(this);
    ...

    public void componentHidden(ComponentEvent e) {
        displayMessage("componentHidden event from "
            + e.getComponent().getClass().getName());
    }

    public void componentMoved(ComponentEvent e) {
        displayMessage("componentMoved event from "
            + e.getComponent().getClass().getName());
    }

    public void componentResized(ComponentEvent e) {
        displayMessage("componentResized event from "
            + e.getComponent().getClass().getName());
    }

    public void componentShown(ComponentEvent e) {
        displayMessage("componentShown event from "
            + e.getComponent().getClass().getName());
    }
}

class ComponentPanel extends JPanel ... {
    ...
    ComponentPanel(ComponentEventDemo listener) {
        ...//after creating the label and check box:
```

```
        label.addComponentListener(listener);
        checkbox.addComponentListener(listener);
    }
    ...
}
```

The Component Event API

The `ComponentListener`[1] interface and its corresponding adapter class, `Component-Adapter`,[2] contain four methods.

void componentHidden(ComponentEvent)
> Called after the listened-to component is hidden as the result of calling the `setVisible` method.

void componentMoved(ComponentEvent)
> Called after the listened-to component moves, relative to its container. For example, if a window is moved, the window fires a component-moved event, but the components it contains do not.

void componentResized(ComponentEvent)
> Called after the listened-to component's size (rectangular bounds) changes.

void componentShown(ComponentEvent)
> Called after the listened-to component becomes visible as the result of calling the `set-Visible` method.

Each component event method has a single parameter: a `ComponentEvent` object. The `ComponentEvent` class defines the following useful method.

Component getComponent()
> Returns the component that fired the event. You can use this instead of the `getSource` method.

Examples that Use Component Listeners

The following table lists an example that uses component listeners.

Table 173   Example that Uses Component Listeners

Example	Where Described	Notes
ComponentEventDemo.java	This section	Reports all component events that occur on several components, to demonstrate the circumstances under which component events are fired.

---

[1]   API documentation for `ComponentListener` is available on this book's CD-ROM and online at http://java.sun.com/products/jdk/1.2/docs/api/java/awt/event/ComponentListener.html

[2]   http://java.sun.com/products/jdk/1.2/docs/api/java/awt/event/ComponentAdapter.html

How to Write a Container Listener

Container events are fired by a `Container` just after a component is added to or removed from the container. These events are for notification only—no container listener need be present for components to be successfully added or removed.

The following applet demonstrates container events. By clicking Add a button or Remove a button, you can add components to or remove them from a panel at the bottom of the applet. Each time a component is added to or removed from the panel, the panel fires a container event, and the panel's container listener is notified. The listener displays descriptive messages in the text area at the top of the applet.

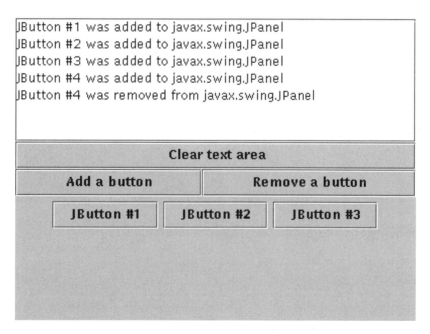

Figure 149 The `ContainerEventDemo` applet. You can see this applet online at `http://java.sun.com/docs/books/tutorial/uiswing/events/ContainerEventDemo.html`

Try this:

1. Click Add a button. You'll see a button appear near the bottom of the applet. The container listener (in this example, an instance of ContainerEventDemo) reacts to the resulting component-added event by displaying "Button #1 was added to java.awt.Panel" at the top of the applet.

2. Click Remove a button. This removes the most recently added button from the panel, causing the container listener to receive a component-removed event.

You can find the applet's code in ContainerEventDemo.java (page 829). Here is the applet's container event–handling code:

```java
public class ContainerEventDemo ... implements ContainerListener ... {
    ...//where initialization occurs:
    buttonPanel = new JPanel();
    buttonPanel.addContainerListener(this);
    ...

    public void componentAdded(ContainerEvent e) {
        displayMessage(" added to ", e);
    }

    public void componentRemoved(ContainerEvent e) {
        displayMessage(" removed from ", e);
    }

    void displayMessage(String action, ContainerEvent e) {
        display.append(((JButton)e.getChild()).getText()
                    + " was"
                    + action
                    + e.getContainer().getClass().getName()
                    + newline);
    }
    ...
}
```

The Container Event API

The ContainerListener[1] interface and its corresponding adapter class, Container-Adapter,[2] contain two methods.

---

[1] API documentation for ContainerListener is available on this book's CD-ROM and online at http://java.sun.com/products/jdk/1.2/docs/api/java/awt/event/ContainerListener.html

[2] http://java.sun.com/products/jdk/1.2/docs/api/java/awt/event/ContainerAdapter.html

void componentAdded(ContainerEvent)
Called just after a component is added to the listened-to container.

void componentRemoved(ContainerEvent)
Called just after a component is removed from the listened-to container.

Each container event method has a single parameter: a ContainerEvent object. The ContainerEvent class defines two useful methods.

Component getChild()
Returns the component whose addition or removal triggered this event.

Container getContainer()
Returns the container that fired this event. You can use this instead of the getSource method.

Examples that Use Container Listeners

The following table lists an example that uses container listeners.

Table 174   Example that Uses Container Listeners

Example	Where Described	Notes
ContainerEventDemo.java	This section	Reports all container events that occur on a single panel, to demonstrate the circumstances under which container events are fired.

How to Write a Document Listener

A Swing <u>text component</u> (page 275) uses a <u>Document</u>[1] to hold and edit its text. Document events occur when the content of a document changes in any way. You attach a document listener to a text component's document rather than to the text component itself.

The following applet demonstrates document events on two plain text components.

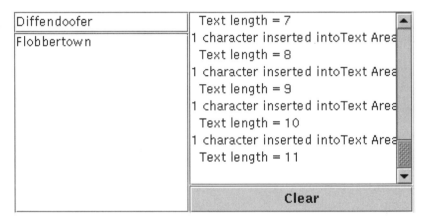

Figure 150 The `DocumentEventDemo` applet. You can see this applet online at `http://` `java.sun.com/docs/books/tutorial/uiswing/events/` `DocumentEventDemo.html`

Try this:

1. Type in the text field at the upper left of the applet or the text area beneath the text field. One document event is fired for each character typed.

2. Delete text by pressing the backspace key. One document event is fired for each press of the backspace key.

---

[1] API documentation for `Document` is available on this book's CD-ROM and online at http://java.sun.com/ products/jdk/1.2/docs/api/javax/swing/text/Document.html

3. Select text and then delete it by pressing the backspace key or by using a keyboard command, such as Control-X (cut). One document event is fired for the entire deletion.

4. Copy text from one text component into the other using keyboard commands such as Control-C (copy) and Control-V (paste). One document event is fired for the entire paste operation, regardless of the length of the text pasted. If text is selected in the target text component before the paste command is issued, an additional document event is fired because the selected text is deleted first.

You can find the applet's code in <u>DocumentEventDemo.java</u> (page 832). Here is the applet's document event–handling code.

```
public class DocumentEventDemo ... {
    ...//where initialization occurs:
    textField = new JTextField(20);
    textField.addActionListener(new MyTextActionListener());
    textField.getDocument().addDocumentListener(
                            new MyDocumentListener());
    textField.getDocument().putProperty("name", "Text Field");
    textArea = new JTextArea();
    textArea.getDocument().addDocumentListener(
                            new MyDocumentListener());
    textArea.getDocument().putProperty("name", "Text Area");
    ...
}

class MyDocumentListener implements DocumentListener {
    final String newline = ("/n");
    public void insertUpdate(DocumentEvent e) {
        updateLog(e, "inserted into");
    }

    public void removeUpdate(DocumentEvent e) {
        updateLog(e, "removed from");
    }

    public void changedUpdate(DocumentEvent e) {
        //Plain text components don't fire these events
    }

    public void updateLog(DocumentEvent e, String action) {
        Document doc = (Document)e.getDocument();
        int changeLength = e.getLength();
        displayArea.append(
            changeLength + " character" +
            ((changeLength == 1) ? " " : "s ") +
            action + " " + doc.getProperty("name") + "." + newline +
            "  Text length = " + doc.getLength() + newline);
    }
}
```

Document listeners shouldn't modify the contents of the document; the change is already complete by the time the listener is notified of the change. Instead write a custom document that overrides the `insertString` or `remove` methods, or both. See <u>Listening for Changes on a Document</u> (page 286) for details.

The Document Event API

The `DocumentListener` interface contains these three methods.

void changedUpdate(DocumentEvent)
> Called when the style of some of the text in the listened-to document changes. This sort of event is fired only from a `StyledDocument`—a `PlainDocument` does not fire these events.

void insertUpdate(DocumentEvent)
> Called when text is inserted into the listened-to document.

void removeUpdate(DocumentEvent)
> Called when text is removed from the listened-to document.

Each document event method has a single parameter: an instance of a class that implements the <u>DocumentEvent</u>[1] interface. Typically the object passed into this method will be an instance of <u>DefaultDocumentEvent</u>,[2] which is defined in `AbstractDocument`.

To get the document that fired the event, you can use `DocumentEvent`'s `getDocument` method. Note that as an interface, `DocumentEvent` does not inherit from `EventObject`. Thus it does not inherit the `getSource` method.

In addition to `getDocument`, the `DocumentEvent` interface requires these methods:

int getLength()
> Returns the length of the change.

int getOffset()
> Returns the location within the document of the first character changed.

ElementChange getChange(Element)
> Returns details about what elements in the document have changed and how. <u>ElementChange</u>[3] is an interface defined within the `DocumentEvent` interface.

---

[1] API documentation for `DocumentEvent` is available on this book's CD-ROM and online at http://java.sun.com/products/jdk/1.2/docs/api/javax/swing/event/DocumentEvent.html

[2] http://java.sun.com/products/jdk/1.2/docs/api/javax/swing/text/AbstractDocument.DefaultDocumentEvent.html

[3] http://java.sun.com/products/jdk/1.2/docs/api/javax/swing/event/DocumentEvent.ElementChange.html

`EventType getType()`

Returns the type of change that occurred. `EventType`,[1] a class defined within the `Docu-mentEvent` interface, enumerates the possible changes that can occur on a document: insert text, remove text, and change text style.

Examples that Use Document Listeners

The following table lists the examples that use document listeners.

Table 175   Examples that Use Document Listeners

Example	Where Described	Notes
`DocumentEventDemo.java`	This section	Reports all document events that occur on the documents for both a text field and a text area. One listener listens to both text components and uses a client property on the document to determine which component fired the event.
`TextComponentDemo.java`	Listening for Changes on a Document (page 286)	Updates a change log every time text in the listened-to document changes. The document in this example supports styled text, so `changedUpdate` gets called in this example.
`TextFieldDemo.java`	Using a Document Listener on a Text Field (page 304)	Registers one document listener on three text fields. The listener computes a numeric value based on numeric values entered into the three text fields by the user.

----

[1]   http://java.sun.com/products/jdk/1.2/docs/api/javax/swing/event/DocumentEvent.EventType.html

How to Write a Focus Listener

Many components—even those operated primarily with the mouse, such as buttons—can be operated with the keyboard. For a key press to affect a component, the component must have the keyboard focus.

From the user's point of view, the component with the keyboard focus is generally prominent—with a thicker border than usual, for example—and the window containing the component is also more prominent than other windows on-screen. These visual cues let the user know to which component any typing will go. At most one component in the window system can have the keyboard focus.

Focus events are fired whenever a component gains or loses the *keyboard focus*. Exactly how components gain the focus depends on the window system. Typically the user sets the focus by clicking a window or a component, by tabbing between components, or by otherwise interacting with a component. Once the focus is in a window (the window is *activated*), a program can use the `Component requestFocus` method to request that a specific component get the focus.

The following applet demonstrates focus events. By clicking the top button in the applet, you can bring up a window that contains a variety of components. A focus listener listens for focus events on each component in the window, including the window itself, which is an instance of a `JFrame` subclass called `FocusWindow`.

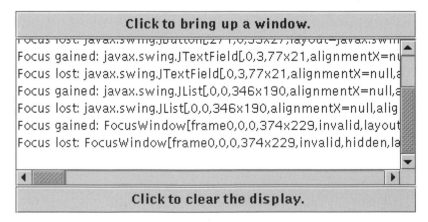

Figure 151 The `FocusEventDemo` applet. You can see this applet online at `http://java.sun.com/docs/books/tutorial/uiswing/events/FocusEventDemo.html`

Try this:

Bring up the Focus Event Window by clicking the top button in the applet, as shown in Figure 152.

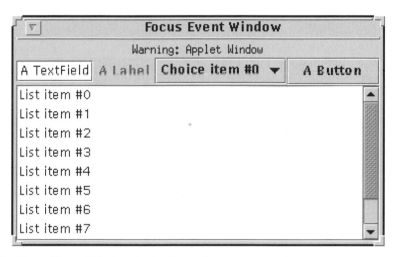

Figure 152 The Focus Event Window in the `FocusEventDemo` applet.

1. If necessary, click the Focus Event Window so that its contents can gain the keyboard focus. You'll see a "Focus gained" message in the applet's display area. The way in which its window gets the focus and which components get the focus are system dependent by default. You can detect when the window gets or loses the focus by implementing a window listener and listening for window activation or deactivation events.

2. Click the button at the right of the Focus Event Window and then click in another component, such as the text field. Note that when the focus changes from one component to another, the first component fires a focus-lost event before the second component fires a focus-gained event.

3. Select an item from the combo box. The combo box does not fire a focus-gained event, even though it appears to have the focus. Now select another component in the Focus Event Window. The combo box does not fire a focus-lost event either.

4. Try changing the focus by pressing Tab or Shift-Tab. Most systems let you use the Tab key to cycle through components that are able to get the focus.

5. Iconify the Focus Event Window. You should see a "Focus lost" message for the component that last had the focus.

You can find the applet's code in <u>FocusEventDemo.java</u> (page 834). Here is the applet's focus event–handling code:

```
public class FocusEventDemo ... implements FocusListener ... {
    ...//where initialization occurs
    window = new FocusWindow(this);
    ...

    public void focusGained(FocusEvent e) {
        displayMessage("Focus gained", e);
    }

    public void focusLost(FocusEvent e) {
        displayMessage("Focus lost", e);
    }

    void displayMessage(String prefix, FocusEvent e) {
        display.append(prefix
                    + ": "
                    + e.getComponent()
                    + newline);
    }
    ...
}

class FocusWindow extends JFrame {
    ...
    public FocusWindow(FocusListener listener) {
        super("Focus Demo Window");
        this.addFocusListener(listener);
        ...
        JLabel label = new JLabel("A Label");
        label.addFocusListener(listener);
        ...
        JComboBox choice = new JComboBox(/* list of items */);
        ...
        choice.addFocusListener(listener);
        ...
        JButton button = new JButton("A Button");
        button.addFocusListener(listener);
        ...
        JList list = new JList(/* list of items */);
        ...
        list.addFocusListener(listener);
    }
}
```

The Focus Event API

The FocusListener[1] interface and its corresponding adapter class, FocusAdapter,[2] contain two methods.

void focusGained(FocusEvent)
Called just after the listened-to component gets the focus.

void focusLost(FocusEvent)
Called just after the listened-to component loses the focus.

Each focus event method has a single parameter: a FocusEvent[3] object. The FocusEvent class defines the following method.

boolean isTemporary()
Returns true if a focus-lost event is temporary. You'll need to use this method if you're implementing a component that can indicate that it will get the focus if its window regains the focus.

The getComponent method, which FocusEvent inherits from ComponentEvent,[4] returns the component that fired the focus event.

Examples that Use Focus Listeners

The following table lists an example that uses focus listeners.

Table 176   Example that Uses Focus Listeners

Example	Where Described	Notes
FocusEventDemo.java	This section	Reports all focus events that occur on several components to demonstrate the circumstances under which focus events are fired.

---

[1] API documentation for FocusListener is available on this book's CD-ROM and online at
     http://java.sun.com/products/jdk/1.2/docs/api/java/awt/event/FocusListener.html

[2] http://java.sun.com/products/jdk/1.2/docs/api/java/awt/event/FocusAdapter.html

[3] http://java.sun.com/products/jdk/1.2/docs/api/java/awt/event/FocusEvent.html

[4] http://java.sun.com/products/jdk/1.2/docs/api/java/awt/event/ComponentEvent.html

How to Write an Internal Frame Listener

Internal frame events are to `JInternalFrame`[1] what window events are to `JFrame`. Like window events, internal frame events notify listeners that the "window" has been shown for the first time, disposed of, iconified, deiconified, activated, or deactivated. Before using internal frame events, please familiarize yourself with How to Write a Window Listener (page 521).

The application shown in Figure 153 demonstrates internal frame events. The application listens for internal frame events from the Event Generator frame, displaying a message that describes each event.

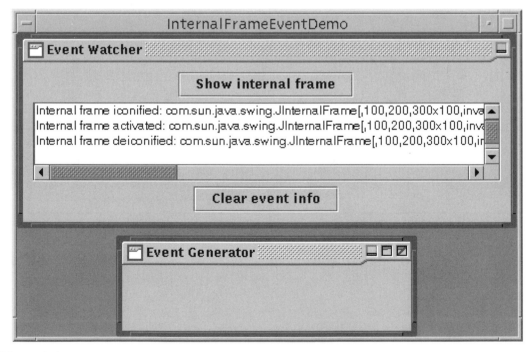

Figure 153 The `InternalFrameEventDemo` application.

---

[1] For more information on `JInternalFrame`, see How to Use Internal Frames (page 143).

Try this:

1. Compile and run `InternalFrameEventDemo`.[1] The source file is <u>Internal-FrameEventDemo.java</u> (page 836).
2. Bring up the Event Generator internal frame by clicking the applet's top button. You should see an "Internal frame opened" message in the display area.
3. Try various operations to see what happens. For example, click the Event Generator so that it gets activated. Click the Event Watcher so that the Event Generator gets deactivated. Click the Event Generator's decorations to iconify, maximize, minimize, and close the window.

Here is the event–handling code for internal frames:

```
public class InternalFrameEventDemo ...
        implements InternalFrameListener ... {
    ...
    protected void createListenedToWindow() {
        listenedToWindow = new JInternalFrame("Event Generator",
                            true,  //resizable
                            true,  //closable
                            true,  //maximizable
                            true); //iconifiable
        listenedToWindow.setDefaultCloseOperation(
                            WindowConstants.DISPOSE_ON_CLOSE);
        ...
    }

    public void internalFrameClosing(InternalFrameEvent e) {
        displayMessage("Internal frame closing", e);
    }

    public void internalFrameClosed(InternalFrameEvent e) {
        displayMessage("Internal frame closed", e);
        listenedToWindow = null;
    }

    public void internalFrameOpened(InternalFrameEvent e) {
        displayMessage("Internal frame opened", e);
    }

    public void internalFrameIconified(InternalFrameEvent e) {
        displayMessage("Internal frame iconified", e);
    }
```

---

[1] See the chapter <u>Getting Started with Swing</u> (page 3) if you need help compiling or running this application.

```
    public void internalFrameDeiconified(InternalFrameEvent e) {
        displayMessage("Internal frame deiconified", e);
    }

    public void internalFrameActivated(InternalFrameEvent e) {
        displayMessage("Internal frame activated", e);
    }

    public void internalFrameDeactivated(InternalFrameEvent e) {
        displayMessage("Internal frame deactivated", e);
    }

    void displayMessage(String prefix, InternalFrameEvent e) {
        String s = prefix + ": " + e.getSource();
        display.append(s + newline);
    }

    public void actionPerformed(ActionEvent e) {
        if (e.getActionCommand().equals(SHOW)) {
            ...
            if (listenedToWindow == null) {
                createListenedToWindow();
                listenedToWindow.addInternalFrameListener(this);
                ...
            }
        }
    ...
    }
}
```

The Internal Frame Event API

The <u>InternalFrameListener</u>[1] interface and its corresponding adapter class, <u>Internal-FrameAdapter</u>,[2] contain these methods.

void internalFrameOpened(InternalFrameEvent)
Called just after the listened-to internal frame has been shown for the first time.

void internalFrameClosing(InternalFrameEvent)
Called in response to a user request that the listened-to internal frame be closed. By default JInternalFrame hides the window when the user closes it. You can use the JInternalFramesetDefaultCloseOperation method to specify another option, which must be either DISPOSE_ON_CLOSE or DO_NOTHING_ON_CLOSE (both defined in

---

[1] API documentation for InternalFrameListener is available on this book's CD-ROM and online at
     http://java.sun.com/products/jdk/1.2/docs/api/javax/swing/event/InternalFrameListener.html
[2] http://java.sun.com/products/jdk/1.2/docs/api/javax/swing/event/InternalFrameAdapter.html

`WindowConstants`, an interface that `JInternalFrame` implements). Or by implementing an `internalFrameClosing` method in the internal frame's listener, you can add custom behavior, such as bringing up dialogs or saving data, to internal frame closing.[1]

void `internalFrameClosed(InternalFrameEvent)`
Called just after the listened-to internal frame has been disposed of.

void `internalFrameIconified(InternalFrameEvent)`
void `internalFrameDeiconified(InternalFrameEvent)`
Called just after the listened-to internal frame is iconified or deiconified, respectively.

void `internalFrameActivated(InternalFrameEvent)`
void `internalFrameDeactivated(InternalFrameEvent)`
Called just after the listened-to internal frame is activated or deactivated, respectively.

Each internal frame event method has a single parameter: an <u>`InternalFrameEvent`</u>[2] object. The `InternalFrameEvent` class defines no generally useful methods. To get the internal frame that fired the event, use the `getSource` method, which `InternalFrameEvent` inherits from `EventObject`.

Examples that Use Internal Frame Listeners

No other source files currently contain internal frame listeners. However, internal frame listeners are similar to window listeners, and many Swing programs have window listeners.

Table 177 Examples that Use Internal Frame Listeners

Example	Where Described	Notes
`InternalFrameEventDemo.java`	This section	Reports all internal frame events that occur on one internal frame, to demonstrate the circumstances under which internal frame events are fired.
`FrameDemo.java`	<u>How to Make Frames</u> (page 82)	One of many examples that listens for window-closing events, so that the application can exit when its only window is closed.
`SliderDemo.java`	<u>How to Use Sliders</u> (page 248)	Listens for window iconify and deiconify events, so that it can stop the animation when the window isn't visible.

---

[1] The correlation between internal frame closing events and window closing events is not perfect. For more information search http://developer.java.sun.com for information about bug #4138031.

[2] API documentation for `InternalFrameEvent` is available on this book's CD-ROM and online at   http://java.sun.com/products/jdk/1.2/docs/api/javax/swing/event/InternalFrameEvent.html

How to Write an Item Listener

Item events are fired by components that implement the <u>ItemSelectable</u>[1] interface. Generally ItemSelectable components maintain on/off state for one or more items. The Swing components that fire item events include <u>check boxes</u> (page 177), <u>check box menu items</u> (page 226), and <u>combo boxes</u> (page 192).

Here is some item event–handling code taken from <u>ComponentEventDemo.java</u> (page 827):

```
...
//where initialization occurs
checkbox.addItemListener(this);
...

public void itemStateChanged(ItemEvent e) {
    if (e.getStateChange() == ItemEvent.SELECTED) {
        label.setVisible(true);
        label.revalidate();
        label.repaint();
    } else {
        label.setVisible(false);
    }
}
```

The Item Event API

The <u>ItemListener</u>[2] interface has just one method, so it has no corresponding adapter class.

void itemStateChanged(ItemEvent)
Called just after a state change in the listened-to component.

The itemStateChanged method has a single parameter: an <u>ItemEvent</u>[3] object. The Item-Event class defines the following handy methods.

---

[1] API documentation for ItemSelectable is available on this book's CD-ROM and online at
   http://java.sun.com/products/jdk/1.2/docs/api/java/awt/ItemSelectable.html
[2] http://java.sun.com/products/jdk/1.2/docs/api/java/awt/event/ItemListener.html
[3] http://java.sun.com/products/jdk/1.2/docs/api/java/awt/event/ItemEvent.html

`Object getItem()`

Returns the component-specific object associated with the item whose state changed. Often this is a `String` containing the text on the selected item.

`ItemSelectable getItemSelectable()`

Returns the component that fired the item event. You can use this instead of the get-Source method.

`int getStateChange()`

Returns the new state of the item. The `ItemEvent` class defines two states: SELECTED and DESELECTED.

Examples that Use Item Listeners

The following table lists some of examples that use item listeners.

Table 178   Examples that Use Item Listeners

Example	Where Described	Notes
ComponentEventDemo.java	This section and How to Write a Component Listener (page 466)	Listens for item events on a check box, which determines whether a label is visible.
CheckBoxDemo.java	How to Use Check Boxes (page 177)	Four check boxes share one item listener, which uses `getItemSelected` to determine which check box fired the event.
MenuDemo.java	How to Use Menus (page 226)	Listens for item events on a check box menu item.

How to Write a Key Listener

Key events tell you when the user is typing at the keyboard. Specifically, the component with the keyboard focus fires key events when the user presses or releases keyboard keys. For information about focus, see the focus discussion in How to Write a Focus Listener (page 476). Alternatives to key-event listeners include keyboard-generated actions (page 68), custom documents (page 282), and document listeners (page 472).

You can be notified about two basic kinds of key events: the typing of a Unicode character and the pressing or releasing of a key on the keyboard. The first kind of event is called a *key-typed* event. The second kind are *key-pressed* and *key-released* events.

In general, you should try to handle only key-typed events unless you need to know when the user presses keys that don't correspond to characters. For example, if you want to know when the user types a Unicode character—whether as the result of pressing one key as "a," or from pressing several keys in sequence—you should handle key-typed events. On the other hand, if you want to know when the user presses the F1 key, you need to handle key-pressed events.

Note: To fire keyboard events, a component *must* have the keyboard focus.

To make a component get the keyboard focus, follow these steps:

1. Make sure that the component's `isFocusTraversable` method returns `true`. This lets the user tab to your component. For example, you can enable keyboard focus for a custom `JLabel` subclass by overriding the `isFocusTraversable` method to return `true`.

2. Make sure that the component requests the focus when appropriate. For custom components, you'll probably need to implement a mouse listener that calls the `requestFocus` method when the component is clicked.

The following applet demonstrates key events. It consists of a text field that you can type into, followed by a text area that displays a message every time the text field fires a key event. A button at the bottom of the applet lets you clear both the text field and the text area.

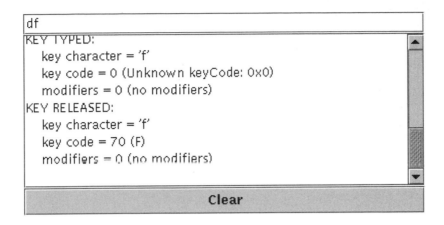

Figure 154 The KeyEventDemo applet.

Try this:

1. Click in the applet's text field so that it gets the keyboard focus.

2. Type a lowercase "a" by pressing and releasing the A key on the keyboard. The text field fires three events: a key-pressed event, a key-typed event, and a key-released event. Note that the key-typed event doesn't have key code information; key-typed events also don't have modifier information.

3. Click the Clear button. You might want to do this after each of the following steps.

4. Press and release the Shift key. The text field fires two events: a key pressed and a key released. The text field doesn't fire a key-typed event, because the Shift key by itself doesn't correspond to any character.

5. Type an uppercase A by pressing the Shift and A keys. You'll see the following events, although perhaps not in this order: key pressed (Shift), key pressed (A), key typed (A), key released (A), key released (Shift).

6. Type an uppercase A by pressing and releasing the Caps Lock key and then pressing the A key. You should see the following events: key pressed (Caps Lock), key pressed (A), key typed (A), key released (A). Note that the Caps Lock key doesn't fire a key-released event until you press and release it again. The same is true of other state keys, such as Scroll Lock and Num Lock.

7. Press and hold the A key. Does it automatically repeat? If so, you'll see the same kinds of events that you would have seen if you pressed and released the A key repeatedly.

You can find the applet's code in <u>KeyEventDemo.java</u> (page 839). Here is the applet's key event–handling code:

```
public class KeyEventDemo ...  implements KeyListener ... {
    ...//where initialization occurs:
    typingArea = new JTextField(20);
    typingArea.addKeyListener(this);
    ...

    /** Handle the key typed event from the text field. */
    public void keyTyped(KeyEvent e) {
        displayInfo(e, "KEY TYPED: ");
    }

    /** Handle the key pressed event from the text field. */
    public void keyPressed(KeyEvent e) {
        displayInfo(e, "KEY PRESSED: ");
    }

    /** Handle the key released event from the text field. */
    public void keyReleased(KeyEvent e) {
        displayInfo(e, "KEY RELEASED: ");
    }

    ...
    protected void displayInfo(KeyEvent e, String s){
        ...
        char c = e.getKeyChar();
        int keyCode = e.getKeyCode();
        int modifiers = e.getModifiers();
        ...
        tmpString = KeyEvent.getKeyModifiersText(modifiers);
        ...//display information about the KeyEvent...
    }
}
```

The Key Event API

The <u>KeyListener</u>[1] interface and its corresponding adapter class, <u>KeyAdapter</u>,[2] contain three methods.

void keyTyped(KeyEvent)
    Called just after the user types a Unicode character into the listened-to component.

---

[1]   API documentation for KeyListener is available on this book's CD-ROM and online at
    http://java.sun.com/products/jdk/1.2/docs/api/java/awt/event/KeyListener.html
[2]   http://java.sun.com/products/jdk/1.2/docs/api/java/awt/event/KeyAdapter.html

`void keyPressed(KeyEvent)`
    Called just after the user presses a key while the listened-to component has the focus.

`void keyReleased(KeyEvent)`
    Called just after the user releases a key while the listened-to component has the focus.

Each key event method has a single parameter: a <u>`KeyEvent`</u>[1] object. The `KeyEvent` class defines the following useful methods:

`int getKeyChar()`
`void setKeyChar(char)`
    Get or set the Unicode character associated with this event.

`int getKeyCode()`
`void setKeyCode(int)`
    Get or set the key code associated with this event. The key code identifies the particular key on the keyboard that the user pressed or released. The `KeyEvent` class defines many key code constants for commonly seen keys. For example, `VK_A` specifies the key labeled A, and `VK_ESCAPE` specifies the Escape key.

`void setModifiers(int)`
    Sets the state of the modifier keys for this event. You can get the state of the modifier keys using the `InputEventgetModifiers` method.

`String getKeyText()`
`String getKeyModifiersText()`
    Return text descriptions of the event's key code and modifier keys, respectively.

The `KeyEvent` class inherits many useful methods from <u>`InputEvent`</u>[2] and <u>`Compo-nentEvent`</u>.[3] The following methods are described in <u>The Mouse Event API</u> (page 500):

- `Component getComponent()`
- `void consume()`
- `int getWhen()`
- `boolean isAltDown()`
- `boolean isControlDown()`
- `boolean isMetaDown()`
- `boolean isShiftDown()`
- `int getModifiers()`

---

[1] API documentation for `KeyEvent` is available on this book's CD-ROM and online at http://java.sun.com/products/jdk/1.2/docs/api/java/awt/event/KeyEvent.html

[2] http://java.sun.com/products/jdk/1.2/docs/api/java/awt/event/InputEvent.html

[3] http://java.sun.com/products/jdk/1.2/docs/api/java/awt/event/ComponentEvent.html

Examples that Use Key Listeners

The following table lists an example that uses key listeners.

Table 179   Example that Uses Key Listeners

Example	Where Described	Notes
`KeyEventDemo.java`	This section	Reports all key events that occur on a text field, to demonstrate the circumstances under which key events are fired.

How to Write a List Data Listener

List data events occur when the contents of a mutable <u>list</u> (page 218) change. The list's model fires these events, the list does not. So you have to register a list data listener with the list model. If you haven't explicitly created a list with a mutable list model, your list is immutable, and its model will not fire these events.

The applet shown in Figure 155 demonstrates list data events on a mutable list.

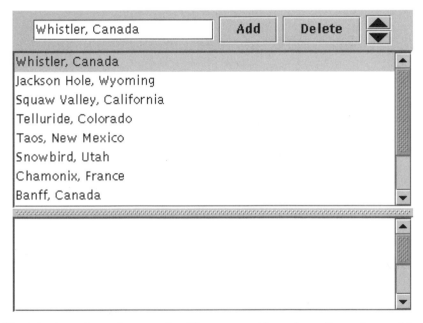

Figure 155 The ListDataEventDemo applet. You can see this applet online at http:// java.sun.com/docs/books/tutorial/uiswing/events/ListDataEventDemo.html

Try this:

1. Type in the name of your favorite ski resort and click the Add button.
2. Select a few contiguous items in the list and click the Delete button.
3. Select one item and use the arrow buttons to move it up or down in the list.

You can find the applet's code in <u>ListDataEventDemo.java</u> (page 840). Here's the applet code that registers a list data listener on the list model and implements the listener:

```java
//...where member variables are declared...
    private DefaultListModel listModel;
    ...

    //Create and populate the list model
    listModel = new DefaultListModel();
    ...
    listModel.addListDataListener(new MyListDataListener());
    ...

class MyListDataListener implements ListDataListener {
    public void contentsChanged(ListDataEvent e) {
        log.append("contentsChanged: " + e.getIndex0() +
            ", " + e.getIndex1() + newline);
    }

    public void intervalAdded(ListDataEvent e) {
        log.append("intervalAdded: " + e.getIndex0() +
            ", " + e.getIndex1() + newline);
    }

    public void intervalRemoved(ListDataEvent e) {
        log.append("intervalRemoved: " + e.getIndex0() +
            ", " + e.getIndex1() + newline);
    }
}
```

The List Data Event API

The ListDataListener interface contains these three methods.

void intervalAdded(ListDataEvent)
Called when one or more items have been added to the list.

void intervalRemoved(ListDataEvent)
Called when one or more items have been removed from the list.

void contentsChanged(ListDataEvent)
Called when the contents of one or more items in the list have changed.

Each list selection event method has a single parameter: a ListDataEvent[1] object. To get the source of a ListDataEvent, use the getSource method, which ListDataEvent inherits from EventObject.[2]

The ListDataEvent class defines the following handy methods.

int getIndex0()
> Returns the index of the first item whose value has changed.

int getIndex1()
> Returns the index of the last item whose value has changed.

Examples that Use List Data Listeners

The following table lists an example that uses list data listeners.

Table 180   Example that Uses List Data Listeners

Example	Where Described	Notes
ListDataEventDemo.java	This section	Reports all list data events that occur on a list.

---

[1] API documentation for ListDataEvent is available on this book's CD-ROM and online at
   http://java.sun.com/products/jdk/1.2/docs/api/javax/swing/event/ListDataEvent.html
[2] http://java.sun.com/products/jdk/1.2/docs/api/java/util/EventObject.html

How to Write a List Selection Listener

List selection events occur when the selection in a <u>list</u> (page 218) or a <u>table</u> (page 254) is either changing or has just changed. List selection events are fired from an object that implements the `ListSelectionModel`[1] interface. To get a list or a table's list selection model object, use the `getSelectionModel` method.

To detect list selection events, you register a listener on the appropriate list selection model object. The `JList` class also gives you the option of registering a listener on the list itself rather than directly on the list selection model.

This section looks at an example that shows how to listen to list selection events on a selection model. <u>The List Selection Event API</u> (page 496) lists examples that listen on the list directly.

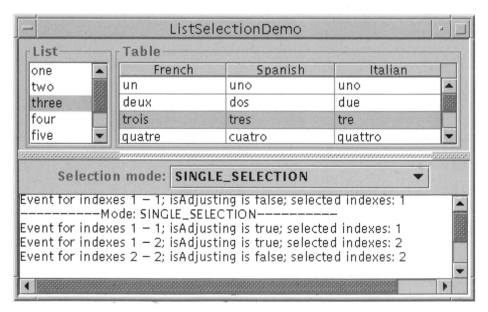

Figure 156 The `ListSelectionDemo` application.

---

[1] API documentation for `ListSelectionModel` is available on this book's CD-ROM and online at
http://java.sun.com/products/jdk/1.2/docs/api/javax/swing/ListSelectionModel.html

The selection model is shared by a list and a table. You can dynamically change the selection mode to any of the three supported modes:

- Single-selection mode
- Single-interval selection mode
- Multiple-interval selection mode

Figure 156 shows the `ListSelectionDemo` in action.

Try this:

1. Compile and run the application.[1] The main source file is <u>`ListSelectionEvent-Demo.java`</u> (page 844).
2. Select and deselect items in the list and the table. The mouse and keyboard commands required to select items depend on the look and feel. For the Java Look & Feel, for example, click the left mouse button to begin a selection, use the Shift key to extend a selection contiguously, and use the Control key to extend a selection discontiguously. Dragging the mouse moves or extends the selection, depending on the list selection mode.

Here's the `ListSelectionDemo.java` code that sets up the selection model and adds a listener to it:

```
.../where the member variables are defined
JList list;
JTable table;

    .../in the init method:
    listSelectionModel = list.getSelectionModel();
    listSelectionModel.addListSelectionListener(
                        new SharedListSelectionHandler());
    ...
    table.setSelectionModel(listSelectionModel);
```

And here's the code for the listener, which works for all the possible selection modes:

```
class SharedListSelectionHandler implements ListSelectionListener {
    public void valueChanged(ListSelectionEvent e) {
        ListSelectionModel lsm = (ListSelectionModel)e.getSource();
        int firstIndex = e.getFirstIndex();
        int lastIndex = e.getLastIndex();
        boolean isAdjusting = e.getValueIsAdjusting();
        output.append("Event for indexes "
                        + firstIndex + " - " + lastIndex
```

---

[1]   See the chapter <u>Getting Started with Swing</u> (page 3) if you need help compiling or running this application.

```
                           + "; isAdjusting is " + isAdjusting
                           + "; selected indexes:");
            if (lsm.isSelectionEmpty()) {
                output.append(" <none>");
            } else {
                // Find out which indexes are selected.
                int minIndex = lsm.getMinSelectionIndex();
                int maxIndex = lsm.getMaxSelectionIndex();
                for (int i = minIndex; i <= maxIndex; i++) {
                    if (lsm.isSelectedIndex(i)) {
                        output.append(" " + i);
                    }
                }
            }
            output.append(newline);
    }
}
```

This valueChanged method displays the first and last indices reported by the event, the value of the event's isAdjusting flag, and the indices currently selected.

Note that the first and last indices reported by the event indicate the inclusive range of items for which the selection has changed. If the selection mode is multiple-interval selection, some items within the range might not have changed. The isAdjusting flag is true if the user is still manipulating the selection and false if the user has finished changing the selection.

The ListSelectionEvent object passed into valueChanged indicates only that the selection has changed. The event contains no information about the current selection. So this method queries the selection model to figure out the current selection.

The List Selection Event API

The ListSelectionListener interface has just one method, so it has no corresponding adapter class.

void valueChanged(ListSelectionEvent)
    Called when the selection in the listened-to component is changing, as well as just after the selection has changed.

Each list selection event method has a single parameter: a <u>ListSelectionEvent</u>[1] object. The event object tells the listener that the selection changed. One list selection event can indicate a change in selection on multiple, discontiguous items in the list.

---

[1] API documentation for ListSelectionEvent is available on this book's CD-ROM and online at
    http://java.sun.com/products/jdk/1.2/docs/api/javax/swing/event/ListSelectionEvent.html

To get the source of a ListSelectionEvent, use the getSource method, which ListSe-lectionEvent inherits from EventObject.[1] If you register a list selection listener on a list directly, the source for each event is the list. Otherwise the source is the selection model.

The ListSelectionEvent class defines the following handy methods.

int getFirstIndex()
   Returns the index of the first item whose selection value has changed. Note that for multiple-interval selection, the first and last items are guaranteed to have changed, but items between them might not have.

int getLastIndex()
   Returns the index of the last item whose selection value has changed. Note that for multiple-interval selection, the first and last items are guaranteed to have changed, but items between them might not have.

int getValueIsAdjusting()
   Returns true if the selection is still changing. Many list selection listeners are interested only in the final state of the selection and can ignore list selection events when this method returns true.

Examples that Use List Selection Listeners

The following table lists the examples that use list selection listeners.

Table 181   Examples that Use List Selection Listeners

Example	Where Described	Notes
ListSelectionDemo.java	This section	Reports all list selection events that occur on a list and on a table. The table and the list share a list selection model, so only one listener is required. Lets the user dynamically change the selection mode.
SplitPaneDemo.java	How to Use Lists (page 218)	Listens to events on a single-selection list (not on the list's selection model).
SimpleTableSelection-Demo.java	How to Use Tables (page 254)	Uses two list selection listeners on one table. One listener listens to list selection events on table columns; the other listens to list selection events on table rows.

---

[1] http://java.sun.com/products/jdk/1.2/docs/api/java/util/EventObject.html

How to Write a Mouse Listener

Mouse events tell you when the user uses the mouse (or similar input device) to interact with a component. Mouse events occur when the cursor enters or exits a component's on-screen area and when the user presses or releases the mouse button. Because tracking the cursor's motion involves significantly more system overhead than does tracking other mouse events, mouse-motion events are separated into a separate listener type (see How to Write a Mouse-Motion Listener (page 503)). If your program needs to detect both mouse events and mouse-motion events, you can use Swing's convenient `MouseInputAdapter` class, which implements both `MouseListener` and `MouseMotionListener`.

The following applet contains a mouse listener. At the top of the applet is a blank area (implemented, strangely enough, by a class named `BlankArea`). The mouse listener listens for events both on the `BlankArea` and on its container, which is an instance of `MouseEvent-Demo`. Each time a mouse event occurs, a descriptive message is displayed under the blank area. By moving the cursor on top of the blank area and occasionally pressing mouse buttons, you can fire mouse events.

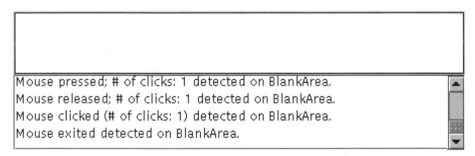

Figure 157 The `MouseEventDemo` applet. You can see this applet online at `http://java.sun.com/docs/books/tutorial/uiswing/events/MouseEventDemo.html`

Try this:

1. Move the cursor into the gray rectangle at the top of the applet. You'll see one or more mouse-entered events.

2. Press and hold the mouse button. You'll see a mouse-pressed event. You might see some extra mouse events, such as mouse-exited and then mouse-entered.

3. Release the mouse button. You'll see a mouse-released event. If you didn't move the mouse, a mouse-clicked event will follow.

4. Press and hold the mouse button, and then drag the mouse so that the cursor ends up outside the applet's area. Release the mouse button. You'll see a mouse-pressed event, followed by a mouse-exited event, followed by a mouse-released event. You are *not* notified of the cursor's motion. To get mouse-motion events, you need to implement a mouse-motion listener.

You can find the applet's code in MouseEventDemo.java (page 847) and BlankArea.java (page 827). Here is the applet's mouse event–handling code:

```
public class MouseEventDemo ... implements MouseListener {
...//where initialization occurs:
      //Register for mouse events on blankArea and applet (panel).
      blankArea.addMouseListener(this);
      addMouseListener(this);
   ...

   public void mousePressed(MouseEvent e) {
      saySomething("Mouse pressed (# of clicks: "
                  + e.getClickCount() + ")", e);
   }

   public void mouseReleased(MouseEvent e) {
      saySomething("Mouse released (# of clicks: "
                  + e.getClickCount() + ")", e);
   }

   public void mouseEntered(MouseEvent e) {
      saySomething("Mouse entered", e);
   }

   public void mouseExited(MouseEvent e) {
      saySomething("Mouse exited", e);
   }

   public void mouseClicked(MouseEvent e) {
      saySomething("Mouse clicked (# of clicks: "
                  + e.getClickCount() + ")", e);
   }

   void saySomething(String eventDescription, MouseEvent e) {
      textArea.append(eventDescription + " detected on "
                  + e.getComponent().getClass().getName()
                  + "." + newline);
   }
}
```

The Mouse Event API

The `MouseListener`[1] interface and its corresponding adapter class, `MouseAdapter`,[2] contain these methods.

void `mouseClicked(MouseEvent)`
 Called just after the user clicks the listened-to component.

void `mouseEntered(MouseEvent)`
 Called just after the cursor enters the bounds of the listened-to component.

void `mouseExited(MouseEvent)`
 Called just after the cursor exits the bounds of the listened-to component.

void `mousePressed(MouseEvent)`
 Called just after the user presses a mouse button while the cursor is over the listened-to component.

void `mouseReleased(MouseEvent)`
 Called just after the user releases a mouse button after a mouse press over the listened-to component.

One complication affects mouse-entered, mouse-exited, and mouse-released events. When the user drags (presses and holds the mouse button and then moves the mouse), the component that the cursor was over when the drag started is the one that receives all subsequent mouse and mouse-motion events up to and including the mouse button release. That means that no other component will receive a single mouse event—not even a mouse-released event—while the drag is occurring.

Each mouse event method has a single parameter: a `MouseEvent`[3] object. The `MouseEvent` class defines the following useful methods.

int `getClickCount()`
 Returns the number of quick, consecutive clicks the user has made (including this event). For example, returns 2 for a double-click.

int `getX()`
int `getY()`
Point `getPoint()`
 Return the (x,y) position at which the event occurred, relative to the component that fired the event.

---

[1] API documentation for `MouseListener` is available on this book's CD-ROM and online at
  http://java.sun.com/products/jdk/1.2/docs/api/java/awt/event/MouseListener.html
[2] http://java.sun.com/products/jdk/1.2/docs/api/java/awt/event/MouseAdapter.html
[3] http://java.sun.com/products/jdk/1.2/docs/api/java/awt/event/MouseEvent.html

`boolean isPopupTrigger()`

Returns `true` if the mouse event should cause a popup menu to appear. Popup triggers are platform dependent; if your program uses popup menus, you should call `isPopup-Trigger` for all mouse-pressed and mouse-released events fired by components over which the popup can appear. See <u>Bringing Up a Popup Menu</u> (page 232) for more information about popup menus.

The `MouseEvent` class inherits the following handy method from <u>ComponentEvent</u>.[1]

`Component getComponent`

Returns the component that fired the event. You can use this method instead of the `get-Source` method.

The `MouseEvent` class inherits many useful methods from <u>InputEvent</u>.[2]

`int getWhen()`

Returns the time stamp of when this event occurred. The higher the time stamp, the more recently the event occurred.

`boolean isAltDown()`
`boolean isControlDown()`
`boolean isMetaDown()`
`boolean isShiftDown()`

Returns the state of individual modifier keys at the time the event was fired.

`int getModifiers()`

Returns the state of all the modifier keys and mouse buttons when the event was fired. You can use this method to determine which mouse button was pressed (or newly released) when a mouse event was fired. The `InputEvent` class defines these constants for use with the `getModifiers` method: `ALT_MASK`, `BUTTON1_MASK`, `BUTTON2__MASK`, `BUTTON3_MASK`, `CTRL_MASK`, `META_MASK`, and `SHIFT_MASK`. For example, the following expression is `true` if the right mouse button was pressed:

```
(mouseEvent.getModifiers()
        & InputEvent.BUTTON3_MASK) == InputEvent.BUTTON3_MASK
```

The <u>SwingUtilities</u>[3] class contains convenience methods for determining whether a particular mouse button has been pressed:

```
static boolean isLeftMouseButton(MouseEvent)
static boolean isMiddleMouseButton(MouseEvent)
static boolean isRightMouseButton(MouseEvent)
```

---

[1] API documentation for this class is available on this book's CD-ROM and online at http://java.sun.com/products/jdk/1.2/docs/api/java/awt/event/ComponentEvent.html

[2] http://java.sun.com/products/jdk/1.2/docs/api/java/awt/event/InputEvent.html

[3] http://java.sun.com/products/jdk/1.2/docs/api/javax/swing/SwingUtilities.html

Examples that Use Mouse Listeners

The following table lists the examples that use mouse listeners.

Table 182   Examples that Use Mouse Listeners

Example	Where Described	Notes
`MouseEventDemo.java`	This section	Reports all mouse events that occur within a blank panel, to demonstrate the circumstances under which mouse events are fired.
`Coordinates-Demo.java`	Overview of Custom Painting (page 537)	An applet that draws a small circle where the user clicks the mouse. The applet also reports the x,y location of the mouse click.
`SelectionDemo.java`	Overview of Custom Painting (page 537)	An applet that lets the user drag a rectangle to select a portion of an image. Uses a subclass of `MouseInputAdapter` to listen to both mouse events and mouse-motion events.
`GlassPaneDemo.java`	How to Use Root Panes (page 158)	Uses a subclass of `MouseInputAdapter` to listen to mouse events and mouse-motion events on the root pane's glass pane. Redispatches the events to underlying components.
`TableSorter.java`	How to Use Tables (page 254)	Listens to mouse events on a table header. Sorts data in the selected column.
`MovingLabels.java`	Moving an Image Across the Screen (page 565)	Stops and starts an animation in response to mouse clicks.
`PopupMenuDemo.java`	How to Use Menus (page 226)	Displays a popup menu in response to mouse clicks.
`ListDemo.java`	How to Use Lists (page 218)	Listens for double mouse clicks on a list. Double-clicks act as an accelerator for selecting an item in the list and pressing a mouse button.

How to Write a Mouse-Motion Listener

Mouse-motion events tell you when the user uses the mouse (or a similar input device) to move the onscreen cursor. For information on listening for other kinds of mouse events, such as clicks, see <u>How to Write a Mouse Listener</u> (page 498). If your program needs to detect both mouse events and mouse-motion events, you can use Swing's convenient `MouseInput-Adapter` class, which implements both `MouseListener` and `MouseMotionListener`.

The following applet contains a mouse-motion listener and is exactly like the applet in <u>How to Write a Mouse Listener</u> (page 498), except for substituting `MouseMotionListener` for `MouseListener`, implementing the `mouseDragged` and `mouseMoved` methods instead of the mouse listener methods, and displaying coordinates instead of numbers of clicks. You can find the applet's code in <u>MouseMotionEventDemo.java</u> (page 848) and <u>BlankArea.java</u> (page 827).

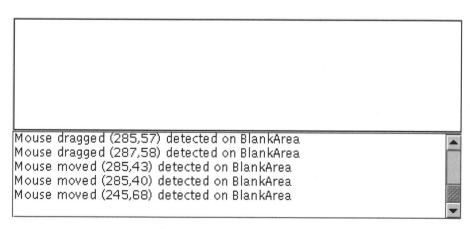

Figure 158 The `MouseMotionEventDemo` applet.

Try this:

1. Move the cursor into the gray rectangle at the top of the applet. You'll see one or more mouse-moved events.

2. Press and hold the mouse button, and then move the mouse so that the cursor is outside the light gray rectangle. You'll see mouse-dragged events.

Here is the code that implements the mouse-motion event handling:

```
public class MouseMotionEventDemo extends JApplet
                              implements MouseMotionListener {
    //...in initialization code:
        //Register for mouse events on blankArea and applet.
        blankArea.addMouseMotionListener(this);
        addMouseMotionListener(this);
    ...

    public void mouseMoved(MouseEvent e) {
        saySomething("Mouse moved", e);
    }

    public void mouseDragged(MouseEvent e) {
        saySomething("Mouse dragged", e);
    }

    void saySomething(String eventDescription, MouseEvent e) {
        textArea.append(eventDescription
                    + " (" + e.getX() + "," + e.getY() + ")"
                    + " detected on "
                    + e.getComponent().getClass().getName()
                    + newline);
    }
}
```

A more interesting example is `SelectionDemo`, which is discussed in <u>Arguments to the repaint Method</u> (page 540). The program draws a rectangle illustrating the user's current dragging. To do this, the program must implement an event handler for three kinds of mouse events: mouse presses, mouse drags, and mouse releases. To be informed of all of these events, the handler must implement both the `MouseListener` and the `MouseMotionListener` interfaces and be registered as both a mouse listener and a mouse-motion listener. To avoid having to define empty methods, the handler doesn't implement either listener interface directly. Instead it extends `MouseInputAdapter`, as the following code snippet shows.

```
...//where initialization occurs:
    MyListener myListener = new MyListener();
    addMouseListener(myListener);
    addMouseMotionListener(myListener);
...

class MyListener extends MouseInputAdapter {
```

```java
public void mousePressed(MouseEvent e) {
    int x = e.getX();
    int y = e.getY();
    currentRect = new Rectangle(x, y, 0, 0);
    updateDrawableRect(getWidth(), getHeight());
    repaint();
}

public void mouseDragged(MouseEvent e) {
    updateSize(e);
}

public void mouseReleased(MouseEvent e) {
    updateSize(e);
}

void updateSize(MouseEvent e) {
    int x = e.getX();
    int y = e.getY();
    ...
    repaint(...);
}
}
```

The Mouse-Motion Event API

The `MouseMotionListener`[1] interface and its corresponding adapter class, `MouseMotion-Adapter`,[2] contain these methods.

void mouseDragged(MouseEvent)

Called in response to the user's moving the mouse while holding a mouse button down. This event is fired by the component that fired the most recent mouse-pressed event, even if the cursor is no longer over that component.

void mouseMoved(MouseEvent)

Called in response to the user's moving the mouse with no mouse buttons pressed. This event is fired by the component that's currently under the cursor.

Each mouse-motion event method has a single parameter—and it's *not* called `Mouse-MotionEvent`! Instead each mouse-motion event method has a `MouseEvent` argument. See The Mouse Event API (page 500) for information about using `MouseEvent` objects.

---

[1] API documentation for `MouseMotionListener` is available on this book's CD-ROM and online at
http://java.sun.com/products/jdk/1.2/docs/api/java/awt/event/MouseMotionListener.html

[2] http://java.sun.com/products/jdk/1.2/docs/api/java/awt/event/MouseMotionAdapter.html

Examples that Use Mouse-Motion Listeners

The following table lists the examples that use mouse-motion listeners.

Table 183   Examples that Use Mouse-Motion Listeners

Example	Where Described	Notes
`MouseMotionEventDemo.java`	This section	Reports all mouse motion events that occur within a blank panel to demonstrate the circumstances under which mouse-motion events are fired.
`LayeredPaneDemo.java` and `LayeredPaneDemo2.java`	How to Use Layered Panes (page 150)	Move an image of Duke around within a layered pane in response to mouse motion events.
`SelectionDemo.java`	Arguments to the repaint Method (page 540)	An applet that lets the user drag a rectangle to select a portion of an image. Uses a subclass of `MouseInputAdapter` to listen to both mouse events and mouse-motion events.
`GlassPaneDemo.java`	How to Use Root Panes (page 158)	Uses a subclass of `MouseInputAdapter` to listen to mouse events and mouse-motion events on the root pane's glass pane. Redispatches the events to underlying components.

How to Write a Table Model Listener

Each JTable[1] object has a table model that holds its data. When a table model listener is registered on the table model, the listener is notified every time the table model's data changes. The JTable itself automatically uses a table model listener to make its GUI reflect the current state of the table model. You register a table model listener by using the TableModeladdTableModelListener method.

The Table Model Event API

The TableModelListener[2] interface contains a single method and thus has no corresponding adapter class. Here is the lone TableModelListener method.

void tableChanged(TableModelEvent)
Called when the structure of or data in the table has changed.

The tableChanged method's argument is a TableModelEvent[3] object that specifies which cells changed and how, in general, they changed. You can query the TableModelEvent by using the following methods.

int getFirstRow()
Returns the index of the first row that changed. TableModelEvent.HEADER_ROW specifies the table header.

int getLastRow()
The last row that changed. Again, HEADER_ROW is a possible value.

int getColumn()
Returns the index of the column that changed. The constant TableModelEvent.ALL_COLUMNS specifies that all the columns might have changed.

int getType()
Specifies what happened to the changed cells. The returned value is one of the following: TableModelEvent.INSERT, TableModelEvent.DELETE, or TableModelEvent.UPDATE.

---

[1] See How to Use Tables (page 254) for more information on JTable.
[2] API documentation for TableModelListener is available on this book's CD-ROM and online at http://java.sun.com/products/jdk/1.2/docs/api/javax/swing/event/TableModelListener.html
[3] http://java.sun.com/products/jdk/1.2/docs/api/javax/swing/event/TableModelEvent.html

Also useful is the `getSource` method, which `TableModelEvent` inherits from <u>EventObject</u>.[1]

Examples that Use Table Model Listeners

The following table lists the examples that use table model listeners.

Table 184   Examples that Use Table Model Listeners

Example	Where Described	Notes
`TableMap.java`	<u>Sorting and Otherwise Manipulating Data</u> (page 269)	This superclass for data-manipulating table models implements a table model that sits between a table data model and a `JTable`. The `TableMap` listens for table model events from the data model and then simply forwards them to its table model listeners, such as the `JTable`.
`TableSorter.java`	<u>Sorting and Otherwise Manipulating Data</u> (page 269)	A sorting table model implemented as a subclass of `TableMap`. In addition to forwarding table model events, the `tableChanged` method keeps track of the number of rows.
`SharedModelDemo.java`	–	Does *not* implement a table model listener, but instead it implements a combined list and table model.

---

[1] API documentation for `EventObject` is available on this book's CD-ROM and online at http://java.sun.com/products/jdk/1.2/docs/api/java/util/EventObject.html

How to Write a Tree Expansion Listener

When using a <u>tree</u> (page 320), you might sometimes need to react when a branch becomes expanded or collapsed. For example, you might need to load or save data. Or you might need to prevent the user from expanding a particular node.

Two kinds of listeners report expansion and collapse occurrences: tree expansion listeners and tree-will-expand listeners. This section discusses the former. A tree expansion listener detects when an expansion or collapse has happened. In general, you should implement a tree expansion listener unless you might need to prevent an expansion or collapse from happening.

Tree-will-expand listeners are discussed in <u>How to Write a Tree-Will-Expand Listener</u> (page 516). That type of listener detects when an expansion or collapse is about to happen.

The following applet demonstrates a simple tree expansion listener. The text area at the bottom of the applet displays a message every time a tree expansion event occurs. It's a straightforward, boring applet. To see a more interesting version that can veto expansions, go to <u>How to Write a Tree-Will-Expand Listener</u> (page 516).

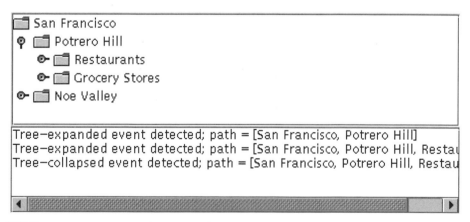

Figure 159 The `TreeExpandEventDemo` applet. You can see this applet online at `http://java.sun.com/docs/books/tutorial/uiswing/events/TreeExpandEventDemo.html`

The following code shows how the program handles expansion events. You can find all of the applet's source code in <u>TreeExpandEventDemo.java</u> (page 851).

```java
public class TreeExpandEventDemo ... {
    ...
    void saySomething(String eventDescription, TreeExpansionEvent e) {
        textArea.append(eventDescription + "; "
                        + "path = " + e.getPath()
                        + newline);
    }

    class DemoArea ... implements TreeExpansionListener {
        ...
        public DemoArea() {
            ...
            tree.addTreeExpansionListener(this);
            ...
        }
        ...

        // Required by TreeExpansionListener interface.
        public void treeExpanded(TreeExpansionEvent e) {
            saySomething("Tree-expanded event detected", e);
        }

        // Required by TreeExpansionListener interface.
        public void treeCollapsed(TreeExpansionEvent e) {
            saySomething("Tree-collapsed event detected", e);
        }
    }
}
```

The Tree Expansion Event API

The <u>TreeExpansionListener</u>[1] interface contains two methods.

void treeCollapsed(TreeExpansionEvent)
    Called just after a tree node collapses.

void treeExpanded(TreeExpansionEvent)
    Called just after a tree node expands.

---

[1] API documentation for TreeExpansionListener is available on this book's CD-ROM and online at http://java.sun.com/products/jdk/1.2/docs/api/javax/swing/event/TreeExpansionListener.html

Both methods have a single parameter: a `TreeExpansionEvent`[1] object. The `TreeExpansionEvent` class defines the following method.

TreePath getPath()
    Returns a `TreePath`[2] object that identifies each node from the root of the tree to the collapsed/expanded node, inclusive.

Another useful method is `getSource`, which `TreeExpansionEvent` inherits from `EventObject`.[3]

Examples that Use Tree Expansion Listeners

The following table lists the examples that use tree expansion listeners.

Table 185   Examples that Use Tree Expansion Listeners

Example	Where Described	Notes
`TreeExpandEventDemo.java`	This section	Displays a message whenever a tree expansion event occurs.
`TreeExpandEventDemo2.java`	How to Write a Tree-Will-Expand Listener (page 516)	Adds a tree-will-expand listener to `TreeExpandEventDemo`.

---

[1] http://java.sun.com/products/jdk/1.2/docs/api/javax/swing/event/TreeExpansionEvent.html
[2] API documentation for `TreePath` is available on this book's CD-ROM and online at http://java.sun.com/products/jdk/1.2/docs/api/javax/swing/tree/TreePath.html
[3] http://java.sun.com/products/jdk/1.2/docs/api/java/util/EventObject.html

How to Write a Tree Model Listener

Implementing a tree model listener enables you to detect when the data displayed by a tree changes. You might use a tree model listener to detect when the user edits tree nodes. To see an example and discussion of doing so, read Dynamically Changing a Tree (page 329).

The Tree Model Event API

The TreeModelListener[1] interface contains four methods.

void treeNodesChanged(TreeModelEvent)
Called when one or more sibling nodes have changed.

void treeNodesInserted(TreeModelEvent)
Called after nodes have been inserted into the tree.

void treeNodesRemoved(TreeModelEvent)
Called after nodes have been removed from the tree.

void treeNodesStructureChanged(TreeModelEvent)
Called after the tree's structure has drastically changed.

Each tree model event method has a single parameter: a TreeModelEvent object. The TreeModelEvent class defines the following useful methods.

int[] getChildIndices()
For treeNodesChanged, treeNodesInserted, and treeNodesRemoved, returns the indices of the changed, inserted, or deleted nodes, respectively. Returns nothing useful for treeStructureChanged.

Object[] getChildren()
Returns the objects corresponding to the child indices.

Object[] getPath()
Returns the path to the parent of the changed, inserted, or deleted nodes. For treeStructureChanged, returns the path to the node beneath which the structure has changed.

---

[1] API documentation for this class is available on this book's CD-ROM and online at http://java.sun.com/products/jdk/1.2/docs/api/javax/swing/event/TreeModelListener.html

TreePath getTreePath()
   Returns the same thing as getPath but as a <u>TreePath</u>[1] object.

Also useful is the getSource method, which TreeModelEvent inherits from <u>EventOb-ject</u>.[2]

Examples that Use Tree Model Listeners

The DynamicTree example implements a tree model listener to detect when the user has edited a node's data. You can find the listener's code in <u>DynamicTree.java</u> (page 646). The example also relies on <u>DynamicTreeDemo.java</u> (page 648). The code is discussed in <u>Dynamically Changing a Tree</u> (page 329).

---

[1] API documentation for TreePath is available on this book's CD-ROM and online at http://java.sun.com/products/jdk/1.2/docs/api/javax/swing/tree/TreePath.html
[2] http://java.sun.com/products/jdk/1.2/docs/api/java/util/EventObject.html

How to Write a Tree Selection Listener

To detect when the user selects a node in a tree, you need to register a tree selection listener. Here is an example, taken from the `TreeDemo` example discussed in <u>Responding to Node Selection</u> (page 323), of detecting node selection in a tree that can have at most one node selected at a time:

```
tree.addTreeSelectionListener(new TreeSelectionListener() {
    public void valueChanged(TreeSelectionEvent e) {
        DefaultMutableTreeNode node = (DefaultMutableTreeNode)
                         tree.getLastSelectedPathComponent();
        if (node == null) return;
        Object nodeInfo = node.getUserObject();
        ...
        /* React to the node selection. */
        ...
    }
});
```

To specify that the tree should support single selection, the program uses this code:

```
tree.getSelectionModel().setSelectionMode
    (TreeSelectionModel.SINGLE_TREE_SELECTION);
```

The <u>TreeSelectionModel</u>[1] interface defines three values for the selection mode.

DISCONTIGUOUS_TREE_SELECTION
The default mode for the default tree selection model. With this mode, any combination of nodes can be selected.

SINGLE_TREE_SELECTION
The mode used by the preceding example. At most one node can be selected at a time.

CONTIGUOUS_TREE_SELECTION
Allows only nodes in adjoining rows to be selected.

---

[1] API documentation for this class is available on this book's CD-ROM and online at http://java.sun.com/products/jdk/1.2/docs/api/javax/swing/tree/TreeSelectionModel.html

The Tree Selection Event API

The `TreeSelectionListener`[1] interface contains a single method and thus has no corresponding adapter class. Here is the lone `TreeSelectionListener` method:

void valueChanged(TreeSelectionEvent)
  Called whenever the selection changes.

The `valueChanged` method has a single parameter: an `TreeSelectionEvent`[2] object. The `TreeSelectionEvent` class defines several methods for returning the path or paths of the selection. As the preceding code example shows, you can also use `JTree` methods, such as `getLastSelectedPathComponent`, to get the current selection.

If you need to find the object that fired the tree selection event, you can use the `getSource` method, which `TableSelectionEvent` inherits from `EventObject`.[3]

Examples that Use Tree Selection Listeners

The `TreeDemo` example, as well as `TreeIconDemo`, which adds to it, uses a tree selection listener. The listener responds to node clicks by showing the appropriate HTML document. You can find the source code for `TreeDemo` in `TreeDemo.java` (page 763) and a full discussion of the program in How to Use Trees (page 320).

---

[1] API documentation for `TreeSelectionListener` is available on this book's CD-ROM and online at
    http://java.sun.com/products/jdk/1.2/docs/api/javax/swing/event/TreeSelectionListener.html
[2] http://java.sun.com/products/jdk/1.2/docs/api/javax/swing/event/TreeSelectionEvent.html
[3] http://java.sun.com/products/jdk/1.2/docs/api/java/util/EventObject.html

How to Write a Tree-Will-Expand Listener

As explained in <u>How to Write a Tree Expansion Listener</u> (page 509), you can use a tree-will-expand listener to prevent a tree node from expanding or collapsing. To be notified just *after* an expansion or a collapse occurs, you should use a tree expansion listener instead.

The following applet adds a tree-will-expand listener to the `TreeExpandEventDemo` example discussed in <u>How to Write a Tree Expansion Listener</u> (page 509). The new code demonstrates the ability of tree-will-expand listeners to veto node expansions and collapses: It asks for confirmation each time you try to expand a node.

Figure 160 The `TreeExpandEventDemo` applet.

Try this:

1. Click the graphic to the left of the Potrero Hill node. This tells the tree that you want to expand the node. A dialog will appear, asking you whether you really want to expand the node.

2. Click Expand or dismiss the dialog. Messages in the text area tell you that both a tree-will-expand event and a tree-expanded event have occurred. At the end of each message is the path to the expanded node.

3. Try to expand another node, but this time click the Cancel Expansion button in the dialog. The node does not expand. Messages in the text area tell you that a tree-will-expand event occurred and that you canceled a tree expansion.

4. Collapse the Potrero Hill node. The node collapses without a dialog appearing, because the event handler's `treeWillCollapse` method lets the collapse occur, uncontested.

The following snippet shows the code that this program adds to `TreeExpandEventDemo`. The boldface line prevents the tree expansion from happening. You can find all of the applet's source code in <u>`TreeExpandEventDemo2.java`</u> (page 853).

```java
public class TreeExpandEventDemo2 ... {
    ...
    class DemoArea ... implements ... TreeWillExpandListener {
        ...
        public DemoArea() {
            ...
            tree.addTreeWillExpandListener(this);
            ...
        }
        ...

        // Required by TreeWillExpandListener interface.
        public void treeWillExpand(TreeExpansionEvent e)
                    throws ExpandVetoException {
            saySomething("Tree-will-expand event detected", e);
            //...show a dialog...
            if (/* user said to cancel the expansion */) {
                //Cancel expansion.
                saySomething("Tree expansion cancelled", e);
                throw new ExpandVetoException(e);
            }
        }

        // Required by TreeWillExpandListener interface.
        public void treeWillCollapse(TreeExpansionEvent e) {
            saySomething("Tree-will-collapse event detected", e);
        }
        ...
    }
}
```

The Tree-Will-Expand Event API

The `TreeWillExpandListener`[1] interface contains two methods.

`void treeWillCollapse(TreeExpansionEvent)`
> Called just before a tree node collapses. To prevent the collapse from occurring, your implementation of this method should throw an `ExpandVetoException`[2] event.

`void treeWillExpand(TreeExpansionEvent)`
> Called just before a tree node expands. To prevent the expansion from occurring, your implementation of this method should throw an `ExpandVetoException` event.

See The Tree Expansion Event API (page 510) for information about the `TreeExpansion-Event` argument for the preceding methods.

Examples that Use Tree-Will-Expand Listeners

`TreeExpandEventDemo2.java` (page 853), featured in this section, is our only example that uses a tree-will-expand listener.

---

[1] API documentation for this class is available on this book's CD-ROM and online at http://java.sun.com/
     products/jdk/1.2/docs/api/javax/swing/event/TreeWillExpandListener.html
[2] API documentation for `ExpandVetoException` is available on this book's CD-ROM and online at
     http://java.sun.com/products/jdk/1.2/docs/api/javax/swing/tree/ExpandVetoException.html

How to Write an Undoable Edit Listener

Undoable edit events occur when an operation that can be undone occurs on a component. Currently only text components fire undoable edit events—and then only indirectly. The text component's document fires the events. For text components, undoable operations include inserting characters, deleting characters, and modifying the style of text. Programs typically listen to undoable edit events to assist in the implementation of undo and redo commands.

Here is the undoable edit event–handling code from an application called `TextComponent-Demo`:

```
...
//where initialization occurs
document.addUndoableEditListener(new MyUndoableEditListener());
...

protected class MyUndoableEditListener implements UndoableEditListener {
    public void undoableEditHappened(UndoableEditEvent e) {
        //Remember the edit and update the menus
        undo.addEdit(e.getEdit());
        undoAction.updateUndoState();
        redoAction.updateRedoState();
    }
}
```

You can find the full source code for the program and instructions for compiling and running it in General Rules for Using Text Components (page 282). For a discussion about the undoable edit listener aspect of the program, see Implementing Undo and Redo (page 292).

The Undoable Edit Event API

The `UndoableEditListener`[1] interface has just one method, so it has no corresponding adapter class.

---

[1] API documentation for this class is available on this book's CD-ROM and online at http://java.sun.com/products/jdk/1.2/docs/api/javax/swing/event/UndoableEditListener.html

`void undoableEditHappened(UndoableEditEvent)`

Called when an undoable event occurs on the listened-to component.

The undoableEditHappened method has a single parameter: an <u>UndoableEditEvent</u>[1] object. To get the document that fired the event, use the getSource method, which UndoableEditEvent inherits from EventObject.

The UndoableEditEvent class defines one method, which returns an object that contains detailed information about the edit that occurred.

`UndoableEdit getEdit()`

Returns an <u>UndoableEdit</u>[2] object that represents the edit that occurred and contains information about and commands for undoing or redoing the edit.

Examples that Use Undoable Edit Listeners

The following table lists the examples that use undoable edit listeners.

Table 186   Examples that Use Undoable Edit Listeners

Example	Where Described	Notes
TextComponentDemo.java	<u>Implementing Undo and Redo</u> (page 292)	Implements undo and redo on a text pane with help from an undoable edit listener.

---

[1] API documentation for UndoableEditEvent is available on this book's CD-ROM and online at
http://java.sun.com/products/jdk/1.2/docs/api/javax/swing/event/UndoableEditEvent.html
[2] http://java.sun.com/products/jdk/1.2/docs/api/javax/swing/undo/UndoableEdit.html

How to Write a Window Listener

Window events are fired by a window, such as a frame or a dialog, just after the window is opened, closed, iconified, deiconified, activated, or deactivated. *Opening* a window means showing it for the first time; *closing* it means removing the window from the screen. *Iconifying* a window means substituting a small icon on the desktop for the window; *deiconifying* means the opposite. A window is *activated* if it or a component it contains has the keyboard focus; *deactivation* occurs when the window and all of its contents lose the keyboard focus. If you want to be notified when a window is made visible or hidden, you should register a component listener on the window.

The most common use of window listeners is implementing custom window-closing behavior. For example, you might use a window listener to save data before closing the window or to exit the program when the last window closes.

You don't necessarily need to implement a window listener to specify what a window should do when the user closes it. When the user closes a window, the window becomes invisible by default. You can specify different behavior—disposing of the window, for example—by using the `JFrame` or the `JDialogsetDefaultCloseOperation` method. If you decide to implement a window-closing handler, you might want to use `setDefaultCloseOperation(WindowConstants.DO_NOTHING_ON_CLOSE)` to specify that your window listener takes care of all window-closing duties.

See How to Make Frames (page 82) for an example of a handler for window-closing events. Within that section, Responding to Window-Closing Events (page 84) has details on how to use `setDefaultCloseOperation`.

Another common use of window listeners is to stop threads and release resources when a window is iconified and to start them up again when the window is deiconified. This way, you can avoid unnecessarily using the processor or other resources. For example, when a window that contains animation is iconified, the window should stop its animation thread and free any large buffers. When the window is deiconified, it can start the thread again and recreate the buffers.

The following applet demonstrates window events. Clicking the top button in the applet brings up a small window. The controlling class listens for window events from the window, displaying a message whenever it detects a window event. You can find the applet's code in `WindowEventDemo.java` (page 855).

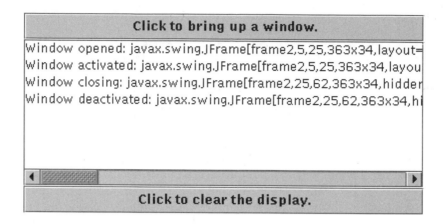

Figure 161 The `WindowEventDemo` applet. You can see this applet online at `http://java.sun.com/docs/books/tutorial/uiswing/events/WindowEventDemo.html`

Try this:

1. Bring up the Window Demo Window by clicking the applet's top button. The first time you click this button, the message "Window opened" will appear in the applet's display area.

2. Click the window if it doesn't already have the focus. Do you see a "Window activated" message in the applet's display area?

3. Iconify the window, using the window controls. You'll see a "Window iconified" message in the applet's display area.

4. Deiconify the window. You'll see a "Window deiconified" message in the applet's display area.

5. Close the window, using the window controls. You'll see "Window closing" in the applet's display area. Because the window-closing event handler invokes `setVisible(false)` instead of `dispose()`, you won't see the message "Window closed".

Here is the applet's window event–handling code:

```
public class WindowEventDemo ... implements WindowListener {
    ...//where initialization occurs:
        //Create but don't show window.
        window = new JFrame("Window Event Window");
        window.addWindowListener(this);
        window.getContentPane().add(new JLabel(ActionListener),
                                BorderLayout.CENTER);
        window.pack();
    ...
```

```java
    public void windowClosing(WindowEvent e) {
        window.setVisible(false);
        displayMessage("Window closing", e);
    }

    public void windowClosed(WindowEvent e) {
        displayMessage("Window closed", e);
    }

    public void windowOpened(WindowEvent e) {
        displayMessage("Window opened", e);
    }

    public void windowIconified(WindowEvent e) {
        displayMessage("Window iconified", e);
    }

    public void windowDeiconified(WindowEvent e) {
        displayMessage("Window deiconified", e);
    }

    public void windowActivated(WindowEvent e) {
        displayMessage("Window activated", e);
    }

    public void windowDeactivated(WindowEvent e) {
        displayMessage("Window deactivated", e);
    }

    void displayMessage(String prefix, WindowEvent e) {
        display.append(prefix
                        + ": "
                        + e.getWindow()
                        + newline);
    }
    ...
}
```

The Window Event API

The `WindowListener`[1] interface and its corresponding adapter class, `WindowAdapter`,[2] contain these methods.

---

[1] API documentation for `WindowListener` is available on this book's CD-ROM and online at
http://java.sun.com/products/jdk/1.2/docs/api/java/awt/event/WindowListener.html

[2] http://java.sun.com/products/jdk/1.2/docs/api/java/awt/event/WindowAdapter.html

void windowOpened(WindowEvent)
Called just after the listened-to window has been shown for the first time.

void windowClosing(WindowEvent)
Called in response to a user request that the listened-to window be closed. To close the window, the listener should invoke the window's `dispose` or `setVisible(false)` method.

void windowClosed(WindowEvent)
Called just after the listened-to window has closed.

void windowIconified(WindowEvent)
void windowDeiconified(WindowEvent)
Called just after the listened-to window is iconified or deiconified, respectively.

void windowActivated(WindowEvent)
void windowDeactivated(WindowEvent)
Called just after the listened-to window is activated or deactivated, respectively.

Each window event method has a single parameter: a `WindowEvent`[1] object. The `Window-Event` class defines one method.

Window getWindow()
Returns the window that fired the event. You can use this instead of the `getSource` method.

Examples that Use Window Listeners

The following table lists the examples that use window listeners.

Table 187   Examples that Use Window Listeners

Example	Where Described	Notes
WindowEventDemo.java	This section	Reports all window events that occur on one window, to demonstrate the circumstances under which window events are fired.
FrameDemo.java	How to Make Frames (page 82)	One of many examples that listens for window-closing events, so that the application can exit when its only window is closed.

---

[1]   API documentation for `WindowEvent` is available on this book's CD-ROM and online at http://java.sun.com/products/jdk/1.2/docs/api/java/awt/event/WindowEvent.html

Table 187   Examples that Use Window Listeners

Example	Where Described	Notes
ComponentEventDemo.java	How to Write a Component Listener (page 466)	Listens for window-closing events on a frame displayed by an applet. This way, the applet knows whether to reopen the window when the user leaves and returns to the applet's page.
FlowWindow.java	How to Use FlowLayout (page 366)	Disposes a frame displayed by an applet when the user closes the frame.
SliderDemo.java	How to Use Sliders (page 248)	Listens for window iconify and deiconify events, so that it can stop the animation when the window isn't visible.
InternalFrameEventDemo.java	How to Write an Internal Frame Listener (page 480)	Reports all internal frame events that occur on one internal frame, to demonstrate the circumstances under which internal frame events are fired. Internal frame events are similar to window events.
TextComponentDemo.java	General Rules for Using Text Components (page 282)	Contains a text pane that requests the keyboard focus in response to window-activated events.
DialogDemo.java and CustomDialog.java	General Rules for Using Text Components (page 282)	Uses setDefaultCloseOperation instead of a window listener to determine what action to take when the user closes the window.

26

Summary of Listener API

IN the table that follows, the first column gives the name of the listener interface. The second column names the corresponding adapter class, if any. [1] The third column lists the methods that the listener interface contains and shows the type of the event object passed into the method. Typically the listener, the adapter, and the event type have the same name prefix, but this is not always the case.

To see which Swing components can fire which kinds of events, see Listeners Supported by Swing Components (page 453).

Table 188   Summary of Listener API

Listener Interface	Adapter Class	Listener Methods
ActionListener	None	actionPerformed(ActionEvent)
AncestorListener	None	ancestorAdded(AncestorEvent) ancestorMoved(AncestorEvent) ancestorRemoved(AncestorEvent)
CaretListener	None	caretUpdate(CaretEvent)
CellEditorListener	None	editingStopped(ChangeEvent) editingCanceled(ChangeEvent)
ChangeListener	None	stateChanged(ChangeEvent)
ComponentListener	Component-Adapter	componentHidden(ComponentEvent) componentMoved(ComponentEvent) componentResized(ComponentEvent) componentShown(ComponentEvent)

---

[1]   For a discussion of using adapters, see Using Adapters and Inner Classes to Handle Events (page 449).

Table 188 Summary of Listener API

Listener Interface	Adapter Class	Listener Methods
ContainerListener	Container-Adapter	componentAdded(ContainerEvent) componentRemoved(ContainerEvent)
DocumentListener	None	changedUpdate(DocumentEvent) insertUpdate(DocumentEvent) removeUpdate(DocumentEvent)
FocusListener	FocusAdapter	focusGained(FocusEvent) focusLost(FocusEvent)
HyperlinkListener	None	hyperlinkUpdate(HyperlinkEvent)
InternalFrameListener	Internal-FrameAdapter	internalFrameActivated(Internal-FrameEvent) internalFrameClosed(InternalFrameEvent) internalFrameClosing(InternalFrameEvent) internalFrameDeactivated(Internal-FrameEvent) internalFrameDeiconified(Internal-FrameEvent) internalFrameIconified(Internal-FrameEvent) internalFrameOpened(InternalFrameEvent)
ItemListener	None	itemStateChanged(ItemEvent)
KeyListener	KeyAdapter	keyPressed(KeyEvent) keyReleased(KeyEvent) keyTyped(KeyEvent)
ListDataListener	None	contentsChanged(ListDataEvent) intervalAdded(ListDataEvent) intervalRemoved(ListDataEvent)
ListSelectionListener	None	valueChanged(ListSelectionEvent)
MenuDragMouseListener	None	menuDragMouseDragged(MenuDragMouseEvent) menuDragMouseEntered(MenuDragMouseEvent) menuDragMouseExited(MenuDragMouseEvent) menuDragMouseReleased(MenuDragMouseEvent)
MenuKeyListener	None	menuKeyPressed(MenuKeyEvent) menuKeyReleased(MenuKeyEvent) menuKeyTyped(MenuKeyEvent)
MenuListener	None	menuCanceled(MenuEvent) menuDeselected(MenuEvent) menuSelected(MenuEvent)

Table 188   Summary of Listener API

Listener Interface	Adapter Class	Listener Methods
MouseInputListener	MouseInput-Adapter	mouseClicked(MouseEvent) mouseEntered(MouseEvent) mouseExited(MouseEvent) mousePressed(MouseEvent) mouseReleased(MouseEvent) mouseDragged(MouseEvent) mouseMoved(MouseEvent)
MouseListener	MouseAdapter	mouseClicked(MouseEvent) mouseEntered(MouseEvent) mouseExited(MouseEvent) mousePressed(MouseEvent) mouseReleased(MouseEvent)
MouseMotionListener	MouseMotion-Adapter	mouseDragged(MouseEvent) mouseMoved(MouseEvent)
PopupMenuListener	None	popupMenuCanceled(PopupMenuEvent) popupMenuWillBecomeInvisible(Popup-MenuEvent) popupMenuWillBecomeVisible(Popup-MenuEvent)
TableColumnModelLis-tener	None	columnAdded(TableColumnModelEvent) columnMoved(TableColumnModelEvent) columnRemoved(TableColumnModelEvent) columnMarginChanged(ChangeEvent) columnSelectionChanged(ListSelection-Event)
TableModelListener	None	tableChanged(TableModelEvent)
TreeExpansionListener	None	treeCollapsed(TreeExpansionEvent) treeExpanded(TreeExpansionEvent)
TreeModelListener	None	treeNodesChanged(TreeModelEvent) treeNodesInserted(TreeModelEvent) treeNodesRemoved(TreeModelEvent) treeStructureChanged(TreeModelEvent)
TreeSelectionListener	None	valueChanged(TreeSelectionEvent)
TreeWillExpandListener	None	treeWillCollapse(TreeExpansionEvent) treeWillExpand(TreeExpansionEvent)
UndoableEditListener	None	undoableEditHappened(UndoableEditEvent)
WindowListener	Window-Adapter	windowActivated(WindowEvent) windowClosed(WindowEvent) windowClosing(WindowEvent) windowDeactivated(WindowEvent) windowDeiconified(WindowEvent) windowIconified(WindowEvent) windowOpened(WindowEvent)

Solving Common Event-Handling Problems

THIS chapter discusses problems that you might encounter while handling events.

Problem: I'm trying to handle certain events from a component, but the component isn't generating the events it should.

- First, make sure you registered the right kind of listener to detect the events. See whether another kind of listener might detect the kind of events you need.

- Make sure you registered the listener on the right object.

- Did you implement the event handler correctly? For example, if you extended an adapter class, then make sure you used the right method signature. Make sure each event-handling method is `public void`, that the name is spelled right and that the argument is of the right type.

- If you still think that the component isn't generating the events it should, check the Java Developer Connection[1] to see whether this is a known bug.

Problem: My combo box isn't generating low-level events, such as focus events.

- Combo boxes are compound components—components implemented using multiple components. For this reason, combo boxes don't fire the low-level events that simple components fire. For more information, see Handling Events on a Combo Box (page 194).

---

[1] You can find the *Java Developer Connection* online at http://developer.java.sun.com

Problem: The document for an editor pane (or text pane) isn't firing document events.

- The document instance for an editor pane or text pane might change when loading text from a URL. Thus, your listeners might be listening for events on an unused document. For example, if you load an editor pane or text pane with HTML that was previously loaded with plain text, the document will change to an HTMLDocument instance. If your program dynamically loads text into an editor pane or text pane, make sure the code adjusts for possible changes to the document (re-register document listeners on the new document, and so on).

If you don't see your problem in this list, see <u>Solving Common Component Problems</u> (page 337).

Working with Graphics

YOU might not need to read this lesson at all. Many programs get by with no custom graphics. If they display images, they do so using <u>icons</u>[1] in standard Swing components such as <u>labels</u>[2] and <u>buttons</u>.[3] To display styled text, perhaps with embedded images and components, they use <u>text components</u>.[4] To customize the edges of components, they use <u>borders</u>.[5]

If you can't find a component that paints what you need onscreen, then read on. This lesson teaches you how to display text, simple shapes, and images, using API that works with both JDK 1.1 and Java 2. Our examples create custom components, but you might also use this API when creating a custom border or icon implementation. This lesson finishes with information about animation.

Note: If you're using only Java™ 2 (version 1.2, not JDK 1.1) you should read not only the relevant sections in this lesson, but also the *2D Graphics* trail in the book *The Java™ Tutorial Continued* and online at `http://java.sun.com/docs/books/tutorial/2d/index.html`. That trail covers the Java 2D Graphics API, which provides much more functionality than the graphics primitives described in this lesson.

---

[1] See <u>How to Use Icons</u> (page 417) for more information.
[2] See <u>How to Use Labels</u> (page 212) for more information.
[3] See <u>How to Use Buttons, Check Boxes, and Radio Buttons</u>(page 169) for more information.
[4] See <u>How to Use Text Components</u> (page 275) for more information.
[5] See <u>How to Use Borders</u> (page 408) for more information.

Overview of Custom Painting (page 537)
This chapter gives you the information you need to start implementing custom painting in components.

Using Graphics Primitives (page 545)
This chapter teaches you how to paint simple shapes and to display text effectively. The chapter includes examples of using the `Graphics`, `Font`, and `FontMetrics` classes.

Using Images (page 555)
This chapter discusses how the Java platform supports images and tells you how to load and to display images.

Performing Animation (page 561)
Many programs perform animation, whether it's the classic cartoon-style animation of Duke waving or simply moving static images across the screen. This chapter tells you how to perform animation, using a `Timer` object to implement an animation loop.

Solving Common Graphics Problems (page 573)
This chapter describes some common problems of graphics programs, along with possible solutions to these problems.

Overview of Custom Painting

IF you haven't read the chapter <u>Painting</u> (page 41), please do so right now. That chapter describes how Swing components are painted—essential information if you're going to write custom painting code.

Before you implement a component that performs custom painting, first make sure that you really need to do so. You might be able to use the text and image capabilities of labels, buttons, or text components instead. And remember, you can use borders to customize the outside edges of a component.

If you really need to perform custom painting, you need to decide which superclass to use. We recommend that you extend either `JPanel` or a more specialized `JComponent` descendant. For example, if you're creating a custom button class, you should probably implement it by extending a button class, such as `JButton` or `JToggleButton`. That way you'll inherit the state management provided by those classes. If you're creating a component that paints on top of an image, you might want to create a `JLabel` subclass. On the other hand, if you're implementing a component that generates and displays a graph on top of a blank or transparent background, you might want to use a `JPanel` subclass.

When implementing custom painting code, keep two things in mind:

- Your custom painting code belongs in a method named `paintComponent`.
- You can—and probably should—use a border to paint the outside edges of your component.

An Example of Custom Painting

The following code gives an example of custom painting. It shows an image twice, once at its natural size and once very wide.

```
class ImagePanel extends JPanel {
    ...
    public void paintComponent(Graphics g) {
        super.paintComponent(g); //paint background
        //Draw image at its natural size first.
        g.drawImage(image, 0, 0, this); //85x62 image
        //Now draw the image scaled.
        g.drawImage(image, 90, 0, 300, 62, this);
    }
}
```

Figure 162 shows the result.

Figure 162 You can see this applet online at `http://java.sun.com/docs/books/tutorial/ uiswing/painting/ImageDisplay.html`

The code example is from <u>ImageDisplayer.java</u> (page 866), which is further discussed in <u>Displaying Images</u> (page 559). The example demonstrates a few rules that apply to all components that perform custom painting:

- The painting code does something that no standard Swing component does. If we just wanted to display the figure once, at its natural size, we would have used a `JLabel` object instead of the custom component.

- The custom component is a `JPanel` subclass. This is a common superclass for custom components.

- All of the custom painting code is in a method called `paintComponent`.

- Before performing any custom painting, the component paints its background by invoking `super.paintComponent`. If we remove that call, either our custom painting code must paint the component's background, or we must invoke `setOpaque(false)` on the component. Doing the latter would inform the Swing painting system that the components behind the nonopaque component might be visible and should be painted.

One thing this component does *not* do is take borders into account. Not only does it not use a border, but it also doesn't adjust its painting coordinates to take a border into account. A production-quality component would adjust to borders, as described next.

The Coordinate System

Each component has its own integer coordinate system, ranging from (0,0) to (*width* −1, *height* −1), with each unit representing the size of one pixel. As the following figure shows, the upper-left corner of a component's painting area is (0,0). The *X* coordinate increases to the right, and the *Y* coordinate increases downward.

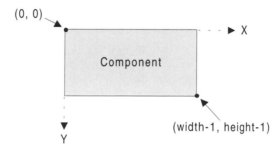

Figure 163 A component's coordinate system.

When painting a component, you must take into account not only the component's size but also the size of the component's border, if any. For example, a border that paints a one-pixel line around a component changes the top leftmost corner from (0,0) to (1,1) and reduces the width and the height of the painting area by two pixels each (one pixel per side).[1] The following figure demonstrates this.

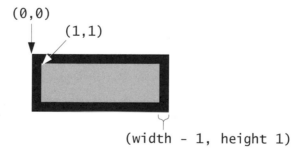

Figure 164 The border draws inside the component's edges.

---

[1] Actually, the border increases the component's size by the amount needed to draw itself. From the component's point of view, however, its display area is less than its full width and height.

You get a component's width and height by using its `getWidth` and `getHeight` methods. To determine the border size, use the `getInsets` method. A component might use the following code to determine the width and height available for custom painting:

```
public void paintComponent(Graphics g) {
    ...
    Insets insets = getInsets();
    int currentWidth = getWidth() - insets.left - insets.right;
    int currentHeight = getHeight() - insets.top - insets.bottom;
    ...
    .../* First painting occurs at (x,y), where x is at least
       insets.left, and y is at least insets.height. */...
}
```

To familiarize yourself with the coordinate system, you can play with the following applet. Wherever you click on or inside the framed area, a dot is painted, and the label below lists the click's coordinates. The dot is obscured if you click on the border, because the component's border is painted after the component performs its custom painting. If we didn't want this effect, an easy solution would be to move the border from the component into a new `JPanel` object that contains the component.

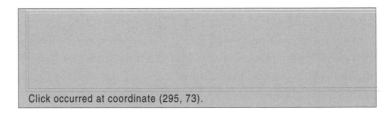

Click occurred at coordinate (295, 73).

Figure 165 You can see this applet online at `http://java.sun.com/docs/books/tutorial/uiswing/painting/CoordinatesDemo.html`

The program is implemented in <u>CoordinatesDemo.java</u> (page 861). Although we don't discuss this example's code anywhere, it's very similar to the code in the `RectangleDemo` program, which is discussed a little later, in <u>Painting Shapes</u> (page 545).

Arguments to the repaint Method

Remember that calling a component's `repaint` method requests that the component be scheduled to paint itself. When the painting system is unable to keep up with the pace of repaint requests, it might combine multiple requests into a single paint request to the component.

The repaint method has two useful forms.

void repaint()
Requests that the entire component be repainted.

void repaint(int, int, int, int)
Requests that only the specified part of the component be repainted. The arguments specify first the *X* and *Y* coordinates at the upper left of the area to be repainted and then the area's width and height.

Although using the four-argument form of repaint method often isn't practical, it can help painting performance significantly. The program in the following picture uses the four-argument repaint method when requesting frequent repaints to display the user's current selection area. Doing so avoids repainting the parts of the component that haven't changed since the previous painting operation.

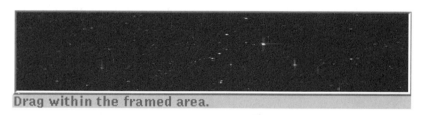

Drag within the framed area.

Figure 166 The SelectionDemo applet.

The program is implemented in SelectionDemo.java (page 879). Here is the code that calculates the area to be repainted and then paints it:

```
class SelectionArea extends JLabel {
    ...
    public SelectionArea(ImageIcon image, ...) {
        super(image); //Makes this component display an image.
        ...
    }
    ...//In a mouse-dragged event handler:
        Rectangle totalRepaint =
                    rectToDraw.union(previousRectDrawn);
        repaint(totalRepaint.x, totalRepaint.y,
                totalRepaint.width, totalRepaint.height);
    ...
    public void paintComponent(Graphics g) {
        super.paintComponent(g); //paints background and image
```

```
        ...
        //Paint a rectangle on top of the image.
        g.setColor(Color.white);
        g.drawRect(rectToDraw.x, rectToDraw.y,
                rectToDraw.width - 1, rectToDraw.height - 1);
        ...
    }
    ...
}
```

As you can see, the custom component extends JLabel so that it inherits the ability to display an image. The user can select a rectangular area by dragging the mouse. The component continuously displays a rectangle indicating the size of the current selection. To improve rendering speed, the component's mouse-dragged event handler specifies a painting area to the repaint method.

By limiting the area to be repainted, the event handlers avoid unnecessarily repainting the image outside of that area. For this small image there's no noticeable performance benefit to this strategy. However, for a large image there might be a real benefit. And if instead of painting an image from a file, you had to compute what to paint under the rectangle—for example, computing shapes in a draw program—using knowledge of the paint area to limit the computation you perform might improve performance significantly.

The area specified to repaint must include not only the area to be painted but also any area that needs to be erased. Otherwise old painting remains visible until it happens to be erased by other painting. The preceding code calculates the total area to be repainted by taking the union of the rectangle to be painted with the rectangle that was previously painted.

The painting area specified to repaint is reflected in the Graphics object passed into the paintComponent method. You can use the getClipBounds method to determine which rectangular area to paint. Here is an example of using the clip bounds:

```
public void paintComponent(Graphics g) {
    Rectangle clipRect = g.getClipBounds();
    if (clipRect != null) {
        //If it's more efficient, draw only the area
        //specified by clipRect.
        //Top-leftmost point = (clipRect.x, clipRect.y)
        //Width, height = clipRect.width, clipRect.height
    } else {
        //Paint the entire component.
    }
}
```

The Graphics Object

The Graphics[1] object passed into the paintComponent method provides both a context for painting and methods for performing the painting. The methods, which we discuss in detail a little later, have such names as drawImage, drawString, drawRect, and fillRect.

The graphics context consists of state, such as the current painting color, the current font, and (as you've already seen) the current painting area. The color and the font are initialized to the foreground color and font of the component just before the invocation of paintComponent. You can get them by using the getColor and the getFont methods and can set them by using the setColor and the setFont methods.

You can safely ignore the current painting area, if you like. It has no effect on the component's coordinate system, and any painting outside the area is ignored. However, if your painting code involves complex operations that can be simplified if the painting area is reduced, you should use your knowledge of the painting area to help you improve painting performance. As shown by the previous code example, you get the painting area's rectangular bounds from the Graphics object by invoking the getClipBounds method.

You can reduce the painting area in two ways. The first is to specify repaint with arguments whenever possible. The other is to implement paintComponent so that it invokes the Graphics object's setClip method. If you use setClip, be sure to restore the original painting area before returning. Otherwise the component could be painted improperly. Here's an example of reducing and then restoring the painting area:

```
Rectangle oldClipBounds = g.getClipBounds();
Rectangle clipBounds = new Rectangle(...);
g.setClip(clipBounds);
...//Perform custom painting...
g.setClip(oldClipBounds);
```

When writing your painting code, keep in mind that you can't depend on any graphics context except what's provided by the Graphics object. For example, you can't rely on the painting area you specify with repaint being exactly the same as the painting area used in the subsequent call to paintComponent. For one thing, multiple repaint requests can be coalesced into a single paintComponent call, with the painting area adjusted accordingly. For another, the painting system occasionally calls paintComponent on its own, without any repaint request from your program. As an example, the painting system invokes a component's paintComponent method when it first shows the component's GUI. Also, when the GUI is covered by another window and then becomes uncovered, the painting system invokes the paintComponent method, with the painting area equal to the newly uncovered area.

---

[1] API documentation for Graphics is available on this book's CD-ROM and online at http://java.sun.com/products/jdk/1.2/docs/api/java/awt/Graphics.html

The Swing Painting Methods

The `paintComponent` method is one of three methods that `JComponent` objects use to paint themselves. The three methods are invoked in this order:

1. `paintComponent`—the main method for painting. By default it first paints the background if the component is opaque. Then it performs any custom painting.

2. `paintBorder`—tells the component's border, if any, to paint. *Do not invoke or override this method.*

3. `paintChildren`—tells any components contained by this component to paint themselves. *Do not invoke or override this method.*

Note: Don't override or invoke the method that calls the `paintXxx` methods: the `paint` method. Although overriding `paint` was legitimate in pre-Swing components, it's generally not a good thing to do in components that descend from `JComponent`. Unless you're careful, overriding `paint` is likely to confuse the painting system, which relies on the `JComponent` implementation of the `paint` method for correct painting, performance enhancements, and features such as double buffering.

The standard Swing components delegate their look-and-feel-specific painting to an object called a *UI delegate*. When such a component's `paintComponent` method is called, the method asks the UI delegate to paint the component. Generally the UI delegate first checks whether the component is opaque and, if so, paints the entire background of the component. Then the UI delegate performs any look-and-feel-specific painting.

The reason that we recommend extending `JPanel` instead of `JComponent` is that the `JComponent` class doesn't currently set up a UI delegate—only its subclasses do. This means that if you extend `JComponent`, your component's background won't be painted unless you paint it yourself. When you extend `JPanel` and invoke `super.paintComponent` at the top of your `paintComponent` method, however, then the panel's UI delegate paints the component's background if the component is opaque.

If you need more information about painting, see the article "Painting inAWT and Swing" in *The Swing Connection*. The article discusses in depth the intricacies of painting. *The Swing Connection* is available on the CD-ROM that accompanies this book and online at

```
http://java.sun.com/products/jfc/tsc/index.html
```

Using Graphics Primitives

THIS chapter provides the details you'll need to generate primitive graphics and text.

- Painting Shapes (page 545)
  This section tells you how to paint shapes, such as lines, rectangles, ovals, arcs, and polygons.
- Working with Text (page 550)
  This section tells you how to use paint text by using the Graphics drawString method. The section also tells you how to use Font and FontMetrics objects to get information about a font's size characteristics.

Painting Shapes

The Graphics[1] class defines methods for painting the following kinds of shapes:

- Lines (drawLine)
- Rectangles (drawRect and fillRect)
- Raised or lowered rectangles (draw3DRect and fill3DRect)
- Round-edged rectangles (drawRoundRect and fillRoundRect)
- Ovals (drawOval and fillOval)
- Arcs (drawArc and fillArc)
- Polygons (drawPolygon, drawPolyline, and fillPolygon)

---

[1] API documentation for Graphics is available on this book's CD-ROM and online at http://java.sun.com/products/jdk/1.2/docs/api/java/awt/Graphics.html

Here is an example of painting the outline of a rectangle:

```
g.drawRect(x, y, rectWidth - 1, rectHeight - 1);
```

Here is an example of painting a filled rectangle of the same size.

```
g.fillRect(x, y, rectWidth, rectHeight);
```

Note that for the `drawRect` method, you must specify one pixel less than the desired width and height. The reason is that the painting system draws lines just below the specified rectangle, instead of within the specified rectangle. The same rule of specifying one less than the desired width applies to other `drawXxx` methods, such as `draw3DRect`. For the `fillXxx` methods, on the other hand, you specify exactly the desired width and height in pixels.

Java 2 Note: If you are using the Java 2 platform, you can use the new Java 2D API, which allows you to create virtually any kind of geometric shape and to specify line styles, line sizes, and fancy fill patterns. To learn how to take advantage of this new functionality, see the *2D Graphics* trail. The 2D trail is available in the book, *The Java™ Tutorial Continued* and online at `http://java.sun.com/docs/books/tutorial/2d/index.html`. In particular, see the "Stroking and Filling Graphics Primitives" and "Shapes" lessons, which present a Java 2D implementation of the program presented in "Example 2: A Shape Sampler."

Example 1: Simple Rectangle Painting

Here's a picture of a program that's almost the same as the `CoordinatesDemo` program shown in <u>The Coordinate System</u> (page 539). Like `CoordinatesDemo`, this program paints a rectangle wherever the user clicks. However, this program's rectangle is larger and has a darker gray fill. Here is a picture of its GUI.

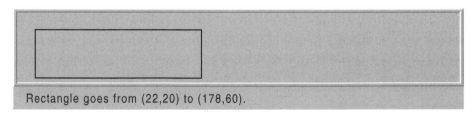

Figure 167 The `RectangleDemo` applet.

The program features two components. The larger one is a custom component implemented by a class named `RectangleArea`. This component paints the beveled border and everything inside it, including the gray rectangle. The other component is a label that appears at the bottom of the GUI, under the custom component. The label describes the program's current state.

You can find the program's code in RectangleDemo.java (page 877). Here is the painting-related code for the custom component:

```
class RectangleArea extends JPanel {
    ...
    int rectWidth = 50;
    int rectHeight = 50;
    ...
    public RectangleArea(...) {
        ...
        Border raisedBevel = BorderFactory.createRaisedBevelBoder();
        Border loweredBevel = BorderFactory.createLoweredBevel Border();
        Border compound = BorderFactory.createCompoundBorder
                            (raisedBevel, loweredBevel);
        setBorder(compound);
        ...
    }
    ...
    public void paintComponent(Graphics g) {
        super.paintComponent(g);   //paint background
        //Paint a filled rectangle at user's chosen point.
        if (point != null) {
            g.drawRect(point.x, point.y, rectWidth - 1, rectHeight - 1);
            g.setColor(Color.yellow);
            g.fillRect(point.x + 1, point.y + 1,
                    rectWidth - 2, rectHeight - 2);
            controller.updateLabel(point);
        }
    }
}
```

The component's implementation of paintComponent uses the fillRect method to paint a rectangle outline 50 pixels by 50 pixels, filled with a gray rectangle 48 pixels by 48 pixels. Note the differences in the arguments specified to drawRect and fillRect.

Note: It's perfectly legal to specify *x*, *y*, height, or width values that are negative or cause a result larger than the painting area. Values outside the painting area don't matter too much, because they're clipped to the painting area. You just won't see part of the shape. Negative height or width results in the shape not being painted at all.

For a little more information about this example, see <u>The Coordinate System</u> (page 539), which features the CoordinatesDemo example on which RectangleDemo is based.

Example 2: A Shape Sampler

The ShapesDemo program demonstrates all of the shapes you can draw and fill, using API supported with both JDK 1.1 and Java 2. Figure 168 shows its GUI.

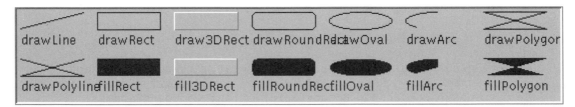

Figure 168 The ShapesDemo applet.

Note: Unless the default font is very small, some of the strings displayed by ShapesDemo overlap with other strings. A fix for this problem is demonstrated in <u>Getting Information About a Font: FontMetrics</u> (page 551).

You can find the code for the entire program in <u>ShapesDemo.java</u> (page 882). The following snippet is just the code that paints the geometric shapes, where the boldface lines are the invocations of painting methods. The rectHeight and rectWidth variables specify the size, in pixels, of the rectangle that contains the shape to be drawn. The x and y variables are changed for every shape, so that the shapes aren't painted on top of each other. The bg and fg variables are <u>Color</u>[1] objects that specify the component's background and foreground colors, respectively.

```
Color fg3D = Color.lightGray;
...
// drawLine(x1, y1, x2, y2)
g.drawLine(x, y+rectHeight-1, x + rectWidth, y);
...
// drawRect(x, y, w, h)
g.drawRect(x, y, rectWidth, rectHeight);
...
// draw3DRect(x, y, w, h, raised)
```

---

[1] API documentation for Color is available on this book's CD-ROM and online at http://java.sun.com/products/jdk/1.2/docs/api/java/awt/Color.html

```
g.setColor(fg3D);
g.draw3DRect(x, y, rectWidth, rectHeight, true);
g.setColor(fg);
...
// drawRoundRect(x, y, w, h, arcw, arch)
g.drawRoundRect(x, y, rectWidth, rectHeight, 10, 10);
...
// drawOval(x, y, w, h)
g.drawOval(x, y, rectWidth, rectHeight);
...
// drawArc(x, y, w, h, startAngle, arcAngle)
g.drawArc(x, y, rectWidth, rectHeight, 90, 135);
...
// drawPolygon(xPoints, yPoints, numPoints)
int x1Points[] = {x, x+rectWidth, x, x+rectWidth};
int y1Points[] = {y, y+rectHeight, y+rectHeight, y};
g.drawPolygon(x1Points, y1Points, x1Points.length);
...
// drawPolyline(xPoints, yPoints, numPoints)
// Note: drawPolygon would close the polygon.
int x2Points[] = {x, x+rectWidth, x, x+rectWidth};
int y2Points[] = {y, y+rectHeight, y+rectHeight, y};
g.drawPolyline(x2Points, y2Points, x2Points.length);
...
// fillRect(x, y, w, h)
g.fillRect(x, y, rectWidth, rectHeight);
...
// fill3DRect(x, y, w, h, raised)
g.setColor(fg3D);
g.fill3DRect(x, y, rectWidth, rectHeight, true);
g.setColor(fg);
...
// fillRoundRect(x, y, w, h, arcw, arch)
g.fillRoundRect(x, y, rectWidth, rectHeight, 10, 10);
...
// fillOval(x, y, w, h)
g.fillOval(x, y, rectWidth, rectHeight);
...
// fillArc(x, y, w, h, startAngle, arcAngle)
g.fillArc(x, y, rectWidth, rectHeight, 90, 135);
...
// fillPolygon(xPoints, yPoints, numPoints)
int x3Points[] = {x, x+rectWidth, x, x+rectWidth};
int y3Points[] = {y, y+rectHeight, y+rectHeight, y};
g.fillPolygon(x3Points, y3Points, x3Points.length);
...
```

Working with Text

Support for working with primitive text is spread among the AWT <u>Graphics</u>,[1] <u>Font</u>,[2] and <u>FontMetrics</u>[3] classes. Of course, you can save yourself a lot of trouble by using a text-drawing component instead—a <u>label</u> (page 212) or a <u>text component</u> (page 275), for instance.

Note: If you are using the Java 2 platform, you can use the full-featured text support in the Java 2D API. See the "Text" section in the *2D Graphics* trail for more information. The 2D trail is available in the book, *The Java*[TM] *Tutorial Continued* and online at `http://java.sun.com/docs/books/tutorial/2d/index.html`. However, we still recommend that you avoid drawing your own text and use a standard Swing component whenever possible.

Painting Text

The Graphics class provides three methods for painting text: drawBytes, drawChars, and drawString. Here is an example of code that paints a string to the screen:

```
g.drawString("Hello World!", x, y);
```

For the text painting methods, x and y are integers that specify the position of the *lower-left* corner of the text. To be precise, the y coordinate specifies the *baseline* of the text—the line that most letters rest on—which doesn't include room for the tails (*descenders*) on letters such as "y". Be sure to make y large enough to allow vertical space for the text but small enough to allow room for descenders.

Here's a figure that shows the baseline, as well as the ascender and descender lines. You'll learn more about ascenders and descenders a bit later.

Figure 169 The baseline, ascender, and descender lines.

---

[1] API documentation for Graphics is available on this book's CD-ROM and online at http://java.sun.com/products/jdk/1.2/docs/api/java/awt/Graphics.html
[2] http://java.sun.com/products/jdk/1.2/docs/api/java/awt/Font.html
[3] http://java.sun.com/products/jdk/1.2/docs/api/java/awt/FontMetrics.html

Here is a picture of a simple applet that illustrates what can happen when you're not careful about where you position your text.

drawString() at (2,30)

Figure 170 You can find the TextXY applet online at `http://java.sun.com/docs/books/`
`tutorial/uiswing/painting/TextXY.html`

The top string is probably cut off, since its y argument is 5, which leaves only 5 pixels above the baseline for the string—not enough for most fonts. The middle string probably shows up just fine, unless you have a huge default font. Most of the letters in the bottom string display fine, except for letters with descenders. All descenders in the bottom string are cut off, since the code that displays this string doesn't allow room for them. You can find the applet's source code in TextXY.java (page 884).

Note: The text-painting methods' interpretation of x and y is different from that of the shape-painting methods. When painting a shape (such as a rectangle), x and y specify the *upper*-left corner of the shape's bounding rectangle, not the *lower*-left corner.

Getting Information About a Font: FontMetrics

The shape-painting example from Example 2: A Shape Sampler (page 548) could be improved by choosing a font that's smaller than the usual default font. The following example does this and also enlarges the shapes to take up the space freed by the font's smaller height. Here is a picture of the improved applet.

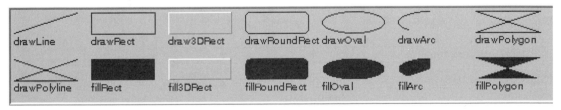

Figure 171 You can find the FontDemo applet online at `http://java.sun.com/docs/books/`
`tutorial/uiswing/painting/FontDemo.html`

You can find its code in <u>FontDemo.java</u> (page 863). The example chooses the appropriate font by using a FontMetrics object to get details of the font's size. For example, the following loop ensures that the longest string displayed by the applet ("drawRoundRect") fits within the space each shape is allotted:

```
boolean fontFits = false;
Font currentFont = biggestFont;
FontMetrics currentMetrics = getFontMetrics(currentFont);
int size = currentFont.getSize();
String name = currentFont.getName();
int style = currentFont.getStyle();
while (!fontFits) {
    if ((currentMetrics.getHeight() <= maxCharHeight)
       && (currentMetrics.stringWidth(longString)
          <= xSpace)) {
        fontFits = true;
    } else {
        if (size <= minFontSize) {
        fontFits = true;
    } else {
        currentFont = new Font(name, style, --size);
        currentMetrics = getFontMetrics(currentFont);
    }
}
```

The code in the preceding example uses the Graphics getFont, setFont, and getFont-Metrics methods to get and set the current font and to get the FontMetrics object that corresponds to the font. From the FontMetrics getHeight and stringWidth(String) methods, the code gets vertical and horizontal size information about the font.

The following figure shows some of the information that a FontMetrics object can provide about a font's size.

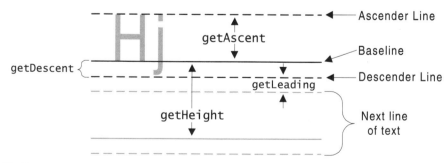

Figure 172 Some of the information FontMetrics can provide about a font's size.

Here's a summary of the `FontMetrics` methods that return information about a font's vertical size.

int getAscent(), int getMaxAscent()

The `getAscent` method returns the number of pixels between the ascender line and the baseline. Generally the ascender line represents the typical height of capital letters. Specifically the ascent and descent values are chosen by the font's designer to represent the correct text "color," or density of ink, so that the text appears as the designer planned it. The ascent typically provides enough room for almost all of the characters in the font, except, perhaps, for accents on capital letters. The `getMaxAscent` method accounts for these exceptionally tall characters.

int getDescent(), int getMaxDescent()

The `getDescent` method returns the number of pixels between the baseline and the descender line. In most fonts all characters fall within the descender line at their lowest point. Just in case, though, you can use the `getMaxDescent` method to get a distance guaranteed to encompass all characters.

int getHeight()

Returns the number of pixels normally found between the baseline of one line of text and the baseline of the next line of text. Note that this includes an allowance for leading.

int getLeading()

Returns the suggested distance, in pixels, between one line of text and the next. Specifically the leading is the distance between the descender line of one line of text and the ascender line of the next line of text. By the way, *leading* is pronounced *LEDD-ing*.

Note that the font size (returned by the `Font` class `getSize` method) is an abstract measurement that corresponds, theoretically, to the ascent plus the descent. Practically, however, the font designer decides exactly how tall a "12-point" font (for example) is. For example, 12-point Times is often slightly shorter than 12-point Helvetica. Typically font size is measured in *points*, which are approximately 1/72 of an inch.

The following list shows the methods that `FontMetrics` provides to return information about the horizontal size of a font's characters. These methods take into account the spacing around each character. More precisely, each method returns *not* the number of pixels taken up by a particular character (or characters) but rather the number of pixels by which the *current point* will be advanced when that character (or characters) is shown. We call this the *advance width* to distinguish it from the character or text width.

int getMaxAdvance()

The advance width, in pixels, of the widest character in the font.

`int bytesWidth(byte[], int, int)`

The advance width of the text represented by the specified array of bytes. The first integer argument specifies the starting offset of the data within the byte array. The second integer argument specifies the maximum number of bytes to check.

`int charWidth(int), int charWidth(char)`

The advance width of the specified character.

`int charsWidth(char[], int, int)`

The advance width of the string represented by the specified character array.

`int stringWidth(String)`

The advance width of the specified string.

`int[] getWidths()`

The advance width of each of the first 256 characters in the font.

Using Images

The following is an image.

Figure 173 A sample image of Duke.

The next few pages provide the details you'll need to work with images. You'll learn how to load, display, and manipulate them.

Note: Although the API this chapter describes is valid for both JDK 1.1 and the Java 2 platform, we recommend that you use Swing's built-in icon support instead. It's described in How to Use Icons (page 417). If Swing icons aren't sufficient and you're writing a program for Java 2, consider using the Java 2D API, which is described in the *2D Graphics* trail. The 2D trail is available in the book *The Java*[TM] *Tutorial Continued* and online at `http://java.sun.com/docs/books/tutorial/2d/index.html`.

Support for using images is spread across several packages. Every image is represented by a `java.awt.Image` object. In addition to the `Image` class, the `java.awt` package provides other basic image support, such as the `Graphics drawImage` methods, the `Toolkit getImage` methods, and the `MediaTracker` class. In `java.applet` the `Applet getImage` methods make it easy for applets to load images by using URLs. Finally, the `java.awt.image` package provides interfaces and classes that let you create, manipulate, and observe images.

The AWT makes it easy to load images in either of two formats: GIF and JPEG. The `Applet` and `Toolkit` classes provide `getImage` methods that work for either format. You use them like this:

```
myImage = getImage(URL); //in a method in an Applet subclass only
```
or
```
myImage = Toolkit.getDefaultToolkit().getImage(filenameOrURL);
```

The `getImage` methods return immediately, so that you don't have to wait for an image to be loaded before going on to perform other operations in your program. Although this improves performance, some programs require more control or information about image loading. You can track image-loading status either by using the `MediaTracker` class or by implementing the `imageUpdate` method, which is defined by the `ImageObserver` interface.

This section will also tell you how to create images on the fly by using the `MemoryImage-Source` class.

It's easy to display an image by using the `Graphics` object that's passed into your `paint-Component` method. You simply invoke a `drawImage` method on the `Graphics` object. For example:

```
g.drawImage(myImage, 0, 0, this);
```

This section explains the four forms of `drawImage`, two of which scale the image. Like `get-Image`, `drawImage` is asynchronous, returning immediately even if the image hasn't been fully loaded or painted yet.

Loading Images

This section describes how to get the `Image` object corresponding to an image. As long as the image data is in GIF or JPEG format and you know its filename or URL, it's easy to get an `Image` object for it: Just use one of the `Applet` or `Toolkit` `getImage` methods. The `getIm-age` methods return immediately, without checking whether the image data exists. The loading of image data normally doesn't start until the first time the program tries to paint the image.

For many programs this invisible background loading works well. Others, though, need to keep track of the progress of the image loading. This section explains how to do so by using the `MediaTracker` class and the `ImageObserver` interface.

Note: The ImageIcon class automatically uses a MediaTracker to load images. See <u>How to Use Icons</u> (page 417) for more information on ImageIcon.

Finally, this section tells you how to create images on the fly, using a class such as Memory-ImageSource.

Using the getImage Methods

This section discusses first the Toolkit getImage methods and then the Applet getImage methods.

The Toolkit class declares two getImage methods:

- Image getImage(URL url)
- Image getImage(String filename)

Here are examples of using the Toolkit getImage methods. Although every Java application and applet can use these methods, applets are subject to the usual security restrictions. In particular, untrusted applets can't successfully specify a filename to getImage, because untrusted applets can't load data from the local file system. You can find information about restrictions on untrusted applets in <u>Security Restrictions</u>.[1]

```
Toolkit toolkit = Toolkit.getDefaultToolkit();
Image image1 = toolkit.getImage("imageFile.gif");
Image image2 = toolkit.getImage(new URL(
                       "http://java.sun.com/graphics/people.gif"));
```

The Applet class supplies two getImage methods:

- Image getImage(URL url)
- Image getImage(URL url, String name)

Only applets can use the Applet getImage methods. Moreover, the Applet getImage methods don't work until the applet has a full context (AppletContext). Therefore, these methods *do not work* if called in a constructor or in a statement that declares an instance variable. You should instead call getImage from a method such as init.

This following code examples show you how to use the Applet getImage methods. See <u>Creating</u> a GUI[2] for an explanation of the getCodeBase and the getDocumentBase methods.

---

[1] The "Security Restrictions" lesson is included in the *Security* trail in the book, *The Java*[TM] *Tutorial Continued* and online at http://java.sun.com/docs/books/tutorial/security1.2/index.html

[2] The "Creating a GUI" section is included in the *Writing Applets* trail in the book, *The Java*[TM] *Tutorial: Second Edition* and online at http://java.sun.com/docs/books/tutorial/applet/practical/gui.html

```
//In a method in an Applet subclass:
Image image1 = getImage(getCodeBase(), "imageFile.gif");
Image image2 = getImage(getDocumentBase(), "anImageFile.jpeg");
Image image3 = getImage(new URL(
                           "http://java.sun.com/graphics/people.gif"));
```

Requesting and Tracking Image Loading: MediaTracker and ImageObserver

You can track image loading in two ways: the `MediaTracker`[1] class and the `ImageObserver`[2] interface. The `MediaTracker` class is sufficient for many programs. You just create a `MediaTracker` instance, tell it to track one or more images, and then ask the `MediaTracker` the status of those images, as needed. An example is explained in <u>Improving the Appearance and Performance of Image Animation</u> (page 569).

The animation example shows two particularly useful `MediaTracker` features: requesting that the data for a group of images be loaded and waiting for a group of images to be loaded. To request that the image data for a group of images be loaded, you can use the forms of `checkID` and `checkAll` that take a boolean argument. Setting the boolean argument to `true` starts loading the data for any images that aren't yet being loaded. Or you can request that the image data be loaded and wait for it, using the `waitForID` and `waitForAll` methods.

The `ImageObserver` interface lets you keep even closer track of image loading than `MediaTracker` allows. The `Component` class uses it so that components are repainted as the images they display are loaded. To use the `ImageObserver` interface, you implement the `ImageObserver` `imageUpdate` method and make sure that the implementing object is registered as the image observer. Usually this registration happens when you specify an `ImageObserver` to the `drawImage` method, as described in a later section. The `imageUpdate` method is called whenever information about an image becomes available.

If you browse the `MediaTracker` API documentation, you might notice that the `Component` class defines two useful-looking methods: `checkImage` and `prepareImage`. The `MediaTracker` class has made these methods largely unnecessary.

Creating Images with MemoryImageSource

With the help of an image producer, such as the `MemoryImageSource`[3] class, you can construct images from scratch. The following code example calculates a 100 x 100 image repre-

---

[1] API documentation for `MediaTracker` is available on this book's CD-ROM and online at
      http://java.sun.com/products/jdk/1.2/docs/api/java/awt/MediaTracker.html

[2] http://java.sun.com/products/jdk/1.2/docs/api/java/awt/image.ImageObserver.html

[3] http://java.sun.com/products/jdk/1.2/docs/api/java/awt/image.MemoryImageSource.html

senting a fade from black to blue along the *X* axis and a fade from black to red along the *Y* axis:

```
int w = 100;
int h = 100;
int[] pix = new int[w * h];
int index = 0;
for (int y = 0; y < h; y++) {
    int red = (y * 255) / (h - 1);
    for (int x = 0; x < w; x++) {
        int blue = (x * 255) / (w - 1);
        pix[index++] = (255 << 24) | (red << 16) | blue;
    }
}
Image img = createImage(new MemoryImageSource(w, h, pix, 0, w));
```

Displaying Images

Here is a code example that displays an image at its normal size in the upper-left corner of the component area (0, 0):

```
g.drawImage(image, 0, 0, this);
```

Here is a code example that displays an image scaled to be 300 pixels wide and 62 pixels tall, starting at the coordinates (90, 0):

```
g.drawImage(myImage, 90, 0, 300, 62, this);
```

The following snapshot shows an applet that loads a single image and displays it twice, using both of the preceding code snippets. You can find the program's full code in ImageDis-player.java (page 866).

Figure 174 You can find the ImageDisplayer applet online at http://java.sun.com/docs/
books/tutorial/uiswing/painting/ImageDisplayer.html

The Graphics class declares the following drawImage methods. They all return a boolean value, although this value is rarely used. The return value is true if the image has been completely loaded and thus completely painted; otherwise it's false.

- boolean drawImage(Image img, int x, int y, ImageObserver observer)
- boolean drawImage(Image img, int x, int y, int width, int height,
                    ImageObserver observer)
- boolean drawImage(Image img, int x, int y, Color bgcolor,
                    ImageObserver observer)
- boolean drawImage(Image img, int x, int y, int width, int height,
                    Color bgcolor, ImageObserver observer)

The drawImage methods have the following arguments.

Image img

The image to paint.

int x, int y

The coordinates of the upper-left corner of the image.

int width, int height

The width and height, in pixels, of the image.

Color bgcolor

The color to paint underneath the image. This can be useful if the image contains transparent pixels and you know that the image will be displayed against a solid background of the indicated color.

ImageObserver observer

An object that implements the ImageObserver interface. This registers the object as the image observer so that it's notified whenever new information about the image becomes available. Most components can simply specify this.

The reason why components can specify this as the image observer is that the Component class implements the ImageObserver interface. Its implementation invokes the repaint method as the image data is loaded, which is usually what you want to happen.

The drawImage method returns after displaying the image data that has been loaded, so far. If you want to make sure that drawImage paints only complete images, you must track image loading. See Requesting and Tracking Image Loading: MediaTracker and ImageObserver (page 558) for information on tracking image loading.

Performing Animation

$\mathbf{A}$LL forms of animation create some kind of perceived motion by showing successive frames at a relatively high speed. Computer animation usually shows 10–20 frames per second. By comparison, traditional hand-drawn animation uses anywhere from 8 frames per second (for poor-quality animation) to 12 frames per second (for standard animation) to 24 frames per second (for short bursts of smooth, realistic motion). This chapter tells you everything you need to know to write a program that performs animation.

Note: Check out existing animation tools and applets, such as `AnimatorApplication.java` (page 886), to see if you can use them instead of writing your own program.

Creating an Animation Loop with Timer (page 562)
The most important step in creating a program that animates is to set up the framework correctly. Except for animation performed only in direct response to external events, such as the user's dragging an onscreen object, a program that performs animation needs an animation loop.

The animation loop is responsible for keeping track of the current frame and for requesting periodic screen updates. For applets and many applications, you need a separate thread to run the animation loop. This section contains a sample applet and a sample application that both use a `Timer` object to implement the animation loop. You can use these examples as templates for your own animation.

Moving an Image Across the Screen (page 565)
The simplest form of image animation involves moving an unchanging image across the screen. In the traditional animation world, this is known as *cutout animation*, since it can be accomplished by cutting a shape out of paper and moving the shape in front of the camera.

561

<u>Displaying a Sequence of Images</u> (page 568)
This section tells you how to perform classic cartoon-style animation, given a sequence of images.

<u>Improving the Appearance and Performance of Image Animation</u> (page 569)
This section tells you how to use `MediaTracker` so that you can delay displaying an animation until all of its images are loaded. You'll also get some hints on improving applet animation performance by combining image files and by using a compression scheme.

Creating an Animation Loop with Timer

Every program that performs animation by painting at regular intervals needs an animation loop. Generally this loop should be in its own thread. It should *never* be in the `paintComponent` method, since that would take over the event-dispatching thread, which is in charge of painting and event handling.

The `Timer`[1] class makes implementing an animation loop easy. This section provides two `Timer`-based templates for performing animation: one for applets and the other for applications. The applet version is pictured in Figure 175. When running the applet, you can click on it to stop the animation. Click again to restart it.

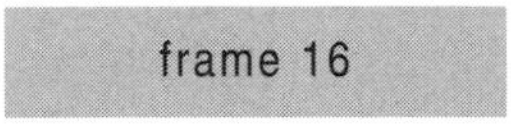

Figure 175 You can see the `AnimatorAppletTimer` online at `http://java.sun.com/docs/`
`books/tutorial/uiswing/painting/AnimatorAppletTimer.html`

The animation the template performs is a bit boring: It simply displays the current frame number, using a default rate of 10 frames per second. The next few sections build on this example, showing you how to animate images.

You can find the code for the applet version of the animation template in <u>AnimatorApplet-</u><u>Timer.java</u> (page 858). The code for the application version is in <u>AnimatorApplication-</u><u>Timer.java</u> (page 860). The rest of this section explains the templates' common code. Here is a summary of what both templates do:

```
public class AnimatorClass ... implements ActionListener {
    int frameNumber = -1;
    Timer timer;
    boolean frozen = false;
    JLabel label;
```

---

[1]   See <u>How to Use Timers</u> (page 436) for more information.

```
//In initialization code:
    //From user-specified frames-per-second value, determine
    //how long to delay between frames.
    ...
    //Set up a timer that calls this object's action handler.
    timer = new Timer(delay, this);
    ...
    //Set up the components in the GUI.

public synchronized void startAnimation() {
    ...
    timer.start();
    ...
}

public synchronized void stopAnimation() {
    ...
    timer.stop();
    ...
}

public void actionPerformed(ActionEvent e) {
    //Advance the animation frame.
    frameNumber++;
    //Request that the frame be painted.
    label.setText("Frame " + frameNumber);
}
...
//When the application's GUI appears:
    startAnimation();
    ...
}
```

Initializing Instance Variables

The animation templates use four instance variables. The first (frameNumber) represents the current frame. It's initialized to –1, even though the first frame number is 0. The reason is that the frame number is incremented at the start of the animation loop, before the first frame is painted.

The second instance variable (timer) is the Timer object that implements the animation loop. It's initialized to fire an action event every delay milliseconds.

The delay variable is a local variable that's initialized by using a *frames per second* number provided by the user. The following code converts frames per second into the number of milliseconds between frames:

```
delay = (fps > 0) ? (1000 / fps) : 100;
```

The ? : notation in the previous code snippet is shorthand for if else. If the user provides a number of frames per second greater than 0, the delay is 1,000 milliseconds divided by the number of frames per second. Otherwise, the delay between frames is 100 milliseconds (ten frames per second).

The third instance variable (frozen) is a boolean value that's initialized to false. The templates set it to true when the user requests that the animation stop. You'll see more about this later in this section.

The fourth instance variable (label) is a reference to the component that performs the painting.

The Animation Loop

The Timer object implements the animation loop by continuously firing action events every delay milliseconds. In response to each action event, the actionPerformed method advances the frame number and requests that the current frame of animation be painted. For more information about timers, see How to Use Timers (page 436).

Behaving Politely

Two more features of the animation templates belong in the category of polite behavior. One feature is allowing the user to explicitly stop (and restart) the animation while the applet or application is still visible. Animation can be quite distracting, and it's a good idea to give the user the power to stop the animation in order to concentrate on something else. This feature is implemented by overriding the mousePressed method so that it stops or starts the timer, depending on the program's current state. Here's the code that implements this:

```
...//In initialization code:
boolean frozen = false;
...

public synchronized void startAnimation() {
    if (frozen) {
        //Do nothing.  The user has requested that we
        //stop changing the image.
    } else {
        //Start animating!
        ...
        timer.start();
        ...
    }
```

```
    public synchronized void stopAnimation() {
        ...
        timer.stop();
        ...
    }
    ...
    //In a mouse listener registered on the animating component:
    public void mousePressed(MouseEvent e) {
        if (frozen) {
            frozen = false;
            startAnimation();
        } else {
            frozen = true;
            stopAnimation();
        }
    }
}
```

The second feature is suspending the animation whenever the applet or application is known not to be visible. For the applet animation template, this is achieved by implementing the Applet stop and start methods to call stopAnimation and startAnimation, respectively. For the application animation template, this is achieved by implementing a window event handler that reacts to iconification and deiconification by, again, calling stopAnimation and startAnimation, respectively.

In both templates, if the user hasn't frozen the animation, when the program detects that the animation isn't visible, it tells the timer to stop. When the user revisits the animation, the program restarts the timer, unless the user has explicitly requested that the animation be stopped.

Moving an Image Across the Screen

This section features an applet that moves one image (a rocketship) in front of a background image (a field of stars). You could implement this example in one of two ways—using either one label per image or one custom component that paints both images. Because this lesson features painting, this section features the custom-component approach, as implemented in MovingImageTimer.java (page 869).

Note: An alternate implementation that uses labels and a layered pane is in MovingLabels.java (page 872).

The applet uses the following two images.

rocketship.gif:[1]

starfield.gif:

Here's a picture of the applet's GUI. Remember that you can click on the applet to stop or start the animation.

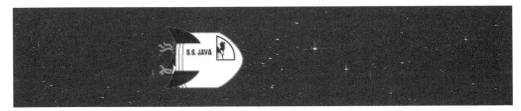

Figure 176 You can see the `MovingImageTimer` applet online at `http://java.sun.com/docs/ books/tutorial/uiswing/painting/MovingImageTimer.html`

Note: The rocketship image has a transparent background, which makes the rocketship image appear to have a rocketship shape, no matter what color background it's painted on top of. If the rocketship background weren't transparent, you'd see not the illusion of a rocketship moving through space, but rather a rocketship on top of a rectangle moving through space.

The code for performing this animation isn't complex. Essentially, it's the applet animation template plus a few additional lines of code. The additional code loads the images, paints the background image, and then uses a simple algorithm to determine where to paint the moving image.

---

[1] You can find the images by visiting: http://java.sun.com/docs/books/tutorial/uiswing/components/ example-swing/index.html

Here is the new code:

```
.../Where the images are initialized:
static String fgFile = "images/rocketship.gif";
static String bgFile = "images/starfield.gif";
...
Image bgImage = getImage(getCodeBase(), bgFile);
Image fgImage = getImage(getCodeBase(), fgFile);
...
public void paintComponent(Graphics g) {
    super.paintComponent(g); //paint any space not covered
                             //by the background image
    int compWidth = getWidth();
    int compHeight = getHeight();
    //Paint background image if we have a valid width and height.
    imageWidth = background.getWidth(this);
    imageHeight = background.getHeight(this);
    if ((imageWidth > 0) && (imageHeight > 0)) {
        g.drawImage(background,
                (compWidth - imageWidth)/2,
                (compHeight - imageHeight)/2, this);
    }
    //Paint foreground image if we have a valid width and height.
    imageWidth = foreground.getWidth(this);
    imageHeight = foreground.getHeight(this);
    if ((imageWidth > 0) && (imageHeight > 0)) {
        g.drawImage(foreground,
                ((frameNumber*5)
                  % (imageWidth + compWidth))
                  - imageWidth,
                (compHeight - imageHeight)/2, this);
    }
}
```

You might think that this program doesn't need to clear the background, since it uses a background image. However, clearing the background is still necessary. One reason is that the applet usually starts painting before the images are fully loaded. If the rocketship image loaded before the background image, you would see parts of multiple rocketships until the background image loaded. Another reason is that if the applet painting area were wider than the background image, you'd see multiple rocketships to either side of the background image.

You could solve the first problem by delaying all painting until both images were fully loaded. The second problem could be solved by scaling the background image to fit the entire applet area. You'll learn how to wait for images to be fully loaded in Improving the Appearance and Performance of Image Animation (page 569). Scaling is described in Displaying Images (page 559).

Displaying a Sequence of Images

The example in this section gives you the basics of displaying an image sequence. The next section has hints for improving the appearance and the performance of this animation. This section shows only applet code. The code for an application would be similar, except that you would use different code to load the images, as described in <u>Loading Images</u> (page 556).

Figure 177 shows the ten images this applet uses.

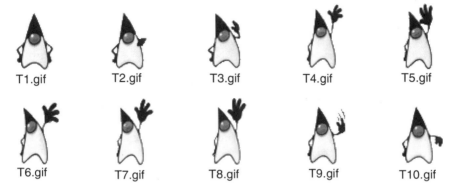

Figure 177   The ten images used in the `ImageSequence` applet.

Here's a picture of what the applet looks like. Remember that you can click on the applet to stop or to start the animation.

Figure 178   You can find this applet online at `http://java.sun.com/docs/books/tutorial/`
`uiswing/painting/ImageSequenceTimer.html`

The code for this example, in <u>`ImageSequenceTimer.java`</u> (page 867), is even simpler than for the previous example, which moved an image. Here is the code that differs significantly from the moving-image example:

```
. . .//In initialization code:
Image[] images = new Image[10];
for (int i = 1; i <= 10; i++) {
    images[i-1] = getImage(getCodeBase(), "images/duke/T"+i+".gif");
}
```

```
. . .//In the paintComponent method:
g.drawImage(images[ImageSequenceTimer.frameNumber % 10],
            0, 0, this);
```

Another way to implement this example would be to use a label to display the image. Instead of having custom painting code, the program would use the setIcon method to change the image displayed.

Improving the Appearance and Performance of Image Animation

You might have noticed two things about the previous animation.

- While the images were loading, the program displayed some images partially and others not at all.
- Loading the images took a long time.

The problem of displaying partial images is easy to fix, using the MediaTracker class. MediaTracker also can decrease the amount of time that loading images takes. Another way to deal with the problem of slow image loading is to change the image format somehow.

Note: The ImageIcon class provided by Swing automatically uses a MediaTracker to download image data as soon as an ImageIcon is created. For more information, see How to Use Icons (page 417).

Using MediaTracker to Download Images and Delay Image Display

The MediaTracker class lets you easily download data for a group of images and find out when the images are fully loaded. Ordinarily an image's data isn't downloaded until the image is painted for the first time. To request that the data for a group of images be preloaded asynchronously, use one of the following MediaTracker methods: checkID(*anInt*, true) or checkAll(true). To load data synchronously (waiting for the data to arrive), use the waitForID or the waitForAll method. The MediaTracker methods that load data use several background threads to download the data, which can speed up downloading.

To check on the status of image loading, you can use the MediaTracker statusID or statusAll method. To simply check whether any image data remains to be loaded, you can use the checkID or the checkAll method.

In `MTImageSequenceTimer.java` (page 874) is a modified version of the sample applet that uses the `MediaTracker` `waitForAll` and the `checkAll` methods. Until every image is fully loaded, this applet simply displays a "Please wait..." message. See the MediaTracker[1] API documentation for an example that paints a background image immediately but delays painting the animated images.

Here is a picture of the `MTImageSequenceTimer` applet:

Figure 179 You can see the MTImageSequenceTimer applet online at `http://java.sun.com/` `docs/books/tutorial/uiswing/painting/MTImageSequenceTimer.html`

Following is the changed code, which uses a `MediaTracker` to help delay image display. Differences are marked in a boldface type.

```
...//Where instance variables are declared:
MediaTracker tracker;
tracker = new MediaTracker(this);

...//In the init method:
for (int i = 1; i <= 10; i++) {
    images[i-1] = getImage(getCodeBase(), "images/duke/T"+i+".gif");
}

...//In the buildUI method, which is called by init and main,
   //allowing us to run the sample as an applet or an application:
for (int i = 1; i <= 10; i++) {
    tracker.addImage(dukes[i-1], 0);
}

...//At the beginning of the actionPerformed method:
try {
    //Start downloading the images. Wait until they're loaded.
    tracker.waitForAll();
} catch (InterruptedException e) {}
```

---

[1]   API documentation for `MediaTracker` is available on this book's CD-ROM and online at
http://java.sun.com/products/jdk/1.2/docs/api/java/awt/MediaTracker.html

```
...//In the paintComponent method:
//If not all the images are loaded, just clear the background
//and display a status string.
if (!tracker.checkAll()) {
    g.clearRect(0, 0, d.width, d.height);
    g.drawString("Please wait...", 0, d.height/2);
}

//If all images are loaded, paint.
else {
    ...//same code as before...
}
```

Speeding Up Image Loading

Whether or not you use MediaTracker, loading images using URLs (as applets usually do) usually takes a long time. Most of the time is taken up by initiating HTTP connections. Each image file requires a separate HTTP connection, and each connection can take several seconds to initiate.

The key to avoiding this performance hit is to put the images in a single file. You can do this using a JAR file, as described in the section "Combining an Applet's Files into a Single File" of the *Writing Applets* trail[1] and the lesson "Using JAR Files: The Basics" in the *JAR Files* trail.[2]

Another strategy that might help performance is to combine a group of images into a single image file. One simple way to do this is to create an image strip—a file that contains several images in a row. Here's an example of an image strip.

Figure 180 An example of an image strip.

---

[1] You can find this section in the book, *The Java™ Tutorial: Second Edition* and online at http://java.sun.com/docs/books/tutorial/applet/appletsonly/html.html#jar

[2] You can find this lesson in the book, *The Java™ Tutorial Continued* and online at http://java.sun.com/docs/books/tutorial/jar/basics/index.html

To paint an image from the strip, you first set the painting area to the size of one image. Then you paint the image strip, shifted to the left, if necessary, so that only the image you want appears within the painting area. For example:

```
//imageStrip is the Image object representing the image strip.
//imageWidth is the size of an individual image in the strip.
//imageNumber is the number (from 0 to numImages) of the image //to paint.
int stripWidth = imageStrip.getWidth(this);
int stripHeight = imageStrip.getHeight(this);
int imageWidth = stripWidth / numImages;
g.clipRect(0, 0, imageWidth, stripHeight);
g.drawImage(imageStrip, -imageNumber*imageWidth, 0, this);
```

If you want image loading to be faster still, you should look into image-compression schemes, especially ones that perform interframe compression.

Solving Common Graphics Problems

Problem: I don't know where to put my painting code.

- Painting code belongs in the `paintComponent` method of any component descended from `JComponent`. See <u>Overview of Custom Painting</u> (page 537) for details.

Problem: The stuff I paint does not show up.

- Check whether your component is showing up at all. <u>Solving Common Component Problems</u> (page 337) should help you with this.

- Check whether your component is obscured by another component. For example, you shouldn't put painting code in a `JFrame` or `JDialog` subclass because it will be covered by the applet's frame or content pane.

Problem: The background of my applet shows up, but the foreground stuff does not show up.

- Did you make the mistake of performing painting directly in a `JApplet` subclass? If so, your contents will be covered by the content pane that is automatically created for every `JApplet` instance. Instead create another class that performs the painting and then add that class to the `JApplet`'s content pane. See <u>Painting</u> (page 41) for more information on how painting in Swing works.

Problem: My component's foreground shows up, but its background is invisible. The result is that one or more components directly behind my component are unexpectedly visible.

- Make sure that your component is opaque. `JPanel`s, for example, are opaque by default. To make other components, such as `JLabel`s, opaque, you must invoke `setOpaque(true)` on them.

- If your custom component extends `JPanel` or a more specialized `JComponent` descendant, you can paint the background by invoking `super.paintComponent` before painting the contents of your component.

- You can paint the background yourself, using this code at the top of a custom component's `paintComponent` method:

```
g.setColor(getBackground());
g.fillRect(0, 0, getWidth(), getHeight());
g.setColor(getForeground());
```

Problem: I used `setBackground` to set my component's background color, but it seemed to have no effect.

- Most likely your component isn't painting its background, either because it's not opaque or your custom painting code doesn't paint the background. If you set the background color for a `JLabel`, for example, you must also invoke `setOpaque(true)` on the label to make the label's background be painted. For more help, see the preceding problem.

Problem: I'm using the exact same code as a tutorial example, but it doesn't work. Why?

- Is the code executed in the exact same method as the tutorial example? For example, if the tutorial example has the code in the example's `paintComponent` method, this method might be the only place where the code is guaranteed to work.

Problem: How do I paint thick lines? Patterns?

- The Java 2D API provides extensive support for implementing line widths and styles, as well as patterns for use in filling and stroking shapes. See the *2D Graphics* trail for more information on using the Java 2D API. The 2D trail is available in the book, *The Java™ Tutorial Continued* and online at `http://java.sun.com/docs/books/tutorial/2d/index.html`.

If you don't see your problem in this list, see <u>Solving Common Component Problems</u> (page 337).

Converting to Swing

THIS lesson tells you how to convert your AWT-based programs to use the Swing components. If a program was written for JDK^{TM} 1.0—meaning that instead of using the event listening system introduced in JDK 1.1, it uses methods such as handleEvent and action—you should convert the program to the newer event system first.[1]

Why to Convert (page 577)
Swing components provide many benefits to programmers and end users. For a list of Swing features, see <u>Features and Concepts</u> (page 25). Another good resource is the section <u>How Are Swing Components Different from AWT Components?</u> (page 9). Unless you have a good reason not to convert, we urge you to convert to Swing components as soon as possible.

How to Convert (page 579)
This chapter outlines a procedure for converting your programs. The good news is that converting 1.1 AWT-based programs can be pretty straightforward. The bad news is that we don't know of any automatic tools for doing so.

Conversion Resources (page 587)
This chapter provides several resources, including examples, to help you with your conversion.

Solving Common Conversion Problems (page 603)
Like the name says, this chapter lists some common gotchas, along with their solutions.

---

[1] For information and instructions on updating 1.0 programs, refer to "Migrating to 1.1," a lesson found in the book, *The Java^{TM} Tutorial: Second Edition*, and online at http://java.sun.com/docs/books/tutorial/post1.0/converting/index.html

575

Why to Convert

THE strongest reason to convert to Swing components is that they offer many benefits to programmers and end users.

- The rich set of ready-made components means that you can easily add some snazzy features to your programs—image buttons, tool bars, tabbed panes, HTML display, images in menu items, color choosers: The list goes on and on.

- You might be able to replace or to reimplement some custom components with more reliable, extensible Swing components.

- Having separate data and state models makes the Swing components highly customizable and enables sharing data between components.

- Swing's Pluggable Look & Feel architecture gives you a wide choice of look-and-feel options. Besides the usual platform-specific looks and feels, you can use the Java Look & Feel, add an accessory look and feel (such as an audio "look and feel"), or use a third-party look and feel.

- Swing components have built-in support for accessibility, which makes your programs automatically usable with assistive technologies.

- The Swing components will continue to be enhanced in the future.

It's reasonable to put off converting if you don't think that your users will be able run Swing programs conveniently. For example, if your program is an applet and you want anyone on the Internet to be able to use it, you have to consider how many Web surfers have browsers that can run Swing programs. As of this writing, the major browsers don't have built-in Swing support; the user must add it by downloading and installing Java Plug-in. Go to the Java Plug-in home page to find additional documentation. [1]

---

[1] http://java.sun.com/products/plugin/index.html

You have the choice of upgrading to the Java^TM 2 platform when you convert to the Swing components. However, you don't need to decide right now whether to upgrade. Programs written with JDK 1.1 and Swing generally work just fine in the Java 2 platform. For information about new and improved features of the Java 2 platform, see <u>Tables of JDK Features</u>.[1]

---

[1] The "Tables of JDK Features" section is available in the "Overview" trail in *The Java^TM Tutorial Continued* book and online at http://java.sun.com/docs/books/tutorial/overview/tables.html

How to Convert

THIS chapter presents steps you can follow to convert a program to use the Swing components. Each step applies to all programs—applications and applets alike—unless noted otherwise.

Step 1: Save a copy of the original program.

Copy all of the program's files, including the `.java` files and the `.class` files. You will need this copy for several reasons.

- You'll need to refer to the source during the conversion process.

- After conversion, you should run both versions of your program side by side to compare them.

- After conversion, you can compare the source code of both versions to apply what you learned to other programs you need to convert.

- Some of your program's users might not be willing or able to immediately update their VM to a version that supports the Swing classes. If you want to keep them as customers, you'll need to keep providing the old AWT-based program in the interim.

Step 2: Remove all references to the java.awt package.

This step puts the compiler to work for you. By removing all imports and other code that references the `java.awt` package, you make the compiler tell you each time you use a class from that package. It's OK to use some AWT classes—layout managers, for example—but your program should use no AWT components. Here are a couple of examples of what to delete:

```
//import java.awt.*;      //temporarily remove this import
```

or

```
//import java.awt.Button; //temporarily remove this import
import java.awt.Color;    //it's OK to leave this in, since
                          //Color isn't a component
...
/*java.awt.*/Frame = new /*java.awt.*/Frame(...);
```

Without the references to `java.awt`, the compiler generates a "not found" error every place your program uses an AWT component. This makes it easier for you to find and to replace AWT components with their Swing equivalents. In <u>Step 9</u> (page 583), you will add back the imports for the AWT classes that you really need.

Step 3: If your program is an applet, remove the java.applet.* import statement (if present) and any references to java.applet.Applet.

You don't need to refer to the old `Applet` class, because your converted applet will be a subclass of the `JApplet` class, which is itself a subclass of `Applet`. If your program uses `AppletContext`, `AppletStub`, or `AudioClip`, of course you'll need to import those classes from the `java.applet` package. Here's an example of what to do:

```
//import java.applet.*;        //temporarily remove this import
import java.applet.AppletContext;    //add this if necessary
```

Step 4: Import the main Swing package.

Add the following import statement to your program:

```
import javax.swing.*;
```

This imports all of the Swing components, as well as some of Swing's other classes. If you want, you can be more meticulous and add one import statement per Swing class you use.

Step 5: Be aware of thread safety issues!

Before you go on remind yourself of this important fact: *Although AWT is designed to be thread safe, Swing is not.* You must take this into consideration when converting your programs.

Most programs modify components in event-handling methods and painting methods, which are called from the event-dispatching thread. Modifying a component in those methods is safe. However, if your program modifies a component anywhere else—such as in the main thread after the GUI is visible or in code called by a thread you have created—you must take explicit action to make it thread safe.

This tutorial contains two sections about Swing and threads. First, <u>Threads and Swing</u> (page 45) provides conceptual coverage. Next, <u>How to Use Threads</u> (page 431) contains practical information and examples.

Step 6: Change each AWT component to its closest Swing equivalent.

The table provided in <u>Swing Replacements for AWT Components</u> (page 587) lists each AWT component and its closest Swing equivalent. Use that section as a guide for choosing a replacement for each AWT component used in your program.

In the best case the AWT component and its Swing replacement are source-compatible, and a simple name change is all that's required. For example, to convert from an AWT button to a Swing button, you just change all occurrences of `Button` to `JButton` in your program. Here's an example:

AWT Code:	`Button button = new Button("A Button");` `button.addActionListener(this);`
Swing Code:	`JButton button = new JButton ("A Button");` `button.addActionListener(this);`

Some Swing components are not source-compatible with the AWT component they replace. So for some AWT components, you have to rewrite some code when replacing them with Swing components. <u>Conversion Resources</u> (page 587) has information to help you with conversions that require more than a simple name change.

While looking at that section, take notes on changes you might want to make later to take advantage of Swing features. For example, you might want to put images in your buttons or to share data models between two components. Before making optional changes, though, we recommend that you make the minimal changes necessary to convert your program to Swing. Once you've successfully run the Swing version of your program, you'll be better able to judge how optional changes might improve your program.

Step 7: Change calls to the add and setLayout methods.

In programs that use AWT components, you add components directly to frames, dialogs, and applets. Similarly you set the layout manager directly on those containers. In contrast, when you use the Swing versions of those containers, you add components to (and set the layout manager on) something called a *content pane*. Here's an example of converting some simple, typical code:

AWT Code:	`frame.add(panel, BorderLayout.CENTER);`
Swing Code:	`frame.getContentPane().add(panel, BorderLayout.CENTER);`

Here is a slightly more complex example:

AWT Code:	`frame.setLayout(new FlowLayout());`
	`frame.add(button);`
	`frame.add(label);`
	`frame.add(textField);`

Swing Code:	`Container contentPane = frame.getContentPane();`
	`contentPane.setLayout(new FlowLayout());`
	`contentPane.add(button);`
	`contentPane.add(label);`
	`contentPane.add(textField);`

Here is an example of converting an applet. Note that the default layout manager for a content pane is `BorderLayout`—not the `FlowLayout` used by `Applet`.

AWT Code:	`setLayout(new BorderLayout());`
	`add(button, BorderLayout.NORTH);`
	`add(panel, BorderLayout.CENTER);`

Swing Code:	`Container contentPane = getContentPane();`
	`contentPane.add(button, BorderLayout.NORTH);`
	`contentPane.add(panel, BorderLayout.CENTER);`

For more information about content panes, see <u>Components and Containment Hierarchies</u> (page 29). For more information about converting applets, refer to <u>Converting Applets</u> (page 590).

Step 8: Move painting code out of the paint and update methods.

For Swing components, custom painting code goes in the `paintComponent` method. Other ways to paint are using standard or custom icons (which generally are used to display pictures) and borders. If your component has painting code that draws the component's edge, you might well be able to replace that code with a border. If your custom painting code performs double buffering, you can probably remove the double-buffering code, since `JComponents` automatically perform double buffering.

If your program has a `Frame`, `Dialog`, or `Applet` subclass that implements `update` or `paint`, you need to move the painting code into another component entirely. The reason is that each of these containers is covered by a content pane, which hides any painting the container might do. Exactly which component the painting code should move to depends on the type of painting. If the container's painting can be performed by an icon, the component can be a standard label with an icon. Otherwise the component should generally be a `JPanel` subclass that either performs the painting in its `paintComponent` method or uses a border to do the painting. You then add the component to the frame, dialog, or applet's content pane, as described in <u>Step 7</u> (page 581) .

See <u>Working with Graphics</u> (page 533) for details about painting.

Step 9: Use the compiler to find any other needed changes.

After you've modified the source code as indicated in the previous steps, use the compiler to *try* to compile your program. You can find instructions in <u>Compiling and Running Swing Programs</u> (page 11). During this step, you are getting the compiler to help you identify any conversions you might have overlooked. Don't expect your program to compile the first time!

The compiler can help you do the following:

- Find each AWT component that you forgot to convert to its Swing equivalent. If you removed all of the `java.awt` import statements from your program as suggested in <u>Step 2</u> (page 579), the compiler displays an error message like this for each AWT component remaining in your program:

  ```
  TextEventDemo.java:23:Class Button not found in type declaration.
  Button button = new Button("Clear");
  ^
  ```

- Identify which AWT classes your program still needs. If you removed all of the `java.awt` import statements from your program, the compiler displays an error message like this for AWT classes you still need:

  ```
  TextEventDemo.java:17:Class BorderLayout not found in type
  declaration.
  BorderLayout layout = new BorderLayout();
  ^
  ```

The AWT classes you might still need in a Swing program are layout managers, graphics-related objects, such as `Color` and `Point`, and other noncomponent classes. You can import them, using one import statement each. Or, if you're sure that you've replaced all of the AWT components with Swing components, import the entire `java.awt` package again.

- Locate any source incompatibilities between the AWT component and its Swing replacement. These typically show up as compiler errors about undefined methods. For example, although AWT text components have an `addTextListener` method, Swing text components don't. The compiler generates an error message like the following one indicating that `JTextField` doesn't have such a method.

  ```
  TextEventDemo.java:22: Method addTextListener(TextEventDemo.
  MyTextListener) not found in class javax.swing.JTextField.
  textField.addTextListener(new MyTextListener("Text Field"));
  ^
  ```

- Remove uses of deprecated API. If the compiler issues a deprecation warning, recompile with the `-deprecation` flag to get details. You can find information about what deprecation means, as well as a list of alternatives to API deprecated in JDK 1.1, in

Migrating to 1.1.[1] Also, the API documentation for the deprecated class or method should have information about what to use instead.

Fix all problems reported by the compiler until the program compiles.

Step 10: Run the Swing program.

Run the program as described in Compiling and Running Swing Programs (page 11). If you forgot to modify any calls to add or setLayout, the runtime system displays a message like this:

```
java.lang.Error: javax.swing.JFrame.add() use
  javax.swing.JFrame.getContentPane() instead
        at javax.swing.JFrame.createRootPaneException(Compiled Code)
        at javax.swing.JFrame.addImpl(Compiled Code)
        at AppletDemo.main(Compiled Code)
```

Go back to the source, search for add or setLayout, fix the problem, and then compile and run again.

Step 11: Compare the Swing version to the AWT version, and make any improvements that Swing enables.

Although you might want the AWT and Swing versions of your program to be similar, be open to improvements offered by Swing. One difference you'll probably notice is that, unless your copy of the JDK has a swing.properties file that specifies otherwise, your converted program uses a new look and feel: the Java Look & Feel. You can specify another look and feel if you like. For more information, see How to Set the Look and Feel (page 428).

You might be able to improve your program's GUI by using features available only to Swing components or by using the Swing components that have no AWT equivalents. Components completely new to Swing include color choosers, editable combo boxes, progress bars, split panes, tabbed panes, tables, tool tips, and trees. Features available only to Swing components include borders, which are especially useful for panels, and icons, which you can add to many components, such as labels and buttons. You might also be able to replace a component you wrote yourself with a standard or customized Swing component.

---

[1] "Migrating to 1.1" is a lesson found in the book, *The Java*[TM] *Tutorial: Second Edition*, and online at
http://java.sun.com/docs/books/tutorial/post1.0/converting/index.html

Step 12: Clean up!

Now is the time to clean up your code. If you hacked any code together to get around some of AWT's deficiencies or bugs, clean it up now! Go through the tutorial sections and examples that are relevant to your program, and make sure that you use Swing features correctly. Review your program's accessibility to make sure that your program does all it can to support assistive technologies.

Conversion Resources

IF you haven't already read <u>How Are Swing Components Different from AWT Components?</u> (page 9), consider reading it now. It provides useful background and architectural information that can put the conversion process in perspective.

Swing Replacements for AWT Components

Use the following table as a guide for choosing a Swing replacement for each AWT component used in your program.

Table 189   Swing Replacements for AWT Components

AWT Component	Closest Swing Equivalent	Notes
`java.applet.Applet`	`JApplet`	AWT applets and Swing applets differ in several ways. See <u>Converting Applets</u> (page 590).
`Button`	`JButton`	A Swing button can include an image and/or text.
`Canvas`	`JPanel`, `JLabel`, or another appropriate Swing component	Your choice depends on what the program uses the canvas for. See <u>Converting Canvases (Custom Components)</u> (page 591) for a discussion of your conversion options.
`Checkbox`	`JCheckBox` or `JRadioButton`	Note that the "B" is capitalized in the Swing class name but not in the AWT class name.

Table 189   Swing Replacements for AWT Components

AWT Component	Closest Swing Equivalent	Notes
CheckboxMenuItem	JCheckBoxMenuItem	Note that the "B" is capitalized in the Swing class name but not in the AWT class name. Also note that Swing menu components are true components.
Choice	JComboBox	Replace a Choice with an uneditable (the default) JComboBox. You might have to rewrite code that handles item events. Refer to <u>Converting Choices</u> (page 592).
Dialog	JDialog or JOptionPane	AWT-based programs add components directly to a dialog and directly set its layout manager. In contrast, Swing-based programs add components to and set the layout manager on a JDialog's content pane.
FileDialog	JFileChooser	FileDialog is a dialog while JFileChooser is a component that you can place in any top-level container. For convenience, JFileChooser provides methods that make it easy to display a file chooser in a dialog.
Frame	JFrame	AWT-based programs add components directly to a frame and directly set its layout manager. In contrast, Swing-based programs add components to and set the layout manager on a JFrame's content pane.
Label	JLabel	A Swing label can include an image and/or text. To support accessibility, use setLabelFor to associate each label with the component it describes, if any.
List	JList	AWT lists and Swing lists differ in many ways. See <u>Converting Lists</u> (page 592) for information and examples. If you'd like your list to display multiple columns of information, consider upgrading to a table. If the list contains hierarchical information, consider using a tree.
Menu	JMenu	Swing menu components are true components.
MenuBar	JMenuBar	Swing menu components are true components.
MenuItem	JMenuItem	Swing menu components are true components.
Panel	JPanel	You can easily add borders to Swing panels.
PopupMenu	JPopupMenu	Swing menu components are true components.

Table 189 Swing Replacements for AWT Components

AWT Component	Closest Swing Equivalent	Notes
Scrollbar	JScrollPane or JSlider or JProgressBar	Although Swing has a ScrollBar class, you don't usually use it directly.
ScrollPane	JScrollPane	You can add custom decorations, including row and column headers, to Swing scroll panes.
TextArea	JTextArea	Typically requires some recoding to convert. See Converting Text Components (page 593) for information and examples.
TextField	JTextField	For simple uses JTextField is source-compatible with TextField. If you use text listeners you need to modify your code to use a custom document or document listener instead. If you need a password field, use JPasswordField instead. See Converting Text Components (page 593) for information about nontrivial conversions and examples.
Window	JWindow or JToolTip	You might be able to substitute a nonwindow component, such as a JLabel, and use a layered pane.

General Conversion Tips

This section gives you conversion tips for dealing with empty space, painting, and images.

Empty Space

If you use the Java Look & Feel, your Swing program might have less space between components than the previous version. If you want to add more space, you can do it by using any combination of layout managers, empty borders, and invisible spacer components. See Putting Space Between Components (page 35) for more information. You can also use the setMargin method for text components.

Converting Painting Code

AWT components perform painting in the paint and the update methods. Swing components use the paintComponent method instead. To take advantage of automatic background painting, your implementation of paintComponent should call super.paintComponent, first thing. See Overview of Custom Painting (page 537) for details.

Note that Swing components automatically use double buffering to make their painting smooth. If the program that you're converting implements double buffering explicitly, this is a unique opportunity to delete some code! For example, the AWT-based animation program ImageSequence.java (page 918) paints to an off-screen image and then paints the image to the screen all at once. Its Swing counterpart, ImageSequenceTimer.java (page 867), simply puts its paint code in the custom component's paintComponent method, and double buffering is handled automatically. During the conversion process, we removed offImage, off-Graphics, and all code that referred to them.

If your painting code puts a title or edges around the component, consider replacing it with a border. For example, you can easily create a box around a group of components by adding the components to a JPanel and making the panel have a border. The AWT-based program CoordinatesDemo uses a class called FramedArea that exists solely to put a frame around the coordinate area. The Swing version of this program, CoordinatesDemo.java (page 861), uses a border instead and deletes the FramedArea class.

Converting Images

Although you can use Image objects in Swing programs, you might want to convert some or all of them into Icon objects. The main reason is that Swing components that can display images—labels, buttons, cell renderers in tables and trees and lists, tabbed panes, menus, and so on—do so by using Icon objects. Another reason is that Icon objects have built-in accessibility support.

You can convert an Image into an icon in one of two ways. The first way is to use new ImageIcon(anImage). The second is to create an ImageIcon, using the same data source that you used to create the Image. When you use the second way, the constructor automatically loads the image data, returning when the image is ready to use.

Component-Specific Conversion Tips

This section has tips for converting AWT applet, canvas, choice, list, and text components to their Swing equivalents.

Converting Applets

As mentioned in Step 7 (page 581) of the conversion instructions, AWT programs add components directly to the Applet object and directly set the applet's layout manager. Swing applets, on the other hand, add components to and set the layout manager on the JApplet's content pane. So to convert an applet, you must make the source code changes described in that section.

Furthermore, whereas FlowLayout is the default layout manager for AWT applets, Border-Layout is the default layout manager for Swing applets. This has two repercussions:

1. If you want to use a FlowLayout, the Swing version of your program must use set-Layout on the content pane to specify it.

2. If you specified BorderLayout in your AWT applet, you can remove the setLayout statement from the Swing version.

As <u>Step 8</u> (page 582) says, don't paint directly in a JApplet, because it will be covered by the applet's content pane. Instead of seeing your painting, you'll just see a blank area. The solution is to have a custom component do the painting, and add it to the content pane. See the instructions for converting canvases for tips on choosing a class for the custom component, and moving the paint code to the appropriate method.

Be very aware of thread issues when converting your applet. Because the stop and the start methods aren't called from the event-dispatching thread, you should use SwingUtilities.invokeLater in those methods whenever you make a change that might result on a call on a component. See <u>Threads and Swing</u> (page 45) and <u>How to Use Threads</u> (page 431) for more information.

Finally, your applet's users will probably use Java Plug-in to run your applet. So you will need to convert the <APPLET> tag to an OBJECT/EMBED tag. An automatic HTML converter can be found at the Java Plug-in site.[1]

Converting Canvases (Custom Components)

Before converting a custom component, check whether you can use a standard Swing component. For example, if your custom component simply displays an image, perhaps with some text, you can use a Swing label. If your custom component implements a button with an image, you can use a Swing button instead. If you've implemented a tree or a grid, consider using a Swing tree or a table.

If no Swing component has the functionality you need, we recommend that you change the superclass of your custom component from Canvas to JPanel. Then move the drawing code from paint or update to a method named paintComponent. At the top of that method, you should insert super.paintComponent(g). Remove all code related to double buffering, since Swing provides that automatically. For more information about implementing painting in custom Swing components, refer to <u>Working with Graphics</u> (page 533).

JPanel is not the only possible superclass for custom components. You can use a more specialized superclass, such as JLabel or AbstractToggleButton. Or you can use a less

---

[1] http://java.sun.com/products/plugin/index.html

specialized superclass, such as `Component`, `Container`, or `JComponent`. Extending `JComponent` instead of `Component` or `Container` gives you automatic double buffering and access to Swing features such as borders. Extending `JPanel` instead of `JComponent` buys you automatic background painting, which you can turn off, if you like, with `setOpaque(false)`.

Converting Choices

AWT choices are equivalent to uneditable Swing combo boxes. Although both choices and combo boxes fire item events, the conditions under which the events are fired differ. A choice fires one item event each time the user selects an item from its menu. The Swing combo box component fires one item event each time the state of an item changes. Thus a combo box fires two item events when the user chooses a new item from the combo box: one because the currently selected item's state changed to deselected and one because the chosen item's state changed to selected. Furthermore, although a choice fires an item event when the user chooses the already selected item, a combo box fires no events in this case.

You have a couple of options.

- If you want to be notified when the user chooses an already selected item, use an action listener instead of an item listener. Although choices fire only item events, combo boxes fire action events as well.

- If you're interested in item events but care only about one per selection, use the event object's `getStateChanged` method to determine whether you're interested in a particular event.

Converting Lists

AWT lists and Swing lists differ in many ways.

- Populating a Swing list is different from populating an AWT list, because a standard Swing list is immutable—you cannot add items to or remove items from it. To populate a Swing list, create a vector, an array, or a data model with the initial items in it.

AWT Code:	```List spanish = new List();```
	```spanish.addItem("uno");```
	```spanish.addItem("dos");```
	```spanish.addItem("tres");```
	```spanish.addItem("cuatro");```

Swing Code:	```String[] listData = { "uno",```
	``` "dos",```
	``` "tres",```
	``` "cuatro" };```
	```JList spanish = new JList(listData);```

If you want a mutable list, you need to provide the list with a custom `ListModel` that is mutable. Refer to <u>Adding Items to and Removing Items from a List</u> (page 221) for details and an example.

- AWT lists provide scroll bars automatically. If you want scrolling capability for a Swing list, you need to put the list in a scroll pane. Remember to change the arguments to the `add` method so that it adds the scroll pane, rather than the actual list, to the container. If you are using a `GridBagLayout`, make sure that you then apply the constraints to the scroll pane rather than to the list.

AWT Code:	```List spanish = new List();``` ```somecontainer.add(spanish);```

Swing Code:	```JList spanish = new JList(listData);```
	```JScrollPane scrollPane = new JScrollPane(spanish);```
	```somecontainer.add(scrollPane);```

- Although `List` generates action events, `JList` doesn't. To listen for changes to the selection on a `JList`, use a `ListSelectionListener`. To listen for single, double, or triple clicks, use a mouse listener.
- A Swing list supports three selection modes, not two.

For an example of converting a program that contains a list, refer to <u>Converting ListDemo</u> (page 600).

Converting Text Components

The Swing text components have much richer functionality than their AWT counterparts. You can easily display styled text, such as HTML text, using an editor pane or a text pane. For information on what Swing text components have to offer, see <u>How to Use Text Components</u> (page 275).

When converting a text area, be aware that Swing text areas aren't automatically placed in scroll panes. You normally should put the Swing text area in a scroll pane and set the scroll pane's preferred size. If you forget to set the preferred size of the scroll pane, depending on the layout manager you use, the scroll pane might grow each time a line of text is added to the text area—and the user won't see scroll bars.

When you add a text area to a scroll pane, remember to make these other changes to your program:

- Change the `add` call to add the scroll pane, instead of the text area, to the container.
- If you are using a `GridBagLayout`, make sure that you then apply the constraints to the scroll pane rather than to the text area.

Swing text components support different listeners than do AWT text components. For example, Swing text components don't have an `addTextListener` method. Instead you should use a custom document or register a document listener. If you have a key event listener registered on an AWT text component, you should probably replace it with a custom document. Documents and document listeners are discussed in <u>General Rules for Using Text Components</u> (page 282), and examples of implementing custom documents are in <u>Creating a Validated Text Field</u> (page 299).

For an example of converting an AWT text component to a Swing text component, including how to convert text listeners, refer to <u>Converting TextEventDemo</u> (page 597).

Some Conversion Examples

This section provides the AWT and Swing versions of several program examples and talks about the interesting aspects of the conversion. Here is an overview of each program.

ButtonDemoApplet

A simple applet that uses three buttons. In our conversion we added mnemonics and icons.

AnimatorApplication

An application that uses custom painting to perform a simple animation. Our first conversion just made the application work. The second pass made the application use Swing features, such as labels and the `Timer` class.

TextEventDemo

An applet that illustrates using listeners on text components. We added no new features during this conversion.

Converter

An application that converts distance measurements between U.S. and metric. We made many changes in this program, taking advantage of such Swing features as data models, borders, and `BoxLayout`.

ListDemo

An application to demonstrate the use of lists. The conversion was fairly straightforward, but again we did more than necessary. We took advantage of some new Swing features, including tables, split panes, and models.

The discussions don't analyze the conversions line by line. However, you can see the differences between the AWT and Swing versions of each program by using a program, such as UNIX's `diff` utility, to compare both versions of the source code.

Converting ButtonDemoApplet

The first AWT-to-Swing conversion example we'll look at is a simple applet that contains three buttons. The first snapshot shows the AWT version of the applet running. The second shows the Swing version.

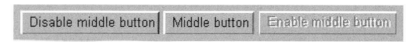

Figure 181 AWT version (Win32 platform).

Figure 182 Swing version (any platform, using Java Look & Feel).

You'll notice that the programs look different.

1. The button edges are different. In the AWT version, running on Win32, the buttons appear raised. In the Swing version, which uses the Java Look & Feel, the button edges appear etched.

2. The button font is different in the two versions.

3. The buttons in the Swing applet have icons as well as text.

4. The buttons in the Swing applet have underlined letters, which lets the user know the mnemonic for each button.

5. The Swing applet is bigger.

Differences 1 and 2 exist simply because the Win32 AWT implementation and the Java Look & Feel used by the Swing program draw buttons differently and have different default fonts. The Java Look & Feel is the default look and feel, which works on all platforms. However, your program or the user can specify another preference.

Differences 3 and 4 exist because we chose to take advantage of two Swing button features not supported by AWT buttons: images and mnemonics.

The final difference is a side effect of the previous four differences. We had to modify the <APPLET> tag so that the browser would reserve enough space for the larger Swing version. After determining the text of the <APPLET> tag, we ran an HTML converter to create the somewhat complex <OBJECT> and <EMBED> tags required by Java Plug-in.

Although the programs look somewhat different, they behave the same. When you click the left button, it disables the middle button and itself and enables the right button. When you click the right button, it disables itself and enables the middle and left buttons.

The following table links to the complete source code and an HTML file containing a sample <APPLET> tag for each version of the program. Compare the code and the <APPLET> tags to see the differences between the two programs.

	Source Code	**HTML Code**
AWT:	`ButtonDemoApplet.java`	`ButtonDemoApplet.html`

Swing:	`ButtonDemoApplet.java`
	`left.gif`
	`middle.gif`
	`right.gif`
		`ButtonDemoApplet.html`

Converting AnimatorApplication

`AnimatorApplication` is a template for animation programs. This particular implementation "animates" a string by changing the string periodically. The program can be easily modified to animate images in the same manner.

This section discusses two solutions to converting the animator program. The first solution takes a minimalist approach: The code is changed only as necessary to get the program to run with Swing. The second solution is more complete: It changes the code to adjust for differences in the way the AWT and Swing programs paint and to take advantage of the Swing timer support.

The AWT `AnimatorApplication` class extends `Frame`. Its `paint` method uses `drawString` to paint a string in the frame. A thread periodically wakes up, changes the string to the next value, and repaints the frame.

Both Swing versions of the `AnimatorApplication` class extend `JFrame`.

The minimalist version of the program paints the same way the AWT version paints—by calling the `drawString` method. However, in Swing the painting code belongs in a method named `paintComponent`. Furthermore because a `JFrame` has a content pane, the painting done in its `paintComponent` method has no effect (the content pane just paints right over it). So the painting code must move out of the frame. Instead the program defines a `JPanel` subclass, `AnimappPanel`, to do the painting and uses an instance of `AnimappPanel` as the `JFrame`'s content pane.

The second solution is a more complete Swing solution. Instead of using a thread that sleeps periodically, the second solution uses Swing's `Timer` class. Additionally, this solution uses a

`JLabel` instead of creating a `JPanel` subclass to draw a string. Replacing the custom component with a label isn't essential for this program, but it is something you might well do in your own programs.

Here are the three versions to compare:

	Source Code
AWT:	`AnimatorApplication.java`
Minimalist Swing Solution:	`AnimatorApplication.java`
More Complete Swing Solution:	`AnimatorApplicationTimer.java`

Converting TextEventDemo

Here's a snapshot of the Swing version of the `TextEventDemo` applet. The AWT version looks similar.

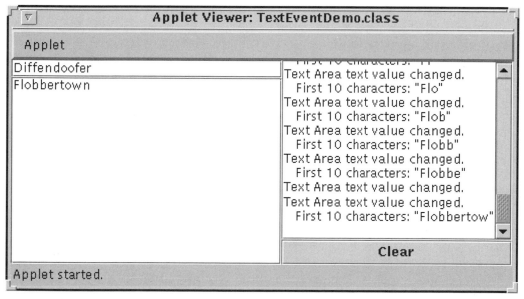

Figure 183 The `SwingTextEventDemo` applet.

This program has a text field and a text area on the left, both of which are editable. The program listens for changes to the text on the text field and the text area and logs changes in the uneditable text area on the right.

AWT text areas support scrolling directly. Swing text areas don't. So the Swing version of this example creates a `JScrollPane` for each text area. The program uses a `GridBagLayout` to position the components. During the first pass of the conversion, we forgot to change the `setConstraints` call to set the constraints on the scroll pane instead of the text area and ended up with a tiny scroll pane.

The AWT version of this program registers a text listener with `addTextListener` to listen for changes on the text components. The text listener implements a single method, called `textValueChanged`.

Swing text components do not have an `addTextListener` method. Instead the Swing version of this program has to register a document listener on each text component's document. A document listener implements three methods: `insertUpdate`, `removeUpdate`, and `changedUpdate`. These methods allow a program to listen for specific types of changes.

Here's the code and <APPLET> tags to compare:

	Source Code	**HTML Code**
AWT:	`TextEventDemo.java`	`TextEventDemo.html`
Swing:	`TextEventDemo.java`	`TextEventDemo.html`

Converting Converter

The `Converter` application changes distance measurements between metric and U.S. units. Here are snapshots of the AWT and Swing versions of the program.

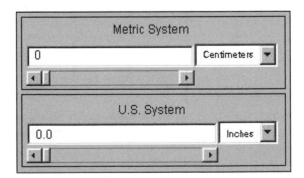

Figure 184 The AWT Converter.

Here's the source code for both versions:

Table 190 Converter Source Code for AWT and Swing Versions

AWT Converter Source	Swing Converter Source
Converter.java (page 914) ConversionPanel.java (page 912) Unit.java (page 924)	Converter.java (page 894) ConversionPanel.java (page 892) Unit.java (page 908) ConverterRangeModel.java (page 896) FollowerRangeModel.java (page 900) DecimalField.java (page 900) FormattedDocument.java (page 902)

The main method for both versions is in the Converter class. Both versions use two instances of ConversionPanel—one for the metric system controls and one for the U.S. system controls. The Converter program keeps several instances of Unit, each of which contains a multiplier for a particular conversion.

The Swing version of the program has four additional classes. These provide custom data models for the text fields and the sliders.

The Anatomy of a Swing-Based Program (page 51) dissects the Swing version of the Converter program. Read that section to familiarize yourself with the program before proceeding.

The Swing version of this program takes advantage of the Swing API and improves on the AWT version in these ways:

- Draws a line border around and provides a text label for each ConversionPanel with a titled border. In the AWT version the ConversionPanel has to draw its own line border and uses an AWT Label for the panel's label.

- Uses a custom document for the text fields, ensuring that the user enters only valid data. In the AWT version the user can enter invalid data, such as characters, into the text fields.

- Provides a custom data model to contain the current value. This ensures that the current value for the program is kept in only one place.

- Uses Swing's BoxLayout class to lay out the components within each ConversionPanel. This makes the layout code simpler, compared to the code for the layout manager previously used (GridBagLayout).

Converting ListDemo

Our final conversion example converts a program that uses lists. The AWT version of this example is fairly simple. Here's its GUI.

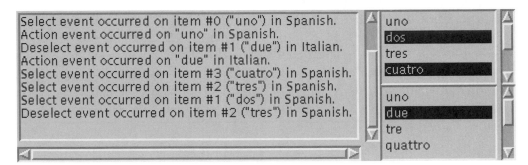

Figure 185 The AWT version of the ListDemo applet.

This applet contains two lists: one that allows single selection and one that allows multiple, discontiguous selections.

When converting this program, we got a little carried away. Rather than doing a basic conversion, we decided to show off the power of Swing's model-view split. The Swing version of the program can be run as an application and is shown next.

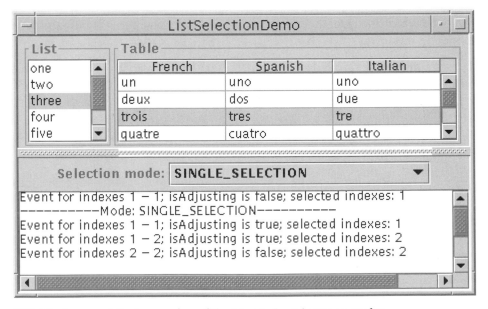

Figure 186 The improved Swing version of the ListSelectionDemo applet.

This program contains a single list alongside a table. The list and the table share a list selection model. Thus selecting an item in the list selects the corresponding row in the table, and vice versa. Furthermore, this program lets the user change the selection mode dynamically.

	Source Code	HTML Code
AWT:	`ListDemo.java` (page 920)	`ListDemo.html` (page 922)
Swing:	`ListSelectionDemo.java` (page 903)	None (implemented as an application)

Not leaving well enough alone, we modified `ListSelectionDemo` so that, in addition to sharing the selection model, the list and the table share the same data model. This new example is called `SharedModelDemo`. You can find its code in `SharedModelDemo.java` (page 706).

Solving Common Conversion Problems

Problem: I'm seeing weird problems that are either intermittent or dependent on timing.

- Does your main thread modify the GUI after it's visible? If so, either move the code so that it executes before the GUI is shown, or execute the GUI-modifying code in the event-dispatching thread.

- Does your program have multiple threads or query/modify the GUI in response to messages from other programs? If so, you should ensure that all GUI-related code is executed in the event-dispatching thread.

- If your program is an applet that implements the stop and start methods, make sure that any GUI work performed by those methods is executed in the event-dispatching thread.

- The preceding suggestions assume that your problem is caused by code that isn't thread safe. See <u>Threads and Swing</u> (page 45) for information about thread safety, and <u>How to Use Threads</u> (page 431) for information about API you can use to help make your programs thread safe.

Problem: My applet/dialog/frame is blank.

- Does the applet/frame/dialog perform custom drawing? If so, you need to move the custom drawing code out of the `JApplet`/`JDialog`/`JFrame` subclass and into a custom component that you add to the content pane. For more information, see <u>Step 8</u> (page 582) of the 12-step conversion plan.

- Do you either set the applet/frame/dialog's content pane or add components to the existing content pane? You should. See <u>Using Top-Level Containers</u> (page 77) for more information.

Problem: In the Swing version of my program, the list/text component is missing its scroll bars.

- Swing list and text components don't have automatic scroll bars. Instead, you need to add the list or text component to a scroll pane, as described in Component-Specific Conversion Tips (page 590).

Problem: Although I'm using the same grid bag layout code as before, one scrollable component is tiny.

- Make sure you set constraints on the scroll pane, rather than on its client.

Problem: I'm not getting the kinds of events I expected for the Swing component I'm using.

- Read both the conversion tips and how-to section for the component you're using. Chances are that the relevant event details are covered in those sections.

- If you think the problem might be a bug, search the bug database at the Java Developer Connection at `http://developer.java.sun.com/`

If you can't find your problem in this chapter, we might have included it in one of our other problem-solving sections:

Appendices

APPENDIX A

Code Examples

THIS appendix lists every complete example program featured in this tutorial. It also includes a few HTML files that you might need to copy.

Each example lists the section(s) in which it is explained, the names of any source or associated files that comprise the example, and the location of each source file on our Web site. Note that all of these files are also included on the CD-ROM that accompanies this book.

The *Examples Index* has tables for each lesson that list the files and images used in each example and give the URL where you can run the applet examples. These tables are included on the CD-ROM and are available online here:

```
http://java.sun.com/docs/books/tutorial/uiswing/examples.html
```

Getting Started with Swing

Complete examples in <u>Getting Started with Swing</u> (page 3):

AppletDemo.java, 608
HelloSwingApplet.java, 610
SwingApplication.java, 610

EXAMPLE: *AppletDemo.java*

**Where
Explained:**
*Running
Swing Applets*
(page 17)

SOURCE CODE: *http://java.sun.com/docs/books/tutorial/uiswing/start/example-swing/
AppletDemo.java*

```java
/*
 * Swing 1.1 version (compatible with both JDK 1.1 and Java 2).
 */
import javax.swing.*;
import java.awt.*;
import java.awt.event.*;
import java.net.URL;

public class AppletDemo extends JApplet implements ActionListener {
    protected JButton b1, b2, b3;

    protected static final String DISABLE = "disable";
    protected static final String ENABLE = "enable";

    protected String leftButtonFilename = "images/right.gif";
    protected String middleButtonFilename = "images/middle.gif";
    protected String rightButtonFilename = "images/left.gif";

    private boolean inAnApplet = true;
    URL codeBase; //used for applet version only

    //Hack to avoid ugly message about system event access check.
    public AppletDemo() {
        this(true);
    }

    public AppletDemo(boolean inAnApplet) {
        this.inAnApplet = inAnApplet;
        if (inAnApplet) {
            getRootPane().putClientProperty("defeatSystemEventQueueCheck",
                                            Boolean.TRUE);
        }
    }

    public void init() {
        setContentPane(makeContentPane());
    }

    public Container makeContentPane() {
        ImageIcon leftButtonIcon;
        ImageIcon middleButtonIcon;
        ImageIcon rightButtonIcon;

        if (inAnApplet) {
            URL leftButtonURL = getURL(leftButtonFilename);
            URL middleButtonURL = getURL(middleButtonFilename);
            URL rightButtonURL = getURL(rightButtonFilename);

            leftButtonIcon = new ImageIcon(leftButtonURL);
            middleButtonIcon = new ImageIcon(middleButtonURL);
            rightButtonIcon = new ImageIcon(rightButtonURL);
        } else {
            leftButtonIcon = new ImageIcon(leftButtonFilename);
            middleButtonIcon = new ImageIcon(middleButtonFilename);
            rightButtonIcon = new ImageIcon(rightButtonFilename);
        }

        b1 = new JButton("Disable middle button", leftButtonIcon);
```

```
        b1.setVerticalTextPosition(AbstractButton.CENTER);
        b1.setHorizontalTextPosition(AbstractButton.LEFT);
        b1.setMnemonic(KeyEvent.VK_D);
        b1.setActionCommand(DISABLE);

        b2 = new JButton("Middle button", middleButtonIcon);
        b2.setVerticalTextPosition(AbstractButton.BOTTOM);
        b2.setHorizontalTextPosition(AbstractButton.CENTER);
        b2.setMnemonic(KeyEvent.VK_M);

        b3 = new JButton("Enable middle button", rightButtonIcon);
        //Use the default text position of CENTER, RIGHT.
        b3.setMnemonic(KeyEvent.VK_E);
        b3.setActionCommand(ENABLE);
        b3.setEnabled(false);

        //Listen for actions on buttons 1 and 3.
        b1.addActionListener(this);
        b3.addActionListener(this);

        b1.setToolTipText("Click this button to disable the middle button.");
        b2.setToolTipText("This middle button does nothing when you click it.");
       b3.setToolTipText("Click this button to enable the middle button.");

        //Add Components to a JPanel, using the default FlowLayout.
        JPanel pane = new JPanel();
        pane.add(b1);
        pane.add(b2);
        pane.add(b3);
        pane.setBackground(new Color(255,255,204));
        pane.setBorder(BorderFactory.createMatteBorder(1,1,2,2,Color.black));

        return pane;
    }

    public void actionPerformed(ActionEvent e) {
        if (e.getActionCommand().equals(DISABLE)) {
            b2.setEnabled(false);
            b1.setEnabled(false);
            b3.setEnabled(true);
        } else {
            b2.setEnabled(true);
            b1.setEnabled(true);
            b3.setEnabled(false);
        }
    }

    protected URL getURL(String filename) {
        URL url = null;
        if (codeBase == null) {
            codeBase = getCodeBase();
        }

        try {
            url = new URL(codeBase, filename);
        } catch (java.net.MalformedURLException e) {
            System.out.println("Couldn't create image: badly specified URL");
            return null;
        }

        return url;
    }

    public static void main(String[] args) {
        JFrame frame = new JFrame("Application version: AppletDemo");
        frame.addWindowListener(new WindowAdapter() {
```

```
        public void windowClosing(WindowEvent e) {
            System.exit(0);
        }
    });

    AppletDemo applet = new AppletDemo(false);
    frame.setContentPane(applet.makeContentPane());
    frame.pack();
    frame.setVisible(true);
    }
}
```

EXAMPLE: *HelloSwingApplet.java*

Where Explained:
Running Swing Applets
(page 17)

SOURCE CODE: *http://java.sun.com/docs/books/tutorial/uiswing/start/example-swing/ HelloSwingApplet.java*

```
import javax.swing.*;            //This is the final package name.
//import com.sun.java.swing.*;  //Used by JDK 1.2 Beta 4 and all
                                //Swing releases before Swing 1.1 Beta 3.
import java.awt.*;

public class HelloSwingApplet extends JApplet {

    // This is a hack to avoid an ugly error message in 1.1.
    public HelloSwingApplet() {
        getRootPane().putClientProperty("defeatSystemEventQueueCheck",
                                        Boolean.TRUE);
    }

    public void init() {
        JLabel label = new JLabel("You are successfully running a Swing applet!");
        label.setHorizontalAlignment(JLabel.CENTER);

        //Add border.  Should use createLineBorder, but then the bottom
        //and left lines don't appear -- seems to be an off-by-one error.
        label.setBorder(BorderFactory.createMatteBorder(1,1,2,2,Color.black));
        getContentPane().add(label, BorderLayout.CENTER);
    }
}
```

EXAMPLE: *SwingApplication.java*

Where Explained:
Compiling and Running Swing Programs
(page 11)

SOURCE CODE: *http://java.sun.com/docs/books/tutorial/uiswing/start/example-swing/ HelloSwingApplication.java*

```
import javax.swing.*;            //This is the final package name.
//import com.sun.java.swing.*;  //Used by JDK 1.2 Beta 4 and all
                                //Swing releases before Swing 1.1 Beta 3.
import java.awt.*;
import java.awt.event.*;

public class SwingApplication {
    private static String labelPrefix = "Number of button clicks: ";
    private int numClicks = 0;

    public Component createComponents() {
        final JLabel label = new JLabel(labelPrefix + "0     ");

        JButton button = new JButton("I'm a Swing button!");
```

```
        button.setMnemonic('i');
        button.addActionListener(new ActionListener() {
            public void actionPerformed(ActionEvent e) {
                numClicks++;
                label.setText(labelPrefix + numClicks);
            }
        });
        label.setLabelFor(button);

        /*
         * An easy way to put space between a top-level container
         * and its contents is to put the contents in a JPanel
         * that has an "empty" border.
         */
        JPanel pane = new JPanel();
        pane.setBorder(BorderFactory.createEmptyBorder(
                                        30, //top
                                        30, //left
                                        10, //bottom
                                        30) //right
                                        );
        pane.setLayout(new GridLayout(0, 1));
        pane.add(button);
        pane.add(label);

        return pane;
    }

    public static void main(String[] args) {
        try {
            UIManager.setLookAndFeel(UIManager.getCrossPlatformLookAndFeelClassName());
        } catch (Exception e) { }

        //Create the top-level container and add contents to it.
        JFrame frame = new JFrame("SwingApplication");
        SwingApplication app = new SwingApplication();
        Component contents = app.createComponents();
        frame.getContentPane().add(contents, BorderLayout.CENTER);

        //Finish setting up the frame, and show it.
        frame.addWindowListener(new WindowAdapter() {
            public void windowClosing(WindowEvent e) {
                System.exit(0);
            }
        });
        frame.pack();
        frame.setVisible(true);
    }
}
```

Features and Concepts

Complete examples in <u>Features and Concepts</u> (page 25):

EXAMPLE: *ConversionPanel.java*

Where Explained:

The Anatomy of a Swing-Based Program
(page 51)

Main Source File: <u>Converter.java</u> *(page 614)*

SOURCE CODE: *http://java.sun.com/docs/books/tutorial/uiswing/overview/example-swing/ConversionPanel.java*

```java
/*
 * Swing 1.1 version (compatible with both JDK 1.1 and Java 2).
 */

import javax.swing.*;
import javax.swing.event.*;
import java.awt.*;
import java.awt.event.*;
import java.util.*;
import java.text.NumberFormat;

public class ConversionPanel extends JPanel {
    DecimalField textField;
    JComboBox unitChooser;
    JSlider slider;
    ConverterRangeModel sliderModel;
    Converter controller;
    Unit[] units;
    String title;
    final static boolean DEBUG = false;
    final static boolean COLORS = false;
    final static int MAX = 10000;

    ConversionPanel(Converter myController, String myTitle, Unit[] myUnits,
                                        ConverterRangeModel myModel) {
        if (COLORS) {
            setBackground(Color.cyan);
        }
        setBorder(BorderFactory.createCompoundBorder(
                    BorderFactory.createTitledBorder(myTitle),
                    BorderFactory.createEmptyBorder(5,5,5,5)));

        //Save arguments in instance variables.
        controller = myController;
        units = myUnits;
        title = myTitle;
        sliderModel = myModel;
```

```
        //Add the text field.  It initially displays "0" and needs
        //to be at least 10 columns wide.
        NumberFormat numberFormat = NumberFormat.getNumberInstance();
        numberFormat.setMaximumFractionDigits(2);
        textField = new DecimalField(0, 10, numberFormat);
        textField.setValue(sliderModel.getDoubleValue());
        textField.addActionListener(new ActionListener() {
            public void actionPerformed(ActionEvent e) {
                sliderModel.setDoubleValue(textField.getValue());
            }
        });

        //Add the combo box.
        unitChooser = new JComboBox();
        for (int i = 0; i < units.length; i++) { //Populate it.
            unitChooser.addItem(units[i].description);
        }
        unitChooser.setSelectedIndex(0);
        sliderModel.setMultiplier(units[0].multiplier);
        unitChooser.addActionListener(new ActionListener() {
            public void actionPerformed(ActionEvent e) {
                //Set new maximums for the sliders.
                int i = unitChooser.getSelectedIndex();
                sliderModel.setMultiplier(units[i].multiplier);
                controller.resetMaxValues(false);
            }
        });

        //Add the slider.
        slider = new JSlider(sliderModel);
        sliderModel.addChangeListener(new ChangeListener() {
            public void stateChanged(ChangeEvent e) {
                textField.setValue(sliderModel.getDoubleValue());
            }
        });

        //Make the textfield/slider group a fixed size.
        JPanel unitGroup = new JPanel() {
            public Dimension getMinimumSize() {
                return getPreferredSize();
            }
            public Dimension getPreferredSize() {
                return new Dimension(150,
                                     super.getPreferredSize().height);
            }
            public Dimension getMaximumSize() {
                return getPreferredSize();
            }
        };
        if (COLORS) {
            unitGroup.setBackground(Color.blue);
        }
        unitGroup.setBorder(BorderFactory.createEmptyBorder(
                                          0,0,0,5));
        unitGroup.setLayout(new BoxLayout(unitGroup,
                                     BoxLayout.Y_AXIS));
        unitGroup.add(textField);
        unitGroup.add(slider);

        setLayout(new BoxLayout(this, BoxLayout.X_AXIS));
        add(unitGroup);
        add(unitChooser);
        unitGroup.setAlignmentY(TOP_ALIGNMENT);
        unitChooser.setAlignmentY(TOP_ALIGNMENT);
    }
```

```java
/**
 * Returns the multiplier (units/meter) for the currently
 * selected unit of measurement.
 */
public double getMultiplier() {
    return sliderModel.getMultiplier();
}

public double getValue() {
    return sliderModel.getDoubleValue();
}
}
```

**Where
Explained:**
*The Anatomy of
a Swing-Based
Program*
(page 51)

EXAMPLE: *Converter.java*

Associated File(s): ConversionPanel.java *(page 612)*,
ConverterRangeModel.java *(page 617)*, DecimalField.java
(page 620), FollowerRange.java *(page 620)*,
FormattedDocument.java *(page 622)*, Unit.java *(page 623)*

SOURCE CODE:　*http://java.sun.com/docs/books/tutorial/uiswing/overview/example-swing/
Converter.java*

```java
/*
 * Swing 1.1 version (compatible with both JDK 1.1 and Java 2).
 */

import javax.swing.*;
import javax.swing.event.*;
import java.awt.*;
import java.awt.event.*;
import java.util.*;

public class Converter {
    ConversionPanel metricPanel, usaPanel;
    Unit[] metricDistances = new Unit[3];
    Unit[] usaDistances = new Unit[4];
    final static boolean COLORS = false;
    final static boolean DEBUG = false;
    final static String LOOKANDFEEL = null;
    ConverterRangeModel dataModel = new ConverterRangeModel();
    JPanel mainPane;

    /**
     * Create the ConversionPanels (one for metric, another for U.S.).
     * I used "U.S." because although Imperial and U.S. distance
     * measurements are the same, this program could be extended to
     * include volume measurements, which aren't the same.
     *
     * Put the ConversionPanels into a frame, and bring up the frame.
     */
    public Converter() {
        //Create Unit objects for metric distances, and then
        //instantiate a ConversionPanel with these Units.
        metricDistances[0] = new Unit("Centimeters", 0.01);
        metricDistances[1] = new Unit("Meters", 1.0);
        metricDistances[2] = new Unit("Kilometers", 1000.0);
        metricPanel = new ConversionPanel(this, "Metric System",
                                          metricDistances,
                                          dataModel);
```

```
        //Create Unit objects for U.S. distances, and then
        //instantiate a ConversionPanel with these Units.
        usaDistances[0] = new Unit("Inches", 0.0254);
        usaDistances[1] = new Unit("Feet", 0.305);
        usaDistances[2] = new Unit("Yards", 0.914);
        usaDistances[3] = new Unit("Miles", 1613.0);
        usaPanel = new ConversionPanel(this, "U.S. System",
                                        usaDistances,
                                        new FollowerRangeModel(dataModel));

        //Create a JPanel, and add the ConversionPanels to it.
        mainPane = new JPanel();
        if (COLORS) {
            mainPane.setBackground(Color.red);
        }
        mainPane.setLayout(new GridLayout(2,1,5,5));
        mainPane.setBorder(BorderFactory.createEmptyBorder(5,5,5,5));
        mainPane.add(metricPanel);
        mainPane.add(usaPanel);
        resetMaxValues(true);
    }

    public void resetMaxValues(boolean resetCurrentValues) {
        double metricMultiplier = metricPanel.getMultiplier();
        double usaMultiplier = usaPanel.getMultiplier();
        int maximum = ConversionPanel.MAX;

        if (metricMultiplier > usaMultiplier) {
            maximum = (int)(ConversionPanel.MAX *
                    (usaMultiplier/metricMultiplier));
        }

        if (DEBUG) {
            System.out.println("in Converter resetMaxValues");
            System.out.println("  metricMultiplier = "
                            + metricMultiplier
                    + "; usaMultiplier = "
                            + usaMultiplier
                    + "; maximum = "
                            + maximum);
        }

        dataModel.setMaximum(maximum);

        if (resetCurrentValues) {
            dataModel.setDoubleValue(maximum);
        }
    }

    private static void initLookAndFeel() {
        String lookAndFeel = null;

        if (LOOKANDFEEL != null) {
            if (LOOKANDFEEL.equals("Metal")) {
                lookAndFeel = UIManager.getCrossPlatformLookAndFeelClassName();
            } else if (LOOKANDFEEL.equals("System")) {
                lookAndFeel = UIManager.getSystemLookAndFeelClassName();
            } else if (LOOKANDFEEL.equals("Mac")) {
                lookAndFeel = "com.sun.java.swing.plaf.mac.MacLookAndFeel";
                //PENDING: check!
            } else if (LOOKANDFEEL.equals("Windows")) {
                lookAndFeel =
                        "com.sun.java.swing.plaf.windows.WindowsLookAndFeel";
```

```java
            } else if (LOOKANDFEEL.equals("Motif")) {
                lookAndFeel = "com.sun.java.swing.plaf.motif.MotifLookAndFeel";
            }

            if (DEBUG) {
                System.out.println("About to request look and feel: "
                                    + lookAndFeel);
            }

            try {
                UIManager.setLookAndFeel(lookAndFeel);
            } catch (ClassNotFoundException e) {
                System.err.println("Couldn't find class for specified look and "
                                    + " feel: " + lookAndFeel);
                System.err.println("Did you include the L&F library in "
                                    + "the class path?");
                System.err.println("Using the default look and feel.");
            } catch (UnsupportedLookAndFeelException e) {
                System.err.println("Can't use the specified look and feel ("
                                    + lookAndFeel
                                    + ") on this platform.");
                System.err.println("Using the default look and feel.");
            } catch (Exception e) {
                System.err.println("Couldn't get specified look and feel ("
                                    + lookAndFeel
                                    + "), for some reason.");
                System.err.println("Using the default look and feel.");
                e.printStackTrace();
            }
        }
    }

    public static void main(String[] args) {
        initLookAndFeel();
        Converter converter = new Converter();

        //Create a new window.
        JFrame f = new JFrame("Converter");
        f.addWindowListener(new WindowAdapter() {
            public void windowClosing(WindowEvent e) {
                System.exit(0);
            }
        });

        //Add the JPanel to the window and display the window.
        //We can use a JPanel for the content pane because JPanel is opaque.
        f.setContentPane(converter.mainPane);
        if (COLORS) {
            //This has no effect, since the JPanel completely
            //covers the content pane.
            f.getContentPane().setBackground(Color.green);
        }

        f.pack();
        f.setVisible(true);
    }
}
```

EXAMPLE: *ConverterRangeModel.java*

Main Source File: `Converter.java` *(page 614)*

SOURCE CODE: *http://java.sun.com/docs/books/tutorial/uiswing/overview/example-*
swing/ConverterRangeModel.java

Where Explained: *The Anatomy of a Swing-Based Program* (page 51)

```java
/*
 * Swing 1.1 version (compatible with both JDK 1.1 and Java 2).
 */

import javax.swing.*;
import javax.swing.event.*;

/**
 * Based on the source code for DefaultBoundedRangeModel,
 * this class stores its value as a double, rather than
 * an int.  The minimum value and extent are always 0.
 **/
public class ConverterRangeModel implements BoundedRangeModel {
    protected ChangeEvent changeEvent = null;
    protected EventListenerList listenerList = new EventListenerList();

    protected int maximum = 10000;
    protected int minimum = 0;
    protected int extent = 0;
    protected double value = 0.0;
    protected double multiplier = 1.0;
    protected boolean isAdjusting = false;
    final static boolean DEBUG = false;

    public ConverterRangeModel() {
    }

    public double getMultiplier() {
        if (DEBUG) {
            System.out.println("In ConverterRangeModel getMultiplier");
        }
        return multiplier;
    }

    public void setMultiplier(double multiplier) {
        if (DEBUG) {
            System.out.println("In ConverterRangeModel setMultiplier");
        }
        this.multiplier = multiplier;
        fireStateChanged();
    }

    public int getMaximum() {
        if (DEBUG) {
            System.out.println("In ConverterRangeModel getMaximum");
        }
        return maximum;
    }

    public void setMaximum(int newMaximum) {
        if (DEBUG) {
            System.out.println("In ConverterRangeModel setMaximum");
        }
        setRangeProperties(value, extent, minimum, newMaximum, isAdjusting);
    }
```

```java
public int getMinimum() {
    return (int)minimum;
}

public void setMinimum(int newMinimum) {
    System.out.println("In ConverterRangeModel setMinimum");
    //Do nothing.
}

public int getValue() {
    if (DEBUG) {
        System.out.println("In ConverterRangeModel getValue");
    }
    return (int)getDoubleValue();
}

public void setValue(int newValue) {
    if (DEBUG) {
        System.out.println("In ConverterRangeModel setValue");
    }
    setDoubleValue((double)newValue);
}

public double getDoubleValue() {
    if (DEBUG) {
        System.out.println("In ConverterRangeModel getDoubleValue");
    }
    return value;
}

public void setDoubleValue(double newValue) {
    if (DEBUG) {
        System.out.println("In ConverterRangeModel setDoubleValue");
    }
    setRangeProperties(newValue, extent, minimum, maximum, isAdjusting);
}

public int getExtent() {
    return (int)extent;
}

public void setExtent(int newExtent) {
    //Do nothing.
}

public boolean getValueIsAdjusting() {
    return isAdjusting;
}

public void setValueIsAdjusting(boolean b) {
    setRangeProperties(value, extent, minimum, maximum, b);
}

public void setRangeProperties(int newValue,
                               int newExtent,
                               int newMin,
                               int newMax,
                               boolean newAdjusting) {
    System.out.println("In ConverterRangeModel setRangeProperties");
    setRangeProperties((double)newValue,
                       newExtent,
                       newMin,
                       newMax,
                       newAdjusting);
}
```

```java
public void setRangeProperties(double newValue,
                               int unusedExtent,
                               int unusedMin,
                               int newMax,
                               boolean newAdjusting) {
    if (DEBUG) {
        System.out.println("setRangeProperties(): " + "newValue = " + newValue
                         + "; newMax = " + newMax);
    }
    if (newMax <= minimum) {
        newMax = minimum + 1;
        if (DEBUG) {
            System.out.println("maximum raised by 1 to " + newMax);
        }
    }
    if (Math.round(newValue) > newMax) { //allow some rounding error
        newValue = newMax;
        if (DEBUG) {
            System.out.println("value lowered to " + newMax);
        }
    }

    boolean changeOccurred = false;
    if (newValue != value) {
        if (DEBUG) {
            System.out.println("value set to " + newValue);
        }
        value = newValue;
        changeOccurred = true;
    }
    if (newMax != maximum) {
        if (DEBUG) {
            System.out.println("maximum set to " + newMax);
        }
        maximum = newMax;
        changeOccurred = true;
    }
    if (newAdjusting != isAdjusting) {
        maximum = newMax;
        isAdjusting = newAdjusting;
        changeOccurred = true;
    }

    if (changeOccurred) {
        fireStateChanged();
    }
}

/*
 * The rest of this is event handling code copied from
 * DefaultBoundedRangeModel.
 */
public void addChangeListener(ChangeListener l) {
    listenerList.add(ChangeListener.class, l);
}

public void removeChangeListener(ChangeListener l) {
    listenerList.remove(ChangeListener.class, l);
}

protected void fireStateChanged() {
    Object[] listeners = listenerList.getListenerList();
    for (int i = listeners.length - 2; i >= 0; i -=2 ) {
        if (listeners[i] == ChangeListener.class) {
            if (changeEvent == null) {
                changeEvent = new ChangeEvent(this);
            }
```

```
                    ((ChangeListener)listeners[i+1]).stateChanged(changeEvent);
                }
            }
        }
    }
```

EXAMPLE: *DecimalField.java*

Where Explained:

The Anatomy of a Swing-Based Program
(page 51)

Main Source File: Converter.java *(page 614)*

SOURCE CODE: *http://java.sun.com/docs/books/tutorial/uiswing/overview/example-swing/
                DecimalField.java*

```java
import javax.swing.*;
import javax.swing.text.*;

import java.awt.Toolkit;
import java.text.*;

public class DecimalField extends JTextField {
    private NumberFormat format;

    public DecimalField(double value, int columns, NumberFormat f) {
        super(columns);
        setDocument(new FormattedDocument(f));
        format = f;
        setValue(value);
    }

    public double getValue() {
        double retVal = 0.0;

        try {
            retVal = format.parse(getText()).doubleValue();
        } catch (ParseException e) {
            // This should never happen because insertString allows
            // only properly formatted data to get in the field.
            Toolkit.getDefaultToolkit().beep();
            System.err.println("getValue: could not parse: " + getText());
        }
        return retVal;
    }

    public void setValue(double value) {
        setText(format.format(value));
    }
}
```

EXAMPLE: *FollowerRange.java*

Where Explained:

The Anatomy of a Swing-Based Program
(page 51)

Main Source File: Converter.java *(page 614)*

SOURCE CODE: *http://java.sun.com/docs/books/tutorial/uiswing/overview/example-swing/
                FollowerRangeModel.java*

```java
/*
 * Swing 1.1 version (compatible with both JDK 1.1 and Java 2).
 */
```

```java
import javax.swing.*;
import javax.swing.event.*;

public class FollowerRangeModel extends ConverterRangeModel
                              implements ChangeListener {
    ConverterRangeModel dataModel;

    public FollowerRangeModel(ConverterRangeModel dataModel) {
        this.dataModel = dataModel;
        dataModel.addChangeListener(this);
    }

    public void stateChanged(ChangeEvent e) {
        fireStateChanged();
    }

    public int getMaximum() {
        int modelMax = dataModel.getMaximum();
        double multiplyBy = dataModel.getMultiplier()/multiplier;
        if (DEBUG) {
            System.out.println("In FollowerRangeModel getMaximum");
            System.out.println("  dataModel.getMaximum = " + modelMax
                            + "; multiply by " + multiplyBy
                            + "; result: " + modelMax*multiplyBy);
        }
        return (int)(modelMax * multiplyBy);
    }

    public void setMaximum(int newMaximum) {
        dataModel.setMaximum((int)(newMaximum *
                (multiplier/dataModel.getMultiplier())));
    }

    public int getValue() {
        return (int)getDoubleValue();
    }

    public void setValue(int newValue) {
        setDoubleValue((double)newValue);
    }

    public double getDoubleValue() {
        return dataModel.getDoubleValue()
                * dataModel.getMultiplier()
                / multiplier;
    }

    public void setDoubleValue(double newValue) {
        dataModel.setDoubleValue(
                newValue * multiplier
                / dataModel.getMultiplier());
    }

    public int getExtent() {
        return super.getExtent();
    }

    public void setExtent(int newExtent) {
        super.setExtent(newExtent);
    }

    public void setRangeProperties(int value,
                                   int extent,
                                   int min,
                                   int max,
                                   boolean adjusting) {
        double multiplyBy = multiplier/dataModel.getMultiplier();
```

```
            dataModel.setRangeProperties(value*multiplyBy,
                                extent, min,
                                (int)(max*multiplyBy),
                                adjusting);
        }
    }
```

EXAMPLE: *FormattedDocument.java*

Where Explained:

The Anatomy of a Swing-Based Program
(page 51)

Main Source File: <u>Converter.java</u> *(page 614)*

SOURCE CODE: *http://java.sun.com/docs/books/tutorial/uiswing/overview/example-swing/ FormattedDocument.java*

```java
import javax.swing.*;
import javax.swing.text.*;

import java.awt.Toolkit;
import java.text.*;
import java.util.Locale;

public class FormattedDocument extends PlainDocument {
    private Format format;

    public FormattedDocument(Format f) {
        format = f;
    }

    public Format getFormat() {
        return format;
    }

    public void insertString(int offs, String str, AttributeSet a)
        throws BadLocationException {

        String currentText = getText(0, getLength());
        String beforeOffset = currentText.substring(0, offs);
        String afterOffset = currentText.substring(offs, currentText.length());
        String proposedResult = beforeOffset + str + afterOffset;

        try {
            format.parseObject(proposedResult);
            super.insertString(offs, str, a);
        } catch (ParseException e) {
            Toolkit.getDefaultToolkit().beep();
            System.err.println("insertString: could not parse: "
                            + proposedResult);
        }
    }

    public void remove(int offs, int len) throws BadLocationException {
        String currentText = getText(0, getLength());
        String beforeOffset = currentText.substring(0, offs);
        String afterOffset = currentText.substring(len + offs,
                                        currentText.length());
        String proposedResult = beforeOffset + afterOffset;

        try {
            if (proposedResult.length() != 0)
                format.parseObject(proposedResult);
            super.remove(offs, len);
```

```
        } catch (ParseException e) {
            Toolkit.getDefaultToolkit().beep();
            System.err.println("remove: could not parse: " +
                        proposedResult);
        }
    }
}
```

EXAMPLE: *Unit.java*

Main Source File: Converter.java *(page 614)*

SOURCE CODE: *http://java.sun.com/docs/books/tutorial/uiswing/overview/example-
swing/Unit.java*

```
public class Unit {
    String description;
    double multiplier;

    Unit(String description, double multiplier) {
        super();
        this.description = description;
        this.multiplier = multiplier;
    }

    public String toString() {
        String s = "Meters/" + description + " = " + multiplier;
        return s;
    }
}
```

**Where
Explained:**
*The Anatomy of
a Swing-Based
Program*
(page 51)

Using Swing Components

Complete examples in <u>Using Swing Components</u> (page 57):

EXAMPLE: *ButtonDemo.java*

SOURCE CODE: *http://java.sun.com/docs/books/tutorial/uiswing/components/example-swing/ButtonDemo.java*

```java
import java.awt.*;
import java.awt.event.*;
import javax.swing.AbstractButton;
import javax.swing.JButton;
import javax.swing.JPanel;
import javax.swing.JFrame;
import javax.swing.ImageIcon;

public class ButtonDemo extends JPanel
                        implements ActionListener {
    protected JButton b1, b2, b3;

    public ButtonDemo() {
        ImageIcon leftButtonIcon = new ImageIcon("images/right.gif");
        ImageIcon middleButtonIcon = new ImageIcon("images/middle.gif");
        ImageIcon rightButtonIcon = new ImageIcon("images/left.gif");

        b1 = new JButton("Disable middle button", leftButtonIcon);
        b1.setVerticalTextPosition(AbstractButton.CENTER);
        b1.setHorizontalTextPosition(AbstractButton.LEFT);
        b1.setMnemonic(KeyEvent.VK_D);
        b1.setActionCommand("disable");

        b2 = new JButton("Middle button", middleButtonIcon);
        b2.setVerticalTextPosition(AbstractButton.BOTTOM);
        b2.setHorizontalTextPosition(AbstractButton.CENTER);
        b2.setMnemonic(KeyEvent.VK_M);

        b3 = new JButton("Enable middle button", rightButtonIcon);
        //Use the default text position of CENTER, RIGHT.
        b3.setMnemonic(KeyEvent.VK_E);
        b3.setActionCommand("enable");
        b3.setEnabled(false);

        //Listen for actions on buttons 1 and 3.
        b1.addActionListener(this);
        b3.addActionListener(this);

        b1.setToolTipText("Click this button to disable the middle button.");
        b2.setToolTipText("This middle button does nothing when you click it.");
        b3.setToolTipText("Click this button to enable the middle button.");

        //Add Components to this container, using the default FlowLayout.
        add(b1);
        add(b2);
        add(b3);
    }

    public void actionPerformed(ActionEvent e) {
        if (e.getActionCommand().equals("disable")) {
            b2.setEnabled(false);
            b1.setEnabled(false);
            b3.setEnabled(true);
        } else {
            b2.setEnabled(true);
            b1.setEnabled(true);
            b3.setEnabled(false);
        }
    }
}
```

Where Explained:
The Button API (page 173)

```
public static void main(String[] args) {
    JFrame frame = new JFrame("ButtonDemo");

    frame.addWindowListener(new WindowAdapter() {
        public void windowClosing(WindowEvent e) {
            System.exit(0);
        }
    });

    frame.getContentPane().add(new ButtonDemo(), BorderLayout.CENTER);
    frame.pack();
    frame.setVisible(true);
}
}
```

EXAMPLE: *CheckBoxDemo.java*

Where Explained:

How to Use Check Boxes
(page 177)

SOURCE CODE: *http://java.sun.com/docs/books/tutorial/uiswing/components/example-swing/CheckBoxDemo.java*

```
import java.awt.*;
import java.awt.event.*;
import javax.swing.*;

public class CheckBoxDemo extends JPanel {
    JCheckBox chinButton;
    JCheckBox glassesButton;
    JCheckBox hairButton;
    JCheckBox teethButton;

    /*
     * Four accessory choices provide for 16 different
     * combinations. The image for each combination is
     * contained in a separate image file whose name indicates
     * the accessories. The filenames are "geek-XXXX.gif"
     * where XXXX can be one of the following 16 choices.
     * The "choices" StringBuffer contains the string that
     * indicates the current selection and is used to generate
     * the file name of the image to display.

        ----                // zero accessories

        c---                // one accessory
        -g--
        --h-
        ---t

        cg--                // two accessories
        c-h-
        c--t
        -gh-
        -g-t
        --ht

        -ght                // three accessories
        c-ht
        cg-t
        cgh-

        cght                // all accessories
     */

    StringBuffer choices;
```

```java
JLabel pictureLabel;

public CheckBoxDemo() {

    // Create the check boxes
    chinButton = new JCheckBox("Chin");
    chinButton.setMnemonic(KeyEvent.VK_C);
    chinButton.setSelected(true);

    glassesButton = new JCheckBox("Glasses");
    glassesButton.setMnemonic(KeyEvent.VK_G);
    glassesButton.setSelected(true);

    hairButton = new JCheckBox("Hair");
    hairButton.setMnemonic(KeyEvent.VK_H);
    hairButton.setSelected(true);

    teethButton = new JCheckBox("Teeth");
    teethButton.setMnemonic(KeyEvent.VK_T);
    teethButton.setSelected(true);

    // Register a listener for the check boxes.
    CheckBoxListener myListener = new CheckBoxListener();
    chinButton.addItemListener(myListener);
    glassesButton.addItemListener(myListener);
    hairButton.addItemListener(myListener);
    teethButton.addItemListener(myListener);

    // Indicates what's on the geek.
    choices = new StringBuffer("cght");

    // Set up the picture label
    pictureLabel = new JLabel(new ImageIcon(
                                  "images/geek/geek-"
                                  + choices.toString()
                                  + ".gif"));
    pictureLabel.setToolTipText(choices.toString());

    // Put the check boxes in a column in a panel
    JPanel checkPanel = new JPanel();
    checkPanel.setLayout(new GridLayout(0, 1));
    checkPanel.add(chinButton);
    checkPanel.add(glassesButton);
    checkPanel.add(hairButton);
    checkPanel.add(teethButton);

    setLayout(new BorderLayout());
    add(checkPanel, BorderLayout.WEST);
    add(pictureLabel, BorderLayout.CENTER);
    setBorder(BorderFactory.createEmptyBorder(20,20,20,20));
}


/** Listens to the check boxes. */
class CheckBoxListener implements ItemListener {
    public void itemStateChanged(ItemEvent e) {
        int index = 0;
        char c = '-';
        Object source = e.getItemSelectable();

        if (source == chinButton) {
            index = 0;
            c = 'c';
        } else if (source == glassesButton) {
            index = 1;
            c = 'g';
```

```
                } else if (source == hairButton) {
                    index = 2;
                    c = 'h';
                } else if (source == teethButton) {
                    index = 3;
                    c = 't';
                }

                if (e.getStateChange() == ItemEvent.DESELECTED)
                    c = '-';

                choices.setCharAt(index, c);
                pictureLabel.setIcon(new ImageIcon(
                                         "images/geek/geek-"
                                         + choices.toString()
                                         + ".gif"));
                pictureLabel.setToolTipText(choices.toString());
            }
        }

        public static void main(String s[]) {
            JFrame frame = new JFrame("CheckBoxDemo");
            frame.addWindowListener(new WindowAdapter() {
                public void windowClosing(WindowEvent e) {
                    System.exit(0);
                }
            });

            frame.setContentPane(new CheckBoxDemo());
            frame.pack();
            frame.setVisible(true);
        }

    }
```

EXAMPLE: *ColorChooserDemo.java*

Where Explained:

How to Use Color Choosers (page 184)

SOURCE CODE: *http://java.sun.com/docs/books/tutorial/uiswing/components/example-swing/ColorChooserDemo.java*

```java
import java.awt.*;
import java.awt.event.*;
import javax.swing.*;
import javax.swing.event.*;
import javax.swing.colorchooser.*;

public class ColorChooserDemo extends JFrame {
    public ColorChooserDemo() {
        super("ColorChooserDemo");

        //Set up the banner at the top of the window
        final JLabel banner = new JLabel("Welcome to the Tutorial Zone!",
                                         JLabel.CENTER);
        banner.setForeground(Color.yellow);
        banner.setBackground(Color.blue);
        banner.setOpaque(true);
        banner.setFont(new Font("SansSerif", Font.BOLD, 24));
        banner.setPreferredSize(new Dimension(100, 65));

        JPanel bannerPanel = new JPanel(new BorderLayout());
        bannerPanel.add(banner, BorderLayout.CENTER);
        bannerPanel.setBorder(BorderFactory.createTitledBorder("Banner"));
```

```
        //Set up color chooser for setting text color
        final JColorChooser tcc = new JColorChooser(banner.getForeground());
        tcc.getSelectionModel().addChangeListener(
            new ChangeListener() {
                public void stateChanged(ChangeEvent e) {
                    Color newColor = tcc.getColor();
                    banner.setForeground(newColor);
                }
            }
        );
        tcc.setBorder(BorderFactory.createTitledBorder(
                                        "Choose Text Color"));

        //Add the components to the demo frame
        Container contentPane = getContentPane();
        contentPane.add(bannerPanel, BorderLayout.CENTER);
        contentPane.add(tcc, BorderLayout.SOUTH);
    }

    public static void main(String[] args) {
        JFrame frame = new ColorChooserDemo();
        frame.addWindowListener(new WindowAdapter() {
            public void windowClosing(WindowEvent e) {System.exit(0);}
        });

        frame.pack();
        frame.setVisible(true);
    }
}
```

EXAMPLE: *ColorChooserDemo2.java*

SOURCE CODE: *http://java.sun.com/docs/books/tutorial/uiswing/components/example-swing/ColorChooserDemo2.java*

Where Explained:
How to Use Color Choosers (page 184)

```
import java.awt.*;
import java.awt.event.*;
import javax.swing.*;
import javax.swing.event.*;
import javax.swing.colorchooser.*;

public class ColorChooserDemo2 extends JFrame {
    public ColorChooserDemo2() {
        super("ColorChooserDemo2");

        //Set up banner to use as custom preview panel
        final JLabel banner = new JLabel("Welcome to the Tutorial Zone!",
                                        JLabel.CENTER);
        banner.setForeground(Color.yellow);
        banner.setBackground(Color.blue);
        banner.setOpaque(true);
        banner.setFont(new Font("SansSerif", Font.BOLD, 24));
        banner.setPreferredSize(new Dimension(100, 65));

        JPanel bannerPanel = new JPanel(new BorderLayout());
        bannerPanel.add(banner, BorderLayout.CENTER);
        bannerPanel.setBorder(BorderFactory.createTitledBorder("Banner"));

        //Set up color chooser for setting background color
        JPanel panel = new JPanel();
        JButton bcc = new JButton("Show Color Chooser...");
        bcc.addActionListener(
            new ActionListener() {
```

```java
        public void actionPerformed(ActionEvent e) {
            Color newColor = JColorChooser.showDialog(
                                        ColorChooserDemo2.this,
                                        "Choose Background Color",
                                        banner.getBackground());
            if (newColor != null) {
                banner.setBackground(newColor);
            }
        }
    }
);
panel.add(bcc);
panel.setBorder(BorderFactory.createTitledBorder(
                        "Choose Background Color"));

//Set up color chooser for setting text color
final JColorChooser tcc = new JColorChooser();
tcc.getSelectionModel().addChangeListener(
    new ChangeListener() {
        public void stateChanged(ChangeEvent e) {
            Color newColor = tcc.getColor();
            banner.setForeground(newColor);
        }
    }
);
tcc.setBorder(BorderFactory.createTitledBorder("Choose Text Color"));

//Remove the preview panel
//XXXXXX: bug #4166059, in Swing 1.1 beta 2 and earlier
//setPreviewPanel throws an exception. no known workaround.
tcc.setPreviewPanel(new JPanel());

//Override the chooser panels with our own
AbstractColorChooserPanel panels[] = { new CrayonPanel() };
tcc.setChooserPanels(panels);
tcc.setColor(banner.getForeground());

Container contentPane = getContentPane();
contentPane.add(bannerPanel, BorderLayout.NORTH);
contentPane.add(panel, BorderLayout.CENTER);
contentPane.add(tcc, BorderLayout.SOUTH);
}

public static void main(String[] args) {

    JFrame frame = new ColorChooserDemo2();

    frame.addWindowListener(new WindowAdapter() {
        public void windowClosing(WindowEvent e) {
            System.exit(0);
        }
    });

    frame.pack();
    frame.setVisible(true);
}
}
```

EXAMPLE: *ComboBoxDemo.java*

Where Explained:

How to Use Combo Boxes (page 192)

SOURCE CODE: *http://java.sun.com/docs/books/tutorial/uiswing/components/example-swing/ComboBoxDemo.java*

```java
import java.awt.*;
import java.awt.event.*;
import javax.swing.*;

public class ComboBoxDemo extends JPanel {
    JLabel picture;

    public ComboBoxDemo() {
        String[] petStrings = { "Bird", "Cat", "Dog", "Rabbit", "Pig" };

        // Create the combo box, select the pig
        JComboBox petList = new JComboBox(petStrings);
        petList.setSelectedIndex(4);
        petList.addActionListener(new ActionListener() {
            public void actionPerformed(ActionEvent e) {
                JComboBox cb = (JComboBox)e.getSource();
                String petName = (String)cb.getSelectedItem();
                picture.setIcon(new ImageIcon("images/" + petName + ".gif"));
            }
        });

        // Set up the picture
        picture = new JLabel(new ImageIcon("images/" +
                                petStrings[petList.getSelectedIndex()] +
                                ".gif"));
        picture.setBorder(BorderFactory.createEmptyBorder(10,0,0,0));

        // The preferred size is hard-coded to be the width of the
        // widest image and the height of the tallest image + the border.
        // A real program would compute this.
        picture.setPreferredSize(new Dimension(177, 122+10));

        // Layout the demo
        setLayout(new BorderLayout());
        add(petList, BorderLayout.NORTH);
        add(picture, BorderLayout.SOUTH);
        setBorder(BorderFactory.createEmptyBorder(20,20,20,20));
    }

    public static void main(String s[]) {
        JFrame frame = new JFrame("ComboBoxDemo");

        frame.addWindowListener(new WindowAdapter() {
            public void windowClosing(WindowEvent e) {System.exit(0);}
        });

        frame.setContentPane(new ComboBoxDemo());
        frame.pack();
        frame.setVisible(true);
    }
}
```

EXAMPLE: *ComboBoxDemo2.java*

**Where
Explained:**
*How to Use
Combo Boxes*
(page 192)

SOURCE CODE: *http://java.sun.com/docs/books/tutorial/uiswing/components/example-swing/
ComboBoxDemo2.java*

```java
import java.awt.*;
import java.awt.event.*;
import javax.swing.*;
import javax.swing.border.*;
import java.util.*;
import java.text.*;

public class ComboBoxDemo2 extends JPanel {
    static JFrame frame;
    JLabel result;
    String currentPattern;

    public ComboBoxDemo2() {
        String[] patternExamples = {
                    "dd MMMMM yyyy",
                    "dd.MM.yy",
                    "MM/dd/yy",
                    "yyyy.MM.dd G 'at' hh:mm:ss z",
                    "EEE, MMM d, ''yy",
                    "h:mm a",
                    "H:mm:ss:SSS",
                    "K:mm a,z",
                    "yyyy.MMMMM.dd GGG hh:mm aaa"
                    };

        currentPattern = patternExamples[0];

        // Set up the UI for selecting a pattern.
        JLabel patternLabel1 = new JLabel("Enter the pattern string or");
        JLabel patternLabel2 = new JLabel("select one from the list:");

        JComboBox patternList = new JComboBox(patternExamples);
        patternList.setEditable(true);
        patternList.setAlignmentX(Component.LEFT_ALIGNMENT);
        patternList.addActionListener(new ActionListener() {
            public void actionPerformed(ActionEvent e) {
                JComboBox cb = (JComboBox)e.getSource();
                String newSelection = (String)cb.getSelectedItem();
                currentPattern = newSelection;
                reformat();
            }
        });

        // Create the UI for displaying result
        JLabel resultLabel = new JLabel("Current Date/Time", JLabel.LEFT);
        result = new JLabel(" ");
        result.setForeground(Color.black);
        result.setBorder(BorderFactory.createCompoundBorder(
            BorderFactory.createLineBorder(Color.black),
            BorderFactory.createEmptyBorder(5,5,5,5)
        ));

        // Lay out everything
        JPanel patternPanel = new JPanel();
        patternPanel.setLayout(new BoxLayout(patternPanel, BoxLayout.Y_AXIS));
        patternPanel.add(patternLabel1);
        patternPanel.add(patternLabel2);
        patternPanel.add(patternList);
        JPanel resultPanel = new JPanel();
```

```
        resultPanel.setLayout(new GridLayout(0, 1));
        resultPanel.add(resultLabel);
        resultPanel.add(result);

        setLayout(new BoxLayout(this, BoxLayout.Y_AXIS));
        patternPanel.setAlignmentX(Component.LEFT_ALIGNMENT);
        resultPanel.setAlignmentX(Component.LEFT_ALIGNMENT);

        add(patternPanel);
        add(Box.createRigidArea(new Dimension(0, 10)));
        add(resultPanel);

        setBorder(BorderFactory.createEmptyBorder(10,10,10,10));

        reformat();
    } // constructor

    /** Formats and displays today's date. */
    public void reformat() {
        Date today = new Date();
        SimpleDateFormat formatter =
          new SimpleDateFormat(currentPattern);
        try {
            String dateString = formatter.format(today);
            result.setForeground(Color.black);
            result.setText(dateString);
        } catch (IllegalArgumentException iae) {
            result.setForeground(Color.red);
            result.setText("Error: " + iae.getMessage());
        }
    }

    public static void main(String s[]) {
        frame = new JFrame("ComboBoxDemo2");
        frame.addWindowListener(new WindowAdapter() {
            public void windowClosing(WindowEvent e) {
                System.exit(0);
            }
        });

        frame.setContentPane(new ComboBoxDemo2());
        frame.pack();
        frame.setVisible(true);
    }
}
```

EXAMPLE: *Corner.java*

Main Source File: ScrollDemo.java *(page 702)*

SOURCE CODE: *http://java.sun.com/docs/books/tutorial/uiswing/components/example-swing/Corner.java*

```
import java.awt.*;
import javax.swing.*;

public class Corner extends JComponent {
    public void paintComponent(Graphics g) {
        // Fill me with dirty brown/orange.
        g.setColor(new Color(230, 163, 4));
        g.fillRect(0, 0, getWidth(), getHeight());
    }
}
```

Where Explained:

How to Use Scroll Panes (page 112)

Where Explained:
How to Use Color Choosers
(page 184)

EXAMPLE: *CrayonPanel.java*

Main Source File: ColorChooserDemo2.java *(page 629)*

SOURCE CODE: *http://java.sun.com/docs/books/tutorial/uiswing/components/example-swing/ CrayonPanel.java*

```java
import java.awt.*;
import java.awt.event.*;
import javax.swing.*;
import javax.swing.border.*;
import javax.swing.event.*;
import javax.swing.colorchooser.*;

public class CrayonPanel extends AbstractColorChooserPanel {
    JToggleButton redCrayon;
    JToggleButton yellowCrayon;
    JToggleButton greenCrayon;
    JToggleButton blueCrayon;

    public CrayonPanel() {
        super();
    }

    public void updateChooser() {
        Color color = getColorFromModel();
        if (color.equals(Color.red)) {
            redCrayon.setSelected(true);
        } else if (color.equals(Color.yellow)) {
            yellowCrayon.setSelected(true);
        } else if (color.equals(Color.green)) {
            greenCrayon.setSelected(true);
        } else if (color.equals(Color.blue)) {
            blueCrayon.setSelected(true);
        }
    }

    protected void buildChooser() {
        setLayout(new GridLayout(0, 1));

        CrayonListener cl = new CrayonListener();
        ButtonGroup boxOfCrayons = new ButtonGroup();
        Border border = BorderFactory.createEmptyBorder(4,4,4,4);

        redCrayon = new JToggleButton(new ImageIcon("images/red.gif"));
        redCrayon.setActionCommand("red");
        redCrayon.addActionListener(cl);
        redCrayon.setBorder(border);
        boxOfCrayons.add(redCrayon);
        add(redCrayon);

        yellowCrayon = new JToggleButton(new ImageIcon("images/yellow.gif"));
        yellowCrayon.setActionCommand("yellow");
        yellowCrayon.addActionListener(cl);
        yellowCrayon.setBorder(border);
        boxOfCrayons.add(yellowCrayon);
        add(yellowCrayon);

        greenCrayon = new JToggleButton(new ImageIcon("images/green.gif"));
        greenCrayon.setActionCommand("green");
        greenCrayon.addActionListener(cl);
        greenCrayon.setBorder(border);
        boxOfCrayons.add(greenCrayon);
        add(greenCrayon);
```

```
            blueCrayon = new JToggleButton(new ImageIcon("images/blue.gif"));
            blueCrayon.setActionCommand("blue");
            blueCrayon.addActionListener(cl);
            blueCrayon.setBorder(border);
            boxOfCrayons.add(blueCrayon);
            add(blueCrayon);
        }

        class CrayonListener implements ActionListener {
            public void actionPerformed(ActionEvent e) {
                Color newColor = null;
                JToggleButton source = (JToggleButton)e.getSource();
                if (source.getActionCommand().equals("green"))
                    newColor = Color.green;
                else if (source.getActionCommand().equals("red"))
                    newColor = Color.red;
                else if (source.getActionCommand().equals("yellow"))
                    newColor = Color.yellow;
                else if (source.getActionCommand().equals("blue"))
                    newColor = Color.blue;
                getColorSelectionModel().setSelectedColor(newColor);
            }
        }

        public String getDisplayName() {
            return "Crayons";
        }

        public Icon getSmallDisplayIcon() {
            return null;
        }

        public Icon getLargeDisplayIcon() {
            return null;
        }
    }
```

EXAMPLE: *CustomComboBoxDemo.java*

SOURCE CODE: *http://java.sun.com/docs/books/tutorial/uiswing/components/example-swing/CustomComboBoxDemo.java*

```
import java.awt.*;
import java.awt.event.*;
import javax.swing.*;

public class CustomComboBoxDemo extends JPanel {
    ImageIcon images[];

    public CustomComboBoxDemo() {
        //Load the pet images
        String[] petStrings = {"Bird", "Cat", "Dog", "Rabbit", "Pig"};
        images = new ImageIcon[petStrings.length];
        for (int i = 0; i < petStrings.length; i++) {
            images[i] = new ImageIcon("images/" + petStrings[i] + ".gif");
            images[i].setDescription(petStrings[i]);
        }

        // Create the combo box
        JComboBox petList = new JComboBox(images);
        ComboBoxRenderer renderer= new ComboBoxRenderer();
        renderer.setPreferredSize(new Dimension(200, 130));
        petList.setRenderer(renderer);
        petList.setMaximumRowCount(3);
```

Where Explained:

Providing a Custom Renderer (page 196)

```
            // Layout the demo
            setLayout(new BorderLayout());
            add(petList, BorderLayout.NORTH);
            setBorder(BorderFactory.createEmptyBorder(20,20,20,20));
        }

        public static void main(String s[]) {
            JFrame frame = new JFrame("CustomComboBoxDemo");
            frame.addWindowListener(new WindowAdapter() {
                public void windowClosing(WindowEvent e) {System.exit(0);}
            });

            frame.getContentPane().add(new CustomComboBoxDemo(),
                                       BorderLayout.CENTER);
            frame.pack();
            frame.setVisible(true);
        }

        class ComboBoxRenderer extends JLabel implements ListCellRenderer {
            public ComboBoxRenderer() {
                setOpaque(true);
                setHorizontalAlignment(CENTER);
                setVerticalAlignment(CENTER);
            }

            public Component getListCellRendererComponent(
                                          JList list,
                                          Object value,
                                          int index,
                                          boolean isSelected,
                                          boolean cellHasFocus) {
                if (isSelected) {
                    setBackground(list.getSelectionBackground());
                    setForeground(list.getSelectionForeground());
                } else {
                    setBackground(list.getBackground());
                    setForeground(list.getForeground());
                }

                ImageIcon icon = (ImageIcon)value;
                setText(icon.getDescription());
                setIcon(icon);
                return this;
            }
        }
    }
}
```

EXAMPLE: *CustomDialog.java*

Where Explained:

Stopping Automatic Dialog Closing (page 95)

SOURCE CODE: *http://java.sun.com/docs/books/tutorial/uiswing/components/example-swing/ CustomDialog.java*

```
import javax.swing.JOptionPane;
import javax.swing.JDialog;
import javax.swing.JTextField;
import java.beans.*; //Property change stuff
import java.awt.*;
import java.awt.event.*;

class CustomDialog extends JDialog {
    private String typedText = null;

    private String magicWord;
    private JOptionPane optionPane;
```

```java
public String getValidatedText() {
    return typedText;
}

public CustomDialog(Frame aFrame, String aWord, DialogDemo parent) {
    super(aFrame, true);
    final DialogDemo dd = parent;

    magicWord = aWord.toUpperCase();
    setTitle("Quiz");

    final String msgString1 = "What was Dr. SEUSS's real last name?";
    final String msgString2 = "(The answer is \"" + magicWord
                                + "\".)";
    final JTextField textField = new JTextField(10);
    Object[] array = {msgString1, msgString2, textField};

    final String btnString1 = "Enter";
    final String btnString2 = "Cancel";
    Object[] options = {btnString1, btnString2};

    optionPane = new JOptionPane(array,
                            JOptionPane.QUESTION_MESSAGE,
                            JOptionPane.YES_NO_OPTION,
                            null,
                            options,
                            options[0]);
    setContentPane(optionPane);
    setDefaultCloseOperation(DO_NOTHING_ON_CLOSE);
    addWindowListener(new WindowAdapter() {
            public void windowClosing(WindowEvent we) {
            /*
             * Instead of directly closing the window,
             * we're going to change the JOptionPane's
             * value property.
             */
                optionPane.setValue(new Integer(
                                JOptionPane.CLOSED_OPTION));
        }
    });

    textField.addActionListener(new ActionListener() {
        public void actionPerformed(ActionEvent e) {
            optionPane.setValue(btnString1);
        }
    });

    optionPane.addPropertyChangeListener(new PropertyChangeListener() {
        public void propertyChange(PropertyChangeEvent e) {
            String prop = e.getPropertyName();

            if (isVisible()
             && (e.getSource() == optionPane)
             && (prop.equals(JOptionPane.VALUE_PROPERTY) ||
               prop.equals(JOptionPane.INPUT_VALUE_PROPERTY))) {
                Object value = optionPane.getValue();

                if (value == JOptionPane.UNINITIALIZED_VALUE) {
                    //ignore reset
                    return;
                }

                // Reset the JOptionPane's value.
                // If you don't do this, then if the user
                // presses the same button next time, no
                // property change event will be fired.
```

```
                          optionPane.setValue(
                                  JOptionPane.UNINITIALIZED_VALUE);

                          if (value.equals(btnString1)) {
                                  typedText = textField.getText();
                              String ucText = typedText.toUpperCase();
                              if (ucText.equals(magicWord)) {
                                  // we're done; dismiss the dialog
                                  setVisible(false);
                              } else {
                                  // text was invalid
                                  textField.selectAll();
                                  JOptionPane.showMessageDialog(
                                          CustomDialog.this,
                                          "Sorry, \"" + typedText + "\" "
                                          + "isn't a valid response.\n"
                                          + "Please enter "
                                          + magicWord + ".",
                                          "Try again",
                                          JOptionPane.ERROR_MESSAGE);
                                  typedText = null;
                              }
                          } else { // user closed dialog or clicked cancel
                              dd.setLabel("It's OK.  "
                                      + "We won't force you to type "
                                      + magicWord + ".");
                              typedText = null;
                              setVisible(false);
                          }
                      }
                  }
              });
          }
      }
```

EXAMPLE: *DecimalField.java*

Where Explained:

Creating a Validated Text Field (page 299)

Main Source File: `TextFieldDemo.java` *(page 751)*

SOURCE CODE: *http://java.sun.com/docs/books/tutorial/uiswing/components/example-swing/DecimalField.java*

```
import javax.swing.*;
import javax.swing.text.*;

import java.awt.Toolkit;
import java.text.*;

public class DecimalField extends JTextField {
    private NumberFormat format;

    public DecimalField(double value, int columns, NumberFormat f) {
        super(columns);
        setDocument(new FormattedDocument(f));
        format = f;
        setValue(value);
    }

    public double getValue() {
        double retVal = 0.0;
```

```
        try {
            retVal = format.parse(getText()).doubleValue();
        } catch (ParseException e) {
            // This should never happen because insertString allows
            // only properly formatted data to get in the field.
            Toolkit.getDefaultToolkit().beep();
            System.err.println("getValue: could not parse: " + getText());
        }
        return retVal;
    }

    public void setValue(double value) {
        setText(format.format(value));
    }
}
```

EXAMPLE: *DialogDemo.java*

SOURCE CODE: *http://java.sun.com/docs/books/tutorial/uiswing/components/example-swing/DialogDemo.java*

Where Explained:
How to Make Dialogs (page 87)

```
import javax.swing.JOptionPane;
import javax.swing.JDialog;
import javax.swing.JButton;
import javax.swing.JRadioButton;
import javax.swing.ButtonGroup;
import javax.swing.JLabel;
import javax.swing.ImageIcon;
import javax.swing.BoxLayout;
import javax.swing.BorderFactory;
import javax.swing.border.Border;
import javax.swing.JTabbedPane;
import javax.swing.JPanel;
import javax.swing.JFrame;
import java.beans.*; //Property change stuff
import java.awt.*;
import java.awt.event.*;

public class DialogDemo extends JPanel {
    JLabel label;
    ImageIcon icon = new ImageIcon("images/middle.gif");
    JFrame frame;
    String simpleDialogDesc = "Some simple message dialogs";
    String iconDesc = "A JOptionPane has its choice of icons";
    String moreDialogDesc = "Some more dialogs";
    CustomDialog customDialog;

    public DialogDemo(JFrame frame) {
        this.frame = frame;
        customDialog = new CustomDialog(frame, "geisel", this);
        customDialog.pack();

        //create the components
        JPanel frequentPanel = createSimpleDialogBox();
        JPanel featurePanel = createFeatureDialogBox();
        JPanel iconPanel = createIconDialogBox();
        label = new JLabel("Click the \"Show it!\" button"
                            + " to bring up the selected dialog.",
                            JLabel.CENTER);

        //lay them out
        Border padding = BorderFactory.createEmptyBorder(20,20,5,20);
        frequentPanel.setBorder(padding);
```

```
            featurePanel.setBorder(padding);
            iconPanel.setBorder(padding);

            JTabbedPane tabbedPane = new JTabbedPane();
            tabbedPane.addTab("Simple Modal Dialogs", null,
                              frequentPanel,
                              simpleDialogDesc); //tooltip text
            tabbedPane.addTab("More Dialogs", null,
                              featurePanel,
                              moreDialogDesc); //tooltip text
            tabbedPane.addTab("Dialog Icons", null,
                              iconPanel,
                              iconDesc); //tooltip text

            setLayout(new BorderLayout());
            add(tabbedPane, BorderLayout.CENTER);
            add(label, BorderLayout.SOUTH);
            label.setBorder(BorderFactory.createEmptyBorder(10,10,10,10));
        }

        void setLabel(String newText) {
            label.setText(newText);
        }

        private JPanel createSimpleDialogBox() {
            final int numButtons = 4;
            JRadioButton[] radioButtons = new JRadioButton[numButtons];
            final ButtonGroup group = new ButtonGroup();

            JButton showItButton = null;

            final String defaultMessageCommand = "default";
            final String yesNoCommand = "yesno";
            final String yeahNahCommand = "yeahnah";
            final String yncCommand = "ync";

            radioButtons[0] = new JRadioButton("OK (in the L&F's words)");
            radioButtons[0].setActionCommand(defaultMessageCommand);

            radioButtons[1] = new JRadioButton("Yes/No (in the L&F's words)");
            radioButtons[1].setActionCommand(yesNoCommand);

            radioButtons[2] = new JRadioButton("Yes/No "
                           + "(in the programmer's words)");
            radioButtons[2].setActionCommand(yeahNahCommand);

            radioButtons[3] = new JRadioButton("Yes/No/Cancel "
                              + "(in the programmer's words)");
            radioButtons[3].setActionCommand(yncCommand);

            for (int i = 0; i < numButtons; i++) {
                group.add(radioButtons[i]);
            }
            radioButtons[0].setSelected(true);

            showItButton = new JButton("Show it!");
            showItButton.addActionListener(new ActionListener() {
                public void actionPerformed(ActionEvent e) {
                    String command = group.getSelection().getActionCommand();

                    //ok dialog
                    if (command == defaultMessageCommand) {
                        JOptionPane.showMessageDialog(frame,
                                "Eggs aren't supposed to be green.");
```

```
            //yes/no dialog
            } else if (command == yesNoCommand) {
                int n = JOptionPane.showConfirmDialog(
                        frame, "Would you like green eggs and ham?",
                        "An Inane Question",
                        JOptionPane.YES_NO_OPTION);
                if (n == JOptionPane.YES_OPTION) {
                    setLabel("Ewww!");
                } else if (n == JOptionPane.NO_OPTION) {
                    setLabel("Me neither!");
                } else {
                    setLabel("Come on -- tell me!");
                }

            //yes/no (not in those words)
            } else if (command == yeahNahCommand) {
                Object[] options = {"Yes, please", "No way!"};
                int n = JOptionPane.showOptionDialog(frame,
                                "Would you like green eggs and ham?",
                                "A Silly Question",
                                JOptionPane.YES_NO_OPTION,
                                JOptionPane.QUESTION_MESSAGE,
                                null,
                                options,
                                options[0]);
                if (n == JOptionPane.YES_OPTION) {
                    setLabel("You're kidding!");
                } else if (n == JOptionPane.NO_OPTION) {
                    setLabel("I don't like them, either.");
                } else {
                    setLabel("Come on -- 'fess up!");
                }

            //yes/no/cancel (not in those words)
            } else if (command == yncCommand) {
                Object[] options = {"Yes, please",
                                    "No, thanks",
                                    "No eggs, no ham!"};
                int n = JOptionPane.showOptionDialog(frame,
                                "Would you like some green eggs to go "
                                + "with that ham?",
                                "A Silly Question",
                                JOptionPane.YES_NO_CANCEL_OPTION,
                                JOptionPane.QUESTION_MESSAGE,
                                null,
                                options,
                                options[2]);
                if (n == JOptionPane.YES_OPTION) {
                    setLabel("Here you go: green eggs and ham!");
                } else if (n == JOptionPane.NO_OPTION) {
                    setLabel("OK, just the ham, then.");
                } else if (n == JOptionPane.CANCEL_OPTION) {
                    setLabel("Well, I'm certainly not going to eat them!");
                } else {
                    setLabel("Please tell me what you want!");
                }
            }
            return;
        }
    });

    return createPane(simpleDialogDesc + ":",
                    radioButtons,
                    showItButton);
}
```

```
        //number of buttons *must* be even
        private JPanel create2ColPane(String description,
                                      JRadioButton[] radioButtons,
                                      JButton showButton) {
            JLabel label = new JLabel(description);
            int numPerColumn = radioButtons.length/2;

            JPanel grid = new JPanel();
            grid.setLayout(new GridLayout(0, 2));
            for (int i = 0; i < numPerColumn; i++) {
                grid.add(radioButtons[i]);
                grid.add(radioButtons[i + numPerColumn]);
            }

            JPanel box = new JPanel();
            box.setLayout(new BoxLayout(box, BoxLayout.Y_AXIS));
            box.add(label);
            grid.setAlignmentX(0.0f);
            box.add(grid);

            JPanel pane = new JPanel();
            pane.setLayout(new BorderLayout());
            pane.add(box, BorderLayout.NORTH);
            pane.add(showButton, BorderLayout.SOUTH);

            return pane;
        }

        private JPanel createPane(String description,
                                  JRadioButton[] radioButtons,
                                  JButton showButton) {

            int numChoices = radioButtons.length;
            JPanel box = new JPanel();
            JLabel label = new JLabel(description);

            box.setLayout(new BoxLayout(box, BoxLayout.Y_AXIS));
            box.add(label);

            for (int i = 0; i < numChoices; i++) {
                box.add(radioButtons[i]);
            }

            JPanel pane = new JPanel();
            pane.setLayout(new BorderLayout());
            pane.add(box, BorderLayout.NORTH);
            pane.add(showButton, BorderLayout.SOUTH);
            return pane;
        }

        /*
         * These dialogs are implemented using showMessageDialog, but
         * you can specify the icon (using similar code) for any other
         * kind of dialog, as well.
         */
        private JPanel createIconDialogBox() {
            JButton showItButton = null;

            final int numButtons = 6;
            JRadioButton[] radioButtons = new JRadioButton[numButtons];
            final ButtonGroup group = new ButtonGroup();

            final String plainCommand = "plain";
            final String infoCommand = "info";
            final String questionCommand = "question";
            final String errorCommand = "error";
```

```
final String warningCommand = "warning";
final String customCommand = "custom";

radioButtons[0] = new JRadioButton("Plain (no icon)");
radioButtons[0].setActionCommand(plainCommand);

radioButtons[1] = new JRadioButton("Information icon");
radioButtons[1].setActionCommand(infoCommand);

radioButtons[2] = new JRadioButton("Question icon");
radioButtons[2].setActionCommand(questionCommand);

radioButtons[3] = new JRadioButton("Error icon");
radioButtons[3].setActionCommand(errorCommand);

radioButtons[4] = new JRadioButton("Warning icon");
radioButtons[4].setActionCommand(warningCommand);

radioButtons[5] = new JRadioButton("Custom icon");
radioButtons[5].setActionCommand(customCommand);

for (int i = 0; i < numButtons; i++) {
    group.add(radioButtons[i]);
}
radioButtons[0].setSelected(true);

showItButton = new JButton("Show it!");
showItButton.addActionListener(new ActionListener() {
    public void actionPerformed(ActionEvent e) {
        String command = group.getSelection().getActionCommand();

        //no icon
        if (command == plainCommand) {
            JOptionPane.showMessageDialog(frame,
                        "Eggs aren't supposed to be green.",
                        "A plain message",
                        JOptionPane.PLAIN_MESSAGE);
        //information icon
        } else if (command == infoCommand) {
            JOptionPane.showMessageDialog(frame,
                        "Eggs aren't supposed to be green.",
                        "Inane informational dialog",
                        JOptionPane.INFORMATION_MESSAGE);

    //XXX: It doesn't make sense to make a question with
    //XXX: only one button.
    //XXX: See "Yes/No (but not in those words)" for a better solution.
        //question icon
        } else if (command == questionCommand) {
            JOptionPane.showMessageDialog(frame,
                        "You shouldn't use a message dialog "
                        + "(like this)\n"
                        + "for a question, OK?",
                        "Inane question",
                        JOptionPane.QUESTION_MESSAGE);
        //error icon
        } else if (command == errorCommand) [
            JOptionPane.showMessageDialog(frame,
                        "Eggs aren't supposed to be green.",
                        "Inane error",
                        JOptionPane.ERROR_MESSAGE);
        //warning icon
        } else if (command == warningCommand) {
            JOptionPane.showMessageDialog(frame,
                        "Eggs aren't supposed to be green.",
                        "Inane warning",
                        JOptionPane.WARNING_MESSAGE);
```

```
                    //custom icon
                    } else if (command == customCommand) {
                        JOptionPane.showMessageDialog(frame,
                                            "Eggs aren't supposed to be green.",
                                            "Inane custom dialog",
                                            JOptionPane.INFORMATION_MESSAGE,
                                            icon);
                    }
                }
            });

            return create2ColPane(iconDesc + ":",
                            radioButtons,
                            showItButton);
    }

    private JPanel createFeatureDialogBox() {
        final int numButtons = 4;
        JRadioButton[] radioButtons = new JRadioButton[numButtons];
        final ButtonGroup group = new ButtonGroup();

        JButton showItButton = null;

        final String pickOneCommand = "pickone";
        final String nonAutoCommand = "nonautooption";
        final String customOptionCommand = "customoption";
        final String nonModalCommand = "nonmodal";

        radioButtons[0] = new JRadioButton("Pick one of several choices");
        radioButtons[0].setActionCommand(pickOneCommand);

        radioButtons[1] = new JRadioButton("Non-auto-closing dialog");
        radioButtons[1].setActionCommand(nonAutoCommand);

        radioButtons[2] = new JRadioButton("Input-validating dialog "
                                    + "(with custom message area)");
        radioButtons[2].setActionCommand(customOptionCommand);

        radioButtons[3] = new JRadioButton("Non-modal dialog");
        radioButtons[3].setActionCommand(nonModalCommand);

        for (int i = 0; i < numButtons; i++) {
            group.add(radioButtons[i]);
        }
        radioButtons[0].setSelected(true);

        showItButton = new JButton("Show it!");
        showItButton.addActionListener(new ActionListener() {
            public void actionPerformed(ActionEvent e) {
                String command = group.getSelection().getActionCommand();

                //pick one of many
                //XXX: There are some layout problems with this kind
                //XXX: of dialog, partly since this dialog has a two-
                //XXX: line label, and partly since it uses a combo
                //XXX: box that must remain within the window's bounds.
                if (command == pickOneCommand) {
                    Object[] possibilities = {"ham", "spam", "yam"};
                    String s = (String)JOptionPane.showInputDialog(
                                        frame,
                                        "Complete the sentence:\n"
                                        + "\"Green eggs and...\"",
                                        "Customized Dialog",
                                        JOptionPane.PLAIN_MESSAGE,
                                        icon,
                                        possibilities,
                                        "ham");
```

```
        if (s != null) {
            s = s.trim();
            if (s.length() > 0) {
                setLabel("Green eggs and... " + s + "!");
                return;
            }
        }
        setLabel("Come on, finish the sentence!");

    //non-auto-closing dialog
    } else if (command == nonAutoCommand) {
        final JOptionPane optionPane = new JOptionPane(
                    "The only way to close this dialog is by\n"
                    + "pressing one of the following buttons.\n"
                    + "Do you understand?",
                    JOptionPane.QUESTION_MESSAGE,
                    JOptionPane.YES_NO_OPTION);

        // You can't use pane.createDialog() because that
        // method sets up the JDialog with a property change
        // listener that automatically closes the window
        // when a button is clicked.
        final JDialog dialog = new JDialog(frame,
                                "Click a button",
                                true);
        dialog.setContentPane(optionPane);
        dialog.setDefaultCloseOperation(
            JDialog.DO_NOTHING_ON_CLOSE);
        dialog.addWindowListener(new WindowAdapter() {
            public void windowClosing(WindowEvent we) {
                setLabel("Thwarted user attempt to close window.");
            }
        });
        optionPane.addPropertyChangeListener(
            new PropertyChangeListener() {
                public void propertyChange(PropertyChangeEvent e) {
                    String prop = e.getPropertyName();

                    if (dialog.isVisible()
                     && (e.getSource() == optionPane)
                     && (prop.equals(JOptionPane.VALUE_PROPERTY) ||
                        prop.equals(JOptionPane.INPUT_VALUE_PROPERTY))) {
                        //If you were going to check something
                        //before closing the window, you'd do
                        //it here.
                        dialog.setVisible(false);
                    }
                }
            });
        dialog.pack();
        dialog.setLocationRelativeTo(frame);
        dialog.setVisible(true);

        int value = ((Integer)optionPane.getValue()).intValue();
        if (value == JOptionPane.YES_OPTION) {
            setLabel("Good.");
        } else if (value == JOptionPane.NO_OPTION) {
            setLabel("Try using the window decorations "
                    + "to close the non-auto-closing dialog. "
                    + "You can't!");
        } else {
            setLabel("Something's wrong -- this shouldn't happen.");
        }

    //non-auto-closing dialog with custom message area
    //NOTE: if you don't intend to check the input,
    //then just use showInputDialog instead.
```

```
            } else if (command == customOptionCommand) {
                customDialog.setLocationRelativeTo(frame);
                customDialog.setVisible(true);

                String s = customDialog.getValidatedText();
                if (s != null) {
                    //The text is valid.
                    setLabel("Congratulations!   " + "You entered \""
                            + s + "\".");
                }

            //non-modal dialog
            } else if (command == nonModalCommand) {
                //Create the dialog.
                JDialog dialog = new JDialog(frame, "A Non-Modal Dialog");

                //Add contents to it.
                JLabel label = new JLabel("This is a non-modal dialog");
                label.setHorizontalAlignment(JLabel.CENTER);
                Container contentPane = dialog.getContentPane();
                contentPane.add(label, BorderLayout.CENTER);

                //Show it.
                dialog.setSize(new Dimension(300, 150));
                dialog.setLocationRelativeTo(frame);
                dialog.setVisible(true);
            }
        }
    });

    return createPane(moreDialogDesc + ":",
                    radioButtons,
                    showItButton);
}

public static void main(String[] args) {
    JFrame frame = new JFrame("DialogDemo");

    Container contentPane = frame.getContentPane();
    contentPane.setLayout(new GridLayout(1,1));
    contentPane.add(new DialogDemo(frame));

    frame.addWindowListener(new WindowAdapter() {
        public void windowClosing(WindowEvent e) {
            System.exit(0);
        }
    });

    frame.pack();
    frame.setVisible(true);
}
}
```

EXAMPLE: *DynamicTree.java*

Where Explained:

Dynamically Changing a Tree (page 329)

Associated File(s): <u>DynamicTreeDemo.java</u> *(page 648)*

SOURCE CODE: *http://java.sun.com/docs/books/tutorial/uiswing/components/example-swing/ DynamicTree.java*

```
/*
 * This code is based on an example provided by Richard Stanford, a tutorial reader.
 */
```

```
import java.awt.*;
import javax.swing.*;
import javax.swing.tree.*;
import javax.swing.event.*;

public class DynamicTree extends JPanel {
    protected DefaultMutableTreeNode rootNode;
    protected DefaultTreeModel treeModel;
    protected JTree tree;
    private Toolkit toolkit = Toolkit.getDefaultToolkit();

    public DynamicTree() {
        rootNode = new DefaultMutableTreeNode("Root Node");
        treeModel = new DefaultTreeModel(rootNode);
        treeModel.addTreeModelListener(new MyTreeModelListener());

        tree = new JTree(treeModel);
        tree.setEditable(true);
        tree.getSelectionModel().setSelectionMode
                (TreeSelectionModel.SINGLE_TREE_SELECTION);
        tree.setShowsRootHandles(true);

        JScrollPane scrollPane = new JScrollPane(tree);
        setLayout(new GridLayout(1,0));
        add(scrollPane);
    }

    /** Remove all nodes except the root node. */
    public void clear() {
        rootNode.removeAllChildren();
        treeModel.reload();
    }

    /** Remove the currently selected node. */
    public void removeCurrentNode() {
        TreePath currentSelection = tree.getSelectionPath();
        if (currentSelection != null) {
            DefaultMutableTreeNode currentNode = (DefaultMutableTreeNode)
                        (currentSelection.getLastPathComponent());
            MutableTreeNode parent = (MutableTreeNode)(currentNode.getParent());
            if (parent != null) {
                treeModel.removeNodeFromParent(currentNode);
                return;
            }
        }

        // Either there was no selection, or the root was selected.
        toolkit.beep();
    }

    /** Add child to the currently selected node. */
    public DefaultMutableTreeNode addObject(Object child) {
        DefaultMutableTreeNode parentNode = null;
        TreePath parentPath = tree.getSelectionPath();

        if (parentPath == null) {
            parentNode = rootNode;
        } else {
            parentNode = (DefaultMutableTreeNode)
                        (parentPath.getLastPathComponent());
        }

        return addObject(parentNode, child, true);
    }

    public DefaultMutableTreeNode addObject(DefaultMutableTreeNode parent,
                                            Object child) {
        return addObject(parent, child, false);
    }
```

```java
    public DefaultMutableTreeNode addObject(DefaultMutableTreeNode parent,
                                            Object child,
                                            boolean shouldBeVisible) {
        DefaultMutableTreeNode childNode =
                new DefaultMutableTreeNode(child);

        if (parent == null) {
            parent = rootNode;
        }

        treeModel.insertNodeInto(childNode, parent,
                                 parent.getChildCount());

        // Make sure the user can see the lovely new node.
        if (shouldBeVisible) {
            tree.scrollPathToVisible(new TreePath(childNode.getPath()));
        }
        return childNode;
    }

    class MyTreeModelListener implements TreeModelListener {
        public void treeNodesChanged(TreeModelEvent e) {
            DefaultMutableTreeNode node;
            node = (DefaultMutableTreeNode)
                    (e.getTreePath().getLastPathComponent());

            /*
             * If the event lists children, then the changed
             * node is the child of the node we've already
             * gotten.  Otherwise, the changed node and the
             * specified node are the same.
             */
            try {
                int index = e.getChildIndices()[0];
                node = (DefaultMutableTreeNode)
                        (node.getChildAt(index));
            } catch (NullPointerException exc) {}

            System.out.println("The user has finished editing the node.");
            System.out.println("New value: " + node.getUserObject());
        }
        public void treeNodesInserted(TreeModelEvent e) {
        }
        public void treeNodesRemoved(TreeModelEvent e) {
        }
        public void treeStructureChanged(TreeModelEvent e) {
        }
    }
}
```

EXAMPLE: *DynamicTreeDemo.java*

Where Explained:

Dynamically Changing a Tree (page 329)

Associated File(s): DynamicTree.java *(page 646)*

SOURCE CODE: *http://java.sun.com/docs/books/tutorial/uiswing/components/example-swing/ DynamicTreeDemo.java*

```java
/*
 * This code is based on an example provided by Richard Stanford, a tutorial reader.
 */

import java.awt.*;
import java.awt.event.*;
```

```java
import javax.swing.*;
import javax.swing.tree.*;

public class DynamicTreeDemo extends JPanel {
    private int newNodeSuffix = 1;

    public DynamicTreeDemo(JFrame frame) {
        //create the components
        final DynamicTree treePanel = new DynamicTree();
        populateTree(treePanel);

        JButton addButton = new JButton("Add");
        addButton.addActionListener(new ActionListener() {
            public void actionPerformed(ActionEvent e) {
                treePanel.addObject("New Node " + newNodeSuffix++);
            }
        });

        JButton removeButton = new JButton("Remove");
        removeButton.addActionListener(new ActionListener() {
            public void actionPerformed(ActionEvent e) {
                treePanel.removeCurrentNode();
            }
        });

        JButton clearButton = new JButton("Clear");
        clearButton.addActionListener(new ActionListener() {
            public void actionPerformed(ActionEvent e) {
                treePanel.clear();
            }
        });

        //Lay everything out.
        setLayout(new BorderLayout());
        treePanel.setPreferredSize(new Dimension(300, 150));
        add(treePanel, BorderLayout.CENTER);

        JPanel panel = new JPanel();
        panel.setLayout(new GridLayout(0,1));
        panel.add(addButton);
        panel.add(removeButton);
        panel.add(clearButton);
        add(panel, BorderLayout.EAST);
    }

    public void populateTree(DynamicTree treePanel) {
        String p1Name = new String("Parent 1");
        String p2Name = new String("Parent 2");
        String c1Name = new String("Child 1");
        String c2Name = new String("Child 2");

        DefaultMutableTreeNode p1, p2;

        p1 = treePanel.addObject(null, p1Name);
        p2 = treePanel.addObject(null, p2Name);

        treePanel.addObject(p1, c1Name);
        treePanel.addObject(p1, c2Name);

        treePanel.addObject(p2, c1Name);
        treePanel.addObject(p2, c2Name);
    }

    public static void main(String[] args) {
        JFrame frame = new JFrame("DynamicTreeDemo");
```

```
                    Container contentPane = frame.getContentPane();
                    contentPane.setLayout(new GridLayout(1,1));
                    contentPane.add(new DynamicTreeDemo(frame));

                    frame.addWindowListener(new WindowAdapter() {
                        public void windowClosing(WindowEvent e) {
                            System.exit(0);
                        }
                    });

                    frame.pack();
                    frame.setVisible(true);
                }
            }
```

EXAMPLE: *FileChooserDemo.java*

**Where
Explained:**

*How to Use
File Choosers*
(page 200)

SOURCE CODE: *http://java.sun.com/docs/books/tutorial/uiswing/components/example-
swing/FileChooserDemo.java*

```
import java.io.*;
import java.awt.*;
import java.awt.event.*;
import javax.swing.*;
import javax.swing.filechooser.*;

public class FileChooserDemo extends JFrame {
    static private final String newline = "\n";

    public FileChooserDemo() {
        super("FileChooserDemo");

        //Create the log first, because the action listeners
        //need to refer to it.
        final JTextArea log = new JTextArea(5,20);
        log.setMargin(new Insets(5,5,5,5));
        log.setEditable(false);
        JScrollPane logScrollPane = new JScrollPane(log);

        //Create a file chooser
        final JFileChooser fc = new JFileChooser();

        //Create the open button
        ImageIcon openIcon = new ImageIcon("images/open.gif");
        JButton openButton = new JButton("Open a File...", openIcon);
        openButton.addActionListener(new ActionListener() {
            public void actionPerformed(ActionEvent e) {
                int returnVal = fc.showOpenDialog(FileChooserDemo.this);

                if (returnVal == JFileChooser.APPROVE_OPTION) {
                    File file = fc.getSelectedFile();
                    //this is where a real application would open the file.
                    log.append("Opening: " + file.getName() + "." + newline);
                } else {
                    log.append("Open command cancelled by user." + newline);
                }
            }
        });

        //Create the save button
        ImageIcon saveIcon = new ImageIcon("images/save.gif");
        JButton saveButton = new JButton("Save a File...", saveIcon);
        saveButton.addActionListener(new ActionListener() {
```

```java
        public void actionPerformed(ActionEvent e) {
            int returnVal = fc.showSaveDialog(FileChooserDemo.this);

            if (returnVal == JFileChooser.APPROVE_OPTION) {
                File file = fc.getSelectedFile();
                //this is where a real application would save the file.
                log.append("Saving: " + file.getName() + "." + newline);
            } else {
                log.append("Save command cancelled by user." + newline);
            }
        }
    });

    //For layout purposes, put the buttons in a separate panel
    JPanel buttonPanel = new JPanel();
    buttonPanel.add(openButton);
    buttonPanel.add(saveButton);

    //Explicitly set the focus sequence.
    openButton.setNextFocusableComponent(saveButton);
    saveButton.setNextFocusableComponent(openButton);

    //Add the buttons and the log to the frame
    Container contentPane = getContentPane();
    contentPane.add(buttonPanel, BorderLayout.NORTH);
    contentPane.add(logScrollPane, BorderLayout.CENTER);
}

public static void main(String[] args) {
    JFrame frame = new FileChooserDemo();

    frame.addWindowListener(new WindowAdapter() {
        public void windowClosing(WindowEvent e) {
            System.exit(0);
        }
    });

    frame.pack();
    frame.setVisible(true);
}
}
```

EXAMPLE: FileChooserDemo2.java

Associated File(s): ImageFilter.java *(page 667)*, ImageFileView.java *(page 666)*, ImagePreview.java *(page 667)*, Utils.java *(page 777)*

SOURCE CODE: *http://java.sun.com/docs/books/tutorial/uiswing/components/example-swing/FileChooserDemo2.java*

Where Explained:
Another Example: FileChooser-Demo2
(page 203)

```java
import java.io.*;
import java.awt.*;
import java.awt.event.*;
import javax.swing.*;
import javax.swing.filechooser.*;

public class FileChooserDemo2 extends JFrame {
    static private String newline = "\n";

    public FileChooserDemo2() {
        super("FileChooserDemo2");
```

```
            //Create the log first, because the action listener
            //needs to refer to it.
            final JTextArea log = new JTextArea(5,20);
            log.setMargin(new Insets(5,5,5,5));
            log.setEditable(false);
            JScrollPane logScrollPane = new JScrollPane(log);

            JButton sendButton = new JButton("Attach...");
            sendButton.addActionListener(new ActionListener() {
                public void actionPerformed(ActionEvent e) {
                    JFileChooser fc = new JFileChooser();
                    fc.addChoosableFileFilter(new ImageFilter());
                    fc.setFileView(new ImageFileView());
                    fc.setAccessory(new ImagePreview(fc));

                    int returnVal = fc.showDialog(FileChooserDemo2.this,
                                                  "Attach");

                    if (returnVal == JFileChooser.APPROVE_OPTION) {
                        File file = fc.getSelectedFile();
                        log.append("Attaching file: " + file.getName()
                                   + "." + newline);
                    } else {
                        log.append("Attachment cancelled by user." + newline);
                    }
                }
            });

            Container contentPane = getContentPane();
            contentPane.add(sendButton, BorderLayout.NORTH);
            contentPane.add(logScrollPane, BorderLayout.CENTER);
        }

        public static void main(String[] args) {
            JFrame frame = new FileChooserDemo2();
            frame.addWindowListener(new WindowAdapter() {
                public void windowClosing(WindowEvent e) {
                    System.exit(0);
                }
            });

            frame.pack();
            frame.setVisible(true);
        }
    }
```

EXAMPLE: *FormattedDocument.java*

Where Explained:

Creating a Validated Text Field (page 299)

Main Source File: `TextFieldDemo.java` *(page 751)*

SOURCE CODE: *http://java.sun.com/docs/books/tutorial/uiswing/components/example-swing/ FormattedDocument.java*

```
import javax.swing.*;
import javax.swing.text.*;

import java.awt.Toolkit;
import java.text.*;
import java.util.Locale;

public class FormattedDocument extends PlainDocument {
    private Format format;
```

```
public FormattedDocument(Format f) {
    format = f;
}

public Format getFormat() {
    return format;
}

public void insertString(int offs, String str, AttributeSet a)
    throws BadLocationException {

    String currentText = getText(0, getLength());
    String beforeOffset = currentText.substring(0, offs);
    String afterOffset = currentText.substring(offs, currentText.length());
    String proposedResult = beforeOffset + str + afterOffset;

    try {
        format.parseObject(proposedResult);
        super.insertString(offs, str, a);
    } catch (ParseException e) {
        Toolkit.getDefaultToolkit().beep();
        System.err.println("insertString: could not parse: "
                            + proposedResult);
    }
}

public void remove(int offs, int len) throws BadLocationException {
    String currentText = getText(0, getLength());
    String beforeOffset = currentText.substring(0, offs);
    String afterOffset = currentText.substring(len + offs,
                                        currentText.length());
    String proposedResult = beforeOffset + afterOffset;

    try {
        if (proposedResult.length() != 0)
            format.parseObject(proposedResult);
        super.remove(offs, len);
    } catch (ParseException e) {
        Toolkit.getDefaultToolkit().beep();
        System.err.println("remove: could not parse: " + proposedResult);
    }
}
}
```

EXAMPLE: *FrameDemo.java*

SOURCE CODE: *http://java.sun.com/docs/books/tutorial/uiswing/components/example-swing/FrameDemo.java*

```
import java.awt.*;
import java.awt.event.*;
import javax.swing.*;

public class FrameDemo {
    public static void main(String s[]) {
        JFrame frame = new JFrame("FrameDemo");

        frame.addWindowListener(new WindowAdapter() {
            public void windowClosing(WindowEvent e) {
                System.exit(0);
            }
        });
```

Where Explained:
How to Make Frames
(page 82)

```
                    JLabel emptyLabel = new JLabel("");
                    emptyLabel.setPreferredSize(new Dimension(175, 100));
                    frame.getContentPane().add(emptyLabel, BorderLayout.CENTER);

                    frame.pack();
                    frame.setVisible(true);
                }
            }
```

EXAMPLE: *Framework.java*

Where Explained:
How to Make Frames
(page 82)

SOURCE CODE: *http://java.sun.com/docs/books/tutorial/uiswing/components/example-swing/ Framework.java*

```java
import javax.swing.JFrame;
import javax.swing.JMenuBar;
import javax.swing.JMenu;
import javax.swing.JMenuItem;

import javax.swing.JOptionPane;

import java.awt.*;
import java.awt.event.*;

public class Framework extends WindowAdapter {
    public int numWindows = 0;
    private Point lastLocation = null;
    private int maxX = 500;
    private int maxY = 500;

    public Framework() {
        Dimension screenSize = Toolkit.getDefaultToolkit().getScreenSize();
        maxX = screenSize.width - 50;
        maxY = screenSize.height - 50;
        makeNewWindow();
    }

    public void makeNewWindow() {
        JFrame frame = new MyFrame(this);
        numWindows++;
        System.out.println("Number of windows: " + numWindows);

        if (lastLocation != null) {
            //Move the window over and down 40 pixels.
            lastLocation.translate(40, 40);
            if ((lastLocation.x > maxX) || (lastLocation.y > maxY)) {
                lastLocation.setLocation(0, 0);
            }
            frame.setLocation(lastLocation);
        } else {
            lastLocation = frame.getLocation();
        }

        System.out.println("Frame location: " + lastLocation);
        frame.setVisible(true);
    }

    //This method must be evoked from the event-dispatching thread.
    public void quit(JFrame frame) {
        if (quitConfirmed(frame)) {
            System.out.println("Quitting.");
            System.exit(0);
        }
        System.out.println("Quit operation not confirmed; staying alive.");
    }
```

```
        private boolean quitConfirmed(JFrame frame) {
            String s1 = "Quit";
            String s2 = "Cancel";
            Object[] options = {s1, s2};
            int n = JOptionPane.showOptionDialog(frame,
                    "Windows are still open.\nDo you really want to quit?",
                    "Quit Confirmation",
                    JOptionPane.YES_NO_OPTION,
                    JOptionPane.QUESTION_MESSAGE,
                    null,
                    options,
                    s1);
            if (n == JOptionPane.YES_OPTION) {
                return true;
            } else {
                return false;
            }
        }

        public void windowClosed(WindowEvent e) {
            numWindows--;
            System.out.println("Number of windows = " + numWindows);
            if (numWindows <= 0) {
                System.out.println("All windows gone.  Bye bye!");
                System.exit(0);
            }
        }

        public static void main(String[] args) {
            Framework framework = new Framework();
        }
    }

class MyFrame extends JFrame {
    protected Dimension defaultSize = new Dimension(200, 200);
    protected Framework framework = null;

    public MyFrame(Framework controller) {
        super("New Frame");
        framework = controller;
        setDefaultCloseOperation(DISPOSE_ON_CLOSE);
        addWindowListener(framework);

        JMenu menu = new JMenu("Window");
        menu.setMnemonic(KeyEvent.VK_W);
        JMenuItem item = null;
        //close
        item = new JMenuItem("Close");
        item.setMnemonic(KeyEvent.VK_C);
        item.addActionListener(new ActionListener() {
            public void actionPerformed(ActionEvent e) {
                System.out.println("Close window");
                MyFrame.this.setVisible(false);
                MyFrame.this.dispose();
            }
        });
        menu.add(item);

        //new
        item = new JMenuItem("New");
        item.setMnemonic(KeyEvent.VK_N);
        item.addActionListener(new ActionListener() {
            public void actionPerformed(ActionEvent e) {
                System.out.println("New window");
                framework.makeNewWindow();
            }
        });
        menu.add(item);
```

```
        //quit
        item = new JMenuItem("Quit");
        item.setMnemonic(KeyEvent.VK_Q);
        item.addActionListener(new ActionListener() {
            public void actionPerformed(ActionEvent e) {
                System.out.println("Quit request");
                framework.quit(MyFrame.this);
            }
        });
        menu.add(item);

        JMenuBar menuBar = new JMenuBar();
        menuBar.add(menu);
        setJMenuBar(menuBar);

        setSize(defaultSize);
    }
}
```

EXAMPLE: *GenealogyExample.java*

Where Explained:

Creating a Data Model (page 331)

Main Source File: GenealogyModel.java *(page 658)*

SOURCE CODE: *http://java.sun.com/docs/books/tutorial/uiswing/components/example-swing/GenealogyExample.java*

```
/*
 * An example provided by tutorial reader Olivier Berlanger.
 */
import javax.swing.*;
import java.awt.*;
import java.awt.event.*;

public class GenealogyExample extends JFrame {
    GenealogyTree tree;

    public GenealogyExample() {
        super("Genealogy tree demo");
        // add window listener
        addWindowListener(new WindowAdapter() {
                public void windowClosing(WindowEvent e) {
                    System.exit(0);
                }
            });
        // construct the panel with the toggle buttons
        JRadioButton showDescendant =
                new JRadioButton("Show descendants", true);
        final JRadioButton showAncestor =
                new JRadioButton("Show ancestors");
        ButtonGroup bGroup = new ButtonGroup();
        bGroup.add(showDescendant);
        bGroup.add(showAncestor);
        ActionListener al = new ActionListener() {
            public void actionPerformed(ActionEvent ae) {
                if (ae.getSource() == showAncestor) {
                    tree.showAncestor(true);
                }
                else {
                    tree.showAncestor(false);
                }
            }
        };
```

```
        showDescendant.addActionListener(al);
        showAncestor.addActionListener(al);
        JPanel buttonPanel = new JPanel();
        buttonPanel.add(showDescendant);
        buttonPanel.add(showAncestor);

        // construct the tree
        tree = new GenealogyTree(getGenealogyGraph());
        JScrollPane scrollPane = new JScrollPane(tree);
        scrollPane.setPreferredSize(new Dimension(200, 200));

        // construct the content pane
        JPanel contentPane = new JPanel(new BorderLayout());
        contentPane.add(buttonPanel, BorderLayout.NORTH);
        contentPane.add(scrollPane, BorderLayout.CENTER);
        setContentPane(contentPane);
    }

    /**
     * Constructs the genealogy graph used by the model.
     */
    public Person getGenealogyGraph() {
        //the greatgrandparent generation
        Person a1 = new Person("Jack (great-granddaddy)");
        Person a2 = new Person("Jean (great-granny)");
        Person a3 = new Person("Albert (great-granddaddy)");
        Person a4 = new Person("Rae (great-granny)");
        Person a5 = new Person("Paul (great-granddaddy)");
        Person a6 = new Person("Josie (great-granny)");

        //the grandparent generation
        Person b1 = new Person("Peter (grandpa)");
        Person b2 = new Person("Zoe (grandma)");
        Person b3 = new Person("Simon (grandpa)");
        Person b4 = new Person("James (grandpa)");
        Person b5 = new Person("Bertha (grandma)");
        Person b6 = new Person("Veronica (grandma)");
        Person b7 = new Person("Anne (grandma)");
        Person b8 = new Person("Renee (grandma)");
        Person b9 = new Person("Joseph (grandpa)");

        //the parent generation
        Person c1 = new Person("Isabelle (mom)");
        Person c2 = new Person("Frank (dad)");
        Person c3 = new Person("Louis (dad)");
        Person c4 = new Person("Laurence (dad)");
        Person c5 = new Person("Valerie (mom)");
        Person c6 = new Person("Marie (mom)");
        Person c7 = new Person("Helen (mom)");
        Person c8 = new Person("Mark (dad)");
        Person c9 = new Person("Oliver (dad)");

        //the youngest generation
        Person d1 = new Person("Clement (boy)");
        Person d2 = new Person("Colin (boy)");

        Person.linkFamily(a1,a2,new Person[] {b1,b2,b3,b4});
        Person.linkFamily(a3,a4,new Person[] {b5,b6,b7});
        Person.linkFamily(a5,a6,new Person[] {b8,b9});
        Person.linkFamily(b3,b6,new Person[] {c1,c2,c3});
        Person.linkFamily(b4,b5,new Person[] {c4,c5,c6});
        Person.linkFamily(b8,b7,new Person[] {c7,c8,c9});
        Person.linkFamily(c4,c7,new Person[] {d1,d2});

        return a1;
    }
```

```
public static void main(String[] args) {
    // create a frame
    JFrame mainFrame = new GenealogyExample();
    mainFrame.pack();
    mainFrame.setVisible(true);
}
}
```

EXAMPLE: GenealogyModel.java

Associated File(s): GenealogyTree.java *(page 660)*, Person.java *(page 691)*, GenealogyExample.java *(page 656)*

Where Explained:
Creating a Data Model
(page 331)

```
import javax.swing.event.*;
import javax.swing.tree.*;
import java.util.Vector;

public class GenealogyModel implements TreeModel {
    private boolean showAncestors;
    private Vector treeModelListeners = new Vector();
    private Person rootPerson;

    public GenealogyModel(Person root) {
        showAncestors = false;
        rootPerson = root;
    }

    /**
     * Used to toggle between show ancestors/show descendant and
     * to change the root of the tree.
     */
    public void showAncestor(boolean b, Object newRoot) {
        showAncestors = b;
        Person oldRoot = rootPerson;
        if (newRoot != null) {
            rootPerson = (Person)newRoot;
        }
        fireTreeStructureChanged(oldRoot);
    }


//////////////// Fire events //////////////////////////////////////////////

    /**
     * The only event raised by this model is TreeStructureChanged with the
     * root as path, i.e. the whole tree has changed.
     */
    protected void fireTreeStructureChanged(Person oldRoot) {
        int len = treeModelListeners.size();
        TreeModelEvent e = new TreeModelEvent(this, new Object[] {oldRoot});
        for (int i = 0; i < len; i++) {
            ((TreeModelListener)treeModelListeners.elementAt(i)).
                    treeStructureChanged(e);
        }
    }

//////////////// TreeModel interface implementation ///////////////////////
```

```java
/**
 * Adds a listener for the TreeModelEvent posted after the tree changes.
 */
public void addTreeModelListener(TreeModelListener l) {
    treeModelListeners.addElement(l);
}

/**
 * Returns the child of parent at index index in the parent's child array.
 */
public Object getChild(Object parent, int index) {
    Person p = (Person)parent;
    if (showAncestors) {
        if ((index > 0) && (p.getFather() != null)) {
            return p.getMother();
        }
        return p.getFather();
    }
    return p.getChildAt(index);
}

/**
 * Returns the number of children of parent.
 */
public int getChildCount(Object parent) {
    Person p = (Person)parent;
    if (showAncestors) {
        int count = 0;
        if (p.getFather() != null) {
            count++;
        }
        if (p.getMother() != null) {
            count++;
        }
        return count;
    }
    return p.getChildCount();
}

/**
 * Returns the index of child in parent.
 */
public int getIndexOfChild(Object parent, Object child) {
    Person p = (Person)parent;
    if (showAncestors) {
        int count = 0;
        Person father = p.getFather();
        if (father != null) {
            count++;
            if (father == child) {
                return 0;
            }
        }
        if (p.getMother() != child) {
            return count;
        }
        return -1;
    }
    return p.getIndexOfChild((Person)child);
}

/**
 * Returns the root of the tree.
 */
public Object getRoot() {
    return rootPerson;
}
```

```
/**
 * Returns true if node is a leaf.
 */
public boolean isLeaf(Object node) {
    Person p = (Person)node;
    if (showAncestors) {
        return ((p.getFather() == null)
            && (p.getMother() == null));
    }
    return p.getChildCount() == 0;
}

/**
 * Removes a listener previously added with addTreeModelListener().
 */
public void removeTreeModelListener(TreeModelListener l) {
    treeModelListeners.removeElement(l);
}

/**
 * Messaged when the user has altered the value for the item
 * identified by path to newValue.  Not used by this model.
 */
public void valueForPathChanged(TreePath path, Object newValue) {
    System.out.println("*** valueForPathChanged : "
                        + path + " --> " + newValue);
}
}
```

**Where
Explained:**

*Creating a
Data Model*
(page 331)

EXAMPLE: *GenealogyTree.java*

Main Source File: <u>GenealogyModel.java</u> *(page 658)*

SOURCE CODE: *http://java.sun.com/docs/books/tutorial/uiswing/components/example-
                swing/GenealogyTree.java*

```
import javax.swing.*;
import javax.swing.tree.*;

public class GenealogyTree extends JTree {
    GenealogyModel model;

    public GenealogyTree(Person graphNode) {
        super(new GenealogyModel(graphNode));
        getSelectionModel().setSelectionMode(
                TreeSelectionModel.SINGLE_TREE_SELECTION);
        DefaultTreeCellRenderer renderer = new DefaultTreeCellRenderer();
        Icon personIcon = null;
        renderer.setLeafIcon(personIcon);
        renderer.setClosedIcon(personIcon);
        renderer.setOpenIcon(personIcon);
        setCellRenderer(renderer);
    }

    /**
     * Get the selected item in the tree, and call showAncestor with this
     * item on the model.
     */
    public void showAncestor(boolean b) {
        Object newRoot = null;
        TreePath path = getSelectionModel().getSelectionPath();
```

```
            if (path != null) {
                newRoot = path.getLastPathComponent();
            }
            ((GenealogyModel)getModel()).showAncestor(b, newRoot);
        }
    }
```

EXAMPLE: *GlassPaneDemo.java*

SOURCE CODE: *http://java.sun.com/docs/books/tutorial/uiswing/components/example-swing/GlassPaneDemo.java*

Where Explained:
The Glass Pane (page 159)

```java
import javax.swing.*;
import javax.swing.event.MouseInputAdapter;
import java.awt.*;
import java.awt.event.*;

public class GlassPaneDemo {
    static private MyGlassPane myGlassPane;

    public static void main(String[] args) {
        JFrame frame = new JFrame("GlassPaneDemo");
        frame.addWindowListener(new WindowAdapter() {
            public void windowClosing(WindowEvent e) {
                System.exit(0);
            }
        });

        JCheckBox changeButton =
                new JCheckBox("Glass pane \"visible\"");
        changeButton.setSelected(false);
        changeButton.addItemListener(new ItemListener() {
            public void itemStateChanged(ItemEvent e) {
                myGlassPane.setVisible(e.getStateChange()
                                == ItemEvent.SELECTED);
            }
        });

        //Set up the content pane, where the "main GUI" lives.
        Container contentPane = frame.getContentPane();
        contentPane.setLayout(new FlowLayout());
        contentPane.add(changeButton);
        contentPane.add(new JButton("Button 1"));
        contentPane.add(new JButton("Button 2"));

        //Set up the menu bar, which appears above the content pane.
        JMenuBar menuBar = new JMenuBar();
        JMenu menu = new JMenu("Menu");
        menu.add(new JMenuItem("Do nothing"));
        menuBar.add(menu);
        frame.setJMenuBar(menuBar);

        //Set up the glass pane, which appears over both menu bar
        //and content pane.
        myGlassPane = new MyGlassPane(changeButton, menuBar,
                                frame.getContentPane());
        frame.setGlassPane(myGlassPane);

        frame.pack();
        frame.setVisible(true);
    }
}
```

```
/**
 * We have to provide our own glass pane so that it can paint.
 */
class MyGlassPane extends JComponent {
    Point point;

    public void paint(Graphics g) {
        if (point != null) {
            g.setColor(Color.red);
            g.fillOval(point.x - 10, point.y - 10, 20, 20);
        }
    }

    public void setPoint(Point p) {
        point = p;
    }

    public MyGlassPane(AbstractButton aButton,
                       JMenuBar menuBar,
                       Container contentPane) {
        CBListener listener = new CBListener(aButton, menuBar,
                                             this, contentPane);
        addMouseListener(listener);
        addMouseMotionListener(listener);
    }
}

/**
 * Listen for all events that our check box is likely to be
 * interested in.  Redispatch them to the check box.
 */
class CBListener extends MouseInputAdapter {
    Toolkit toolkit;
    Component liveButton;
    JMenuBar menuBar;
    MyGlassPane glassPane;
    Container contentPane;
    boolean inDrag = false;

    public CBListener(Component liveButton, JMenuBar menuBar,
                      MyGlassPane glassPane, Container contentPane) {
        toolkit = Toolkit.getDefaultToolkit();
        this.liveButton = liveButton;
        this.menuBar = menuBar;
        this.glassPane = glassPane;
        this.contentPane = contentPane;
    }

    public void mouseMoved(MouseEvent e) {
        redispatchMouseEvent(e, false);
    }

    /*
     * We must forward at least the mouse drags that started
     * with mouse presses over the check box.  Otherwise,
     * when the user presses the check box then drags off,
     * the check box isn't disarmed -- it keeps its dark
     * gray background or whatever its L&F uses to indicate
     * that the button is currently being pressed.
     */
    public void mouseDragged(MouseEvent e) {
        redispatchMouseEvent(e, false);
    }
```

```
public void mouseClicked(MouseEvent e) {
    redispatchMouseEvent(e, false);
}

public void mouseEntered(MouseEvent e) {
    redispatchMouseEvent(e, false);
}

public void mouseExited(MouseEvent e) {
    redispatchMouseEvent(e, false);
}

public void mousePressed(MouseEvent e) {
    redispatchMouseEvent(e, false);
}

public void mouseReleased(MouseEvent e) {
    redispatchMouseEvent(e, true);
    inDrag = false;
}

private void redispatchMouseEvent(MouseEvent e,
                                  boolean repaint) {
    boolean inButton = false;
    boolean inMenuBar = false;
    Point glassPanePoint = e.getPoint();
    Component component = null;
    Container container = contentPane;
    Point containerPoint = SwingUtilities.convertPoint(
                                    glassPane,
                                    glassPanePoint,
                                    contentPane);

    int eventID = e.getID();

    if (containerPoint.y < 0) {
        inMenuBar = true;
        container = menuBar;
        containerPoint = SwingUtilities.convertPoint(
                                    glassPane,
                                    glassPanePoint,
                                    menuBar);
        testForDrag(eventID);
    }

    //XXX: If the event is from a component in a popped-up menu,
    //XXX: then the container should probably be the menu's
    //XXX: JPopupMenu, and containerPoint should be adjusted
    //XXX: accordingly.
    component = SwingUtilities.getDeepestComponentAt(
                                    container,
                                    containerPoint.x,
                                    containerPoint.y);

    if (component == null) {
        return;
    }

    if (component.equals(liveButton)) {
        inButton = true;
        testForDrag(eventID);
    }

    if (inMenuBar || inButton || inDrag) {
        Point componentPoint = SwingUtilities.convertPoint(
                                    glassPane,
                                    glassPanePoint,
                                    component);
```

```
                    component.dispatchEvent(new MouseEvent(component,
                                                           eventID,
                                                           e.getWhen(),
                                                           e.getModifiers(),
                                                           componentPoint.x,
                                                           componentPoint.y,
                                                           e.getClickCount(),
                                                           e.isPopupTrigger()));
                }

                if (repaint) {
                    toolkit.beep();
                    glassPane.setPoint(glassPanePoint);
                    glassPane.repaint();
                }
            }
        }

        private void testForDrag(int eventID) {
            if (eventID == MouseEvent.MOUSE_PRESSED) {
                inDrag = true;
            }
        }
    }
}
```

EXAMPLE: *HtmlDemo.java*

**Where
Explained:**
*Using HTML
on a Label*
(page 213)

SOURCE CODE: *http://java.sun.com/docs/books/tutorial/uiswing/components/example-swing/
                HtmlDemo.java*

```java
import javax.swing.*;
import java.awt.*;
import java.awt.event.*;

public class HtmlDemo extends JPanel {

    JLabel theLabel;
    JTextArea htmlTextArea;

    public HtmlDemo() {
        String initialText = "<html>\n" +
                "Color and font test:\n" +
                "<ul>\n" +
                "<li><font color=red>red</font>\n" +
                "<li><font color=blue>blue</font>\n" +
                "<li><font color=green>green</font>\n" +
                "<li><font size=-2>small</font>\n" +
                "<li><font size=+2>large</font>\n" +
                "<li><i>italic</i>\n" +
                "<li><b>bold</b>\n" +
                "</ul>\n";

        htmlTextArea = new JTextArea(10, 20);
        htmlTextArea.setText(initialText);
        JScrollPane scrollPane = new JScrollPane(htmlTextArea);

        JButton changeTheLabel = new JButton("Change the label");
        changeTheLabel.setMnemonic(KeyEvent.VK_C);
        changeTheLabel.addActionListener(new ActionListener() {
            public void actionPerformed(ActionEvent e) {
                try {
                    theLabel.setText(htmlTextArea.getText());
```

```java
            } catch (Throwable exc) {
                JOptionPane.showMessageDialog(
                        HtmlDemo.this,
                        "The HTML you specified was invalid.");
            }
        }
    });
    changeTheLabel.setAlignmentX(Component.CENTER_ALIGNMENT);

    theLabel = new JLabel(initialText) {
        public Dimension getPreferredSize() {
            return new Dimension(200, 200);
        }
        public Dimension getMinimumSize() {
            return new Dimension(200, 200);
        }
        public Dimension getMaximumSize() {
            return new Dimension(200, 200);
        }
    };
    theLabel.setVerticalAlignment(SwingConstants.CENTER);
    theLabel.setHorizontalAlignment(SwingConstants.CENTER);

    JPanel leftPanel = new JPanel();
    leftPanel.setLayout(new BoxLayout(leftPanel, BoxLayout.Y_AXIS));
    leftPanel.setBorder(BorderFactory.createCompoundBorder(
            BorderFactory.createTitledBorder(
                "Edit the HTML, then click the button"),
            BorderFactory.createEmptyBorder(10,10,10,10)));
    leftPanel.add(scrollPane);
    leftPanel.add(Box.createRigidArea(new Dimension(0,10)));
    leftPanel.add(changeTheLabel);

    JPanel rightPanel = new JPanel();
    rightPanel.setLayout(new BoxLayout(rightPanel, BoxLayout.Y_AXIS));
    rightPanel.setBorder(BorderFactory.createCompoundBorder(
                BorderFactory.createTitledBorder("A label with HTML"),
                BorderFactory.createEmptyBorder(10,10,10,10)));
    rightPanel.add(theLabel);

    setLayout(new BoxLayout(this, BoxLayout.X_AXIS));
    setBorder(BorderFactory.createEmptyBorder(10,10,10,10));
    add(leftPanel);
    add(Box.createRigidArea(new Dimension(10,0)));
    add(rightPanel);
}

public static void main(String args[]) {
    JFrame f = new JFrame("HtmlDemo");

    f.addWindowListener(new WindowAdapter() {
        public void windowClosing(WindowEvent e) {
            System.exit(0);
        }
    });

    f.getContentPane().add(new HtmlDemo());
    f.pack();
    f.setVisible(true);
}
}
```

EXAMPLE: *ImageFileView.java*

Where Explained:

Another Example: FileChooser- Demo2
(page 203)

Main Source File: `FileChooserDemo2.java` *(page 651)*

SOURCE CODE: *http://java.sun.com/docs/books/tutorial/uiswing/components/example-swing/ ImageFileView.java*

```java
import java.io.File;
import javax.swing.*;
import javax.swing.filechooser.*;

public class ImageFileView extends FileView {
    ImageIcon jpgIcon = new ImageIcon("images/jpgIcon.gif");
    ImageIcon gifIcon = new ImageIcon("images/gifIcon.gif");
    ImageIcon tiffIcon = new ImageIcon("images/tiffIcon.gif");

    public String getName(File f) {
        return null; // let the L&F FileView figure this out
    }

    public String getDescription(File f) {
        return null; // let the L&F FileView figure this out
    }

    public Boolean isTraversable(File f) {
        return null; // let the L&F FileView figure this out
    }

    public String getTypeDescription(File f) {
        String extension = Utils.getExtension(f);
        String type = null;

        if (extension != null) {
            if (extension.equals(Utils.jpeg) ||
                extension.equals(Utils.jpg)) {
                type = "JPEG Image";
            } else if (extension.equals(Utils.gif)){
                type = "GIF Image";
            } else if (extension.equals(Utils.tiff) ||
                       extension.equals(Utils.tif)) {
                type = "TIFF Image";
            }
        }
        return type;
    }

    public Icon getIcon(File f) {
        String extension = Utils.getExtension(f);
        Icon icon = null;

        if (extension != null) {
            if (extension.equals(Utils.jpeg) ||
                extension.equals(Utils.jpg)) {
                icon = jpgIcon;
            } else if (extension.equals(Utils.gif)) {
                icon = gifIcon;
            } else if (extension.equals(Utils.tiff) ||
                       extension.equals(Utils.tif)) {
                icon = tiffIcon;
            }
        }
        return icon;
    }
}
```

EXAMPLE: *ImageFilter.java*

Main Source File: `FileChooserDemo2.java` *(page 651)*

SOURCE CODE: *http://java.sun.com/docs/books/tutorial/uiswing/components/example-swing/ImageFilter.java*

```java
import java.io.File;
import javax.swing.*;
import javax.swing.filechooser.*;

public class ImageFilter extends FileFilter {

    // Accept all directories and all gif, jpg, or tiff files.
    public boolean accept(File f) {
        if (f.isDirectory()) {
            return true;
        }

        String extension = Utils.getExtension(f);
        if (extension != null) {
            if (extension.equals(Utils.tiff) ||
                extension.equals(Utils.tif) ||
                extension.equals(Utils.gif) ||
                extension.equals(Utils.jpeg) ||
                extension.equals(Utils.jpg)) {
                    return true;
            } else {
                return false;
            }
        }

        return false;
    }

    // The description of this filter
    public String getDescription() {
        return "Just Images";
    }
}
```

Where Explained: *Another Example: FileChooser-Demo2* (page 203)

EXAMPLE: *ImagePreview.java*

Main Source File: `FileChooserDemo2.java` *(page 651)*

SOURCE CODE: *http://java.sun.com/docs/books/tutorial/uiswing/components/example-swing/ImagePreview.java*

```java
import javax.swing.*;
import java.beans.*;
import java.awt.*;
import java.io.File;

public class ImagePreview extends JComponent
                          implements PropertyChangeListener {
    ImageIcon thumbnail = null;
    File file = null;
```

Where Explained: *Another Example: FileChooser-Demo2* (page 203)

```
    public ImagePreview(JFileChooser fc) {
        setPreferredSize(new Dimension(100, 50));
        fc.addPropertyChangeListener(this);
    }

    public void loadImage() {
        if (file == null) {
            return;
        }

        ImageIcon tmpIcon = new ImageIcon(file.getPath());
        if (tmpIcon.getIconWidth() > 90) {
            thumbnail = new ImageIcon(tmpIcon.getImage().
                            getScaledInstance(90, -1,
                                    Image.SCALE_DEFAULT));
        } else {
            thumbnail = tmpIcon;
        }
    }

    public void propertyChange(PropertyChangeEvent e) {
        String prop = e.getPropertyName();
        if (prop.equals(JFileChooser.SELECTED_FILE_CHANGED_PROPERTY)) {
            file = (File) e.getNewValue();
            if (isShowing()) {
                loadImage();
                repaint();
            }
        }
    }

    public void paintComponent(Graphics g) {
        if (thumbnail == null) {
            loadImage();
        }
        if (thumbnail != null) {
            int x = getWidth()/2 - thumbnail.getIconWidth()/2;
            int y = getHeight()/2 - thumbnail.getIconHeight()/2;

            if (y < 0) {
                y = 0;
            }

            if (x < 5) {
                x = 5;
            }
            thumbnail.paintIcon(this, g, x, y);
        }
    }
}
```

EXAMPLE: *InternalFrameDemo.java*

**Where
Explained:**

*How to Use
Internal
Frames*
(page 143)

Associated File(s): <u>MyInternalFrame.java</u> *(page 689)*

SOURCE CODE: *http://java.sun.com/docs/books/tutorial/uiswing/components/example-
                  swing/InternalFrameDemo.java*

```
import javax.swing.JInternalFrame;
import javax.swing.JDesktopPane;
import javax.swing.JMenu;
import javax.swing.JMenuItem;
```

```java
import javax.swing.JMenuBar;
import javax.swing.JFrame;
import java.awt.event.*;
import java.awt.*;

public class InternalFrameDemo extends JFrame {
    JDesktopPane desktop;

    public InternalFrameDemo() {
        super("InternalFrameDemo");

        //Make the big window be indented 50 pixels from each edge
        //of the screen.
        int inset = 50;
        Dimension screenSize = Toolkit.getDefaultToolkit().getScreenSize();
        setBounds(inset, inset,
                screenSize.width - inset*2,
                screenSize.height-inset*2);

        //Quit this app when the big window closes.
        addWindowListener(new WindowAdapter() {
            public void windowClosing(WindowEvent e) {
                System.exit(0);
            }
        });

        //Set up the GUI.
        desktop = new JDesktopPane(); //a specialized layered pane
        createFrame(); //Create first window
        setContentPane(desktop);
        setJMenuBar(createMenuBar());

        //Make dragging faster:
        desktop.putClientProperty("JDesktopPane.dragMode", "outline");
    }

    protected JMenuBar createMenuBar() {
        JMenuBar menuBar = new JMenuBar();

        JMenu menu = new JMenu("Document");
        menu.setMnemonic(KeyEvent.VK_D);
        JMenuItem menuItem = new JMenuItem("New");
        menuItem.setMnemonic(KeyEvent.VK_N);
        menuItem.addActionListener(new ActionListener() {
            public void actionPerformed(ActionEvent e) {
                createFrame();
            }
        });
        menu.add(menuItem);
        menuBar.add(menu);

        return menuBar;
    }

    protected void createFrame() {
        MyInternalFrame frame = new MyInternalFrame();
        desktop.add(frame);
        try {
            frame.setSelected(true);
        } catch (java.beans.PropertyVetoException e) {}
    }

    public static void main(String[] args) {
        InternalFrameDemo frame = new InternalFrameDemo();
        frame.setVisible(true);
    }
}
```

EXAMPLE: *LabelDemo.java*

Where Explained:
How to Use Labels
(page 212)

SOURCE CODE: *http://java.sun.com/docs/books/tutorial/uiswing/components/example-swing/LabelDemo.java*

```java
import java.awt.GridLayout;
import java.awt.event.WindowAdapter;
import java.awt.event.WindowEvent;
import javax.swing.JLabel;
import javax.swing.JPanel;
import javax.swing.JFrame;
import javax.swing.ImageIcon;

public class LabelDemo extends JPanel {
    JLabel label1, label2, label3;

    public LabelDemo() {
        ImageIcon icon = new ImageIcon("images/middle.gif",
                                "a pretty but meaningless splat");
        setLayout(new GridLayout(3,1));      //3 rows, 1 column

        label1 = new JLabel("Image and Text",
                            icon,
                            JLabel.CENTER);
        //Set the position of the text, relative to the icon:
        label1.setVerticalTextPosition(JLabel.BOTTOM);
        label1.setHorizontalTextPosition(JLabel.CENTER);

        label2 = new JLabel("Text-Only Label");

        label3 = new JLabel(icon);

        //Add labels to the JBufferedPane.
        add(label1);
        add(label2);
        add(label3);
    }

    public static void main(String[] args) {
        /*
         * Create a window.  Use JFrame since this window will include
         * lightweight components.
         */
        JFrame frame = new JFrame("LabelDemo");

        frame.addWindowListener(new WindowAdapter() {
            public void windowClosing(WindowEvent e) {
                System.exit(0);
            }
        });

        frame.setContentPane(new LabelDemo());
        frame.pack();
        frame.setVisible(true);
    }
}
```

EXAMPLE: *LayeredPaneDemo.java*

Where Explained:
How to Use Layered Panes (page 150)

SOURCE CODE: *http://java.sun.com/docs/books/tutorial/uiswing/components/example-swing/LayeredPaneDemo.java*

```java
import javax.swing.*;
import javax.swing.border.*;
import javax.accessibility.*;

import java.awt.*;
import java.awt.event.*;

public class LayeredPaneDemo extends JFrame {
    private String[] layerStrings = { "Yellow (0)", "Magenta (1)",
                                      "Cyan (2)", "Red (3)",
                                      "Green (4)" };
    private Color[] layerColors = { Color.yellow, Color.magenta,
                                    Color.cyan, Color.red,
                                    Color.green };

    private JLayeredPane layeredPane;
    private JLabel dukeLabel;

    public LayeredPaneDemo()    {
        super("LayeredPaneDemo");

        //Create and load the duke icon.
        final ImageIcon icon = new ImageIcon("images/dukeWaveRed.gif");

        //Create and set up the layered pane.
        layeredPane = new JLayeredPane();
        layeredPane.setPreferredSize(new Dimension(300, 310));
        layeredPane.setBorder(BorderFactory.createTitledBorder(
                                "Move the Mouse to Move Duke"));
        layeredPane.addMouseMotionListener(new MouseMotionAdapter() {
            final int XFUDGE = 40;
            final int YFUDGE = 57;
            public void mouseEntered(MouseEvent e) {
                dukeLabel.setLocation(e.getX()-XFUDGE, e.getY()-YFUDGE);
            }
            public void mouseMoved(MouseEvent e) {
                dukeLabel.setLocation(e.getX()-XFUDGE, e.getY()-YFUDGE);
            }
        });

        //This is the origin of the first label added.
        Point origin = new Point(10, 20);

        //This is the offset for computing the origin for the next label.
        int offset = 35;

        //Add several overlapping, colored labels to the layered pane
        //using absolute positioning/sizing.
        for (int i = 0; i < layerStrings.length; i++) {
            JLabel label = createColoredLabel(layerStrings[i],
                                              layerColors[i], origin);
            layeredPane.add(label, new Integer(i));
            origin.x += offset;
            origin.y += offset;
        }

        //Create and add the Duke label to the layered pane.
        dukeLabel = new JLabel(icon);
```

```
                    dukeLabel.setBounds(15, 225,
                                        icon.getIconWidth(),
                                        icon.getIconHeight());
                    layeredPane.add(dukeLabel, new Integer(2), 0);

                    //Add control pane and layered pane to frame.
                    Container contentPane = getContentPane();
                    contentPane.setLayout(new BoxLayout(contentPane,
                                                BoxLayout.Y_AXIS));
                    contentPane.add(Box.createRigidArea(new Dimension(0, 10)));
                    contentPane.add(createControlPanel());
                    contentPane.add(Box.createRigidArea(new Dimension(0, 10)));
                    contentPane.add(layeredPane);
        }

        //Create and set up a colored label.
        private JLabel createColoredLabel(String text,
                                          Color color,
                                          Point origin) {
            JLabel label = new JLabel(text);
            label.setVerticalAlignment(JLabel.TOP);
            label.setHorizontalAlignment(JLabel.CENTER);
            label.setOpaque(true);
            label.setBackground(color);
            label.setForeground(Color.black);
            label.setBorder(BorderFactory.createLineBorder(Color.black));
            label.setBounds(origin.x, origin.y, 140, 140);
            return label;
        }

        //Create the control pane for the top of the frame.
        private JPanel createControlPanel() {
            final JCheckBox onTop = new JCheckBox("Top Position in Layer");
            onTop.setSelected(true);
            onTop.addActionListener(new ActionListener() {
                public void actionPerformed(ActionEvent e) {
                    if (onTop.isSelected())
                        layeredPane.moveToFront(dukeLabel);
                    else
                        layeredPane.moveToBack(dukeLabel);
                }
            });

            final JComboBox layerList = new JComboBox(layerStrings);
            layerList.setSelectedIndex(2);     //Cyan layer
            layerList.addActionListener(new ActionListener () {
                public void actionPerformed(ActionEvent e) {
                    int position = onTop.isSelected() ? 0 : 1;
                    layeredPane.setLayer(dukeLabel,
                                        layerList.getSelectedIndex(),
                                        position);
                }
            });

            JPanel controls = new JPanel();
            controls.add(layerList);
            controls.add(onTop);
            controls.setBorder(BorderFactory.createTitledBorder(
                                "Choose Duke's Layer and Position"));
            return controls;
        }

        public static void main(String[] args) {
            JFrame frame = new LayeredPaneDemo();
```

```
        frame.addWindowListener(new WindowAdapter() {
            public void windowClosing(WindowEvent e) {
                System.exit(0);
            }
        });

        frame.pack();
        frame.setVisible(true);
    }
}
```

EXAMPLE: *LayeredPaneDemo2.java*

SOURCE CODE: *http://java.sun.com/docs/books/tutorial/uiswing/components/example-swing/LayeredPaneDemo2.java*

Where Explained: *Laying Out Components in a Layered Pane* (page 154)

```
import javax.swing.*;
import javax.swing.border.*;
import javax.accessibility.*;

import java.awt.*;
import java.awt.event.*;

public class LayeredPaneDemo2 extends JFrame {
    private String[] layerStrings = { "Yellow (0)", "Magenta (1)",
                                      "Cyan (2)", "Red (3)",
                                      "Green (4)", "Blue (5)" };
    private Color[] layerColors = { Color.yellow, Color.magenta,
                                    Color.cyan, Color.red,
                                    Color.green, Color.blue };

    private JLayeredPane layeredPane;
    private JLabel dukeLabel;

    public LayeredPaneDemo2()    {
        super("LayeredPaneDemo2");

        //Create and load the duke icon
        final ImageIcon icon = new ImageIcon("images/dukeWaveRed.gif");

        //Create and set up the layered pane
        layeredPane = new JLayeredPane();
        layeredPane.setPreferredSize(new Dimension(300, 310));
        layeredPane.setBorder(BorderFactory.createTitledBorder(
                                "Move the Mouse to Move Duke"));
        layeredPane.addMouseMotionListener(new MouseMotionAdapter() {
            final int XFUDGE = 40;
            final int YFUDGE = 57;
            public void mouseEntered(MouseEvent e) {
                dukeLabel.setLocation(e.getX()-XFUDGE, e.getY()-YFUDGE);
            }
            public void mouseMoved(MouseEvent e) {
                dukeLabel.setLocation(e.getX()-XFUDGE, e.getY()-YFUDGE);
            }
        });

        layeredPane.setLayout(new GridLayout(2,3));

        //Add several overlapping, colored labels to the layered pane
        //using absolute positioning/sizing.
        for (int i = 0; i < layerStrings.length; i++) {
            JLabel label = createColoredLabel(layerStrings[i], layerColors[i]);
```

```
                layeredPane.add(label, new Integer(i));
        }

        //Create and add the Duke label to the layered pane
        dukeLabel = new JLabel(icon);
        dukeLabel.setBounds(15, 225,
                            icon.getIconWidth(),
                            icon.getIconHeight());
        layeredPane.add(dukeLabel, new Integer(2), 0);

        //Add control pane and layered pane to frame
        Container contentPane = getContentPane();
        contentPane.setLayout(new BoxLayout(contentPane,
                            BoxLayout.Y_AXIS));
        contentPane.add(Box.createRigidArea(new Dimension(0, 10)));
        contentPane.add(createControlPanel());
        contentPane.add(Box.createRigidArea(new Dimension(0, 10)));
        contentPane.add(layeredPane);
    }

    //Create and set up a colored label
    private JLabel createColoredLabel(String text, Color color) {
        JLabel label = new JLabel(text);
        label.setVerticalAlignment(JLabel.TOP);
        label.setHorizontalAlignment(JLabel.CENTER);
        label.setOpaque(true);
        label.setBackground(color);
        label.setForeground(Color.black);
        label.setBorder(BorderFactory.createLineBorder(Color.black));
        label.setPreferredSize(new Dimension(140, 140));
        return label;
    }

    //Create the control pane for the top of the frame.
    private JPanel createControlPanel() {

        final JCheckBox onTop = new JCheckBox("Top Position in Layer");
        onTop.setSelected(true);
        onTop.addActionListener(new ActionListener() {
            public void actionPerformed(ActionEvent e) {
                if (onTop.isSelected())
                    layeredPane.moveToFront(dukeLabel);
                else
                    layeredPane.moveToBack(dukeLabel);
            }
        });

        final JComboBox layerList = new JComboBox(layerStrings);
        layerList.setSelectedIndex(2);     //cyan layer
        layerList.addActionListener(new ActionListener () {
            public void actionPerformed(ActionEvent e) {
                int position = onTop.isSelected() ? 0 : 1;
                layeredPane.setLayer(dukeLabel,
                                    layerList.getSelectedIndex(),
                                    position);
            }
        });

        JPanel controls = new JPanel();
        controls.add(layerList);
        controls.add(onTop);
        controls.setBorder(BorderFactory.createTitledBorder(
                            "Choose Duke's Layer and Position"));
        return controls;
    }
```

```
        public static void main(String[] args) {
            JFrame frame = new LayeredPaneDemo2();

            frame.addWindowListener(new WindowAdapter() {
                public void windowClosing(WindowEvent e) {
                    System.exit(0);
                }
            });

            frame.pack();
            frame.setVisible(true);
        }
    }
```

EXAMPLE: *LimitedPlainDocument.java*

Associated File(s): `TextComponentDemo.java` *(page 744)*

SOURCE CODE: *http://java.sun.com/docs/books/tutorial/uiswing/components/example-swing/LimitedPlainDocument.java*

```java
import javax.swing.*;
import javax.swing.text.*;

import java.awt.Toolkit;

public class LimitedPlainDocument extends PlainDocument {

    int maxCharacters;

    public LimitedPlainDocument(int maxChars) {
        maxCharacters = maxChars;
    }

    public void insertString(int offs, String str, AttributeSet a)
        throws BadLocationException {

        //This rejects the entire insertion if it would make
        //the contents too long. Another option would be
        //to truncate the inserted string so the contents
        //would be exactly maxCharacters in length.
        if ((getLength() + str.length()) <= maxCharacters)
            super.insertString(offs, str, a);
        else
            Toolkit.getDefaultToolkit().beep();
    }
}
```

Where Explained:
General Rules for Using Text Components (page 282)

EXAMPLE: *LimitedStyledDocument.java*

Main Source File: `TextComponentDemo.java` *(page 744)*

SOURCE CODE: *http://java.sun.com/docs/books/tutorial/uiswing/components/example-swing/LimitedStyledDocument.java*

```java
import javax.swing.*;
import javax.swing.text.*;
import java.awt.Toolkit;
```

Where Explained:
General Rules for Using Text Components (page 282)

```
public class LimitedStyledDocument extends DefaultStyledDocument {
    int maxCharacters;

    public LimitedStyledDocument(int maxChars) {
        maxCharacters = maxChars;
    }

    public void insertString(int offs, String str, AttributeSet a)
        throws BadLocationException {

        //This rejects the entire insertion if it would make
        //the contents too long. Another option would be
        //to truncate the inserted string so the contents
        //would be exactly maxCharacters in length.
        if ((getLength() + str.length()) <= maxCharacters)
            super.insertString(offs, str, a);
        else
            Toolkit.getDefaultToolkit().beep();
    }
}
```

EXAMPLE: *ListDemo.java*

Where Explained:

Adding Items to and Removing Items from a List (page 221)

SOURCE CODE: *http://java.sun.com/docs/books/tutorial/uiswing/components/example-swing/ ListDemo.java*

```
import java.awt.*;
import java.awt.event.*;
import javax.swing.*;
import javax.swing.event.*;

public class ListDemo extends JFrame
                      implements ListSelectionListener {
    private JList list;
    private DefaultListModel listModel;

    private static final String hireString = "Hire";
    private static final String fireString = "Fire";
    private JButton fireButton;
    private JTextField employeeName;

    public ListDemo() {
        super("ListDemo");

        listModel = new DefaultListModel();
        listModel.addElement("Alison Huml");
        listModel.addElement("Kathy Walrath");
        listModel.addElement("Lisa Friendly");
        listModel.addElement("Mary Campione");

        //Create the list and put it in a scroll pane
        list = new JList(listModel);
        list.setSelectionMode(ListSelectionModel.SINGLE_SELECTION);
        list.setSelectedIndex(0);
        list.addListSelectionListener(this);
        JScrollPane listScrollPane = new JScrollPane(list);

        JButton hireButton = new JButton(hireString);
        hireButton.setActionCommand(hireString);
        hireButton.addActionListener(new HireListener());

        fireButton = new JButton(fireString);
        fireButton.setActionCommand(fireString);
        fireButton.addActionListener(new FireListener());
```

```java
        employeeName = new JTextField(10);
        employeeName.addActionListener(new HireListener());
        String name = listModel.getElementAt(
                                list.getSelectedIndex()).toString();
        employeeName.setText(name);

        //Create a panel that uses FlowLayout (the default).
        JPanel buttonPane = new JPanel();
        buttonPane.add(employeeName);
        buttonPane.add(hireButton);
        buttonPane.add(fireButton);

        Container contentPane = getContentPane();
        contentPane.add(listScrollPane, BorderLayout.CENTER);
        contentPane.add(buttonPane, BorderLayout.SOUTH);
    }

    class FireListener implements ActionListener {
        public void actionPerformed(ActionEvent e) {
            //This method can be called only if
            //there's a valid selection
            //so go ahead and remove whatever's selected.
            int index = list.getSelectedIndex();
            listModel.remove(index);

            int size = listModel.getSize();

            if (size == 0) {
            //Nobody's left, disable firing.
                fireButton.setEnabled(false);

            } else {
            //Adjust the selection.
                if (index == listModel.getSize())//removed item in last position
                    index--;
                list.setSelectedIndex(index);    //otherwise select same index
            }
        }
    }

    //This listener is shared by the text field and the hire button
    class HireListener implements ActionListener {
        public void actionPerformed(ActionEvent e) {

            //User didn't type in a name...
            if (employeeName.getText().equals("")) {
                Toolkit.getDefaultToolkit().beep();
                return;
            }

            int index = list.getSelectedIndex();
            int size = listModel.getSize();

            //If no selection or if item in last position is selected,
            //add the new hire to end of list, and select new hire.
            if (index == -1 || (index+1 == size)) {
                listModel.addElement(employeeName.getText());
                list.setSelectedIndex(size);

            //Otherwise insert the new hire after the current selection,
            //and select new hire.
            } else {
                listModel.insertElementAt(employeeName.getText(), index+1);
                list.setSelectedIndex(index+1);
            }
        }
    }
}
```

```
        public void valueChanged(ListSelectionEvent e) {
            if (e.getValueIsAdjusting() == false) {

                if (list.getSelectedIndex() == -1) {
                //No selection, disable fire button.
                    fireButton.setEnabled(false);
                    employeeName.setText("");

                } else {
                //Selection, update text field.
                    fireButton.setEnabled(true);
                    String name = list.getSelectedValue().toString();
                    employeeName.setText(name);
                }
            }
        }

        public static void main(String s[]) {
            JFrame frame = new ListDemo();

            frame.addWindowListener(new WindowAdapter() {
                public void windowClosing(WindowEvent e) {
                    System.exit(0);
                }
            });

            frame.pack();
            frame.setVisible(true);
        }
    }
```

EXAMPLE: *ListDialog.java*

**Where
Explained:**

*JButton
Features*
(page 172)

SOURCE CODE: *http://java.sun.com/docs/books/tutorial/uiswing/components/example-
              swing/ListDialog.java*

```
import javax.swing.*;
import java.awt.*;
import java.awt.event.*;

/**
 * Use this modal dialog to let the user choose one string from a long
 * list.  See the main method for an example of using ListDialog.  The
 * basics:
 * <pre>
    String[] choices = {"A", "long", "array", "of", "strings"};
    ListDialog.initialize(componentInControllingFrame, choices,
                          "Dialog Title",
                          "A description of the list:");
    String selectedName = ListDialog.showDialog(locatorComponent,
                                                initialSelection);
 * </pre>
 */
public class ListDialog extends JDialog {
    private static ListDialog dialog;
    private static String value = "";
    private JList list;

    /**
     * Set up the dialog.  The first argument can be null,
     * but it really should be a component in the dialog's
     * controlling frame.
     */
```

```
public static void initialize(Component comp,
                              String[] possibleValues,
                              String title,
                              String labelText) {
    Frame frame = JOptionPane.getFrameForComponent(comp);
    dialog = new ListDialog(frame, possibleValues,
                            title, labelText);
}

/**
 * Show the initialized dialog.  The first argument should
 * be null if you want the dialog to come up in the center
 * of the screen.  Otherwise, the argument should be the
 * component on top of which the dialog should appear.
 */
public static String showDialog(Component comp, String initialValue) {
    if (dialog != null) {
        dialog.setValue(initialValue);
        dialog.setLocationRelativeTo(comp);
        dialog.setVisible(true);
    } else {
        System.err.println("ListDialog requires you to call initialize "
                           + "before calling showDialog.");
    }
    return value;
}

private void setValue(String newValue) {
    value = newValue;
    list.setSelectedValue(value, true);
}

private ListDialog(Frame frame, Object[] data, String title,
                   String labelText) {
    super(frame, title, true);

    //buttons
    JButton cancelButton = new JButton("Cancel");
    final JButton setButton = new JButton("Set");
    cancelButton.addActionListener(new ActionListener() {
        public void actionPerformed(ActionEvent e) {
            ListDialog.dialog.setVisible(false);
        }
    });
    setButton.addActionListener(new ActionListener() {
        public void actionPerformed(ActionEvent e) {
            ListDialog.value = (String)(list.getSelectedValue());
            ListDialog.dialog.setVisible(false);
        }
    });
    getRootPane().setDefaultButton(setButton);

    //main part of the dialog
    list = new JList(data);
    list.setSelectionMode(ListSelectionModel.SINGLE_INTERVAL_SELECTION);
    list.addMouseListener(new MouseAdapter() {
        public void mouseClicked(MouseEvent e) {
            if (e.getClickCount() == 2) {
                setButton.doClick();
            }
        }
    });
    JScrollPane listScroller = new JScrollPane(list);
    listScroller.setPreferredSize(new Dimension(250, 80));
    //XXX: Must do the following, too, or else the scroller thinks
    //XXX: it's taller than it is:
    listScroller.setMinimumSize(new Dimension(250, 80));
    listScroller.setAlignmentX(LEFT_ALIGNMENT);
```

```
        //Create a container so that we can add a title around
        //the scroll pane.  Can't add a title directly to the
        //scroll pane because its background would be white.
        //Lay out the label and scroll pane from top to button.
        JPanel listPane = new JPanel();
        listPane.setLayout(new BoxLayout(listPane, BoxLayout.Y_AXIS));
        JLabel label = new JLabel(labelText);
        label.setLabelFor(list);
        listPane.add(label);
        listPane.add(Box.createRigidArea(new Dimension(0,5)));
        listPane.add(listScroller);
        listPane.setBorder(BorderFactory.createEmptyBorder(10,10,10,10));

        //Lay out the buttons from left to right.
        JPanel buttonPane = new JPanel();
        buttonPane.setLayout(new BoxLayout(buttonPane, BoxLayout.X_AXIS));
        buttonPane.setBorder(BorderFactory.createEmptyBorder(0, 10, 10, 10));
        buttonPane.add(Box.createHorizontalGlue());
        buttonPane.add(cancelButton);
        buttonPane.add(Box.createRigidArea(new Dimension(10, 0)));
        buttonPane.add(setButton);

        //Put everything together, using the content pane's BorderLayout.
        Container contentPane = getContentPane();
        contentPane.add(listPane, BorderLayout.CENTER);
        contentPane.add(buttonPane, BorderLayout.SOUTH);

        pack();
    }

    /**
     * This is here so that you can view ListDialog even if you
     * haven't written the code to include it in a program.
     */
    public static void main(String[] args) {
        String[] names = {"Arlo", "Cosmo", "Elmo", "Hugo",
                          "Jethro", "Laszlo", "Milo", "Nemo",
                          "Otto", "Ringo", "Rocco", "Rollo"};
        JFrame f = new JFrame("Name That Baby");
        f.addWindowListener(new WindowAdapter() {
            public void windowClosing(WindowEvent e) {
                System.exit(0);
            }
        });

        JLabel intro = new JLabel("The chosen name:");

        final JLabel name = new JLabel("Cosmo");
        intro.setLabelFor(name);
        name.setForeground(Color.black);

        JButton button = new JButton("Pick a new name...");
        ListDialog.initialize(f, names, "Name Chooser",
                              "Baby names ending in O:");
        button.addActionListener(new ActionListener() {
            public void actionPerformed(ActionEvent e) {
                String selectedName = ListDialog.showDialog(null,
                                                    name.getText());
                name.setText(selectedName);
            }
        });

        JPanel contentPane = new JPanel();
        f.setContentPane(contentPane);
        contentPane.setLayout(new BoxLayout(contentPane, BoxLayout.Y_AXIS));
        contentPane.setBorder(BorderFactory.createEmptyBorder(20,20,20,20));
```

```
        contentPane.add(intro);
        contentPane.add(name);
        contentPane.add(Box.createRigidArea(new Dimension(0,10)));
        contentPane.add(button);
        intro.setAlignmentX(JComponent.CENTER_ALIGNMENT);
        name.setAlignmentX(JComponent.CENTER_ALIGNMENT);
        button.setAlignmentX(JComponent.CENTER_ALIGNMENT);

        f.pack();
        f.setVisible(true);
    }
}
```

EXAMPLE: *LongTask.java*

Main Source File: `ProgressBarDemo.java` *(page 695)*

SOURCE CODE: *http://java.sun.com/docs/books/tutorial/uiswing/components/example-swing/LongTask.java*

Where Explained:

How to Monitor Progress (page 239)

```java
/** Uses a SwingWorker to perform a time-consuming (and utterly fake) task. */
public class LongTask {
    private int lengthOfTask;
    private int current = 0;
    private String statMessage;

    LongTask() {
        //Compute length of task...
        //In a real program, this would figure out
        //the number of bytes to read or whatever.
        lengthOfTask = 1000;
    }

    /**
     * Called from ProgressBarDemo to start the task.
     */
    void go() {
        current = 0;
        final SwingWorker worker = new SwingWorker() {
            public Object construct() {
                return new ActualTask();
            }
        };
    }

    /**
     * Called from ProgressBarDemo to find out how much work needs
     * to be done.
     */
    int getLengthOfTask() {
        return lengthOfTask;
    }

    /**
     * Called from ProgressBarDemo to find out how much has been done.
     */
    int getCurrent() {
        return current;
    }

    void stop() {
        current = lengthOfTask;
    }
```

```
/**
 * Called from ProgressBarDemo to find out if the task has completed.
 */
boolean done() {
    if (current >= lengthOfTask)
        return true;
    else
        return false;
}

String getMessage() {
    return statMessage;
}

/**
 * The actual long running task.  This runs in a SwingWorker thread.
 */
class ActualTask {
    ActualTask () {
        //Fake a long task,
        //making a random amount of progress every second.
        while (current < lengthOfTask) {
            try {
                Thread.sleep(1000); //sleep for a second
                current += Math.random() * 100; //make some progress
                if (current > lengthOfTask) {
                    current = lengthOfTask;
                }
                statMessage = "Completed " + current +
                              " out of " + lengthOfTask + ".";
            } catch (InterruptedException e) {}
        }
    }
}
}
```

EXAMPLE: *MenuDemo.java*

Where Explained:

Handling Events from Menu Items (page 229)

SOURCE CODE: *http://java.sun.com/docs/books/tutorial/uiswing/components/example-swing/ MenuDemo.java*

```
import java.awt.*;
import java.awt.event.*;
import javax.swing.JMenu;
import javax.swing.JMenuItem;
import javax.swing.JCheckBoxMenuItem;
import javax.swing.JRadioButtonMenuItem;
import javax.swing.ButtonGroup;
import javax.swing.JMenuBar;
import javax.swing.KeyStroke;
import javax.swing.ImageIcon;

import javax.swing.JTextArea;
import javax.swing.JScrollPane;
import javax.swing.JFrame;

/*
 * This class adds event handling to MenuLookDemo.
 */
public class MenuDemo extends JFrame
                      implements ActionListener, ItemListener {
    JTextArea output;
    JScrollPane scrollPane;
    String newline = "\n";
```

```
public MenuDemo() {
    JMenuBar menuBar;
    JMenu menu, submenu;
    JMenuItem menuItem;
    JRadioButtonMenuItem rbMenuItem;
    JCheckBoxMenuItem cbMenuItem;

    addWindowListener(new WindowAdapter() {
        public void windowClosing(WindowEvent e) {
            System.exit(0);
        }
    });

    //Add regular components to the window, using the default BorderLayout.
    Container contentPane = getContentPane();
    output = new JTextArea(5, 30);
    output.setEditable(false);
    scrollPane = new JScrollPane(output);
    contentPane.add(scrollPane, BorderLayout.CENTER);

    //Create the menu bar.
    menuBar = new JMenuBar();
    setJMenuBar(menuBar);

    //Build the first menu.
    menu = new JMenu("A Menu");
    menu.setMnemonic(KeyEvent.VK_A);
    menu.getAccessibleContext().setAccessibleDescription(
            "The only menu in this program that has menu items");
    menuBar.add(menu);

    //a group of JMenuItems
    menuItem = new JMenuItem("A text-only menu item",
                            KeyEvent.VK_T);
    //menuItem.setMnemonic(KeyEvent.VK_T); //used constructor instead
    menuItem.setAccelerator(KeyStroke.getKeyStroke(
            KeyEvent.VK_1, ActionEvent.ALT_MASK));
    menuItem.getAccessibleContext().setAccessibleDescription(
            "This doesn't really do anything");
    menuItem.addActionListener(this);
    menu.add(menuItem);

    menuItem = new JMenuItem("Both text and icon",
                            new ImageIcon("images/middle.gif"));
    menuItem.setMnemonic(KeyEvent.VK_B);
    menuItem.addActionListener(this);
    menu.add(menuItem);

    menuItem = new JMenuItem(new ImageIcon("images/middle.gif"));
    menuItem.setMnemonic(KeyEvent.VK_D);
    menuItem.addActionListener(this);
    menu.add(menuItem);

    //a group of radio button menu items
    menu.addSeparator();
    ButtonGroup group = new ButtonGroup();
    rbMenuItem = new JRadioButtonMenuItem("A radio button menu item");
    rbMenuItem.setSelected(true);
    rbMenuItem.setMnemonic(KeyEvent.VK_R);
    group.add(rbMenuItem);
    rbMenuItem.addActionListener(this);
    menu.add(rbMenuItem);
    rbMenuItem = new JRadioButtonMenuItem("Another one");
    rbMenuItem.setMnemonic(KeyEvent.VK_O);
    group.add(rbMenuItem);
    rbMenuItem.addActionListener(this);
    menu.add(rbMenuItem);
```

```
            //a group of check box menu items
            menu.addSeparator();
            cbMenuItem = new JCheckBoxMenuItem("A check box menu item");
            cbMenuItem.setMnemonic(KeyEvent.VK_C);
            cbMenuItem.addItemListener(this);
            menu.add(cbMenuItem);
            cbMenuItem = new JCheckBoxMenuItem("Another one");
            cbMenuItem.setMnemonic(KeyEvent.VK_H);
            cbMenuItem.addItemListener(this);
            menu.add(cbMenuItem);

            //a submenu
            menu.addSeparator();
            submenu = new JMenu("A submenu");
            submenu.setMnemonic(KeyEvent.VK_S);

            menuItem = new JMenuItem("An item in the submenu");
            menuItem.setAccelerator(KeyStroke.getKeyStroke(
                    KeyEvent.VK_2, ActionEvent.ALT_MASK));
            menuItem.addActionListener(this);
            submenu.add(menuItem);

            menuItem = new JMenuItem("Another item");
            menuItem.addActionListener(this);
            submenu.add(menuItem);
            menu.add(submenu);

            //Build second menu in the menu bar.
            menu = new JMenu("Another Menu");
            menu.setMnemonic(KeyEvent.VK_N);
            menu.getAccessibleContext().setAccessibleDescription(
                    "This menu does nothing");
            menuBar.add(menu);
        }

        public void actionPerformed(ActionEvent e) {
            JMenuItem source = (JMenuItem)(e.getSource());
            String s = "Action event detected."
                        + newline
                        + "    Event source: " + source.getText()
                        + " (an instance of " + getClassName(source) + ")";
            output.append(s + newline);
        }

        public void itemStateChanged(ItemEvent e) {
            JMenuItem source = (JMenuItem)(e.getSource());
            String s = "Item event detected."
                        + newline
                        + "    Event source: " + source.getText()
                        + " (an instance of " + getClassName(source) + ")"
                        + newline
                        + "    New state: "
                        + ((e.getStateChange() == ItemEvent.SELECTED) ?
                          "selected":"unselected");
            output.append(s + newline);
        }

    // Returns just the class name -- no package info.
    protected String getClassName(Object o) {
        String classString = o.getClass().getName();
        int dotIndex = classString.lastIndexOf(".");
        return classString.substring(dotIndex+1);
    }
```

```
    public static void main(String[] args) {
        MenuDemo window = new MenuDemo();

        window.setTitle("MenuDemo");
        window.setSize(450, 260);
        window.setVisible(true);
    }
}
```

EXAMPLE: *MenuGlueDemo.java*

SOURCE CODE: *http://java.sun.com/docs/books/tutorial/uiswing/components/example-swing/MenuGlueDemo.java*

Where Explained: *Customizing Menu Layout* (page 234)

```
import java.awt.*;
import java.awt.event.*;
import javax.swing.*;

/**
 * @author ges
 * @author kwalrath
 */
public class MenuGlueDemo extends JFrame {
    protected JMenuBar menuBar;

    public MenuGlueDemo() {
        super("MenuGlueDemo");
        menuBar = new JMenuBar();
        setJMenuBar(menuBar);
        addNewMenu("Menu 1");
        addNewMenu("Menu 2");
        menuBar.add(Box.createHorizontalGlue());
        addNewMenu("Menu 3");

        addWindowListener(new WindowAdapter() {
            public void windowClosing(WindowEvent e) {
                System.exit(0);
            }
        });
    }

    public void addNewMenu(String title) {
        JMenu m = (JMenu)menuBar.add(new JMenu(title));
        m.add("Menu item");
        m.add("Menu item");
        m.add("Menu item");
    }

    public static void main(String args[]) {
        MenuGlueDemo f = new MenuGlueDemo();
        f.setSize(300, 50);
        f.setVisible(true);
    }
}
```

EXAMPLE: *MenuLayoutDemo.java*

Where Explained:

Customizing Menu Layout (page 234)

SOURCE CODE: *http://java.sun.com/docs/books/tutorial/uiswing/components/example-swing/MenuLayoutDemo.java*

```java
import java.awt.*;
import java.awt.event.*;
import javax.swing.*;

/** @author ges */

public class MenuLayoutDemo extends JFrame {
    protected JMenuBar menuBar;

    public MenuLayoutDemo() {
        super("MenuLayoutDemo");
        menuBar = new JMenuBar();
        menuBar.setLayout(new BoxLayout(menuBar, BoxLayout.Y_AXIS));
        addNewMenu("Menu 1");
        addNewMenu("Menu 2");
        addNewMenu("Menu 3");
        getContentPane().add(menuBar, BorderLayout.WEST);

        addWindowListener(new WindowAdapter() {
            public void windowClosing(WindowEvent e) {
                System.exit(0);
            }
        });
    }

    public void addNewMenu(String title) {
        JMenu m = (JMenu)menuBar.add(new HorizontalMenu(title));
        m.add("Menu item");
        m.add("Menu item");
        m.add("Menu item");
        JMenu m1 = (JMenu)m.add(new HorizontalMenu("Submenu"));
        m1.add("Submenu item");
        m1.add("Submenu item");
    }

    public static void main(String args[]) {
        MenuLayoutDemo f = new MenuLayoutDemo();
        f.pack();
        f.setVisible(true);
    }

    class HorizontalMenu extends JMenu {
        HorizontalMenu(String label) {
            super(label);
            JPopupMenu pm = getPopupMenu();
            pm.setLayout(new BoxLayout(pm, BoxLayout.X_AXIS));
            setMinimumSize(getPreferredSize());
        }

        public void setPopupMenuVisible(boolean b) {
            boolean isVisible = isPopupMenuVisible();
            if (b != isVisible) {
                if ((b==true) && isShowing()) {
                    // Set location of popupMenu (pulldown or pullright)
                    // Perhaps this should be dictated by L&F
                    int x = 0;
                    int y = 0;
                    Container parent = getParent();
```

```
                    if (parent instanceof JPopupMenu) {
                        x = 0;
                        y = getHeight();
                    } else {
                        x = getWidth();
                        y = 0;
                    }
                    getPopupMenu().show(this, x, y);
                } else {
                    getPopupMenu().setVisible(false);
                }
            }
        }
    }
}
```

EXAMPLE: *MenuLookDemo.java*

**Where
Explained:**
*Creating
Menus*
(page 227)

SOURCE CODE: *http://java.sun.com/docs/books/tutorial/uiswing/components/example-swing/MenuLookDemo.java*

```java
import java.awt.*;
import java.awt.event.*;
import javax.swing.JMenu;
import javax.swing.JMenuItem;
import javax.swing.JCheckBoxMenuItem;
import javax.swing.JRadioButtonMenuItem;
import javax.swing.ButtonGroup;
import javax.swing.JMenuBar;
import javax.swing.KeyStroke;
import javax.swing.ImageIcon;

import javax.swing.JTextArea;
import javax.swing.JScrollPane;
import javax.swing.JFrame;

/*
 * This class exists solely to show you what menus look like.
 * It has no menu-related event handling.
 */
public class MenuLookDemo extends JFrame {
    JTextArea output;
    JScrollPane scrollPane;

    public MenuLookDemo() {
        JMenuBar menuBar;
        JMenu menu, submenu;
        JMenuItem menuItem;
        JCheckBoxMenuItem cbMenuItem;
        JRadioButtonMenuItem rbMenuItem;

        addWindowListener(new WindowAdapter() {
            public void windowClosing(WindowEvent e) {
                System.exit(0);
            }
        });

        //Add regular components to the window, using the default BorderLayout.
        Container contentPane = getContentPane();
        output = new JTextArea(5, 30);
        output.setEditable(false);
        scrollPane = new JScrollPane(output);
        contentPane.add(scrollPane, BorderLayout.CENTER);
```

```
//Create the menu bar.
menuBar = new JMenuBar();
setJMenuBar(menuBar);

//Build the first menu.
menu = new JMenu("A Menu");
menu.setMnemonic(KeyEvent.VK_A);
menu.getAccessibleContext().setAccessibleDescription(
        "The only menu in this program that has menu items");
menuBar.add(menu);

//a group of JMenuItems
menuItem = new JMenuItem("A text-only menu item",
                        KeyEvent.VK_T);
//menuItem.setMnemonic(KeyEvent.VK_T); //used constructor instead
menuItem.setAccelerator(KeyStroke.getKeyStroke(
        KeyEvent.VK_1, ActionEvent.ALT_MASK));
menuItem.getAccessibleContext().setAccessibleDescription(
        "This doesn't really do anything");
menu.add(menuItem);

menuItem = new JMenuItem("Both text and icon",
                        new ImageIcon("images/middle.gif"));
menuItem.setMnemonic(KeyEvent.VK_B);
menu.add(menuItem);

menuItem = new JMenuItem(new ImageIcon("images/middle.gif"));
menuItem.setMnemonic(KeyEvent.VK_D);
menu.add(menuItem);

//a group of radio button menu items
menu.addSeparator();
ButtonGroup group = new ButtonGroup();

rbMenuItem = new JRadioButtonMenuItem("A radio button menu item");
rbMenuItem.setSelected(true);
rbMenuItem.setMnemonic(KeyEvent.VK_R);
group.add(rbMenuItem);
menu.add(rbMenuItem);

rbMenuItem = new JRadioButtonMenuItem("Another one");
rbMenuItem.setMnemonic(KeyEvent.VK_O);
group.add(rbMenuItem);
menu.add(rbMenuItem);

//a group of check box menu items
menu.addSeparator();
cbMenuItem = new JCheckBoxMenuItem("A check box menu item");
cbMenuItem.setMnemonic(KeyEvent.VK_C);
menu.add(cbMenuItem);

cbMenuItem = new JCheckBoxMenuItem("Another one");
cbMenuItem.setMnemonic(KeyEvent.VK_H);
menu.add(cbMenuItem);

//a submenu
menu.addSeparator();
submenu = new JMenu("A submenu");
submenu.setMnemonic(KeyEvent.VK_S);

menuItem = new JMenuItem("An item in the submenu");
menuItem.setAccelerator(KeyStroke.getKeyStroke(
        KeyEvent.VK_2, ActionEvent.ALT_MASK));
submenu.add(menuItem);
```

```
        menuItem = new JMenuItem("Another item");
        submenu.add(menuItem);
        menu.add(submenu);

        //Build second menu in the menu bar.
        menu = new JMenu("Another Menu");
        menu.setMnemonic(KeyEvent.VK_N);
        menu.getAccessibleContext().setAccessibleDescription(
                "This menu does nothing");
        menuBar.add(menu);
    }

    public static void main(String[] args) {
        MenuLookDemo window = new MenuLookDemo();

        window.setTitle("MenuLookDemo");
        window.setSize(450, 260);
        window.setVisible(true);
    }
}
```

EXAMPLE: *MyInternalFrame.java*

Associated File(s): <u>InternalFrameDemo.java</u> *(page 668)*

SOURCE CODE: *http://java.sun.com/docs/books/tutorial/uiswing/components/example-swing/MyInternalFrame.java*

```
    import javax.swing.JInternalFrame;

    import java.awt.event.*;
    import java.awt.*;

    public class MyInternalFrame extends JInternalFrame {
        static int openFrameCount = 0;
        static final int xOffset = 30, yOffset = 30;

        public MyInternalFrame() {
            super("Document #" + (++openFrameCount),
                    true, //resizable
                    true, //closable
                    true, //maximizable
                    true);//iconifiable

            //...Create the GUI and put it in the window...

            //...Then set the window size or call pack...
            setSize(300,300);

            //Set the window's location.
            setLocation(xOffset*openFrameCount, yOffset*openFrameCount);
        }
    }
```

Where Explained: *How to Use Internal Frames* (page 143)

Where Explained:

Creating a Validated Text Field
(page 299)

EXAMPLE: *PasswordDemo.java*

SOURCE CODE: *http://java.sun.com/docs/books/tutorial/uiswing/components/example-swing/PasswordDemo.java*

```java
import javax.swing.*;
import java.awt.*;
import java.awt.event.*;

public class PasswordDemo {
    public static void main(String[] argv) {
        final JFrame f = new JFrame("PasswordDemo");

        JLabel label = new JLabel("Enter the password: ");
        JPasswordField passwordField = new JPasswordField(10);
        passwordField.setEchoChar('#');
        passwordField.addActionListener(new ActionListener() {
            public void actionPerformed(ActionEvent e) {
                JPasswordField input = (JPasswordField)e.getSource();
                char[] password = input.getPassword();
                if (isPasswordCorrect(password)) {
                    JOptionPane.showMessageDialog(f,
                        "Success! You typed the right password.");
                } else {
                    JOptionPane.showMessageDialog(f,
                        "Invalid password. Try again.",
                        "Error Message",
                        JOptionPane.ERROR_MESSAGE);
                }
            }
        });

        JPanel contentPane = new JPanel(new BorderLayout());
        contentPane.setBorder(BorderFactory.createEmptyBorder(20, 20, 20, 20));
        contentPane.add(label, BorderLayout.WEST);
        contentPane.add(passwordField, BorderLayout.CENTER);

        f.setContentPane(contentPane);
        f.addWindowListener(new WindowAdapter() {
            public void windowClosing(WindowEvent e) { System.exit(0); }
        });
        f.pack();
        f.setVisible(true);
    }

    private static boolean isPasswordCorrect(char[] input) {
        char[] correctPassword = { 'b', 'u', 'g', 'a', 'b', 'o', 'o' };
        if (input.length != correctPassword.length)
            return false;
        for (int i = 0;  i < input.length; i ++)
            if (input[i] != correctPassword[i])
                return false;
        return true;
    }
}
```

EXAMPLE: *Person.java*

Main Source File: GenealogyModel.java *(page 658)*

SOURCE CODE: *http://java.sun.com/docs/books/tutorial/uiswing/components/example-swing/Person.java*

Where Explained:

Creating a Data Model (page 331)

```java
import java.util.Vector;

public class Person {
    Person father;
    Person mother;
    Vector children;
    private String name;

    public Person(String name) {
        this.name = name;
        mother = father = null;
        children = new Vector();
    }

    /**
     *   Link together all members of a family.
     *
     *   @param pa the father
     *   @param ma the mother
     *   @param kids the children
     */
    public static void linkFamily(Person pa,
                                  Person ma,
                                  Person[] kids) {
        int len = kids.length;
        Person kid = null;
        for (int i = 0; i < len; i++) {
            kid = kids[i];
            pa.children.addElement(kid);
            ma.children.addElement(kid);
            kid.father = pa;
            kid.mother = ma;
        }
    }

/// getter methods ///////////////////////////////////

    public String toString() { return name; }
    public String getName() { return name; }
    public Person getFather() { return father; }
    public Person getMother() { return mother; }
    public int getChildCount() { return children.size(); }
    public Person getChildAt(int i) {
        return (Person)children.elementAt(i);
    }
    public int getIndexOfChild(Person kid) {
        return children.indexOf(kid);
    }
}
```

**Where
Explained:**

*Bringing Up a
Popup Menu*
(page 232)

EXAMPLE: *PopupMenuDemo.java*

SOURCE CODE: *http://java.sun.com/docs/books/tutorial/uiswing/components/example-swing/
PopupMenuDemo.java*

```java
import java.awt.*;
import java.awt.event.*;
import javax.swing.JPopupMenu;
import javax.swing.JMenu;
import javax.swing.JMenuItem;
import javax.swing.JCheckBoxMenuItem;
import javax.swing.JRadioButtonMenuItem;
import javax.swing.ButtonGroup;
import javax.swing.JMenuBar;
import javax.swing.KeyStroke;
import javax.swing.ImageIcon;

import javax.swing.JTextArea;
import javax.swing.JScrollPane;
import javax.swing.JFrame;

/*
 * This class adds popup menus to MenuDemo.
 */
public class PopupMenuDemo extends JFrame
                          implements ActionListener, ItemListener {
    JTextArea output;
    JScrollPane scrollPane;
    String newline = "\n";
    JPopupMenu popup;

    public PopupMenuDemo() {
        JMenuBar menuBar;
        JMenu menu, submenu;
        JMenuItem menuItem;
        JRadioButtonMenuItem rbMenuItem;
        JCheckBoxMenuItem cbMenuItem;

        addWindowListener(new WindowAdapter() {
            public void windowClosing(WindowEvent e) {
                System.exit(0);
            }
        });

        //Add regular components to the window, using the default BorderLayout.
        Container contentPane = getContentPane();
        output = new JTextArea(5, 30);
        output.setEditable(false);
        scrollPane = new JScrollPane(output);
        contentPane.add(scrollPane, BorderLayout.CENTER);

        //Create the menu bar.
        menuBar = new JMenuBar();
        setJMenuBar(menuBar);

        //Build the first menu.
        menu = new JMenu("A Menu");
        menu.setMnemonic(KeyEvent.VK_A);
        menu.getAccessibleContext().setAccessibleDescription(
                "The only menu in this program that has menu items");
        menuBar.add(menu);

        //a group of JMenuItems
        menuItem = new JMenuItem("A text-only menu item", KeyEvent.VK_T);
```

```
//menuItem.setMnemonic(KeyEvent.VK_T); //used constructor instead
menuItem.setAccelerator(KeyStroke.getKeyStroke(
                                KeyEvent.VK_1, ActionEvent.ALT_MASK));
menuItem.getAccessibleContext().setAccessibleDescription(
        "This doesn't really do anything");
menuItem.addActionListener(this);
menu.add(menuItem);
menuItem = new JMenuItem("Both text and icon",
                        new ImageIcon("images/middle.gif"));
menuItem.setMnemonic(KeyEvent.VK_B);
menuItem.addActionListener(this);
menu.add(menuItem);
menuItem = new JMenuItem(new ImageIcon("images/middle.gif"));
menuItem.setMnemonic(KeyEvent.VK_D);
menuItem.addActionListener(this);
menu.add(menuItem);

//a group of radio button menu items
menu.addSeparator();
ButtonGroup group = new ButtonGroup();
rbMenuItem = new JRadioButtonMenuItem("A radio button menu item");
rbMenuItem.setSelected(true);
rbMenuItem.setMnemonic(KeyEvent.VK_R);
group.add(rbMenuItem);
rbMenuItem.addActionListener(this);
menu.add(rbMenuItem);
rbMenuItem = new JRadioButtonMenuItem("Another one");
rbMenuItem.setMnemonic(KeyEvent.VK_O);
group.add(rbMenuItem);
rbMenuItem.addActionListener(this);
menu.add(rbMenuItem);

//a group of check box menu items
menu.addSeparator();
cbMenuItem = new JCheckBoxMenuItem("A check box menu item");
cbMenuItem.setMnemonic(KeyEvent.VK_C);
cbMenuItem.addItemListener(this);
menu.add(cbMenuItem);
cbMenuItem = new JCheckBoxMenuItem("Another one");
cbMenuItem.setMnemonic(KeyEvent.VK_H);
cbMenuItem.addItemListener(this);
menu.add(cbMenuItem);

//a submenu
menu.addSeparator();
submenu = new JMenu("A submenu");
submenu.setMnemonic(KeyEvent.VK_S);

menuItem = new JMenuItem("An item in the submenu");
menuItem.setAccelerator(KeyStroke.getKeyStroke(
                                KeyEvent.VK_2,
                                ActionEvent.ALT_MASK));
menuItem.addActionListener(this);
submenu.add(menuItem);

menuItem = new JMenuItem("Another item");
menuItem.addActionListener(this);
submenu.add(menuItem);
menu.add(submenu);

//Build second menu in the menu bar.
menu = new JMenu("Another Menu");
menu.setMnemonic(KeyEvent.VK_N);
menu.getAccessibleContext().setAccessibleDescription(
                                "This menu does nothing");
menuBar.add(menu);
```

```
        //Create the popup menu.
        popup = new JPopupMenu();
        menuItem = new JMenuItem("A popup menu item");
        menuItem.addActionListener(this);
        popup.add(menuItem);
        menuItem = new JMenuItem("Another popup menu item");
        menuItem.addActionListener(this);
        popup.add(menuItem);

        //Add listener to components that can bring up popup menus.
        MouseListener popupListener = new PopupListener();
        output.addMouseListener(popupListener);
        scrollPane.addMouseListener(popupListener);
        menuBar.addMouseListener(popupListener);
    }

    public void actionPerformed(ActionEvent e) {
        JMenuItem source = (JMenuItem)(e.getSource());
        String s = "Action event detected."
                    + newline
                    + "    Event source: " + source.getText()
                    + " (an instance of " + getClassName(source) + ")";
        output.append(s + newline);
    }

    public void itemStateChanged(ItemEvent e) {
        JMenuItem source = (JMenuItem)(e.getSource());
        String s = "Item event detected."
                    + newline
                    + "    Event source: " + source.getText()
                    + " (an instance of " + getClassName(source) + ")"
                    + newline
                    + "    New state: "
                    + ((e.getStateChange() == ItemEvent.SELECTED) ?
                      "selected":"unselected");
        output.append(s + newline);
    }

    // Returns just the class name -- no package info.
    protected String getClassName(Object o) {
        String classString = o.getClass().getName();
        int dotIndex = classString.lastIndexOf(".");
        return classString.substring(dotIndex+1);
    }

    public static void main(String[] args) {
        PopupMenuDemo window = new PopupMenuDemo();

        window.setTitle("PopupMenuDemo");
        window.setSize(450, 260);
        window.setVisible(true);
    }

    class PopupListener extends MouseAdapter {
        public void mousePressed(MouseEvent e) {
            maybeShowPopup(e);
        }

        public void mouseReleased(MouseEvent e) {
            maybeShowPopup(e);
        }

        private void maybeShowPopup(MouseEvent e) {
            if (e.isPopupTrigger()) {
                popup.show(e.getComponent(), e.getX(), e.getY());
            }
        }
    }
}
```

EXAMPLE: *ProgressBarDemo.java*

Associated File(s): LongTask.java *(page 681)*, SwingWorker.java *(page 720)*

Where Explained: *How to Monitor Progress* (page 239)

SOURCE CODE: *http://java.sun.com/docs/books/tutorial/uiswing/components/example-swing/ProgressBarDemo.java*

```java
import java.awt.*;
import java.awt.event.*;
import javax.swing.*;

public class ProgressBarDemo extends JFrame {
    public final static int ONE_SECOND = 1000;

    private JProgressBar progressBar;
    private Timer timer;
    private JButton startButton;
    private LongTask task;
    private JTextArea taskOutput;
    private String newline = "\n";

    public ProgressBarDemo() {
        super("ProgressBarDemo");
        task = new LongTask();

        //Create the demo's UI.
        startButton = new JButton("Start");
        startButton.setActionCommand("start");
        startButton.addActionListener(new ButtonListener());

        progressBar = new JProgressBar(0, task.getLengthOfTask());
        progressBar.setValue(0);
        progressBar.setStringPainted(true);

        taskOutput = new JTextArea(5, 20);
        taskOutput.setMargin(new Insets(5,5,5,5));
        taskOutput.setEditable(false);

        JPanel panel = new JPanel();
        panel.add(startButton);
        panel.add(progressBar);

        JPanel contentPane = new JPanel();
        contentPane.setLayout(new BorderLayout());
        contentPane.add(panel, BorderLayout.NORTH);
        contentPane.add(new JScrollPane(taskOutput), BorderLayout.CENTER);
        contentPane.setBorder(BorderFactory.createEmptyBorder(20, 20, 20, 20));
        setContentPane(contentPane);

        //Create a timer.
        timer = new Timer(ONE_SECOND, new ActionListener() {
            public void actionPerformed(ActionEvent evt) {
                progressBar.setValue(task.getCurrent());
                taskOutput.append(task.getMessage() + newline);
                taskOutput.setCaretPosition(taskOutput.getDocument().getLength());
                if (task.done()) {
                    Toolkit.getDefaultToolkit().beep();
                    timer.stop();
                    startButton.setEnabled(true);
                    progressBar.setValue(progressBar.getMinimum());
                }
            }
        });
    }
```

```
/**
 * The actionPerformed method in this class
 * is called when the user presses the start button.
 */
class ButtonListener implements ActionListener {
    public void actionPerformed(ActionEvent evt) {
        startButton.setEnabled(false);
        task.go();
        timer.start();
    }
}

public static void main(String[] args) {
    JFrame frame = new ProgressBarDemo();
    frame.addWindowListener(new WindowAdapter() {
        public void windowClosing(WindowEvent e) {
            System.exit(0);
        }
    });

    frame.pack();
    frame.setVisible(true);
}
}
```

EXAMPLE: *ProgressMonitorDemo.java*

**Where
Explained:**

*How to Moni-
tor Progress*
(page 239)

SOURCE CODE: *http://java.sun.com/docs/books/tutorial/uiswing/components/example-swing/
ProgressMonitorDemo.java*

```
import java.awt.*;
import java.awt.event.*;
import javax.swing.*;

public class ProgressMonitorDemo extends JFrame {
    public final static int ONE_SECOND = 1000;

    private ProgressMonitor progressMonitor;
    private Timer timer;
    private JButton startButton;
    private LongTask task;
    private JTextArea taskOutput;
    private String newline = "\n";

    public ProgressMonitorDemo() {
        super("ProgressMonitorDemo");
        task = new LongTask();

        //Create the demo's UI.
        startButton = new JButton("Start");
        startButton.setActionCommand("start");
        startButton.addActionListener(new ButtonListener());

        taskOutput = new JTextArea(5, 20);
        taskOutput.setMargin(new Insets(5,5,5,5));
        taskOutput.setEditable(false);

        JPanel contentPane = new JPanel();
        contentPane.setLayout(new BorderLayout());
        contentPane.add(startButton, BorderLayout.NORTH);
        contentPane.add(new JScrollPane(taskOutput), BorderLayout.CENTER);
        contentPane.setBorder(BorderFactory.createEmptyBorder(20, 20, 20, 20));
        setContentPane(contentPane);
```

```
            //Create a timer.
            timer = new Timer(ONE_SECOND, new TimerListener());
    }

    /**
     * The actionPerformed method in this class
     * is called each time the Timer "goes off".
     */
    class TimerListener implements ActionListener {
        public void actionPerformed(ActionEvent evt) {
            if (progressMonitor.isCanceled() || task.done()) {
                progressMonitor.close();
                task.stop();
                Toolkit.getDefaultToolkit().beep();
                timer.stop();
                if (task.done()) {
                    taskOutput.append("Task completed." + newline);
                }
                startButton.setEnabled(true);
            } else {
                progressMonitor.setNote(task.getMessage());
                progressMonitor.setProgress(task.getCurrent());
                taskOutput.append(task.getMessage() + newline);
                taskOutput.setCaretPosition(
                    taskOutput.getDocument().getLength());
            }
        }
    }

    /**
     * The actionPerformed method in this class
     * is called when the user presses the start button.
     */
    class ButtonListener implements ActionListener {
        public void actionPerformed(ActionEvent evt) {
            progressMonitor = new ProgressMonitor(ProgressMonitorDemo.this,
                                    "Running a Long Task",
                                    "", 0, task.getLengthOfTask());
            progressMonitor.setProgress(0);
            progressMonitor.setMillisToDecideToPopup(2 * ONE_SECOND);

            startButton.setEnabled(false);
            task.go();
            timer.start();
        }
    }

    public static void main(String[] args) {
        JFrame frame = new ProgressMonitorDemo();
        frame.addWindowListener(new WindowAdapter() {
            public void windowClosing(WindowEvent e) {
                System.exit(0);
            }
        });

        frame.pack();
        frame.setVisible(true);
    }
}
```

**Where
Explained:**

*How to Use
Radio Buttons*
(page 180)

EXAMPLE: *RadioButtonDemo.java*

SOURCE CODE: *http://java.sun.com/docs/books/tutorial/uiswing/components/example-swing/
RadioButtonDemo.java*

```java
import java.awt.*;
import java.awt.event.*;
import javax.swing.*;

public class RadioButtonDemo extends JPanel {
    static JFrame frame;

    static String birdString = "Bird";
    static String catString = "Cat";
    static String dogString = "Dog";
    static String rabbitString = "Rabbit";
    static String pigString = "Pig";

    JLabel picture;

    public RadioButtonDemo() {
        // Create the radio buttons.
        JRadioButton birdButton = new JRadioButton(birdString);
        birdButton.setMnemonic(KeyEvent.VK_B);
        birdButton.setActionCommand(birdString);
        birdButton.setSelected(true);

        JRadioButton catButton = new JRadioButton(catString);
        catButton.setMnemonic(KeyEvent.VK_C);
        catButton.setActionCommand(catString);

        JRadioButton dogButton = new JRadioButton(dogString);
        dogButton.setMnemonic(KeyEvent.VK_D);
        dogButton.setActionCommand(dogString);

        JRadioButton rabbitButton = new JRadioButton(rabbitString);
        rabbitButton.setMnemonic(KeyEvent.VK_R);
        rabbitButton.setActionCommand(rabbitString);

        JRadioButton pigButton = new JRadioButton(pigString);
        pigButton.setMnemonic(KeyEvent.VK_P);
        pigButton.setActionCommand(pigString);

        // Group the radio buttons.
        ButtonGroup group = new ButtonGroup();
        group.add(birdButton);
        group.add(catButton);
        group.add(dogButton);
        group.add(rabbitButton);
        group.add(pigButton);

        // Register a listener for the radio buttons.
        RadioListener myListener = new RadioListener();
        birdButton.addActionListener(myListener);
        catButton.addActionListener(myListener);
        dogButton.addActionListener(myListener);
        rabbitButton.addActionListener(myListener);
        pigButton.addActionListener(myListener);

        // Set up the picture label
        picture = new JLabel(new ImageIcon("images/"
                                    + birdString
                                    + ".gif"));
```

```
        // The preferred size is hard-coded to be the width of the
        // widest image and the height of the tallest image.
        // A real program would compute this.
        picture.setPreferredSize(new Dimension(177, 122));


        // Put the radio buttons in a column in a panel
        JPanel radioPanel = new JPanel();
        radioPanel.setLayout(new GridLayout(0, 1));
        radioPanel.add(birdButton);
        radioPanel.add(catButton);
        radioPanel.add(dogButton);
        radioPanel.add(rabbitButton);
        radioPanel.add(pigButton);

        setLayout(new BorderLayout());
        add(radioPanel, BorderLayout.WEST);
        add(picture, BorderLayout.CENTER);
        setBorder(BorderFactory.createEmptyBorder(20,20,20,20));
    }

    /** Listens to the radio buttons. */
    class RadioListener implements ActionListener {
        public void actionPerformed(ActionEvent e) {
            picture.setIcon(new ImageIcon("images/"
                                       + e.getActionCommand()
                                       + ".gif"));
        }
    }

    public static void main(String s[]) {
        frame = new JFrame("RadioButtonDemo");
        frame.addWindowListener(new WindowAdapter() {
            public void windowClosing(WindowEvent e) {System.exit(0);}
        });

        frame.getContentPane().add(new RadioButtonDemo(), BorderLayout.CENTER);
        frame.pack();
        frame.setVisible(true);
    }
}
```

EXAMPLE: *Rule.java*

Main Source File: ScrollDemo.java *(page 702)*

SOURCE CODE: *http://java.sun.com/docs/books/tutorial/uiswing/components/example-swing/Rule.java*

Where Explained: *How to Use Scroll Panes* (page 112)

```
import java.awt.*;
import javax.swing.*;

public class Rule extends JComponent {
    public static final int INCH = Toolkit.getDefaultToolkit().
            getScreenResolution();
    public static final int HORIZONTAL = 0;
    public static final int VERTICAL = 1;
    public static final int SIZE = 35;

    public int orientation;
    public boolean isMetric;
    private int increment;
    private int units;
```

```java
public Rule(int o, boolean m) {
    orientation = o;
    isMetric = m;
    setIncrementAndUnits();
}

public void setIsMetric(boolean isMetric) {
    this.isMetric = isMetric;
    setIncrementAndUnits();
    repaint();
}

private void setIncrementAndUnits() {
    if (isMetric) {
        units = (int)((double)INCH / (double)2.54); // dots per centimeter
        increment = units;
    } else {
        units = INCH;
        increment = units / 2;
    }
}

public boolean isMetric() {
    return this.isMetric;
}

public int getIncrement() {
    return increment;
}

public void setPreferredHeight(int ph) {
    setPreferredSize(new Dimension(SIZE, ph));
}

public void setPreferredWidth(int pw) {
    setPreferredSize(new Dimension(pw, SIZE));
}

public void paintComponent(Graphics g) {
    Rectangle drawHere = g.getClipBounds();

    // Fill clipping area with dirty brown/orange.
    g.setColor(new Color(230, 163, 4));
    g.fillRect(drawHere.x, drawHere.y, drawHere.width, drawHere.height);

    // Do the ruler labels in a small font that's black.
    g.setFont(new Font("SansSerif", Font.PLAIN, 10));
    g.setColor(Color.black);

    // Some vars we need.
    int end = 0;
    int start = 0;
    int tickLength = 0;
    String text = null;

    // Use clipping bounds to calculate first tick and last tick location.
    if (orientation == HORIZONTAL) {
        start = (drawHere.x / increment) * increment;
        end = (((drawHere.x + drawHere.width) / increment) + 1)
                * increment;
    } else {
        start = (drawHere.y / increment) * increment;
        end = (((drawHere.y + drawHere.height) / increment) + 1)
                * increment;
    }
```

```
                    // Make a special case of 0 to display the number
                    // within the rule and draw a units label.
                    if (start == 0) {
                        text = Integer.toString(0) + (isMetric ? " cm" : " in");
                        tickLength = 10;
                        if (orientation == HORIZONTAL) {
                            g.drawLine(0, SIZE-1, 0, SIZE-tickLength-1);
                            g.drawString(text, 2, 21);
                        } else {
                            g.drawLine(SIZE-1, 0, SIZE-tickLength-1, 0);
                            g.drawString(text, 9, 10);
                        }
                        text = null;
                        start = increment;
                    }

                    // ticks and labels
                    for (int i = start; i < end; i += increment) {
                        if (i % units == 0)  {
                            tickLength = 10;
                            text = Integer.toString(i/units);
                        } else {
                            tickLength = 7;
                            text = null;
                        }

                        if (tickLength != 0) {
                            if (orientation == HORIZONTAL) {
                                g.drawLine(i, SIZE-1, i, SIZE-tickLength-1);
                                if (text != null)
                                    g.drawString(text, i-3, 21);
                            } else {
                                g.drawLine(SIZE-1, i, SIZE-tickLength-1, i);
                                if (text != null)
                                    g.drawString(text, 9, i+3);
                            }
                        }
                    }
                }
            }
        }
```

EXAMPLE: *ScrollablePicture.java*

Main Source File: <u>ScrollDemo.java</u> *(page 702)*

SOURCE CODE: *http://java.sun.com/docs/books/tutorial/uiswing/components/example-swing/ScrollablePicture.java*

```
import java.awt.*;
import java.awt.event.*;
import javax.swing.*;
import javax.swing.border.*;

public class ScrollablePicture extends JLabel implements Scrollable {

    private int maxUnitIncrement = 1;

    public ScrollablePicture(ImageIcon i, int m) {
        super(i);
        maxUnitIncrement = m;
    }
```

Where Explained:

How to Use Scroll Panes (page 112)

```
    public Dimension getPreferredScrollableViewportSize() {
        return getPreferredSize();
    }

    public int getScrollableUnitIncrement(Rectangle visibleRect,
                                          int orientation,
                                          int direction) {
        //Get the current position.
        int currentPosition = 0;
        if (orientation == SwingConstants.HORIZONTAL)
            currentPosition = visibleRect.x;
        else
            currentPosition = visibleRect.y;

        //Return the number of pixels between currentPosition
        //and the nearest tick mark in the indicated direction.
        if (direction < 0) {
            int newPosition = currentPosition -
                              (currentPosition / maxUnitIncrement) *
                               maxUnitIncrement;
            return (newPosition == 0) ? maxUnitIncrement : newPosition;
        } else {
            return ((currentPosition / maxUnitIncrement) + 1) *
                    maxUnitIncrement - currentPosition;
        }
    }

    public int getScrollableBlockIncrement(Rectangle visibleRect,
                                           int orientation,
                                           int direction) {
        if (orientation == SwingConstants.HORIZONTAL)
            return visibleRect.width - maxUnitIncrement;
        else
            return visibleRect.height - maxUnitIncrement;
    }

    public boolean getScrollableTracksViewportWidth() {
        return false;
    }

    public boolean getScrollableTracksViewportHeight() {
        return false;
    }

    public void setMaxUnitIncrement(int pixels) {
        maxUnitIncrement = pixels;
    }
}
```

EXAMPLE: *ScrollDemo.java*

Where Explained:
How to Use Scroll Panes
(page 112)

Associated File(s): ScrollablePicture.java *(page 701)*, Rule.java *(page 699)*, and Corner.java *(page 633)*

SOURCE CODE: *http://java.sun.com/docs/books/tutorial/uiswing/components/example-swing/ScrollDemo.java*

```
import java.awt.*;
import java.awt.event.*;
import javax.swing.*;
import javax.swing.border.*;
```

```java
public class ScrollDemo extends JPanel {
    private Rule columnView;
    private Rule rowView;
    private JToggleButton isMetric;
    private ScrollablePicture picture;

    public ScrollDemo() {
        // Start loading the image icon now.
        ImageIcon david = new ImageIcon("images/youngdad.jpeg");

        // Create the row and column headers.
        columnView = new Rule(Rule.HORIZONTAL, true);
        columnView.setPreferredWidth(david.getIconWidth());
        rowView = new Rule(Rule.VERTICAL, true);
        rowView.setPreferredHeight(david.getIconHeight());

        // Create the corners.
        JPanel buttonCorner = new JPanel();
        isMetric = new JToggleButton("cm", true);
        isMetric.setFont(new Font("SansSerif", Font.PLAIN, 11));
        isMetric.setMargin(new Insets(2,2,2,2));
        isMetric.addItemListener(new UnitsListener());
        buttonCorner.add(isMetric); //Use the default FlowLayout

        // Set up the scroll pane.
        picture = new ScrollablePicture(david, columnView.getIncrement());
        JScrollPane pictureScrollPane = new JScrollPane(picture);
        pictureScrollPane.setPreferredSize(new Dimension(300, 250));
        pictureScrollPane.setViewportBorder(
                BorderFactory.createLineBorder(Color.black));

        pictureScrollPane.setColumnHeaderView(columnView);
        pictureScrollPane.setRowHeaderView(rowView);

        pictureScrollPane.setCorner(JScrollPane.UPPER_LEFT_CORNER,
                                buttonCorner);
        pictureScrollPane.setCorner(JScrollPane.LOWER_LEFT_CORNER,
                                new Corner());
        pictureScrollPane.setCorner(JScrollPane.UPPER_RIGHT_CORNER,
                                new Corner());

        // Put it in this panel.
        setLayout(new BoxLayout(this, BoxLayout.X_AXIS));
        add(pictureScrollPane);
        setBorder(BorderFactory.createEmptyBorder(20,20,20,20));
    }

    class UnitsListener implements ItemListener {
        public void itemStateChanged(ItemEvent e) {
            if (e.getStateChange() == ItemEvent.SELECTED) {
                // Turn it to metric.
                rowView.setIsMetric(true);
                columnView.setIsMetric(true);
            } else {
                // Turn it to inches.
                rowView.setIsMetric(false);
                columnView.setIsMetric(false);
            }
            picture.setMaxUnitIncrement(rowView.getIncrement());
        }
    }

    public static void main(String s[]) {
        JFrame frame = new JFrame("ScrollDemo");
        frame.addWindowListener(new WindowAdapter() {
            public void windowClosing(WindowEvent e) {
```

```
                          System.exit(0);
                  }
            });

            frame.setContentPane(new ScrollDemo());
            frame.pack();
            frame.setVisible(true);
        }
    }
```

EXAMPLE: *ScrollDemo2.java*

**Where
Explained:**
*Dynamically
Changing the
Client's Size*
(page 122)

SOURCE CODE: *http://java.sun.com/docs/books/tutorial/uiswing/components/example-swing/
                    ScrollDemo2.java*

```java
/*
 * This code is based on an example provided by John Vella,
 * a tutorial reader.
 */

import javax.swing.*;
import javax.swing.event.MouseInputAdapter;
import java.awt.*;
import java.awt.event.*;
import java.util.*;

public class ScrollDemo2 extends JPanel {
    private Dimension size; // indicates size taken up by graphics
    private Vector objects; // rectangular coordinates used to draw graphics

    private final Color colors[] = {
        Color.red, Color.blue, Color.green, Color.orange,
        Color.cyan, Color.magenta, Color.darkGray, Color.yellow};
    private final int color_n = colors.length;

    JPanel drawingArea;

    public ScrollDemo2() {
        setOpaque(true);
        size = new Dimension(0,0);
        objects = new Vector();

        //Set up the instructions.
        JLabel instructionsLeft = new JLabel(
                    "Click left mouse button to place a circle.");
        JLabel instructionsRight = new JLabel(
                    "Click right mouse button to clear drawing area.");
        JPanel instructionPanel = new JPanel(new GridLayout(0,1));
        instructionPanel.add(instructionsLeft);
        instructionPanel.add(instructionsRight);

        //Set up the drawing area.
        drawingArea = new JPanel() {
            protected void paintComponent(Graphics g) {
                super.paintComponent(g);

                Rectangle rect;
                for (int i = 0; i < objects.size(); i++) {
                    rect = (Rectangle)objects.elementAt(i);
                    g.setColor(colors[(i % color_n)]);
                    g.fillOval(rect.x, rect.y, rect.width, rect.height);
                }
            }
        };
```

```
        drawingArea.setBackground(Color.white);
        drawingArea.addMouseListener(new MyMouseListener());

        //Put the drawing area in a scroll pane.
        JScrollPane scroller = new JScrollPane(drawingArea);
        scroller.setPreferredSize(new Dimension(200,200));

        //Layout this demo.
        setLayout(new BorderLayout());
        add(instructionPanel, BorderLayout.NORTH);
        add(scroller, BorderLayout.CENTER);
    }

    class MyMouseListener extends MouseInputAdapter {
        final int W = 100;
        final int H = 100;

        public void mouseReleased(MouseEvent e) {
            boolean changed = false;
            if (SwingUtilities.isRightMouseButton(e)) {
                // This will clear the graphic objects.
                objects.removeAllElements();
                size.width=0;
                size.height=0;
                changed = true;
            } else {
                int x = e.getX() - W/2;
                int y = e.getY() - H/2;
                if (x < 0) x = 0;
                if (y < 0) y = 0;
                Rectangle rect = new Rectangle(x, y, W, H);
                objects.addElement(rect);
                drawingArea.scrollRectToVisible(rect);

                int this_width = (x + W + 2);
                if (this_width > size.width)
                    {size.width = this_width; changed=true;}

                int this_height = (y + H + 2);
                if (this_height > size.height)
                    {size.height = this_height; changed=true;}
            }
            if (changed) {
                //Update client's preferred size because
                //the area taken up by the graphics has
                //gotten larger or smaller (if cleared).
                drawingArea.setPreferredSize(size);

                //Let the scroll pane know to update itself
                //and its scrollbars.
                drawingArea.revalidate();
            }
            drawingArea.repaint();
        }
    }

    public static void main (String args[]) {
        JFrame frame = new JFrame("ScrollDemo2");
        frame.addWindowListener(new WindowAdapter() {
            public void windowClosing(WindowEvent e) {System.exit(0);}
        });

        frame.setContentPane(new ScrollDemo2());
        frame.pack();
        frame.setVisible(true);
    }
}
```

EXAMPLE: *SharedModelDemo.java*

Where Explained:
How to Use Lists
(page 218)

SOURCE CODE: *http://java.sun.com/docs/books/tutorial/uiswing/components/example-swing/*
SharedModelDemo.java

```java
import javax.swing.*;
import javax.swing.event.*;
import javax.swing.table.*;

import java.util.*;
import java.awt.*;
import java.awt.event.*;

public class SharedModelDemo extends JPanel {
    JTextArea output;
    JList list;
    JTable table;
    String newline = "\n";
    ListSelectionModel listSelectionModel;

    public SharedModelDemo() {
        super(new BorderLayout());

        Vector data = new Vector(7);
        String[] columnNames = { "French", "Spanish", "Italian" };
        String[] oneData =     { "un",      "uno",     "uno"    };
        String[] twoData =     { "deux",    "dos",     "due"    };
        String[] threeData =   { "trois",   "tres",    "tre"    };
        String[] fourData =    { "quatre",  "cuatro",  "quattro" };
        String[] fiveData =    { "cinq",    "cinco",   "cinque" };
        String[] sixData =     { "six",     "seis",    "sei"    };
        String[] sevenData =   { "sept",    "siete",   "sette"  };

        //Build the model.
        SharedDataModel dataModel = new SharedDataModel(columnNames);
        dataModel.addElement(oneData);
        dataModel.addElement(twoData);
        dataModel.addElement(threeData);
        dataModel.addElement(fourData);
        dataModel.addElement(fiveData);
        dataModel.addElement(sixData);
        dataModel.addElement(sevenData);

        list = new JList(dataModel);
        list.setCellRenderer(new DefaultListCellRenderer() {
            public Component getListCellRendererComponent(JList l,
                                                          Object value,
                                                          int i,
                                                          boolean s,
                                                          boolean f) {

                String[] array = (String[])value;
                return super.getListCellRendererComponent(l,
                                                          array[0],
                                                          i, s, f);
            }
        });

        listSelectionModel = list.getSelectionModel();
        listSelectionModel.addListSelectionListener(
                            new SharedListSelectionHandler());
        JScrollPane listPane = new JScrollPane(list);

        table = new JTable(dataModel);
        table.setSelectionModel(listSelectionModel);
        JScrollPane tablePane = new JScrollPane(table);
```

```
//Build control area (use default FlowLayout).
JPanel controlPane = new JPanel();
String[] modes = { "SINGLE_SELECTION",
                   "SINGLE_INTERVAL_SELECTION",
                   "MULTIPLE_INTERVAL_SELECTION" };

final JComboBox comboBox = new JComboBox(modes);
comboBox.setSelectedIndex(2);
comboBox.addActionListener(new ActionListener() {
    public void actionPerformed(ActionEvent e) {
        String newMode = (String)comboBox.getSelectedItem();
        if (newMode.equals("SINGLE_SELECTION")) {
            listSelectionModel.setSelectionMode(
                ListSelectionModel.SINGLE_SELECTION);
        } else if (newMode.equals("SINGLE_INTERVAL_SELECTION")) {
            listSelectionModel.setSelectionMode(
                ListSelectionModel.SINGLE_INTERVAL_SELECTION);
        } else {
            listSelectionModel.setSelectionMode(
                ListSelectionModel.MULTIPLE_INTERVAL_SELECTION);
        }
        output.append("----------"
                        + "Mode: " + newMode
                        + "----------" + newline);
    }
});
controlPane.add(new JLabel("Selection mode:"));
controlPane.add(comboBox);

//Build output area.
output = new JTextArea(10, 40);
output.setEditable(false);
JScrollPane outputPane = new JScrollPane(output,
                ScrollPaneConstants.VERTICAL_SCROLLBAR_ALWAYS,
                ScrollPaneConstants.HORIZONTAL_SCROLLBAR_ALWAYS);

//Do the layout.
JSplitPane splitPane = new JSplitPane(JSplitPane.VERTICAL_SPLIT);
add(splitPane, BorderLayout.CENTER);

JPanel topHalf = new JPanel();
topHalf.setLayout(new BoxLayout(topHalf, BoxLayout.X_AXIS));
JPanel listContainer = new JPanel(new GridLayout(1,1));
listContainer.setBorder(BorderFactory.createTitledBorder(
                                "List"));
listContainer.add(listPane);
JPanel tableContainer = new JPanel(new GridLayout(1,1));
tableContainer.setBorder(BorderFactory.createTitledBorder(
                                "Table"));
tableContainer.add(tablePane);
tablePane.setPreferredSize(new Dimension(300, 100));
topHalf.setBorder(BorderFactory.createEmptyBorder(5,5,0,5));
topHalf.add(listContainer);
topHalf.add(tableContainer);

topHalf.setMinimumSize(new Dimension(400, 50));
topHalf.setPreferredSize(new Dimension(400, 110));
splitPane.add(topHalf);

JPanel bottomHalf = new JPanel(new BorderLayout());
bottomHalf.add(controlPane, BorderLayout.NORTH);
bottomHalf.add(outputPane, BorderLayout.CENTER);
//XXX: next line needed if bottomHalf is a scroll pane:
//bottomHalf.setMinimumSize(new Dimension(400, 50));
bottomHalf.setPreferredSize(new Dimension(450, 135));
splitPane.add(bottomHalf);
}
```

```java
public static void main(String[] args) {
    JFrame frame = new JFrame("SharedModelDemo");
    frame.addWindowListener(new WindowAdapter() {
        public void windowClosing(WindowEvent e) {
            System.exit(0);
        }
    });

    frame.setContentPane(new SharedModelDemo());
    frame.pack();
    frame.setVisible(true);
}

class SharedListSelectionHandler implements ListSelectionListener {
    public void valueChanged(ListSelectionEvent e) {
        ListSelectionModel lsm = (ListSelectionModel)e.getSource();

        int firstIndex = e.getFirstIndex();
        int lastIndex = e.getLastIndex();
        boolean isAdjusting = e.getValueIsAdjusting();
        output.append("Event for indexes "
                      + firstIndex + " - " + lastIndex
                      + "; isAdjusting is " + isAdjusting
                      + "; selected indexes:");

        if (lsm.isSelectionEmpty()) {
            output.append(" <none>");
        } else {
            // Find out which indexes are selected.
            int minIndex = lsm.getMinSelectionIndex();
            int maxIndex = lsm.getMaxSelectionIndex();
            for (int i = minIndex; i <= maxIndex; i++) {
                if (lsm.isSelectedIndex(i)) {
                    output.append(" " + i);
                }
            }
        }
        output.append(newline);
    }
}

class SharedDataModel extends DefaultListModel
                      implements TableModel {
    public String[] columnNames;

    public SharedDataModel(String[] columnNames) {
        super();
        this.columnNames = columnNames;
    }

    public void rowChanged(int row) {
        fireContentsChanged(this, row, row);
    }

    private TableModel tableModel = new AbstractTableModel() {
        public String getColumnName(int column) {
            return columnNames[column];
        }
        public int getRowCount() {
            return size();
        }
        public int getColumnCount() {
            return columnNames.length;
        }
        public Object getValueAt(int row, int column) {
            String[] rowData = (String [])elementAt(row);
            return rowData[column];
        }
```

```
                    public boolean isCellEditable(int row, int column) {
                        return true;
                    }
                    public void setValueAt(Object value, int row, int column) {
                        String newValue = (String)value;
                        String[] rowData = (String [])elementAt(row);
                        rowData[column] = newValue;
                        fireTableCellUpdated(row, column); //table event
                        rowChanged(row);                    //list event
                    }
                };

                //Implement the TableModel interface.
                public int getRowCount() {
                    return tableModel.getRowCount();
                }
                public int getColumnCount() {
                    return tableModel.getColumnCount();
                }
                public String getColumnName(int columnIndex) {
                    return tableModel.getColumnName(columnIndex);
                }
                public Class getColumnClass(int columnIndex) {
                    return tableModel.getColumnClass(columnIndex);
                }
                public boolean isCellEditable(int rowIndex, int columnIndex) {
                    return tableModel.isCellEditable(rowIndex, columnIndex);
                }
                public Object getValueAt(int rowIndex, int columnIndex) {
                    return tableModel.getValueAt(rowIndex, columnIndex);
                }
                public void setValueAt(Object aValue, int rowIndex, int columnIndex) {
                    tableModel.setValueAt(aValue, rowIndex, columnIndex);
                }
                public void addTableModelListener(TableModelListener l) {
                    tableModel.addTableModelListener(l);
                }
                public void removeTableModelListener(TableModelListener l) {
                    tableModel.removeTableModelListener(l);
                }
            }
        }
```

EXAMPLE: *SimpleTableDemo.java*

SOURCE CODE: *http://java.sun.com/docs/books/tutorial/uiswing/components/example-swing/SimpleTableDemo.java*

Where Explained:

Creating a Simple Table (page 254)

```
import javax.swing.JTable;
import javax.swing.JScrollPane;
import javax.swing.JPanel;
import javax.swing.JFrame;
import java.awt.*;
import java.awt.event.*;

public class SimpleTableDemo extends JFrame {
    private boolean DEBUG = true;

    public SimpleTableDemo() {
        super("SimpleTableDemo");
```

```java
        Object[][] data = {
            {"Mary", "Campione",
             "Snowboarding", new Integer(5), new Boolean(false)},
            {"Alison", "Huml",
             "Rowing", new Integer(3), new Boolean(true)},
            {"Kathy", "Walrath",
             "Chasing toddlers", new Integer(2), new Boolean(false)},
            {"Mark", "Andrews",
             "Speed reading", new Integer(20), new Boolean(true)},
            {"Angela", "Lih",
             "Teaching high school", new Integer(4), new Boolean(false)}
        };

        String[] columnNames = {"First Name",
                                "Last Name",
                                "Sport",
                                "# of Years",
                                "Vegetarian"};

        final JTable table = new JTable(data, columnNames);
        table.setPreferredScrollableViewportSize(new Dimension(500, 70));

        if (DEBUG) {
            table.addMouseListener(new MouseAdapter() {
                public void mouseClicked(MouseEvent e) {
                    printDebugData(table);
                }
            });
        }

        //Create the scroll pane and add the table to it.
        JScrollPane scrollPane = new JScrollPane(table);

        //Add the scroll pane to this window.
        getContentPane().add(scrollPane, BorderLayout.CENTER);

        addWindowListener(new WindowAdapter() {
            public void windowClosing(WindowEvent e) {
                System.exit(0);
            }
        });
    }

    private void printDebugData(JTable table) {
        int numRows = table.getRowCount();
        int numCols = table.getColumnCount();
        javax.swing.table.TableModel model = table.getModel();

        System.out.println("Value of data: ");
        for (int i=0; i < numRows; i++) {
            System.out.print("    row " + i + ":");
            for (int j=0; j < numCols; j++) {
                System.out.print("  " + model.getValueAt(i, j));
            }
            System.out.println();
        }
        System.out.println("--------------------------");
    }

    public static void main(String[] args) {
        SimpleTableDemo frame = new SimpleTableDemo();
        frame.pack();
        frame.setVisible(true);
    }
}
```

EXAMPLE: *SimpleTableSelectionDemo.java*

SOURCE CODE: *http://java.sun.com/docs/books/tutorial/uiswing/components/example-swing/SimpleTableSelectionDemo.java*

Where Explained: *Detecting User Selections* (page 259)

```java
import javax.swing.JTable;
import javax.swing.ListSelectionModel;
import javax.swing.event.ListSelectionListener;
import javax.swing.event.ListSelectionEvent;
import javax.swing.JScrollPane;
import javax.swing.JPanel;
import javax.swing.JFrame;
import java.awt.*;
import java.awt.event.*;

public class SimpleTableSelectionDemo extends JFrame {
    private boolean DEBUG = false;
    private boolean ALLOW_COLUMN_SELECTION = false;
    private boolean ALLOW_ROW_SELECTION = true;

    public SimpleTableSelectionDemo() {
        super("SimpleTableSelectionDemo");

        Object[][] data = {
            {"Mary", "Campione",
             "Snowboarding", new Integer(5), new Boolean(false)},
            {"Alison", "Huml",
             "Rowing", new Integer(3), new Boolean(true)},
            {"Kathy", "Walrath",
             "Chasing toddlers", new Integer(2), new Boolean(false)},
            {"Mark", "Andrews",
             "Speed reading", new Integer(20), new Boolean(true)},
            {"Angela", "Lih",
             "Teaching high school", new Integer(4), new Boolean(false)}
        };

        String[] columnNames = {"First Name",
                                "Last Name",
                                "Sport",
                                "# of Years",
                                "Vegetarian"};

        final JTable table = new JTable(data, columnNames);
        table.setPreferredScrollableViewportSize(new Dimension(500, 70));

        table.setSelectionMode(ListSelectionModel.SINGLE_SELECTION);
        if (ALLOW_ROW_SELECTION) { // true by default
            ListSelectionModel rowSM = table.getSelectionModel();
            rowSM.addListSelectionListener(new ListSelectionListener() {
                public void valueChanged(ListSelectionEvent e) {
                    ListSelectionModel lsm = (ListSelectionModel)e.getSource();
                    if (lsm.isSelectionEmpty()) {
                        System.out.println("No rows are selected.");
                    } else {
                        int selectedRow = lsm.getMinSelectionIndex();
                        System.out.println("Row " + selectedRow
                                            + " is now selected.");
                    }
                }
            });
        } else {
            table.setRowSelectionAllowed(false);
        }
```

```java
        if (ALLOW_COLUMN_SELECTION) { // false by default
            if (ALLOW_ROW_SELECTION) {
                //We allow both row and column selection, which
                //implies that we *really* want to allow individual
                //cell selection.
                table.setCellSelectionEnabled(true);
            }
            table.setColumnSelectionAllowed(true);
            ListSelectionModel colSM =
                table.getColumnModel().getSelectionModel();
            colSM.addListSelectionListener(new ListSelectionListener() {
                public void valueChanged(ListSelectionEvent e) {
                    ListSelectionModel lsm = (ListSelectionModel)e.getSource();
                    if (lsm.isSelectionEmpty()) {
                        System.out.println("No columns are selected.");
                    } else {
                        int selectedCol = lsm.getMinSelectionIndex();
                        System.out.println("Column " + selectedCol
                                          + " is now selected.");
                    }
                }
            });
        }

        if (DEBUG) {
            table.addMouseListener(new MouseAdapter() {
                public void mouseClicked(MouseEvent e) {
                    printDebugData(table);
                }
            });
        }

        //Create the scroll pane and add the table to it.
        JScrollPane scrollPane = new JScrollPane(table);

        //Add the scroll pane to this window.
        getContentPane().add(scrollPane, BorderLayout.CENTER);

        addWindowListener(new WindowAdapter() {
            public void windowClosing(WindowEvent e) {
                System.exit(0);
            }
        });
    }

    private void printDebugData(JTable table) {
        int numRows = table.getRowCount();
        int numCols = table.getColumnCount();
        javax.swing.table.TableModel model = table.getModel();

        System.out.println("Value of data: ");
        for (int i=0; i < numRows; i++) {
            System.out.print("    row " + i + ":");
            for (int j=0; j < numCols; j++) {
                System.out.print("  " + model.getValueAt(i, j));
            }
            System.out.println();
        }
        System.out.println("--------------------------");
    }

    public static void main(String[] args) {
        SimpleTableSelectionDemo frame = new SimpleTableSelectionDemo();
        frame.pack();
        frame.setVisible(true);
    }
}
```

EXAMPLE: *SliderDemo.java*

SOURCE CODE: *http://java.sun.com/docs/books/tutorial/uiswing/components/example-swing/SliderDemo.java*

**Where
Explained:**
*How to Use
Sliders*
(page 248)

```java
import java.awt.*;
import java.awt.event.*;
import javax.swing.*;
import javax.swing.event.*;

public class SliderDemo extends JFrame
                        implements ActionListener {
    //Set up animation parameters.
    static final int FPS_INIT = 15;      //initial frames per second
    int frameNumber = 0;
    int delay;
    Timer timer;
    boolean frozen = false;

    //This label uses ImageIcon to show the doggy pictures.
    JLabel picture;

    public SliderDemo(String windowTitle) {
        super(windowTitle);
        delay = 1000 / FPS_INIT;

        //Create the slider and its label
        JLabel sliderLabel = new JLabel("Frames Per Second", JLabel.CENTER);
        sliderLabel.setAlignmentX(Component.CENTER_ALIGNMENT);

        JSlider framesPerSecond = new JSlider(JSlider.HORIZONTAL,
                                     0, 30, FPS_INIT);
        framesPerSecond.addChangeListener(new SliderListener());

        //Turn on labels at major tick marks.
        framesPerSecond.setMajorTickSpacing(10);
        framesPerSecond.setMinorTickSpacing(1);
        framesPerSecond.setPaintTicks(true);
        framesPerSecond.setPaintLabels(true);
        framesPerSecond.setBorder(
                BorderFactory.createEmptyBorder(0,0,10,0));

        //Create the label for the animation.
        picture = new JLabel(new ImageIcon("images/doggy/T"
                                    + frameNumber
                                    + ".gif"),
                         JLabel.CENTER);
        picture.setAlignmentX(Component.CENTER_ALIGNMENT);
        picture.setBorder(BorderFactory.createCompoundBorder(
                BorderFactory.createLoweredBevelBorder(),
                BorderFactory.createEmptyBorder(10,10,10,10)));

        //Put everything in the content pane.
        JPanel contentPane = new JPanel();
        contentPane.setLayout(new BoxLayout(contentPane, BoxLayout.Y_AXIS));
        contentPane.add(sliderLabel);
        contentPane.add(framesPerSecond);
        contentPane.add(picture);
        contentPane.setBorder(BorderFactory.createEmptyBorder(10,10,10,10));
        setContentPane(contentPane);

        //Set up a timer that calls this object's action handler.
        timer = new Timer(delay, this);
```

```
        timer.setInitialDelay(delay * 10); //pauses animation after frames
                                     //0 and 6 by restarting the timer
        timer.setCoalesce(true);

        //Add a listener for window events
        addWindowListener(new WindowAdapter() {
            public void windowIconified(WindowEvent e) {
                stopAnimation();
            }
            public void windowDeiconified(WindowEvent e) {
                startAnimation();
            }
            public void windowClosing(WindowEvent e) {
                System.exit(0);
            }
        });

    }

    /** Listens to the slider. */
    class SliderListener implements ChangeListener {
        public void stateChanged(ChangeEvent e) {
            JSlider source = (JSlider)e.getSource();
            if (!source.getValueIsAdjusting()) {
                int fps = (int)source.getValue();
                if (fps == 0) {
                    if (!frozen) stopAnimation();
                } else {
                    delay = 1000 / fps;
                    timer.setDelay(delay);
                    timer.setInitialDelay(delay * 10);
                    if (frozen) startAnimation();
                }
            }
        }
    }

    public void startAnimation() {
        //Start (or restart) animating!
        timer.start();
        frozen = false;
    }

    public void stopAnimation() {
        //Stop the animating thread.
        timer.stop();
        frozen = true;
    }

    //Called when the Timer fires
    public void actionPerformed(ActionEvent e) {
        //Advance the animation frame.
        if (frameNumber==13) {
            frameNumber = 0;
        } else {
            frameNumber++;
        }
        //XXX no caching?
        picture.setIcon(new ImageIcon("images/doggy/T" + frameNumber + ".gif"));
        if (frameNumber==0 || frameNumber==6) {
            timer.restart();
        }
    }

    public static void main(String[] args) {
        SliderDemo animator = new SliderDemo("SliderDemo");
```

```
            animator.pack();
            animator.setVisible(true);
            animator.startAnimation();
        }
    }
```

EXAMPLE: *SliderDemo2.java*

**Where
Explained:**
*How to Use
Sliders*
(page 248)

SOURCE CODE: *http://java.sun.com/docs/books/tutorial/uiswing/components/example-
swing/SliderDemo2.java*

```java
import java.awt.*;
import java.awt.event.*;
import javax.swing.*;
import javax.swing.event.*;
import java.util.Hashtable;

public class SliderDemo2 extends JFrame
                         implements ActionListener {
    //Set up animation parameters.
    static final int FPS_INIT = 15;    //initial frames per second
    int frameNumber = 0;
    int delay;
    Timer timer;
    boolean frozen = false;

    //This label uses ImageIcon to show the doggy pictures.
    JLabel picture;

    public SliderDemo2(String windowTitle) {
        super(windowTitle);
        delay = 1000 / FPS_INIT;

        //Create the slider.
        JSlider framesPerSecond = new JSlider(JSlider.VERTICAL,
                                      0, 30, FPS_INIT);
        framesPerSecond.addChangeListener(new SliderListener());
        framesPerSecond.setMajorTickSpacing(10);
        framesPerSecond.setPaintTicks(true);

        //Create the label table.
        Hashtable labelTable = new Hashtable();
        //PENDING: could use images, but we don't have any good ones.
        labelTable.put(new Integer( 0 ),
                   new JLabel("Stop") );
                   //new JLabel(new ImageIcon("images/stop.gif")) );
        labelTable.put(new Integer( 3 ),
                   new JLabel("Slow") );
                   //new JLabel(new ImageIcon("images/slow.gif")) );
        labelTable.put(new Integer( 30 ),
                   new JLabel("Fast") );
                   //new JLabel(new ImageIcon("images/fast.gif")) );
        framesPerSecond.setLabelTable(labelTable);

        framesPerSecond.setPaintLabels(true);
        framesPerSecond.setBorder(
                BorderFactory.createEmptyBorder(0,0,0,10));

        //Create the label for the animation.
        picture = new JLabel(new ImageIcon("images/doggy/T"
                                      + frameNumber
                                      + ".gif"),
                             JLabel.CENTER);
```

```java
        picture.setAlignmentX(Component.CENTER_ALIGNMENT);
        picture.setBorder(BorderFactory.createCompoundBorder(
                BorderFactory.createLoweredBevelBorder(),
                BorderFactory.createEmptyBorder(10,10,10,10)));

        //Put everything in the content pane.
        JPanel contentPane = new JPanel();
        contentPane.setLayout(new BorderLayout());
        contentPane.add(framesPerSecond, BorderLayout.WEST);
        contentPane.add(picture, BorderLayout.CENTER);
        contentPane.setBorder(BorderFactory.createEmptyBorder(10,10,10,10));
        setContentPane(contentPane);

        //Set up a timer that calls this object's action handler.
        timer = new Timer(delay, this);
        timer.setInitialDelay(delay * 10); //pauses animation after frames
                                        //0 and 6 by restarting the timer
        timer.setCoalesce(true);

        //Add a listener for window events
        addWindowListener(new WindowAdapter() {
            public void windowIconified(WindowEvent e) {
                stopAnimation();
            }
            public void windowDeiconified(WindowEvent e) {
                startAnimation();
            }
            public void windowClosing(WindowEvent e) {
                System.exit(0);
            }
        });
    }

    /** Listens to the slider. */
    class SliderListener implements ChangeListener {
        public void stateChanged(ChangeEvent e) {
            JSlider source = (JSlider)e.getSource();
            if (!source.getValueIsAdjusting()) {
                int fps = (int)source.getValue();
                if (fps == 0) {
                    if (!frozen) stopAnimation();
                } else {
                    delay = 1000 / fps;
                    timer.setDelay(delay);
                    timer.setInitialDelay(delay * 10);
                    if (frozen) startAnimation();
                }
            }
        }
    }

    public void startAnimation() {
        //Start (or restart) animating!
        timer.start();
        frozen = false;
    }

    public void stopAnimation() {
        //Stop the animating thread.
        timer.stop();
        frozen = true;
    }

    //Called when the Timer fires
    public void actionPerformed(ActionEvent e) {
```

```
            //Advance the animation frame.
            if (frameNumber==13) {
                frameNumber = 0;
            } else {
                framcNumber++;
            }
            //XXX no caching?
            picture.setIcon(new ImageIcon("images/doggy/T"
                                            + frameNumber
                                            + ".gif"));
            if (frameNumber==0 || frameNumber==6) {
                timer.restart();
            }
        }

    public static void main(String[] args) {
        SliderDemo2 animator = new SliderDemo2("SliderDemo2");
        animator.pack();
        animator.setVisible(true);
        animator.startAnimation();
    }
}
```

EXAMPLE: *SplitPaneDemo.java*

SOURCE CODE: *http://java.sun.com/docs/books/tutorial/uiswing/components/example-swing/SplitPaneDemo.java*

Where Explained:

How to Use Split Panes (page 127)

```java
import java.awt.*;
import java.awt.event.*;
import javax.swing.*;
import javax.swing.event.*;

import java.util.*;

//SplitPaneDemo itself is not a visible component.
public class SplitPaneDemo implements ListSelectionListener {
    private Vector imageNames;
    private JLabel picture;
    private JList list;
    private JSplitPane splitPane;

    public SplitPaneDemo() {
        //Read image names from a properties file
        ResourceBundle imageResource;
        try {
            imageResource = ResourceBundle.getBundle("imagenames");
            String imageNamesString = imageResource.getString("images");
            imageNames = parseList(imageNamesString);
        } catch (MissingResourceException e) {
            System.err.println();
            System.err.println("Can't find the properties file " +
                                "that contains the image names.");
            System.err.println("Its name should be imagenames.properties, " +
                                "and it should");
            System.err.println("contain a single line that specifies " +
                                "one or more image");
            System.err.println("files to be found in a directory " +
                                "named images.  Example:");
            System.err.println();
            System.err.println("    images=Bird.gif Cat.gif Dog.gif");
            System.err.println();
            System.exit(1);
        }
```

```
        //Create the list of images and put it in a scroll pane
        list = new JList(imageNames);
        list.setSelectionMode(ListSelectionModel.SINGLE_SELECTION);
        list.setSelectedIndex(0);
        list.addListSelectionListener(this);
        JScrollPane listScrollPane = new JScrollPane(list);

        //Set up the picture label and put it in a scroll pane
        ImageIcon firstImage = new ImageIcon("images/" +
                               (String)imageNames.firstElement());
        picture = new JLabel(firstImage);
        picture.setPreferredSize(new Dimension(firstImage.getIconWidth(),
                                        firstImage.getIconHeight())));
        JScrollPane pictureScrollPane = new JScrollPane(picture);

        //Create a split pane with the two scroll panes in it
        splitPane = new JSplitPane(JSplitPane.HORIZONTAL_SPLIT,
                             listScrollPane, pictureScrollPane);
        splitPane.setOneTouchExpandable(true);
        splitPane.setDividerLocation(150);

        //Provide minimum sizes for the two components in the split pane
        Dimension minimumSize = new Dimension(100, 50);
        listScrollPane.setMinimumSize(minimumSize);
        pictureScrollPane.setMinimumSize(minimumSize);

        //Provide a preferred size for the split pane
        splitPane.setPreferredSize(new Dimension(400, 200));
    }

    //Used by SplitPaneDemo2
    public JList getImageList() {
        return list;
    }

    public JSplitPane getSplitPane() {
        return splitPane;
    }

    public void valueChanged(ListSelectionEvent e) {
        if (e.getValueIsAdjusting())
            return;

        JList theList = (JList)e.getSource();
        if (theList.isSelectionEmpty()) {
            picture.setIcon(null);
        } else {
            int index = theList.getSelectedIndex();
            ImageIcon newImage = new ImageIcon("images/" +
                                (String)imageNames.elementAt(index));
            picture.setIcon(newImage);
            picture.setPreferredSize(new Dimension(newImage.getIconWidth(),
                                        newImage.getIconHeight() ));
            picture.revalidate();
        }
    }

    protected static Vector parseList(String theStringList) {
        Vector v = new Vector(10);
        StringTokenizer tokenizer = new StringTokenizer(theStringList, " ");
        while (tokenizer.hasMoreTokens()) {
            String image = tokenizer.nextToken();
            v.addElement(image);
        }
        return v;
    }
```

```java
    public static void main(String s[]) {
        JFrame frame = new JFrame("SplitPaneDemo");

        frame.addWindowListener(new WindowAdapter() {
            public void windowClosing(WindowEvent e) {System.exit(0);}
        });

        SplitPaneDemo splitPaneDemo = new SplitPaneDemo();
        frame.getContentPane().add(splitPaneDemo.getSplitPane());
        frame.pack();
        frame.setVisible(true);
    }
}
```

EXAMPLE: *SplitPaneDemo2.java*

SOURCE CODE: *http://java.sun.com/docs/books/tutorial/uiswing/components/example-swing/SplitPaneDemo2.java*

Where Explained: *Nesting Split Panes* (page 130)

```java
import java.awt.*;
import java.awt.event.*;
import javax.swing.*;
import javax.swing.event.*;

import java.util.*;

public class SplitPaneDemo2 extends JFrame
                            implements ListSelectionListener {
    private JLabel label;

    public SplitPaneDemo2() {
        super("SplitPaneDemo2");

        //Create an instance of SplitPaneDemo
        SplitPaneDemo splitPaneDemo = new SplitPaneDemo();
        JSplitPane top = splitPaneDemo.getSplitPane();
        splitPaneDemo.getImageList().addListSelectionListener(this);

        //XXXX: Bug #4131528, borders on nested split panes accumulate.
        //Workaround: Set the border on any split pane within
        //another split pane to null. Components within nested split
        //panes need to have their own border for this to work well.
        top.setBorder(null);

        //Create a regular old label
        label = new JLabel("Click on an image name in the list.",
                    JLabel.CENTER);

        //Create a split pane and put "top" (a split pane)
        //and JLabel instance in it.
        JSplitPane splitPane = new JSplitPane(JSplitPane.VERTICAL_SPLIT,
                                    top, label);
        splitPane.setOneTouchExpandable(true);
        splitPane.setDividerLocation(180);

        //Provide minimum sizes for the two components in the split pane
        top.setMinimumSize(new Dimension(100, 50));
        label.setMinimumSize(new Dimension(100, 30));

        //Add the split pane to this frame
        getContentPane().add(splitPane);
    }
```

```
public void valueChanged(ListSelectionEvent e) {
    if (e.getValueIsAdjusting())
        return;

    JList theList = (JList)e.getSource();
    if (theList.isSelectionEmpty()) {
        label.setText("Nothing selected.");
    } else {
        int index = theList.getSelectedIndex();
        label.setText("Selected image number " + index);
    }
}

public static void main(String s[]) {
    JFrame frame = new SplitPaneDemo2();

    frame.addWindowListener(new WindowAdapter() {
        public void windowClosing(WindowEvent e) {System.exit(0);}
    });

    frame.pack();
    frame.setVisible(true);
}
}
```

EXAMPLE: *SwingWorker.java*

Where Explained:

Using the SwingWorker Class
(page 432)

Main Source File: ProgressBarDemo.java *(page 695),* IconDemoApplet.java *(page 816)*

SOURCE CODE: *http://java.sun.com/docs/books/tutorial/uiswing/components/example-swing/ SwingWorker.java*

```
//import com.sun.java.swing.SwingUtilities;  //old package name
import javax.swing.SwingUtilities;  //new package name

/**
 * An abstract class that you subclass to perform
 * GUI-related work in a dedicated thread.
 * For instructions on using this class, see
 * http://java.sun.com/products/jfc/swingdoc-current/threads2.html
 */
public abstract class SwingWorker {
    private Object value;  // see getValue(), setValue()
    private Thread thread;

    /**
     * Class to maintain reference to current worker thread
     * under separate synchronization control.
     */
    private static class ThreadVar {
        private Thread thread;
        ThreadVar(Thread t) { thread = t; }
        synchronized Thread get() { return thread; }
        synchronized void clear() { thread = null; }
    }

    private ThreadVar threadVar;

    /**
     * Get the value produced by the worker thread, or null if it
     * hasn't been constructed yet.
     */
```

```
protected synchronized Object getValue() {
    return value;
}

/**
 * Set the value produced by worker thread
 */
private synchronized void setValue(Object x) {
    value = x;
}

/**
 * Compute the value to be returned by the <code>get</code> method.
 */
public abstract Object construct();

/**
 * Called on the event dispatching thread (not on the worker thread)
 * after the <code>construct</code> method has returned.
 */
public void finished() {
}

/**
 * A new method that interrupts the worker thread.  Call this method
 * to force the worker to abort what it's doing.
 */
public void interrupt() {
    Thread t = threadVar.get();
    if (t != null) {
        t.interrupt();
    }
    threadVar.clear();
}

/**
 * Return the value created by the <code>construct</code> method.
 * Returns null if either the constructing thread or
 * the current thread was interrupted before a value was produced.
 *
 * @return the value created by the <code>construct</code> method
 */
public Object get() {
    while (true) {
        Thread t = threadVar.get();
        if (t == null) {
            return getValue();
        }
        try {
            t.join();
        }
        catch (InterruptedException e) {
            Thread.currentThread().interrupt(); // propagate
            return null;
        }
    }
}

/**
 * Start a thread that will call the <code>construct</code> method
 * and then exit.
 */
public SwingWorker() {
    final Runnable doFinished = new Runnable() {
        public void run() { finished(); }
    };
```

```
                      Runnable doConstruct = new Runnable() {
                          public void run() {
                              try {
                                  setValue(construct());
                              }
                              finally {
                                  threadVar.clear();
                              }

                              SwingUtilities.invokeLater(doFinished);
                          }
                      };

                      Thread t = new Thread(doConstruct);
                      threadVar = new ThreadVar(t);
                      t.start();
                  }
              }
```

EXAMPLE: *TabbedPaneDemo.java*

SOURCE CODE: *http://java.sun.com/docs/books/tutorial/uiswing/components/example-swing/ TabbedPaneDemo.java*

Where Explained:

How to Use Tabbed Panes
(page 134)

```
import javax.swing.JTabbedPane;
import javax.swing.ImageIcon;
import javax.swing.JLabel;
import javax.swing.JPanel;
import javax.swing.JFrame;

import java.awt.*;
import java.awt.event.*;

public class TabbedPaneDemo extends JPanel {
    public TabbedPaneDemo() {
        ImageIcon icon = new ImageIcon("images/middle.gif");
        JTabbedPane tabbedPane = new JTabbedPane();

        Component panel1 = makeTextPanel("Blah");
        tabbedPane.addTab("One", icon, panel1, "Does nothing");
        tabbedPane.setSelectedIndex(0);

        Component panel2 = makeTextPanel("Blah blah");
        tabbedPane.addTab("Two", icon, panel2, "Does twice as much nothing");

        Component panel3 = makeTextPanel("Blah blah blah");
        tabbedPane.addTab("Three", icon, panel3, "Still does nothing");

        Component panel4 = makeTextPanel("Blah blah blah blah");
        tabbedPane.addTab("Four", icon, panel4, "Does nothing at all");

        //Add the tabbed pane to this panel.
        setLayout(new GridLayout(1, 1));
        add(tabbedPane);
    }

    protected Component makeTextPanel(String text) {
        JPanel panel = new JPanel(false);
        JLabel filler = new JLabel(text);
        filler.setHorizontalAlignment(JLabel.CENTER);
        panel.setLayout(new GridLayout(1, 1));
        panel.add(filler);
        return panel;
    }
```

```
        public static void main(String[] args) {
            JFrame frame = new JFrame("TabbedPaneDemo");
            frame.addWindowListener(new WindowAdapter() {
                public void windowClosing(WindowEvent e) {System.exit(0);}
            });

            frame.getContentPane().add(new TabbedPaneDemo(),
                                    BorderLayout.CENTER);
            frame.setSize(400, 125);
            frame.setVisible(true);
        }
    }
```

EXAMPLE: *TableDemo.java*

SOURCE CODE: *http://java.sun.com/docs/books/tutorial/uiswing/components/example-swing/TableDemo.java*

```
    import javax.swing.JTable;
    import javax.swing.table.AbstractTableModel;
    import javax.swing.JScrollPane;
    import javax.swing.JFrame;
    import javax.swing.SwingUtilities;
    import javax.swing.JOptionPane;
    import java.awt.*;
    import java.awt.event.*;

    public class TableDemo extends JFrame {
        private boolean DEBUG = true;

        public TableDemo() {
            super("TableDemo");

            MyTableModel myModel = new MyTableModel();
            JTable table = new JTable(myModel);
            table.setPreferredScrollableViewportSize(new Dimension(500, 70));

            //Create the scroll pane and add the table to it.
            JScrollPane scrollPane = new JScrollPane(table);

            //Add the scroll pane to this window.
            getContentPane().add(scrollPane, BorderLayout.CENTER);

            addWindowListener(new WindowAdapter() {
                public void windowClosing(WindowEvent e) {
                    System.exit(0);
                }
            });
        }

        class MyTableModel extends AbstractTableModel {
            final String[] columnNames = {"First Name",
                                        "Last Name",
                                        "Sport",
                                        "# of Years",
                                        "Vegetarian"};
            final Object[][] data = {
                {"Mary", "Campione",
                 "Snowboarding", new Integer(5), new Boolean(false)},
                {"Alison", "Huml",
                 "Rowing", new Integer(3), new Boolean(true)},
                {"Kathy", "Walrath",
                 "Chasing toddlers", new Integer(2), new Boolean(false)},
```

**Where
Explained:**
*Creating a
Table Model*
(page 259)

```
        {"Mark", "Andrews",
         "Speed reading", new Integer(20), new Boolean(true)},
        {"Angela", "Lih",
         "Teaching high school", new Integer(4), new Boolean(false)}
    };

    public int getColumnCount() {
        return columnNames.length;
    }

    public int getRowCount() {
        return data.length;
    }

    public String getColumnName(int col) {
        return columnNames[col];
    }

    public Object getValueAt(int row, int col) {
        return data[row][col];
    }

    /*
     * JTable uses this method to determine the default renderer/
     * editor for each cell.  If we didn't implement this method,
     * then the last column would contain text ("true"/"false"),
     * rather than a check box.
     */
    public Class getColumnClass(int c) {
        return getValueAt(0, c).getClass();
    }

    /*
     * Don't need to implement this method unless your table's
     * editable.
     */
    public boolean isCellEditable(int row, int col) {
        //Note that the data/cell address is constant,
        //no matter where the cell appears onscreen.
        if (col < 2) {
            return false;
        } else {
            return true;
        }
    }

    /*
     * Don't need to implement this method unless your table's
     * data can change.
     */
    public void setValueAt(Object value, int row, int col) {
        if (DEBUG) {
            System.out.println("Setting value at " + row + "," + col
                               + " to " + value
                               + " (an instance of "
                               + value.getClass() + ")");
        }

        if (data[0][col] instanceof Integer) {
            //If we don't do something like this, the column
            //switches to contain Strings.
            //XXX: See TableEditDemo.java for a better solution!!!
            try {
                data[row][col] = new Integer((String)value);
                fireTableCellUpdated(row, col);
```

```
                    } catch (NumberFormatException e) {
                        JOptionPane.showMessageDialog(TableDemo.this,
                            "The \"" + getColumnName(col)
                            + "\" column accepts only integer values.");
                    }
                } else {
                    data[row][col] = value;
                    fireTableCellUpdated(row, col);
                }

                if (DEBUG) {
                    System.out.println("New value of data:");
                    printDebugData();
                }
            }
        }

        private void printDebugData() {
            int numRows = getRowCount();
            int numCols = getColumnCount();

            for (int i=0; i < numRows; i++) {
                System.out.print("    row " + i + ":");
                for (int j=0; j < numCols; j++) {
                    System.out.print("  " + data[i][j]);
                }
                System.out.println();
            }
            System.out.println("--------------------------");
        }
    }

    public static void main(String[] args) {
        TableDemo frame = new TableDemo();
        frame.pack();
        frame.setVisible(true);
    }
}
```

EXAMPLE: *TableDialogEditDemo.java*

Associated File(s): <u>WholeNumberField.java</u> *(page 777)*

SOURCE CODE: *http://java.sun.com/docs/books/tutorial/uiswing/components/example-swing/TableDialogEditDemo.java*

```
import javax.swing.JTable;
import javax.swing.table.AbstractTableModel;
import javax.swing.DefaultCellEditor;
import javax.swing.table.TableCellRenderer;

import javax.swing.JLabel;
import javax.swing.JDialog;
import javax.swing.JButton;
import javax.swing.JCheckBox;
import javax.swing.JColorChooser;
import javax.swing.BorderFactory;
import javax.swing.border.Border;

import javax.swing.JScrollPane;
import javax.swing.JFrame;
import javax.swing.SwingUtilities;
import java.awt.*;
import java.awt.event.*;
```

Where Explained:

Specifying Other Editors (page 266)

```
/**
 * This is like TableEditDemo, except that it substitutes a
 * Favorite Color column for the Last Name column and specifies
 * a custom cell renderer and editor for the color data.
 */
public class TableDialogEditDemo extends JFrame {
    private boolean DEBUG = false;

    public TableDialogEditDemo() {
        super("TableDialogEditDemo");

        MyTableModel myModel = new MyTableModel();
        JTable table = new JTable(myModel);
        table.setPreferredScrollableViewportSize(new Dimension(500, 70));

        //Create the scroll pane and add the table to it.
        JScrollPane scrollPane = new JScrollPane(table);

        //Set up renderer and editor for the Favorite Color column.
        setUpColorRenderer(table);
        setUpColorEditor(table);

        //Set up real input validation for integer data.
        setUpIntegerEditor(table);

        //Add the scroll pane to this window.
        getContentPane().add(scrollPane, BorderLayout.CENTER);

        addWindowListener(new WindowAdapter() {
            public void windowClosing(WindowEvent e) {
                System.exit(0);
            }
        });
    }

    class ColorRenderer extends JLabel
                        implements TableCellRenderer {
        Border unselectedBorder = null;
        Border selectedBorder = null;
        boolean isBordered = true;

        public ColorRenderer(boolean isBordered) {
            super();
            this.isBordered = isBordered;
            setOpaque(true); //MUST do this for background to show up.
        }

        public Component getTableCellRendererComponent(
                            JTable table, Object color,
                            boolean isSelected, boolean hasFocus,
                            int row, int column) {
            setBackground((Color)color);
            if (isBordered) {
                if (isSelected) {
                    if (selectedBorder == null) {
                        selectedBorder = BorderFactory.createMatteBorder(2,5,2,5,
                                                table.getSelectionBackground());
                    }
                    setBorder(selectedBorder);
                } else {
                    if (unselectedBorder == null) {
                        unselectedBorder = BorderFactory.createMatteBorder(2,5,2,5,
                                                table.getBackground());
                    }
                    setBorder(unselectedBorder);
                }
```

```
                }
            return this;
        }
    }

    private void setUpColorRenderer(JTable table) {
        table.setDefaultRenderer(Color.class,
                              new ColorRenderer(true));
    }

    //Set up the editor for the Color cells.
    private void setUpColorEditor(JTable table) {
        //First, set up the button that brings up the dialog.
        final JButton button = new JButton("") {
            public void setText(String s) {
                //Button never shows text -- only color.
            }
        };
        button.setBackground(Color.white);
        button.setBorderPainted(false);
        button.setMargin(new Insets(0,0,0,0));

        //Now create an editor to encapsulate the button, and
        //set it up as the editor for all Color cells.
        final ColorEditor colorEditor = new ColorEditor(button);
        table.setDefaultEditor(Color.class, colorEditor);

        //Set up the dialog that the button brings up.
        final JColorChooser colorChooser = new JColorChooser();
        ActionListener okListener = new ActionListener() {
            public void actionPerformed(ActionEvent e) {
                colorEditor.currentColor = colorChooser.getColor();
            }
        };
        final JDialog dialog = JColorChooser.createDialog(button,
                                      "Pick a Color",
                                      true,
                                      colorChooser,
                                      okListener,
                                      null); //XXXDoublecheck this is OK

        //Here's the code that brings up the dialog.
        button.addActionListener(new ActionListener() {
            public void actionPerformed(ActionEvent e) {
                button.setBackground(colorEditor.currentColor);
                colorChooser.setColor(colorEditor.currentColor);
                //Without the following line, the dialog comes up
                //in the middle of the screen.
                //dialog.setLocationRelativeTo(button);
                dialog.show();
            }
        });
    }

/*
 * The editor button that brings up the dialog.
 * We extend DefaultCellEditor for convenience,
 * even though it mean we have to create a dummy
 * check box.  Another approach would be to copy
 * the implementation of TableCellEditor methods
 * from the source code for DefaultCellEditor.
 */
class ColorEditor extends DefaultCellEditor {
    Color currentColor = null;
```

```java
    public ColorEditor(JButton b) {
        super(new JCheckBox()); //Unfortunately, the constructor expects a
                                //check box, combo box, or text field.
        editorComponent = b;
        setClickCountToStart(1); //This is usually 1 or 2.

        //Must do this so that editing stops when appropriate.
        b.addActionListener(new ActionListener() {
            public void actionPerformed(ActionEvent e) {
                fireEditingStopped();
            }
        });
    }

    protected void fireEditingStopped() {
        super.fireEditingStopped();
    }

    public Object getCellEditorValue() {
        return currentColor;
    }

    public Component getTableCellEditorComponent(JTable table,
                                                 Object value,
                                                 boolean isSelected,
                                                 int row,
                                                 int column) {
        ((JButton)editorComponent).setText(value.toString());
        currentColor = (Color)value;
        return editorComponent;
    }
}

private void setUpIntegerEditor(JTable table) {
    //Set up the editor for the integer cells.
    final WholeNumberField integerField = new WholeNumberField(0, 5);
    integerField.setHorizontalAlignment(WholeNumberField.RIGHT);

    DefaultCellEditor integerEditor =
        new DefaultCellEditor(integerField) {
            //Override DefaultCellEditor's getCellEditorValue method
            //to return an Integer, not a String:
            public Object getCellEditorValue() {
                return new Integer(integerField.getValue());
            }
        };
    table.setDefaultEditor(Integer.class, integerEditor);
}


class MyTableModel extends AbstractTableModel {
    final String[] columnNames = {"First Name",
                                  "Favorite Color",
                                  "Sport",
                                  "# of Years",
                                  "Vegetarian"};
    final Object[][] data = {
        {"Mary", new Color(153, 0, 153),
         "Snowboarding", new Integer(5), new Boolean(false)},
        {"Alison", new Color(51, 51, 153),
         "Rowing", new Integer(3), new Boolean(true)},
        {"Kathy", new Color(51, 102, 51),
         "Chasing toddlers", new Integer(2), new Boolean(false)},
        {"Mark", Color.blue,
         "Speed reading", new Integer(20), new Boolean(true)},
        {"Philip", Color.pink,
         "Pool", new Integer(7), new Boolean(false)}
    };
```

```java
public int getColumnCount() {
    return columnNames.length;
}

public int getRowCount() {
    return data.length;
}

public String getColumnName(int col) {
    return columnNames[col];
}

public Object getValueAt(int row, int col) {
    return data[row][col];
}

/*
 * JTable uses this method to determine the default renderer/
 * editor for each cell.  If we didn't implement this method,
 * then the last column would contain text ("true"/"false"),
 * rather than a check box.
 */
public Class getColumnClass(int c) {
    return getValueAt(0, c).getClass();
}

/*
 * Don't need to implement this method unless your table's
 * editable.
 */
public boolean isCellEditable(int row, int col) {
    //Note that the data/cell address is constant,
    //no matter where the cell appears onscreen.
    if (col < 1) {
        return false;
    } else {
        return true;
    }
}

public void setValueAt(Object value, int row, int col) {
    if (DEBUG) {
        System.out.println("Setting value at " + row + "," + col
                           + " to " + value
                           + " (an instance of "
                           + value.getClass() + ")");
    }

    data[row][col] = value;
    fireTableCellUpdated(row, col);

    if (DEBUG) {
        System.out.println("New value of data:");
        printDebugData();
    }
}

private void printDebugData() {
    int numRows = getRowCount();
    int numCols = getColumnCount();

    for (int i=0; i < numRows; i++) {
        System.out.print("    row " + i + ":");
        for (int j=0; j < numCols; j++) {
            System.out.print("  " + data[i][j]);
        }
```

```
                             System.out.println();
                         }
                         System.out.println("-------------------------");
                    }
                }

                public static void main(String[] args) {
                    TableDialogEditDemo frame = new TableDialogEditDemo();
                    frame.pack();
                    frame.setVisible(true);
                }
            }
```

EXAMPLE: *TableEditDemo.java*

**Where
Explained:**
*Validating
User-Entered
Text* (page 265)

SOURCE CODE: *http://java.sun.com/docs/books/tutorial/uiswing/components/example-swing/
                TableEditDemo.java*

```java
import javax.swing.JTable;
import javax.swing.table.AbstractTableModel;

import javax.swing.DefaultCellEditor;

import javax.swing.JScrollPane;
import javax.swing.JFrame;
import javax.swing.SwingUtilities;
import java.awt.*;
import java.awt.event.*;

/**
 * This is exactly like TableDemo, except that it uses a
 * custom cell editor to validate integer input.
 */
public class TableEditDemo extends JFrame {
    private boolean DEBUG = true;

    public TableEditDemo() {
        super("TableEditDemo");

        MyTableModel myModel = new MyTableModel();
        JTable table = new JTable(myModel);
        table.setPreferredScrollableViewportSize(new Dimension(500, 70));

        //Create the scroll pane and add the table to it.
        JScrollPane scrollPane = new JScrollPane(table);

        //Set up real input validation for the integer column.
        setUpIntegerEditor(table);

        //Add the scroll pane to this window.
        getContentPane().add(scrollPane, BorderLayout.CENTER);

        addWindowListener(new WindowAdapter() {
            public void windowClosing(WindowEvent e) {
                System.exit(0);
            }
        });
    }

    private void setUpIntegerEditor(JTable table) {
        //Set up the editor for the integer cells.
        final WholeNumberField integerField = new WholeNumberField(0, 5);
        integerField.setHorizontalAlignment(WholeNumberField.RIGHT);
```

```
    DefaultCellEditor integerEditor =
        new DefaultCellEditor(integerField) {
            //Override DefaultCellEditor's getCellEditorValue method
            //to return an Integer, not a String:
            public Object getCellEditorValue() {
                return new Integer(integerField.getValue());
            }
        };
    table.setDefaultEditor(Integer.class, integerEditor);
}

class MyTableModel extends AbstractTableModel {
    final String[] columnNames = {"First Name",
                                  "Last Name",
                                  "Sport",
                                  "# of Years",
                                  "Vegetarian"};
    final Object[][] data = {
        {"Mary", "Campione",
         "Snowboarding", new Integer(5), new Boolean(false)},
        {"Alison", "Huml",
         "Rowing", new Integer(3), new Boolean(true)},
        {"Kathy", "Walrath",
         "Chasing toddlers", new Integer(2), new Boolean(false)},
        {"Mark", "Andrews",
         "Speed reading", new Integer(20), new Boolean(true)},
        {"Angela", "Lih",
         "Teaching high school", new Integer(4), new Boolean(false)}
    };

    public int getColumnCount() {
        return columnNames.length;
    }

    public int getRowCount() {
        return data.length;
    }

    public String getColumnName(int col) {
        return columnNames[col];
    }

    public Object getValueAt(int row, int col) {
        return data[row][col];
    }

    /*
     * JTable uses this method to determine the default renderer/
     * editor for each cell.  If we didn't implement this method,
     * then the last column would contain text ("true"/"false"),
     * rather than a check box.
     */
    public Class getColumnClass(int c) {
        return getValueAt(0, c).getClass();
    }

    /*
     * Don't need to implement this method unless your table's
     * editable.
     */
    public boolean isCellEditable(int row, int col) {
        //Note that the data/cell address is constant,
        //no matter where the cell appears onscreen.
        if (col < 2) {
            return false;
```

```
            } else {
                return true;
            }
        }

        public void setValueAt(Object value, int row, int col) {
            if (DEBUG) {
                System.out.println("Setting value at " + row + "," + col
                                    + " to " + value
                                    + " (an instance of "
                                    + value.getClass() + ")");
            }

            data[row][col] = value;
            fireTableCellUpdated(row, col);

            if (DEBUG) {
                System.out.println("New value of data:");
                printDebugData();
            }
        }

        private void printDebugData() {
            int numRows = getRowCount();
            int numCols = getColumnCount();

            for (int i=0; i < numRows; i++) {
                System.out.print("    row " + i + ":");
                for (int j=0; j < numCols; j++) {
                    System.out.print("  " + data[i][j]);
                }
                System.out.println();
            }
            System.out.println("--------------------------");
        }
    }

    public static void main(String[] args) {
        TableEditDemo frame = new TableEditDemo();
        frame.pack();
        frame.setVisible(true);
    }
}
```

EXAMPLE: *TableMap.java*

Where Explained:
Sorting and Otherwise Manipulating Data
(page 269)

SOURCE CODE: *http://java.sun.com/docs/books/tutorial/uiswing/components/example-swing/TableMap.java*

```
/**
 * In a chain of data manipulators some behaviour is common. TableMap
 * provides most of this behavior and can be subclassed by filters
 * that only need to override a handful of specific methods. TableMap
 * implements TableModel by routing all requests to its model, and
 * TableModelListener by routing all events to its listeners. Inserting
 * a TableMap which has not been subclassed into a chain of table filters
 * should have no effect.
 *
 * @author Philip Milne */

import javax.swing.table.*;
import javax.swing.event.TableModelListener;
import javax.swing.event.TableModelEvent;
```

```
    public class TableMap extends AbstractTableModel
                          implements TableModelListener {
        protected TableModel model;

        public TableModel getModel() {
            return model;
        }

        public void setModel(TableModel model) {
            this.model = model;
            model.addTableModelListener(this);
        }

        // By default, implement TableModel by forwarding all messages
        // to the model.

        public Object getValueAt(int aRow, int aColumn) {
            return model.getValueAt(aRow, aColumn);
        }

        public void setValueAt(Object aValue, int aRow, int aColumn) {
            model.setValueAt(aValue, aRow, aColumn);
        }

        public int getRowCount() {
            return (model == null) ? 0 : model.getRowCount();
        }

        public int getColumnCount() {
            return (model == null) ? 0 : model.getColumnCount();
        }

        public String getColumnName(int aColumn) {
            return model.getColumnName(aColumn);
        }

        public Class getColumnClass(int aColumn) {
            return model.getColumnClass(aColumn);
        }

        public boolean isCellEditable(int row, int column) {
            return model.isCellEditable(row, column);
        }
//
// Implementation of the TableModelListener interface,
//
        // By default forward all events to all the listeners.
        public void tableChanged(TableModelEvent e) {
            fireTableChanged(e);
        }
    }
```

EXAMPLE: *TableRenderDemo.java*

SOURCE CODE: *http://java.sun.com/docs/books/tutorial/uiswing/components/example-swing/TableRenderDemo.java*

```
import javax.swing.JTable;
import javax.swing.table.AbstractTableModel;
import javax.swing.table.TableColumn;
import javax.swing.DefaultCellEditor;
import javax.swing.table.TableCellRenderer;
import javax.swing.table.DefaultTableCellRenderer;
```

Where Explained:

Setting and Changing Column Widths (page 256)

```java
import javax.swing.JScrollPane;
import javax.swing.JComboBox;
import javax.swing.JFrame;
import javax.swing.SwingUtilities;
import javax.swing.JOptionPane;
import java.awt.*;
import java.awt.event.*;

public class TableRenderDemo extends JFrame {
    private boolean DEBUG = true;

    public TableRenderDemo() {
        super("TableRenderDemo");

        MyTableModel myModel = new MyTableModel();
        JTable table = new JTable(myModel);
        table.setPreferredScrollableViewportSize(new Dimension(500, 70));

        //Create the scroll pane and add the table to it.
        JScrollPane scrollPane = new JScrollPane(table);

        //Set up column sizes.
        initColumnSizes(table, myModel);

        //Fiddle with the Sport column's cell editors/renderers.
        setUpSportColumn(table.getColumnModel().getColumn(2));

        //Add the scroll pane to this window.
        getContentPane().add(scrollPane, BorderLayout.CENTER);

        addWindowListener(new WindowAdapter() {
            public void windowClosing(WindowEvent e) {
                System.exit(0);
            }
        });
    }

    /*
     * This method picks good column sizes.
     * If all column heads are wider than the column's cells'
     * contents, then you can just use column.sizeWidthToFit().
     */
    private void initColumnSizes(JTable table, MyTableModel model) {
        TableColumn column = null;
        Component comp = null;
        int headerWidth = 0;
        int cellWidth = 0;
        Object[] longValues = model.longValues;

        for (int i = 0; i < 5; i++) {
            column = table.getColumnModel().getColumn(i);

            comp = column.getHeaderRenderer().
                          getTableCellRendererComponent(
                              null, column.getHeaderValue(),
                              false, false, 0, 0);
            headerWidth = comp.getPreferredSize().width;

            comp = table.getDefaultRenderer(model.getColumnClass(i)).
                          getTableCellRendererComponent(
                              table, longValues[i],
                              false, false, 0, i);
            cellWidth = comp.getPreferredSize().width;
```

```
                    if (DEBUG) {
                        System.out.println("Initializing width of column "
                                            + i + ". "
                                            + "headerWidth = " + headerWidth
                                            + "; cellWidth = " + cellWidth);
                    }

                    //XXX: Before Swing 1.1 Beta 2, use setMinWidth instead.
                    column.setPreferredWidth(Math.max(headerWidth, cellWidth));
            }
        }

        public void setUpSportColumn(TableColumn sportColumn) {
            //Set up the editor for the sport cells.
            JComboBox comboBox = new JComboBox();
            comboBox.addItem("Snowboarding");
            comboBox.addItem("Rowing");
            comboBox.addItem("Chasing toddlers");
            comboBox.addItem("Speed reading");
            comboBox.addItem("Teaching high school");
            comboBox.addItem("None");
            sportColumn.setCellEditor(new DefaultCellEditor(comboBox));

            //Set up tool tips for the sport cells.
            DefaultTableCellRenderer renderer =
                    new DefaultTableCellRenderer();
            renderer.setToolTipText("Click for combo box");
            sportColumn.setCellRenderer(renderer);

            //Set up tool tip for the sport column header.
            TableCellRenderer headerRenderer = sportColumn.getHeaderRenderer();
            if (headerRenderer instanceof DefaultTableCellRenderer) {
                ((DefaultTableCellRenderer)headerRenderer).setToolTipText(
                        "Click the sport to see a list of choices");
            }
        }
    }

    class MyTableModel extends AbstractTableModel {
        final String[] columnNames = {"First Name",
                                      "Last Name",
                                      "Sport",
                                      "# of Years",
                                      "Vegetarian"};
        final Object[][] data = {
            {"Mary", "Campione",
             "Snowboarding", new Integer(5), new Boolean(false)},
            {"Alison", "Huml",
             "Rowing", new Integer(3), new Boolean(true)},
            {"Kathy", "Walrath",
             "Chasing toddlers", new Integer(2), new Boolean(false)},
            {"Mark", "Andrews",
             "Speed reading", new Integer(20), new Boolean(true)},
            {"Angela", "Lih",
             "Teaching high school", new Integer(4), new Boolean(false)}
        };
        public final Object[] longValues = {"Angela", "Andrews",
                                            "Teaching high school",
                                            new Integer(20), Boolean.TRUE};

        public int getColumnCount() {
            return columnNames.length;
        }

        public int getRowCount() {
            return data.length;
        }
```

```java
public String getColumnName(int col) {
    return columnNames[col];
}

public Object getValueAt(int row, int col) {
    return data[row][col];
}

/*
 * JTable uses this method to determine the default renderer/
 * editor for each cell.  If we didn't implement this method,
 * then the last column would contain text ("true"/"false"),
 * rather than a check box.
 */
public Class getColumnClass(int c) {
    return getValueAt(0, c).getClass();
}

/*
 * Don't need to implement this method unless your table's
 * editable.
 */
public boolean isCellEditable(int row, int col) {
    //Note that the data/cell address is constant,
    //no matter where the cell appears onscreen.
    if (col < 2) {
        return false;
    } else {
        return true;
    }
}

/*
 * Don't need to implement this method unless your table's
 * data can change.
 */
public void setValueAt(Object value, int row, int col) {
    if (DEBUG) {
        System.out.println("Setting value at " + row + "," + col
                           + " to " + value
                           + " (an instance of "
                           + value.getClass() + ")");
    }

    if (data[0][col] instanceof Integer) {
        //If we don't do something like this, the column
        //switches to contain Strings.
        try {
            data[row][col] = new Integer((String)value);
            fireTableCellUpdated(row, col);
        } catch (NumberFormatException e) {
            JOptionPane.showMessageDialog(TableRenderDemo.this,
                "The \"" + getColumnName(col)
                + "\" column accepts only integer values.");
        }
    } else {
        data[row][col] = value;
        fireTableCellUpdated(row, col);
    }

    if (DEBUG) {
        System.out.println("New value of data:");
        printDebugData();
    }
}
```

```
        private void printDebugData() {
            int numRows = getRowCount();
            int numCols = getColumnCount();

            for (int i=0; i < numRows; i++) {
                System.out.print("    row " + i + ":");
                for (int j=0; j < numCols; j++) {
                    System.out.print("  " + data[i][j]);
                }
                System.out.println();
            }
            System.out.println("-------------------------");
        }
    }

    public static void main(String[] args) {
        TableRenderDemo frame = new TableRenderDemo();
        frame.pack();
        frame.setVisible(true);
    }
}
```

EXAMPLE: *TableSorter.java*

SOURCE CODE: *http://java.sun.com/docs/books/tutorial/uiswing/components/example-swing/TableSorter.java*

Where Explained:
Further Customizing Table Display and Event Handling (page 267)

```
/**
 * A sorter for TableModels. The sorter has a model (conforming to TableModel)
 * and itself implements TableModel. TableSorter does not store or copy
 * the data in the TableModel, instead it maintains an array of
 * integers which it keeps the same size as the number of rows in its
 * model. When the model changes it notifies the sorter that something
 * has changed eg. "rowsAdded" so that its internal array of integers
 * can be reallocated. As requests are made of the sorter (like
 * getValueAt(row, col) it redirects them to its model via the mapping
 * array. That way the TableSorter appears to hold another copy of the table
 * with the rows in a different order. The sorting algorthm used is stable
 * which means that it does not move around rows when its comparison
 * function returns 0 to denote that they are equivalent.
 *
 * @author Philip Milne
 */

import java.util.*;

import javax.swing.table.TableModel;
import javax.swing.event.TableModelEvent;

// Imports for picking up mouse events from the JTable.

import java.awt.event.MouseAdapter;
import java.awt.event.MouseEvent;
import java.awt.event.InputEvent;
import javax.swing.JTable;
import javax.swing.table.JTableHeader;
import javax.swing.table.TableColumnModel;

public class TableSorter extends TableMap {
    int             indexes[];
    Vector          sortingColumns = new Vector();
    boolean         ascending = true;
    int compares;
```

```java
public TableSorter() {
    indexes = new int[0]; // for consistency
}

public TableSorter(TableModel model) {
    setModel(model);
}

public void setModel(TableModel model) {
    super.setModel(model);
    reallocateIndexes();
}

public int compareRowsByColumn(int row1, int row2, int column) {
    Class type = model.getColumnClass(column);
    TableModel data = model;

    // Check for nulls.

    Object o1 = data.getValueAt(row1, column);
    Object o2 = data.getValueAt(row2, column);

    // If both values are null, return 0.
    if (o1 == null && o2 == null) {
        return 0;
    } else if (o1 == null) { // Define null less than everything.
        return -1;
    } else if (o2 == null) {
        return 1;
    }

    /*
     * We copy all returned values from the getValue call in case
     * an optimised model is reusing one object to return many
     * values.  The Number subclasses in the JDK are immutable and
     * so will not be used in this way but other subclasses of
     * Number might want to do this to save space and avoid
     * unnecessary heap allocation.
     */

    if (type.getSuperclass() == java.lang.Number.class) {
        Number n1 = (Number)data.getValueAt(row1, column);
        double d1 = n1.doubleValue();
        Number n2 = (Number)data.getValueAt(row2, column);
        double d2 = n2.doubleValue();

        if (d1 < d2) {
            return -1;
        } else if (d1 > d2) {
            return 1;
        } else {
            return 0;
        }
    } else if (type == java.util.Date.class) {
        Date d1 = (Date)data.getValueAt(row1, column);
        long n1 = d1.getTime();
        Date d2 = (Date)data.getValueAt(row2, column);
        long n2 = d2.getTime();

        if (n1 < n2) {
            return -1;
        } else if (n1 > n2) {
            return 1;
        } else {
            return 0;
        }
```

```
        } else if (type == String.class) {
            String s1 = (String)data.getValueAt(row1, column);
            String s2   = (String)data.getValueAt(row2, column);
            int result = s1.compareTo(s2);

            if (result < 0) {
                return -1;
            } else if (result > 0) {
                return 1;
            } else {
                return 0;
            }
        } else if (type == Boolean.class) {
            Boolean bool1 = (Boolean)data.getValueAt(row1, column);
            boolean b1 = bool1.booleanValue();
            Boolean bool2 = (Boolean)data.getValueAt(row2, column);
            boolean b2 = bool2.booleanValue();

            if (b1 == b2) {
                return 0;
            } else if (b1) { // Define false < true
                return 1;
            } else {
                return -1;
            }
        } else {
            Object v1 = data.getValueAt(row1, column);
            String s1 = v1.toString();
            Object v2 = data.getValueAt(row2, column);
            String s2 = v2.toString();
            int result = s1.compareTo(s2);

            if (result < 0) {
                return -1;
            } else if (result > 0) {
                return 1;
            } else {
        return 0;
            }
        }
    }

    public int compare(int row1, int row2) {
        compares++;
        for (int level = 0; level < sortingColumns.size(); level++) {
            Integer column = (Integer)sortingColumns.elementAt(level);
            int result = compareRowsByColumn(row1, row2, column.intValue());
            if (result != 0) {
                return ascending ? result : -result;
            }
        }
        return 0;
    }

    public void reallocateIndexes() {
        int rowCount = model.getRowCount();

        // Set up a new array of indexes with the right number of elements
        // for the new data model.
        indexes = new int[rowCount];

        // Initialise with the identity mapping.
        for (int row = 0; row < rowCount; row++) {
            indexes[row] = row;
        }
    }
```

```java
public void tableChanged(TableModelEvent e) {
    //System.out.println("Sorter: tableChanged");
    reallocateIndexes();

    super.tableChanged(e);
}

public void checkModel() {
    if (indexes.length != model.getRowCount()) {
        System.err.println("Sorter not informed of a change in model.");
    }
}

public void sort(Object sender) {
    checkModel();

    compares = 0;
    // n2sort();
    // qsort(0, indexes.length-1);
    shuttlesort((int[])indexes.clone(), indexes, 0, indexes.length);
    //System.out.println("Compares: "+compares);
}

public void n2sort() {
    for (int i = 0; i < getRowCount(); i++) {
        for (int j = i+1; j < getRowCount(); j++) {
            if (compare(indexes[i], indexes[j]) == -1) {
                swap(i, j);
            }
        }
    }
}

// This is a home-grown implementation which we have not had time
// to research - it may perform poorly in some circumstances. It
// requires twice the space of an in-place algorithm and makes
// NlogN assigments shuttling the values between the two
// arrays. The number of compares appears to vary between N-1 and
// NlogN depending on the initial order but the main reason for
// using it here is that, unlike qsort, it is stable.
public void shuttlesort(int from[], int to[], int low, int high) {
    if (high - low < 2) {
        return;
    }
    int middle = (low + high)/2;
    shuttlesort(to, from, low, middle);
    shuttlesort(to, from, middle, high);

    int p = low;
    int q = middle;

    /* This is an optional short-cut; at each recursive call,
    check to see if the elements in this subset are already
    ordered.  If so, no further comparisons are needed; the
    sub-array can just be copied.  The array must be copied rather
    than assigned otherwise sister calls in the recursion might
    get out of sinc.  When the number of elements is three they
    are partitioned so that the first set, [low, mid), has one
    element and and the second, [mid, high), has two. We skip the
    optimisation when the number of elements is three or less as
    the first compare in the normal merge will produce the same
    sequence of steps. This optimisation seems to be worthwhile
    for partially ordered lists but some analysis is needed to
    find out how the performance drops to Nlog(N) as the initial
    order diminishes - it may drop very quickly.  */
```

```
            if (high - low >= 4 && compare(from[middle-1], from[middle]) <= 0) {
                for (int i = low; i < high; i++) {
                    to[i] = from[i];
                }
                return;
            }

            // A normal merge.

            for (int i = low; i < high; i++) {
                if (q >= high || (p < middle && compare(from[p], from[q]) <= 0)) {
                    to[i] = from[p++];
                }
                else {
                    to[i] = from[q++];
                }
            }
        }

        public void swap(int i, int j) {
            int tmp = indexes[i];
            indexes[i] = indexes[j];
            indexes[j] = tmp;
        }

        // The mapping only affects the contents of the data rows.
        // Pass all requests to these rows through the mapping array: "indexes".

        public Object getValueAt(int aRow, int aColumn) {
            checkModel();
            return model.getValueAt(indexes[aRow], aColumn);
        }

        public void setValueAt(Object aValue, int aRow, int aColumn) {
            checkModel();
            model.setValueAt(aValue, indexes[aRow], aColumn);
        }

        public void sortByColumn(int column) {
            sortByColumn(column, true);
        }

        public void sortByColumn(int column, boolean ascending) {
            this.ascending = ascending;
            sortingColumns.removeAllElements();
            sortingColumns.addElement(new Integer(column));
            sort(this);
            super.tableChanged(new TableModelEvent(this));
        }

        // There is nowhere else to put this.
        // Add a mouse listener to the Table to trigger a table sort
        // when a column heading is clicked in the JTable.
        public void addMouseListenerToHeaderInTable(JTable table) {
            final TableSorter sorter = this;
            final JTable tableView = table;
            tableView.setColumnSelectionAllowed(false);
            MouseAdapter listMouseListener = new MouseAdapter() {
                public void mouseClicked(MouseEvent e) {
                    TableColumnModel columnModel = tableView.getColumnModel();
                    int viewColumn = columnModel.getColumnIndexAtX(e.getX());
                    int column = tableView.convertColumnIndexToModel(viewColumn);
                    if (e.getClickCount() == 1 && column != -1) {
                        //System.out.println("Sorting ...");
                        int shiftPressed = e.getModifiers()&InputEvent.SHIFT_MASK;
```

```
                            boolean ascending = (shiftPressed == 0);
                            sorter.sortByColumn(column, ascending);
                        }
                    }
                };
                JTableHeader th = tableView.getTableHeader();
                th.addMouseListener(listMouseListener);
            }
        }
```

EXAMPLE: *TableSorterDemo.java*

**Where
Explained:**

*Sorting and
Otherwise
Manipulating
Data*
(page 269)

SOURCE CODE: *http://java.sun.com/docs/books/tutorial/uiswing/components/example-
swing/TableSorterDemo.java*

```java
import javax.swing.JTable;
import javax.swing.table.AbstractTableModel;
import javax.swing.JScrollPane;
import javax.swing.JFrame;
import javax.swing.SwingUtilities;
import javax.swing.JOptionPane;
import java.awt.*;
import java.awt.event.*;

public class TableSorterDemo extends JFrame {
    private boolean DEBUG = true;

    public TableSorterDemo() {
        super("TableSorterDemo");

        MyTableModel myModel = new MyTableModel();
        TableSorter sorter = new TableSorter(myModel); //ADDED THIS
        //JTable table = new JTable(myModel);          //OLD
        JTable table = new JTable(sorter);             //NEW
        sorter.addMouseListenerToHeaderInTable(table); //ADDED THIS
        table.setPreferredScrollableViewportSize(new Dimension(500, 70));

        //Create the scroll pane and add the table to it.
        JScrollPane scrollPane = new JScrollPane(table);

        //Add the scroll pane to this window.
        getContentPane().add(scrollPane, BorderLayout.CENTER);

        addWindowListener(new WindowAdapter() {
            public void windowClosing(WindowEvent e) {
                System.exit(0);
            }
        });
    }

    class MyTableModel extends AbstractTableModel {
        final String[] columnNames = {"First Name",
                                      "Last Name",
                                      "Sport",
                                      "# of Years",
                                      "Vegetarian"};
        final Object[][] data = {
            {"Mary", "Campione",
             "Snowboarding", new Integer(5), new Boolean(false)},
            {"Alison", "Huml",
             "Rowing", new Integer(3), new Boolean(true)},
            {"Kathy", "Walrath",
             "Chasing toddlers", new Integer(2), new Boolean(false)},
```

```
            {"Mark", "Andrews",
             "Speed reading", new Integer(20), new Boolean(true)},
            {"Angela", "Lih",
             "Teaching high school", new Integer(4), new Boolean(false)}
    };

    public int getColumnCount() {
        return columnNames.length;
    }

    public int getRowCount() {
        return data.length;
    }

    public String getColumnName(int col) {
        return columnNames[col];
    }

    public Object getValueAt(int row, int col) {
        return data[row][col];
    }

    /*
     * JTable uses this method to determine the default renderer/
     * editor for each cell.  If we didn't implement this method,
     * then the last column would contain text ("true"/"false"),
     * rather than a check box.
     */
    public Class getColumnClass(int c) {
        return getValueAt(0, c).getClass();
    }

    /*
     * Don't need to implement this method unless your table's
     * editable.
     */
    public boolean isCellEditable(int row, int col) {
        //Note that the data/cell address is constant,
        //no matter where the cell appears onscreen.
        if (col < 2) {
            return false;
        } else {
            return true;
        }
    }

    /*
     * Don't need to implement this method unless your table's
     * data can change.
     */
    public void setValueAt(Object value, int row, int col) {
        if (DEBUG) {
            System.out.println("Setting value at " + row + "," + col
                               + " to " + value
                               + " (an instance of "
                               + value.getClass() + ")");
        }

        if (data[0][col] instanceof Integer) {
            //If we don't do something like this, the column
            //switches to contain Strings.
            try {
                data[row][col] = new Integer((String)value);
                fireTableCellUpdated(row, col);
```

```
                    } catch (NumberFormatException e) {
                        JOptionPane.showMessageDialog(TableSorterDemo.this,
                            "The \"" + getColumnName(col)
                            + "\" column accepts only integer values.");
                    }
                } else {
                    data[row][col] = value;
                    fireTableCellUpdated(row, col);
                }

                if (DEBUG) {
                    System.out.println("New value of data:");
                    printDebugData();
                }
            }

            private void printDebugData() {
                int numRows = getRowCount();
                int numCols = getColumnCount();

                for (int i=0; i < numRows; i++) {
                    System.out.print("    row " + i + ":");
                    for (int j=0; j < numCols; j++) {
                        System.out.print("  " + data[i][j]);
                    }
                    System.out.println();
                }
                System.out.println("-------------------------");
            }
        }

        public static void main(String[] args) {
            TableSorterDemo frame = new TableSorterDemo();
            frame.pack();
            frame.setVisible(true);
        }
    }
```

EXAMPLE: *TextComponentDemo.java*

Where Explained:

General Rules for Using Text Components
(page 282)

Associated File(s): `LimitedStyledDocument.java` *(page 675)*,
`LimitedPlainDocument.java` *(page 675)*

SOURCE CODE: *http://java.sun.com/docs/books/tutorial/uiswing/components/example-swing/TextComponentDemo.java*

```
import java.awt.*;
import java.awt.event.*;
import java.util.Hashtable;
import javax.swing.*;
import javax.swing.text.*;
import javax.swing.event.*;
import javax.swing.undo.*;

public class TextComponentDemo extends JFrame {
    JTextPane textPane;
    LimitedStyledDocument lsd;
    JTextArea changeLog;
    String newline = "\n";
    static final int MAX_CHARACTERS = 300;
    Hashtable actions;
```

```java
//undo helpers
protected UndoAction undoAction;
protected RedoAction redoAction;
protected UndoManager undo = new UndoManager();

public TextComponentDemo() {
    //some initial setup
    super("TextComponentDemo");

    //Create the document for the text area.
    lsd = new LimitedStyledDocument(MAX_CHARACTERS);

    //Create the text pane and configure it.
    textPane = new JTextPane(lsd);  //All right! No 60's jokes.
    textPane.setCaretPosition(0);
    textPane.setMargin(new Insets(5,5,5,5));
    JScrollPane scrollPane = new JScrollPane(textPane);
    scrollPane.setPreferredSize(new Dimension(200, 200));

    //Create the text area for the status log and configure it.
    changeLog = new JTextArea(5, 30);
    changeLog.setEditable(false);
    JScrollPane scrollPaneForLog = new JScrollPane(changeLog);

    //Create a split pane for the change log and the text area.
    JSplitPane splitPane = new JSplitPane(
                                 JSplitPane.VERTICAL_SPLIT,
                                 scrollPane, scrollPaneForLog);
    splitPane.setOneTouchExpandable(true);

    //Create the status area.
    JPanel statusPane = new JPanel(new GridLayout(1, 1));
    CaretListenerLabel caretListenerLabel =
            new CaretListenerLabel("Caret Status");
    statusPane.add(caretListenerLabel);

    //Add the components to the frame.
    JPanel contentPane = new JPanel(new BorderLayout());
    contentPane.add(splitPane, BorderLayout.CENTER);
    contentPane.add(statusPane, BorderLayout.SOUTH);
    setContentPane(contentPane);

    //Set up the menu bar.
    createActionTable(textPane);
    JMenu editMenu = createEditMenu();
    JMenu styleMenu = createStyleMenu();
    JMenuBar mb = new JMenuBar();
    mb.add(editMenu);
    mb.add(styleMenu);
    setJMenuBar(mb);

    //Add some key bindings to the keymap.
    addKeymapBindings();

    //Put the initial text into the text pane.
    initDocument();

    //Start watching for undoable edits and caret changes.
    lsd.addUndoableEditListener(new MyUndoableEditListener());
    textPane.addCaretListener(caretListenerLabel);
    lsd.addDocumentListener(new MyDocumentListener());
}
```

```java
//This listens for and reports caret movements.
protected class CaretListenerLabel extends JLabel implements CaretListener {
    public CaretListenerLabel (String label) {
        super(label);
    }

    public void caretUpdate(CaretEvent e) {
        //Get the location in the text.
        int dot = e.getDot();
        int mark = e.getMark();
        if (dot == mark) {  // no selection
            try {
                Rectangle caretCoords = textPane.modelToView(dot);
                //Convert it to view coordinates.
                setText("caret: text position: " + dot
                        + ", view location = ["
                        + caretCoords.x + ", "
                        + caretCoords.y + "]"
                        + newline);
            } catch (BadLocationException ble) {
                setText("caret: text position: " + dot + newline);
            }
        } else if (dot < mark) {
            setText("selection from: " + dot
                    + " to " + mark + newline);
        } else {
            setText("selection from: " + mark
                    + " to " + dot + newline);
        }
    }
}

//This one listens for edits that can be undone.
protected class MyUndoableEditListener
                implements UndoableEditListener {
    public void undoableEditHappened(UndoableEditEvent e) {
        //Remember the edit and update the menus.
        undo.addEdit(e.getEdit());
        undoAction.updateUndoState();
        redoAction.updateRedoState();
    }
}

//And this one listens for any changes to the document.
protected class MyDocumentListener
                implements DocumentListener {
    public void insertUpdate(DocumentEvent e) {
        displayEditInfo(e);
    }
    public void removeUpdate(DocumentEvent e) {
        displayEditInfo(e);
    }
    public void changedUpdate(DocumentEvent e) {
        displayEditInfo(e);
    }
    private void displayEditInfo(DocumentEvent e) {
        Document doc = (Document)e.getDocument();
        int changeLength = e.getLength();
        changeLog.append(e.getType().toString() + ": " +
            changeLength + " character" +
            ((changeLength == 1) ? ". " : "s. ") +
            " Text length = " + doc.getLength() + "." + newline);
    }
}
```

```
//Add a couple of emacs key bindings to the key map for navigation.
protected void addKeymapBindings() {
    //Add a new key map to the keymap hierarchy.
    Keymap keymap = textPane.addKeymap("MyEmacsBindings",
                                       textPane.getKeymap());

    //Ctrl-b to go backward one character
    Action action = getActionByName(DefaultEditorKit.backwardAction);
    KeyStroke key = KeyStroke.getKeyStroke(KeyEvent.VK_B, Event.CTRL_MASK);
    keymap.addActionForKeyStroke(key, action);

    //Ctrl-f to go forward one character
    action = getActionByName(DefaultEditorKit.forwardAction);
    key = KeyStroke.getKeyStroke(KeyEvent.VK_F, Event.CTRL_MASK);
    keymap.addActionForKeyStroke(key, action);

    //Ctrl-p to go up one line
    action = getActionByName(DefaultEditorKit.upAction);
    key = KeyStroke.getKeyStroke(KeyEvent.VK_P, Event.CTRL_MASK);
    keymap.addActionForKeyStroke(key, action);

    //Ctrl-n to go down one line
    action = getActionByName(DefaultEditorKit.downAction);
    key = KeyStroke.getKeyStroke(KeyEvent.VK_N, Event.CTRL_MASK);
    keymap.addActionForKeyStroke(key, action);

    textPane.setKeymap(keymap);
}

//Create the edit menu.
protected JMenu createEditMenu() {
    JMenu menu = new JMenu("Edit");

    //Undo and redo are actions of our own creation.
    undoAction = new UndoAction();
    menu.add(undoAction);

    redoAction = new RedoAction();
    menu.add(redoAction);

    menu.addSeparator();

    //These actions come from the default editor kit.
    //Get the ones we want and stick them in the menu.
    menu.add(getActionByName(DefaultEditorKit.cutAction));
    menu.add(getActionByName(DefaultEditorKit.copyAction));
    menu.add(getActionByName(DefaultEditorKit.pasteAction));

    menu.addSeparator();

    menu.add(getActionByName(DefaultEditorKit.selectAllAction));
    return menu;
}

//Create the style menu.
protected JMenu createStyleMenu() {
    JMenu menu = new JMenu("Style");

    Action action = new StyledEditorKit.BoldAction();
    action.putValue(Action.NAME, "Bold");
    menu.add(action);

    action = new StyledEditorKit.ItalicAction();
    action.putValue(Action.NAME, "Italic");
    menu.add(action);
```

```
            action = new StyledEditorKit.UnderlineAction();
            action.putValue(Action.NAME, "Underline");
            menu.add(action);

            menu.addSeparator();

            menu.add(new StyledEditorKit.FontSizeAction("12", 12));
            menu.add(new StyledEditorKit.FontSizeAction("14", 14));
            menu.add(new StyledEditorKit.FontSizeAction("18", 18));

            menu.addSeparator();

            menu.add(new StyledEditorKit.FontFamilyAction("Serif",
                                                "Serif"));
            menu.add(new StyledEditorKit.FontFamilyAction("SansSerif",
                                                "SansSerif"));

            menu.addSeparator();

            menu.add(new StyledEditorKit.ForegroundAction("Red",
                                                Color.red));
            menu.add(new StyledEditorKit.ForegroundAction("Green",
                                                Color.green));
            menu.add(new StyledEditorKit.ForegroundAction("Blue",
                                                Color.blue));
            menu.add(new StyledEditorKit.ForegroundAction("Black",
                                                Color.black));

            return menu;
        }

        protected void initDocument() {
            String initString[] =
                    { "Use the mouse to place the caret.",
                      "Use the edit menu to cut, copy, paste, and select text.",
                      "Also to undo and redo changes.",
                      "Use the style menu to change the style of the text.",
                      "Use these emacs key bindings to move the caret:",
                      "ctrl-f, ctrl-b, ctrl-n, ctrl-p." };

            SimpleAttributeSet[] attrs = initAttributes(initString.length);

            try {
                for (int i = 0; i < initString.length; i ++) {
                    lsd.insertString(lsd.getLength(), initString[i] + newline,
                            attrs[i]);
                }
            } catch (BadLocationException ble) {
                System.err.println("Couldn't insert initial text.");
            }
        }

        protected SimpleAttributeSet[] initAttributes(int length) {
            //Hard-code some attributes.
            SimpleAttributeSet[] attrs = new SimpleAttributeSet[length];

            attrs[0] = new SimpleAttributeSet();
            StyleConstants.setFontFamily(attrs[0], "SansSerif");
            StyleConstants.setFontSize(attrs[0], 16);

            attrs[1] = new SimpleAttributeSet(attrs[0]);
            StyleConstants.setBold(attrs[1], true);

            attrs[2] = new SimpleAttributeSet(attrs[0]);
            StyleConstants.setItalic(attrs[2], true);
```

```
        attrs[3] = new SimpleAttributeSet(attrs[0]);
        StyleConstants.setFontSize(attrs[3], 20);

        attrs[4] = new SimpleAttributeSet(attrs[0]);
        StyleConstants.setFontSize(attrs[4], 12);

        attrs[5] = new SimpleAttributeSet(attrs[0]);
        StyleConstants.setForeground(attrs[5], Color.red);

        return attrs;
    }

    //The following two methods allow us to find an
    //action provided by the editor kit by its name.
    private void createActionTable(JTextComponent textComponent) {
        actions = new Hashtable();
        Action[] actionsArray = textComponent.getActions();
        for (int i = 0; i < actionsArray.length; i++) {
            Action a = actionsArray[i];
            actions.put(a.getValue(Action.NAME), a);
        }
    }

    private Action getActionByName(String name) {
        return (Action)(actions.get(name));
    }

    class UndoAction extends AbstractAction {
        public UndoAction() {
            super("Undo");
            setEnabled(false);
        }

        public void actionPerformed(ActionEvent e) {
            try {
                undo.undo();
            } catch (CannotUndoException ex) {
                System.out.println("Unable to undo: " + ex);
                ex.printStackTrace();
            }
            updateUndoState();
            redoAction.updateRedoState();
        }

        protected void updateUndoState() {
            if (undo.canUndo()) {
                setEnabled(true);
                putValue(Action.NAME, undo.getUndoPresentationName());
            } else {
                setEnabled(false);
                putValue(Action.NAME, "Undo");
            }
        }
    }

    class RedoAction extends AbstractAction {
        public RedoAction() {
            super("Redo");
            setEnabled(false);
        }

        public void actionPerformed(ActionEvent e) {
            try {
                undo.redo();
            } catch (CannotRedoException ex) {
                System.out.println("Unable to redo: " + ex);
                ex.printStackTrace();
            }
```

```
                    updateRedoState();
                    undoAction.updateUndoState();
                }

                protected void updateRedoState() {
                    if (undo.canRedo()) {
                        setEnabled(true);
                        putValue(Action.NAME, undo.getRedoPresentationName());
                    } else {
                        setEnabled(false);
                        putValue(Action.NAME, "Redo");
                    }
                }
            }
        }

        //The standard main method.
        public static void main(String[] args) {
            final TextComponentDemo frame = new TextComponentDemo();
            frame.addWindowListener(new WindowAdapter() {
                public void windowClosing(WindowEvent e) {
                    System.exit(0);
                }
                public void windowActivated(WindowEvent e) {
                    frame.textPane.requestFocus();
                }
            });

            frame.pack();
            frame.setVisible(true);
        }
    }
```

EXAMPLE: *TextDemo.java*

**Where
Explained:**
*How to Use
Text Fields*
(page 298)

SOURCE CODE: *http://java.sun.com/docs/books/tutorial/uiswing/components/example-swing/
TextDemo.java*

```
/*
 * Swing 1.1 version (compatible with both JDK 1.1 and Java 2).
 */

import java.awt.*;
import java.awt.event.*;
import javax.swing.*;

public class TextDemo extends JApplet implements ActionListener {
    JTextField textField;
    JTextArea textArea;
    String newline = "\n";

    //Hack to avoid annoying error message (1.1).
    public TextDemo() {
        getRootPane().putClientProperty("defeatSystemEventQueueCheck",
                                        Boolean.TRUE);
    }

    public void init() {
        textField = new JTextField(20);
        textField.addActionListener(this);

        textArea = new JTextArea(5, 20);
        textArea.setEditable(false);
```

```
        JScrollPane scrollPane = new JScrollPane(textArea,
                        JScrollPane.VERTICAL_SCROLLBAR_ALWAYS,
                        JScrollPane.HORIZONTAL_SCROLLBAR_ALWAYS);

        //Add Components to the Applet.
        GridBagLayout gridBag = new GridBagLayout();
        Container contentPane = getContentPane();
        contentPane.setLayout(gridBag);
        GridBagConstraints c = new GridBagConstraints();
        c.gridwidth = GridBagConstraints.REMAINDER;

        c.fill = GridBagConstraints.HORIZONTAL;
        gridBag.setConstraints(textField, c);
        contentPane.add(textField);

        c.fill = GridBagConstraints.BOTH;
        c.weightx = 1.0;
        c.weighty = 1.0;
        gridBag.setConstraints(scrollPane, c);
        contentPane.add(scrollPane);
    }

    public void actionPerformed(ActionEvent evt) {
        String text = textField.getText();
        textArea.append(text + newline);
        textField.selectAll();
    }
}
```

EXAMPLE: *TextFieldDemo.java*

Associated File(s): <u>DecimalField.java</u> *(page 638)*, <u>FormattedDocument.java</u> *(page 652)*, <u>WholeNumberField.java</u> *(page 777)*

SOURCE CODE: *http://java.sun.com/docs/books/tutorial/uiswing/components/example-swing/TextFieldDemo.java*

Where Explained:
Creating a Validated Text Field (page 299)

```
import java.awt.*;
import java.awt.event.*;

import javax.swing.*;
import javax.swing.event.*;
import javax.swing.text.*;

import java.text.*;

public class TextFieldDemo extends JFrame {
    //Values for the text fields
    private double amount = 100000;
    private double rate = 7.5;   //7.5 %
    private int numPeriods = 30;
    private double payment = 0.0;

    //Labels to identify the text fields
    private JLabel amountLabel;
    private JLabel rateLabel;
    private JLabel numPeriodsLabel;
    private JLabel paymentLabel;

    //Strings for the labels
    private static String amountString = "Loan Amount: ";
    private static String rateString = "APR (%): ";
```

```java
    private static String numPeriodsString = "Years: ";
    private static String paymentString = "Monthly Payment: ";

    //Text fields for data entry
    private DecimalField amountField;
    private DecimalField rateField;
    private WholeNumberField numPeriodsField;
    private DecimalField paymentField;

    //Formats to format and parse numbers
    private NumberFormat moneyFormat;
    private NumberFormat percentFormat;
    private DecimalFormat paymentFormat;

    private boolean focusIsSet = false;

    public TextFieldDemo() {
        super("TextFieldDemo");

        setUpFormats();

        payment = computePayment(amount, rate, numPeriods);

        //Create the labels.
        amountLabel = new JLabel(amountString);
        rateLabel = new JLabel(rateString);
        numPeriodsLabel = new JLabel(numPeriodsString);
        paymentLabel = new JLabel(paymentString);

        //Create the text fields and set them up.
        MyDocumentListener myDocumentListener = new MyDocumentListener();

        amountField = new DecimalField(amount, 10, moneyFormat);
        amountField.getDocument().addDocumentListener(myDocumentListener);
        amountField.getDocument().putProperty("name", "amount");

        rateField = new DecimalField(rate, 10, percentFormat);
        rateField.getDocument().addDocumentListener(myDocumentListener);
        rateField.getDocument().putProperty("name", "rate");

        numPeriodsField = new WholeNumberField(numPeriods, 10);
        numPeriodsField.getDocument().addDocumentListener(myDocumentListener);
        numPeriodsField.getDocument().putProperty("name", "numPeriods");

        paymentField = new DecimalField(payment, 10, paymentFormat);
        paymentField.setEditable(false);
        paymentField.setForeground(Color.red);

        //Tell accessibility tools about label/textfield pairs.
        amountLabel.setLabelFor(amountField);
        rateLabel.setLabelFor(rateField);
        numPeriodsLabel.setLabelFor(numPeriodsField);
        paymentLabel.setLabelFor(paymentField);

        //Layout the labels in a panel.
        JPanel labelPane = new JPanel();
        labelPane.setLayout(new GridLayout(0, 1));
        labelPane.add(amountLabel);
        labelPane.add(rateLabel);
        labelPane.add(numPeriodsLabel);
        labelPane.add(paymentLabel);

        //Layout the text fields in a panel.
        JPanel fieldPane = new JPanel();
        fieldPane.setLayout(new GridLayout(0, 1));
        fieldPane.add(amountField);
```

```
        fieldPane.add(rateField);
        fieldPane.add(numPeriodsField);
        fieldPane.add(paymentField);

        //Put the panels in another panel, labels on left,
        //text fields on right.
        JPanel contentPane = new JPanel();
        contentPane.setBorder(BorderFactory.createEmptyBorder(20, 20, 20, 20));
        contentPane.setLayout(new BorderLayout());
        contentPane.add(labelPane, BorderLayout.CENTER);
        contentPane.add(fieldPane, BorderLayout.EAST);

        setContentPane(contentPane);
    }

    class MyDocumentListener implements DocumentListener {
        public void insertUpdate(DocumentEvent e) {
            calculateValue(e);
        }
        public void removeUpdate(DocumentEvent e) {
            calculateValue(e);
        }
        public void changedUpdate(DocumentEvent e) {
            // we won't ever get this with PlainDocument
        }
        private void calculateValue(DocumentEvent e) {
            Document whatsup = e.getDocument();
            if (whatsup.getProperty("name").equals("amount"))
                amount = amountField.getValue();
            else if (whatsup.getProperty("name").equals("rate"))
                rate = rateField.getValue();
            else if (whatsup.getProperty("name").equals("numPeriods"))
                numPeriods = numPeriodsField.getValue();
            payment = computePayment(amount, rate, numPeriods);
            paymentField.setValue(payment);
        }
    }

    public static void main(String[] args) {
        final TextFieldDemo demo = new TextFieldDemo();

        demo.addWindowListener(new WindowAdapter() {
            public void windowClosing(WindowEvent e) {
                System.exit(0);
            }

            //Whenever window gets the focus, let the
            //TextFieldDemo set the initial focus.
            public void windowActivated(WindowEvent e) {
                demo.setFocus();
            }
        });
        demo.pack();
        demo.setVisible(true);
    }

    private void setFocus() {
        if (!focusIsSet) {
            amountField.requestFocus();
            focusIsSet = true;
        }
    }

    // Compute the monthly payment based on the loan amount,
    // APR, and length of loan.
    double computePayment(double loanAmt, double rate, int numPeriods) {
        double I, partial1, denominator, answer;
```

```
        I = rate / 100.0 / 12.0;          // get monthly rate from annual
        numPeriods *= 12;           // get number of months
        partial1 = Math.pow((1 + I), (0.0 - numPeriods));
        denominator = (1 - partial1) / I;
        answer = (-1 * loanAmt) / denominator;
        return answer;
    }

    // Create and set up number formats. These objects also
    // parse numbers input by user.
    private void setUpFormats() {
        moneyFormat = NumberFormat.getNumberInstance();
        //XXXX: Workaround. With an empty positive suffix
        //the format allows letters in the number.
        ((DecimalFormat)moneyFormat).setPositiveSuffix(" ");

        percentFormat = NumberFormat.getNumberInstance();
        percentFormat.setMinimumFractionDigits(3);
        //XXXX: Workaround. With an empty positive suffix
        //the format allows letters in the number.
        ((DecimalFormat)percentFormat).setPositiveSuffix(" ");

        paymentFormat = (DecimalFormat)NumberFormat.getNumberInstance();
        paymentFormat.setMaximumFractionDigits(2);
        paymentFormat.setNegativePrefix("(");
        paymentFormat.setNegativeSuffix(")");
    }
}
```

EXAMPLE: *TextSamplerDemo.java*

Associated File(s): TextSamplerDemo.html *(page 758)*

SOURCE CODE: *http://java.sun.com/docs/books/tutorial/uiswing/components/example-swing/TextSamplerDemo.java*

Where Explained:

An Example that Uses Each Text Component (page 276)

```
/*
 * Swing 1.1 version (compatible with both JDK 1.1 and Java 2).
 */

import javax.swing.*;
import javax.swing.text.*;

import java.awt.*;                //for layout managers
import java.awt.event.*;         //for action and window events

import java.net.URL;
import java.io.IOException;

public class TextSamplerDemo extends JFrame
                             implements ActionListener {
    private String newline = "\n";
    protected static final String textFieldString = "JTextField";
    protected static final String passwordFieldString = "JPasswordField";

    protected JLabel actionLabel;

    public TextSamplerDemo() {
        super("TextSamplerDemo");

        //Create a regular text field.
        JTextField textField = new JTextField(10);
```

```
textField.setActionCommand(textFieldString);
textField.addActionListener(this);

//Create a password field.
JPasswordField passwordField = new JPasswordField(10);
passwordField.setActionCommand(passwordFieldString);
passwordField.addActionListener(this);

//Create some labels for the fields.
JLabel textFieldLabel = new JLabel(textFieldString + ": ");
textFieldLabel.setLabelFor(textField);
JLabel passwordFieldLabel = new JLabel(passwordFieldString + ": ");
passwordFieldLabel.setLabelFor(passwordField);

//Create a label to put messages during an action event.
actionLabel = new JLabel("Type text and then Return in a field.");
actionLabel.setBorder(BorderFactory.createEmptyBorder(10,0,0,0));

//Lay out the text controls and the labels.
JPanel textControlsPane = new JPanel();
GridBagLayout gridbag = new GridBagLayout();
GridBagConstraints c = new GridBagConstraints();

textControlsPane.setLayout(gridbag);

JLabel[] labels = {textFieldLabel, passwordFieldLabel};
JTextField[] textFields = {textField, passwordField};
addLabelTextRows(labels, textFields, gridbag, textControlsPane);

c.gridwidth = GridBagConstraints.REMAINDER; //last
c.anchor = GridBagConstraints.WEST;
c.weightx = 1.0;
gridbag.setConstraints(actionLabel, c);
textControlsPane.add(actionLabel);
textControlsPane.setBorder(
        BorderFactory.createCompoundBorder(
                    BorderFactory.createTitledBorder("Text Fields"),
                    BorderFactory.createEmptyBorder(5,5,5,5)));

//Create a text area.
JTextArea textArea = new JTextArea(
        "This is an editable JTextArea " +
        "that has been initialized with the setText method. " +
        "A text area is a \"plain\" text component, " +
        "which means that although it can display text " +
        "in any font, all of the text is in the same font."
);
textArea.setFont(new Font("Serif", Font.ITALIC, 16));
textArea.setLineWrap(true);
textArea.setWrapStyleWord(true);
JScrollPane areaScrollPane = new JScrollPane(textArea);
areaScrollPane.setVerticalScrollBarPolicy(
                JScrollPane.VERTICAL_SCROLLBAR_ALWAYS);
areaScrollPane.setPreferredSize(new Dimension(250, 250));
areaScrollPane.setBorder(
    BorderFactory.createCompoundBorder(
        BorderFactory.createCompoundBorder(
                    BorderFactory.createTitledBorder("Plain Text"),
                    BorderFactory.createEmptyBorder(5,5,5,5)),
        areaScrollPane.getBorder()));

//Create an editor pane.
JEditorPane editorPane = createEditorPane();
JScrollPane editorScrollPane = new JScrollPane(editorPane);
editorScrollPane.setVerticalScrollBarPolicy(
                JScrollPane.VERTICAL_SCROLLBAR_ALWAYS);
editorScrollPane.setPreferredSize(new Dimension(250, 145));
```

```java
        //Create a text pane.
        JTextPane textPane = createTextPane();
        JScrollPane paneScrollPane = new JScrollPane(textPane);
        paneScrollPane.setVerticalScrollBarPolicy(
                        JScrollPane.VERTICAL_SCROLLBAR_ALWAYS);
        paneScrollPane.setPreferredSize(new Dimension(250, 155));

        //Put the editor pane and the text pane in a split pane.
        JSplitPane splitPane = new JSplitPane(JSplitPane.VERTICAL_SPLIT,
                                              editorScrollPane,
                                              paneScrollPane);
        splitPane.setOneTouchExpandable(true);
        JPanel rightPane = new JPanel();
        rightPane.add(splitPane);
        rightPane.setBorder(BorderFactory.createCompoundBorder(
                    BorderFactory.createTitledBorder("Styled Text"),
                    BorderFactory.createEmptyBorder(5,5,5,5)));


        //Put everything in the applet.
        JPanel leftPane = new JPanel();
        BoxLayout leftBox = new BoxLayout(leftPane, BoxLayout.Y_AXIS);
        leftPane.setLayout(leftBox);
        leftPane.add(textControlsPane);
        leftPane.add(areaScrollPane);

        JPanel contentPane = new JPanel();
        BoxLayout box = new BoxLayout(contentPane, BoxLayout.X_AXIS);
        contentPane.setLayout(box);
        contentPane.add(leftPane);
        contentPane.add(rightPane);
        setContentPane(contentPane);
    }

    private void addLabelTextRows(JLabel[] labels,
                                  JTextField[] textFields,
                                  GridBagLayout gridbag,
                                  Container container) {
        GridBagConstraints c = new GridBagConstraints();
        c.anchor = GridBagConstraints.EAST;
        int numLabels = labels.length;

        for (int i = 0; i < numLabels; i++) {
            c.gridwidth = GridBagConstraints.RELATIVE; //next-to-last
            c.fill = GridBagConstraints.NONE;      //reset to default
            c.weightx = 0.0;                       //reset to default
            gridbag.setConstraints(labels[i], c);
            container.add(labels[i]);

            c.gridwidth = GridBagConstraints.REMAINDER;     //end row
            c.fill = GridBagConstraints.HORIZONTAL;
            c.weightx = 1.0;
            gridbag.setConstraints(textFields[i], c);
            container.add(textFields[i]);
        }
    }

    public void actionPerformed(ActionEvent e) {
        String prefix = "You typed \"";
        if (e.getActionCommand().equals(textFieldString)) {
            JTextField source = (JTextField)e.getSource();
            actionLabel.setText(prefix + source.getText() + "\"");
        } else {
            JPasswordField source = (JPasswordField)e.getSource();
            actionLabel.setText(prefix + new String(source.getPassword())
                                + "\"");
        }
    }
```

```java
private JEditorPane createEditorPane() {
    JEditorPane editorPane = new JEditorPane();
    editorPane.setEditable(false);
    String s = null;
    try {
        s = "file:"
            + System.getProperty("user.dir")
            + System.getProperty("file.separator")
            + "TextSamplerDemoHelp.html";
        URL helpURL = new URL(s);
        displayURL(helpURL, editorPane);
    } catch (Exception e) {
        System.err.println("Couldn't create help URL: " + s);
    }

    return editorPane;
}

private void displayURL(URL url, JEditorPane editorPane) {
    try {
        editorPane.setPage(url);
    } catch (IOException e) {
        System.err.println("Attempted to read a bad URL: " + url);
    }
}

private JTextPane createTextPane() {
    JTextPane textPane = new JTextPane();
    String[] initString =
            { "This is an editable JTextPane, ",//regular
              "another ",//italic
              "styled ",//bold
              "text ",//small
              "component, ",//large
              "which supports embedded components..." + newline,//regular
              " " + newline,//button
              "...and embedded icons..." + newline,//regular
              " ",       //icon
              newline + "JTextPane is a subclass of JEditorPane that " +
                "uses a StyledEditorKit and StyledDocument, and provides " +
                "cover methods for interacting with those objects."
             };

    String[] initStyles =
            { "regular", "italic", "bold", "small", "large",
              "regular", "button", "regular", "icon",
              "regular"
            };

    initStylesForTextPane(textPane);

    Document doc = textPane.getDocument();

    try {
        for (int i=0; i < initString.length; i++) {
            doc.insertString(doc.getLength(), initString[i],
                            textPane.getStyle(initStyles[i]));
        }
    } catch (BadLocationException ble) {
        System.err.println("Couldn't insert initial text.");
    }

    return textPane;
}
```

```java
protected void initStylesForTextPane(JTextPane textPane) {
    //Initialize some styles.
    Style def = StyleContext.getDefaultStyleContext().
                            getStyle(StyleContext.DEFAULT_STYLE);

    Style regular = textPane.addStyle("regular", def);
    StyleConstants.setFontFamily(def, "SansSerif");

    Style s = textPane.addStyle("italic", regular);
    StyleConstants.setItalic(s, true);

    s = textPane.addStyle("bold", regular);
    StyleConstants.setBold(s, true);

    s = textPane.addStyle("small", regular);
    StyleConstants.setFontSize(s, 10);

    s = textPane.addStyle("large", regular);
    StyleConstants.setFontSize(s, 16);

    s = textPane.addStyle("icon", regular);
    StyleConstants.setAlignment(s, StyleConstants.ALIGN_CENTER);
    StyleConstants.setIcon(s, new ImageIcon("images/Pig.gif"));

    s = textPane.addStyle("button", regular);
    StyleConstants.setAlignment(s, StyleConstants.ALIGN_CENTER);
    JButton button = new JButton(new ImageIcon("images/sound.gif"));
    button.setMargin(new Insets(0,0,0,0));
    button.addActionListener(new ActionListener() {
        public void actionPerformed(ActionEvent e) {
            Toolkit.getDefaultToolkit().beep();
        }
    });
    StyleConstants.setComponent(s, button);
}

public static void main(String[] args) {
    JFrame frame = new TextSamplerDemo();

    frame.addWindowListener(new WindowAdapter() {
        public void windowClosing(WindowEvent e) {
            System.exit(0);
        }
    });

    frame.pack();
    frame.setVisible(true);
}
}
```

EXAMPLE: TextSamplerDemo.html

Main Source File: <u>TextSamplerDemo.java</u> *(page 754)*

```html
<html>
<body>
<img src="images/dukeWaveRed.gif" width="64" height="64">
This is an uneditable <code>JEditorPane</code>,
which was <em>initialized</em>
with <strong>HTML</strong> text <font size=-2>from</font> a
<font size=+2>URL</font>.
<p>
```

```
An editor pane uses specialized editor kits
to read, write, display, and edit text of
different formats.
The Swing text package includes editor kits
for plain text, HTML, and RTF.
You can also develop
custom editor kits for other formats.
</body>
</html>
```

EXAMPLE: *ToolBarDemo.java*

SOURCE CODE: *http://java.sun.com/docs/books/tutorial/uiswing/components/example-swing/ToolBarDemo.java*

Where Explained:
How to Use Tool Bars (page 138)

```java
import javax.swing.JToolBar;
import javax.swing.JButton;
import javax.swing.ImageIcon;

import javax.swing.JFrame;
import javax.swing.JTextArea;
import javax.swing.JScrollPane;
import javax.swing.JPanel;

import java.awt.*;
import java.awt.event.*;

public class ToolBarDemo extends JFrame {
    protected JTextArea textArea;
    protected String newline = "\n";

    public ToolBarDemo() {
        //Do frame stuff.
        super("ToolBarDemo");
        addWindowListener(new WindowAdapter() {
            public void windowClosing(WindowEvent e) {
                System.exit(0);
            }
        });

        //Create the toolbar.
        JToolBar toolBar = new JToolBar();
        addButtons(toolBar);

        //Create the text area used for output.
        textArea = new JTextArea(5, 30);
        JScrollPane scrollPane = new JScrollPane(textArea);

        //Lay out the content pane.
        JPanel contentPane = new JPanel();
        contentPane.setLayout(new BorderLayout());
        contentPane.setPreferredSize(new Dimension(400, 100));
        contentPane.add(toolBar, BorderLayout.NORTH);
        contentPane.add(scrollPane, BorderLayout.CENTER);
        setContentPane(contentPane);
    }

    protected void addButtons(JToolBar toolBar) {
        JButton button = null;

        //first button
        button = new JButton(new ImageIcon("images/left.gif"));
        button.setToolTipText("This is the left button");
```

```
        button.addActionListener(new ActionListener() {
            public void actionPerformed(ActionEvent e) {
                displayResult("Action for first button");
            }
        });
        toolBar.add(button);

        //second button
        button = new JButton(new ImageIcon("images/middle.gif"));
        button.setToolTipText("This is the middle button");
        button.addActionListener(new ActionListener() {
            public void actionPerformed(ActionEvent e) {
                displayResult("Action for second button");
            }
        });
        toolBar.add(button);

        //third button
        button = new JButton(new ImageIcon("images/right.gif"));
        button.setToolTipText("This is the right button");
        button.addActionListener(new ActionListener() {
            public void actionPerformed(ActionEvent e) {
                displayResult("Action for third button");
            }
        });
        toolBar.add(button);
    }

    protected void displayResult(String actionDescription) {
        textArea.append(actionDescription + newline);
    }

    public static void main(String[] args) {
        ToolBarDemo frame = new ToolBarDemo();
        frame.pack();
        frame.setVisible(true);
    }
}
```

EXAMPLE: *ToolBarDemo2.java*

**Where
Explained:**
*How to Use
Tool Bars*
(page 138)

SOURCE CODE: *http://java.sun.com/docs/books/tutorial/uiswing/components/example-
swing/ToolBarDemo2.java*

```
import javax.swing.JToolBar;
import javax.swing.JButton;
import javax.swing.ImageIcon;

import javax.swing.JTextField;

import javax.swing.JFrame;
import javax.swing.JTextArea;
import javax.swing.JScrollPane;
import javax.swing.JPanel;

import java.awt.*;
import java.awt.event.*;

public class ToolBarDemo2 extends JFrame {
    protected JTextArea textArea;
    protected String newline = "\n";

    public ToolBarDemo2() {
```

```
        //Do frame stuff.
        super("ToolBarDemo2");
        addWindowListener(new WindowAdapter() {
            public void windowClosing(WindowEvent e) {
                System.exit(0);
            }
        });

        //Create the toolbar.
        JToolBar toolBar = new JToolBar();
        toolBar.setFloatable(false);
        addButtons(toolBar);

        //Create the text area used for output.
        textArea = new JTextArea(5, 30);
        JScrollPane scrollPane = new JScrollPane(textArea);

        //Lay out the content pane.
        JPanel contentPane = new JPanel();
        contentPane.setLayout(new BorderLayout());
        contentPane.setPreferredSize(new Dimension(400, 100));
        contentPane.add(toolBar, BorderLayout.NORTH);
        contentPane.add(scrollPane, BorderLayout.CENTER);
        setContentPane(contentPane);
    }

    protected void addButtons(JToolBar toolBar) {
        JButton button = null;

        //first button
        button = new JButton(new ImageIcon("images/left.gif"));
        button.setToolTipText("This is the left button");
        button.addActionListener(new ActionListener() {
            public void actionPerformed(ActionEvent e) {
                displayResult("Action for first button");
            }
        });
        toolBar.add(button);

        //second button
        button = new JButton(new ImageIcon("images/middle.gif"));
        button.setToolTipText("This is the middle button");
        button.addActionListener(new ActionListener() {
            public void actionPerformed(ActionEvent e) {
                displayResult("Action for second button");
            }
        });
        toolBar.add(button);

        //third button
        button = new JButton(new ImageIcon("images/right.gif"));
        button.setToolTipText("This is the right button");
        button.addActionListener(new ActionListener() {
            public void actionPerformed(ActionEvent e) {
                displayResult("Action for third button");
            }
        });
        toolBar.add(button);

        //separator
        toolBar.addSeparator();

        //fourth button
        button = new JButton("Another button");
        button.addActionListener(new ActionListener() {
```

```
                        public void actionPerformed(ActionEvent e) {
                            displayResult("Action for fourth button");
                        }
                    });
                    toolBar.add(button);

                    //fifth component is NOT a button!
                    JTextField textField = new JTextField("A text field");
                    //Action handler implementation would go here.
                    toolBar.add(textField);
                }

                protected void displayResult(String actionDescription) {
                    textArea.append(actionDescription + newline);
                }

                public static void main(String[] args) {
                    ToolBarDemo2 frame = new ToolBarDemo2();
                    frame.pack();
                    frame.setVisible(true);
                }
            }
```

EXAMPLE: *TopLevelDemo.java*

**Where
Explained:**

*Using Top-
Level Contain-
ers* (page 77)

SOURCE CODE: *http://java.sun.com/docs/books/tutorial/uiswing/components/example-
                swing/TopLevelDemo.java*

```java
import java.awt.*;
import java.awt.event.*;
import javax.swing.*;

public class TopLevelDemo {
    public static void main(String s[]) {
        JFrame frame = new JFrame("TopLevelDemo");

        frame.addWindowListener(new WindowAdapter() {
            public void windowClosing(WindowEvent e) {
                System.exit(0);
            }
        });

        JLabel yellowLabel = new JLabel("");
        yellowLabel.setOpaque(true);
        yellowLabel.setBackground(Color.yellow);
        yellowLabel.setPreferredSize(new Dimension(200, 180));

        JMenuBar cyanMenuBar = new JMenuBar();
        cyanMenuBar.setOpaque(true);
        cyanMenuBar.setBackground(Color.cyan);
        cyanMenuBar.setPreferredSize(new Dimension(200, 20));

        frame.setJMenuBar(cyanMenuBar);
        frame.getContentPane().add(yellowLabel, BorderLayout.CENTER);

        frame.pack();
        frame.setVisible(true);
    }
}
```

EXAMPLE: *TreeDemo.java*

SOURCE CODE: *http://java.sun.com/docs/books/tutorial/uiswing/components/example-swing/TreeDemo.java*

Where Explained: *How to Use Trees* (page 320)

```java
import javax.swing.JTree;
import javax.swing.tree.DefaultMutableTreeNode;
import javax.swing.event.TreeSelectionListener;
import javax.swing.event.TreeSelectionEvent;
import javax.swing.tree.TreeSelectionModel;
import java.net.URL;
import java.io.IOException;
import javax.swing.JEditorPane;
import javax.swing.JScrollPane;
import javax.swing.JSplitPane;
import javax.swing.JFrame;
import java.awt.*;
import java.awt.event.*;

public class TreeDemo extends JFrame {
    private JEditorPane htmlPane;
    private static boolean DEBUG = false;
    private URL helpURL;

    //Optionally play with line styles.  Possible values are
    //"Angled", "Horizontal", and "None" (the default).
    private boolean playWithLineStyle = false;
    private String lineStyle = "Angled";

    public TreeDemo() {
        super("TreeDemo");

        //Create the nodes.
        DefaultMutableTreeNode top = new DefaultMutableTreeNode(
                                            "The Java Series");
        createNodes(top);

        //Create a tree that allows one selection at a time.
        final JTree tree = new JTree(top);
        tree.getSelectionModel().setSelectionMode
                (TreeSelectionModel.SINGLE_TREE_SELECTION);

        //Listen for when the selection changes.
        tree.addTreeSelectionListener(new TreeSelectionListener() {
            public void valueChanged(TreeSelectionEvent e) {
                DefaultMutableTreeNode node = (DefaultMutableTreeNode)
                                tree.getLastSelectedPathComponent();

                if (node == null) return;

                Object nodeInfo = node.getUserObject();
                if (node.isLeaf()) {
                    BookInfo book = (BookInfo)nodeInfo;
                    displayURL(book.bookURL);
                    if (DEBUG) {
                        System.out.print(book.bookURL + ": \n    ");
                    }
                } else {
                    displayURL(helpURL);
                }
                if (DEBUG) {
                    System.out.println(nodeInfo.toString());
                }
            }
        });
```

```
        if (playWithLineStyle) {
            tree.putClientProperty("JTree.lineStyle", lineStyle);
        }

        //Create the scroll pane and add the tree to it.
        JScrollPane treeView = new JScrollPane(tree);

        //Create the HTML viewing pane.
        htmlPane = new JEditorPane();
        htmlPane.setEditable(false);
        initHelp();
        JScrollPane htmlView = new JScrollPane(htmlPane);

        //Add the scroll panes to a split pane.
        JSplitPane splitPane = new JSplitPane(JSplitPane.VERTICAL_SPLIT);
        splitPane.setTopComponent(treeView);
        splitPane.setBottomComponent(htmlView);

        Dimension minimumSize = new Dimension(100, 50);
        htmlView.setMinimumSize(minimumSize);
        treeView.setMinimumSize(minimumSize);
        splitPane.setDividerLocation(100); //XXX: ignored in some releases
                                    //of Swing. bug 4101306
        //workaround for bug 4101306:
        //treeView.setPreferredSize(new Dimension(100, 100));

        splitPane.setPreferredSize(new Dimension(500, 300));

        //Add the split pane to this frame.
        getContentPane().add(splitPane, BorderLayout.CENTER);
    }

    private class BookInfo {
        public String bookName;
        public URL bookURL;
        public String prefix = "file:"
                            + System.getProperty("user.dir")
                            + System.getProperty("file.separator");
        public BookInfo(String book, String filename) {
            bookName = book;
            try {
                bookURL = new URL(prefix + filename);
            } catch (java.net.MalformedURLException exc) {
                System.err.println("Attempted to create a BookInfo "
                                    + "with a bad URL: " + bookURL);
                bookURL = null;
            }
        }

        public String toString() {
            return bookName;
        }
    }

    private void initHelp() {
        String s = null;
        try {
            s = "file:"
                + System.getProperty("user.dir")
                + System.getProperty("file.separator")
                + "TreeDemoHelp.html";
            if (DEBUG) {
                System.out.println("Help URL is " + s);
            }
            helpURL = new URL(s);
            displayURL(helpURL);
```

```
        } catch (Exception e) {
            System.err.println("Couldn't create help URL: " + s);
        }
    }

    private void displayURL(URL url) {
        try {
            htmlPane.setPage(url);
        } catch (IOException e) {
            System.err.println("Attempted to read a bad URL: " + url);
        }
    }

    private void createNodes(DefaultMutableTreeNode top) {
        DefaultMutableTreeNode category = null;
        DefaultMutableTreeNode book = null;

        category = new DefaultMutableTreeNode("Books for Java Programmers");
        top.add(category);

        //original Tutorial
        book = new DefaultMutableTreeNode(new BookInfo
            ("The Java Tutorial: Object-Oriented Programming for the Internet",
             "tutorial.html"));
        category.add(book);

        //Tutorial Continued
        book = new DefaultMutableTreeNode(new BookInfo
            ("The Java Tutorial Continued: The Rest of the JDK",
             "tutorialcont.html"));
        category.add(book);

        //JFC Swing Tutorial
        book = new DefaultMutableTreeNode(new BookInfo
            ("The JFC Swing Tutorial: A Guide to Constructing GUIs",
             "swingtutorial.html"));
        category.add(book);

        //Arnold/Gosling
        book = new DefaultMutableTreeNode(new BookInfo
            ("The Java Programming Language", "arnold.html"));
        category.add(book);

        //FAQ
        book = new DefaultMutableTreeNode(new BookInfo(
            "The Java FAQ", "faq.html"));
        category.add(book);

        //Chan/Lee
        book = new DefaultMutableTreeNode(new BookInfo
            ("The Java Class Libraries: An Annotated Reference",
             "chanlee.html"));
        category.add(book);

        //Threads
        book = new DefaultMutableTreeNode(new BookInfo
            ("Concurrent Programming in Java: Design Principles and Patterns",
                "thread.html"));
        category.add(book);

        category = new DefaultMutableTreeNode("Books for Java Implementers");
        top.add(category);

        //VM
        book = new DefaultMutableTreeNode(new BookInfo
            ("The Java Virtual Machine Specification", "vm.html"));
        category.add(book);
```

```
                    //Language Spec
                    book = new DefaultMutableTreeNode(new BookInfo
                        ("The Java Language Specification",
                         "jls.html"));
                    category.add(book);
                }

                public static void main(String[] args) {
                    JFrame frame = new TreeDemo();

                    frame.addWindowListener(new WindowAdapter() {
                        public void windowClosing(WindowEvent e) {
                            System.exit(0);
                        }
                    });

                    frame.pack();
                    frame.setVisible(true);
                }
            }
```

EXAMPLE: *TreeIconDemo.java*

Where Explained:

Customizing a Tree's Display (page 324)

SOURCE CODE: *http://java.sun.com/docs/books/tutorial/uiswing/components/example-swing/TreeIconDemo.java*

```java
import javax.swing.JTree;
import javax.swing.tree.DefaultMutableTreeNode;
import javax.swing.event.TreeSelectionListener;
import javax.swing.event.TreeSelectionEvent;
import javax.swing.tree.TreeSelectionModel;
import javax.swing.tree.DefaultTreeCellRenderer;
import javax.swing.ImageIcon;
import java.net.URL;
import java.io.IOException;
import javax.swing.JEditorPane;
import javax.swing.JScrollPane;
import javax.swing.JSplitPane;
import javax.swing.JFrame;
import java.awt.*;
import java.awt.event.*;

public class TreeIconDemo extends JFrame {
    private JEditorPane htmlPane;
    private static boolean DEBUG = false;
    private URL helpURL;

    public TreeIconDemo() {
        super("TreeIconDemo");

        //Create the nodes.
        DefaultMutableTreeNode top = new DefaultMutableTreeNode("The Java Series");
        createNodes(top);

        //Create a tree that allows one selection at a time.
        final JTree tree = new JTree(top);
        tree.getSelectionModel().setSelectionMode
                (TreeSelectionModel.SINGLE_TREE_SELECTION);

        /*
         * Set the icon for leaf nodes.
         * Note: In the Swing 1.0.x release, we used
         * swing.plaf.basic.BasicTreeCellRenderer.
         */
```

```
        DefaultTreeCellRenderer renderer = new DefaultTreeCellRenderer();
        renderer.setLeafIcon(new ImageIcon("images/middle.gif"));
        tree.setCellRenderer(renderer);

        //Listen for when the selection changes.
        tree.addTreeSelectionListener(new TreeSelectionListener() {
            public void valueChanged(TreeSelectionEvent e) {
                DefaultMutableTreeNode node = (DefaultMutableTreeNode)
                                tree.getLastSelectedPathComponent();

                if (node == null) return;

                Object nodeInfo = node.getUserObject();
                if (node.isLeaf()) {
                    BookInfo book = (BookInfo)nodeInfo;
                    displayURL(book.bookURL);
                    if (DEBUG) {
                        System.out.print(book.bookURL + ": \n    ");
                    }
                } else {
                    displayURL(helpURL);
                }
                if (DEBUG) {
                    System.out.println(nodeInfo.toString());
                }
            }
        });

        //Create the scroll pane and add the tree to it.
        JScrollPane treeView = new JScrollPane(tree);

        //Create the HTML viewing pane.
        htmlPane = new JEditorPane();
        htmlPane.setEditable(false);
        initHelp();
        JScrollPane htmlView = new JScrollPane(htmlPane);

        //Add the scroll panes to a split pane.
        JSplitPane splitPane = new JSplitPane(JSplitPane.VERTICAL_SPLIT);
        splitPane.setTopComponent(treeView);
        splitPane.setBottomComponent(htmlView);
        Dimension minimumSize = new Dimension(100, 50);
        htmlView.setMinimumSize(minimumSize);
        treeView.setMinimumSize(minimumSize);
        splitPane.setDividerLocation(100); //XXX: ignored in some releases
                                           //of Swing. bug 4101306
        //workaround for bug 4101306:
        //treeView.setPreferredSize(new Dimension(100, 100));

        splitPane.setPreferredSize(new Dimension(500, 300));

        //Add the split pane to this frame.
        getContentPane().add(splitPane, BorderLayout.CENTER);
    }

    private class BookInfo {
        public String bookName;
        public URL bookURL;
        public String prefix = "file:"
                            + System.getProperty("user.dir")
                            + System.getProperty("file.separator");
        public BookInfo(String book, String filename) {
            bookName = book;
            try {
                bookURL = new URL(prefix + filename);
```

```
            } catch (java.net.MalformedURLException exc) {
                System.err.println("Attempted to create a BookInfo "
                                   + "with a bad URL: " + bookURL);
                bookURL = null;
            }
        }

        public String toString() {
            return bookName;
        }
    }

    private void initHelp() {
        String s = null;
        try {
            s = "file:"
                + System.getProperty("user.dir")
                + System.getProperty("file.separator")
                + "TreeDemoHelp.html";
            if (DEBUG) {
                System.out.println("Help URL is " + s);
            }
            helpURL = new URL(s);
            displayURL(helpURL);
        } catch (Exception e) {
            System.err.println("Couldn't create help URL: " + s);
        }
    }

    private void displayURL(URL url) {
        try {
            htmlPane.setPage(url);
        } catch (IOException e) {
            System.err.println("Attempted to read a bad URL: " + url);
        }
    }

    private void createNodes(DefaultMutableTreeNode top) {
        DefaultMutableTreeNode category = null;
        DefaultMutableTreeNode book = null;

        category = new DefaultMutableTreeNode("Books for Java Programmers");
        top.add(category);

        //original Tutorial
        book = new DefaultMutableTreeNode(new BookInfo
            ("The Java Tutorial: Object-Oriented Programming for the Internet",
            "tutorial.html"));
        category.add(book);

        //Tutorial Continued
        book = new DefaultMutableTreeNode(new BookInfo
            ("The Java Tutorial Continued: The Rest of the JDK",
            "tutorialcont.html"));
        category.add(book);

        //JFC Swing Tutorial
        book = new DefaultMutableTreeNode(new BookInfo
            ("The JFC Swing Tutorial: A Guide to Constructing GUIs",
            "swingtutorial.html"));
        category.add(book);

        //Arnold/Gosling
        book = new DefaultMutableTreeNode(new BookInfo
            ("The Java Programming Language", "arnold.html"));
        category.add(book);
```

```
        //FAQ
        book = new DefaultMutableTreeNode(new BookInfo(
            "The Java FAQ", "faq.html"));
        category.add(book);

        //Chan/Lee
        book = new DefaultMutableTreeNode(new BookInfo
            ("The Java Class Libraries: An Annotated Reference",
             "chanlee.html"));
        category.add(book);

        //Threads
        book = new DefaultMutableTreeNode(new BookInfo
            ("Concurrent Programming in Java: Design Principles and Patterns",
             "thread.html"));
        category.add(book);

        category = new DefaultMutableTreeNode("Books for Java Implementers");
        top.add(category);

        //VM
        book = new DefaultMutableTreeNode(new BookInfo
            ("The Java Virtual Machine Specification",
             "vm.html"));
        category.add(book);

        //Language Spec
        book = new DefaultMutableTreeNode(new BookInfo
            ("The Java Language Specification",
             "jls.html"));
        category.add(book);
    }

    public static void main(String[] args) {
        JFrame frame = new TreeIconDemo();

        frame.addWindowListener(new WindowAdapter() {
            public void windowClosing(WindowEvent e) {
                System.exit(0);
            }
        });

        frame.pack();
        frame.setVisible(true);
    }
}
```

EXAMPLE: *TreeIconDemo2.java*

Where Explained: *Customizing a Tree's Display* (page 324)

SOURCE CODE: *http://java.sun.com/docs/books/tutorial/uiswing/components/example-swing/TreeIconDemo2.java*

```
import javax.swing.JTree;
import javax.swing.tree.DefaultMutableTreeNode;
import javax.swing.event.TreeSelectionListener;
import javax.swing.event.TreeSelectionEvent;
import javax.swing.tree.TreeSelectionModel;
import javax.swing.tree.DefaultTreeCellRenderer;
import javax.swing.ImageIcon;
import javax.swing.ToolTipManager;
import java.net.URL;
import java.io.IOException;
import javax.swing.JEditorPane;
```

```java
import javax.swing.JScrollPane;
import javax.swing.JSplitPane;
import javax.swing.JFrame;
import java.awt.*;
import java.awt.event.*;

public class TreeIconDemo2 extends JFrame {
    private JEditorPane htmlPane;
    private static boolean DEBUG = false;
    private URL helpURL;

    public TreeIconDemo2() {
        super("TreeIconDemo2");

        //Create the nodes.
        DefaultMutableTreeNode top = new DefaultMutableTreeNode(
                                        "The Java Series");
        createNodes(top);

        //Create a tree that allows one selection at a time.
        final JTree tree = new JTree(top);
        tree.getSelectionModel().setSelectionMode
                (TreeSelectionModel.SINGLE_TREE_SELECTION);

        //Enable tool tips.
        ToolTipManager.sharedInstance().registerComponent(tree);

        /*
         * Set the icon for leaf nodes.
         * Note: In the Swing 1.0.x release, we used
         * swing.plaf.basic.BasicTreeCellRenderer.
         */
        tree.setCellRenderer(new MyRenderer());

        //Listen for when the selection changes.
        tree.addTreeSelectionListener(new TreeSelectionListener() {
            public void valueChanged(TreeSelectionEvent e) {
                DefaultMutableTreeNode node = (DefaultMutableTreeNode)
                                tree.getLastSelectedPathComponent();

                if (node == null) return;

                Object nodeInfo = node.getUserObject();
                if (node.isLeaf()) {
                    BookInfo book = (BookInfo)nodeInfo;
                    displayURL(book.bookURL);
                    if (DEBUG) {
                        System.out.print(book.bookURL + ":  \n    ");
                    }
                } else {
                    displayURL(helpURL);
                }
                if (DEBUG) {
                    System.out.println(nodeInfo.toString());
                }
            }
        });

        //Create the scroll pane and add the tree to it.
        JScrollPane treeView = new JScrollPane(tree);

        //Create the HTML viewing pane.
        htmlPane = new JEditorPane();
        htmlPane.setEditable(false);
        initHelp();
        JScrollPane htmlView = new JScrollPane(htmlPane);
```

```java
            //Add the scroll panes to a split pane.
            JSplitPane splitPane = new JSplitPane(JSplitPane.VERTICAL_SPLIT);
            splitPane.setTopComponent(treeView);
            splitPane.setBottomComponent(htmlView);
            Dimension minimumSize = new Dimension(100, 50);
            htmlView.setMinimumSize(minimumSize);
            treeView.setMinimumSize(minimumSize);
            splitPane.setDividerLocation(100); //XXX: ignored in some releases
                                               //of Swing. bug 4101306
            //workaround for bug 4101306:
            //treeView.setPreferredSize(new Dimension(100, 100));

            splitPane.setPreferredSize(new Dimension(500, 300));

            //Add the split pane to this frame.
            getContentPane().add(splitPane, BorderLayout.CENTER);
        }

        private class BookInfo {
            public String bookName;
            public URL bookURL;
            public String prefix = "file:"
                                   + System.getProperty("user.dir")
                                   + System.getProperty("file.separator");
            public BookInfo(String book, String filename) {
                bookName = book;
                try {
                    bookURL = new URL(prefix + filename);
                } catch (java.net.MalformedURLException exc) {
                    System.err.println("Attempted to create a BookInfo "
                                       + "with a bad URL: " + bookURL);
                    bookURL = null;
                }
            }

            public String toString() {
                return bookName;
            }
        }

        private void initHelp() {
            String s = null;
            try {
                s = "file:"
                    + System.getProperty("user.dir")
                    + System.getProperty("file.separator")
                    + "TreeDemoHelp.html";
                if (DEBUG) {
                    System.out.println("Help URL is " + s);
                }
                helpURL = new URL(s);
                displayURL(helpURL);
            } catch (Exception e) {
                System.err.println("Couldn't create help URL: " + s);
            }
        }

        private void displayURL(URL url) {
            try {
                htmlPane.setPage(url);
            } catch (IOException e) {
                System.err.println("Attempted to read a bad URL: " + url);
            }
        }
```

```java
private void createNodes(DefaultMutableTreeNode top) {
    DefaultMutableTreeNode category = null;
    DefaultMutableTreeNode book = null;

    category = new DefaultMutableTreeNode("Books for Java Programmers");
    top.add(category);

    //original Tutorial
    book = new DefaultMutableTreeNode(new BookInfo
        ("The Java Tutorial: Object-Oriented Programming for the Internet",
         "tutorial.html"));
    category.add(book);

    //Tutorial Continued
    book = new DefaultMutableTreeNode(new BookInfo
        ("The Java Tutorial Continued: The Rest of the JDK",
         "tutorialcont.html"));
    category.add(book);

    //JFC Swing Tutorial
    book = new DefaultMutableTreeNode(new BookInfo
        ("The JFC Swing Tutorial: A Guide to Constructing GUIs",
         "swingtutorial.html"));
    category.add(book);

    //Arnold/Gosling
    book = new DefaultMutableTreeNode(new BookInfo
        ("The Java Programming Language", "arnold.html"));
    category.add(book);

    //FAQ
    book = new DefaultMutableTreeNode(new BookInfo(
        "The Java FAQ", "faq.html"));
    category.add(book);

    //Chan/Lee
    book = new DefaultMutableTreeNode(new BookInfo
        ("The Java Class Libraries: An Annotated Reference",
         "chanlee.html"));
    category.add(book);

    //Threads
    book = new DefaultMutableTreeNode(new BookInfo
        ("Concurrent Programming in Java: Design Principles and Patterns",
         "thread.html"));
    category.add(book);

    category = new DefaultMutableTreeNode("Books for Java Implementers");
    top.add(category);

    //VM
    book = new DefaultMutableTreeNode(new BookInfo
        ("The Java Virtual Machine Specification",
         "vm.html"));
    category.add(book);

    //Language Spec
    book = new DefaultMutableTreeNode(new BookInfo
        ("The Java Language Specification",
         "jls.html"));
    category.add(book);
}

public static void main(String[] args) {
    JFrame frame = new TreeIconDemo2();
```

```
        frame.addWindowListener(new WindowAdapter() {
            public void windowClosing(WindowEvent e) {
                System.exit(0);
            }
        });

        frame.pack();
        frame.setVisible(true);
    }

    private class MyRenderer extends DefaultTreeCellRenderer {
        ImageIcon tutorialIcon;

        public MyRenderer() {
            tutorialIcon = new ImageIcon("images/middle.gif");
        }

        public Component getTreeCellRendererComponent(
                        JTree tree,
                        Object value,
                        boolean sel,
                        boolean expanded,
                        boolean leaf,
                        int row,
                        boolean hasFocus) {

            super.getTreeCellRendererComponent(
                        tree, value, sel,
                        expanded, leaf, row,
                        hasFocus);
            if (leaf && isTutorialBook(value)) {
                setIcon(tutorialIcon);
                setToolTipText("This book is in the Tutorial series.");
            } else {
                setToolTipText(null);
            }

            return this;
        }

        protected boolean isTutorialBook(Object value) {
            DefaultMutableTreeNode node =
                    (DefaultMutableTreeNode)value;
            BookInfo nodeInfo =
                    (BookInfo)(node.getUserObject());
            String title = nodeInfo.bookName;
            if (title.indexOf("Tutorial") >= 0) {
                return true;
            }

            return false;
        }
    }
}
```

EXAMPLE: *TumbleItem.java*

SOURCE CODE: *http://java.sun.com/docs/books/tutorial/uiswing/components/example-swing/TumbleItem.java*

Where Explained: *How to Make Applets* (page 99)

```
import javax.swing.*;
import java.awt.*;
import java.awt.event.*;
import java.net.*;
```

```java
/**
 * @author jag
 * @author mem
 * @author kwalrath
 */

public class TumbleItem extends JApplet
                        implements ActionListener {
    int loopslot = -1;   //the current frame number

    String dir;          //the directory relative to the codebase
                         //from which the images are loaded

    Timer timer;         //the timer animating the images

    int pause;           //the length of the pause between revs

    int offset;          //how much to offset between loops
    int off;             //the current offset
    int speed;           //animation speed
    int nimgs;           //number of images to animate
    int width;           //width of the applet's content pane
    JComponent contentPane; //the applet's content pane

    ImageIcon imgs[];    //the images
    int maxWidth;        //width of widest image
    boolean finishedLoading = false;
    JLabel statusLabel;
    static Color[] labelColor = { Color.black, Color.black,
                                  Color.black, Color.black,
                                  Color.black, Color.white,
                                  Color.white, Color.white,
                                  Color.white, Color.white };

    public void init() {
        //Get the applet parameters.
        String at = getParameter("img");
        dir = (at != null) ? at : "images/tumble";
        at = getParameter("pause");
        pause = (at != null) ? Integer.valueOf(at).intValue() : 1900;
        at = getParameter("offset");
        offset = (at != null) ? Integer.valueOf(at).intValue() : 0;
        at = getParameter("speed");
        speed = (at != null) ? (1000 / Integer.valueOf(at).intValue()) : 100;
        at = getParameter("nimgs");
        nimgs = (at != null) ? Integer.valueOf(at).intValue() : 16;
        at = getParameter("maxwidth");
        maxWidth = (at != null) ? Integer.valueOf(at).intValue() : 0;

        //Animate from right to left if offset is negative.
        width = getSize().width;
        if (offset < 0) {
            off = width - maxWidth;
        }

        //Custom component to draw the current image
        //at a particular offset.
        contentPane = new JPanel() {
            public void paintComponent(Graphics g) {
                super.paintComponent(g);

                if (finishedLoading &&
                    (loopslot > -1) && (loopslot < nimgs)) {
                    imgs[loopslot].paintIcon(this, g, off, 0);
                }
            }
        };
```

```
        contentPane.setBackground(Color.white);
        setContentPane(contentPane);

        //Put a "Loading Images..." label in the middle of
        //the content pane.  To center the label's text in
        //the applet, put it in the center part of a
        //BorderLayout-controlled container, and center-align
        //the label's text.
        statusLabel = new JLabel("Loading Images...",
                                 JLabel.CENTER);
        statusLabel.setForeground(labelColor[0]);
        contentPane.setLayout(new BorderLayout());
        contentPane.add(statusLabel, BorderLayout.CENTER);

        //Set up the timer that will perform the animation.
        //Don't start it until all the images are loaded.
        timer = new Timer(speed, this);
        timer.setInitialDelay(pause);
        timer.setCoalesce(false);

        //Loading the images can take quite a while, so to
        //avoid staying in init() (and thus not being able
        //to show the "Loading Images..." label, we'll
        //load the images in a SwingWorker thread.
        imgs = new ImageIcon[nimgs];
        timer.start(); //Start the animation.
        final SwingWorker worker = new SwingWorker() {
            public Object construct() {
                URL baseURL = getCodeBase();
                String prefix = dir + "/T";
                //Images are numbered 1 to nimgs,
                //but fill array from 0 to nimgs-1.
                for (int i = 0; i < nimgs; i++) {
                    imgs[i] = new ImageIcon(getURL(baseURL,
                                     prefix + (i+1) + ".gif"));
                }
                finishedLoading = true;
                return imgs;
            }
            public void finished() {
                //Remove the "Loading images" label.
                contentPane.removeAll();
                contentPane.repaint();
                loopslot = -1;
            }
        };
    }

    //Update the the loopslot (frame number) and the offset.
    //If it's the last frame, restart the timer to get a long
    //pause between loops.
    public void actionPerformed(ActionEvent e) {
        loopslot++;

        if (!finishedLoading) {
            int colorIndex = loopslot % labelColor.length;
            try {
                statusLabel.setForeground(labelColor[colorIndex]);
            } catch (NullPointerException exc) {}
            return;
        }

        if (loopslot >= nimgs) {
            loopslot = 0;
            off += offset;
```

```java
            if (off < 0) {
                off = width - maxWidth;
            } else if (off + maxWidth > width) {
                off = 0;
            }
        }

        contentPane.repaint();

        if (loopslot == nimgs - 1) {
            timer.restart();
        }
    }

    public void start() {
        if (finishedLoading && (nimgs > 1)) {
            timer.restart();
        }
    }

    public void stop() {
        timer.stop();
    }

    protected URL getURL(URL codeBase, String filename) {
        URL url = null;

        try {
            url = new URL(codeBase, filename);
        } catch (java.net.MalformedURLException e) {
            System.out.println("Couldn't create image: badly specified URL");
            return null;
        }

        return url;
    }

    public String getAppletInfo() {
        return "Title: TumbleItem v1.2, 23 Jul 1997\n"
                + "Author: James Gosling\n"
                + "A simple Item class to play an image loop.";
    }

    public String[][] getParameterInfo() {
        String[][] info = {
            {"img", "string", "the directory containing the images to loop"},
            {"pause", "int", "pause between complete loops; default is 3900"},
            {"offset", "int", "offset of each image to simulate left (-) or "
                            + "right (+) motion; default is 0 (no motion)"},
            {"speed", "int", "the speed at which the frames are looped; "
                            + "default is 100"},
            {"nimgs", "int", "the number of images to be looped; default is 16"},
            {"maxwidth", "int", "the maximum width of any image in the loop; "
                            + "default is 0"}
        };
        return info;
    }
}
```

EXAMPLE: *Utils.java*

Main Source File: `FileChooserDemo2.java` *(page 651)*

SOURCE CODE: *http://java.sun.com/docs/books/tutorial/uiswing/components/example-swing/Utils.java*

```java
import java.io.File;

public class Utils {

    public final static String jpeg = "jpeg";
    public final static String jpg = "jpg";
    public final static String gif = "gif";
    public final static String tiff = "tiff";
    public final static String tif = "tif";

    /*
     * Get the extension of a file.
     */
    public static String getExtension(File f) {
        String ext = null;
        String s = f.getName();
        int i = s.lastIndexOf('.');

        if (i > 0 &&  i < s.length() - 1) {
            ext = s.substring(i+1).toLowerCase();
        }
        return ext;
    }
}
```

Where Explained: *Another Example: FileChooser-Demo2 (page 203)*

EXAMPLE: *WholeNumberField.java*

Main Source File: `TableEditDemo.java` *(page 730),*
`TextFieldDemo.java` *(page 751)*

SOURCE CODE: *http://java.sun.com/docs/books/tutorial/uiswing/components/example-swing/WholeNumberField.java*

```java
import javax.swing.*;
import javax.swing.text.*;

import java.awt.Toolkit;
import java.text.NumberFormat;
import java.text.ParseException;
import java.util.Locale;

public class WholeNumberField extends JTextField {
    private Toolkit toolkit;
    private NumberFormat integerFormatter;

    public WholeNumberField(int value, int columns) {
        super(columns);
        toolkit = Toolkit.getDefaultToolkit();
        integerFormatter = NumberFormat.getNumberInstance(Locale.US);
        integerFormatter.setParseIntegerOnly(true);
        setValue(value);
    }
```

Where Explained: *How to Use Text Fields (page 298)*

```
        public int getValue() {
            int retVal = 0;
            try {
                retVal = integerFormatter.parse(getText()).intValue();
            } catch (ParseException e) {
                // This should never happen because insertString allows
                // only properly formatted data to get in the field.
                toolkit.beep();
            }
            return retVal;
        }

        public void setValue(int value) {
            setText(integerFormatter.format(value));
        }

        protected Document createDefaultModel() {
            return new WholeNumberDocument();
        }

        protected class WholeNumberDocument extends PlainDocument {
            public void insertString(int offs,
                                     String str,
                                     AttributeSet a)
                    throws BadLocationException {
                char[] source = str.toCharArray();
                char[] result = new char[source.length];
                int j = 0;

                for (int i = 0; i < result.length; i++) {
                    if (Character.isDigit(source[i]))
                        result[j++] = source[i];
                    else {
                        toolkit.beep();
                        System.err.println("insertString: " + source[i]);
                    }
                }
                super.insertString(offs, new String(result, 0, j), a);
            }
        }
    }
}
```

Laying Out Components

Complete examples in <u>Laying Out Components</u> (page 341):

EXAMPLE: *AlignmentDemo.java*

SOURCE CODE: *http://java.sun.com/docs/books/tutorial/uiswing/layout/example-swing/ AlignmentDemo.java*

Where Explained:

Fixing Alignment Problems (page 357)

```
/*
 * Shows how to specify alignments when you're using
 * a BoxLayout for components with maximum sizes
 * and different default alignments.
 */

import javax.swing.*;
import javax.swing.border.*;
import java.awt.*;
import java.awt.event.*;

public class AlignmentDemo extends JFrame {
    public AlignmentDemo() {
        super("AlignmentDemo");

        JTabbedPane tabbedPane = new JTabbedPane();

        JPanel buttonRow = new JPanel();
        //Use default FlowLayout.
        buttonRow.add(createButtonRow(false));
        buttonRow.add(createButtonRow(true));
        tabbedPane.addTab("Altering alignments", buttonRow);

        JPanel labelAndComponent = new JPanel();
```

```java
        //Use default FlowLayout.
        labelAndComponent.add(createLabelAndComponent(false));
        labelAndComponent.add(createLabelAndComponent(true));
        tabbedPane.addTab("X alignment mismatch", labelAndComponent);

        JPanel buttonAndComponent = new JPanel();
        //Use default FlowLayout.
        buttonAndComponent.add(createYAlignmentExample(false));
        buttonAndComponent.add(createYAlignmentExample(true));
        tabbedPane.addTab("Y alignment mismatch", buttonAndComponent);

        //Add tabbedPane to this frame.
        getContentPane().add(tabbedPane, BorderLayout.CENTER);
    }

    protected JPanel createButtonRow(boolean changeAlignment) {
        JButton button1 = new JButton("A JButton",
                             new ImageIcon("images/middle.gif"));
        button1.setVerticalTextPosition(AbstractButton.BOTTOM);
        button1.setHorizontalTextPosition(AbstractButton.CENTER);

        JButton button2 = new JButton("Another JButton",
                             new ImageIcon("images/geek-cght.gif"));
        button2.setVerticalTextPosition(AbstractButton.BOTTOM);
        button2.setHorizontalTextPosition(AbstractButton.CENTER);

        String title;
        if (changeAlignment) {
            title = "Desired";
            button1.setAlignmentY(BOTTOM_ALIGNMENT);
            button2.setAlignmentY(BOTTOM_ALIGNMENT);
        } else {
            title = "Default";
        }

        JPanel pane = new JPanel();
        pane.setBorder(BorderFactory.createTitledBorder(title));
        pane.setLayout(new BoxLayout(pane, BoxLayout.X_AXIS));
        pane.add(button1);
        pane.add(button2);
        return pane;
    }

    protected JPanel createLabelAndComponent(boolean doItRight) {
        JPanel pane = new JPanel();

        JComponent component = new JPanel();
        Dimension size = new Dimension(150,100);
        component.setMaximumSize(size);
        component.setPreferredSize(size);
        component.setMinimumSize(size);
        TitledBorder border = new TitledBorder(
                                 new LineBorder(Color.black),
                                 "A JPanel",
                                 TitledBorder.CENTER,
                                 TitledBorder.BELOW_TOP);
        border.setTitleColor(Color.black);
        component.setBorder(border);

        JLabel label = new JLabel("This is a JLabel");
        String title;
        if (doItRight) {
            title = "Matched";
            label.setAlignmentX(CENTER_ALIGNMENT);
        } else {
            title = "Mismatched";
        }
```

```java
        pane.setBorder(BorderFactory.createTitledBorder(title));
        pane.setLayout(new BoxLayout(pane, BoxLayout.Y_AXIS));
        pane.add(label);
        pane.add(component);
        return pane;
    }

    protected JPanel createYAlignmentExample(boolean doItRight) {
        JPanel pane = new JPanel();
        String title;

        JComponent component1 = new JPanel();
        Dimension size = new Dimension(100, 50);
        component1.setMaximumSize(size);
        component1.setPreferredSize(size);
        component1.setMinimumSize(size);
        TitledBorder border = new TitledBorder(
                            new LineBorder(Color.black),
                            "A JPanel",
                            TitledBorder.CENTER,
                            TitledBorder.BELOW_TOP);
        border.setTitleColor(Color.black);
        component1.setBorder(border);

        JComponent component2 = new JPanel();
        size = new Dimension(100, 50);
        component2.setMaximumSize(size);
        component2.setPreferredSize(size);
        component2.setMinimumSize(size);
        border = new TitledBorder(new LineBorder(Color.black),
                            "A JPanel",
                            TitledBorder.CENTER,
                            TitledBorder.BELOW_TOP);
        border.setTitleColor(Color.black);
        component2.setBorder(border);

        if (doItRight) {
            title = "Matched";
        } else {
            component1.setAlignmentY(TOP_ALIGNMENT);
            title = "Mismatched";
        }

        pane.setBorder(BorderFactory.createTitledBorder(title));
        pane.setLayout(new BoxLayout(pane, BoxLayout.X_AXIS));
        pane.add(component1);
        pane.add(component2);
        return pane;
    }

    public static void main(String[] args) {
        JFrame frame = new AlignmentDemo();
        frame.addWindowListener(new WindowAdapter() {
            public void windowClosing(WindowEvent e) {
                System.exit(0);
            }
        });

        frame.pack();
        frame.setVisible(true);
    }
}
```

EXAMPLE: *BLDComponent.java*

**Where
Explained:**

*How to Use
BoxLayout*
(page 350)

Main Source File: BoxLayoutDemo.java *(page 787)*

SOURCE CODE: *http://java.sun.com/docs/books/tutorial/uiswing/layout/example-swing/
BLDComponent.java*

```
import java.awt.*;
import java.awt.event.*;
import javax.swing.*;

/** A rectangle that has a fixed size. */
class BLDComponent extends JComponent {
    private Color normalHue;
    private final Dimension preferredSize;
    private String name;
    private boolean restrictMaximumSize;
    private boolean printSize;

    public BLDComponent(float alignmentX, float hue, int shortSideSize,
                        boolean restrictSize,
                        boolean printSize,
                        String name) {
        this.name = name;
        this.restrictMaximumSize = restrictSize;
        this.printSize = printSize;
        setAlignmentX(alignmentX);
        normalHue = Color.getHSBColor(hue, 0.4f, 0.85f);
        preferredSize = new Dimension(shortSideSize*2, shortSideSize);

        MouseListener l = new MouseAdapter() {
            public void mousePressed(MouseEvent e) {
                int width = getWidth();
                float alignment = (float)(e.getX())
                                  / (float)width;

                // Round to the nearest 1/10th.
                int tmp = Math.round(alignment * 10.0f);
                alignment = (float)tmp / 10.0f;

                setAlignmentX(alignment);
                revalidate(); // this GUI needs relayout
                repaint();
            }
        };
        addMouseListener(l);
    }

    /**
     * Our BLDComponents are completely opaque, so we override
     * this method to return true.  This lets the painting
     * system know that it doesn't need to paint any covered
     * part of the components underneath this component.  The
     * end result is possibly improved painting performance.
     */
    public boolean isOpaque() {
        return true;
    }

    public void paint(Graphics g) {
        int width = getWidth();
        int height = getHeight();
        float alignmentX = getAlignmentX();
```

```
        g.setColor(normalHue);
        g.fill3DRect(0, 0, width, height, true);

        /* Draw a vertical white line at the alignment point.*/
        // XXX: This code is probably not the best.
        g.setColor(Color.white);
        int x = (int)(alignmentX * (float)width) - 1;
        g.drawLine(x, 0, x, height - 1);

        /* Say what the alignment point is. */
        g.setColor(Color.black);
        g.drawString(Float.toString(alignmentX), 3, height - 3);

        if (printSize) {
            System.out.println("BLDComponent " + name + ": size is "
                               + width + "x" + height
                               + "; preferred size is "
                               + getPreferredSize().width + "x"
                               + getPreferredSize().height);
        }
    }

    public Dimension getPreferredSize() {
        return preferredSize;
    }

    public Dimension getMinimumSize() {
        return preferredSize;
    }

    public Dimension getMaximumSize() {
        if (restrictMaximumSize) {
            return preferredSize;
        } else {
            return super.getMaximumSize();
        }
    }

    public void setSizeRestriction(boolean restrictSize) {
        restrictMaximumSize = restrictSize;
    }

}
```

EXAMPLE: AppletButton.java

Associated File(s): <u>BorderWindow.java</u> *(page 786)*, <u>BoxWindow.java</u> *(page 788)*, <u>CardWindow.java</u> *(page 789)*, <u>CustomWindow.java</u> *(page 791)*, <u>DiagonalLayout.java</u> *(page 791)*, <u>FlowWindow.java</u> *(page 794)*, <u>GridBagWindow.java</u> *(page 801)*, <u>NoneWindow.java</u> *(page 803)*, <u>TabWindow.java</u> *(page 804)*

Where Explained:
How to Use CardLayout (page 363)

SOURCE CODE: *http://java.sun.com/docs/books/tutorial/uiswing/layout/example-swing/ AppletButton.java*

```
/*
 * Swing 1.1 version (compatible with both JDK 1.1 and Java 2)..
 */

import java.awt.*;
import java.awt.event.*;
import javax.swing.*;
```

```java
public class AppletButton extends JApplet implements Runnable, ActionListener {
    int frameNumber = 1;
    String windowClass;
    String buttonText;
    String windowTitle;
    int requestedWidth = 0;
    int requestedHeight = 0;
    JButton button;
    Thread windowThread;
    JLabel label;
    boolean pleaseShow = false;
    boolean shouldInitialize = true;
    Class windowClassObject;

    public void init() {
        //Look up the parameters we need right away.
        windowClass = getParameter("WINDOWCLASS");
        if (windowClass == null) {
            windowClass = "TestWindow";
        }
        buttonText = getParameter("BUTTONTEXT");
        if (buttonText == null) {
            buttonText = "Click here to bring up a " + windowClass;
        }

        //Set up the button and label this applet displays.
        button = new JButton(buttonText);
        button.addActionListener(this);
        label = new JLabel("", JLabel.CENTER);

        //Add the button and label to this applet.
        Container contentPane = getContentPane();
        contentPane.setLayout(new GridLayout(2,0));
        contentPane.add(button);
        contentPane.add(label);
    }

    public void start() {
        if (windowThread == null) {
            windowThread = new Thread(this, "Bringing Up " + windowClass);
            windowThread.start();
        }
    }

    public void stop() {
        windowThread = null;
    }

    public synchronized void run() {
        Object object = null;
        JFrame window = null;
        String name = null;

        if (shouldInitialize) {
            //Look up the rest of the parameters.
            windowTitle = getParameter("WINDOWTITLE");
            if (windowTitle == null) {
                windowTitle = windowClass;
            }
            String windowWidthString = getParameter("WINDOWWIDTH");
            if (windowWidthString != null) {
                try {
                    requestedWidth = Integer.parseInt(windowWidthString);
                } catch (NumberFormatException e) {
                    //Use default width.
                }
            }
```

```
            String windowHeightString = getParameter("WINDOWHEIGHT");
            if (windowHeightString != null) {
                try {
                    requestedHeight = Integer.parseInt(windowHeightString);
                } catch (NumberFormatException e) {
                    //Use default height.
                }
            }

            //Make sure the window class exists.
            try {
                windowClassObject = Class.forName(windowClass);
            } catch (Exception e) {
                //The specified class isn't anywhere that we can find.
                label.setText("Bad parameter: Couldn't find class "
                              + windowClass);
                button.setEnabled(false);
                return;
            }

            //Create an invisible instance.
            window = createWindow(windowTitle);
            if (window == null) {
                return;
            }

            shouldInitialize = false;
        }

        Thread currentThread = Thread.currentThread();
        while (currentThread == windowThread) {

            //Wait until we're asked to show a window.
            while (pleaseShow == false) {
                try {
                    wait();
                } catch (InterruptedException e) {
                }
            }

            //We've been asked to bring up a window.
            pleaseShow = false;

            //Create another window if necessary.
            if (window == null) {
                window = createWindow(windowTitle + ": "
                                      + ++frameNumber);
            }

            window.setVisible(true);
            label.setText("");
            window = null;
        } //end thread loop
    }

    private JFrame createWindow(String title) {
        Object object = null;
        JFrame window = null;

        //Instantiate the window class.
        try {
            object = windowClassObject.newInstance();
        } catch (Exception e) {
            label.setText("Bad parameter: Can't instantiate "
                          + windowClassObject);
            button.setEnabled(false);
            return null;
        }
```

```
                //Make sure it's a frame.
                try {
                    window = (JFrame)object;
                } catch (Exception e) {
                    label.setText("Bad parameter: "
                                    + windowClassObject +
                                    " isn't a JFrame subclass.");
                    button.setEnabled(false);
                    return null;
                }

                window.setTitle(title);

                //Set its size.
                window.pack();
                if ((requestedWidth > 0)
                  | (requestedHeight > 0)) {
                    window.setSize(Math.max(requestedWidth,
                                            window.getSize().width),
                                   Math.max(requestedHeight,
                                            window.getSize().height));
                }

                return window;
            }

        /* Signal the window thread to build a window. */
        public synchronized void actionPerformed(ActionEvent event) {
            label.setText("Please wait while the window comes up...");
            pleaseShow = true;
            notify();
        }
    }

    class TestWindow extends JFrame {
        public TestWindow() {
            setDefaultCloseOperation(DISPOSE_ON_CLOSE);
        }
    }
}
```

EXAMPLE: *BorderWindow.java*

Where Explained:

How to Use BorderLayout (page 347)

Associated File(s): `AppletButton.java` *(page 783)*

SOURCE CODE: *http://java.sun.com/docs/books/tutorial/uiswing/layout/example-swing/ BorderWindow.java*

```
/*
 * Swing 1.1 version (compatible with both JDK 1.1 and Java 2)..
 */

import java.awt.*;
import java.awt.event.*;
import javax.swing.*;

public class BorderWindow extends JFrame {
    boolean inAnApplet = true;

    public BorderWindow() {
        Container contentPane = getContentPane();
        //Use the content pane's default BorderLayout.
        //contentPane.setLayout(new BorderLayout()); //unnecessary
```

```
        contentPane.add(new JButton("Button 1 (NORTH)"),
                        BorderLayout.NORTH);
        contentPane.add(new JButton("2 (CENTER)"),
                        BorderLayout.CENTER);
        contentPane.add(new JButton("Button 3 (WEST)"),
                        BorderLayout.WEST);
        contentPane.add(new JButton("Long-Named Button 4 (SOUTH)"),
                        BorderLayout.SOUTH);
        contentPane.add(new JButton("Button 5 (EAST)"),
                        BorderLayout.EAST);

        addWindowListener(new WindowAdapter() {
            public void windowClosing(WindowEvent e) {
                if (inAnApplet) {
                    dispose();
                } else {
                    System.exit(0);
                }
            }
        });
    }

    public static void main(String args[]) {
        BorderWindow window = new BorderWindow();
        window.inAnApplet = false;

        window.setTitle("BorderLayout");
        window.pack();
        window.setVisible(true);
    }
}
```

EXAMPLE: *BoxLayoutDemo.java*

Associated File(s): BLDComponent.java *(page 782)*

SOURCE CODE: *http://java.sun.com/docs/books/tutorial/uiswing/layout/example-swing/ BoxLayoutDemo.java*

Where Explained:
How to Use BoxLayout (page 350)

```
import java.awt.*;
import java.awt.event.*;
import javax.swing.*;

public class BoxLayoutDemo {
    protected static int NUM_COMPONENTS = 3;
    protected static float[] xAlignment = {Component.LEFT_ALIGNMENT,
                                           Component.CENTER_ALIGNMENT,
                                           Component.RIGHT_ALIGNMENT};
    protected static float[] hue = {0.0f, 0.33f, 0.67f};
    protected static boolean restrictSize = true;
    protected static boolean sizeIsRandom = false;
    protected static BLDComponent[] bldComponent =
        new BLDComponent[NUM_COMPONENTS];

    public static void main(String[] args) {
        final JPanel panel = new JPanel();
        panel.setLayout(new BoxLayout(panel, BoxLayout.Y_AXIS));

        //Create the rectangles.
        int shortSideSize = 15;
        for (int i = 0; i < NUM_COMPONENTS; i++) {
            if (sizeIsRandom) {
                shortSideSize = (int)(30.0 * Math.random()) + 30;
```

```
        } else {
            shortSideSize += 10;
        }
        bldComponent[i] = new BLDComponent(xAlignment[i], hue[i], shortSideSize,
                                           restrictSize, sizeIsRandom,
                                           String.valueOf(i));
        panel.add(bldComponent[i]);
    }

    //Create the instructions.
    JLabel label = new JLabel("Click a rectangle to change its X alignment.");
    JCheckBox cb = new JCheckBox("Restrict maximum rectangle size.");
    cb.setSelected(restrictSize);
    cb.addItemListener(new ItemListener() {
        public void itemStateChanged(ItemEvent e) {
            if (e.getStateChange() == ItemEvent.SELECTED) {
                restrictSize = true;
            } else {
                restrictSize = false;
            }
            notifyBLDComponents();
        }
    });

    JFrame f = new JFrame("BoxLayoutDemo");
    Container contentPane = f.getContentPane();
    contentPane.add(panel, BorderLayout.CENTER);
    panel.setBorder(BorderFactory.createLineBorder(Color.red));

    Box box = Box.createVerticalBox();
    box.add(label);
    box.add(cb);

    contentPane.add(box, BorderLayout.SOUTH);
    f.addWindowListener(new WindowAdapter() {
        public void windowClosing(WindowEvent e) {
            System.exit(0);
        }
    });
    f.pack();
    f.setVisible(true);
}

static public void notifyBLDComponents() {
    for (int i = 0; i < NUM_COMPONENTS; i++) {
        bldComponent[i].setSizeRestriction(restrictSize);
    }
    bldComponent[0].revalidate();
}
}
```

EXAMPLE: BoxWindow.java

Where Explained:

How to Use BoxLayout (page 350)

Associated File(s): <u>AppletButton.java</u> *(page 783)*

SOURCE CODE: *http://java.sun.com/docs/books/tutorial/uiswing/layout/example-swing/ BoxWindow.java*

```
/*
 * Swing 1.1 version (compatible with both JDK 1.1 and Java 2)..
 */
```

```java
import java.awt.*;
import java.awt.event.*;
import javax.swing.*;

public class BoxWindow extends JFrame {
    boolean inAnApplet = true;

    public BoxWindow() {
        Container contentPane = getContentPane();
        contentPane.setLayout(new BoxLayout(contentPane,
                                            BoxLayout.Y_AXIS));

        addAButton("Button 1", contentPane);
        addAButton("2", contentPane);
        addAButton("Button 3", contentPane);
        addAButton("Long-Named Button 4", contentPane);
        addAButton("Button 5", contentPane);

        addWindowListener(new WindowAdapter() {
            public void windowClosing(WindowEvent e) {
                if (inAnApplet) {
                    dispose();
                } else {
                    System.exit(0);
                }
            }
        });
    }

    private void addAButton(String text, Container container) {
        JButton button = new JButton(text);
        button.setAlignmentX(Component.CENTER_ALIGNMENT);
        container.add(button);
    }

    public static void main(String args[]) {
        BoxWindow window = new BoxWindow();
        window.inAnApplet = false;

        window.setTitle("BoxLayout");
        window.pack();
        window.setVisible(true);
    }
}
```

EXAMPLE: *CardWindow.java*

Associated File(s): AppletButton.java *(page 783)*

**Where
Explained:**
*How to Use
CardLayout*
(page 363)

SOURCE CODE: *http://java.sun.com/docs/books/tutorial/uiswing/layout/example-swing/
CardWindow.java*

```java
/*
 * Swing 1.1 version (compatible with both JDK 1.1 and Java 2)..
 */
import java.awt.*;
import java.awt.event.*;
import javax.swing.*;

public class CardWindow extends JFrame
                        implements ItemListener {
    boolean inAnApplet = true;
```

```
JPanel cards;
final static String BUTTONPANEL = "JPanel with JButtons";
final static String TEXTPANEL = "JPanel with JTextField";

public CardWindow() {
    Container contentPane = getContentPane();

    //Put the JComboBox in a JPanel to get a nicer look.
    String comboBoxItems[] = { BUTTONPANEL, TEXTPANEL };
    JPanel cbp = new JPanel();
    JComboBox c = new JComboBox(comboBoxItems);
    c.setEditable(false);
    c.addItemListener(this);
    cbp.add(c);

    //Use the default layout manager, BorderLayout
    contentPane.add(cbp, BorderLayout.NORTH);

    cards = new JPanel();
    cards.setLayout(new CardLayout());

    JPanel p1 = new JPanel();
    p1.add(new JButton("Button 1"));
    p1.add(new JButton("Button 2"));
    p1.add(new JButton("Button 3"));

    JPanel p2 = new JPanel();
    p2.add(new JTextField("TextField", 20));

    cards.add(p1, BUTTONPANEL);
    cards.add(p2, TEXTPANEL);
    contentPane.add(cards, BorderLayout.CENTER);

    addWindowListener(new WindowAdapter() {
        public void windowClosing(WindowEvent e) {
            if (inAnApplet) {
                dispose();
            } else {
                System.exit(0);
            }
        }
    });
}

public void itemStateChanged(ItemEvent evt) {
    CardLayout cl = (CardLayout)(cards.getLayout());
    cl.show(cards, (String)evt.getItem());
}

public static void main(String args[]) {
    CardWindow window = new CardWindow();
    window.inAnApplet = false;

    window.setTitle("CardLayout");
    window.pack();
    window.setVisible(true);
}
}
```

EXAMPLE: *CustomWindow.java*

Associated File(s): AppletButton.java *(page 783)*, DiagonalLayout.java *(page 791)*

SOURCE CODE: *http://java.sun.com/docs/books/tutorial/uiswing/layout/example-swing/ CustomWindow.java*

Where Explained:
Creating a Custom Layout Manager (page 379)

```java
/*
 * Swing 1.1 version (compatible with both JDK 1.1 and Java 2).
 */

import java.awt.*;
import java.awt.event.*;
import javax.swing.*;

public class CustomWindow extends JFrame {
    boolean inAnApplet = true;

    public CustomWindow() {
        Container contentPane = getContentPane();
        contentPane.setLayout(new DiagonalLayout());

        contentPane.add(new JButton("Button 1"));
        contentPane.add(new JButton("Button 2"));
        contentPane.add(new JButton("Button 3"));
        contentPane.add(new JButton("Button 4"));
        contentPane.add(new JButton("Button 5"));

        addWindowListener(new WindowAdapter() {
            public void windowClosing(WindowEvent e) {
                if (inAnApplet) {
                    dispose();
                } else {
                    System.exit(0);
                }
            }
        });
    }

    public static void main(String args[]) {
        CustomWindow window = new CustomWindow();
        window.inAnApplet = false;

        window.setTitle("Custom Layout Manager");
        window.pack();
        window.setVisible(true);
    }
}
```

EXAMPLE: *DiagonalLayout.java*

Main Source File: CustomWindow.java *(page 791)*

SOURCE CODE: *http://java.sun.com/docs/books/tutorial/uiswing/layout/example-swing/ DiagonalLayout.java*

Where Explained:
Creating a Custom Layout Manager (page 379)

```java
/*
 * 1.1 version.  For the 1.2 version, you would probably
 * change getSize() to getWidth() or getHeight().
 */
```

```java
import java.awt.*;
import java.util.Vector;

public class DiagonalLayout implements LayoutManager {
    private int vgap;
    private int minWidth = 0, minHeight = 0;
    private int preferredWidth = 0, preferredHeight = 0;
    private boolean sizeUnknown = true;

    public DiagonalLayout() {
        this(5);
    }

    public DiagonalLayout(int v) {
        vgap = v;
    }

    /* Required by LayoutManager. */
    public void addLayoutComponent(String name, Component comp) {
    }

    /* Required by LayoutManager. */
    public void removeLayoutComponent(Component comp) {
    }

    private void setSizes(Container parent) {
        int nComps = parent.getComponentCount();
        Dimension d = null;

        //Reset preferred/minimum width and height.
        preferredWidth = 0;
        preferredHeight = 0;
        minWidth = 0;
        minHeight = 0;

        for (int i = 0; i < nComps; i++) {
            Component c = parent.getComponent(i);
            if (c.isVisible()) {
                d = c.getPreferredSize();

                if (i > 0) {
                    preferredWidth += d.width/2;
                    preferredHeight += vgap;
                } else {
                    preferredWidth = d.width;
                }
                preferredHeight += d.height;

                minWidth = Math.max(c.getMinimumSize().width, minWidth);
                minHeight = preferredHeight;
            }
        }
    }

    /* Required by LayoutManager. */
    public Dimension preferredLayoutSize(Container parent) {
        Dimension dim = new Dimension(0, 0);
        int nComps = parent.getComponentCount();

        setSizes(parent);

        //Always add the container's insets!
        Insets insets = parent.getInsets();
        dim.width = preferredWidth + insets.left + insets.right;
        dim.height = preferredHeight + insets.top + insets.bottom;
        sizeUnknown = false;

        return dim;
    }
```

```
/* Required by LayoutManager. */
public Dimension minimumLayoutSize(Container parent) {
    Dimension dim = new Dimension(0, 0);
    int nComps = parent.getComponentCount();

    //Always add the container's insets!
    Insets insets = parent.getInsets();
    dim.width = minWidth
                + insets.left + insets.right;
    dim.height = minHeight
                + insets.top + insets.bottom;

    sizeUnknown = false;

    return dim;
}

/* Required by LayoutManager. */
/*
 * This is called when the panel is first displayed,
 * and every time its size changes.
 * Note: You CAN'T assume preferredLayoutSize or
 * minimumLayoutSize will be called -- in the case
 * of applets, at least, they probably won't be.
 */
public void layoutContainer(Container parent) {
    Insets insets = parent.getInsets();
    int maxWidth = parent.getSize().width
                    - (insets.left + insets.right);
    int maxHeight = parent.getSize().height
                    - (insets.top + insets.bottom);
    int nComps = parent.getComponentCount();
    int previousWidth = 0, previousHeight = 0;
    int x = 0, y = insets.top;
    int rowh = 0, start = 0;
    int xFudge = 0, yFudge = 0;
    boolean oneColumn = false;

    // Go through the components' sizes, if neither
    // preferredLayoutSize nor minimumLayoutSize has
    // been called.
    if (sizeUnknown) {
        setSizes(parent);
    }

    if (maxWidth <= minWidth) {
        oneColumn = true;
    }

    if (maxWidth != preferredWidth) {
        xFudge = (maxWidth - preferredWidth)/(nComps - 1);
    }

    if (maxHeight > preferredHeight) {
        yFudge = (maxHeight - preferredHeight)/(nComps - 1);
    }

    for (int i = 0 ; i < nComps ; i++) {
        Component c = parent.getComponent(i);
        if (c.isVisible()) {
            Dimension d = c.getPreferredSize();
             // increase x and y, if appropriate
            if (i > 0) {
                if (!oneColumn) {
                    x += previousWidth/2 + xFudge;
                }
                y += previousHeight + vgap + yFudge;
            }
```

```
                                // If x is too large,
                                if ((!oneColumn) &&
                                    (x + d.width) >
                                    (parent.getSize().width - insets.right)) {
                                    // reduce x to a reasonable number.
                                    x = parent.getSize().width
                                        - insets.bottom - d.width;
                                }

                                // If y is too large,
                                if ((y + d.height)
                                    > (parent.getSize().height - insets.bottom)) {
                                    // do nothing.
                                    // Another choice would be to do what we do to x.
                                }

                                // Set the component's size and position.
                                c.setBounds(x, y, d.width, d.height);

                                previousWidth = d.width;
                                previousHeight = d.height;
                            }
                        }
                    }

                    public String toString() {
                        String str = "";
                        return getClass().getName() + "[vgap=" + vgap + str + "]";
                    }
                }
```

EXAMPLE: *FlowWindow.java*

Where Explained:

How to Use FlowLayout (page 366)

Associated File(s): <u>AppletButton.java</u> *(page 783)*

SOURCE CODE: *http://java.sun.com/docs/books/tutorial/uiswing/layout/example-swing/ FlowWindow.java*

```
/*
 * Swing 1.1 version (compatible with both JDK 1.1 and Java 2).
 */

import java.awt.*;
import java.awt.event.*;
import javax.swing.*;

public class FlowWindow extends JFrame {
    boolean inAnApplet = true;

    public FlowWindow() {
        Container contentPane = getContentPane();
        contentPane.setLayout(new FlowLayout());

        contentPane.add(new JButton("Button 1"));
        contentPane.add(new JButton("2"));
        contentPane.add(new JButton("Button 3"));
        contentPane.add(new JButton("Long-Named Button 4"));
        contentPane.add(new JButton("Button 5"));

        addWindowListener(new WindowAdapter() {
            public void windowClosing(WindowEvent e) {
                if (inAnApplet) {
                    dispose();
```

```
                    } else {
                        System.exit(0);
                    }
                }
            });
        }

    public static void main(String args[]) {
        FlowWindow window = new FlowWindow();
        window.inAnApplet = false;

        window.setTitle("FlowLayout");
        window.pack();
        window.setVisible(true);
    }
}
```

EXAMPLE: *GraphPaperLayout.java*

Associated File(s): <u>GraphPaperTest.java</u> *(page 800)*

SOURCE CODE: *http://java.sun.com/docs/books/tutorial/uiswing/layout/example-swing/*
                    GraphPaperLayout.java

Where Explained: *Creating a Custom Layout Manager* (page 379)

```java
import java.awt.*;
import java.util.Hashtable;

/**
 * The <code>GraphPaperLayout</code> class is a layout manager that
 * lays out a container's components in a rectangular grid, similar
 * to GridLayout.  Unlike GridLayout, however, components can take
 * up multiple rows and/or columns.  The layout manager acts as a
 * sheet of graph paper.  When a component is added to the layout
 * manager, the location and relative size of the component are
 * simply supplied by the constraints as a Rectangle.
 * <p><code><pre>
 * import java.awt.*;
 * import java.applet.Applet;
 * public class ButtonGrid extends Applet {
 *     public void init() {
 *         setLayout(new GraphPaperLayout(new Dimension(5,5)));
 *         // Add a 1x1 Rect at (0,0)
 *         add(new Button("1"), new Rectangle(0,0,1,1));
 *         // Add a 2x1 Rect at (2,0)
 *         add(new Button("2"), new Rectangle(2,0,2,1));
 *         // Add a 1x2 Rect at (1,1)
 *         add(new Button("3"), new Rectangle(1,1,1,2));
 *         // Add a 2x2 Rect at (3,2)
 *         add(new Button("4"), new Rectangle(3,2,2,2));
 *         // Add a 1x1 Rect at (0,4)
 *         add(new Button("5"), new Rectangle(0,4,1,1));
 *         // Add a 1x2 Rect at (2,3)
 *         add(new Button("6"), new Rectangle(2,3,1,2));
 *     }
 * }
 * </pre></code>
 *
 * @author     Michael Martak
 */
```

```java
public class GraphPaperLayout implements LayoutManager2 {
    int hgap;                //horizontal gap
    int vgap;                //vertical gap
    Dimension gridSize; //grid size in logical units (n x m)
    Hashtable compTable; //constraints (Rectangles)

    /**
     * Creates a graph paper layout with a default of a 1 x 1 graph, with no
     * vertical or horizontal padding.
     */
    public GraphPaperLayout() {
        this(new Dimension(1,1));
    }

    /**
     * Creates a graph paper layout with the given grid size, with no vertical
     * or horizontal padding.
     */
    public GraphPaperLayout(Dimension gridSize) {
        this(gridSize, 0, 0);
    }

    /**
     * Creates a graph paper layout with the given grid size and padding.
     * @param gridSize size of the graph paper in logical units (n x m)
     * @param hgap horizontal padding
     * @param vgap vertical padding
     */
    public GraphPaperLayout(Dimension gridSize, int hgap, int vgap) {
        if ((gridSize.width <= 0) || (gridSize.height <= 0)) {
            throw new IllegalArgumentException(
                "dimensions must be greater than zero");
        }
        this.gridSize = new Dimension(gridSize);
        this.hgap = hgap;
        this.vgap = vgap;
        compTable = new Hashtable();
    }

    /**
     * @return the size of the graph paper in logical units (n x m)
     */
    public Dimension getGridSize() {
        return new Dimension( gridSize );
    }

    /**
     * Set the size of the graph paper in logical units (n x m)
     */
    public void setGridSize( Dimension d ) {
        setGridSize( d.width, d.height );
    }

    /**
     * Set the size of the graph paper in logical units (n x m)
     */
    public void setGridSize( int width, int height ) {
        gridSize = new Dimension( width, height );
    }

    public void setConstraints(Component comp, Rectangle constraints) {
        compTable.put(comp, new Rectangle(constraints));
    }

    /**
     * Adds the specified component with the specified name to
     * the layout.  This does nothing in GraphPaperLayout, since constraints
     * are required.
     */
```

```java
public void addLayoutComponent(String name, Component comp) {
}

/**
 * Removes the specified component from the layout.
 * @param comp the component to be removed
 */
public void removeLayoutComponent(Component comp) {
    compTable.remove(comp);
}

/**
 * Calculates the preferred size dimensions for the specified
 * panel given the components in the specified parent container.
 * @param parent the component to be laid out
 *
 * @see #minimumLayoutSize
 */
public Dimension preferredLayoutSize(Container parent) {
    return getLayoutSize(parent, true);
}

/**
 * Calculates the minimum size dimensions for the specified
 * panel given the components in the specified parent container.
 * @param parent the component to be laid out
 * @see #preferredLayoutSize
 */
public Dimension minimumLayoutSize(Container parent) {
    return getLayoutSize(parent, false);
}

/**
 * Algorithm for calculating layout size (minimum or preferred).
 * <p>
 * The width of a graph paper layout is the largest cell width
 * (calculated in <code>getLargestCellSize()</code> times the number of
 * columns, plus the horizontal padding times the number of columns
 * plus one, plus the left and right insets of the target container.
 * <p>
 * The height of a graph paper layout is the largest cell height
 * (calculated in <code>getLargestCellSize()</code> times the number of
 * rows, plus the vertical padding times the number of rows
 * plus one, plus the top and bottom insets of the target container.
 *
 * @param parent the container in which to do the layout.
 * @param isPreferred true for calculating preferred size, false for
 *                     calculating minimum size.
 * @return the dimensions to lay out the subcomponents of the specified
 *         container.
 * @see java.awt.GraphPaperLayout#getLargestCellSize
 */
protected Dimension getLayoutSize(Container parent, boolean isPreferred) {
    Dimension largestSize = getLargestCellSize(parent, isPreferred);
    Insets insets = parent.getInsets();
    largestSize.width = ( largestSize.width * gridSize.width ) +
        ( hgap * ( gridSize.width + 1 ) ) + insets.left + insets.right;
    largestSize.height = ( largestSize.height * gridSize.height ) +
        ( vgap * ( gridSize.height + 1 ) ) + insets.top + insets.bottom;
    return largestSize;
}

/**
 * Algorithm for calculating the largest minimum or preferred cell size.
 * <p>
 * Largest cell size is calculated by getting the applicable size of each
```

```
 * component and keeping the maximum value, dividing the component's width
 * by the number of columns it is specified to occupy and dividing the
 * component's height by the number of rows it is specified to occupy.
 *
 * @param parent the container in which to do the layout.
 * @param isPreferred true for calculating preferred size, false for
 *                     calculating minimum size.
 * @return the largest cell size required.
 */
protected Dimension getLargestCellSize(Container parent,
                                       boolean isPreferred) {
    int ncomponents = parent.getComponentCount();
    Dimension maxCellSize = new Dimension(0,0);
    for ( int i = 0; i < ncomponents; i++ ) {
        Component c = parent.getComponent(i);
        Rectangle rect = (Rectangle)compTable.get(c);
        if ( c != null && rect != null ) {
            Dimension componentSize;
            if ( isPreferred ) {
                componentSize = c.getPreferredSize();
            } else {
                componentSize = c.getMinimumSize();
            }
            // Note: rect dimensions are already asserted to be > 0 when the
            // component is added with constraints
            maxCellSize.width = Math.max(maxCellSize.width,
                componentSize.width / rect.width);
            maxCellSize.height = Math.max(maxCellSize.height,
                componentSize.height / rect.height);
        }
    }
    return maxCellSize;
}


/**
 * Lays out the container in the specified container.
 * @param parent the component which needs to be laid out
 */
public void layoutContainer(Container parent) {
    synchronized (parent.getTreeLock()) {
        Insets insets = parent.getInsets();
        int ncomponents = parent.getComponentCount();

        if (ncomponents == 0) {
            return;
        }

        // Total parent dimensions
        Dimension size = parent.getSize();
        int totalW = size.width - (insets.left + insets.right);
        int totalH = size.height - (insets.top + insets.bottom);

        // Cell dimensions, including padding
        int totalCellW = totalW / gridSize.width;
        int totalCellH = totalH / gridSize.height;

        // Cell dimensions, without padding
        int cellW = (totalW - ( (gridSize.width + 1) * hgap) )
                / gridSize.width;
        int cellH = (totalH - ( (gridSize.height + 1) * vgap) )
                / gridSize.height;

        for ( int i = 0; i < ncomponents; i++ ) {
            Component c = parent.getComponent(i);
            Rectangle rect = (Rectangle)compTable.get(c);
            if ( rect != null ) {
```

```
                    int x = insets.left + ( totalCellW * rect.x ) + hgap;
                    int y = insets.top + ( totalCellH * rect.y ) + vgap;
                    int w = ( cellW * rect.width ) - hgap;
                    int h = ( cellH * rect.height ) - vgap;
                    c.setBounds(x, y, w, h);
                }
            }
        }
    }

    // LayoutManager2 ////////////////////////////////////////////////////////////

    /**
     * Adds the specified component to the layout, using the specified
     * constraint object.
     * @param comp the component to be added
     * @param constraints  where/how the component is added to the layout.
     */
    public void addLayoutComponent(Component comp, Object constraints) {
        if (constraints instanceof Rectangle) {
            Rectangle rect = (Rectangle)constraints;
            if ( rect.width <= 0 || rect.height <= 0 ) {
                throw new IllegalArgumentException(
                    "cannot add to layout: "
                        + "rectangle must have positive width and height");
            }
            if ( rect.x < 0 || rect.y < 0 ) {
                throw new IllegalArgumentException(
                    "cannot add to layout: rectangle x and y must be >= 0");
            }
            setConstraints(comp, rect);
        } else if (constraints != null) {
            throw new IllegalArgumentException(
                "cannot add to layout: constraint must be a Rectangle");
        }
    }

    /**
     * Returns the maximum size of this component.
     * @see java.awt.Component#getMinimumSize()
     * @see java.awt.Component#getPreferredSize()
     * @see LayoutManager
     */
    public Dimension maximumLayoutSize(Container target) {
        return new Dimension(Integer.MAX_VALUE, Integer.MAX_VALUE);
    }

    /**
     * Returns the alignment along the x axis.  This specifies how
     * the component would like to be aligned relative to other
     * components.  The value should be a number between 0 and 1
     * where 0 represents alignment along the origin, 1 is aligned
     * the furthest away from the origin, 0.5 is centered, etc.
     */
    public float getLayoutAlignmentX(Container target) {
        return 0.5f;
    }

    /**
     * Returns the alignment along the y axis.  This specifies how
     * the component would like to be aligned relative to other
     * components.  The value should be a number between 0 and 1
     * where 0 represents alignment along the origin, 1 is aligned
     * the furthest away from the origin, 0.5 is centered, etc.
     */
```

```
        public float getLayoutAlignmentY(Container target) {
            return 0.5f;
        }

        /**
         * Invalidates the layout, indicating that if the layout manager
         * has cached information it should be discarded.
         */
        public void invalidateLayout(Container target) {
            // Do nothing
        }
    }
```

EXAMPLE: *GraphPaperTest.java*

Where Explained:

Creating a Custom Layout Manager
(page 379)

Main Source File: GraphPaperLayout.java *(page 795)*

SOURCE CODE: *http://java.sun.com/docs/books/tutorial/uiswing/layout/example-swing/*
                GraphPaperTest.java

```java
import javax.swing.*;
import java.awt.*;
import java.awt.event.*;

public class GraphPaperTest extends JPanel {
    public GraphPaperTest() {
        setLayout(new GraphPaperLayout(new Dimension(5,5)));

        // Add a 1x1 Rect at (0,0)
        add(new JButton("1"), new Rectangle(0,0,1,1));

        // Add a 2x1 Rect at (2,0)
        add(new JButton("2"), new Rectangle(2,0,2,1));

        // Add a 1x2 Rect at (1,1)
        add(new JButton("3"), new Rectangle(1,1,1,2));

        // Add a 2x2 Rect at (3,2)
        add(new JButton("4"), new Rectangle(3,2,2,2));

        // Add a 1x1 Rect at (0,4)
        add(new JButton("5"), new Rectangle(0,4,1,1));

        // Add a 1x2 Rect at (2,3)
        add(new JButton("6"), new Rectangle(2,3,1,2));
    }

    public static void main(String[] args) {
        JFrame f = new JFrame("GraphPaperTest");
        f.addWindowListener(new WindowAdapter() {
            public void windowClosing(WindowEvent e) {
                System.exit(0);
            }
        });

        f.getContentPane().add(new GraphPaperTest(),
                               BorderLayout.CENTER);
        f.pack();
        f.setVisible(true);
    }
}
```

EXAMPLE: *GridBagWindow.java*

Associated File(s): AppletButton.java *(page 783)*

SOURCE CODE: *http://java.sun.com/docs/books/tutorial/uiswing/layout/example-swing/*
GridBagWindow.java

**Where
Explained:**

*How to Use
GridBagLay-
out* (page 370)

```java
/*
 * Swing 1.1 version (compatible with both JDK 1.1 and Java 2).
 */

import java.awt.*;
import java.awt.event.*;
import javax.swing.*;

public class GridBagWindow extends JFrame {
    boolean inAnApplet = true;
    final boolean shouldFill = true;
    final boolean shouldWeightX = true;

    public GridBagWindow() {
        JButton button;
        Container contentPane = getContentPane();
        GridBagLayout gridbag = new GridBagLayout();
        GridBagConstraints c = new GridBagConstraints();
        contentPane.setLayout(gridbag);
        if (shouldFill) {
            //natural height, maximum width
            c.fill = GridBagConstraints.HORIZONTAL;
        }

        button = new JButton("Button 1");
        if (shouldWeightX) {
            c.weightx = 0.5;
        }
        c.gridx = 0;
        c.gridy = 0;
        gridbag.setConstraints(button, c);
        contentPane.add(button);

        button = new JButton("2");
        c.gridx = 1;
        c.gridy = 0;
        gridbag.setConstraints(button, c);
        contentPane.add(button);

        button = new JButton("Button 3");
        c.gridx = 2;
        c.gridy = 0;
        gridbag.setConstraints(button, c);
        contentPane.add(button);

        button = new JButton("Long-Named Button 4");
        c.ipady = 40;        //make this component tall
        c.weightx = 0.0;
        c.gridwidth = 3;
        c.gridx = 0;
        c.gridy = 1;
        gridbag.setConstraints(button, c);
        contentPane.add(button);

        button = new JButton("Button 5");
        c.ipady = 0;        //reset to default
```

```
            c.weighty = 1.0;   //request any extra vertical space
            c.anchor = GridBagConstraints.SOUTH; //bottom of space
            c.insets = new Insets(10,0,0,0);  //top padding
            c.gridx = 1;        //aligned with button 2
            c.gridwidth = 2;    //2 columns wide
            c.gridy = 2;        //third row
            gridbag.setConstraints(button, c);
            contentPane.add(button);

            addWindowListener(new WindowAdapter() {
                public void windowClosing(WindowEvent e) {
                    if (inAnApplet) {
                        dispose();
                    } else {
                        System.exit(0);
                    }
                }
            });
        }

        public static void main(String args[]) {
            GridBagWindow window = new GridBagWindow();
            window.inAnApplet = false;

            window.setTitle("GridBagLayout");
            window.pack();
            window.setVisible(true);
        }
    }
```

EXAMPLE: *GridWindow.java*

**Where
Explained:**

*How to Use
GridLayout*
(page 368)

Associated File(s): <u>AppletButton.java</u> *(page 783)*

SOURCE CODE: *http://java.sun.com/docs/books/tutorial/uiswing/layout/example-swing/
GridWindow.java*

```
/*
 * Swing 1.1 version (compatible with both JDK 1.1 and Java 2).
 */

import java.awt.*;
import java.awt.event.*;
import javax.swing.*;

public class GridWindow extends JFrame {
    boolean inAnApplet = true;

    public GridWindow() {
        Container contentPane = getContentPane();

        contentPane.setLayout(new GridLayout(0,2));

        contentPane.add(new JButton("Button 1"));
        contentPane.add(new JButton("2"));
        contentPane.add(new JButton("Button 3"));
        contentPane.add(new JButton("Long-Named Button 4"));
        contentPane.add(new JButton("Button 5"));

        addWindowListener(new WindowAdapter() {
            public void windowClosing(WindowEvent e) {
                if (inAnApplet) {
                    dispose();
```

```
                } else {
                    System.exit(0);
                }
            }
        });
    }

    public static void main(String args[]) {
        GridWindow window = new GridWindow();
        window.inAnApplet = false;

        window.setTitle("GridLayout");
        window.pack();
        window.setVisible(true);
    }
}
```

EXAMPLE: *NoneWindow.java*

Associated File(s): <u>AppletButton.java</u> *(page 783)*

SOURCE CODE: *http://java.sun.com/docs/books/tutorial/uiswing/layout/example-swing/ NoneWindow.java*

```
/*
 * Swing 1.1 version (compatible with both JDK 1.1 and Java 2).
 */

import java.awt.*;
import java.awt.event.*;
import javax.swing.*;

public class NoneWindow extends JFrame {
    boolean inAnApplet = true;
    private boolean laidOut = false;
    private JButton b1, b2, b3;

    public NoneWindow() {
        Container contentPane = getContentPane();
        contentPane.setLayout(null);

        b1 = new JButton("one");
        contentPane.add(b1);
        b2 = new JButton("two");
        contentPane.add(b2);
        b3 = new JButton("three");
        contentPane.add(b3);

        Insets insets = contentPane.getInsets();
        b1.setBounds(25 + insets.left, 5 + insets.top, 75, 20);
        b2.setBounds(55 + insets.left, 35 + insets.top, 75, 20);
        b3.setBounds(150 + insets.left, 15 + insets.top, 75, 30);

        addWindowListener(new WindowAdapter() {
            public void windowClosing(WindowEvent e) {
                if (inAnApplet) {
                    dispose();
                } else {
                    System.exit(0);
                }
            }
        });
    }
```

Where Explained: *Doing Without a Layout Manager (Absolute Positioning)* (page 383)

```
public static void main(String args[]) {
    NoneWindow window = new NoneWindow();
    Insets insets = window.getInsets();
    window.inAnApplet = false;

    window.setTitle("Absolute Positioning");
    window.setSize(250 + insets.left + insets.right,
                    90 + insets.top + insets.bottom);
    window.setVisible(true);
    }
}
```

EXAMPLE: *TabWindow.java*

**Where
Explained:**

*How to Use
CardLayout*
(page 363)

Associated File(s): <u>AppletButton.java</u> *(page 783)*

SOURCE CODE: *http://java.sun.com/docs/books/tutorial/uiswing/layout/example-swing/
                      TabWindow.java*

```
/*
 * Swing 1.1 version (compatible with both JDK 1.1 and Java 2).
 */

import java.awt.*;
import java.awt.event.*;
import javax.swing.*;

public class TabWindow extends JFrame {
    boolean inAnApplet = true;

    final static String BUTTONPANEL = "JPanel with JButtons";
    final static String TEXTPANEL = "JPanel with JTextField";

    public TabWindow() {
        Container contentPane = getContentPane();

        JTabbedPane tabbedPane = new JTabbedPane();

        JPanel p1 = new JPanel() {
            //Force the window to be 400+ pixels wide.
            public Dimension getPreferredSize() {
                Dimension size = super.getPreferredSize();
                size.width = 400;
                return size;
            }
        };
        p1.add(new JButton("Button 1"));
        p1.add(new JButton("Button 2"));
        p1.add(new JButton("Button 3"));
        tabbedPane.addTab(BUTTONPANEL, p1);

        JPanel p2 = new JPanel();
        p2.add(new JTextField("TextField", 20));
        tabbedPane.addTab(TEXTPANEL, p2);

        contentPane.add(tabbedPane, BorderLayout.CENTER);

        addWindowListener(new WindowAdapter() {
            public void windowClosing(WindowEvent e) {
                if (inAnApplet) {
                    dispose();
```

```
                } else {
                    System.exit(0);
                }
            }
        });
    }

    public static void main(String args[]) {
        TabWindow window = new TabWindow();
        window.inAnApplet = false;

        window.setTitle("TabWindow");
        window.pack();
        window.setVisible(true);
    }
}
```

Using Other Swing Features

Complete examples in <u>Using Other Swing Features</u> (page 387):

EXAMPLE: *AccessibleScrollDemo.java*

**Where
Explained:**

Setting Accessible Names and Descriptions on Components
(page 395)

Associated File(s): <u>ScrollablePicture.java</u> *(page 825)*, <u>Rule.java</u> *(page 822)*, <u>Corner.java</u> *(page 815)*

SOURCE CODE: *http://java.sun.com/docs/books/tutorial/uiswing/misc/example-swing/ AccessibleScrollDemo.java*

```
import java.awt.*;
import java.awt.event.*;
import javax.swing.*;
import javax.swing.border.*;

public class AccessibleScrollDemo extends JPanel {
    private Rule columnView;
    private Rule rowView;

    private JToggleButton isMetric;
    private ScrollablePicture picture;

    public AccessibleScrollDemo() {
        //Load the photograph into an image icon.
        ImageIcon david = new ImageIcon("images/youngdad.jpeg");
        david.setDescription("Photograph of David McNabb in his youth.");

        //Create the row and column headers
        columnView = new Rule(Rule.HORIZONTAL, true);
        columnView.setPreferredWidth(david.getIconWidth());
        columnView.getAccessibleContext().setAccessibleName("Column Header");
        columnView.getAccessibleContext().
                setAccessibleDescription("Displays horizontal ruler for " +
                                         "measuring scroll pane client.");
        rowView = new Rule(Rule.VERTICAL, true);
        rowView.setPreferredHeight(david.getIconHeight());
        rowView.getAccessibleContext().setAccessibleName("Row Header");
        rowView.getAccessibleContext().
                setAccessibleDescription("Displays vertical ruler for " +
                                         "measuring scroll pane client.");
```

```
    //Create the corners
    JPanel buttonCorner = new JPanel();
    isMetric = new JToggleButton("cm", true);
    isMetric.setFont(new Font("SansSerif", Font.PLAIN, 11));
    isMetric.setMargin(new Insets(2,2,2,2));
    isMetric.addItemListener(new UnitsListener());
    isMetric.setToolTipText("Toggles rulers' unit of measure " +
                            "between inches and centimeters.");
    buttonCorner.add(isMetric); //Use the default FlowLayout
    buttonCorner.getAccessibleContext().
                setAccessibleName("Upper Left Corner");

    String desc = "Fills the corner of a scroll pane " +
                    "with color for aesthetic reasons.";
    Corner lowerLeft = new Corner();
    lowerLeft.getAccessibleContext()
            setAccessibleName("Lower Left Corner");
    lowerLeft.getAccessibleContext().setAccessibleDescription(desc);

    Corner upperRight = new Corner();
    upperRight.getAccessibleContext().
                setAccessibleName("Upper Right Corner");
    upperRight.getAccessibleContext().setAccessibleDescription(desc);

    //Set up the scroll pane
    picture = new ScrollablePicture(david,
                                    columnView.getIncrement());
    picture.setToolTipText(david.getDescription());
    picture.getAccessibleContext().setAccessibleName(
                                    "Scroll pane client");

    JScrollPane pictureScrollPane = new JScrollPane(picture);
    pictureScrollPane.setPreferredSize(new Dimension(300, 250));
    pictureScrollPane.setViewportBorder(
            BorderFactory.createLineBorder(Color.black));

    pictureScrollPane.setColumnHeaderView(columnView);
    pictureScrollPane.setRowHeaderView(rowView);

    pictureScrollPane.setCorner(JScrollPane.UPPER_LEFT_CORNER,
                                buttonCorner);
    pictureScrollPane.setCorner(JScrollPane.LOWER_LEFT_CORNER,
                                lowerLeft);
    pictureScrollPane.setCorner(JScrollPane.UPPER_RIGHT_CORNER,
                                upperRight);

    //Put it in this panel
    setLayout(new BoxLayout(this, BoxLayout.X_AXIS));
    add(pictureScrollPane);
    setBorder(BorderFactory.createEmptyBorder(20,20,20,20));
}

class UnitsListener implements ItemListener {
    public void itemStateChanged(ItemEvent e) {
        if (e.getStateChange() == ItemEvent.SELECTED) {
            //turn it to metric
            rowView.setIsMetric(true);
            columnView.setIsMetric(true);
        } else {
            //turn it to inches
            rowView.setIsMetric(false);
            columnView.setIsMetric(false);
        }
        picture.setMaxUnitIncrement(rowView.getIncrement());
    }
}
}
```

```
        public static void main(String s[]) {
            JFrame frame = new JFrame("AccessibleScrollDemo");
            frame.addWindowListener(new WindowAdapter() {
                public void windowClosing(WindowEvent e) {
                    System.exit(0);
                }
            });

            frame.setContentPane(new AccessibleScrollDemo());
            frame.pack();
            frame.setVisible(true);
        }
    }
```

EXAMPLE: *ActionDemo.java*

Where Explained:

How to Use Actions (page 389)

SOURCE CODE: *http://java.sun.com/docs/books/tutorial/uiswing/misc/example-swing/ ActionDemo.java*

```
/* Uses actions with a tool bar and a menu. */

import javax.swing.AbstractAction;
import javax.swing.Action;

import javax.swing.JToolBar;
import javax.swing.JButton;
import javax.swing.ImageIcon;

import javax.swing.JMenuItem;
import javax.swing.JCheckBoxMenuItem;
import javax.swing.JMenu;
import javax.swing.JMenuBar;

import javax.swing.JFrame;
import javax.swing.JTextArea;
import javax.swing.JScrollPane;
import javax.swing.JPanel;

import java.awt.*;
import java.awt.event.*;

public class ActionDemo extends JFrame {
    protected JTextArea textArea;
    protected String newline = "\n";
    protected Action leftAction;
    protected Action middleAction;
    protected Action rightAction;

    public ActionDemo() {
        //Do frame stuff.
        super("ActionDemo");
        addWindowListener(new WindowAdapter() {
            public void windowClosing(WindowEvent e) {
                System.exit(0);
            }
        });

        //Create the toolbar and menu.
        JToolBar toolBar = new JToolBar();
        JMenu mainMenu = new JMenu("Menu");
        createActionComponents(toolBar, mainMenu);
```

```
        //Create the text area used for output.
        textArea = new JTextArea(5, 30);
        JScrollPane scrollPane = new JScrollPane(textArea);

        //Lay out the content pane.
        JPanel contentPane = new JPanel();
        contentPane.setLayout(new BorderLayout());
        contentPane.setPreferredSize(new Dimension(400, 150));
        contentPane.add(toolBar, BorderLayout.SOUTH);
        contentPane.add(scrollPane, BorderLayout.CENTER);
        setContentPane(contentPane);

        //Set up the menu bar.
        JMenuBar mb = new JMenuBar();
        mb.add(mainMenu);
        mb.add(createAbleMenu());
        setJMenuBar(mb);
    }

    protected void createActionComponents(JToolBar toolBar,
                                          JMenu mainMenu) {
        JButton button = null;
        JMenuItem menuItem = null;

        //first button and menu item
        leftAction = new AbstractAction("Go left",
                        new ImageIcon("images/left.gif")) {
            public void actionPerformed(ActionEvent e) {
                displayResult("Action for first button/menu item", e);
            }
        };
        button = toolBar.add(leftAction);
        button.setText(""); //an icon-only button
        button.setToolTipText("This is the left button");
        menuItem = mainMenu.add(leftAction);
        menuItem.setIcon(null); //arbitrarily chose not to use icon in menu

        //second button and menu item
        middleAction = new AbstractAction("Do something",
                        new ImageIcon("images/middle.gif")) {
            public void actionPerformed(ActionEvent e) {
                displayResult("Action for second button/menu item", e);
            }
        };
        button = toolBar.add(middleAction);
        button.setText("");
        button.setToolTipText("This is the middle button");
        menuItem = mainMenu.add(middleAction);
        menuItem.setIcon(null); //arbitrarily chose not to use icon in menu

        //third button and menu item
        rightAction = new AbstractAction("Go right",
                        new ImageIcon("images/right.gif")) {
            public void actionPerformed(ActionEvent e) {
                displayResult("Action for third button/menu item", e);
            }
        };
        button = toolBar.add(rightAction);
        button.setText("");
        button.setToolTipText("This is the right button");
        menuItem = mainMenu.add(rightAction);
        menuItem.setIcon(null); //arbitrarily chose not to use icon in menu
    }

    protected JMenu createAbleMenu() {
        JMenu ableMenu = new JMenu("Action State");
        JCheckBoxMenuItem cbmi = null;
```

```
        cbmi = new JCheckBoxMenuItem("First action enabled");
        cbmi.setSelected(true);
        cbmi.addItemListener(new ItemListener() {
            public void itemStateChanged(ItemEvent e) {
                JCheckBoxMenuItem mi = (JCheckBoxMenuItem)(e.getSource());
                boolean selected =
                    (e.getStateChange() == ItemEvent.SELECTED);
                leftAction.setEnabled(selected);
            }
        });
        ableMenu.add(cbmi);

        cbmi = new JCheckBoxMenuItem("Second action enabled");
        cbmi.setSelected(true);
        cbmi.addItemListener(new ItemListener() {
            public void itemStateChanged(ItemEvent e) {
                JCheckBoxMenuItem mi = (JCheckBoxMenuItem)(e.getSource());
                boolean selected =
                    (e.getStateChange() == ItemEvent.SELECTED);
                middleAction.setEnabled(selected);
            }
        });
        ableMenu.add(cbmi);

        cbmi = new JCheckBoxMenuItem("Third action enabled");
        cbmi.setSelected(true);
        cbmi.addItemListener(new ItemListener() {
            public void itemStateChanged(ItemEvent e) {
                JCheckBoxMenuItem mi =
                    (JCheckBoxMenuItem)(e.getSource());
                boolean selected =
                    (e.getStateChange() == ItemEvent.SELECTED);
                rightAction.setEnabled(selected);
            }
        });
        ableMenu.add(cbmi);

        return ableMenu;
    }

    protected void displayResult(String actionDescription,
                                 ActionEvent e) {
        String s = ("Action event detected by: "
                    + actionDescription
                    + newline
                    + "     Event source: " + e.getSource()
                    + newline);
        textArea.append(s);
    }

    public static void main(String[] args) {
        ActionDemo frame = new ActionDemo();
        frame.pack();
        frame.setVisible(true);
    }
}
```

EXAMPLE: *ArrowIcon.java*

Main Source File: CustomIconDemo.java *(page 815)*

SOURCE CODE: *http://java.sun.com/docs/books/tutorial/uiswing/misc/example-swing/ArrowIcon.java*

Where Explained:
Creating a Custom Icon Implementation
(page 424)

```java
import java.awt.*;
import javax.swing.*;

public class ArrowIcon implements Icon, SwingConstants {
    private int width = 9;
    private int height = 18;

    private int[] xPoints = new int[4];
    private int[] yPoints = new int[4];

    public ArrowIcon(int direction) {
        if (direction == LEFT) {
            xPoints[0] = width;
            yPoints[0] = -1;
            xPoints[1] = width;
            yPoints[1] = height;
            xPoints[2] = 0;
            yPoints[2] = height/2;
            xPoints[3] = 0;
            yPoints[3] = height/2 - 1;
        } else /* direction == RIGHT */ {
            xPoints[0] = 0;
            yPoints[0] = -1;
            xPoints[1] = 0;
            yPoints[1] = height;
            xPoints[2] = width;
            yPoints[2] = height/2;
            xPoints[3] = width;
            yPoints[3] = height/2 - 1;
        }
    }

    public int getIconHeight() {
        return height;
    }

    public int getIconWidth() {
        return width;
    }

    public void paintIcon(Component c, Graphics g, int x, int y) {
        int length = xPoints.length;
        int adjustedXPoints[] = new int[length];
        int adjustedYPoints[] = new int[length];

        for (int i = 0; i < length; i++) {
            adjustedXPoints[i] = xPoints[i] + x;
            adjustedYPoints[i] = yPoints[i] + y;
        }

        if (c.isEnabled()) {
            g.setColor(Color.black);
        } else {
            g.setColor(Color.gray);
        }

        g.fillPolygon(adjustedXPoints, adjustedYPoints, length);
    }
}
```

EXAMPLE: *BorderDemo.java*

Where Explained:

How to Use Borders
(page 408)

SOURCE CODE: *http://java.sun.com/docs/books/tutorial/uiswing/misc/example-swing/*
BorderDemo.java

```java
import java.awt.*;
import java.awt.event.*;
import javax.swing.BorderFactory;
import javax.swing.border.Border;
import javax.swing.border.TitledBorder;
import javax.swing.ImageIcon;
import javax.swing.JTabbedPane;
import javax.swing.JLabel;
import javax.swing.JPanel;
import javax.swing.JFrame;
import javax.swing.Box;
import javax.swing.BoxLayout;

public class BorderDemo extends JFrame {
    public BorderDemo() {
        super("BorderDemo");
        Border blackline, etched, raisedbevel, loweredbevel, empty;

        //A border that puts 10 extra pixels at the sides and
        //bottom of each pane.
        Border paneEdge = BorderFactory.createEmptyBorder(0,10,10,10);

        blackline = BorderFactory.createLineBorder(Color.black);
        etched = BorderFactory.createEtchedBorder();
        raisedbevel = BorderFactory.createRaisedBevelBorder();
        loweredbevel = BorderFactory.createLoweredBevelBorder();
        empty = BorderFactory.createEmptyBorder();

        //First pane: simple borders
        JPanel simpleBorders = new JPanel();
        simpleBorders.setBorder(paneEdge);
        simpleBorders.setLayout(new BoxLayout(simpleBorders,
                                   BoxLayout.Y_AXIS));

        addCompForBorder(blackline, "line border",
                           simpleBorders);
        addCompForBorder(etched, "etched border",
                           simpleBorders);
        addCompForBorder(raisedbevel, "raised bevel border",
                           simpleBorders);
        addCompForBorder(loweredbevel, "lowered bevel border",
                           simpleBorders);
        addCompForBorder(empty, "empty border",
                           simpleBorders);

        //Second pane: matte borders
        JPanel matteBorders = new JPanel();
        matteBorders.setBorder(paneEdge);
        matteBorders.setLayout(new BoxLayout(matteBorders,
                                   BoxLayout.Y_AXIS));

        //XXX: We *should* size the component so that the
        //XXX: icons tile OK.  Without that, the icons are
        //XXX: likely to be cut off and look bad.
        ImageIcon icon = new ImageIcon("images/left.gif"); //20x22
        Border border = BorderFactory.createMatteBorder(-1, -1, -1, -1, icon);
        addCompForBorder(border,
                    "matte border (-1,-1,-1,-1,icon)", matteBorders);
```

```
border = BorderFactory.createMatteBorder(1, 5, 1, 1, Color.red);
addCompForBorder(border,
                "matte border (1,5,1,1,Color.red)",
                matteBorders);
border = BorderFactory.createMatteBorder(0, 20, 0, 0, icon);
addCompForBorder(border,
                "matte border (0,20,0,0,icon)",
                matteBorders);

//Third pane: titled borders
JPanel titledBorders = new JPanel();
titledBorders.setBorder(paneEdge);
titledBorders.setLayout(new BoxLayout(titledBorders,
                                      BoxLayout.Y_AXIS));
TitledBorder titled;

titled = BorderFactory.createTitledBorder("title");
addCompForBorder(titled,
                "default titled border"
                + " (default just., default pos.)",
                titledBorders);

titled = BorderFactory.createTitledBorder(
                     blackline, "title");
addCompForTitledBorder(titled,
                     "titled line border"
                       + " (centered, default pos.)",
                     TitledBorder.CENTER,
                     TitledBorder.DEFAULT_POSITION,
                     titledBorders);

titled = BorderFactory.createTitledBorder(etched, "title");
addCompForTitledBorder(titled,
                     "titled etched border"
                       + " (right just., default pos.)",
                     TitledBorder.RIGHT,
                     TitledBorder.DEFAULT_POSITION,
                     titledBorders);

titled = BorderFactory.createTitledBorder(
                loweredbevel, "title");
addCompForTitledBorder(titled,
                     "titled lowered bevel border"
                       + " (default just., above top)",
                     TitledBorder.DEFAULT_JUSTIFICATION,
                     TitledBorder.ABOVE_TOP,
                     titledBorders);

titled = BorderFactory.createTitledBorder(
                empty, "title");
addCompForTitledBorder(titled, "titled empty border"
                       + " (default just., bottom)",
                     TitledBorder.DEFAULT_JUSTIFICATION,
                     TitledBorder.BOTTOM,
                     titledBorders);

//Fourth pane: compound borders
JPanel compoundBorders = new JPanel();
compoundBorders.setBorder(paneEdge);
compoundBorders.setLayout(new BoxLayout(compoundBorders,
                                        BoxLayout.Y_AXIS));
Border redline = BorderFactory.createLineBorder(Color.red);

Border compound;
compound = BorderFactory.createCompoundBorder(
                          raisedbevel, loweredbevel);
```

```
        addCompForBorder(compound, "compound border (two bevels)",
                         compoundBorders);

        compound = BorderFactory.createCompoundBorder(
                                 redline, compound);
        addCompForBorder(compound, "compound border (add a red outline)",
                         compoundBorders);

        titled = BorderFactory.createTitledBorder(
                                 compound, "title",
                                 TitledBorder.CENTER,
                                 TitledBorder.BELOW_BOTTOM);
        addCompForBorder(titled,
                         "titled compound border"
                         + " (centered, below bottom)",
                         compoundBorders);

        JTabbedPane tabbedPane = new JTabbedPane();
        tabbedPane.addTab("Simple", null, simpleBorders, null);
        tabbedPane.addTab("Matte", null, matteBorders, null);
        tabbedPane.addTab("Titled", null, titledBorders, null);
        tabbedPane.addTab("Compound", null, compoundBorders, null);
        tabbedPane.setSelectedIndex(0);

        getContentPane().add(tabbedPane, BorderLayout.CENTER);
    }

    void addCompForTitledBorder(TitledBorder border,
                                String description,
                                int justification,
                                int position,
                                Container container) {
        border.setTitleJustification(justification);
        border.setTitlePosition(position);
        addCompForBorder(border, description,
                         container);
    }

    void addCompForBorder(Border border,
                          String description,
                          Container container) {
        JPanel comp = new JPanel(false);
        JLabel label = new JLabel(description, JLabel.CENTER);
        comp.setLayout(new GridLayout(1, 1));
        comp.add(label);
        comp.setBorder(border);

        container.add(Box.createRigidArea(new Dimension(0, 10)));
        container.add(comp);
    }

    public static void main(String[] args) {
        JFrame frame = new BorderDemo();
        frame.addWindowListener(new WindowAdapter() {
            public void windowClosing(WindowEvent e) {
                System.exit(0);
            }
        });

        frame.pack();
        frame.setVisible(true);
    }
}
```

EXAMPLE: *Corner.java*

Main Source File: AccessibleScrollDemo.java *(page 806)*

SOURCE CODE: *http://java.sun.com/docs/books/tutorial/uiswing/misc/example-swing/ Corner.java*

```java
import java.awt.*;
import javax.swing.*;
import javax.accessibility.*;

public class Corner extends JComponent
                    implements Accessible {

    public void paintComponent(Graphics g) {
        // Fill me with dirty brown/orange.
        g.setColor(new Color(230, 163, 4));
        g.fillRect(0, 0, getWidth(), getHeight());
    }

    public AccessibleContext getAccessibleContext() {
        if (accessibleContext == null) {
            accessibleContext = new AccessibleCorner();
        }
        return accessibleContext;
    }

    protected class AccessibleCorner extends AccessibleJComponent {
        //Inherit everything, override nothing.
    }
}
```

Where Explained: *Setting Accessible Names and Descriptions on Components* (page 395)

EXAMPLE: *CustomIconDemo.java*

Associated File(s): ArrowIcon.java *(page 811)*

SOURCE CODE: *http://java.sun.com/docs/books/tutorial/uiswing/misc/example-swing/ CustomIconDemo.java*

```java
import java.awt.*;
import java.awt.event.*;
import javax.swing.*;

public class CustomIconDemo extends JPanel
                            implements ActionListener {
    protected JButton b1, b2, b3;

    public CustomIconDemo() {
        Icon leftButtonIcon = new ArrowIcon(SwingConstants.RIGHT);
        Icon middleButtonIcon = new ImageIcon("images/middle.gif");
        Icon rightButtonIcon = new ArrowIcon(SwingConstants.LEFT);

        b1 = new JButton("Disable middle button", leftButtonIcon);
        b1.setVerticalTextPosition(AbstractButton.CENTER);
        b1.setHorizontalTextPosition(AbstractButton.LEFT);
        b1.setMnemonic(KeyEvent.VK_D);
        b1.setActionCommand("disable");
```

Where Explained: *How to Use Icons* (page 417)

```
        b2 = new JButton("Middle button", middleButtonIcon);
        b2.setVerticalTextPosition(AbstractButton.BOTTOM);
        b2.setHorizontalTextPosition(AbstractButton.CENTER);
        b2.setMnemonic(KeyEvent.VK_M);

        b3 = new JButton("Enable middle button", rightButtonIcon);
        //Use the default text position of CENTER, RIGHT.
        b3.setMnemonic(KeyEvent.VK_E);
        b3.setActionCommand("enable");
        b3.setEnabled(false);

        //Listen for actions on buttons 1 and 3.
        b1.addActionListener(this);
        b3.addActionListener(this);

        b1.setToolTipText("Click this button to disable the middle button.");
        b2.setToolTipText("This middle button does nothing when you click it.");
        b3.setToolTipText("Click this button to enable the middle button.");

        //Add Components to this container, using the default FlowLayout.
        add(b1);
        add(b2);
        add(b3);
    }

    public void actionPerformed(ActionEvent e) {
        if (e.getActionCommand().equals("disable")) {
            b2.setEnabled(false);
            b1.setEnabled(false);
            b3.setEnabled(true);
        } else {
            b2.setEnabled(true);
            b1.setEnabled(true);
            b3.setEnabled(false);
        }
    }

    public static void main(String[] args) {
        JFrame frame = new JFrame("CustomIconDemo");
        frame.addWindowListener(new WindowAdapter() {
            public void windowClosing(WindowEvent e) {
                System.exit(0);
            }
        });

        frame.getContentPane().add(new CustomIconDemo(),
                                   BorderLayout.CENTER);
        frame.pack();
        frame.setVisible(true);
    }
}
```

EXAMPLE: *IconDemoApplet.java*

Where
Explained:
How to Use
Icons
(page 417)

Associated File(s): <u>Photo.java</u> *(page 821)*, <u>SwingWorker.java</u> *(page 720)*

SOURCE CODE: *http://java.sun.com/docs/books/tutorial/uiswing/misc/example-swing/*
                      IconDemoApplet.java

```
import javax.swing.*;
import java.awt.*;
import java.awt.event.*;
```

```
import java.net.URL;
import java.util.Vector;
import java.util.StringTokenizer;

public class IconDemoApplet extends JApplet
                            implements ActionListener {
    Vector pictures;

    JButton previousButton;
    JButton nextButton;
    JLabel photographLabel;
    JLabel captionLabel;
    JLabel numberLabel;

    int current = 0;
    int widthOfWidest = 0;
    int heightOfTallest = 0;

    String imagedir = null;

    public void init() {
        //Parse the applet parameters
        pictures = parseParameters();

        //If the applet tag doesn't provide an "IMAGE0" parameter,
        //display an error message.
        if (pictures.size() == 0) {
            captionLabel = new JLabel("No images listed in applet tag.");
            captionLabel.setHorizontalAlignment(JLabel.CENTER);
            getContentPane().add(captionLabel);
            return;
        }

        //NOW CREATE THE GUI COMPONENTS

        //A label to identify XX of XX.
        numberLabel = new JLabel("Picture " + (current+1) +
                            " of " + pictures.size());
        numberLabel.setHorizontalAlignment(JLabel.LEFT);
        numberLabel.setBorder(BorderFactory.createEmptyBorder(5, 0, 5, 5));

        //A label for the caption.
        final Photo first = (Photo)pictures.firstElement();
        captionLabel = new JLabel(first.caption);
        captionLabel.setHorizontalAlignment(JLabel.CENTER);
        captionLabel.setBorder(BorderFactory.createEmptyBorder(5, 0, 5, 0));

        //A label for displaying the photographs.
        photographLabel = new JLabel("Loading first image...");
        photographLabel.setHorizontalAlignment(JLabel.CENTER);
        photographLabel.setVerticalAlignment(JLabel.CENTER);
        photographLabel.setVerticalTextPosition(JLabel.CENTER);
        photographLabel.setHorizontalTextPosition(JLabel.CENTER);
        photographLabel.setBorder(BorderFactory.createCompoundBorder(
                    BorderFactory.createLoweredBevelBorder(),
                    BorderFactory.createEmptyBorder(5, 5, 5, 5)
        ));
        photographLabel.setBorder(BorderFactory.createCompoundBorder(
                    BorderFactory.createEmptyBorder(0, 0, 10, 0),
                    photographLabel.getBorder()
        ));

        //Set the preferred size for the picture,
        //with room for the borders.
        Insets i = photographLabel.getInsets();
        photographLabel.setPreferredSize(new Dimension(
                    widthOfWidest+i.left+i.right,
                    heightOfTallest+i.bottom+i.top));
```

```
//Create the next and previous buttons.
ImageIcon nextIcon = new ImageIcon(
        getURL(imagedir + "right.gif"));
ImageIcon dimmedNextIcon = new ImageIcon(
        getURL(imagedir + "dimmedRight.gif"));
ImageIcon previousIcon = new ImageIcon(
        getURL(imagedir + "left.gif"));
ImageIcon dimmedPreviousIcon = new ImageIcon(
        getURL(imagedir + "dimmedLeft.gif"));

previousButton = new JButton("Previous Picture",
                             previousIcon);
previousButton.setDisabledIcon(dimmedPreviousIcon);
previousButton.setVerticalTextPosition(AbstractButton.CENTER);
previousButton.setHorizontalTextPosition(AbstractButton.RIGHT);
previousButton.setMnemonic(KeyEvent.VK_P);
previousButton.setActionCommand("previous");
previousButton.addActionListener(this);
previousButton.setEnabled(false);

nextButton = new JButton("Next Picture", nextIcon);
nextButton.setDisabledIcon(dimmedNextIcon);
nextButton.setVerticalTextPosition(AbstractButton.CENTER);
nextButton.setHorizontalTextPosition(AbstractButton.LEFT);
nextButton.setMnemonic(KeyEvent.VK_N);
nextButton.setActionCommand("next");
nextButton.addActionListener(this);

//Lay out the GUI.
GridBagLayout layout = new GridBagLayout();
GridBagConstraints c = new GridBagConstraints();

Container contentPane = getContentPane();
contentPane.setLayout(layout);

c.gridwidth = GridBagConstraints.REMAINDER;
c.fill = GridBagConstraints.HORIZONTAL;
layout.setConstraints(numberLabel, c);
contentPane.add(numberLabel);

layout.setConstraints(captionLabel, c);
contentPane.add(captionLabel);

c.gridwidth = GridBagConstraints.REMAINDER;
c.fill = GridBagConstraints.BOTH;
layout.setConstraints(photographLabel, c);
contentPane.add(photographLabel);

c.gridwidth = GridBagConstraints.RELATIVE;
c.fill = GridBagConstraints.HORIZONTAL;
layout.setConstraints(previousButton, c);
contentPane.add(previousButton);

c.gridwidth = GridBagConstraints.REMAINDER;
layout.setConstraints(nextButton, c);
contentPane.add(nextButton);

//Start loading the image for the first photograph now.
//The loadImage method uses a SwingWorker
//to load the image in a separate thread.
loadImage(imagedir + first.filename, current);
}
```

```
//User clicked either the next or the previous button.
public void actionPerformed(ActionEvent e) {
    //Show loading message.
    photographLabel.setIcon(null);
    photographLabel.setText("Loading image...");

    //Compute index of photograph to view.
    if (e.getActionCommand().equals("next")) {
        current += 1;
        if (!previousButton.isEnabled())
            previousButton.setEnabled(true);
        if (current == pictures.size() - 1)
            nextButton.setEnabled(false);
    } else {
        current -= 1;
        if (!nextButton.isEnabled())
            nextButton.setEnabled(true);
        if (current == 0)
            previousButton.setEnabled(false);
    }

    //Get the photo object.
    Photo pic = (Photo)pictures.elementAt(current);

    //Update the caption and number labels.
    captionLabel.setText(pic.caption);
    numberLabel.setText("Picture " + (current+1) +
                        " of " + pictures.size());

    //Update the photograph.
    ImageIcon icon = pic.getIcon();
    if (icon == null) {      //haven't viewed this photo before
        loadImage(imagedir + pic.filename, current);
    } else {
        updatePhotograph(current, pic);
    }
}

//Must be invoked from the event-dispatching thread.
private void updatePhotograph(int index, Photo pic) {
    ImageIcon icon = pic.getIcon();

    photographLabel.setToolTipText(pic.filename + ": " +
                                   icon.getIconWidth() + " X " +
                                   icon.getIconHeight());
    photographLabel.setIcon(icon);
    photographLabel.setText("");
}

//Load an image in a separate thread.
private void loadImage(final String imagePath, final int index) {
    final SwingWorker worker = new SwingWorker() {
        ImageIcon icon = null;

        public Object construct() {
            icon = new ImageIcon(getURL(imagePath));
            return icon; //return value not used by this program
        }

        //Runs on the event-dispatching thread.
        public void finished() {
            Photo pic = (Photo)pictures.elementAt(index);
            pic.setIcon(icon);
            if (index == current)
                updatePhotograph(index, pic);
        }
    };
}
```

```java
protected URL getURL(String filename) {
    URL codeBase = this.getCodeBase();
    URL url = null;

    try {
        url = new URL(codeBase, filename);
    } catch (java.net.MalformedURLException e) {
        System.out.println("Couldn't create image: "
                            + "badly specified URL");
        return null;
    }

    return url;
}

protected Vector parseParameters() {
    Vector pix = new Vector(10);     //start with 10, grows if necessary
    int i = 0;                       //parameters index must start at 0
    String paramName = "IMAGE" + i;
    String paramValue;

    while ((paramValue = getParameter(paramName)) != null) {
        Photo pic = new Photo(paramValue, getCaption(i),
                              getWidth(i), getHeight(i));
        pix.addElement(pic);
        i++;
        paramName = "IMAGE" + i;
    }

    //Get the name of the directory that contains the image files.
    imagedir = getParameter("IMAGEDIR");
    if (imagedir != null)
        imagedir = imagedir + "/";

    return pix;
}

protected String getCaption(int i) {
    return getParameter("CAPTION"+i);
}

protected int getWidth(int i) {
    int width = 0;
    String widthString = getParameter("WIDTH"+i);
    if (widthString != null) {
        try {
            width = Integer.parseInt(widthString);
        } catch (NumberFormatException e) {
            width = 0;
        }
    } else {
        width = 0;
    }
    if (width > widthOfWidest)
        widthOfWidest = width;
    return width;
}

protected int getHeight(int i) {
    int height = 0;
    String heightString = getParameter("HEIGHT"+i);
    if (heightString != null) {
        try {
            height = Integer.parseInt(heightString);
        } catch (NumberFormatException e) {
            height = 0;
        }
    }
```

```
        } else {
            height = 0;
        }
        if (height > heightOfTallest)
            heightOfTallest = height;
        return height;
    }

    public String[][] getParameterInfo() {
        String[][] info = {
            {"IMAGEDIR", "string", "directory containing image files" },
            {"IMAGEN", "string", "filename" },
            {"CAPTIONN", "string", "caption" },
            {"WIDTHN", "integer", "width of image" },
            {"HEIGIITN", "integer", "height of image" },
        };
        return info;
    }
}
```

EXAMPLE: *Photo.java*

Main Source File: IconDemoApplet.java *(page 816)*

SOURCE CODE: *http://java.sun.com/docs/books/tutorial/uiswing/misc/example-swing/ Photo.java*

```
import javax.swing.ImageIcon;

public class Photo {
    public String filename;
    public String caption;
    public int width;
    public int height;
    public ImageIcon icon;

    public Photo(String filename, String caption, int w, int h) {
        this.filename = filename;
        if (caption == null)
            this.caption = filename;
        else
            this.caption = caption;
        width = w;
        height = h;
        icon = null;
    }

    public void setIcon(ImageIcon i) {
        icon = i;
    }

    public ImageIcon getIcon() {
        return icon;
    }
}
```

Where Explained:
How to Use Icons (page 417)

**Where
Explained:**

*Setting Accessi-
ble Names and
Descriptions on
Components*
(page 395)

EXAMPLE: *Rule.java*

Main Source File: `AccessibleScrollDemo.java` *(page 806)*

SOURCE CODE: *http://java.sun.com/docs/books/tutorial/uiswing/misc/example-swing/
Rule.java*

```java
import java.awt.*;
import javax.swing.*;
import javax.accessibility.*;
import java.util.Locale;

public class Rule extends JComponent implements Accessible {
    public static final int INCH = Toolkit.getDefaultToolkit().
            getScreenResolution();
    public static final int HORIZONTAL = 0;
    public static final int VERTICAL = 1;
    public static final int SIZE = 35;

    public int orientation;
    public boolean isMetric;
    private int increment;
    private int units;

    public Rule(int o, boolean m) {
        orientation = o;
        isMetric = m;
        setIncrementAndUnits();
    }

    public void setIsMetric(boolean isMetric) {
        if (accessibleContext != null && this.isMetric != isMetric) {
            if (isMetric) {
                accessibleContext.firePropertyChange(
                    AccessibleContext.ACCESSIBLE_STATE_PROPERTY,
                    AccessibleRulerState.INCHES,
                    AccessibleRulerState.CENTIMETERS);
            } else {
                accessibleContext.firePropertyChange(
                    AccessibleContext.ACCESSIBLE_STATE_PROPERTY,
                    AccessibleRulerState.CENTIMETERS,
                    AccessibleRulerState.INCHES);
            }
        }
        this.isMetric = isMetric;
        setIncrementAndUnits();
        repaint();
    }

    private void setIncrementAndUnits() {
        if (isMetric) {
            units = (int)((double)INCH / (double)2.54); // dots per centimeter
            increment = units;
        } else {
            units = INCH;
            increment = units / 2;
        }
    }

    public boolean isMetric() {
        return this.isMetric;
    }

    public int getIncrement() {
        return increment;
    }
```

```java
public void setPreferredHeight(int ph) {
    setPreferredSize(new Dimension(SIZE, ph));
}

public void setPreferredWidth(int pw) {
    setPreferredSize(new Dimension(pw, SIZE));
}

public void paintComponent(Graphics g) {
    Rectangle drawHere = g.getClipBounds();

    // Fill clipping area with dirty brown/orange.
    g.setColor(new Color(230, 163, 4));
    g.fillRect(drawHere.x, drawHere.y, drawHere.width, drawHere.height);

    // Do the ruler labels in a small font that's black.
    g.setFont(new Font("SansSerif", Font.PLAIN, 10));
    g.setColor(Color.black);

    // Some vars we need.
    int end = 0;
    int start = 0;
    int tickLength = 0;
    String text = null;

    // Use clipping bounds to calculate first tick
    // and last tick location.
    if (orientation == HORIZONTAL) {
        start = (drawHere.x / increment) * increment;
        end = (((drawHere.x + drawHere.width) / increment) + 1)
                * increment;
    } else {
        start = (drawHere.y / increment) * increment;
        end = (((drawHere.y + drawHere.height) / increment) + 1)
                * increment;
    }

    // Make a special case of 0 to display the number
    // within the rule and draw a units label.
    if (start == 0) {
        text = Integer.toString(0) + (isMetric ? " cm" : " in");
        tickLength = 10;
        if (orientation == HORIZONTAL) {
            g.drawLine(0, SIZE-1, 0, SIZE-tickLength-1);
            g.drawString(text, 2, 21);
        } else {
            g.drawLine(SIZE-1, 0, SIZE-tickLength-1, 0);
            g.drawString(text, 9, 10);
        }
        text = null;
        start = increment;
    }

    // ticks and labels
    for (int i = start; i < end; i += increment) {
        if (i % units == 0)  {
            tickLength = 10;
            text = Integer.toString(i/units);
        } else {
            tickLength = 7;
            text = null;
        }

        if (tickLength != 0) {
            if (orientation == HORIZONTAL) {
                g.drawLine(i, SIZE-1, i, SIZE-tickLength-1);
                if (text != null)
                    g.drawString(text, i-3, 21);
```

```java
            } else {
                g.drawLine(SIZE-1, i, SIZE-tickLength-1, i);
                if (text != null)
                    g.drawString(text, 9, i+3);
            }
        }
    }
}

public AccessibleContext getAccessibleContext() {
    if (accessibleContext == null) {
        accessibleContext = new AccessibleRuler();
    }
    return accessibleContext;
}

protected class AccessibleRuler extends AccessibleJComponent {
    public AccessibleRole getAccessibleRole() {
        return AccessibleRuleRole.RULER;
    }

    public AccessibleStateSet getAccessibleStateSet() {
        AccessibleStateSet states = super.getAccessibleStateSet();
        if (orientation == VERTICAL) {
            states.add(AccessibleState.VERTICAL);
        } else {
            states.add(AccessibleState.HORIZONTAL);
        }
        if (isMetric) {
            states.add(AccessibleRulerState.CENTIMETERS);
        } else {
            states.add(AccessibleRulerState.INCHES);
        }
        return states;
    }
}
}

class AccessibleRuleRole extends AccessibleRole {
    public static final AccessibleRuleRole RULER
        = new AccessibleRuleRole("ruler");

    protected AccessibleRuleRole(String key) {
        super(key);
    }

    //Should really provide localizable versions of these names.
    public String toDisplayString(String resourceBundleName,
                                  Locale locale) {
        return key;
    }
}

class AccessibleRulerState extends AccessibleState {
    public static final AccessibleRulerState INCHES = new
AccessibleRulerState("inches");
    public static final AccessibleRulerState CENTIMETERS
        = new AccessibleRulerState("centimeters");

    protected AccessibleRulerState(String key) {
        super(key);
    }

    //Should really provide localizable versions of these names.
    public String toDisplayString(String resourceBundleName, Locale locale) {
        return key;
    }
}
```

EXAMPLE: *ScrollablePicture.java*

Main Source File: <u>AccessibleScrollDemo.java</u> *(page 806)*

SOURCE CODE: *http://java.sun.com/docs/books/tutorial/uiswing/misc/example-swing/ ScrollablePicture.java*

Where Explained:

Setting Accessible Names and Descriptions on Components
(page 395)

```java
import java.awt.*;
import java.awt.event.*;
import javax.swing.*;
import javax.swing.border.*;

public class ScrollablePicture extends JLabel implements Scrollable {

    private int maxUnitIncrement = 1;

    public ScrollablePicture(ImageIcon i, int m) {
        super(i);
        maxUnitIncrement = m;
    }

    public Dimension getPreferredScrollableViewportSize() {
        return getPreferredSize();
    }

    public int getScrollableUnitIncrement(Rectangle visibleRect, int orientation,
                                          int direction) {

        int currentPosition = 0;
        if (orientation == SwingConstants.HORIZONTAL)
            currentPosition = visibleRect.x;
        else
            currentPosition = visibleRect.y;

        if (direction < 0) {
            int newPosition = currentPosition -
                              (currentPosition / maxUnitIncrement)
                              * maxUnitIncrement;
            return (newPosition == 0) ? maxUnitIncrement : newPosition;
        } else {
            return ((currentPosition / maxUnitIncrement) + 1) *
                    maxUnitIncrement - currentPosition;
        }
    }

    public int getScrollableBlockIncrement(Rectangle visibleRect, int orientation,
                                           int direction) {
        if (orientation == SwingConstants.HORIZONTAL)
            return visibleRect.width - maxUnitIncrement;
        else
            return visibleRect.height - maxUnitIncrement;
    }

    public boolean getScrollableTracksViewportWidth() {
        return false;
    }

    public boolean getScrollableTracksViewportHeight() {
        return false;
    }

    public void setMaxUnitIncrement(int pixels) {
        maxUnitIncrement = pixels;
    }
}
```

Writing Event Listeners

Complete examples in <u>Writing Event Listeners</u> (page 439):

EXAMPLE: *Beeper.java*

Where Explained:

Some Simple Event-Handling Examples (page 443)

SOURCE CODE: *http://java.sun.com/docs/books/tutorial/uiswing/events/example-swing/ Beeper.java*

```
/*
 * Swing 1.1 version (compatible with both JDK 1.1 and Java 2).
 */
import javax.swing.JApplet;
import javax.swing.JButton;

import java.awt.Toolkit;
import java.awt.BorderLayout;
import java.awt.event.ActionListener;
import java.awt.event.ActionEvent;

public class Beeper extends JApplet
                    implements ActionListener {
    JButton button;

    public void init() {
        button = new JButton("Click Me");
        getContentPane().add(button, BorderLayout.CENTER);
        button.addActionListener(this);
    }

    public void actionPerformed(ActionEvent e) {
        Toolkit.getDefaultToolkit().beep();
    }
}
```

EXAMPLE: *BlankArea.java*

Associated File(s): MouseEventDemo.java *(page 847),*
MouseMotionEventDemo.java *(page 848)*

SOURCE CODE: *http://java.sun.com/docs/books/tutorial/uiswing/events/example-swing/
BlankArea.java*

```java
/*
 * Swing 1.1 version (compatible with both JDK 1.1 and Java 2).
 */

import javax.swing.*;
import java.awt.Dimension;
import java.awt.Color;
import java.awt.Graphics;

public class BlankArea extends JLabel {
    Dimension minSize = new Dimension(100, 100);

    public BlankArea(Color color) {
        setBackground(color);
        setOpaque(true);
        setBorder(BorderFactory.createLineBorder(Color.black));
    }

    public Dimension getMinimumSize() {
        return minSize;
    }

    public Dimension getPreferredSize() {
        return minSize;
    }
}
```

EXAMPLE: *ComponentEventDemo.java*

SOURCE CODE: *http://java.sun.com/docs/books/tutorial/uiswing/events/example-swing/
ComponentEventDemo.java*

```java
/*
 * Swing 1.1 version (compatible with both JDK 1.1 and Java 2).
 */

import javax.swing.*;

import java.awt.Dimension;
import java.awt.BorderLayout;
import java.awt.event.*;

public class ComponentEventDemo extends JApplet
                                implements ComponentListener,
                                           ActionListener {
    JTextArea display;
    JFrame aFrame;
    public boolean showIt = false;
    final static String SHOW = "show";
    final static String CLEAR = "clear";
    String newline = "\n";
```

**Where
Explained:**
*An Example of
Handling
Another Event
Type* (page 445)

**Where
Explained:**
*How to Write a
Component
Listener*
(page 466)

```
public void init() {
    display = new JTextArea();
    display.setEditable(false);
    JScrollPane scrollPane = new JScrollPane(display);
    scrollPane.setPreferredSize(new Dimension(200, 75));
    getContentPane().add(scrollPane, BorderLayout.CENTER);

    JButton b1 = new JButton("Start playing...");
    b1.setActionCommand(SHOW);
    b1.addActionListener(this);
    getContentPane().add(b1, BorderLayout.NORTH);

    JButton b2 = new JButton("Clear");
    b2.setActionCommand(CLEAR);
    b2.addActionListener(this);
    getContentPane().add(b2, BorderLayout.SOUTH);

    aFrame = new JFrame("A Frame");
    ComponentPanel p = new ComponentPanel(this);
    aFrame.addComponentListener(this);
    p.addComponentListener(this);
    aFrame.getContentPane().add(p, BorderLayout.CENTER);
    aFrame.pack();

    aFrame.addWindowListener(new WindowAdapter() {
        // This event handler is executed before the
        // default close operation (hide) is applied.
        public void windowClosing(WindowEvent e) {
            showIt = false;
        }
    });
}

public void actionPerformed(ActionEvent e) {
    if (e.getActionCommand() == SHOW) {
        showIt = true;
        aFrame.setVisible(true);
    } else { //CLEAR
        display.setText("");
    }
}

public void stop() {
    SwingUtilities.invokeLater(new Runnable() {
        public void run() {
            aFrame.setVisible(false);
        }
    });
}

public void start() {
    SwingUtilities.invokeLater(new Runnable() {
        public void run() {
            if (showIt) {
                aFrame.setVisible(true);
            }
        }
    });
}

protected void displayMessage(String message) {
    display.append(message + newline);
}
```

```
    public void componentHidden(ComponentEvent e) {
        displayMessage("componentHidden event from " +
         e.getComponent().getClass().getName());
    }

    public void componentMoved(ComponentEvent e) {
        displayMessage("componentMoved event from "
                        + e.getComponent().getClass().getName());
    }

    public void componentResized(ComponentEvent e) {
        displayMessage("componentResized event from "
                        + e.getComponent().getClass().getName());
    }

    public void componentShown(ComponentEvent e) {
        displayMessage("componentShown event from "
                        + e.getComponent().getClass().getName());
    }
}

class ComponentPanel extends JPanel
                     implements ItemListener {
    JLabel label;
    JCheckBox checkbox;

    ComponentPanel(ComponentEventDemo listener) {
        super(new BorderLayout());

        label = new JLabel("This is a Label", JLabel.CENTER);
        add(label, BorderLayout.CENTER);

        checkbox = new JCheckBox("Label visible", true);
        checkbox.addItemListener(this);
        add(checkbox, BorderLayout.SOUTH);

        label.addComponentListener(listener);
        checkbox.addComponentListener(listener);
    }

    public void itemStateChanged(ItemEvent e) {
        if (e.getStateChange() == ItemEvent.SELECTED) {
            label.setVisible(true);

            //Need to revalidate and repaint, or else the label
            //will probably be drawn in the wrong place.
            label.revalidate();
            label.repaint();

        } else {
            label.setVisible(false);
        }
    }
}
```

EXAMPLE: *ContainerEventDemo.java*

SOURCE CODE: *http://java.sun.com/docs/books/tutorial/uiswing/events/example-swing/
ContainerEventDemo.java*

```
/*
 * Swing 1.1 version (compatible with both JDK 1.1 and Java 2).
 */
```

**Where
Explained:**
*How to Write a
Container
Listener*
(page 469)

```java
import javax.swing.*;

import java.awt.Dimension;
import java.awt.GridBagLayout;
import java.awt.GridBagConstraints;

import java.awt.event.ContainerEvent;
import java.awt.event.ContainerListener;
import java.awt.event.ActionEvent;
import java.awt.event.ActionListener;

import java.util.Vector;

public class ContainerEventDemo extends JApplet
                                 implements ContainerListener,
                                            ActionListener {
    JTextArea display;
    JPanel buttonPanel;
    JButton addButton, removeButton, clearButton;
    Vector buttonList;
    static final String ADD = "add";
    static final String REMOVE = "remove";
    static final String CLEAR = "clear";
    static final String newline = "\n";

    public void init() {
        //Initialize an empty list of buttons.
        buttonList = new Vector(10, 10);

        //Create all the components.
        addButton = new JButton("Add a button");
        addButton.setActionCommand(ADD);
        addButton.addActionListener(this);

        removeButton = new JButton("Remove a button");
        removeButton.setActionCommand(REMOVE);
        removeButton.addActionListener(this);

        buttonPanel = new JPanel();
        buttonPanel.setPreferredSize(new Dimension(200, 75));
        buttonPanel.addContainerListener(this);

        display = new JTextArea();
        display.setEditable(false);
        JScrollPane scrollPane = new JScrollPane(display);
        scrollPane.setPreferredSize(new Dimension(200, 75));

        clearButton = new JButton("Clear text area");
        clearButton.setActionCommand(CLEAR);
        clearButton.addActionListener(this);

        //Lay out the components.
        GridBagLayout gridbag = new GridBagLayout();
        GridBagConstraints c = new GridBagConstraints();
        JPanel contentPane = new JPanel();
        contentPane.setLayout(gridbag);
        c.fill = GridBagConstraints.BOTH; //Fill entire cell.

        c.weighty = 1.0;  //Button area and message area have equal height.
        c.gridwidth = GridBagConstraints.REMAINDER; //end of row
        gridbag.setConstraints(scrollPane, c);
        contentPane.add(scrollPane);

        c.weighty = 0.0;
        gridbag.setConstraints(clearButton, c);
        contentPane.add(clearButton);
```

```
        c.weightx = 1.0;  //Add/remove buttons have equal width.
        c.gridwidth = 1;  //NOT end of row
        gridbag.setConstraints(addButton, c);
        contentPane.add(addButton);

        c.gridwidth = GridBagConstraints.REMAINDER; //end of row
        gridbag.setConstraints(removeButton, c);
        contentPane.add(removeButton);

        c.weighty = 1.0;  //Button area and message area have equal height.
        gridbag.setConstraints(buttonPanel, c);
        contentPane.add(buttonPanel);

        setContentPane(contentPane);
    }

    public void componentAdded(ContainerEvent e) {
        displayMessage(" added to ", e);
    }

    public void componentRemoved(ContainerEvent e) {
        displayMessage(" removed from ", e);
    }

    void displayMessage(String action, ContainerEvent e) {
        display.append(((JButton)e.getChild()).getText()
                        + " was"
                        + action
                        + e.getContainer().getClass().getName()
                        + newline);
    }

    /*
     * This could have been implemented as two or three
     * classes or objects, for clarity.
     */
    public void actionPerformed(ActionEvent e) {
        String command = e.getActionCommand();

        if (command == ADD) {
            JButton newButton = new JButton("JButton #"
                                        + (buttonList.size() + 1));
            buttonList.addElement(newButton);
            buttonPanel.add(newButton);
            buttonPanel.revalidate(); //Make the button show up.

        } else if (command == REMOVE) {
            int lastIndex = buttonList.size() - 1;
            try {
                JButton nixedButton = (JButton)buttonList.elementAt(lastIndex);
                buttonPanel.remove(nixedButton);
                buttonList.removeElementAt(lastIndex);
                buttonPanel.revalidate(); //Make the button disappear.
                buttonPanel.repaint(); //Make the button disappear.
            } catch (ArrayIndexOutOfBoundsException exc) {}
        } else if (command == CLEAR) {
            display.setText("");
        }
    }
}
```

EXAMPLE: *DocumentEventDemo.java*

Where Explained:

How to Write a Document Listener (page 472)

SOURCE CODE: *http://java.sun.com/docs/books/tutorial/uiswing/events/example-swing/ DocumentEventDemo.java*

```java
/*
 * Swing 1.1 version (compatible with both JDK 1.1 and Java 2)
 */
import javax.swing.*;
import javax.swing.text.*;
import javax.swing.event.*;

import java.awt.Dimension;
import java.awt.BorderLayout;
import java.awt.GridBagLayout;
import java.awt.GridBagConstraints;

import java.awt.event.*;

public class DocumentEventDemo extends JApplet
                               implements ActionListener {
    JTextField textField;
    JTextArea textArea;
    JTextArea displayArea;

    public void init() {
        JButton button = new JButton("Clear");
        button.addActionListener(this);

        textField = new JTextField(20);
        textField.addActionListener(new MyTextActionListener());
        textField.getDocument().addDocumentListener(new MyDocumentListener());
        textField.getDocument().putProperty("name", "Text Field");

        textArea = new JTextArea();
        textArea.getDocument().addDocumentListener(new MyDocumentListener());
        textArea.getDocument().putProperty("name", "Text Area");

        JScrollPane scrollPane = new JScrollPane(textArea);
        scrollPane.setPreferredSize(new Dimension(200, 75));

        displayArea = new JTextArea();
        displayArea.setEditable(false);
        JScrollPane displayScrollPane = new JScrollPane(displayArea);
        displayScrollPane.setPreferredSize(new Dimension(200, 75));

        JPanel contentPane = new JPanel();
        GridBagLayout gridbag = new GridBagLayout();
        GridBagConstraints c = new GridBagConstraints();
        contentPane.setLayout(gridbag);

        c.gridx = 0;
        c.gridy = 0;
        c.weightx = 1.0;
        c.fill = GridBagConstraints.HORIZONTAL;
        gridbag.setConstraints(textField, c);
        contentPane.add(textField);

        c.gridx = 0;
        c.gridy = 1;
        c.weightx = 0.0;
        c.gridheight = 2;
```

```
            c.fill = GridBagConstraints.BOTH;
            gridbag.setConstraints(scrollPane, c);
            contentPane.add(scrollPane);

            c.gridx = 1;
            c.gridy = 0;
            c.weightx = 1.0;
            c.weighty = 1.0;
            gridbag.setConstraints(displayScrollPane, c);
            contentPane.add(displayScrollPane);

            c.gridx = 1;
            c.gridy = 2;
            c.weightx = 0.0;
            c.gridheight = 1;
            c.weighty = 0.0;
            c.fill = GridBagConstraints.HORIZONTAL;
            gridbag.setConstraints(button, c);
            contentPane.add(button);

            setContentPane(contentPane);
        }

        class MyDocumentListener implements DocumentListener {
            final String newline = "\n";

            public void insertUpdate(DocumentEvent e) {
                updateLog(e, "inserted into");
            }
            public void removeUpdate(DocumentEvent e) {
                updateLog(e, "removed from");
            }
            public void changedUpdate(DocumentEvent e) {
                //Plain text components don't fire these events.
            }

            public void updateLog(DocumentEvent e, String action) {
                Document doc = (Document)e.getDocument();
                int changeLength = e.getLength();
                displayArea.append(
                    changeLength + " character"
                  + ((changeLength == 1) ? " " : "s ")
                  + action + " " + doc.getProperty("name") + "."
                  + newline
                  + "    Text length = " + doc.getLength() + newline);
            }
        }

        class MyTextActionListener implements ActionListener {
            /** Handle the text field Return. */
            public void actionPerformed(ActionEvent e) {
                int selStart = textArea.getSelectionStart();
                int selEnd = textArea.getSelectionEnd();

                textArea.replaceRange(textField.getText(),
                                      selStart, selEnd);
                textField.selectAll();
            }
        }

        /** Handle button click. */
        public void actionPerformed(ActionEvent e) {
            displayArea.setText("");
            textField.requestFocus();
        }
    }
```

Where
Explained:

How to Write a
Focus Listener
(page 476)

EXAMPLE: *FocusEventDemo.java*

SOURCE CODE: *http://java.sun.com/docs/books/tutorial/uiswing/events/example-swing/*
                FocusEventDemo.java

```java
/*
 * Swing 1.1 version (compatible with both JDK 1.1 and Java 2)
 */

import javax.swing.*;

import java.awt.BorderLayout;
import java.awt.Dimension;
import java.awt.GridBagLayout;
import java.awt.GridBagConstraints;
import java.awt.Insets;

import java.util.Vector;

import java.awt.event.FocusListener;
import java.awt.event.FocusEvent;
import java.awt.event.ActionListener;
import java.awt.event.ActionEvent;
import java.awt.event.WindowEvent;
import java.awt.event.WindowAdapter;

public class FocusEventDemo extends JApplet
                            implements FocusListener,
                                       ActionListener {

    JTextArea display;
    FocusWindow window;
    JButton b1, b2;
    static final String SHOW = "show";
    static final String CLEAR = "clear";
    static final String newline = "\n";

    public void init() {
        b1 = new JButton("Click to bring up a window.");
        b1.setActionCommand(SHOW);
        b1.addActionListener(this);

        b2 = new JButton("Click to clear the display.");
        b2.setActionCommand(CLEAR);
        b2.addActionListener(this);

        display = new JTextArea();
        display.setEditable(false);
        JScrollPane scrollPane = new JScrollPane(display);
        scrollPane.setPreferredSize(new Dimension(375, 125));

        JPanel contentPane = new JPanel();
        contentPane.setLayout(new BorderLayout());
        contentPane.add(b1, BorderLayout.NORTH);
        contentPane.add(scrollPane, BorderLayout.CENTER);
        contentPane.add(b2, BorderLayout.SOUTH);
        setContentPane(contentPane);

        //Create but don't show window.
        window = new FocusWindow(this);
    }
```

```
        public void stop() {
            SwingUtilities.invokeLater(new Runnable() {
                public void run() {
                    window.setVisible(false);
                }
            });
        }

        public void focusGained(FocusEvent e) {
            displayMessage("Focus gained", e);
        }

        public void focusLost(FocusEvent e) {
            displayMessage("Focus lost", e);
        }

        void displayMessage(String prefix, FocusEvent e) {
            display.append(prefix
                            + ": "
                            + e.getComponent()
                            + newline);
        }

        public void actionPerformed(ActionEvent e) {
            if (e.getActionCommand() == SHOW) {
                window.pack();
                window.setVisible(true);
            } else { //CLEAR
                display.setText("");
            }
        }
    }

    class FocusWindow extends JFrame {
        public FocusWindow(FocusListener listener) {
            super("Focus Event Window");
            //We'll use the default close operation -- hiding.

            JPanel contentPane = new JPanel();
            this.addFocusListener(listener);

            GridBagLayout gridbag = new GridBagLayout();
            GridBagConstraints c = new GridBagConstraints();
            contentPane.setLayout(gridbag);

            c.fill = GridBagConstraints.HORIZONTAL;
            c.weightx = 1.0;  //Make column as wide as possible.
            JTextField textField = new JTextField("A TextField");
            textField.setMargin(new Insets(0,2,0,2));
            textField.addFocusListener(listener);
            gridbag.setConstraints(textField, c);
            contentPane.add(textField);

            c.weightx = 0.1;  //Widen every other column a bit, when possible.
            c.fill = GridBagConstraints.NONE;
            JLabel label = new JLabel("A Label");
            label.setBorder(BorderFactory.createEmptyBorder(0,5,0,5));
            label.addFocusListener(listener);
            gridbag.setConstraints(label, c);
            contentPane.add(label);

            //We'll add a focus listener to a choice, but since it's
            //typically implemented as a compound component, we aren't
            //likely to get any events.
            String choiceprefix = "Choice item #";
            final int numItems = 10;
```

```
                Vector vector = new Vector(numItems);
                for (int i = 0; i < numItems; i++) {
                    vector.addElement(choiceprefix + i);
                }
                JComboBox choice = new JComboBox(vector);
                choice.addFocusListener(listener);
                gridbag.setConstraints(choice, c);
                contentPane.add(choice);

                c.gridwidth = GridBagConstraints.REMAINDER;
                JButton button = new JButton("A Button");
                button.addFocusListener(listener);
                gridbag.setConstraints(button, c);
                contentPane.add(button);

                c.weighty = 1.0;    //Make this row as tall as possible.
                c.weightx = 0.0;
                c.fill = GridBagConstraints.BOTH;
                String listprefix = "List item #";
                Vector listVector = new Vector(numItems);
                for (int i = 0; i < numItems; i++) {
                    listVector.addElement(listprefix + i);
                }
                JList list = new JList(listVector);
                JScrollPane scrollPane = new JScrollPane(list);
                list.addFocusListener(listener);
                gridbag.setConstraints(scrollPane, c);
                contentPane.add(scrollPane);

                setContentPane(contentPane);
        }
}
```

EXAMPLE: *InternalFrameEventDemo.java*

**Where
Explained:**

*How to Write
an Internal
Frame Listener*
(page 480)

SOURCE CODE: *http://java.sun.com/docs/books/tutorial/uiswing/events/example-swing/
InternalFrameEventDemo.java*

```
import java.awt.*;
import java.awt.event.*;
import javax.swing.*;
import javax.swing.event.*;

public class InternalFrameEventDemo
                    extends JFrame
                    implements InternalFrameListener,
                                    ActionListener {
    JTextArea display;
    JDesktopPane desktop;
    JInternalFrame displayWindow;
    JInternalFrame listenedToWindow;
    static final String SHOW = "show";
    static final String CLEAR = "clear";
    String newline = "\n";
    static final int desktopWidth = 500;
    static final int desktopHeight = 300;

    public InternalFrameEventDemo(String title) {
        super(title);

        //Set up the GUI.
        desktop = new JDesktopPane();
        desktop.putClientProperty("JDesktopPane.dragMode",
                                    "outline");
```

```
        //Because we use pack, it's not enough to call setSize.
        //We must set the desktop's preferred size.
        desktop.setPreferredSize(new Dimension(desktopWidth, desktopHeight));
        setContentPane(desktop);

        createDisplayWindow();
        desktop.add(displayWindow); //DON'T FORGET THIS!!!
        Dimension displaySize = displayWindow.getSize();
        displayWindow.setSize(desktopWidth, displaySize.height);
    }

    //Create the window that displays event information.
    protected void createDisplayWindow() {
        JButton b1 = new JButton("Show internal frame");
        b1.setActionCommand(SHOW);
        b1.addActionListener(this);

        JButton b2 = new JButton("Clear event info");
        b2.setActionCommand(CLEAR);
        b2.addActionListener(this);

        display = new JTextArea(3, 30);
        display.setEditable(false);
        JScrollPane textScroller = new JScrollPane(display);
        //Have to supply a preferred size, or else the scroll
        //area will try to stay as large as the text area.
        textScroller.setPreferredSize(new Dimension(200, 75));
        textScroller.setMinimumSize(new Dimension(10, 10));

        displayWindow = new JInternalFrame("Event Watcher",
                                    true,  //resizable
                                    false, //not closable
                                    false, //not maximizable
                                    true); //iconifiable
        JPanel contentPane = new JPanel();
        contentPane.setBorder(BorderFactory.createEmptyBorder(10,10,10,10));
        contentPane.setLayout(new BoxLayout(contentPane,
                                    BoxLayout.Y_AXIS));
        b1.setAlignmentX(CENTER_ALIGNMENT);
        contentPane.add(b1);
        contentPane.add(Box.createRigidArea(new Dimension(0, 5)));
        contentPane.add(textScroller);
        contentPane.add(Box.createRigidArea(new Dimension(0, 5)));
        b2.setAlignmentX(CENTER_ALIGNMENT);
        contentPane.add(b2);

        displayWindow.setContentPane(contentPane);
        displayWindow.pack();
    }

    //Create the listened-to window.
    protected void createListenedToWindow() {
        listenedToWindow = new JInternalFrame("Event Generator",
                                        true,  //resizable
                                        true,  //closable
                                        true,  //maximizable
                                        true); //iconifiable
        //The next statement is necessary to work around bug 4138031.
        listenedToWindow.setDefaultCloseOperation(
                            WindowConstants.DISPOSE_ON_CLOSE);
        listenedToWindow.setSize(300, 100);
    }

    public void internalFrameClosing(InternalFrameEvent e) {
        displayMessage("Internal frame closing", e);
    }
```

```java
    public void internalFrameClosed(InternalFrameEvent e) {
        displayMessage("Internal frame closed", e);
        listenedToWindow = null;
    }

    public void internalFrameOpened(InternalFrameEvent e) {
        //XXX: We don't seem to get any of these.
        displayMessage("Internal frame opened", e);
    }

    public void internalFrameIconified(InternalFrameEvent e) {
        displayMessage("Internal frame iconified", e);
    }

    public void internalFrameDeiconified(InternalFrameEvent e) {
        displayMessage("Internal frame deiconified", e);
    }

    public void internalFrameActivated(InternalFrameEvent e) {
        displayMessage("Internal frame activated", e);
    }

    public void internalFrameDeactivated(InternalFrameEvent e) {
        displayMessage("Internal frame deactivated", e);
    }

    void displayMessage(String prefix, InternalFrameEvent e) {
        String s = prefix + ": " + e.getSource();
        display.append(s + newline);
    }

    public void actionPerformed(ActionEvent e) {
        if (e.getActionCommand().equals(SHOW)) {
            //XXX: Can't reuse internal frame (bug 4138031).
            //listenedToWindow.setVisible(true);

            //XXX: Instead, create a new internal frame.
            if (listenedToWindow == null) {
                createListenedToWindow();
                listenedToWindow.addInternalFrameListener(this);
                desktop.add(listenedToWindow);
                listenedToWindow.setLocation(
                    desktopWidth/2 - listenedToWindow.getWidth()/2,
                    desktopHeight - listenedToWindow.getHeight());
            }
        } else {
            display.setText("");
        }
    }

    public static void main(String[] args) {
        JFrame frame = new InternalFrameEventDemo(
                "InternalFrameEventDemo");

        //Quit this app when the big window closes.
        frame.addWindowListener(new WindowAdapter() {
            public void windowClosing(WindowEvent e) {
                System.exit(0);
            }
        });

        frame.pack();
        frame.setVisible(true);
    }
}
```

EXAMPLE: *KeyEventDemo.java*

Where Explained:

How to Write a Key Listener (page 486)

SOURCE CODE: *http://java.sun.com/docs/books/tutorial/uiswing/events/example-swing/ KeyEventDemo.java*

```java
/*
 * Swing 1.1 version (compatible with both JDK 1.1 and Java 2)
 */

import javax.swing.*;
import java.awt.event.*;
import java.awt.BorderLayout;
import java.awt.Dimension;

public class KeyEventDemo extends JApplet implements KeyListener, ActionListener {
    JTextArea displayArea;
    JTextField typingArea;
    static final String newline = "\n";

    public void init() {
        JButton button = new JButton("Clear");
        button.addActionListener(this);

        typingArea = new JTextField(20);
        typingArea.addKeyListener(this);

        displayArea = new JTextArea();
        displayArea.setEditable(false);
        JScrollPane scrollPane = new JScrollPane(displayArea);
        scrollPane.setPreferredSize(new Dimension(375, 125));

        JPanel contentPane = new JPanel();
        contentPane.setLayout(new BorderLayout());
        contentPane.add(typingArea, BorderLayout.NORTH);
        contentPane.add(scrollPane, BorderLayout.CENTER);
        contentPane.add(button, BorderLayout.SOUTH);
        setContentPane(contentPane);
    }

    /** Handle the key typed event from the text field. */
    public void keyTyped(KeyEvent e) {
        displayInfo(e, "KEY TYPED: ");
    }

    /** Handle the key pressed event from the text field. */
    public void keyPressed(KeyEvent e) {
        displayInfo(e, "KEY PRESSED: ");
    }

    /** Handle the key released event from the text field. */
    public void keyReleased(KeyEvent e) {
        displayInfo(e, "KEY RELEASED: ");
    }

    /** Handle the button click. */
    public void actionPerformed(ActionEvent e) {
        //Clear the text components.
        displayArea.setText("");
        typingArea.setText("");

        //Return the focus to the typing area.
        typingArea.requestFocus();
    }
```

```
/*
 * We have to jump through some hoops to avoid
 * trying to print non-printing characters
 * such as Shift.  (Not only do they not print,
 * but if you put them in a String, the characters
 * afterward won't show up in the text area.)
 */
protected void displayInfo(KeyEvent e, String s){
    String charString, keyCodeString, modString, tmpString;

    char c = e.getKeyChar();
    int keyCode = e.getKeyCode();
    int modifiers = e.getModifiers();

    if (Character.isISOControl(c)) {
        charString = "key character = "
                    + "(an unprintable control character)";
    } else {
        charString = "key character = '"
                    + c + "'";
    }

    keyCodeString = "key code = " + keyCode
                    + " ("
                    + KeyEvent.getKeyText(keyCode)
                    + ")";

    modString = "modifiers = " + modifiers;
    tmpString = KeyEvent.getKeyModifiersText(modifiers);
    if (tmpString.length() > 0) {
        modString += " (" + tmpString + ")";
    } else {
        modString += " (no modifiers)";
    }

    displayArea.append(s + newline
                    + "      " + charString + newline
                    + "      " + keyCodeString + newline
                    + "      " + modString + newline);
    }
}
```

EXAMPLE: *ListDataEventDemo.java*

**Where
Explained:**

*How to Write
a List Data
Listener*
(page 491)

SOURCE CODE: *http://java.sun.com/docs/books/tutorial/uiswing/events/example-swing/
                    ListDataEventDemo.java*

```
import java.awt.*;
import java.awt.event.*;
import javax.swing.*;
import javax.swing.event.*;
import java.net.URL;

public class ListDataEventDemo extends JApplet implements ListSelectionListener {
    private JList list;
    private DefaultListModel listModel;

    private static final String addString = "Add";
    private static final String deleteString = "Delete";
    private static final String upString = "Move up";
    private static final String downString = "Move down";
```

```
private JButton addButton;
private JButton deleteButton;
private JButton upButton;
private JButton downButton;

private JTextField nameField;
private JTextArea log;
static private String newline = "\n";

public void init() {
    //Create and populate the list model.
    listModel = new DefaultListModel();
    listModel.addElement("Whistler, Canada");
    listModel.addElement("Jackson Hole, Wyoming");
    listModel.addElement("Squaw Valley, California");
    listModel.addElement("Telluride, Colorado"),
    listModel.addElement("Taos, New Mexico");
    listModel.addElement("Snowbird, Utah");
    listModel.addElement("Chamonix, France");
    listModel.addElement("Banff, Canada");
    listModel.addElement("Arapahoe Basin, Colorado");
    listModel.addElement("Kirkwood, California");
    listModel.addElement("Sun Valley, Idaho");
    listModel.addListDataListener(new MyListDataListener());

    //Create the list and put it in a scroll pane.
    list = new JList(listModel);
    list.setSelectionMode(
        ListSelectionModel.SINGLE_INTERVAL_SELECTION);
    list.setSelectedIndex(0);
    list.addListSelectionListener(this);
    JScrollPane listScrollPane = new JScrollPane(list);

    //Create the list modifying buttons.
    addButton = new JButton(addString);
    addButton.setActionCommand(addString);
    addButton.addActionListener(new AddButtonListener());

    deleteButton = new JButton(deleteString);
    deleteButton.setActionCommand(deleteString);
    deleteButton.addActionListener(
        new DeleteButtonListener());

    upButton = new JButton(
        new ImageIcon(getURL("images/up.gif")));
    upButton.setMargin(new Insets(0,0,0,0));
    upButton.setActionCommand(upString);
    upButton.addActionListener(new UpDownListener());

    downButton = new JButton(
        new ImageIcon(getURL("images/down.gif")));
    downButton.setMargin(new Insets(0,0,0,0));
    downButton.setActionCommand(downString);
    downButton.addActionListener(new UpDownListener());

    JPanel upDownPanel = new JPanel(new GridLayout(2, 1));
    upDownPanel.add(upButton);
    upDownPanel.add(downButton);

    //Create the text field for entering new names.
    nameField = new JTextField(15);
    nameField.addActionListener(new AddButtonListener());
    String name = listModel.getElementAt(list.getSelectedIndex())
                            .toString();
    nameField.setText(name);
```

```
                //Create a control panel (uses the default FlowLayout).
                JPanel buttonPane = new JPanel();
                buttonPane.add(nameField);
                buttonPane.add(addButton);
                buttonPane.add(deleteButton);
                buttonPane.add(upDownPanel);

                //Create the log for reporting list data events.
                log = new JTextArea(10, 20);
                JScrollPane logScrollPane = new JScrollPane(log);

                //Create a split pane for the log and the list.
                JSplitPane splitPane = new JSplitPane(JSplitPane.VERTICAL_SPLIT,
                                            listScrollPane, logScrollPane);

                Container contentPane = getContentPane();
                contentPane.add(buttonPane, BorderLayout.NORTH);
                contentPane.add(splitPane, BorderLayout.CENTER);
            }

        class MyListDataListener implements ListDataListener {
            public void contentsChanged(ListDataEvent e) {
                log.append("contentsChanged: " + e.getIndex0() +
                            ", " + e.getIndex1() + newline);
            }
            public void intervalAdded(ListDataEvent e) {
                log.append("intervalAdded: " + e.getIndex0() +
                            ", " + e.getIndex1() + newline);
            }
            public void intervalRemoved(ListDataEvent e) {
                log.append("intervalRemoved: " + e.getIndex0() +
                            ", " + e.getIndex1() + newline);
            }
        }

        class DeleteButtonListener implements ActionListener {
            public void actionPerformed(ActionEvent e) {
                /*
                 * This method can be called only if
                 * there's a valid selection,
                 * so go ahead and remove whatever's selected.
                 */

                ListSelectionModel lsm = list.getSelectionModel();
                int firstSelected = lsm.getMinSelectionIndex();
                int lastSelected = lsm.getMaxSelectionIndex();
                listModel.removeRange(firstSelected, lastSelected);

                int size = listModel.size();

                if (size == 0) {
                //List is empty: disable delete, up, and down buttons.
                    deleteButton.setEnabled(false);
                    upButton.setEnabled(false);
                    downButton.setEnabled(false);

                } else {
                //Adjust the selection.
                    if (firstSelected == listModel.getSize()) {
                    //Removed item in last position.
                        firstSelected--;
                    }
                    list.setSelectedIndex(firstSelected);
                }
            }
        }
```

```java
/** A listener shared by the text field and add button. */
class AddButtonListener implements ActionListener {
    public void actionPerformed(ActionEvent e) {
        if (nameField.getText().equals("")) {
        //User didn't type in a name...
            Toolkit.getDefaultToolkit().beep();
            return;
        }

        int index = list.getSelectedIndex();
        int size = listModel.getSize();

        //If no selection or if item in last position is selected,
        //add the new one to end of list, and select new one.
        if (index == -1 || (index+1 == size)) {
            listModel.addElement(nameField.getText());
            list.setSelectedIndex(size);

        //Otherwise insert the new one after the current selection,
        //and select new one.
        } else {
            listModel.insertElementAt(nameField.getText(), index+1);
            list.setSelectedIndex(index+1);
        }
    }
}

//Listen for clicks on the up and down arrow buttons.
class UpDownListener implements ActionListener {
    public void actionPerformed(ActionEvent e) {
        //This method can be called only when
        //there's a valid selection,
        //so go ahead and move the list item.
        int moveMe = list.getSelectedIndex();

        if (e.getActionCommand().equals(upString)) {
        //UP ARROW BUTTON
            if (moveMe != 0) {
            //not already at top
                swap(moveMe, moveMe-1);
                list.setSelectedIndex(moveMe-1);
                list.ensureIndexIsVisible(moveMe-1);
            }
        } else {
        //DOWN ARROW BUTTON
            if (moveMe != listModel.getSize()-1) {
            //not already at bottom
                swap(moveMe, moveMe+1);
                list.setSelectedIndex(moveMe+1);
                list.ensureIndexIsVisible(moveMe+1);
            }
        }
    }
}

//Swap two elements in the list.
private void swap(int a, int b) {
    Object aObject = listModel.getElementAt(a);
    Object bObject = listModel.getElementAt(b);
    listModel.set(a, bObject);
    listModel.set(b, aObject);
}

//Listener method for list selection changes.
public void valueChanged(ListSelectionEvent e) {
    if (e.getValueIsAdjusting() == false) {
```

```
        if (list.getSelectedIndex() == -1) {
        //No selection: disable delete, up, and down buttons.
            deleteButton.setEnabled(false);
            upButton.setEnabled(false);
            downButton.setEnabled(false);
            nameField.setText("");

        } else if (list.getSelectedIndices().length > 1) {
        //Multiple selection: disable up and down buttons.
            deleteButton.setEnabled(true);
            upButton.setEnabled(false);
            downButton.setEnabled(false);

        } else {
        //Single selection: permit all operations.
            deleteButton.setEnabled(true);
            upButton.setEnabled(true);
            downButton.setEnabled(true);
            nameField.setText(list.getSelectedValue().toString());
        }
    }
}

protected URL getURL(String filename) {
    URL codeBase = this.getCodeBase();
    URL url = null;

    try {
        url = new URL(codeBase, filename);
    } catch (java.net.MalformedURLException e) {
        System.out.println("Couldn't create image: badly specified URL");
        return null;
    }

    return url;
}
}
```

EXAMPLE: *ListSelectionEventDemo.java*

Where Explained:

How to Write a List Selection Listener (page 494)

SOURCE CODE: *http://java.sun.com/docs/books/tutorial/uiswing/events/example-swing/ ListSelectionDemo.java*

```
import javax.swing.*;
import javax.swing.event.*;
import javax.swing.table.*;

import java.util.*;
import java.awt.*;
import java.awt.event.*;

public class ListSelectionDemo extends JPanel {
    JTextArea output;
    JList list;
    JTable table;
    String newline = "\n";
    ListSelectionModel listSelectionModel;

    public ListSelectionDemo() {
        super(new BorderLayout());

        String[] listData = { "one", "two", "three", "four",
                              "five", "six", "seven" };
```

```
String[] columnNames = { "French", "Spanish", "Italian" };
String[][] tableData = {{"un",      "uno",     "uno"     },
                        {"deux",    "dos",     "due"     },
                        {"trois",   "tres",    "tre"     },
                        { "quatre", "cuatro",  "quattro"},
                        { "cinq",   "cinco",   "cinque" },
                        { "six",    "seis",    "sei"     },
                        { "sept",   "siete",   "sette"  } };

list = new JList(listData);

listSelectionModel = list.getSelectionModel();
listSelectionModel.addListSelectionListener(
        new SharedListSelectionHandler());
JScrollPane listPane = new JScrollPane(list);

table = new JTable(tableData, columnNames);
table.setSelectionModel(listSelectionModel);
JScrollPane tablePane = new JScrollPane(table);

//Build control area (use default FlowLayout).
JPanel controlPane = new JPanel();
String[] modes = { "SINGLE_SELECTION",
                   "SINGLE_INTERVAL_SELECTION",
                   "MULTIPLE_INTERVAL_SELECTION" };

final JComboBox comboBox = new JComboBox(modes);
comboBox.setSelectedIndex(2);
comboBox.addActionListener(new ActionListener() {
    public void actionPerformed(ActionEvent e) {
        String newMode = (String)comboBox.getSelectedItem();
        if (newMode.equals("SINGLE_SELECTION")) {
            listSelectionModel.setSelectionMode(
                ListSelectionModel.SINGLE_SELECTION);
        } else if (newMode.equals("SINGLE_INTERVAL_SELECTION")) {
            listSelectionModel.setSelectionMode(
                ListSelectionModel.SINGLE_INTERVAL_SELECTION);
        } else {
            listSelectionModel.setSelectionMode(
                ListSelectionModel.MULTIPLE_INTERVAL_SELECTION);
        }
        output.append("----------"
                        + "Mode: " + newMode
                        + "----------" + newline);
    }
});
controlPane.add(new JLabel("Selection mode:"));
controlPane.add(comboBox);

//Build output area.
output = new JTextArea(1, 10);
output.setEditable(false);
JScrollPane outputPane = new JScrollPane(output,
                ScrollPaneConstants.VERTICAL_SCROLLBAR_ALWAYS,
                ScrollPaneConstants.HORIZONTAL_SCROLLBAR_AS_NEEDED);

//Do the layout.
JSplitPane splitPane = new JSplitPane(JSplitPane.VERTICAL_SPLIT);
add(splitPane, BorderLayout.CENTER);

JPanel topHalf = new JPanel();
topHalf.setLayout(new BoxLayout(topHalf, BoxLayout.X_AXIS));
JPanel listContainer = new JPanel(new GridLayout(1,1));
listContainer.setBorder(BorderFactory.createTitledBorder(
                                        "List"));
```

```
            listContainer.add(listPane);
            JPanel tableContainer = new JPanel(new GridLayout(1,1));
            tableContainer.setBorder(BorderFactory.createTitledBorder(
                                            "Table"));
            tableContainer.add(tablePane);
            tablePane.setPreferredSize(new Dimension(300, 100));
            topHalf.setBorder(BorderFactory.createEmptyBorder(5,5,0,5));
            topHalf.add(listContainer);
            topHalf.add(tableContainer);

            topHalf.setMinimumSize(new Dimension(400, 50));
            topHalf.setPreferredSize(new Dimension(400, 110));
            splitPane.add(topHalf);

            JPanel bottomHalf = new JPanel(new BorderLayout());
            bottomHalf.add(controlPane, BorderLayout.NORTH);
            bottomHalf.add(outputPane, BorderLayout.CENTER);
            //XXX: next line needed if bottomHalf is a scroll pane:
            //bottomHalf.setMinimumSize(new Dimension(400, 50));
            bottomHalf.setPreferredSize(new Dimension(450, 135));
            splitPane.add(bottomHalf);
        }

        public static void main(String[] args) {
            JFrame frame = new JFrame("ListSelectionDemo");
            frame.addWindowListener(new WindowAdapter() {
                public void windowClosing(WindowEvent e) {
                    System.exit(0);
                }
            });

            frame.setContentPane(new ListSelectionDemo());
            frame.pack();
            frame.setVisible(true);
        }

        class SharedListSelectionHandler implements ListSelectionListener {
            public void valueChanged(ListSelectionEvent e) {
                ListSelectionModel lsm = (ListSelectionModel)e.getSource();

                int firstIndex = e.getFirstIndex();
                int lastIndex = e.getLastIndex();
                boolean isAdjusting = e.getValueIsAdjusting();
                output.append("Event for indexes "
                                + firstIndex + " - " + lastIndex
                                + "; isAdjusting is " + isAdjusting
                                + "; selected indexes:");

                if (lsm.isSelectionEmpty()) {
                    output.append(" <none>");
                } else {
                    // Find out which indexes are selected.
                    int minIndex = lsm.getMinSelectionIndex();
                    int maxIndex = lsm.getMaxSelectionIndex();
                    for (int i = minIndex; i <= maxIndex; i++) {
                        if (lsm.isSelectedIndex(i)) {
                            output.append(" " + i);
                        }
                    }
                }
                output.append(newline);
            }
        }
    }
}
```

EXAMPLE: *MouseEventDemo.java*

Associated File(s): `BlankArea.java` *(page 827)*

SOURCE CODE: *http://java.sun.com/docs/books/tutorial/uiswing/events/example-swing/ MouseEventDemo.java*

Where Explained:

An Example of Handling Another Event Type (page 445)

```java
/*
 * Swing 1.1 version (compatible with both JDK 1.1 and Java 2)
 */

import javax.swing.*;

import java.awt.GridBagLayout;
import java.awt.GridBagConstraints;
import java.awt.Insets;
import java.awt.Color;
import java.awt.Dimension;

import java.awt.event.MouseListener;
import java.awt.event.MouseEvent;

public class MouseEventDemo extends JApplet
                            implements MouseListener {
    BlankArea blankArea;
    JTextArea textArea;
    final static String newline = "\n";

    public void init() {
        GridBagLayout gridbag = new GridBagLayout();
        GridBagConstraints c = new GridBagConstraints();
        JPanel contentPane = new JPanel();
        contentPane.setLayout(gridbag);

        c.fill = GridBagConstraints.BOTH;
        c.gridwidth = GridBagConstraints.REMAINDER;
        c.weightx = 1.0;
        c.weighty = 1.0;

        c.insets = new Insets(1, 1, 1, 1);
        blankArea = new BlankArea(new Color(0.98f, 0.97f, 0.85f));
        gridbag.setConstraints(blankArea, c);
        contentPane.add(blankArea);

        c.insets = new Insets(0, 0, 0, 0);
        textArea = new JTextArea();
        textArea.setEditable(false);
        JScrollPane scrollPane = new JScrollPane(textArea);
        scrollPane.setVerticalScrollBarPolicy(
                JScrollPane.VERTICAL_SCROLLBAR_ALWAYS);
        scrollPane.setPreferredSize(new Dimension(200, 75));
        gridbag.setConstraints(scrollPane, c);
        contentPane.add(scrollPane);

        //Register for mouse events on blankArea and applet.
        blankArea.addMouseListener(this);
        addMouseListener(this);

        setContentPane(contentPane);
    }
```

```
        public void mousePressed(MouseEvent e) {
            saySomething("Mouse pressed (# of clicks: "
                            + e.getClickCount() + ")", e);
        }

        public void mouseReleased(MouseEvent e) {
            saySomething("Mouse released (# of clicks: "
                            + e.getClickCount() + ")", e);
        }

        public void mouseEntered(MouseEvent e) {
            saySomething("Mouse entered", e);
        }

        public void mouseExited(MouseEvent e) {
            saySomething("Mouse exited", e);
        }

        public void mouseClicked(MouseEvent e) {
            saySomething("Mouse clicked (# of clicks: " + e.getClickCount() + ")", e);
        }

        void saySomething(String eventDescription, MouseEvent e) {
            textArea.append(eventDescription + " detected on "
                            + e.getComponent().getClass().getName()
                            + "." + newline);
        }
    }
```

EXAMPLE: *MouseMotionEventDemo.java*

Where Explained:

How to Write a Mouse-Motion Listener
(page 503)

Associated File(s): BlankArea.java *(page 827)*

SOURCE CODE: *http://java.sun.com/docs/books/tutorial/uiswing/events/example-swing/*
                MouseMotionEventDemo.java

```
/*
 * Swing 1.1 version (compatible with both JDK 1.1 and Java 2)
 */

import javax.swing.*;

import java.awt.Color;
import java.awt.Dimension;
import java.awt.Insets;
import java.awt.GridBagLayout;
import java.awt.GridBagConstraints;

import java.awt.event.MouseMotionListener;
import java.awt.event.MouseEvent;

public class MouseMotionEventDemo extends JApplet
                                  implements MouseMotionListener {
    BlankArea blankArea;
    JTextArea textArea;
    static final String newline = "\n";

    public void init() {
        JPanel contentPane = new JPanel();

        GridBagLayout gridbag = new GridBagLayout();
        GridBagConstraints c = new GridBagConstraints();
        contentPane.setLayout(gridbag);
```

```
        c.fill = GridBagConstraints.BOTH;
        c.gridwidth = GridBagConstraints.REMAINDER;
        c.weightx = 1.0;
        c.weighty = 1.0;

        c.insets = new Insets(1, 1, 1, 1);
        blankArea = new BlankArea(new Color(0.98f, 0.97f, 0.85f));
        gridbag.setConstraints(blankArea, c);
        contentPane.add(blankArea);

        c.insets = new Insets(0, 0, 0, 0);
        textArea = new JTextArea();
        textArea.setEditable(false);
        JScrollPane scrollPane = new JScrollPane(textArea,
                JScrollPane.VERTICAL_SCROLLBAR_ALWAYS,
                JScrollPane.HORIZONTAL_SCROLLBAR_AS_NEEDED);
        scrollPane.setPreferredSize(new Dimension(200, 75));
        gridbag.setConstraints(scrollPane, c);
        contentPane.add(scrollPane);

        //Register for mouse events on blankArea and applet.
        blankArea.addMouseMotionListener(this);
        addMouseMotionListener(this);

        setContentPane(contentPane);
    }

    public void mouseMoved(MouseEvent e) {
        saySomething("Mouse moved", e);
    }

    public void mouseDragged(MouseEvent e) {
        saySomething("Mouse dragged", e);
    }

    void saySomething(String eventDescription, MouseEvent e) {
        textArea.append(eventDescription
                        + " (" + e.getX() + "," + e.getY() + ")"
                        + " detected on "
                        + e.getComponent().getClass().getName()
                        + newline);
    }
}
```

EXAMPLE: *MultiListener.java*

SOURCE CODE: *http://java.sun.com/docs/books/tutorial/uiswing/events/example-swing/ MultiListener.java*

```
/*
 * Swing 1.1 version (compatible with both JDK 1.1 and Java 2)
 */

import javax.swing.*;

import java.awt.GridBagLayout;
import java.awt.GridBagConstraints;
import java.awt.Insets;
import java.awt.Dimension;
import java.awt.Color;

import java.awt.event.ActionListener;
import java.awt.event.ActionEvent;
```

Where Explained:

A More Complex Example (page 444)

```java
public class MultiListener extends JApplet
                        implements ActionListener {
    JTextArea topTextArea;
    JTextArea bottomTextArea;
    JButton button1, button2;
    final static String newline = "\n";

    public void init() {
        JLabel l = null;

        GridBagLayout gridbag = new GridBagLayout();
        GridBagConstraints c = new GridBagConstraints();
        JPanel contentPane = new JPanel();
        contentPane.setLayout(gridbag);
        contentPane.setBorder(BorderFactory.createCompoundBorder(
                            BorderFactory.createMatteBorder(
                                        1,1,2,2,Color.black),
                            BorderFactory.createEmptyBorder(5,5,5,5)));

        c.fill = GridBagConstraints.BOTH;
        c.gridwidth = GridBagConstraints.REMAINDER;
        l = new JLabel("What MultiListener hears:");
        gridbag.setConstraints(l, c);
        contentPane.add(l);

        c.weighty = 1.0;
        topTextArea = new JTextArea();
        topTextArea.setEditable(false);
        JScrollPane topScrollPane = new JScrollPane(topTextArea);
        Dimension preferredSize = new Dimension(200, 75);
        topScrollPane.setPreferredSize(preferredSize);
        gridbag.setConstraints(topScrollPane, c);
        contentPane.add(topScrollPane);

        c.weightx = 0.0;
        c.weighty = 0.0;
        l = new JLabel("What Eavesdropper hears:");
        gridbag.setConstraints(l, c);
        contentPane.add(l);

        c.weighty = 1.0;
        bottomTextArea = new JTextArea();
        bottomTextArea.setEditable(false);
        JScrollPane bottomScrollPane = new JScrollPane(bottomTextArea);
        bottomScrollPane.setPreferredSize(preferredSize);
        gridbag.setConstraints(bottomScrollPane, c);
        contentPane.add(bottomScrollPane);

        c.weightx = 1.0;
        c.weighty = 0.0;
        c.gridwidth = 1;
        c.insets = new Insets(10, 10, 0, 10);
        button1 = new JButton("Blah blah blah");
        gridbag.setConstraints(button1, c);
        contentPane.add(button1);

        c.gridwidth = GridBagConstraints.REMAINDER;
        button2 = new JButton("You don't say!");
        gridbag.setConstraints(button2, c);
        contentPane.add(button2);

        button1.addActionListener(this);
        button2.addActionListener(this);

        button2.addActionListener(new Eavesdropper(bottomTextArea));

        setContentPane(contentPane);
    }
```

```
        public void actionPerformed(ActionEvent e) {
            topTextArea.append(e.getActionCommand() + newline);
        }
    }

class Eavesdropper implements ActionListener {
    JTextArea myTextArea;
    public Eavesdropper(JTextArea ta) {
        myTextArea = ta;
    }

    public void actionPerformed(ActionEvent e) {
        myTextArea.append(e.getActionCommand()
                          + MultiListener.newline);
    ]
}
```

EXAMPLE: *TreeExpandEventDemo.java*

Where Explained: *How to Write a Tree Expansion Listener* (page 509)

SOURCE CODE: *http://java.sun.com/docs/books/tutorial/uiswing/events/example-swing/ TreeExpandEventDemo.java*

```
import javax.swing.*;
import javax.swing.tree.*;
import javax.swing.event.*;
import java.awt.*;

public class TreeExpandEventDemo extends JApplet {
    DemoArea demoArea;
    JTextArea textArea;
    final static String newline = "\n";

    public void init() {
        GridBagLayout gridbag = new GridBagLayout();
        GridBagConstraints c = new GridBagConstraints();
        JPanel contentPane = new JPanel();
        contentPane.setLayout(gridbag);

        c.fill = GridBagConstraints.BOTH;
        c.gridwidth = GridBagConstraints.REMAINDER;
        c.weightx = 1.0;
        c.weighty = 1.0;

        c.insets = new Insets(1, 1, 1, 1);
        demoArea = new DemoArea();
        gridbag.setConstraints(demoArea, c);
        contentPane.add(demoArea);

        c.insets = new Insets(0, 0, 0, 0);
        textArea = new JTextArea();
        textArea.setEditable(false);
        JScrollPane scrollPane = new JScrollPane(textArea);
        scrollPane.setVerticalScrollBarPolicy(
            JScrollPane.VERTICAL_SCROLLBAR_ALWAYS);
        scrollPane.setPreferredSize(new Dimension(200, 75));
        gridbag.setConstraints(scrollPane, c);
        contentPane.add(scrollPane);

        setContentPane(contentPane);
    }
```

```java
void saySomething(String eventDescription, TreeExpansionEvent e) {
    textArea.append(eventDescription + "; "
                    + "path = " + e.getPath()
                    + newline);
}

class DemoArea extends JScrollPane
               implements TreeExpansionListener {
    Dimension minSize = new Dimension(100, 100);
    JTree tree;

    public DemoArea() {
        TreeNode rootNode = createNodes();
        tree = new JTree(rootNode);
        tree.addTreeExpansionListener(this);

        setViewportView(tree);
    }

    private TreeNode createNodes() {
        DefaultMutableTreeNode root;
        DefaultMutableTreeNode grandparent;
        DefaultMutableTreeNode parent;
        DefaultMutableTreeNode child;

        root = new DefaultMutableTreeNode("San Francisco");

        grandparent = new DefaultMutableTreeNode("Potrero Hill");
        root.add(grandparent);
        //
        parent = new DefaultMutableTreeNode("Restaurants");
        grandparent.add(parent);
        child = new DefaultMutableTreeNode("Thai Barbeque");
        parent.add(child);
        child = new DefaultMutableTreeNode("Goat Hill Pizza");
        parent.add(child);
        //
        parent = new DefaultMutableTreeNode("Grocery Stores");
        grandparent.add(parent);
        child = new DefaultMutableTreeNode("Good Life Grocery");
        parent.add(child);
        child = new DefaultMutableTreeNode("Safeway");
        parent.add(child);

        grandparent = new DefaultMutableTreeNode("Noe Valley");
        root.add(grandparent);
        //
        parent = new DefaultMutableTreeNode("Restaurants");
        grandparent.add(parent);
        child = new DefaultMutableTreeNode("Hamano Sushi");
        parent.add(child);
        child = new DefaultMutableTreeNode("Hahn's Hibachi");
        parent.add(child);
        //
        parent = new DefaultMutableTreeNode("Grocery Stores");
        grandparent.add(parent);
        child = new DefaultMutableTreeNode("Real Foods");
        parent.add(child);
        child = new DefaultMutableTreeNode("Bell Market");
        parent.add(child);

        return root;
    }

    public Dimension getMinimumSize() {
        return minSize;
    }
```

```
                public Dimension getPreferredSize() {
                    return minSize;
                }

                // Required by TreeExpansionListener interface.
                public void treeExpanded(TreeExpansionEvent e) {
                    saySomething("Tree-expanded event detected", e);
                }

                // Required by TreeExpansionListener interface.
                public void treeCollapsed(TreeExpansionEvent e) {
                    saySomething("Tree-collapsed event detected", e);
                }
            }
        }
```

EXAMPLE: *TreeExpandEventDemo2.java*

SOURCE CODE: *http://java.sun.com/docs/books/tutorial/uiswing/events/example-swing/ TreeExpandEventDemo2.java*

```
import javax.swing.*;
import javax.swing.tree.*;
import javax.swing.event.*;
import java.awt.*;

public class TreeExpandEventDemo2 extends JApplet {
    DemoArea demoArea;
    JTextArea textArea;
    final static String newline = "\n";

    public void init() {
        GridBagLayout gridbag = new GridBagLayout();
        GridBagConstraints c = new GridBagConstraints();
        JPanel contentPane = new JPanel();
        contentPane.setLayout(gridbag);

        c.fill = GridBagConstraints.BOTH;
        c.gridwidth = GridBagConstraints.REMAINDER;
        c.weightx = 1.0;
        c.weighty = 1.0;

        c.insets = new Insets(1, 1, 1, 1);
        demoArea = new DemoArea();
        gridbag.setConstraints(demoArea, c);
        contentPane.add(demoArea);

        c.insets = new Insets(0, 0, 0, 0);
        textArea = new JTextArea();
        textArea.setEditable(false);
        JScrollPane scrollPane = new JScrollPane(textArea);
        scrollPane.setVerticalScrollBarPolicy(
            JScrollPane.VERTICAL_SCROLLBAR_ALWAYS);
        scrollPane.setPreferredSize(new Dimension(200, 75));
        gridbag.setConstraints(scrollPane, c);
        contentPane.add(scrollPane);

        setContentPane(contentPane);
    }

    void saySomething(String eventDescription, TreeExpansionEvent e) {
        textArea.append(eventDescription + "; "
                        + "path = " + e.getPath()
                        + newline);
    }
```

Where Explained:

How to Write a Tree-Will-Expand Listener (page 516)

```java
class DemoArea extends JScrollPane
                implements TreeExpansionListener,
                           TreeWillExpandListener {
    Dimension minSize = new Dimension(100, 100);
    JTree tree;
    Object[] willExpandOptions = {"Cancel Expansion", "Expand"};
    String willExpandText = "A branch node is about to be expanded.\n"
                          + "Click \"Cancel Expansion\" to prevent it.";
    String willExpandTitle = "Tree Will Expand";

    public DemoArea() {
        TreeNode rootNode = createNodes();
        tree = new JTree(rootNode);
        tree.addTreeExpansionListener(this);
        tree.addTreeWillExpandListener(this);

        setViewportView(tree);
    }

    private TreeNode createNodes() {
        DefaultMutableTreeNode root;
        DefaultMutableTreeNode grandparent;
        DefaultMutableTreeNode parent;
        DefaultMutableTreeNode child;

        root = new DefaultMutableTreeNode("San Francisco");

        grandparent = new DefaultMutableTreeNode("Potrero Hill");
        root.add(grandparent);
        //
        parent = new DefaultMutableTreeNode("Restaurants");
        grandparent.add(parent);
        child = new DefaultMutableTreeNode("Thai Barbeque");
        parent.add(child);
        child = new DefaultMutableTreeNode("Goat Hill Pizza");
        parent.add(child);
        //
        parent = new DefaultMutableTreeNode("Grocery Stores");
        grandparent.add(parent);
        child = new DefaultMutableTreeNode("Good Life Grocery");
        parent.add(child);
        child = new DefaultMutableTreeNode("Safeway");
        parent.add(child);

        grandparent = new DefaultMutableTreeNode("Noe Valley");
        root.add(grandparent);
        //
        parent = new DefaultMutableTreeNode("Restaurants");
        grandparent.add(parent);
        child = new DefaultMutableTreeNode("Hamano Sushi");
        parent.add(child);
        child = new DefaultMutableTreeNode("Hahn's Hibachi");
        parent.add(child);
        //
        parent = new DefaultMutableTreeNode("Grocery Stores");
        grandparent.add(parent);
        child = new DefaultMutableTreeNode("Real Foods");
        parent.add(child);
        child = new DefaultMutableTreeNode("Bell Market");
        parent.add(child);

        return root;
    }

    public Dimension getMinimumSize() {
        return minSize;
    }
```

```
        public Dimension getPreferredSize() {
            return minSize;
        }

        // Required by TreeWillExpandListener interface.
        public void treeWillExpand(TreeExpansionEvent e)
                    throws ExpandVetoException {
            saySomething("Tree-will-expand event detected", e);
            int n = JOptionPane.showOptionDialog(
                this, willExpandText, willExpandTitle,
                JOptionPane.YES_NO_OPTION,
                JOptionPane.QUESTION_MESSAGE,
                null,
                willExpandOptions,
                willExpandOptions[1]);
            if (n == 0) {
                //User said cancel expansion.
                saySomething("Tree expansion cancelled", e);
                throw new ExpandVetoException(e);
            }
        }

        // Required by TreeWillExpandListener interface.
        public void treeWillCollapse(TreeExpansionEvent e) {
            saySomething("Tree-will-collapse event detected", e);
        }

        // Required by TreeExpansionListener interface.
        public void treeExpanded(TreeExpansionEvent e) {
            saySomething("Tree-expanded event detected", e);
        }

        // Required by TreeExpansionListener interface.
        public void treeCollapsed(TreeExpansionEvent e) {
            saySomething("Tree-collapsed event detected", e);
        }
    }
}
```

EXAMPLE: *WindowEventDemo.java*

SOURCE CODE: *http://java.sun.com/docs/books/tutorial/uiswing/events/example-swing/
             WindowEventDemo.java*

```
/*
 * Swing 1.1 version (compatible with both JDK 1.1 and Java 2).
 */

import javax.swing.*;

import java.awt.Dimension;
import java.awt.BorderLayout;

import java.awt.event.ActionListener;
import java.awt.event.ActionEvent;
import java.awt.event.WindowEvent;
import java.awt.event.WindowListener;

public class WindowEventDemo extends JApplet
                            implements WindowListener,
                                       ActionListener {
```

**Where
Explained:**
*How to Write a
Window
Listener*
(page 521)

```
JTextArea display;
JFrame window;
JButton b1, b2;
static final String SHOW = "show";
static final String CLEAR = "clear";
final static String newline = "\n";

public void init() {
    b1 = new JButton("Click to bring up a window.");
    b1.setActionCommand(SHOW);
    b1.addActionListener(this);

    b2 = new JButton("Click to clear the display.");
    b2.setActionCommand(CLEAR);
    b2.addActionListener(this);

    display = new JTextArea();
    display.setEditable(false);
    JScrollPane scrollPane = new JScrollPane(display);
    scrollPane.setPreferredSize(new Dimension(200, 75));

    JPanel contentPane = new JPanel();
    contentPane.setLayout(new BorderLayout());
    contentPane.add(b1, BorderLayout.NORTH);
    contentPane.add(scrollPane, BorderLayout.CENTER);
    contentPane.add(b2, BorderLayout.SOUTH);
    setContentPane(contentPane);

    //Create but don't show window.
    window = new JFrame("Window Event Window");
    window.addWindowListener(this);
    JLabel l = new JLabel("The applet listens to this window "
                          + "for window events.");
    window.getContentPane().add(l, BorderLayout.CENTER);
    window.pack();
}

public void stop() {
    window.setVisible(false);
}

public void windowClosing(WindowEvent e) {
    window.setVisible(false);
    displayMessage("Window closing", e);
}

public void windowClosed(WindowEvent e) {
    displayMessage("Window closed", e);
}

public void windowOpened(WindowEvent e) {
    displayMessage("Window opened", e);
}

public void windowIconified(WindowEvent e) {
    displayMessage("Window iconified", e);
}

public void windowDeiconified(WindowEvent e) {
    displayMessage("Window deiconified", e);
}

public void windowActivated(WindowEvent e) {
    displayMessage("Window activated", e);
}
```

```
        public void windowDeactivated(WindowEvent e) {
            displayMessage("Window deactivated", e);
        }

        void displayMessage(String prefix, WindowEvent e) {
            display.append(prefix + ": "  + e.getWindow() + newline);
        }

        public void actionPerformed(ActionEvent e) {
            if (e.getActionCommand() == SHOW) {
                window.pack();
                window.setVisible(true);
            } else {
                display.setText("");
            }
        }
    }
```

Working with Graphics

Complete examples in <u>Working with Graphics</u> (page 533):

EXAMPLE: *AnimatorAppletTimer.java*

**Where
Explained:**

*Creating an
Animation
Loop with
Timer*
(page 562)

SOURCE CODE: *http://java.sun.com/docs/books/tutorial/uiswing/painting/example-swing/
AnimatorAppletTimer.java*

```java
/*
 * Swing 1.1 version (compatible with both JDK 1.1 and Java 2).
 */

import java.awt.*;
import java.awt.event.*;
import javax.swing.*;

/*
 * A template for animation applets.
 */

public class AnimatorAppletTimer extends JApplet
                                 implements ActionListener {
    int frameNumber = -1;
    Timer timer;
    boolean frozen = false;
    JLabel label;

    public void init() {
        String str;
        int fps = 0;

        //How many milliseconds between frames?
        str = getParameter("fps");
        try {
            if (str != null) {
                fps = Integer.parseInt(str);
            }
        } catch (Exception e) {}
```

```
        int delay = (fps > 0) ? (1000 / fps) : 100;

        //Set up a timer that calls this object's action handler.
        timer = new Timer(delay, this);
        timer.setInitialDelay(0);
        timer.setCoalesce(true);

        label = new JLabel("Frame    ", JLabel.CENTER);

        label.addMouseListener(new MouseAdapter() {
            public void mousePressed(MouseEvent e) {
                if (frozen) {
                    frozen = false;
                    startAnimation();
                } else {
                    frozen = true;
                    stopAnimation();
                }
            }
        });

        getContentPane().add(label, BorderLayout.CENTER);
    }

    //Invoked by the browser only.  invokeLater not needed
    //because startAnimation can be called from any thread.
    public void start() {
        startAnimation();
    }

    //Invoked by the browser only.  invokeLater not needed
    //because stopAnimation can be called from any thread.
    public void stop() {
        stopAnimation();
    }

    //Can be invoked from any thread.
    public synchronized void startAnimation() {
        if (frozen) {
            //Do nothing.  The user has requested that we
            //stop changing the image.
        } else {
            //Start animating!
            if (!timer.isRunning()) {
                timer.start();
            }
        }
    }

    //Can be invoked from any thread.
    public synchronized void stopAnimation() {
        //Stop the animating thread.
        if (timer.isRunning()) {
            timer.stop();
        }
    }

    public void actionPerformed(ActionEvent e) {
        //Advance the animation frame.
        frameNumber++;

        //Request that the frame be painted.
        label.setText("Frame " + frameNumber);
    }
}
```

EXAMPLE: *AnimatorApplicationTimer.java*

Where Explained:

Creating an Animation Loop with Timer
(page 562)

SOURCE CODE: *http://java.sun.com/docs/books/tutorial/uiswing/painting/example-swing/ AnimatorApplicationTimer.java*

```java
/*
 * Swing 1.1 version (compatible with both JDK 1.1 and Java 2).
 */

import java.awt.*;
import java.awt.event.*;
import javax.swing.*;

/*
 * A template for animation applications.
 */
public class AnimatorApplicationTimer extends JFrame
                               implements ActionListener {
    int frameNumber = -1;
    Timer timer;
    boolean frozen = false;
    JLabel label;

    AnimatorApplicationTimer(int fps, String windowTitle) {
        super(windowTitle);
        int delay = (fps > 0) ? (1000 / fps) : 100;

        //Set up a timer that calls this object's action handler.
        timer = new Timer(delay, this);
        timer.setInitialDelay(0);
        timer.setCoalesce(true);

        addWindowListener(new WindowAdapter() {
            public void windowIconified(WindowEvent e) {
                stopAnimation();
            }
            public void windowDeiconified(WindowEvent e) {
                startAnimation();
            }
            public void windowClosing(WindowEvent e) {
                System.exit(0);
            }
        });

        label = new JLabel("Frame     ", JLabel.CENTER);
        label.addMouseListener(new MouseAdapter() {
            public void mousePressed(MouseEvent e) {
                if (frozen) {
                    frozen = false;
                    startAnimation();
                } else {
                    frozen = true;
                    stopAnimation();
                }
            }
        });

        getContentPane().add(label, BorderLayout.CENTER);
    }
```

```
        //Can be invoked by any thread (since timer is thread-safe).
        public void startAnimation() {
            if (frozen) {
                //Do nothing.  The user has requested that we
                //stop changing the image.
            } else {
                //Start animating!
                if (!timer.isRunning()) {
                    timer.start();
                }
            }
        }

        //Can be invoked by any thread (since timer is thread-safe).
        public void stopAnimation() {
            //Stop the animating thread.
            if (timer.isRunning()) {
                timer.stop();
            }
        }

        public void actionPerformed(ActionEvent e) {
            //Advance the animation frame.
            frameNumber++;
            label.setText("Frame " + frameNumber);
        }

        public static void main(String args[]) {
            AnimatorApplicationTimer animator = null;
            int fps = 10;

            //Get frames per second from the command line argument.
            if (args.length > 0) {
                try {
                    fps = Integer.parseInt(args[0]);
                } catch (Exception e) {}
            }
            animator = new AnimatorApplicationTimer(fps, "Animator with Timer");
            animator.pack();
            animator.setVisible(true);

            //It's OK to start the animation here because
            //startAnimation can be invoked by any thread.
            animator.startAnimation();
        }
    }
```

EXAMPLE: *CoordinatesDemo.java*

SOURCE CODE: *http://java.sun.com/docs/books/tutorial/uiswing/painting/example-swing/*
CoordinatesDemo.java

**Where
Explained:**

*The Coordinate
System*
(page 539)

```
/*
 * Swing 1.1 version (compatible with both JDK 1.1 and Java 2).
 */

import javax.swing.*;
import javax.swing.border.Border;
import javax.swing.event.*;
import java.awt.*;
import java.awt.event.*;
```

```
/*
 * This displays a framed area.  When the user clicks within
 * the area, this program displays a dot and a string indicating
 * the coordinates where the click occurred.
 */
public class CoordinatesDemo extends JApplet {
    JLabel label;

    //Called only when this is run as an applet.
    public void init() {
        buildUI(getContentPane());
    }

    void buildUI(Container container) {
        container.setLayout(new BoxLayout(container,
                                          BoxLayout.Y_AXIS));

        CoordinateArea coordinateArea = new CoordinateArea(this);
        container.add(coordinateArea);

        label = new JLabel("Click within the framed area.");
        container.add(label);

        //Align the left edges of the components.
        coordinateArea.setAlignmentX(LEFT_ALIGNMENT);
        label.setAlignmentX(LEFT_ALIGNMENT); //redundant
    }

    public void updateLabel(Point point) {
        label.setText("Click occurred at coordinate ("
                      + point.x + ", " + point.y + ").");
    }

    public static void main(String[] args) {
        JFrame f = new JFrame("CoordinatesDemo");
        f.addWindowListener(new WindowAdapter() {
            public void windowClosing(WindowEvent e) {
                System.exit(0);
            }
        });
        CoordinatesDemo controller = new CoordinatesDemo();
        controller.buildUI(f.getContentPane());
        f.pack();
        f.setVisible(true);
    }
}

class CoordinateArea extends JPanel {
    Point point = null;
    CoordinatesDemo controller;
    Dimension preferredSize = new Dimension(400,150);

    public CoordinateArea(CoordinatesDemo controller) {
        this.controller = controller;

        Border raisedBevel = BorderFactory.createRaisedBevelBorder();
        Border loweredBevel = BorderFactory.createLoweredBevelBorder();
        Border compound = BorderFactory.createCompoundBorder
                               (raisedBevel, loweredBevel);
        setBorder(compound);

        addMouseListener(new MouseAdapter() {
            public void mousePressed(MouseEvent e) {
                int x = e.getX();
                int y = e.getY();
                if (point == null) {
                    point = new Point(x, y);
```

```
                    } else {
                        point.x = x;
                        point.y = y;
                    }
                    repaint();
                }
            });
        }

        public Dimension getPreferredSize() {
            return preferredSize;
        }

        public void paintComponent(Graphics g) {
            super.paintComponent(g);   //paint background

            //If user has chosen a point, paint a tiny rectangle on top.
            if (point != null) {
                controller.updateLabel(point);
                g.fillRect(point.x - 1, point.y - 1, 2, 2);
            }
        }
    }
}
```

EXAMPLE: *FontDemo.java*

SOURCE CODE: *http://java.sun.com/docs/books/tutorial/uiswing/painting/example-swing/*
FontDemo.java

Where
Explained:

Getting Infor-
mation About a
Font: FontMet-
rics (page 551)

```
/*
 * Swing 1.1 version (compatible with both JDK 1.1 and Java 2).
 */

import java.awt.*;
import java.awt.event.*;
import javax.swing.*;

/*
 * This is like the ShapesDemo applet, except that it
 * handles fonts more carefully.
 */
public class FontDemo extends JApplet {
    /** Executed only in applet. */
    public void init() {
        FontPanel fontPanel = new FontPanel();
        getContentPane().add(fontPanel, BorderLayout.CENTER);
    }

    /** Executed only in application.*/
    public static void main(String[] args) {
        JFrame f = new JFrame("FontDemo");
        f.addWindowListener(new WindowAdapter() {
            public void windowClosing(WindowEvent e) {
                System.exit(0);
            }
        });
        FontPanel fontPanel = new FontPanel();
        f.getContentPane().add(fontPanel, BorderLayout.CENTER);
        f.setSize(550, 200);
        f.setVisible(true);
    }
}
```

```java
class FontPanel extends JPanel {
    final int maxCharHeight = 17;
    final int minFontSize = 6;
    final int maxFontSize = 14;
    final Color bg = Color.lightGray;
    final Color fg = Color.black;

    Dimension totalSize;
    FontMetrics fontMetrics;
    Font biggestFont = new Font("SansSerif", Font.PLAIN, maxFontSize);

    public FontPanel() {
        //Initialize drawing colors, border, opacity.
        setBackground(bg);
        setForeground(fg);
        setBorder(BorderFactory.createCompoundBorder(
                    BorderFactory.createRaisedBevelBorder(),
                    BorderFactory.createLoweredBevelBorder()));
    }

    FontMetrics pickFont(Graphics g,
                         String longString,
                         int xSpace) {
        boolean fontFits = false;
        Font currentFont = biggestFont;
        FontMetrics currentMetrics = getFontMetrics(currentFont);
        int size = currentFont.getSize();
        String name = currentFont.getName();
        int style = currentFont.getStyle();

        while (!fontFits) {
            if ( (currentMetrics.getHeight() <= maxCharHeight)
              && (currentMetrics.stringWidth(longString)
                  <= xSpace)) {
                fontFits = true;
            } else {
                if (size <= minFontSize) {
                    fontFits = true;
                } else {
                    currentFont = new Font(name, style, --size);
                    currentMetrics = getFontMetrics(currentFont);
                }
            }
        }

        //Must set font in both component and Graphics object.
        g.setFont(currentFont);
        setFont(currentFont);
        return currentMetrics;
    }

    public void paintComponent(Graphics g) {
        super.paintComponent(g);        //clears the background

        Dimension d = getSize();
        Insets insets = getInsets();
        int currentWidth = d.width - insets.left - insets.right;
        int currentHeight = d.height - insets.top - insets.bottom;
        int gridWidth = currentWidth / 7;
        int gridHeight = currentHeight / 2;

        if ( (totalSize == null)
          || (totalSize.width != currentWidth)
          || (totalSize.height != currentHeight) ) {
            totalSize = new Dimension(currentWidth, currentHeight);
            fontMetrics = pickFont(g, "drawRoundRect",
                                   gridWidth);
        }
```

```
Color fg3D = Color.lightGray;
int firstX = insets.left + 3;
int firstY = insets.top + 3;
int x = firstX;
int y = firstY;
int rectWidth = gridWidth - 2*x;
int stringY = gridHeight - 5 - fontMetrics.getDescent();
int rectHeight = stringY - fontMetrics.getMaxAscent() - y - 2;
// drawLine(x1, y1, x2, y2)
g.drawLine(x, y+rectHeight-1, x + rectWidth, y);
g.drawString("drawLine", x, stringY);
x += gridWidth;

// drawRect(x, y, w, h)
g.drawRect(x, y, rectWidth, rectHeight);
g.drawString("drawRect", x, stringY);
x += gridWidth;

// draw3DRect(x, y, w, h, raised)
g.setColor(fg3D);
g.draw3DRect(x, y, rectWidth, rectHeight, true);
g.setColor(fg);
g.drawString("draw3DRect", x, stringY);
x += gridWidth;

// drawRoundRect(x, y, w, h, arcw, arch)
g.drawRoundRect(x, y, rectWidth, rectHeight, 10, 10);
g.drawString("drawRoundRect", x, stringY);
x += gridWidth;

// drawOval(x, y, w, h)
g.drawOval(x, y, rectWidth, rectHeight);
g.drawString("drawOval", x, stringY);
x += gridWidth;

// drawArc(x, y, w, h)
g.drawArc(x, y, rectWidth, rectHeight, 90, 135);
g.drawString("drawArc", x, stringY);
x += gridWidth;

// drawPolygon(xPoints, yPoints, numPoints)
int x1Points[] = {x, x+rectWidth, x, x+rectWidth};
int y1Points[] = {y, y+rectHeight, y+rectHeight, y};
g.drawPolygon(x1Points, y1Points, x1Points.length);
g.drawString("drawPolygon", x, stringY);

// NEW ROW
x = firstX;
y += gridHeight;
stringY += gridHeight;

// drawPolyline(xPoints, yPoints, numPoints)
// Note: drawPolygon would close the polygon.
int x2Points[] = {x, x+rectWidth, x, x+rectWidth};
int y2Points[] = {y, y+rectHeight, y+rectHeight, y};
g.drawPolyline(x2Points, y2Points, x2Points.length);
g.drawString("drawPolyline", x, stringY);
x += gridWidth;

// fillRect(x, y, w, h)
g.fillRect(x, y, rectWidth, rectHeight);
g.drawString("fillRect", x, stringY);
x += gridWidth;
```

```
              // fill3DRect(x, y, w, h, raised)
              g.setColor(fg3D);
              g.fill3DRect(x, y, rectWidth, rectHeight, true);
              g.setColor(fg);
              g.drawString("fill3DRect", x, stringY);
              x += gridWidth;

              // fillRoundRect(x, y, w, h, arcw, arch)
              g.fillRoundRect(x, y, rectWidth, rectHeight, 10, 10);
              g.drawString("fillRoundRect", x, stringY);
              x += gridWidth;

              // fillOval(x, y, w, h)
              g.fillOval(x, y, rectWidth, rectHeight);
              g.drawString("fillOval", x, stringY);
              x += gridWidth;

              // fillArc(x, y, w, h)
              g.fillArc(x, y, rectWidth, rectHeight, 90, 135);
              g.drawString("fillArc", x, stringY);
              x += gridWidth;

              // fillPolygon(xPoints, yPoints, numPoints)
              int x3Points[] = {x, x+rectWidth, x, x+rectWidth};
              int y3Points[] = {y, y+rectHeight, y+rectHeight, y};
              g.fillPolygon(x3Points, y3Points, x3Points.length);
              g.drawString("fillPolygon", x, stringY);
       }
}
```

EXAMPLE: *ImageDisplayer.java*

**Where
Explained:**

*An Example of
Custom Paint-
ing* (page 538)
and
*Displaying
Images*
(page 559)

SOURCE CODE: *http://java.sun.com/docs/books/tutorial/uiswing/painting/example-swing/
                ImageDisplayer.java*

```
/*
 * Swing.
 */

import java.awt.*;
import java.awt.event.*;
import javax.swing.*;

/*
 * This applet displays a single image twice,
 * once at its normal size and once much wider.
 */
public class ImageDisplayer extends JApplet {
    static String imageFile = "images/rocketship.gif";

    public void init() {
        Image image = getImage(getCodeBase(), imageFile);
        ImagePanel imagePanel = new ImagePanel(image);
        getContentPane().add(imagePanel, BorderLayout.CENTER);
    }

    public static void main(String[] args) {
        Image image = Toolkit.getDefaultToolkit().getImage(
                                     ImageDisplayer.imageFile);
        ImagePanel imagePanel = new ImagePanel(image);

        JFrame f = new JFrame("ImageDisplayer");
```

```
        f.addWindowListener(new WindowAdapter() {
            public void windowClosing(WindowEvent e) {
                System.exit(0);
            }
        });

        f.getContentPane().add(imagePanel, BorderLayout.CENTER);
        f.setSize(new Dimension(550,100));
        f.setVisible(true);
    }
}

class ImagePanel extends JPanel {
    Image image;

    public ImagePanel(Image image) {
        this.image = image;
    }

    public void paintComponent(Graphics g) {
        super.paintComponent(g); //paint background

        //Draw image at its natural size first.
        g.drawImage(image, 0, 0, this); //85x62 image

        //Now draw the image scaled.
        g.drawImage(image, 90, 0, 300, 62, this);
    }
}
```

EXAMPLE: *ImageSequenceTimer.java*

SOURCE CODE: *http://java.sun.com/docs/books/tutorial/uiswing/painting/example-swing/
ImageSequenceTimer.java*

**Where
Explained:**

*Displaying a
Sequence of
Images*
(page 568)

```
/*
 * Swing 1.1 version (compatible with both JDK 1.1 and Java 2).
 */

import javax.swing.*;
import java.awt.*;
import java.awt.event.*;

/*
 * This applet displays several images in a row.  However,
 * it doesn't wait for the images to fully load before drawing
 * them, which causes the weird effect of the animation appearing
 * from the top down.
 */

public class ImageSequenceTimer extends JApplet
                                implements ActionListener {
    ImageSQPanel imageSQPanel;
    static int frameNumber = -1;
    int delay;
    Thread animatorThread;
    static boolean frozen = false;
    Timer timer;

    //Invoked only when this is run as an applet.
    public void init() {
        //Get the images.
        Image[] images = new Image[10];
```

```
        for (int i = 1; i <= 10; i++) {
            images[i-1] = getImage(getCodeBase(), "images/T"+i+".gif");
        }
        buildUI(getContentPane(), images);
        startAnimation();
    }

    //Note: Container must use BorderLayout, which is the
    //default layout manager for content panes.
    void buildUI(Container container, Image[] dukes) {
        int fps = 10;

        //How many milliseconds between frames?
        delay = (fps > 0) ? (1000 / fps) : 100;

        //Set up a timer that calls this object's action handler
        timer = new Timer(delay, this);
        timer.setInitialDelay(0);
        timer.setCoalesce(true);

        imageSQPanel = new ImageSQPanel(dukes);
        container.add(imageSQPanel, BorderLayout.CENTER);

        imageSQPanel.addMouseListener(new MouseAdapter() {
            public void mousePressed(MouseEvent e) {
                if (frozen) {
                    frozen = false;
                    startAnimation();
                } else {
                    frozen = true;
                    stopAnimation();
                }
            }
        });
    }

    public void start() {
        startAnimation();
    }

    public void stop() {
        stopAnimation();
    }

    public synchronized void startAnimation() {
        if (frozen) {
            //Do nothing.  The user has requested that we
            //stop changing the image.
        } else {
            //Start animating!
            if (!timer.isRunning()) {
                timer.start();
            }
        }
    }

    public synchronized void stopAnimation() {
        //Stop the animating thread.
        if (timer.isRunning()) {
            timer.stop();
        }
    }

    public void actionPerformed(ActionEvent e) {
        //Advance the animation frame.
        frameNumber++;
```

```
        //Display it.
        imageSQPanel.repaint();
    }

    class ImageSQPanel extends JPanel{
        Image dukesWave[];

        public ImageSQPanel(Image[] dukesWave) {
            this.dukesWave = dukesWave;
        }

        //Draw the current frame of animation.
        public void paintComponent(Graphics g) {
            super.paintComponent(g); //paint background

            //Paint the frame into the image.
            try {
                g.drawImage(dukesWave[ImageSequenceTimer.frameNumber%10],
                            0, 0, this);

            } catch (ArrayIndexOutOfBoundsException e) {
                //On rare occasions, this method can be called
                //when frameNumber is still -1.  Do nothing.
                return;
            }
        }
    }

    //Invoked only when this is run as an application.
    public static void main(String[] args) {
        Image[] waving = new Image[10];

        for (int i = 1; i <= 10; i++) {
            waving[i-1] =
                Toolkit.getDefaultToolkit().getImage(
                    "images/T"+i+".gif");
        }

        JFrame f = new JFrame("ImageSequenceTimer");
        f.addWindowListener(new WindowAdapter() {
            public void windowClosing(WindowEvent e) {
                System.exit(0);
            }
        });

        ImageSequenceTimer controller = new ImageSequenceTimer();
        controller.buildUI(f.getContentPane(), waving);
        controller.startAnimation();
        f.setSize(new Dimension(75, 100));
        f.setVisible(true);
    }
}
```

EXAMPLE: *MovingImageTimer.java*

SOURCE CODE: *http://java.sun.com/docs/books/tutorial/uiswing/painting/example-swing/ MovingImageTimer.java*

```
/*
 * Swing 1.1 version (compatible with both JDK 1.1 and Java 2).
 */
```

Where Explained:
Moving an Image Across the Screen
(page 565)

```java
import javax.swing.*;
import java.awt.*;
import java.awt.event.*;

/*
 * Moves a foreground image in front of a background image.
 * See MovingLabels.java for an alternative implementation
 * that uses two labels instead of doing its own painting.
 */
public class MovingImageTimer extends JApplet
                             implements ActionListener {
    int frameNumber = -1;
    boolean frozen = false;
    Timer timer;
    AnimationPane animationPane;

    static String fgFile = "images/rocketship.gif";
    static String bgFile = "images/starfield.gif";

    //Invoked only when run as an applet.
    public void init() {
        //Get the images.
        Image bgImage = getImage(getCodeBase(), bgFile);
        Image fgImage = getImage(getCodeBase(), fgFile);
        buildUI(getContentPane(), bgImage, fgImage);
    }

    void buildUI(Container container, Image bgImage, Image fgImage) {
        int fps = 10;

        //How many milliseconds between frames?
        int delay = (fps > 0) ? (1000 / fps) : 100;

        //Set up a timer that calls this object's action handler.
        timer = new Timer(delay, this);
        timer.setInitialDelay(0);
        timer.setCoalesce(true);

        animationPane = new AnimationPane(bgImage, fgImage);
        container.add(animationPane, BorderLayout.CENTER);

        animationPane.addMouseListener(new MouseAdapter() {
            public void mousePressed(MouseEvent e) {
                if (frozen) {
                    frozen = false;
                    startAnimation();
                } else {
                    frozen = true;
                    stopAnimation();
                }
            }
        });
    }

    //Invoked by a browser only.
    public void start() {
        startAnimation();
    }

    //Invoked by a browser only.
    public void stop() {
        stopAnimation();
    }

    //Can be invoked from any thread.
    public synchronized void startAnimation() {
```

```
        if (frozen) {
            //Do nothing.  The user has requested that we
            //stop changing the image.
        } else {
            //Start animating!
            if (!timer.isRunning()) {
                timer.start();
            }
        }
    }

    //Can be invoked from any thread.
    public synchronized void stopAnimation() {
        //Stop the animating thread.
        if (timer.isRunning()) {
            timer.stop();
        }
    }

    public void actionPerformed(ActionEvent e) {
        //Advance animation frame.
        frameNumber++;

        //Display it.
        animationPane.repaint();
    }

    class AnimationPane extends JPanel {
        Image background, foreground;

        public AnimationPane(Image background, Image foreground) {
            this.background = background;
            this.foreground = foreground;
        }

        //Draw the current frame of animation.
        public void paintComponent(Graphics g) {
            super.paintComponent(g);   //paint any space not covered
                                       //by the background image
            int compWidth = getWidth();
            int compHeight = getHeight();
            int imageWidth, imageHeight;

            //If we have a valid width and height for the
            //background image, draw it.
            imageWidth = background.getWidth(this);
            imageHeight = background.getHeight(this);
            if ((imageWidth > 0) && (imageHeight > 0)) {
                g.drawImage(background,
                        (compWidth - imageWidth)/2,
                        (compHeight - imageHeight)/2, this);
            }

            //If we have a valid width and height for the
            //foreground image, draw it.
            imageWidth = foreground.getWidth(this);
            imageHeight = foreground.getHeight(this);
            if ((imageWidth > 0) && (imageHeight > 0)) {
                g.drawImage(foreground,
                        ((frameNumber*5)
                          % (imageWidth + compWidth))
                          - imageWidth,
                        (compHeight - imageHeight)/2,
                        this);
            }
        }
    }
}
```

```
        //Invoked only when run as an application.
        public static void main(String[] args) {
            Image bgImage = Toolkit.getDefaultToolkit().getImage(
                                 MovingImageTimer.bgFile);
            Image fgImage = Toolkit.getDefaultToolkit().getImage(
                                 MovingImageTimer.fgFile);

            JFrame f = new JFrame("MovingImageTimer");
            final MovingImageTimer controller = new MovingImageTimer();
            controller.buildUI(f.getContentPane(), bgImage, fgImage);

            f.addWindowListener(new WindowAdapter() {
                public void windowIconified(WindowEvent e) {
                    controller.stopAnimation();
                }
                public void windowDeiconified(WindowEvent e) {
                    controller.startAnimation();
                }
                public void windowClosing(WindowEvent e) {
                    System.exit(0);
                }
            });
            f.setSize(new Dimension(500, 125));
            f.setVisible(true);
            controller.startAnimation();
        }
    }
```

EXAMPLE: *MovingLabels.java*

Where Explained:

Moving an Image Across the Screen
(page 565)

SOURCE CODE: *http://java.sun.com/docs/books/tutorial/uiswing/painting/example-swing/ MovingLabels.java*

```
/*
 * Swing 1.1 version (compatible with both JDK 1.1 and Java 2).
 */

import java.awt.*;
import java.awt.event.*;
import javax.swing.*;

public class MovingLabels extends JApplet
                          implements ActionListener {
    int frameNumber = -1;
    Timer timer;
    boolean frozen = false;

    JLayeredPane layeredPane;
    JLabel bgLabel, fgLabel;
    int fgHeight, fgWidth;
    int bgHeight, bgWidth;
    static String fgFile = "images/rocketship.gif";
    static String bgFile = "images/starfield.gif";

    //Invoked only when run as an applet.
    public void init() {
        Image bgImage = getImage(getCodeBase(), bgFile);
        Image fgImage = getImage(getCodeBase(), fgFile);
        buildUI(getContentPane(), bgImage, fgImage);
    }

    void buildUI(Container container, Image bgImage, Image fgImage) {
        final ImageIcon bgIcon = new ImageIcon(bgImage);
```

```java
        final ImageIcon fgIcon = new ImageIcon(fgImage);
        bgWidth = bgIcon.getIconWidth();
        bgHeight = bgIcon.getIconHeight();
        fgWidth = fgIcon.getIconWidth();
        fgHeight = fgIcon.getIconHeight();

        //Set up a timer that calls this object's action handler
        timer = new Timer(100, this); //delay = 100 ms
        timer.setInitialDelay(0);
        timer.setCoalesce(true);

        //Create a label to display the background image.
        bgLabel = new JLabel(bgIcon);
        bgLabel.setOpaque(true);
        bgLabel.setBounds(0, 0, bgWidth, bgHeight);

        //Create a label to display the foreground image.
        fgLabel = new JLabel(fgIcon);
        fgLabel.setBounds(-fgWidth, -fgHeight, fgWidth, fgHeight);

        //Create the layered pane to hold the labels.
        layeredPane = new JLayeredPane();
        layeredPane.setPreferredSize.new Dimension(bgWidth, bgHeight));
        layeredPane.addMouseListener(new MouseAdapter() {
            public void mousePressed(MouseEvent e) {
                if (frozen) {
                    frozen = false;
                    startAnimation();
                } else {
                    frozen = true;
                    stopAnimation();
                }
            }
        });

        layeredPane.add(bgLabel, 0);  //low layer
        layeredPane.add(fgLabel, 1);  //high layer
        container.add(layeredPane, BorderLayout.CENTER);
    }

    //Invoked by the applet browser only.
    public void start() {
        startAnimation();
    }

    //Invoked by the applet browser only.
    public void stop() {
        stopAnimation();
    }

    public synchronized void startAnimation() {
        if (frozen) {
            //Do nothing.  The user has requested that we
            //stop changing the image.
        } else {
            //Start animating!
            if (!timer.isRunning()) {
                timer.start();
            }
        }
    }

    public synchronized void stopAnimation() {
        //Stop the animating thread.
        if (timer.isRunning()) {
            timer.stop();
        }
    }
```

```java
    public void actionPerformed(ActionEvent e) {
        //Advance animation frame.
        frameNumber++;

        //Display it.
        fgLabel.setLocation(
            ((frameNumber*5)
             % (fgWidth + bgWidth))
            - fgWidth,
            (bgHeight - fgHeight)/2);
    }

    //Invoked only when run as an application.
    public static void main(String[] args) {
        Image bgImage = Toolkit.getDefaultToolkit().getImage(
                            MovingLabels.bgFile);
        Image fgImage = Toolkit.getDefaultToolkit().getImage(
                            MovingLabels.fgFile);
        final MovingLabels movingLabels = new MovingLabels();
        JFrame f = new JFrame("MovingLabels");
        f.addWindowListener(new WindowAdapter() {
            public void windowIconified(WindowEvent e) {
                movingLabels.stopAnimation();
            }
            public void windowDeiconified(WindowEvent e) {
                movingLabels.startAnimation();
            }
            public void windowClosing(WindowEvent e) {
                System.exit(0);
            }
        });
        movingLabels.buildUI(f.getContentPane(), bgImage, fgImage);
        f.setSize(500, 125);
        f.setVisible(true);
        movingLabels.startAnimation();
    }
}
```

EXAMPLE: *MTImageSequenceTimer.java*

Where Explained:
Using Media-Tracker to Download Images and Delay Image Display
(page 569)

SOURCE CODE: *http://java.sun.com/docs/books/tutorial/uiswing/painting/example-swing/ MTImageSequenceTimer.java*

```java
/*
 * Swing 1.1 version (compatible with both JDK 1.1 and Java 2).
 */

import javax.swing.*;
import java.awt.*;
import java.awt.event.*;

/*
 * This applet displays several images in a row.  It preloads
 * the images using MediaTracker, which uses multiple background
 * threads to download the images.  The program displays a
 * "Please wait" message until all the images are fully loaded.
 * Note that the Swing ImageIcon class uses MediaTracker to
 * preload images, so you can often use it instead of using
 * Images and MediaTracker directly.
 */

public class MTImageSequenceTimer extends JApplet
                                  implements ActionListener {
```

```
MTPanel mtPanel;
static int frameNumber = -1;
int delay;
static boolean frozen = false;
Timer timer;
boolean error;
MediaTracker tracker;

//Invoked only when run as an applet.
public void init() {
    //Load the images.
    Image images[] = new Image[10];
    for (int i = 1; i <= 10; i++) {
        images[i-1] = getImage(getCodeBase(), "images/T"+i+".gif");
    }
    buildUI(getContentPane(), images);
    startAnimation();
}

void buildUI(Container container, Image[] dukes) {
    tracker = new MediaTracker(this);
    for (int i = 1; i <= 10; i++) {
        tracker.addImage(dukes[i-1], 0);
        error = tracker.isErrorAny();
    }

    int fps = 10;

    //How many milliseconds between frames?
    delay = (fps > 0) ? (1000 / fps) : 100;

    //Set up a timer that calls this object's action handler.
    timer = new Timer(delay, this);
    timer.setInitialDelay(0);
    timer.setCoalesce(true);

    mtPanel = new MTPanel(dukes);
    container.add(mtPanel, BorderLayout.CENTER);

    mtPanel.addMouseListener(new MouseAdapter() {
        public void mousePressed(MouseEvent e) {
            if (frozen) {
                frozen = false;
                startAnimation();
            } else {
                frozen = true;
                stopAnimation();
            }
        }
    });
}

public void start() {
    startAnimation();
}

public void stop() {
    stopAnimation();
}

public synchronized void startAnimation() {
    if (frozen) {
        //Do nothing.  The user has requested that we
        //stop changing the image.
    } else {
        //Start animating!
```

```java
        if (!timer.isRunning()) {
            timer.start();
        }
    }
}

public synchronized void stopAnimation() {
    //Stop the animating thread.
    if (timer.isRunning()) {
        timer.stop();
    }
}

public void actionPerformed(ActionEvent e) {
    //Start downloading the images. Wait until they're
    //loaded before requesting repaints.
    try {
        tracker.waitForAll();
    } catch (InterruptedException exc) {}

    //Advance the frame.
    frameNumber++;

    //Display it.
    mtPanel.repaint();
}

class MTPanel extends JPanel {
    Image dukesWave[];

    public MTPanel(Image[] dukesWave) {
        this.dukesWave = dukesWave;
    }

    //Draw the current frame of animation.
    public void paintComponent(Graphics g) {
        super.paintComponent(g); //paint the background
        int width = getWidth();
        int height = getHeight();

        //If not all the images are loaded,
        //just display a status string.
        if (!tracker.checkAll()) {
            g.drawString("Please wait...", 0, height/2);
            return;
        }

        //Paint the frame into the image.
        g.drawImage(dukesWave[MTImageSequenceTimer.frameNumber%10],
                0, 0, this);
    }
}

//Invoked only when run as an application.
public static void main(String[] args) {
    Image[] waving = new Image[10];
    for (int i = 1; i <= 10; i++) {
        waving[i-1] =
            Toolkit.getDefaultToolkit().getImage("images/T"+i+".gif");
    }

    JFrame f = new JFrame("MTImageSequenceTimer");
    f.addWindowListener(new WindowAdapter() {
        public void windowClosing(WindowEvent e) {
            System.exit(0);
        }
    });
```

```
        MTImageSequenceTimer controller = new MTImageSequenceTimer();
        controller.buildUI(f.getContentPane(), waving);
        controller.startAnimation();
        f.setSize(new Dimension(75, 100));
        f.setVisible(true);
    }
}
```

EXAMPLE: *RectangleDemo.java*

SOURCE CODE: *http://java.sun.com/docs/books/tutorial/uiswing/painting/example-swing/ RectangleDemo.java*

Where Explained:

Example 1: Simple Rectangle Painting (page 546)

```java
/*
 * Swing 1.1 version (compatible with both JDK 1.1 and Java 2).
 */

import javax.swing.*;
import javax.swing.border.Border;
import javax.swing.event.*;
import java.awt.*;
import java.awt.event.*;

/*
 * Displays a framed area.  When the user clicks within
 * the area, this program displays a filled rectangle
 * and a string indicating the coordinates where the
 * click occurred.
 */

public class RectangleDemo extends JApplet {
    JLabel label;

    //Called only when this is run as an applet.
    public void init() {
        buildUI(getContentPane());
    }

    void buildUI(Container container) {
        container.setLayout(new BoxLayout(container,
                                    BoxLayout.Y_AXIS));

        RectangleArea rectangleArea = new RectangleArea(this);
        container.add(rectangleArea);

        label = new JLabel("Click within the framed area.");
        container.add(label);

        //Align the left edges of the components.
        rectangleArea.setAlignmentX(LEFT_ALIGNMENT);
        label.setAlignmentX(LEFT_ALIGNMENT); //unnecessary, but doesn't hurt
    }

    public void updateLabel(Point point) {
        label.setText("Click occurred at coordinate ("
                    + point.x + ", " + point.y + ").");
    }

    //Called only when this is run as an application.
    public static void main(String[] args) {
        JFrame f = new JFrame("RectangleDemo");
        f.addWindowListener(new WindowAdapter() {
```

```
                public void windowClosing(WindowEvent e) {
                    System.exit(0);
                }
            });
            RectangleDemo controller = new RectangleDemo();
            controller.buildUI(f.getContentPane());
            f.pack();
            f.setVisible(true);
        }
    }

class RectangleArea extends JPanel {
    Point point = null;
    RectangleDemo controller;
    Dimension preferredSize = new Dimension(300,100);
    int rectWidth = 50;
    int rectHeight = 50;

    public RectangleArea(RectangleDemo controller) {
        this.controller = controller;

        Border raisedBevel = BorderFactory.createRaisedBevelBorder();
        Border loweredBevel = BorderFactory.createLoweredBevelBorder();
        Border compound = BorderFactory.createCompoundBorder
                                (raisedBevel, loweredBevel);
        setBorder(compound);

        addMouseListener(new MouseAdapter() {
            public void mousePressed(MouseEvent e) {
                int x = e.getX();
                int y = e.getY();
                if (point == null) {
                    point = new Point(x, y);
                } else {
                    point.x = x;
                    point.y = y;
                }
                repaint();
            }
        });
    }

    public Dimension getPreferredSize() {
        return preferredSize;
    }

    public void paintComponent(Graphics g) {
        super.paintComponent(g);   //paint background

        //Paint a filled rectangle at user's chosen point.
        if (point != null) {
            g.drawRect(point.x, point.y,
                        rectWidth - 1, rectHeight - 1);
            g.setColor(Color.yellow);
            g.fillRect(point.x + 1, point.y + 1,
                        rectWidth - 2, rectHeight - 2);

            controller.updateLabel(point);
        }
    }
}
```

EXAMPLE: *SelectionDemo.java*

Where Explained:
Arguments to the repaint Method
(page 540)

SOURCE CODE: *http://java.sun.com/docs/books/tutorial/uiswing/painting/example-swing/ SelectionDemo.java*

```java
/*
 * 1.1 Swing 1.1 version (compatible with both JDK 1.1 and Java 2).
 */

import javax.swing.*;
import javax.swing.border.Border;
import javax.swing.event.*;
import java.awt.*;
import java.awt.event.*;

/*
 * This displays a framed area.  When the user drags within
 * the area, this program displays a rectangle and a string
 * indicating the bounds of the rectangle.
 */
public class SelectionDemo extends JApplet {
    JLabel label;
    static String starFile = "images/starfield.gif";

    //Called only when this is run as an applet.
    public void init() {
        ImageIcon image = new ImageIcon(getImage(getCodeBase(),
                                                   starFile));
        buildUI(getContentPane(), image);
    }

    void buildUI(Container container, ImageIcon image) {
        container.setLayout(new BoxLayout(container,
                                    BoxLayout.Y_AXIS));

        JPanel framedArea = frameItUp(new SelectionArea(image, this));
        container.add(framedArea);

        label = new JLabel("Drag within the framed area.");
        container.add(label);

        //Align the left edges of the components.
        framedArea.setAlignmentX(LEFT_ALIGNMENT);
        label.setAlignmentX(LEFT_ALIGNMENT); //redundant
    }

    JPanel frameItUp(Component insides) {
        Border raisedBevel, loweredBevel, compound;
        raisedBevel = BorderFactory.createRaisedBevelBorder();
        loweredBevel = BorderFactory.createLoweredBevelBorder();
        compound = BorderFactory.createCompoundBorder
                        (raisedBevel, loweredBevel);

        JPanel framedArea = new JPanel();
        framedArea.setBorder(compound);
        framedArea.setLayout(new GridLayout(1,0));
        framedArea.add(insides);

        return framedArea;
    }

    public void updateLabel(Rectangle rect) {
        int width = rect.width;
        int height = rect.height;
```

```
            //Make the coordinates look OK if a dimension is 0.
            if (width == 0) {
                width = 1;
            }
            if (height == 0) {
                height = 1;
            }

            label.setText("Rectangle goes from ("
                            + rect.x + ", " + rect.y + ") to ("
                            + (rect.x + width - 1) + ", "
                            + (rect.y + height - 1) + ").");
        }

    public static void main(String[] args) {
        JFrame f = new JFrame("SelectionDemo");
        f.addWindowListener(new WindowAdapter() {
            public void windowClosing(WindowEvent e) {
                System.exit(0);
            }
        });
        SelectionDemo controller = new SelectionDemo();
        controller.buildUI(f.getContentPane(),
                            new ImageIcon(starFile));
        f.pack();
        f.setVisible(true);
    }
}

class SelectionArea extends JLabel {
    Rectangle currentRect = null;
    Rectangle rectToDraw = null;
    Rectangle previousRectDrawn = new Rectangle();
    SelectionDemo controller;

    public SelectionArea(ImageIcon image, SelectionDemo controller) {
        super(image); //This component displays an image.
        this.controller = controller;
        setOpaque(true);
        setMinimumSize(new Dimension(10,10)); //don't hog space

        MyListener myListener = new MyListener();
        addMouseListener(myListener);
        addMouseMotionListener(myListener);
    }

    class MyListener extends MouseInputAdapter {
        public void mousePressed(MouseEvent e) {
            int x = e.getX();
            int y = e.getY();
            currentRect = new Rectangle(x, y, 0, 0);
            updateDrawableRect(getWidth(), getHeight());
            repaint();
        }

        public void mouseDragged(MouseEvent e) {
            updateSize(e);
        }

        public void mouseReleased(MouseEvent e) {
            updateSize(e);
        }

        /*
         * Update the size of the current rectangle
         * and call repaint.  Because currentRect
         * always has the same origin, translate it
         * if the width or height is negative.
```

```
     *  For efficiency (though
     *  that isn't an issue for this program),
     *  specify the painting region using arguments
     *  to the repaint() call.
     *
     */
    void updateSize(MouseEvent e) {
        int x = e.getX();
        int y = e.getY();
        currentRect.setSize(x - currentRect.x, y - currentRect.y);
        updateDrawableRect(getWidth(), getHeight());
        Rectangle totalRepaint = rectToDraw.union(previousRectDrawn);
        repaint(totalRepaint.x, totalRepaint.y,
                totalRepaint.width, totalRepaint.height);
    }
}

public void paintComponent(Graphics g) {
    super.paintComponent(g); //paints the background and image

    //If currentRect exists, paint a box on top.
    if (currentRect != null) {
        //Draw a rectangle on top of the image.
// XXX: We used to use XOR mode, but in 1.2, due to bugs 4188795
// XXX: and 4219548, that causes an off-by-one error.
        //g.setXORMode(Color.white); //Color of line varies
                                    //depending on image colors
        g.setColor(Color.white);
        g.drawRect(rectToDraw.x, rectToDraw.y,
                rectToDraw.width - 1, rectToDraw.height - 1);

        controller.updateLabel(rectToDraw);
    }
}

void updateDrawableRect(int compWidth, int compHeight) {
    int x = currentRect.x;
    int y = currentRect.y;
    int width = currentRect.width;
    int height = currentRect.height;

    //Make the width and height positive, if necessary.
    if (width < 0) {
        width = 0 - width;
        x = x - width + 1;
        if (x < 0) {
            width += x;
            x = 0;
        }
    }
    if (height < 0) {
        height = 0 - height;
        y = y - height + 1;
        if (y < 0) {
            height += y;
            y = 0;
        }
    }

    //The rectangle shouldn't extend past the drawing area.
    if ((x + width) > compWidth) {
        width = compWidth - x;
    }
    if ((y + height) > compHeight) {
        height = compHeight - y;
    }
```

```
                    //Update rectToDraw after saving old value.
                    if (rectToDraw != null) {
                        previousRectDrawn.setBounds(
                                    rectToDraw.x, rectToDraw.y,
                                    rectToDraw.width, rectToDraw.height);
                        rectToDraw.setBounds(x, y, width, height);
                    } else {
                        rectToDraw = new Rectangle(x, y, width, height);
                    }
                }
            }
        }
```

EXAMPLE: *ShapesDemo.java*

**Where
Explained:**

*Example 2: A
Shape Sampler*
(page 548)

SOURCE CODE: *http://java.sun.com/docs/books/tutorial/uiswing/painting/example-swing/
                ShapesDemo.java*

```java
/*
 * Swing 1.1 version (compatible with both JDK 1.1 and Java 2).
 */

import javax.swing.*;
import java.awt.*;
import java.awt.event.*;

/*
 * This displays a framed area containing one of
 * each shape you can draw.
 */
public class ShapesDemo extends JApplet {

    //Executed only when this program is run as an applet.
    public void init() {
        ShapesPanel shapesPanel = new ShapesPanel();
        getContentPane().add(shapesPanel, BorderLayout.CENTER);
    }

    //Executed only when this program is run as an applicaiton.
    public static void main(String[] args) {
        JFrame f = new JFrame("ShapesDemo");
        f.addWindowListener(new WindowAdapter() {
            public void windowClosing(WindowEvent e) {
                System.exit(0);
            }
        });

        ShapesPanel shapesPanel = new ShapesPanel();
        f.getContentPane().add(shapesPanel, BorderLayout.CENTER);
        f.setSize(new Dimension(550, 200));
        f.setVisible(true);
    }
}

class ShapesPanel extends JPanel {
    final int maxCharHeight = 15;
    final Color bg = Color.lightGray;
    final Color fg = Color.black;

    public ShapesPanel() {
        //Initialize drawing colors, border, opacity.
        setBackground(bg);
        setForeground(fg);
```

```
        setBorder(BorderFactory.createCompoundBorder(
                BorderFactory.createRaisedBevelBorder(),
                BorderFactory.createLoweredBevelBorder()));
}

public void paintComponent(Graphics g) {
    super.paintComponent(g);        //clears the background

    Insets insets = getInsets();
    int currentWidth = getWidth() - insets.left - insets.right;
    int currentHeight = getHeight() - insets.top - insets.bottom;
    int gridWidth = currentWidth / 7;
    int gridHeight = currentHeight / 2;

    Color fg3D = Color.lightGray;
    int firstX = insets.left + 3;
    int firstY = insets.top + 3;
    int x = firstX;
    int y = firstY;
    int stringY = gridHeight - 7;
    int rectWidth = gridWidth - 2*x;
    int rectHeight = stringY - maxCharHeight - y;

    // drawLine(x1, y1, x2, y2)
    g.drawLine(x, y+rectHeight-1, x + rectWidth, y);
    g.drawString("drawLine", x, stringY);
    x += gridWidth;

    // drawRect(x, y, w, h)
    g.drawRect(x, y, rectWidth, rectHeight);
    g.drawString("drawRect", x, stringY);
    x += gridWidth;

    // draw3DRect(x, y, w, h, raised)
    g.setColor(fg3D);
    g.draw3DRect(x, y, rectWidth, rectHeight, true);
    g.setColor(fg);
    g.drawString("draw3DRect", x, stringY);
    x += gridWidth;

    // drawRoundRect(x, y, w, h, arcw, arch)
    g.drawRoundRect(x, y, rectWidth, rectHeight, 10, 10);
    g.drawString("drawRoundRect", x, stringY);
    x += gridWidth;

    // drawOval(x, y, w, h)
    g.drawOval(x, y, rectWidth, rectHeight);
    g.drawString("drawOval", x, stringY);
    x += gridWidth;

    // drawArc(x, y, w, h)
    g.drawArc(x, y, rectWidth, rectHeight, 90, 135);
    g.drawString("drawArc", x, stringY);
    x += gridWidth;

    // drawPolygon(xPoints, yPoints, numPoints)
    int x1Points[] = {x, x+rectWidth, x, x+rectWidth};
    int y1Points[] = {y, y+rectHeight, y+rectHeight, y};
    g.drawPolygon(x1Points, y1Points, x1Points.length);
    g.drawString("drawPolygon", x, stringY);

    // NEW ROW
    x = firstX;
    y += gridHeight;
    stringY += gridHeight;
```

```
        // drawPolyline(xPoints, yPoints, numPoints)
        // Note: drawPolygon would close the polygon.
        int x2Points[] = {x, x+rectWidth, x, x+rectWidth};
        int y2Points[] = {y, y+rectHeight, y+rectHeight, y};
        g.drawPolyline(x2Points, y2Points, x2Points.length);
        g.drawString("drawPolyline", x, stringY);
        x += gridWidth;

        // fillRect(x, y, w, h)
        g.fillRect(x, y, rectWidth, rectHeight);
        g.drawString("fillRect", x, stringY);
        x += gridWidth;

        // fill3DRect(x, y, w, h, raised)
        g.setColor(fg3D);
        g.fill3DRect(x, y, rectWidth, rectHeight, true);
        g.setColor(fg);
        g.drawString("fill3DRect", x, stringY);
        x += gridWidth;

        // fillRoundRect(x, y, w, h, arcw, arch)
        g.fillRoundRect(x, y, rectWidth, rectHeight, 10, 10);
        g.drawString("fillRoundRect", x, stringY);
        x += gridWidth;

        // fillOval(x, y, w, h)
        g.fillOval(x, y, rectWidth, rectHeight);
        g.drawString("fillOval", x, stringY);
        x += gridWidth;

        // fillArc(x, y, w, h)
        g.fillArc(x, y, rectWidth, rectHeight, 90, 135);
        g.drawString("fillArc", x, stringY);
        x += gridWidth;

        // fillPolygon(xPoints, yPoints, numPoints)
        int x3Points[] = {x, x+rectWidth, x, x+rectWidth};
        int y3Points[] = {y, y+rectHeight, y+rectHeight, y};
        g.fillPolygon(x3Points, y3Points, x3Points.length);
        g.drawString("fillPolygon", x, stringY);
    }
}
```

EXAMPLE: *TextXY.java*

**Where
Explained:**
Painting Text
(page 550)

SOURCE CODE: *http://java.sun.com/docs/books/tutorial/uiswing/painting/example-swing/
                TextXY.java*

```
/*
 * Swing 1.1 version (compatible with both JDK 1.1 and Java 2).
 */

import java.awt.*;
import java.awt.event.*;
import javax.swing.*;

/*
 * Very simple applet that illustrates parameters to text-drawing methods.
 */
public class TextXY extends JApplet {
    //Invoked only when executed as applet.
    public void init() {
        buildUI(getContentPane());
    }
```

```java
public void buildUI(Container container) {
    TextPanel textPanel = new TextPanel();
    container.add(textPanel, BorderLayout.CENTER);
}

class TextPanel extends JPanel {
    public TextPanel() {
        setPreferredSize(new Dimension(400, 100));
    }

    public void paintComponent(Graphics g) {
        super.paintComponent(g);
        g.drawString("drawString() at (2, 5)", 2, 5);
        g.drawString("drawString() at (2, 30)", 2, 30);
        g.drawString("drawString() at (2, height)", 2, getHeight());
    }
}

//Invoked only when executed as application.
public static void main(String[] args) {
    JFrame f = new JFrame("TextXY");
    f.addWindowListener(new WindowAdapter() {
        public void windowClosing(WindowEvent e) {
            System.exit(0);
        }
    });

    TextXY controller = new TextXY();
    controller.buildUI(f.getContentPane());
    f.pack();
    f.setVisible(true);
}
}
```

Converting to Swing

Complete Swing examples in <u>Converting to Swing</u> (page 575):

Complete AWT examples:

EXAMPLE: *AnimatorApplication.java*

**Where
Explained:**

*Converting
Animator-
Application*
(page 596)

AWT Version: <u>AnimatorApplication.java</u> *(page 909)*

Associated File(s): <u>AnimatorApplicationTimer.java</u> *(page 889)*

SOURCE CODE: *http://java.sun.com/docs/books/tutorial/uiswing/converting/example-swing/
AnimatorApplication.java*

```
/*
 * Swing 1.1 version (compatible with both JDK 1.1 and Java 2).
 */
```

```
import java.awt.*;
import java.awt.event.*;
import javax.swing.*;

/*
 * Based on Arthur van Hoff's animation examples, this application
 * can serve as a template for all animation applications.
 */
public class AnimatorApplication extends JFrame
                                 implements Runnable {
    AnimappPanel animappPanel;
    int frameNumber = -1;
    int delay;
    Thread animatorThread;
    boolean frozen = false;

    AnimatorApplication(int fps, String windowTitle) {
        super(windowTitle);
        delay = (fps > 0) ? (1000 / fps) : 100;

        animappPanel = new AnimappPanel();
        getContentPane().add(animappPanel);

        addMouseListener(new MouseAdapter() {
            public void mousePressed(MouseEvent e) {
                if (frozen) {
                    frozen = false;
                    startAnimation();
                } else {
                    frozen = true;
                    stopAnimation();
                }
            }
        });

        addWindowListener(new WindowAdapter() {
            public void windowIconified(WindowEvent e) {
                stopAnimation();
            }
            public void windowDeiconified(WindowEvent e) {
                startAnimation();
            }
            public void windowClosing(WindowEvent e) {
                System.exit(0);
            }
        });
    }

    public void startAnimation() {
        if (frozen) {
            //Do nothing.  The user has requested that we
            //stop changing the image.
        } else {
            //Start animating!
            if (animatorThread == null) {
                animatorThread = new Thread(this);
            }
            animatorThread.start();
        }
    }

    public void stopAnimation() {
        //Stop the animating thread.
        animatorThread = null;
    }
```

```java
    public void run() {
        //Just to be nice, lower this thread's priority
        //so it can't interfere with other processing going on.
        Thread.currentThread().setPriority(Thread.MIN_PRIORITY);

        //Remember the starting time.
        long startTime = System.currentTimeMillis();

        //Remember which thread we are.
        Thread currentThread = Thread.currentThread();

        //This is the animation loop.
        while (currentThread == animatorThread) {
            //Advance the animation frame.
            frameNumber++;

            //Display it.
            repaint();

            //Delay depending on how far we are behind.
            try {
                startTime += delay;
                Thread.sleep(Math.max(0,
                             startTime-System.currentTimeMillis()));
            } catch (InterruptedException e) {
                break;
            }
        }
    }
}

class AnimappPanel extends JPanel {

    public AnimappPanel() {}

    //Draw the current frame of animation.
    public void paintComponent(Graphics g) {
        super.paintComponent(g);
        g.drawString("Frame " + frameNumber, 5, 50);
    }
}

    public static void main(String args[]) {
        AnimatorApplication animator = null;
        int fps = 10;

        // Get frames per second from the command line argument
        if (args.length > 0) {
            try {
                fps = Integer.parseInt(args[0]);
            } catch (Exception e) {}
        }
        animator = new AnimatorApplication(fps, "Animator");
        animator.setSize(200, 60);
        animator.setVisible(true);
        animator.startAnimation();
    }
}
```

EXAMPLE: *AnimatorApplicationTimer.java*

Main Source File: `AnimatorApplication.java` *(page 886)*

SOURCE CODE: *http://java.sun.com/docs/books/tutorial/uiswing/painting/example-swing/*
AnimatorApplicationTimer.java

Where Explained:
Converting Animator- Application (page 596)

```
/*
 * Swing 1.1 version (compatible with both JDK 1.1 and Java 2).
 */

import java.awt.*;
import java.awt.event.*;
import javax.swing.*;

/*
 * Based on Arthur van Hoff's animation examples, this application
 * can serve as a template for all animation applications.
 */
public class AnimatorApplicationTimer extends JFrame implements ActionListener {
    int frameNumber = -1;
    int delay;
    boolean frozen = false;
    JLabel label;
    Timer timer; //Is the priority of this thread too high?
                 //Sometimes I can't interrupt the program easily.

    AnimatorApplicationTimer(int fps, String windowTitle) {
        super(windowTitle);
        delay = (fps > 0) ? (1000 / fps) : 100;

        //Set up a timer that calls this object's action handler.
        timer = new Timer(delay, this);
        timer.setInitialDelay(0);
        timer.setCoalesce(true);

        addWindowListener(new WindowAdapter() {
            public void windowIconified(WindowEvent e) {
                stopAnimation();
            }
            public void windowDeiconified(WindowEvent e) {
                startAnimation();
            }
            public void windowClosing(WindowEvent e) {
                System.exit(0);
            }
        });

        Container contentPane = getContentPane();
        contentPane.addMouseListener(new MouseAdapter() {
            public void mousePressed(MouseEvent e) {
                if (frozen) {
                    frozen = false;
                    startAnimation();
                } else {
                    frozen = true;
                    stopAnimation();
                }
            }
        });

        label = new JLabel("Frame        ", JLabel.CENTER);
        contentPane.add(label, BorderLayout.CENTER);
    }
```

```
public void startAnimation() {
    if (frozen) {
        //Do nothing.  The user has requested that we
        //stop changing the image.
    } else {
        //Start (or restart) animating!
        timer.start();
    }
}

public void stopAnimation() {
    //Stop the animating thread.
    timer.stop();
}

public void actionPerformed(ActionEvent e) {
    //Advance the animation frame.
    frameNumber++;
    label.setText("Frame " + frameNumber);
}

public static void main(String args[]) {
    AnimatorApplicationTimer animator = null;
    int fps = 10;

    // Get frames per second from the command line argument
    if (args.length > 0) {
        try {
            fps = Integer.parseInt(args[0]);
        } catch (Exception e) {}
    }
    animator = new AnimatorApplicationTimer(fps, "Animator with Timer");
    animator.pack();
    animator.setVisible(true);
    animator.startAnimation();
}
}
```

EXAMPLE: *ButtonDemoApplet.java*

Where Explained:

Converting Button-DemoApplet (page 595)

AWT Version: ButtonDemoApplet.java *(page 911)*

SOURCE CODE: *http://java.sun.com/docs/books/tutorial/uiswing/converting/example-swing/ ButtonDemoApplet.java*

```
/*
 * Swing 1.1 version (compatible with both JDK 1.1 and Java 2).
 */

import javax.swing.*;
import java.awt.*;
import java.awt.event.*;
import java.net.URL;

public class ButtonDemoApplet extends JApplet
                              implements ActionListener {

    protected JButton b1, b2, b3;

    protected static final String DISABLE = "disable";
    protected static final String ENABLE = "enable";
```

```java
protected String leftButtonFilename = "images/right.gif";
protected String middleButtonFilename = "images/middle.gif";
protected String rightButtonFilename = "images/left.gif";

public void init() {
    ImageIcon leftButtonIcon = new ImageIcon(
                                getURL(leftButtonFilename));
    ImageIcon middleButtonIcon = new ImageIcon(
                                getURL(middleButtonFilename));
    ImageIcon rightButtonIcon = new ImageIcon(
                                getURL(rightButtonFilename));

    b1 = new JButton("Disable middle button", leftButtonIcon);
    b1.setVerticalTextPosition(AbstractButton.CENTER);
    b1.setHorizontalTextPosition(AbstractButton.LEFT);
    b1.setMnemonic(KeyEvent.VK_D);
    b1.setActionCommand(DISABLE);

    b2 = new JButton("Middle button", middleButtonIcon);
    b2.setVerticalTextPosition(AbstractButton.BOTTOM);
    b2.setHorizontalTextPosition(AbstractButton.CENTER);
    b2.setMnemonic(KeyEvent.VK_M);

    b3 = new JButton("Enable middle button", rightButtonIcon);
    //Use the default text position of CENTER, RIGHT.
    b3.setMnemonic(KeyEvent.VK_E);
    b3.setActionCommand(ENABLE);
    b3.setEnabled(false);

    //Listen for actions on buttons 1 and 3.
    b1.addActionListener(this);
    b3.addActionListener(this);

    //Add Components to a JPanel, using the default FlowLayout.
    JPanel pane = new JPanel();
    pane.add(b1);
    pane.add(b2);
    pane.add(b3);

    //Make the JPanel this applet's content pane.
    setContentPane(pane);
}

public void actionPerformed(ActionEvent e) {
    if (e.getActionCommand().equals(DISABLE)) {
        b2.setEnabled(false);
        b1.setEnabled(false);
        b3.setEnabled(true);
    } else {
        b2.setEnabled(true);
        b1.setEnabled(true);
        b3.setEnabled(false);
    }
}

protected URL getURL(String filename) {
    URL codeBase = getCodeBase();
    URL url = null;

    try {
        url = new URL(codeBase, filename);
    } catch (java.net.MalformedURLException e) {
        System.out.println("Couldn't create image: badly specified URL");
        return null;
    }

    return url;
}
}
```

EXAMPLE: *ButtonDemoApplet.html*

Associated File(s): ButtonDemoApplet.java *(page 890)*

```html
<html>
<body>

<applet code=ButtonDemoApplet.class width=570 height=65>
</applet>

</body>
</html>
```

EXAMPLE: *ConversionPanel.java*

Where Explained:

Converting Converter (page 598)

AWT Version: ConversionPanel.java *(page 912)*

Main Source File: Converter.java *(page 914)*

SOURCE CODE: *http://java.sun.com/docs/books/tutorial/uiswing/overview/example-swing/ ConversionPanel.java*

```java
/*
 * Swing 1.1 version (compatible with both JDK 1.1 and Java 2).
 */

import javax.swing.*;
import javax.swing.event.*;
import java.awt.*;
import java.awt.event.*;
import java.util.*;
import java.text.NumberFormat;

public class ConversionPanel extends JPanel {
    DecimalField textField;
    JComboBox unitChooser;
    JSlider slider;
    ConverterRangeModel sliderModel;
    Converter controller;
    Unit[] units;
    String title;
    final static boolean DEBUG = false;
    final static boolean COLORS = false;
    final static int MAX = 10000;

    ConversionPanel(Converter myController, String myTitle,
                    Unit[] myUnits,
                    ConverterRangeModel myModel) {
        if (COLORS) {
            setBackground(Color.cyan);
        }
        setBorder(BorderFactory.createCompoundBorder(
                        BorderFactory.createTitledBorder(myTitle),
                        BorderFactory.createEmptyBorder(5,5,5,5)));

        //Save arguments in instance variables.
        controller = myController;
        units = myUnits;
        title = myTitle;
        sliderModel = myModel;
```

```java
    //Add the text field.  It initially displays "0" and needs
    //to be at least 10 columns wide.
    NumberFormat numberFormat = NumberFormat.getNumberInstance();
    numberFormat.setMaximumFractionDigits(2);
    textField = new DecimalField(0, 10, numberFormat);
    textField.setValue(sliderModel.getDoubleValue());
    textField.addActionListener(new ActionListener() {
        public void actionPerformed(ActionEvent e) {
            sliderModel.setDoubleValue(textField.getValue());
        }
    });

    //Add the combo box.
    unitChooser = new JComboBox();
    for (int i = 0; i < units.length; i++) { //Populate it.
        unitChooser.addItem(units[i].description);
    }
    unitChooser.setSelectedIndex(0);
    sliderModel.setMultiplier(units[0].multiplier);
    unitChooser.addActionListener(new ActionListener() {
        public void actionPerformed(ActionEvent e) {
            //Set new maximums for the sliders.
            int i = unitChooser.getSelectedIndex();
            sliderModel.setMultiplier(units[i].multiplier);
            controller.resetMaxValues(false);
        }
    });

    //Add the slider.
    slider = new JSlider(sliderModel);
    sliderModel.addChangeListener(new ChangeListener() {
        public void stateChanged(ChangeEvent e) {
            textField.setValue(sliderModel.getDoubleValue());
        }
    });

    //Make the textfield/slider group a fixed size.
    JPanel unitGroup = new JPanel() {
        public Dimension getMinimumSize() {
            return getPreferredSize();
        }
        public Dimension getPreferredSize() {
            return new Dimension(150,
                                 super.getPreferredSize().height);
        }
        public Dimension getMaximumSize() {
            return getPreferredSize();
        }
    };
    if (COLORS) {
        unitGroup.setBackground(Color.blue);
    }
    unitGroup.setBorder(BorderFactory.createEmptyBorder(
                                      0,0,0,5));
    unitGroup.setLayout(new BoxLayout(unitGroup,
                                BoxLayout.Y_AXIS));
    unitGroup.add(textField);
    unitGroup.add(slider);

    setLayout(new BoxLayout(this, BoxLayout.X_AXIS));
    add(unitGroup);
    add(unitChooser);
    unitGroup.setAlignmentY(TOP_ALIGNMENT);
    unitChooser.setAlignmentY(TOP_ALIGNMENT);
}
```

```
/**
 * Returns the multiplier (units/meter) for the currently
 * selected unit of measurement.
 */
public double getMultiplier() {
    return sliderModel.getMultiplier();
}

public double getValue() {
    return sliderModel.getDoubleValue();
}
```
}

EXAMPLE: *Converter.java*

Where Explained:

Converting Converter (page 598)

AWT Version: <u>Converter.java</u> *(page 914)*

Associated File(s): <u>ConversionPanel.java</u> *(page 892)*, <u>ConverterRangeModel.java</u> *(page 896)*, <u>DecimalField.java</u> *(page 900)*, <u>FollowerRangeModel.java</u> *(page 900)*, <u>FormattedDocument.java</u> *(page 902)*, <u>Unit.java</u> *(page 908)*

SOURCE CODE: *http://java.sun.com/docs/books/tutorial/uiswing/overview/example-swing/ Converter.java*

```
/*
 * Swing 1.1 version (compatible with both JDK 1.1 and Java 2).
 */

import javax.swing.*;
import javax.swing.event.*;
import java.awt.*;
import java.awt.event.*;
import java.util.*;

public class Converter {
    ConversionPanel metricPanel, usaPanel;
    Unit[] metricDistances = new Unit[3];
    Unit[] usaDistances = new Unit[4];
    final static boolean COLORS = false;
    final static boolean DEBUG = false;
    final static String LOOKANDFEEL = null;
    ConverterRangeModel dataModel = new ConverterRangeModel();
    JPanel mainPane;

    /**
     * Create the ConversionPanels (one for metric, another for U.S.).
     * I used "U.S." because although Imperial and U.S. distance
     * measurements are the same, this program could be extended to
     * include volume measurements, which aren't the same.
     *
     * Put the ConversionPanels into a frame, and bring up the frame.
     */
    public Converter() {
        //Create Unit objects for metric distances, and then
        //instantiate a ConversionPanel with these Units.
        metricDistances[0] = new Unit("Centimeters", 0.01);
        metricDistances[1] = new Unit("Meters", 1.0);
        metricDistances[2] = new Unit("Kilometers", 1000.0);
        metricPanel = new ConversionPanel(this, "Metric System",
                                          metricDistances, dataModel);
```

```
        //Create Unit objects for U.S. distances, and then
        //instantiate a ConversionPanel with these Units.
        usaDistances[0] = new Unit("Inches", 0.0254);
        usaDistances[1] = new Unit("Feet", 0.305);
        usaDistances[2] = new Unit("Yards", 0.914);
        usaDistances[3] = new Unit("Miles", 1613.0);
        usaPanel = new ConversionPanel(this, "U.S. System",
                                       usaDistances,
                                       new FollowerRangeModel(dataModel));

        //Create a JPanel, and add the ConversionPanels to it.
        mainPane = new JPanel();
        if (COLORS) {
            mainPane.setBackground(Color.red);
        }
        mainPane.setLayout(new GridLayout(2,1,5,5));
        mainPane.setBorder(BorderFactory.createEmptyBorder(5,5,5,5));
        mainPane.add(metricPanel);
        mainPane.add(usaPanel);
        resetMaxValues(true);
    }

    public void resetMaxValues(boolean resetCurrentValues) {
        double metricMultiplier = metricPanel.getMultiplier();
        double usaMultiplier = usaPanel.getMultiplier();
        int maximum = ConversionPanel.MAX;

        if (metricMultiplier > usaMultiplier) {
            maximum = (int)(ConversionPanel.MAX *
                    (usaMultiplier/metricMultiplier));
        }

        if (DEBUG) {
            System.out.println("in Converter resetMaxValues");
            System.out.println("  metricMultiplier = "
                                + metricMultiplier
                        + "; usaMultiplier = "
                                + usaMultiplier
                        + "; maximum = "
                                + maximum);
        }

        dataModel.setMaximum(maximum);

        if (resetCurrentValues) {
            dataModel.setDoubleValue(maximum);
        }
    }

    private static void initLookAndFeel() {
        String lookAndFeel = null;

        if (LOOKANDFEEL != null) {
            if (LOOKANDFEEL.equals("Metal")) {
                lookAndFeel = UIManager.getCrossPlatformLookAndFeelClassName();
            } else if (LOOKANDFEEL.equals("System")) {
                lookAndFeel = UIManager.getSystemLookAndFeelClassName();
            } else if (LOOKANDFEEL.equals("Mac")) {
                lookAndFeel = "com.sun.java.swing.plaf.mac.MacLookAndFeel";
                //PENDING: check!
            } else if (LOOKANDFEEL.equals("Windows")) {
                lookAndFeel =
                        "com.sun.java.swing.plaf.windows.WindowsLookAndFeel";
            } else if (LOOKANDFEEL.equals("Motif")) {
                lookAndFeel = "com.sun.java.swing.plaf.motif.MotifLookAndFeel";
            }
```

```
        if (DEBUG) {
            System.out.println("About to request look and feel: "
                               + lookAndFeel);
        }

        try {
            UIManager.setLookAndFeel(lookAndFeel);
        } catch (ClassNotFoundException e) {
            System.err.println("Couldn't find class for specified "
                               + "look and feel:" + lookAndFeel);
            System.err.println("Did you include the L&F library in "
                               + "the class path?");
            System.err.println("Using the default look and feel.");
        } catch (UnsupportedLookAndFeelException e) {
            System.err.println("Can't use the specified look and feel ("
                               + lookAndFeel + ") on this platform.");
            System.err.println("Using the default look and feel.");
        } catch (Exception e) {
            System.err.println("Couldn't get specified look and feel ("
                               + lookAndFeel + "), for some reason.");
            System.err.println("Using the default look and feel.");
            e.printStackTrace();
        }
    }
}

public static void main(String[] args) {
    initLookAndFeel();
    Converter converter = new Converter();

    //Create a new window.
    JFrame f = new JFrame("Converter");
    f.addWindowListener(new WindowAdapter() {
        public void windowClosing(WindowEvent e) {
            System.exit(0);
        }
    });

    //Add the JPanel to the window and display the window.
    //We can use a JPanel for the content pane because JPanel is opaque.
    f.setContentPane(converter.mainPane);
    if (COLORS) {
        //This has no effect, since the JPanel completely
        //covers the content pane.
        f.getContentPane().setBackground(Color.green);
    }

    f.pack();             //Resizes the window to its natural size.
    f.setVisible(true);
}
}
```

EXAMPLE: *ConverterRangeModel.java*

Where Explained:

Converting Converter (page 598)

Main Source File: Converter.java *(page 894)*

SOURCE CODE: *http://java.sun.com/docs/books/tutorial/uiswing/overview/example-swing/ ConverterRangeModel.java*

```
/*
 * Swing 1.1 version (compatible with both JDK 1.1 and Java 2).
 */
```

```java
import javax.swing.*;
import javax.swing.event.*;

/**
 * Based on the source code for DefaultBoundedRangeModel,
 * this class stores its value as a double, rather than
 * an int.  The minimum value and extent are always 0.
 **/
public class ConverterRangeModel implements BoundedRangeModel {
    protected ChangeEvent changeEvent = null;
    protected EventListenerList listenerList = new EventListenerList();

    protected int maximum = 10000;
    protected int minimum = 0;
    protected int extent = 0;
    protected double value = 0.0;
    protected double multiplier = 1.0;
    protected boolean isAdjusting = false;
    final static boolean DEBUG = false;

    public ConverterRangeModel() {
    }

    public double getMultiplier() {
        if (DEBUG) {
            System.out.println("In ConverterRangeModel getMultiplier");
        }
        return multiplier;
    }

    public void setMultiplier(double multiplier) {
        if (DEBUG) {
            System.out.println("In ConverterRangeModel setMultiplier");
        }
        this.multiplier = multiplier;
        fireStateChanged();
    }

    public int getMaximum() {
        if (DEBUG) {
            System.out.println("In ConverterRangeModel getMaximum");
        }
        return maximum;
    }

    public void setMaximum(int newMaximum) {
        if (DEBUG) {
            System.out.println("In ConverterRangeModel setMaximum");
        }
        setRangeProperties(value, extent, minimum, newMaximum, isAdjusting);
    }

    public int getMinimum() {
        return (int)minimum;
    }

    public void setMinimum(int newMinimum) {
        System.out.println("In ConverterRangeModel setMinimum");
        //Do nothing.
    }

    public int getValue() {
        if (DEBUG) {
            System.out.println("In ConverterRangeModel getValue");
        }
        return (int)getDoubleValue();
    }
```

```java
public void setValue(int newValue) {
    if (DEBUG) {
        System.out.println("In ConverterRangeModel setValue");
    }
    setDoubleValue((double)newValue);
}

public double getDoubleValue() {
    if (DEBUG) {
        System.out.println("In ConverterRangeModel getDoubleValue");
    }
    return value;
}

public void setDoubleValue(double newValue) {
    if (DEBUG) {
        System.out.println("In ConverterRangeModel setDoubleValue");
    }
    setRangeProperties(newValue, extent, minimum, maximum, isAdjusting);
}

public int getExtent() {
    return (int)extent;
}

public void setExtent(int newExtent) {
    //Do nothing.
}

public boolean getValueIsAdjusting() {
    return isAdjusting;
}

public void setValueIsAdjusting(boolean b) {
    setRangeProperties(value, extent, minimum, maximum, b);
}

public void setRangeProperties(int newValue,
                               int newExtent,
                               int newMin,
                               int newMax,
                               boolean newAdjusting) {
    System.out.println("In ConverterRangeModel setRangeProperties");
    setRangeProperties((double)newValue,
                       newExtent,
                       newMin,
                       newMax,
                       newAdjusting);
}

public void setRangeProperties(double newValue,
                               int unusedExtent,
                               int unusedMin,
                               int newMax,
                               boolean newAdjusting) {
    if (DEBUG) {
        System.out.println("setRangeProperties(): "
                            + "newValue = " + newValue
                            + "; newMax = " + newMax);
    }
    if (newMax <= minimum) {
        newMax = minimum + 1;
        if (DEBUG) {
            System.out.println("maximum raised by 1 to " + newMax);
        }
    }
```

```
        if (Math.round(newValue) > newMax) { //allow some rounding error
            newValue = newMax;
            if (DEBUG) {
                System.out.println("value lowered to " + newMax);
            }
        }

        boolean changeOccurred = false;
        if (newValue != value) {
            if (DEBUG) {
                System.out.println("value set to " + newValue);
            }
            value = newValue;
            changeOccurred = true;
        }
        if (newMax != maximum) {
            if (DEBUG) {
                System.out.println("maximum set to " + newMax);
            }
            maximum = newMax;
            changeOccurred = true;
        }
        if (newAdjusting != isAdjusting) {
            maximum = newMax;
            isAdjusting = newAdjusting;
            changeOccurred = true;
        }

        if (changeOccurred) {
            fireStateChanged();
        }
    }

    /*
     * The rest of this is event handling code copied from
     * DefaultBoundedRangeModel.
     */
    public void addChangeListener(ChangeListener l) {
        listenerList.add(ChangeListener.class, l);
    }

    public void removeChangeListener(ChangeListener l) {
        listenerList.remove(ChangeListener.class, l);
    }

    protected void fireStateChanged() {
        Object[] listeners = listenerList.getListenerList();
        for (int i = listeners.length - 2; i >= 0; i -=2 ) {
            if (listeners[i] == ChangeListener.class) {
                if (changeEvent == null) {
                    changeEvent = new ChangeEvent(this);
                }
                ((ChangeListener)listeners[i+1]).stateChanged(changeEvent);
            }
        }
    }
}
```

**Where
Explained:**
*Converting
Converter*
(page 598)

EXAMPLE: *DecimalField.java*

Main Source File: Converter.java *(page 894)*

SOURCE CODE: *http://java.sun.com/docs/books/tutorial/uiswing/overview/example-swing/
DecimalField.java*

```java
import javax.swing.*;
import javax.swing.text.*;

import java.awt.Toolkit;

import java.text.*;

public class DecimalField extends JTextField {

    private NumberFormat format;

    public DecimalField(double value, int columns, NumberFormat f) {
        super(columns);
        setDocument(new FormattedDocument(f));
        format = f;
        setValue(value);
    }

    public double getValue() {
        double retVal = 0.0;

        try {
            retVal = format.parse(getText()).doubleValue();
        } catch (ParseException e) {
            // This should never happen because insertString allows
            // only properly formatted data to get in the field.
            Toolkit.getDefaultToolkit().beep();
            System.err.println("getValue: could not parse: " + getText());
        }
        return retVal;
    }

    public void setValue(double value) {
        setText(format.format(value));
    }
}
```

**Where
Explained:**
*Converting
Converter*
(page 598)

EXAMPLE: *FollowerRangeModel.java*

Main Source File: Converter.java *(page 894)*

SOURCE CODE: *http://java.sun.com/docs/books/tutorial/uiswing/overview/example-swing/
FollowerRangeModel.java*

```java
/*
 * Swing 1.1 version (compatible with both JDK 1.1 and Java 2).
 */

import javax.swing.*;
import javax.swing.event.*;
```

```java
public class FollowerRangeModel extends ConverterRangeModel
                            implements ChangeListener {
    ConverterRangeModel dataModel;

    public FollowerRangeModel(ConverterRangeModel dataModel) {
        this.dataModel = dataModel;
        dataModel.addChangeListener(this);
    }

    public void stateChanged(ChangeEvent e) {
        fireStateChanged();
    }

    public int getMaximum() {
        int modelMax = dataModel.getMaximum();
        double multiplyBy = dataModel.getMultiplier()/multiplier;
        if (DEBUG) {
            System.out.println("In FollowerRangeModel getMaximum");
            System.out.println("  dataModel.getMaximum = " + modelMax
                            + "; multiply by " + multiplyBy
                            + "; result: " + modelMax*multiplyBy);
        }
        return (int)(modelMax * multiplyBy);
    }

    public void setMaximum(int newMaximum) {
        dataModel.setMaximum((int)(newMaximum *
                    (multiplier/dataModel.getMultiplier())));
    }

    public int getValue() {
        return (int)getDoubleValue();
    }

    public void setValue(int newValue) {
        setDoubleValue((double)newValue);
    }

    public double getDoubleValue() {
        return dataModel.getDoubleValue()
                * dataModel.getMultiplier()
                / multiplier;
    }

    public void setDoubleValue(double newValue) {
        dataModel.setDoubleValue(
                    newValue * multiplier
                    / dataModel.getMultiplier());
    }

    public int getExtent() {
        return super.getExtent();
    }

    public void setExtent(int newExtent) {
        super.setExtent(newExtent);
    }

    public void setRangeProperties(int value, int extent, int min,
                                int max, boolean adjusting) {
        double multiplyBy = multiplier/dataModel.getMultiplier();
        dataModel.setRangeProperties(value*multiplyBy, extent, min,
                                (int)(max*multiplyBy),
                                adjusting);
    }
}
```

EXAMPLE: *FormattedDocument.java*

**Where
Explained:**
*Converting
Converter*
(page 598)

Main Source File: Converter.java *(page 894)*

SOURCE CODE: *http://java.sun.com/docs/books/tutorial/uiswing/overview/example-swing/
FormattedDocument.java*

```java
import javax.swing.*;
import javax.swing.text.*;

import java.awt.Toolkit;
import java.text.*;
import java.util.Locale;

// You can attach any format to this document.
// Only text that can be parsed by the format is
// allowed in the document.
// Thus this class is general enough to handle dates,
// integers, percents, money, strings, anything for
// which you have a format.
// You could even write your own phone number or
// SSN format classes to handle those types.
// Textfields that use this type of document.
// are locale-sensitive,
// because the formats provided by the JDK
// are locale-sensitive.

public class FormattedDocument extends PlainDocument {

    private Format format;

    public FormattedDocument(Format f) {
        format = f;
    }

    public Format getFormat() {
        return format;
    }

    public void insertString(int offs, String str, AttributeSet a)
        throws BadLocationException {

        String currentText = getText(0, getLength());
        String beforeOffset = currentText.substring(0, offs);
        String afterOffset = currentText.substring(offs, currentText.length());
        String proposedResult = beforeOffset + str + afterOffset;

        try {
            format.parseObject(proposedResult);
            super.insertString(offs, str, a);
        } catch (ParseException e) {
            Toolkit.getDefaultToolkit().beep();
            System.err.println("insertString: could not parse: " + proposedResult);
        }
    }

    public void remove(int offs, int len) throws BadLocationException {
        String currentText = getText(0, getLength());
        String beforeOffset = currentText.substring(0, offs);
        String afterOffset = currentText.substring(len + offs,
                                                   currentText.length());
        String proposedResult = beforeOffset + afterOffset;
```

```
        try {
            if (proposedResult.length() != 0)
                format.parseObject(proposedResult);
            super.remove(offs, len);
        } catch (ParseException e) {
            Toolkit.getDefaultToolkit().beep();
            System.err.println("remove: could not parse: " + proposedResult);
        }
    }
}
```

EXAMPLE: *ListSelectionDemo.java*

AWT Version: `ListDemo.java` *(page 920)*

SOURCE CODE: *http://java.sun.com/docs/books/tutorial/uiswing/events/example-swing/*
ListSelectionDemo.java

**Where
Explained:**
*Converting
ListDemo*
(page 600)

```java
import javax.swing.*;
import javax.swing.event.*;
import javax.swing.table.*;

import java.util.*;
import java.awt.*;
import java.awt.event.*;

public class ListSelectionDemo extends JApplet {
    JTextArea output;
    JList list;
    JTable table;
    String newline = "\n";
    ListSelectionModel listSelectionModel;

    private boolean inAnApplet = true;

    //Hack to avoid ugly message about system event access check.
    public ListSelectionDemo() {
        this(true);
    }

    public ListSelectionDemo(boolean inAnApplet) {
        this.inAnApplet = inAnApplet;
        if (inAnApplet) {
            getRootPane().putClientProperty("defeatSystemEventQueueCheck",
                                Boolean.TRUE);
        }
    }

    public void init() {
        //newline = System.getProperty("line.separator");

        String[] listData = { "one", "two", "three", "four",
                              "five", "six", "seven" };
        String[] columnNames = { "French", "Spanish", "Italian" };
        String[][] tableData = {{"un",      "uno",     "uno"     },
                                {"deux",    "dos",     "due"     },
                                {"trois",   "tres",    "tre"     },
                                { "quatre", "cuatro",  "quattro"},
                                { "cinq",   "cinco",   "cinque" },
                                { "six",    "seis",    "sei"     },
                                { "sept",   "siete",   "sette"  } };
```

```
list = new JList(listData);

listSelectionModel = list.getSelectionModel();
listSelectionModel.addListSelectionListener(
                        new SharedListSelectionHandler());
JScrollPane listPane = new JScrollPane(list);

table = new JTable(tableData, columnNames);
table.setSelectionModel(listSelectionModel);
JScrollPane tablePane = new JScrollPane(table);

//build control area (use default FlowLayout)
JPanel controlPane = new JPanel();
String[] modes = { "SINGLE_SELECTION",
                   "SINGLE_INTERVAL_SELECTION",
                   "MULTIPLE_INTERVAL_SELECTION" };

final JComboBox comboBox = new JComboBox(modes);
comboBox.setSelectedIndex(2);
comboBox.addActionListener(new ActionListener() {
    public void actionPerformed(ActionEvent e) {
        String newMode = (String)comboBox.getSelectedItem();
        if (newMode.equals("SINGLE_SELECTION")) {
            listSelectionModel.setSelectionMode(
                ListSelectionModel.SINGLE_SELECTION);
        } else if (newMode.equals("SINGLE_INTERVAL_SELECTION")) {
            listSelectionModel.setSelectionMode(
                ListSelectionModel.SINGLE_INTERVAL_SELECTION);
        } else {
            listSelectionModel.setSelectionMode(
                ListSelectionModel.MULTIPLE_INTERVAL_SELECTION);
        }
        output.append("----------"
                      + "Mode: " + newMode
                      + "----------" + newline);
    }
});
controlPane.add(new JLabel("Selection mode:"));
controlPane.add(comboBox);

//build output area
output = new JTextArea(10, 40);
output.setEditable(false);
JScrollPane outputPane = new JScrollPane(output,
                ScrollPaneConstants.VERTICAL_SCROLLBAR_ALWAYS,
                ScrollPaneConstants.HORIZONTAL_SCROLLBAR_ALWAYS);

//do the layout
JSplitPane splitPane = new JSplitPane(JSplitPane.VERTICAL_SPLIT);
getContentPane().add(splitPane, BorderLayout.CENTER);

//XXX: used a Box at first, but you can't call setMinimumSize on it
JPanel topHalf = new JPanel();
topHalf.setLayout(new BoxLayout(topHalf, BoxLayout.X_AXIS));
JPanel listContainer = new JPanel(new GridLayout(1,1));
listContainer.setBorder(BorderFactory.createTitledBorder(
                                    "List"));
listContainer.add(listPane);
JPanel tableContainer = new JPanel(new GridLayout(1,1));
tableContainer.setBorder(BorderFactory.createTitledBorder(
                                    "Table"));
tableContainer.add(tablePane);
tablePane.setPreferredSize(new Dimension(300, 100));
topHalf.setBorder(BorderFactory.createEmptyBorder(5,5,0,5));
topHalf.add(listContainer);
topHalf.add(tableContainer);
```

```
            topHalf.setMinimumSize(new Dimension(400, 50));
            topHalf.setPreferredSize(new Dimension(400, 110));
            splitPane.add(topHalf);

            JPanel bottomHalf = new JPanel(new BorderLayout());
            bottomHalf.add(controlPane, BorderLayout.NORTH);
            bottomHalf.add(outputPane, BorderLayout.CENTER);
            //XXX: the next line is necessary if bottomHalf is a scroll pane:
            //bottomHalf.setMinimumSize(new Dimension(400, 50));
            bottomHalf.setPreferredSize(new Dimension(450, 135));
            splitPane.add(bottomHalf);
    }

    public static void main(String[] args) {
        JFrame frame = new JFrame("ListSelectionDemo");
        frame.addWindowListener(new WindowAdapter() {
            public void windowClosing(WindowEvent e) {
                System.exit(0);
            }
        });

        ListSelectionDemo listDemo = new ListSelectionDemo(false);
        listDemo.init();

        frame.setContentPane(listDemo);
        frame.pack();
        frame.setVisible(true);
    }

    class SharedListSelectionHandler implements ListSelectionListener {
        public void valueChanged(ListSelectionEvent e) {
            ListSelectionModel lsm = (ListSelectionModel)e.getSource();

            int firstIndex = e.getFirstIndex();
            int lastIndex = e.getLastIndex();
            boolean isAdjusting = e.getValueIsAdjusting();
            output.append("Event for indexes "
                            + firstIndex + " - " + lastIndex
                            + "; isAdjusting is " + isAdjusting
                            + "; selected indexes:");

            if (lsm.isSelectionEmpty()) {
                output.append(" <none>");
            } else {
                // Find out which indexes are selected.
                int minIndex = lsm.getMinSelectionIndex();
                int maxIndex = lsm.getMaxSelectionIndex();
                for (int i = minIndex; i <= maxIndex; i++) {
                    if (lsm.isSelectedIndex(i)) {
                        output.append(" " + i);
                    }
                }
            }
            output.append(newline);
        }
    }
}
```

Where Explained:

Converting TextEventDemo (page 597)

EXAMPLE: *TextEventDemo.java*

AWT Version: TextEventDemo.java *(page 922)*

Associated File(s): TextEventDemo.html *(page 908)*

SOURCE CODE: *http://java.sun.com/docs/books/tutorial/uiswing/converting/example-swing/ TextEventDemo.java*

```
/*
 * Swing 1.1 version (compatible with both JDK 1.1 and Java 2).
 */

import javax.swing.*;
import javax.swing.text.*;
import javax.swing.event.*;

import java.awt.Dimension;
import java.awt.BorderLayout;
import java.awt.GridBagLayout;
import java.awt.GridBagConstraints;

import java.awt.event.*;

public class TextEventDemo extends JApplet implements ActionListener {
    JTextField textField;
    JTextArea textArea;
    JTextArea displayArea;

    public void init() {
        JButton button = new JButton("Clear");
        button.addActionListener(this);

        textField = new JTextField(20);
        textField.addActionListener(new MyTextActionListener());
        textField.getDocument().addDocumentListener(
                                 new MyDocumentListener("Text Field"));

        textArea = new JTextArea();
        textArea.getDocument().addDocumentListener(
            new MyDocumentListener("Text Area"));
        JScrollPane scrollPane = new JScrollPane(textArea);
        scrollPane.setPreferredSize(new Dimension(200, 75));

        displayArea = new JTextArea();
        displayArea.setEditable(false);
        JScrollPane displayScrollPane = new JScrollPane(displayArea);
        displayScrollPane.setPreferredSize(new Dimension(200, 75));

        JPanel contentPane = new JPanel();
        GridBagLayout gridbag = new GridBagLayout();
        GridBagConstraints c = new GridBagConstraints();
        contentPane.setLayout(gridbag);
        c.fill = GridBagConstraints.BOTH;
        c.weightx = 1.0;

        /*
         * Hack to get around gridbag's refusal to allow
         * multi-row components in anything but the left column.
         */
        JPanel leftPanel = new JPanel();
        leftPanel.setLayout(new BorderLayout());
```

```
        leftPanel.add(textField, BorderLayout.NORTH);
        leftPanel.add(scrollPane, BorderLayout.CENTER);

        c.gridheight = 2;
        gridbag.setConstraints(leftPanel, c);
        contentPane.add(leftPanel);

        c.weighty = 1.0;
        c.gridwidth = GridBagConstraints.REMAINDER;
        c.gridheight = 1;
        gridbag.setConstraints(displayScrollPane, c);
        contentPane.add(displayScrollPane);

        c.weighty = 0.0;
        gridbag.setConstraints(button, c);
        contentPane.add(button);

        textField.requestFocus();

        setContentPane(contentPane);
    }

    class MyDocumentListener implements DocumentListener {
        String preface;
        String newline;

        public MyDocumentListener(String source) {
            newline = System.getProperty("line.separator");
            preface = source + " text value changed." + newline
                            + "    First 10 characters: \"";
        }

        public void insertUpdate(DocumentEvent e) {
            update(e);
        }

        public void removeUpdate(DocumentEvent e) {
            update(e);
        }
        public void changedUpdate(DocumentEvent e) {
            //You don't get these with a plain text component.
        }
        public void update(DocumentEvent e) {
            Document doc = (Document)e.getDocument();
            int length = doc.getLength();
            String s = null;
            try {
                s = doc.getText(0, (length > 10) ? 10 : length);
            } catch (BadLocationException ex) {
            }
            displayArea.append(preface + s + "\"" + newline);
        }
    }

    class MyTextActionListener implements ActionListener {
        /** Handle the text field Return. */
        public void actionPerformed(ActionEvent e) {
            int selStart = textArea.getSelectionStart();
            int selEnd = textArea.getSelectionEnd();

            textArea.replaceRange(textField.getText(), selStart, selEnd);
            textField.selectAll();
        }
    }

    /** Handle button click. */
```

```
    public void actionPerformed(ActionEvent e) {
        displayArea.setText("");
        textField.requestFocus();
    }
}
```

EXAMPLE: *TextEventDemo.html*

Associated File(s): <u>TextEventDemo.java</u> *(page 906)*

```
<applet code="TextEventDemo.class"
    width=500 height=300
    alt="Your browser understands the applet tag but isn't displaying any
applet.">
</applet>
```

EXAMPLE: *Unit.java*

**Where
Explained:**

*Converting
Converter*
(page 598)

AWT Version: <u>Unit.java</u> *(page 924)*

Main Source File: <u>Converter.java</u> *(page 894)*

SOURCE CODE: *http://java.sun.com/docs/books/tutorial/uiswing/overview/example-swing/
Unit.java*

```
/*
 * Swing 1.1 version (compatible with both JDK 1.1 and Java 2).
 */

public class Unit {
    String description;
    double multiplier;

    Unit(String description, double multiplier) {
        super();
        this.description = description;
        this.multiplier = multiplier;
    }

    public String toString() {
        String s = "Meters/" + description + " = " + multiplier;
        return s;
    }
}
```

AWT Versions

AWT EXAMPLE : *AnimatorApplication.java*

Swing Version: AnimatorApplication.java *(page 886)*

SOURCE CODE: *http://java.sun.com/docs/books/tutorial/uiswing/converting/example-1dot1/AnimatorApplication.java*

```
/*
 * 1.1 version.
 */

import java.awt.*;
import java.awt.event.*;

/*
 * Based on Arthur van Hoff's animation examples, this application
 * can serve as a template for all animation applications.
 */
public class AnimatorApplication extends Frame
                                 implements Runnable {
    int frameNumber = -1;
    int delay;
    Thread animatorThread;
    boolean frozen = false;

    AnimatorApplication(int fps, String windowTitle) {
        super(windowTitle);
        delay = (fps > 0) ? (1000 / fps) : 100;

        addMouseListener(new MouseAdapter() {
            public void mousePressed(MouseEvent e) {
                if (frozen) {
                    frozen = false;
                    startAnimation();
                } else {
                    frozen = true;
                    stopAnimation();
                }
            }
        });

        addWindowListener(new WindowAdapter() {
            public void windowIconified(WindowEvent e) {
                stopAnimation();
            }
            public void windowDeiconified(WindowEvent e) {
                startAnimation();
            }
            public void windowClosing(WindowEvent e) {
                System.exit(0);
            }
        });
    }

    public void startAnimation() {
        if (frozen) {
            //Do nothing.  The user has requested that we
            //stop changing the image.
```

Where Explained:

Converting Animator-Application (page 596)

```java
        } else {
            //Start animating!
            if (animatorThread == null) {
                animatorThread = new Thread(this);
            }
            animatorThread.start();
        }
    }

    public void stopAnimation() {
        //Stop the animating thread.
        animatorThread = null;
    }

    public void run() {
        //Just to be nice, lower this thread's priority
        //so it can't interfere with other processing going on.
        Thread.currentThread().setPriority(Thread.MIN_PRIORITY);

        //Remember the starting time.
        long startTime = System.currentTimeMillis();

        //Remember which thread we are.
        Thread currentThread = Thread.currentThread();

        //This is the animation loop.
        while (currentThread == animatorThread) {
            //Advance the animation frame.
            frameNumber++;

            //Display it.
            repaint();

            //Delay depending on how far we are behind.
            try {
                startTime += delay;
                Thread.sleep(Math.max(0,
                            startTime-System.currentTimeMillis()));
            } catch (InterruptedException e) {
                break;
            }
        }
    }

    //Draw the current frame of animation.
    public void paint(Graphics g) {
        g.drawString("Frame " + frameNumber, 5, 50);
    }

    public static void main(String args[]) {
        AnimatorApplication animator = null;
        int fps = 10;

        // Get frames per second from the command line argument
        if (args.length > 0) {
            try {
                fps = Integer.parseInt(args[0]);
            } catch (Exception e) {}
        }
        animator = new AnimatorApplication(fps, "Animator");
        animator.setSize(200, 60);
        animator.setVisible(true);
        animator.startAnimation();
    }
}
```

AWT EXAMPLE :*ButtonDemoApplet.java*

Swing Version: <u>ButtonDemoApplet.java</u> *(page 890)*

Associated File(s): <u>ButtonDemoApplet.html</u> *(page 912)*

SOURCE CODE: *http://java.sun.com/docs/books/tutorial/uiswing/converting/example-1dot1/ButtonDemoApplet.java*

Where Explained:

Converting Button-DemoApplet (page 595)

```java
/*
 * 1.1 version.
 */

import java.awt.*;
import java.awt.event.ActionListener;
import java.awt.event.ActionEvent;
import java.applet.Applet;

public class ButtonDemoApplet extends Applet
                           implements ActionListener {

    protected Button b1, b2, b3;
    protected static final String DISABLE = "disable";
    protected static final String ENABLE = "enable";

    public void init() {
        b1 = new Button();
        b1.setLabel("Disable middle button");
        b1.setActionCommand(DISABLE);

        b2 = new Button("Middle button");

        b3 = new Button("Enable middle button");
        b3.setEnabled(false);
        b3.setActionCommand(ENABLE);

        //Listen for actions on buttons 1 and 3.
        b1.addActionListener(this);
        b3.addActionListener(this);

        //Add Components to the Applet, using the default FlowLayout.
        add(b1);
        add(b2);
        add(b3);
    }

    public void actionPerformed(ActionEvent e) {
        if (e.getActionCommand().equals(DISABLE)) {
            b2.setEnabled(false);
            b1.setEnabled(false);
            b3.setEnabled(true);
        } else {
            b2.setEnabled(true);
            b1.setEnabled(true);
            b3.setEnabled(false);
        }
    }
}
```

AWT EXAMPLE: *ButtonDemoApplet.html*

Associated File(s): ButtonDemoApplet.java *(page 911)*

```
<html>
<body>

<applet code=ButtonDemoApplet.class width=500 height=35>
</applet>

</body>
</html>
```

AWT EXAMPLE: *ConversionPanel.java*

**Where
Explained:**

*Converting
Converter*
(page 598)

Swing Version: ConversionPanel.java *(page 892)*

Main Source File: Converter.java *(page 914)*

SOURCE CODE: *http://java.sun.com/docs/books/tutorial/uiswing/converting/example-1dot1/
ConversionPanel.java*

```
/*
 * 1.1 version.
 */

import java.awt.*;
import java.awt.event.*;
import java.util.*;
import java.applet.Applet;

public class ConversionPanel extends Panel implements ActionListener,
                                AdjustmentListener,
                                ItemListener {
    TextField textField;
    Choice unitChooser;
    Scrollbar slider;
    int max = 10000;
    int block = 100;
    Converter controller;
    Unit[] units;

    ConversionPanel(Converter myController, String myTitle, Unit[] myUnits) {
        //Initialize this ConversionPanel to use a GridBagLayout.
        GridBagConstraints c = new GridBagConstraints();
        GridBagLayout gridbag = new GridBagLayout();
        setLayout(gridbag);

        //Save arguments in instance variables.
        controller = myController;
        units = myUnits;

        //Set up default layout constraints.
        c.fill = GridBagConstraints.HORIZONTAL;

        //Add the label.  It displays this panel's title, centered.
        Label label = new Label(myTitle, Label.CENTER);
        c.gridwidth = GridBagConstraints.REMAINDER; //It ends a row.
```

```
        gridbag.setConstraints(label, c);
        add(label);

        //Add the text field.  It initially displays "0" and needs
        //to be at least 10 columns wide.
        textField = new TextField("0", 10);
        c.weightx = 1.0;  //Use maximum horizontal space...
        c.gridwidth = 1; //The default value.
        gridbag.setConstraints(textField, c);
        add(textField);
        textField.addActionListener(this);

        //Add the pop-up list (Choice).
        unitChooser = new Choice();
        for (int i = 0; i < units.length; i++) { //Populate it.
            unitChooser.add(units[i].description);
        }
        c.weightx = 0.0; //The default value.
        c.gridwidth = GridBagConstraints.REMAINDER; //End a row.
        gridbag.setConstraints(unitChooser, c);
        add(unitChooser);
        unitChooser.addItemListener(this);

        //Add the slider.  It's horizontal, and it has the maximum
        //value specified by the instance variable max.  Its initial
        //and minimum values are the default (0).  A click increments
        //the value by block units.
        slider = new Scrollbar(Scrollbar.HORIZONTAL);
        slider.setMaximum(max + 10);
        slider.setBlockIncrement(block);
        c.gridwidth = 1; //The default value.
        gridbag.setConstraints(slider, c);
        add(slider);
        slider.addAdjustmentListener(this);
    }

/**
 * Returns the multiplier (units/meter) for the currently
 * selected unit of measurement.
 */
double getMultiplier() {
    int i = unitChooser.getSelectedIndex();
    return units[i].multiplier;
}

/** Draws a box around this panel. */
public void paint(Graphics g) {
    Dimension d = getSize();
    g.drawRect(0,0, d.width - 1, d.height - 1);
}

/**
 * Puts a little breathing space between
 * the panel and its contents, which lets us draw a box
 * in the paint() method.
 * We add more pixels to the right, to work around a
 * Choice bug.
 */
public Insets getInsets() {
    return new Insets(5,5,5,8);
}

/**
 * Gets the current value in the text field.
 * It's guaranteed to be the same as the value
 * in the scroller (subject to rounding, of course).
 */
double getValue() {
    double f;
```

```
        try {
            f = (double)Double.valueOf(textField.getText()).doubleValue();
        } catch (java.lang.NumberFormatException e) {
            f = 0.0;
        }
        return f;
    }

    public void actionPerformed(ActionEvent e) {
        setSliderValue(getValue());
        controller.convert(this);
    }

    public void itemStateChanged(ItemEvent e) {
        controller.convert(this);
    }
    /** Respond to the slider. */
    public void adjustmentValueChanged(AdjustmentEvent e) {
        textField.setText(String.valueOf(e.getValue()));
        controller.convert(this);
    }

    /** Set the values in the slider and text field. */
    void setValue(double f) {
        setSliderValue(f);
        textField.setText(String.valueOf((float)f));
    }

    /** Set the slider value. */
    void setSliderValue(double f) {
        int sliderValue = (int)f;

        if (sliderValue > max)
            sliderValue = max;
        if (sliderValue < 0)
            sliderValue = 0;
        slider.setValue(sliderValue);
    }
}
```

AWT EXAMPLE: *Converter.java*

**Where
Explained:**

*Converting
Converter*
(page 598)

Swing Version: Converter.java *(page 894)*

Associated File(s): ConversionPanel.java *(page 912)*, Unit.java *(page 924)*

SOURCE CODE: *http://java.sun.com/docs/books/tutorial/uiswing/converting/example-1dot1/
                Converter.java*

```
/*
 * 1.1 version.
 */

import java.awt.*;
import java.awt.event.*;
import java.util.*;
import java.applet.Applet;

public class Converter extends Applet {
    ConversionPanel metricPanel, usaPanel;
    Unit[] metricDistances = new Unit[3];
```

```
Unit[] usaDistances = new Unit[4];

/**
 * Create the ConversionPanels (one for metric, another for U.S.).
 * I used "U.S." because although Imperial and U.S. distance
 * measurements are the same, this program could be extended to
 * include volume measurements, which aren't the same.
 */
public void init() {
    //Use a GridLayout with 2 rows, as many columns as necessary,
    //and 5 pixels of padding around all edges of each cell.
    setLayout(new GridLayout(2,0,5,5));

    //Create Unit objects for metric distances, and then
    //instantiate a ConversionPanel with these Units.
    metricDistances[0] = new Unit("Centimeters", 0.01);
    metricDistances[1] = new Unit("Meters", 1.0);
    metricDistances[2] = new Unit("Kilometers", 1000.0);
    metricPanel = new ConversionPanel(this, "Metric System",
                                      metricDistances);

    //Create Unit objects for U.S. distances, and then
    //instantiate a ConversionPanel with these Units.
    usaDistances[0] = new Unit("Inches", 0.0254);
    usaDistances[1] = new Unit("Feet", 0.305);
    usaDistances[2] = new Unit("Yards", 0.914);
    usaDistances[3] = new Unit("Miles", 1613.0);
    usaPanel = new ConversionPanel(this, "U.S. System", usaDistances);

    //Add both ConversionPanels to the Converter.
    add(metricPanel);
    add(usaPanel);
}

/**
 * Does the conversion from metric to U.S., or vice versa, and
 * updates the appropriate ConversionPanel.
 */
void convert(ConversionPanel from) {
    ConversionPanel to;

    if (from == metricPanel)
        to = usaPanel;
    else
        to = metricPanel;

    double multiplier = from.getMultiplier() / to.getMultiplier();
    to.setValue(multiplier * from.getValue());
}

/** Draws a box around this panel. */
public void paint(Graphics g) {
    Dimension d = getSize();
    g.drawRect(0,0, d.width - 1, d.height - 1);
}

/**
 * Puts a little breathing space between
 * the panel and its contents, which lets us draw a box
 * in the paint() method.
 */
public Insets getInsets() {
    return new Insets(5,5,5,5);
}

/** Executed only when this program runs as an application. */
public static void main(String[] args) {
    //Create a new window.
```

```
        Frame f = new Frame("Converter Applet/Application");
        f.addWindowListener(new WindowAdapter() {
            public void windowClosing(WindowEvent e) {
                System.exit(0);
            }
        });

        //Create a Converter instance.
        Converter converter = new Converter();

        //Initialize the Converter instance.
        converter.init();

        //Add the Converter to the window and display the window.
        f.add("Center", converter);
        f.pack();         //Resizes the window to its natural size.
        f.setVisible(true);
    }
}
```

AWT EXAMPLE: *CoordinatesDemo.java*

**Where
Explained:**

*Converting
Converter*
(page 598)

Swing Version: CoordinatesDemo.java *(page 861)*

SOURCE CODE:　*http://java.sun.com/docs/books/tutorial/uiswing/converting/example-1dot1/
CoordinatesDemo.java*

```
/*
 * 1.1 version.
 */

import java.awt.*;
import java.awt.event.*;
import java.applet.Applet;

/*
 * This displays a framed area.  When the user clicks within
 * the area, this program displays a dot and a string indicating
 * the coordinates where the click occurred.
 */
public class CoordinatesDemo extends Applet {
    FramedArea framedArea;
    Label label;

    public void init() {
        GridBagLayout gridBag = new GridBagLayout();
        GridBagConstraints c = new GridBagConstraints();

        setLayout(gridBag);

        framedArea = new FramedArea(this);
        c.fill = GridBagConstraints.BOTH;
        c.weighty = 1.0;
        c.gridwidth = GridBagConstraints.REMAINDER; //end row
        gridBag.setConstraints(framedArea, c);
        add(framedArea);

        label = new Label("Click within the framed area.");
        c.fill = GridBagConstraints.HORIZONTAL;
        c.weightx = 1.0;
        c.weighty = 0.0;
```

```
                gridBag.setConstraints(label, c);
                add(label);
        }

        public void updateLabel(Point point) {
            label.setText("Click occurred at coordinate ("
                            + point.x + ", " + point.y + ").");
        }
}

/* This class exists solely to put a frame around the coordinate area. */
class FramedArea extends Panel {
        public FramedArea(CoordinatesDemo controller) {
            super();

            //Set layout to one that makes its contents as big as possible.
            setLayout(new GridLayout(1,0));

            add(new CoordinateArea(controller));
        }

        public Insets getInsets() {
            return new Insets(4,4,5,5);
        }

        public void paint(Graphics g) {
            Dimension d = getSize();
            Color bg = getBackground();

            g.setColor(bg);
            g.draw3DRect(0, 0, d.width - 1, d.height - 1, true);
            g.draw3DRect(3, 3, d.width - 7, d.height - 7, false);
        }
}

class CoordinateArea extends Canvas {
        Point point = null;
        CoordinatesDemo controller;

        public CoordinateArea(CoordinatesDemo controller) {
            super();
            this.controller = controller;

            addMouseListener(new MouseAdapter() {
                public void mousePressed(MouseEvent e) {
                    int x = e.getX();
                    int y = e.getY();
                    if (point == null) {
                        point = new Point(x, y);
                    } else {
                        point.x = x;
                        point.y = y;
                    }
                    repaint();
                }
            });
        }

        public void paint(Graphics g) {
            //If user has chosen a point, paint a tiny rectangle on top.
            if (point != null) {
                controller.updateLabel(point);
                g.fillRect(point.x - 1, point.y - 1, 2, 2);
            }
        }
}
```

AWT EXAMPLE :*ImageSequence.java*

Where Explained:

Converting Painting Code
(page 589)

Swing Version: `ImageSequenceTimer.java` *(page 867)*

SOURCE CODE: *http://java.sun.com/docs/books/tutorial/uiswing/converting/example-1dot1/ ImageSequence.java*

```java
/*
 * 1.1 version.
 */

import java.awt.*;
import java.awt.event.*;
import java.applet.Applet;

/*
 * This applet displays several images in a row.  It prevents
 * flashing by double buffering.  However, it doesn't wait
 * for the images to fully load before drawing them, which
 * causes the weird effect of the animation appearing from
 * the top down.
 */
public class ImageSequence extends Applet
                           implements Runnable {
    int frameNumber = -1;
    int delay;
    Thread animatorThread;
    boolean frozen = false;

    Image images[];

    Dimension offDimension;
    Image offImage;
    Graphics offGraphics;

    public void init() {
        String str;
        int fps = 10;

        //How many milliseconds between frames?
        str = getParameter("fps");
        try {
            if (str != null) {
                fps = Integer.parseInt(str);
            }
        } catch (Exception e) {}
        delay = (fps > 0) ? (1000 / fps) : 100;

        //Get the images.
        images = new Image[10];
        for (int i = 1; i <= 10; i++) {
            images[i-1] = getImage(getCodeBase(),
                                   "T"+i+".gif");
        }

        addMouseListener(new MouseAdapter() {
            public void mousePressed(MouseEvent e) {
                if (frozen) {
                    frozen = false;
                    start();
                } else {
                    frozen = true;
```

```
                        //Instead of calling stop(), which destroys the
                        //backbuffer, just stop the animating thread.
                        animatorThread = null;
                }
            }
        });
    }

    public void start() {
        if (frozen) {
            //Do nothing.  The user has requested that we
            //stop changing the image.
        } else {
            //Start animating!
            if (animatorThread == null) {
                animatorThread = new Thread(this);
            }
            animatorThread.start();
        }
    }

    public void stop() {
        //Stop the animating thread.
        animatorThread = null;

        //Get rid of the objects necessary for double buffering.
        offGraphics = null;
        offImage = null;
    }

    public void run() {
        //Just to be nice, lower this thread's priority
        //so it can't interfere with other processing going on.
        Thread.currentThread().setPriority(Thread.MIN_PRIORITY);

        //Remember the starting time.
        long startTime = System.currentTimeMillis();

        //Remember which thread we are.
        Thread currentThread = Thread.currentThread();

        //This is the animation loop.
        while (currentThread == animatorThread) {
            //Advance the animation frame.
            frameNumber++;

            //Display it.
            repaint();

            //Delay depending on how far we are behind.
            try {
                startTime += delay;
                Thread.sleep(Math.max(0,
                            startTime-System.currentTimeMillis()));
            } catch (InterruptedException e) {
                break;
            }
        }
    }

    //Draw the current frame of animation.
    public void paint(Graphics g) {
        update(g);
    }
```

```
public void update(Graphics g) {
    Dimension d = getSize();

    //Create the offscreen graphics context,
    //if no good one exists.
    if ( (offGraphics == null)
      || (d.width != offDimension.width)
      || (d.height != offDimension.height) ) {
        offDimension = d;
        offImage = createImage(d.width, d.height);
        offGraphics = offImage.getGraphics();
    }

    //Erase the previous image.
    offGraphics.setColor(getBackground());
    offGraphics.fillRect(0, 0, d.width, d.height);
    offGraphics.setColor(Color.black);

    //Paint the frame into the image.
    try {
        offGraphics.drawImage(images[frameNumber%10],
                              0, 0, this);
    } catch(ArrayIndexOutOfBoundsException e) {
        //On rare occasions, this method can be called
        //when frameNumber is still -1.  Do nothing.
        return;
    }

    //Paint the image onto the screen.
    g.drawImage(offImage, 0, 0, this);
    }
}
```

AWT EXAMPLE :*ListDemo.java*

Where Explained:

Converting ListDemo (page 600)

Swing Version: ListSelectionDemo.java *(page 903)*

Associated File(s): ListDemo.html *(page 922)*

SOURCE CODE: *http://java.sun.com/docs/books/tutorial/uiswing/converting/example-1dot1/ ListDemo.java*

```
/*
 * 1.1 version.
 */

import java.awt.*;
import java.awt.event.*;
import java.applet.Applet;

public class ListDemo extends Applet
                      implements ActionListener,
                                 ItemListener {
    TextArea output;
    List spanish, italian;
    String newline;

    public void init() {
        newline = System.getProperty("line.separator");

        //Build first list, which allows multiple selections.
        spanish = new List(4, true); //prefer 4 items visible
```

```
        spanish.add("uno");
        spanish.add("dos");
        spanish.add("tres");
        spanish.add("cuatro");
        spanish.add("cinco");
        spanish.add("seis");
        spanish.add("siete");
        spanish.addActionListener(this);
        spanish.addItemListener(this);

        //Build second list, which allows one selection at a time.
        italian = new List(); //Defaults to none visible, only one selectable
        italian.add("uno");
        italian.add("due");
        italian.add("tre");
        italian.add("quattro");
        italian.add("cinque");
        italian.add("sei");
        italian.add("sette");
        italian.addActionListener(this);
        italian.addItemListener(this);

        //Add lists to the Applet.
        GridBagLayout gridBag = new GridBagLayout();
        setLayout(gridBag);

        //Can't put text area on right due to GBL bug
        //(can't span rows in any column but the first).
        output = new TextArea(10, 40);
        output.setEditable(false);
        GridBagConstraints tc = new GridBagConstraints();
        tc.fill = GridBagConstraints.BOTH;
        tc.weightx = 1.0;
        tc.weighty = 1.0;
        tc.gridheight = 2;
        gridBag.setConstraints(output, tc);
        add(output);

        GridBagConstraints lc = new GridBagConstraints();
        lc.fill = GridBagConstraints.VERTICAL;
        lc.gridwidth = GridBagConstraints.REMAINDER; //end row
        gridBag.setConstraints(spanish, lc);
        add(spanish);
        gridBag.setConstraints(italian, lc);
        add(italian);
    }

    public void actionPerformed(ActionEvent e) {
        List list = (List)(e.getSource());
        String language = (list == spanish) ?
                        "Spanish" : "Italian";
        output.append("Action event occurred on \""
                        + list.getSelectedItem()  + "\" in "
                        + language + "." + newline);
    }

    public void itemStateChanged(ItemEvent e) {
        List list = (List)(e.getItemSelectable());
        String language = (list == spanish) ?
                        "Spanish" : "Italian";

        int index = ((Integer)(e.getItem())).intValue();
        if (e.getStateChange() == ItemEvent.SELECTED) {
            output.append("Select event occurred on item #"
                        + index + " (\""
                        + list.getItem(index) + "\") in "
                        + language + "." + newline);
```

```
          } else { //the item was deselected
             output.append("Deselect event occurred on item #"
                         + index + " (\""
                         + list.getItem(index) + "\") in "
                         + language + "." + newline);
          }
       }
   }
```

AWT EXAMPLE: *ListDemo.html*

Associated File(s): ListDemo.java *(page 920)*

```
<html>
<body>
   <applet code=ListDemo.class width=500 height=150>
   </applet>
</body>
</html>
```

AWT EXAMPLE: *TextEventDemo.java*

Where Explained:

Converting TextEventDemo (page 597)

Swing Version: TextEventDemo.java *(page 906)*

SOURCE CODE: *http://java.sun.com/docs/books/tutorial/uiswing/converting/example-1dot1/ TextEventDemo.java*

```java
/*
 * 1.1 code.
 */

import java.applet.Applet;
import java.awt.*;
import java.awt.event.*;

public class TextEventDemo extends Applet
                           implements ActionListener {
    TextField textField;
    TextArea textArea;
    TextArea displayArea;

    public void init() {
        Button button = new Button("Clear");
        button.addActionListener(this);

        textField = new TextField(20);
        textField.addActionListener(new MyTextActionListener());
        textField.addTextListener(new MyTextListener("Text Field"));

        textArea = new TextArea(5, 20);
        textArea.addTextListener(new MyTextListener("Text Area"));

        displayArea = new TextArea(5, 20);
        displayArea.setEditable(false);

        GridBagLayout gridbag = new GridBagLayout();
        GridBagConstraints c = new GridBagConstraints();
```

```
        setLayout(gridbag);
        c.fill = GridBagConstraints.BOTH;
        c.weightx = 1.0;

        /*
         * Hack to get around gridbag's refusal to allow
         * multi-row components in anything but the left column.
         */
        Panel leftPanel = new Panel();
        leftPanel.setLayout(new BorderLayout());
        leftPanel.add("North", textField);
        leftPanel.add("Center", textArea);

        c.gridheight = 2;
        gridbag.setConstraints(leftPanel, c);
        add(leftPanel);

        c.weighty = 1.0;
        c.gridwidth = GridBagConstraints.REMAINDER;
        c.gridheight = 1;
        gridbag.setConstraints(displayArea, c);
        add(displayArea);

        c.weighty = 0.0;
        gridbag.setConstraints(button, c);
        add(button);

        textField.requestFocus();
    }

    class MyTextListener implements TextListener {
        String preface;
        String newline;

        public MyTextListener(String source) {
            newline = System.getProperty("line.separator");
            preface = source
                    + " text value changed."
                    + newline
                    + "    First 10 characters: \"";
        }

        public void textValueChanged(TextEvent e) {
            TextComponent tc = (TextComponent)e.getSource();
            String s = tc.getText();
            try {
                s = s.substring(0, 10);
            } catch (StringIndexOutOfBoundsException ex) {
            }

            displayArea.append(preface + s + "\"" + newline);

            //Scroll down, unless the peer still needs to be created.
            if (displayArea.isValid()) {
                displayArea.setCaretPosition(java.lang.Integer.MAX_VALUE);
            }
        }
    }

    class MyTextActionListener implements ActionListener {
        /** Handle the text field Return. */
        public void actionPerformed(ActionEvent e) {
            int selStart = textArea.getSelectionStart();
            int selEnd = textArea.getSelectionEnd();
```

```
                textArea.replaceRange(textField.getText(),
                                  selStart, selEnd);
                textField.selectAll();
            }
        }

        /** Handle button click. */
        public void actionPerformed(ActionEvent e) {
            displayArea.setText("");
            textField.requestFocus();
        }
    }
```

AWT EXAMPLE: *Unit.java*

Where Explained:

Converting Converter (page 598)

Swing Version: Unit.java *(page 908)*

Main Source File: Converter.java *(page 894)*

SOURCE CODE: *http://java.sun.com/docs/books/tutorial/uiswing/converting/example-1dot1/ Unit.java*

```
/*
 * 1.1 version.
 */

public class Unit {
    String description;
    double multiplier;

    Unit(String description, double multiplier) {
        super();
        this.description = description;
        this.multiplier = multiplier;
    }

    public String toString() {
        String s = "Meters/" + description + " = " + multiplier;
        return s;
    }
}
```

Reference

THIS appendix gives details you might find useful when using the Swing API. First, it tells you how to set the class path and environment variables, which can be useful if you're using JFC 1.1 without Java Plug-in. Next, it gives the history of the Swing package names.

This appendix contains the following reference information:

- Platform-Specific Details: Setting the Browser's Class Path (page 925)
- Platform-Specific Details: Setting Environment Variables (page 927)
- Swing Package Names (page 927)

Platform-Specific Details: Setting the Browser's Class Path

This section tells you how to include the JFC 1.1 release in the class path of a 1.1 browser. For example, you can follow these instructions to make the Applet Viewer provided in JDK 1.1 find the JFC 1.1 libraries. If you're using either the Java 2 Platform or Java Plug-in, then stop reading—you don't need this information.

You can make sure a 1.1 browser's class path includes the Swing release in one of two ways:

- Use a browser-specific option to set your browser's class path.
- Set the CLASSPATH environment variable.

Warning: Permanently setting the CLASSPATH environment variable can lead to trouble, since it's easy to forget to update it when you use a different version of the JDK or Swing. Instead, try to specify the class path programmatically, such as with a -classpath command-line option. Or specify it at a shell prompt, rather than saving it in a file.

The following instructions give examples of each approach. For more information on setting the class path, see "Managing Source and Class Files" in the "Learning Java Languages" trail. You can find this trail in *The Java*[TM] *Tutorial* book and online at http://java.sun.com/docs/books/tutorial/java/index.html.

The directory paths used below assume that you have installed both the JDK 1.1 and JFC 1.1 releases under /home/me (for Solaris) or on drive C (for Windows). You should adjust the directory paths to reflect your installation.

Solaris

If you're using the JDK Applet Viewer, then instead of specifying the CLASSPATH environment variable, you can use the -J option of the appletviewer command to specify options to the interpreter. For example:

```
appletviewer -J"-classpath
/home/me/swing-1.1/swing.jar:/home/me/jdk1.1.8/lib/classes.zip"
http://java.sun.com/docs/books/tutorial/uiswing/start/
HelloSwingApplet.atag
```

If you choose to set the CLASSPATH environment variable, use a command like the following:

```
setenv CLASSPATH .:/home/me/swing-1.1/swing.jar
```

Then invoke your browser as usual.

Win32

If you're using the JDK Applet Viewer, then instead of specifying the CLASSPATH environment variable (as described in the next section), you can use the -J option of the appletviewer command. For example:

```
appletviewer -J"-classpath
C:\swing-1.1\swing.jar;c:\jdk1.1.8\lib\classes.zip"
http://java.sun.com/docs/books/tutorial/uiswing/start/
HelloSwingApplet.atag
```

Platform-Specific Details: Setting Environment Variables

This section tells you how to set environment variables, as you might need to do when using JFC 1.1 with JDK 1.1. The directory paths used below assume that you have installed both the JDK and Swing releases under /home/me (for Solaris) or on drive C (for Windows). You should adjust the directory paths to reflect your installation.

Solaris

Set the environment variables with commands like the following:

```
setenv JAVA_HOME /home/me/jdk1.1.8
setenv SWING_HOME /home/me/swing-1.1
```

Windows 95

Open your favorite text editor and add the following to your system's AUTOEXEC.BAT file:

```
set JAVA_HOME=C:\jdk1.1.8
set SWING_HOME=C:\Swing-1.1
set CLASSPATH=.;%JAVA_HOME%\lib\classes.zip;%SWING_HOME%\swing.jar
set PATH=%PATH%;%JAVA_HOME%\bin
```

Windows NT

Double-click the System icon inside the Control Panel. When the System Properties dialog box opens, choose the Environment tab, and place the following in the lower list box, which is labeled "User Variables":

```
JAVA_HOME      C:\jdk1.1.8
SWING_HOME     C:\Swing-1.1
CLASSPATH      .;%JAVA_HOME%\lib\classes.zip;%SWING_HOME%\swing.jar
PATH           %PATH%;%JAVA_HOME%\bin
```

Note: Be careful not to change your system environment variables, which appear in the upper list box.

Swing Package Names

The names of the Swing packages have varied over time. This book uses the final package names, which generally start with javax.swing. If you have code that uses earlier package names, such as com.sun.java.swing, then you will need to convert it.

This section has two parts:

How to Convert to the Final Package Names

Between the Beta 2 and Beta 3 releases of Swing 1.1 API, the names of the Swing packages changed. In Beta 2, for example, the main package was called `com.sun.java.swing`, while in Swing 1.1 Beta 3, the name is `javax.swing`. The same changes occurred between the Beta 4 and RC1 releases of the Java 2 Platform (then codenamed "JDK 1.2").

Converting the package names is easy, although it can be tedious to do by hand when many source files are involved. Fortunately, the Swing team provides a utility called `PackageRenamer` that converts programs to use the final Swing package names. You can find the program at: `http://java.sun.com/products/jfc/PackageRenamer`.

The following table shows how the names have changed:

Table 191 Changes in the Swing Package Names

Old Name (Swing 1.1 Beta 2, JDK 1.2 Beta 4)	New, Final Name (Swing 1.1 [Beta 3 and later], JDK 1.2 RC1)
`com.sun.java.accessibility`	`javax.accessibility`
`com.sun.java.swing`	`javax.swing`
`com.sun.java.swing.border`	`javax.swing.border`
`com.sun.java.swing.colorchooser`	`javax.swing.colorchooser`
`com.sun.java.swing.event`	`javax.swing.event`
`com.sun.java.swing.filechooser`	`javax.swing.filechooser`
`com.sun.java.swing.plaf`	`javax.swing.plaf`
`com.sun.java.swing.plaf.basic`	`javax.swing.plaf.basic`
`com.sun.java.swing.plaf.metal`	`javax.swing.plaf.metal`
`com.sun.java.swing.plaf.motif`	`com.sun.java.swing.plaf.motif` (no change)
`com.sun.java.swing.plaf.multi`	`javax.swing.plaf.multi`
`com.sun.java.swing.plaf.windows`	`com.sun.java.swing.plaf.windows` (no change)
`com.sun.java.swing.table`	`javax.swing.table`

Table 191 Changes in the Swing Package Names

Old Name (Swing 1.1 Beta 2, JDK 1.2 Beta 4)	New, Final Name (Swing 1.1 [Beta 3 and later], JDK 1.2 RC1)
`com.sun.java.swing.text`	`javax.swing.text`
`com.sun.java.swing.text.html`	`javax.swing.text.html`
`com.sun.java.swing.tree`	`javax.swing.tree`
`com.sun.java.swing.undo`	`javax.swing.undo`
`com.sun.java.swing.plaf.mac`	`com.sun.java.swing.plaf.mac` (no change)
`com.sun.java.accessibility.util`	`com.sun.java.accessibility.util` (no change)

Note: The `com.sun.java.accessibility.util` package isn't part of the JFC 1.1 release or the Java 2 Platform. It is distributed separately as part of the Accessibility Utilities. For details, see the *JFC Home Page* online at: `http://java.sun.com/products/jfc/index.html`.

The History of the Swing Package Names

At various times, the Swing API has used the following package names:

- `com.sun.java.swing`
- `java.awt.swing`
- `javax.swing`

In the end, the core Swing API is under the `javax.swing` package, with some additional Sun-provided packages under `com.sun.java.swing`. The previous table gives details of the final package names. Now let's look at how the names have varied over time. The following discussion uses the JDK 1.2 name, which was the previous codename for the Java 2 Platform.

In all the JFC 1.1 releases up through Swing 1.1 Beta 2, the name of the main Swing package was `com.sun.java.swing`. The JFC 1.1 releases were meant to be used with JDK 1.1. There was no built-in JDK 1.2 support for Swing until JDK 1.2 Beta 2.

In the JDK 1.2 Beta 2 and Beta 3 releases, the Swing API was in a new package: `java.awt.swing`. However, some of our customers told us that they wanted the Swing package names to be the same in JFC 1.1 and JDK 1.2, so that they would be able to use the exact same code for both releases.

As a result, in JDK 1.2 Beta 4 the Swing team moved the main Swing package to `com.sun.java.swing`. Unfortunately, many people didn't like this change. One of the reasons for the discontent was that having a core API in a package that didn't begin with "java" seemed to imply that Swing wasn't a core API.

The Swing team reacted by floating a proposal to move the Swing packages to `javax.swing` in both JFC 1.1 and JDK 1.2. The proposal was favorably greeted by the user community, and the new package names were introduced in Swing 1.1 Beta 3 and JDK 1.2 RC1. The right column of the preceding Table 191 on page 928 shows the final package names used in JFC 1.1 (Swing 1.1 and compatible releases) and the Java 2 Platform.

Index

Note: An italic *e* after a page number indicates an entry in Appendix A, *Code Examples*.

? : notation, 564

A

Absolute positioning, 34, 383–384
AbstractAction, 293, 389, 392
AbstractButton, 169–170
AbstractDocument, 311
AbstractTableModel, 260, 271
Accelerators, 231, 232
Accessibility, 398–400
  API for, 6, 69, 393, 406–408
  of components, 395–398
  of custom components, 400–402
  support for, 394–395
  testing for, 402–406
Accessibility Utilities, 928
Accessible interface, 398, 407
AccessibleAction, 398, 407
AccessibleComponent, 398, 399, 407
AccessibleContext, 398, 407
AccessibleHypertext, 399, 407
AccessibleJComponent, 399, 400
AccessibleJLabel, 400
AccessibleRole, 401, 407
AccessibleScrollDemo.java, 396–398,
    402, 404–406, 407, 806–808*e*
AccessibleSelection, 399, 407
AccessibleStateSet, 401–402, 407
AccessibleText, 399, 407
AccessibleValue, 399, 407
Action listeners, 56, 194
Action objects, 49–50
  API for, 391–392
  using, 389–392
Action validation, 265, 300
ActionDemo.java, 142, 179, 238, 319,
    390–391, 392, 427, 808–810*e*

ActionEvent, 232
  API for, 459–460
ActionListener, 37, 38, 389, 459, 527
actionPerformed, 38–39, 152–153, 202,
    222, 241, 293, 294, 299, 300, 459–460,
    564
Activated window, defined, 521
add, 73, 110, 129, 132, 141, 156, 175, 229,
    235, 236, 389, 392
  AWT version of, 581
addActionForKeyStroke, 291, 315
addActionListener, 175, 199, 237, 309,
    389
addCaretListener, 313, 462
addChangeListener, 252
addChoosableFileFilter, 210
addChooserPanel, 188, 190
addComponentListener, 71, 453
addContainerListener, 71
addDocumentListener, 312
addElement, 223
addFocusListener, 71, 453
addInternalFrameListener, 148
addItem, 198
addItemListener, 175, 194, 199, 237
addKeyListener, 71, 453
addKeymap, 291, 292, 315
addLayoutComponent, 379, 380
addListenerTypeListener, 47
addListSelectionListener, 220, 224
addMouseListener, 71, 453
addMouseListenerToHeaderInTable,
    270
addMouseMotionListener, 71, 453
addSeparator, 142, 235, 236
addTab, 134, 135, 317
addTableModelListener, 507

The Addison-Wesley Java™ Series

Ken Arnold · James Gosling

The Java™ Programming Language Second Edition

ISBN 0-201-31006-6

Mary Campione · Kathy Walrath

The Java™ Tutorial Second Edition

Object-Oriented Programming for the Internet

ISBN 0-201-31007-4

Campione · Walrath · Huml · Tutorial Team

The Java™ Tutorial Continued

The Rest of the JDK™

ISBN 0-201-48558-3

Patrick Chan

The Java™ Developers ALMANAC 1999

ISBN 0-201-43298-6

Patrick Chan · Rosanna Lee

The Java™ Class Libraries Second Edition, Volume 2

java.applet java.awt java.beans

ISBN 0-201-31003-1

Patrick Chan · Rosanna Lee · Douglas Kramer

The Java™ Class Libraries Second Edition, Volume 1

java.io java.lang java.math java.net java.text java.util

ISBN 0-201-31002-3

Patrick Chan · Rosanna Lee · Douglas Kramer

The Java™ Class Libraries Second Edition, Volume 1

Supplement for the Java™ 2 Platform Standard Edition, v1.2

ISBN 0-201-48552-4

James Gosling · Bill Joy · Guy Steele

The Java™ Language Specification

ISBN 0-201-63451-1

James Gosling · Frank Yellin · The Java Team

The Java™ Application Programming Interface, Volume 1

Core Packages

ISBN 0-201-63453-8

James Gosling · Frank Yellin · The Java Team

The Java™ Application Programming Interface, Volume 2

Window Toolkit and Applets

ISBN 0-201-63459-7

Li Gong

Inside the Java™ 2 Platform Security Architecture

Cryptography, APIs, and Implementations

ISBN 0-201-31000-7

Jonni Kanerva

The Java™ FAQ

ISBN 0-201-63456-2

Doug Lea

Concurrent Programming in Java™

Design Principles and Patterns

ISBN 0-201-69581-2

Sheng Liang

The Java™ Native Interface

Programmer's Guide and Specification

ISBN 0-201-32577-2

Tim Lindholm · Frank Yellin

The Java™ Virtual Machine Specification Second Edition

ISBN 0-201-43294-3

Henry Sowizral · Kevin Rushforth · Michael Deering

The Java™ 3D API Specification

ISBN 0-201-32576-4

Kathy Walrath · Mary Campione

The JFC™ Swing Tutorial

A Guide to Constructing GUIs

ISBN 0-201-43321-4

White · Fisher · Cattell · Hamilton · Hapner

JDBC™ API Tutorial and Reference, Second Edition

Universal Data Access for the Java™ 2 Platform

ISBN 0-201-43328-1

Please see our web site (http://www.awl.com/cseng/javaseries)
for more information on these titles.

The Java™ Tutorials

The definitive tutorial to the JDK 1.1 and 1.2 class libraries

The Java™ Tutorials are practical, step-by-step guides to writing programs with JDK™ 1.1, 1.2 and the new Swing components. Each book is designed to be read either cover-to-cover or as a quick reference. *The Java™ Tutorials* also provide an example-driven, self-paced approach so that readers can step through and learn about topics with sample programming exercises and example applications.

The Java™ Tutorial, Second Edition
Object-Oriented Programming for the Internet
By Mary Campione and Kathy Walrath
0-201-31007-4 • Paperback • 992 pages w/CD-ROM
A step-by-step reference to writing programs with JDK™ 1.1.

The Java™ Tutorial *Continued*
The Rest of the JDK™
By Mary Campione, Kathy Walrath, Alison Huml, and The Tutorial Team
0-201-48558-3 • Paperback • 976 pages w/CD-ROM
This companion to The Java Tutorial, Second Edition *features new JDK™ 1.2 topics.*

The JFC Swing Tutorial
A Guide to Constructing GUIs
by Kathy Walrath and Mary Campione
0-201-43321-4 • Paperback • 752 pages w/CD-ROM
A guide to creating user interfaces with Swing components.

http://www.javaseries.com
http://java.sun.com/books/Series

✦ Addison-Wesley

Addison-Wesley Computer and Engineering Publishing Group

How to Interact with Us

1. Visit our Web site

http://www.awl.com/cseng

When you think you've read enough, there's always more content for you at Addison-Wesley's web site. Our web site contains a directory of complete product information including:

- Chapters
- Exclusive author interviews
- Links to authors' pages
- Tables of contents
- Source code

You can also discover what tradeshows and conferences Addison-Wesley will be attending, read what others are saying about our titles, and find out where and when you can meet our authors and have them sign your book.

2. Subscribe to Our Email Mailing Lists

Subscribe to our electronic mailing lists and be the first to know when new books are publishing. Here's how it works: Sign up for our electronic mailing at **http://www.awl.com/cseng/mailinglists.html**. Just select the subject areas that interest you and you will receive notification via email when we publish a book in that area.

3. Contact Us via Email

cepubprof@awl.com
Ask general questions about our books.
Sign up for our electronic mailing lists.
Submit corrections for our web site.

bexpress@awl.com
Request an Addison-Wesley catalog.
Get answers to questions regarding your order or our products.

innovations@awl.com
Request a current Innovations Newsletter.

webmaster@awl.com
Send comments about our web site.

mikeh@awl.com
Submit a book proposal.
Send errata for an Addison-Wesley book.

cepubpublicity@awl.com
Request a review copy for a member of the media interested in reviewing new Addison-Wesley titles.

We encourage you to patronize the many fine retailers who stock Addison-Wesley titles. Visit our online directory to find stores near you or visit our online store: **http://store.awl.com/** or call **800-824-7799**.

Addison Wesley Longman
Computer and Engineering Publishing Group
One Jacob Way, Reading, Massachusetts 01867 USA
TEL 781-944-3700 • FAX 781-942-3076

The Java Tutorial CD-ROM

The *Java Tutorial* CD-ROM that accompanies this book is loaded with development kits and documentation, including the content and code of all three books: *The Java Tutorial*, *The Java Tutorial Continued*, and *The JFC Swing Tutorial*. Where the release version is not noted, the most recent release at the time of printing is included.

Table 192   Development Kits on *The Java Tutorial* CD-ROM

Development Kits	Version(s)
Java 2 Platform (formerly JDK 1.2)	Standard, v 1.2
Java Development Kit (JDK)	1.1.8, 1.0.2
Java Runtime Environment (JRE)	Java 2
Java Foundation Classes (JFC) *includes Swing 1.1*	1.1
Beans Development Kit (BDK)	1.1
JavaBeans Activation Framework (JAF)	1.0
Java Servlet Development Kit (JSDK)	2.0
Java Naming and Directory Interface (JNDI)	1.1

Table 193   Documentation on *The Java Tutorial* CD-ROM

Documentation	Version(s)
The Java Tutorial	
Java Programming Language API Documentation	Java 2, 1.1, 1.0.2
JFC 1.1 API Documentation	1.1
The Swing Connection	
The Java Platform White Paper	

Table 194   Products on *The Java Tutorial* CD-ROM

...ducts	Version(s)
...ava Browser	3.0
...Plug-In	1.2
...ojava Compiler	

Table 195   Specifications on *The Java Tutorial* CD-ROM

Specifications
Java 2D Specification
JavaBeans Specification
Servlet Specification
JDBC 1.2 and 2.0 Specifications
Security 1.2 Specification
Java Cryptography Architecture API Specification
Drag & Drop Specification

Table 196   Miscellaneous on *The Java Tutorial* CD-ROM

And more...
Java Code Conventions
Java Programming Language Glossary
100% Pure Java CookBook

The `README.html` file on the CD-ROM is the central HTML page that links you to all of its contents. To view this page, use the `Open Page` command or its equivalent in your Internet browser. On some platforms, you can simply double click on the HTML file to launch it in your browser.

You can check out the latest Sun Microsystems Java™ programming language product releases at: `http://java.sun.com/products/index.html`. If you sign up for the Java Developer Connection,[1] you will receive free, early access to such products, including the latest Java platform.

See this book's Web page at: `http://java.sun.com/docs/books/tutorial/uiswing/index.html` for pointers to the latest versions of this content.

---

[1] http://developer.javasoft.com/index.html